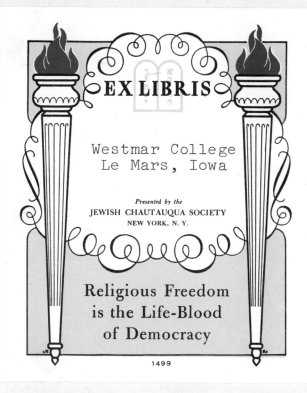

THE SYNOPTIC GOSPELS

LIBRARY OF
BIBLICAL STUDIES

edited by

HARRY M. ORLINSKY

Professor of Bible

Hebrew Union College - Jewish Institute of Religion

New York City

THE SYNOPTIC GOSPELS

EDITED WITH

AN INTRODUCTION AND A COMMENTARY

BY

C. G. MONTEFIORE

HON. D.D. (MANCHESTER)

**PROLEGOMENON
BY**
LOU H. SILBERMAN

IN TWO VOLUMES

VOL. I

Second Edition revised and partly rewritten

KTAV PUBLISHING HOUSE, INC.
NEW YORK
1968

First Published 1927

KTAV PUBLISHING HOUSE, Inc.

New Matter © Copyright 1968

Library of Congress Catalog Card Number: 67-18256
Manufactured in The United States of America

TO

F. G. M.

φίλτρον γὰρ ἀνυσιμώτατον καὶ δεσμὸς ἄλυτος εὐνοίας ἑνωτικῆς ἡ τοῦ ἑνὸς θεοῦ τιμή.

Philo, *De Specialibus Legibus*, Lib. I. (*De Monarchia*)
Chap. VII. (Mangey II. p. 219).

τὸ συγγενὲς οὐχ αἵματι μετρεῖται μόνον, πρυτανευούσης ἀληθείας, ἀλλὰ πράξεων ὁμοιότητι καὶ θήρᾳ τῶν αὐτῶν.

Philo, *De Nobilitate*, Chap. I.
(Mangey II. p. 438).

ואהבת לרעך כמוך · רבי עקיבא אומר זה כלל גדול בתורה · בן עזאי אומר זה
ספר תולדות אדם · זה כלל גדול מזה: אמר רבי תנחומא שלא תאמר הואיל
ונתבזיתי יתבזה חבירי עמי הואיל ונתקללתי יתקלל חבירי עמי · אם עשית כן דע
למי אתה מבזה · בדמות אלהים עשה אותו:

Sifra 89 b on Lev. xix. 18, and Genesis Rabba Chap. xxiv. ad
fin. *Cp.* Bacher, *Die Agada der Tannaiten*, Vol. I. p. 417,
n. 4, p. 422, n. 1. (Ed. 2, 1903.)

σοφία...μία δὲ οὖσα πάντα δύναται, καὶ μένουσα ἐν αὑτῇ τὰ πάντα καινίζει, καὶ κατὰ
γενεὰς εἰς ψυχὰς ὁσίας μεταβαίνουσα φίλους θεοῦ καὶ προφήτας κατασκευάζει.

Wisdom of Solomon, vii. 27.

The Country Parson...as he doth not so study others as to neglect the
grace of God in himself and what the Holy Spirit teacheth him, so doth he
assure himself that God in all ages hath had his servants, to whom he hath
revealed his Truth as well as to him; and that as one Country doth not bear
all things, that there may be a Commerce, so neither hath God opened or
will open all to one, that there may be a traffick in knowledge between
the servants of God for the planting both of love and humility.

George Herbert, *The County Parson*, Chap. IV.
" The Parson's Knowledge."

The Humble, Meek, Merciful, Just, Pious and Devout Souls are everywhere of one Religion; and when Death has taken off the Mask, they will
know one another, though the divers Liveries they wear here makes them
Strangers.

Some Fruits of Solitude, by William Penn.
(Part I. Number 519.)

PROLEGOMENON

I. Some Preliminary Remarks

In 1938, the year of Claude G. Montefiore's death, Gösta Lindeskog published his work *Die Jesusfrage im Neuzeitlichen Judentum*: *Ein Beitrag zur Geschichte der Leben-Jesu-Forschung.*[1] In it he examined, against the background of the political emancipation of the Jews in western Europe and the cultural and religious results of that process, the various ways in which Jewish scholarship, directly and indirectly, came to deal with the rise of Christianity, its literature, and most particularly with its central figure, Jesus. Although there are undoubtedly some gaps in the thirty-four page *"Jüdische Bibliographie,"* its magnitude and detail suggest that not much of significance escaped the author's wide-cast net.

Ideally, the reprinting of Claude G. Montefiore's work *The Synoptic Gospels* might have been the occasion for bringing Lindeskog's study up to date. Indeed, it was this I had in mind when I undertook the task of writing this prolegomenon. But I was soon disabused. If the tragic years of the thirties and forties, during which most of the European centers of Jewish learning, both traditional and modern, were destroyed, added little to the bibliography, the subsequent years, enspirited by the establishment of the State of Israel and the flourishing development of vital Jewish scholarship in its centers of learning, have contributed much. A contemporary writer has noted a rising interest in Jesus and Christianity in the State of Israel which, in our context, is ironic, for Montefiore who, as we shall see,

1

sought to find a way to reclaim Jesus for Judaism, was a staunch and unyielding opponent of Zionism with its program of establishing a Jewish State in Palestine. Other, remaining centers of Jewish learning, too, have made their contributions, and there is little doubt that a sizeable bibliography of studies by American scholars has already come into being.

The discovery of the Qumran materials in the late forties and their publication, albeit after the first flurry all-too slowly, together with other archeological and literary finds whose publication has been prompt, all coming from the period of the Second Commonwealth and the Roman Wars, has livened scholarly interest in the period encompassing the origin and rise of Christianity. The broadening of our knowledge of the varieties of Judaism in the period has made it possible to examine Christianity within a wider range and broader spectrum than was previously possible. When this is joined to the results of the form-critical and redactional-critical approach of contemporary New Testament scholarship, one is no longer required to set a putative normative Judaism, labelled Pharisaism, over against the "teachings of Jesus" in sterile conflict. The richness of the scene and the complex possibilities lying within it have allowed for investigations that a generation ago would not have been imagined.

When set over against this burgeoning scholarship, Montefiore's work (2nd edition, 1927), references to which dominate the concluding pages of Lindeskog's book, represents the end of an era in more than one sense. Six years after its appearance, the destruction of European Jewry began; a process Montefiore seems not to have comprehended, for in November, 1935, he wrote: ". . . if it had not been for German and Austrian anti-Semitism all would have gone well. Each 'one' was bringing 'ten' in his train [apparently a reference to his hoped-for rapprochment of Liberal Judaism and Christianity], till German and Austrian anti-Semitism on the one hand and the defeatist Zionism, on the other, spoilt everything."[2] With the total world upheaval of which these dreadful events were a part, the particular ideas and attitudes that formed Montefiore's life and thought lost their grounding and sadly retreated into the wings of civilization's stage. The following pages are then an attempt to understand and assay this work, and thus to explain and to jutsify the judgment here made.

II. Claude Goldsmid Montefiore

1858-1938

> Today I finished my review
> of Baeck's article on J.
> religious education. This
> review ends with a sharp
> criticism of the great man. I
> hope it is not impertinent.
>
> C. G. M. to Lucy Cohen,[3]
> April 9,1930

The quotation from a letter by Montefiore to his cousin has been set as a motto for this brief introductory interpretation of *The Synoptic Gospels* because it does indeed sum up my own response to the work at hand, critical but, hopefully, not impertinent. I have always had an ambivalent attitude toward Montefiore, at once admiring and impatient. There is a passage in the Introduction to his last work, *A Rabbinic Anthology*[4] (p. xxvii), that I use regularly as a foil in beginning an attempt to interpret the nature of rabbinic Judaism:

> "But, otherwise, as the Rabbis often took all that is said about God in the Hebrew Bible very literally, and as they were so sadly fettered by the burden of regarding every biblical utterance as good and true and inspired, they seem often to talk about God like so many big children. I do not think it is possible to regard all that they say as conscious 'accommodations'. These childishnesses are too constant and simple for that . . .
> It may, indeed, be—I think it is—that to most of us God is less vividly realised, less a constant certainty, than He was to the Rabbis, but He is also, if less human, more divine. Our reserve in speaking of Him is good and healthy.

A certain austerity and restraint in regard to our conception of, and attitude towards Him, make for increased reverence and awe. Is there a touch of over-familiarity in the Rabbinic attitude toward Him?"

I respect the serious religious stance of the concluding lines, save the last, which I find priggish. I am totally impatient with what I know, on the basis of my own studies, to be a wrong-headed interpretation of the rabbinic attitude toward and understanding of Holy Scriptures. But more than that, I am astounded at Montefiore's condescending attitude:

> "Another point to remember in regard to Rabbinic literature is that it comes from men whose outlook was extraordinarily limited. They had no interests outside Religion and The Law. They had lost all historic sense. They had no interest in art, in drama, in *belle lettres,* in poetry, or in science (except, perhaps, in medicine). They had no training in philosophy. How enormously they might have benefited if, under competent teachers, they had been put through a course of Greek philosophy and literature. They had not training in rhetoric or the art of composition."[5]

In other words, they had not been at Balliol when Jowett was Master.

Perhaps the clue to all this, and such a clue is necessary in approaching *The Synoptic Gospels,* for it does not claim to be an objective but a highly personal scholarly work, is to be found in a passage from another letter to Lucy Cohen:

> "Our bringing up was of course much more Jewish than yours, but rather in teaching and observance and atmosphere! not in *persons.* We know *very* few Jews, except our relations. I mean *very* few Jews except our relations come to the house; few, if any. It was teaching, atmosphere, observance, belief. Cosmopolitan is *quite* incorrect. *Un*cosmopolitan and purely English."[6]

Claude Goldsmid Montefiore was, indeed, purely English.

"Two of the foremost Jewish families, the Montefiores and the Goldsmids, were united in him, and his grandmother had been a Rothschild . . . Both families had been established in England since the end of the eighteenth century." His early education was private. He "learnt German (which he spoke perfectly) from his sister's governess, and Hebrew from The Reverend Professor Marks, Senior Minister of The Berkeley Street Synagogue . . . The future Sir Philip Magnus was responsible for his general education, which up to seventeen was wholly on the modern side." His brilliance may be judged by the fact that for university matriculation he learned Greek in eight weeks and "matriculated at The London University thirtieth out of three hundred . . ." In 1878 he went to Balliol College and later took a First Class degree. Lucy Cohen reports: "Balliol and Oxford made a lasting impression on Claude. Jowett's liberal views of the Christian religion affected his own line of thought."[7] Norman Bentwich, writing of the same influence in his Montefiore Memorial Lecture, suggested that the divergence between Montefiore and Solomon Schechter, his tutor, at a later date, in Jewish studies, "was perhaps influenced by their different English University backgrounds. Jowett's Oxford was the home of Liberal Christianity and the theology of the High Church, while Cambridge was the home of the Low Church . . ."[8]

Yet, despite these differences and interests, and despite the varied opportunities open to a young man of wealth and family, Montefiore had already determined while at Oxford, and with Jowett's blessing, to devote himself to Jewish theology and learning. "That was," wrote Bentwich, "a vocation almost unknown to Jews of the leading families."[9] It is this decision that, over and over again, despite my reservation about and quarrels with its fruits, continues to call forth unbounded admiration, deep respect and profound gratitude. In 1882, Montefiore, accompanied by his widowed mother (who had subvened the printing of the authorized translation of the traditional order of Syna-

gogue worship so that it might be available at an inexpensive
cost) and his sister, went to Berlin to study at the *Hochschule
für die Wissenchaft des Judentums,* one of the important centers
of Jewish studies created because of the refusal of German uni-
versities to create faculties of Jewish theology corresponding to
the Catholic and Protestant establishments. Here Solomon
Schechter, who was to play an important role in Montefiore's
scholarly development, became his tutor and returned with him
to England the following year. The importance of the relationship between these two may be seen in the introduction to
Montefiore's Hibbert Lectures of 1892. ("He was the first Jew
to be appointed to that foundation for the study of religion.")[10]
"To Schechter I owe more than I can adequately express. My
whole conception of The Law and its place in the Jewish religion and life is largely the fruit of his teaching and inspiration,
while most of the Rabbinical material on which that conception
rests was put before my notice and explained to me by him."[11]

The two were, however, destined to go their own ways.
Bentwich wrote: "There was a difference of thought which the
rabbis called 'conflicts for Heaven's sake' between them.
Schechter above all else stressed the unity of Israel and the
continuity of tradition of past and present, and resisted any
schism. Montefiore in middle age wanted a radical rethinking
of the Jewish faith and observance in the light of modern
knowledge, and he wanted Jews to consider afresh their relation
to Jesus and the Christian Gospel."[12]

The work before us represents that interest for, as indicated
above, it was not written merely as a scientific study but had,
not in addition to, but as its guiding motive, a more subjective
intention:

> "The object of these notes is by no means to make another
> commentary superfluous even for a Jewish reader. There
> are many points and difficulties in the Gospels about
> which my notes will give no explanation. . . . My main pur-
> pose has been to concentrate attention upon those passages
> in the Gospels which have religious value or interest for
> Jewish readers at the present time. . . . My point of view is

frankly that of a Jew, that is, of some one who stands outside of every form and phase of Christianity. . . . That Jesus did not literally fulfill the Old Testament conditions and characteristics of the 'Messiah' is obvious. Whether he fulfilled them in some higher and spiritual sense I have not discussed."[13]

Again: "My book does not pretend to learning. If it were not for my special point of view, I should have no justification to write upon the Gospels at all . . . If it be asked: 'Why then do you venture to throw your work at the public?' I can only reply that the peculiar point of view to which I have alluded has, I hope, made my book of some interest and use to a few persons, both within and without my religious community . . . This 'peculiar point of view' is that of a Liberal Jew who has not found his profound attachment to Liberal Judaism inconsistent either with a high appreciation of the lives and teachings of many of the ancient Rabbis . . . or with a similar high appreciation of the character and teachings of Jesus . . ."[14]

The particular and peculiar point of view from which Montefiore wrote this work is disclosed as well in a letter to Lucy Cohen written in August, 1906: ". . . I feel that by odd chance I am the only English Jew living who can approach the Gospels fairly impartially, and who *also* has time and inclination to write about them, and if only I were 15 per cent more learned and 80 per cent more able, I could really produce a good book. But in truth, alas, I am not fitted intellectually or spiritually for the job."[15]

The first edition, which he hoped would appear in 1910, actually came forth in 1909. A second edition "revised and partly rewritten" was published in 1927. Of it he wrote to Miss Cohen: "I have had some nice letters about the Gospels. I ought to prepare for a third edition I suppose, and correct all the mistakes and fill up all the gaps. I am not much fit for anything else." Apparently, his correspondent notes, she suggested in reply, "That he had exhausted the topic of the Synoptic Gospels." On August 5, 1927, Montefiore wrote, "I have a disagreeable feeling that you are very right about the Gospels, and yet I feel it with *great* reluctance."[16]

His insistence upon the point of view from which the book was written seems to have met with considerable resistance, for in a note on page 670 of Volume Two of the second edition, Montefiore explained: "I ought to have stated in my Preface that though my 'peculiar point of view' is that of a Liberal Jew, I, nevertheless, speak only for myself, and by no means as a representative of Liberal Judaism. I believe that I hold a higher view of the greatness and originality of the teaching of Jesus than is common among Liberal Jewish writers." That note is, indeed, filled with pathos for it was to the end that "a higher view of the greatness and originality of the teachings of Jesus" be recognized and accepted at least by those of like religious persuasion, that the work had been directed.

Montefiore's awareness of his "peculiar point of view" was wedded to a singular honesty. Thus the original plan for this work contemplated a third volume of critical notes by his friend Israel Abrahams, of whom he wrote:

> "Dr. Abrahams who always made the best of it for the Rabbis and brought out every possible grace and beauty that he could (of him it may be truly said that he wore his apologetics with a difference)."[17]

The project was not carried through as planned, but the material that was expected to go into the notes appeared in the two volumes of Abrahams' *Studies in Pharisaism and the Gospels.* (See Professor Morton Enslin's Prolegomenon to that work as it has appeared in this series.) A further note by Abrahams on *'Am ha'-Areç* did appear at the end of the second volume of the second edition. The same readiness to open his work to criticism is to be found in his last book, *A Rabbinic Anthology,* in which he collaborated with Herbert Loewe who described himself as "an Orthodox Jew . . . but not a fundamentalist."[18] Here each wrote an Introduction from his own point of view, and Loewe was invited to comment on Montefiore's interpretations of rabbinic texts when he felt less than justice had been done.

Montefiore argued in the Preface to the Gospels that for the Jew "the great interest or value of the Synoptic Gospels lies in the *teaching* ascribed to Jesus rather than in the personality or the life . . ."[19]

> ". . . the *teaching* of Jesus abides. The unprejudiced Jew, even remaining a Jew, can find bits of his teaching which go beyond O. T. teaching, or which, at any rate, bring out occasional utterances and teachings of the O. T. more clearly and fully."

In the next sentence, Montefiore discloses the particular nature of his "peculiar point of view", the touchstone of his entire approach to his subject:

> "Jesus links on to the Prophets and sometimes seems to go beyond them."[20]

Recognition of this ought not impair one's Jewish faith, but ought to be a source of delight, Montefiore argues. As to the question arising from a critical examination of the texts in which it is evident that many teachings ascribed to Jesus are indeed not his:

> ". . . the value of the teaching in the Synoptic Gospels does not really depend on whether it was said by Jesus or not . . . in any case, Jesus gave the impetus for the teaching of the Gospel as a whole. It can now be *regarded* as a whole and assessed as a whole. We can just speak of its aroma, its spirit, whether Jesus said everything which is ascribed to him or not."[21]

Thus the emphasis must be on the teachings found in the Gospels, without any real concern for their immediate connection with Jesus. Yet the Gospels are not merely a collection of teachings. "It is the combination of Hebrew and Greek, working on the basis of a great historic figure and genius of a religious enthusiasm and exaltation, and of growing needs and growing worship, which produced the Gospels . . ."[22] The person or personality of Jesus thus intrudes and remains a stumbling block or better yet, a source of embarrassment:

> "With the best will in the world, trying hard to peer through the mist and see the facts as they were, trying hard not to be prejudiced and prepossessed, I cannot see in the life of Jesus as recorded in Mark i-xiii. anything about which to be lost in marvelling admiration or adoration. The character revealed as far as *it is* revealed, appears undoubtedly strong and sweet, firm and tender, ardent and compassionate; but the evidence in Mark i-xiii. for regarding Jesus as the most wonderful and perfect character which ever existed seems to me to be lacking." [23]

But the rub is that, according to his own claim, the Gospels were produced on the basis not of the teachings but "of a great historic figure and genius." The teachings are integral, to be sure, but incidental to the central concern of the Gospels, the person of Jesus. The teachings, too, for Montefiore despite his disclaimer, must be related to a person, and indeed a particular type of person, a prophetic personality, if they are to carry the full import he assigns to them:

> "His freshness and originality, his power and confidence, his assurance of direct divine inspiration, are all points of resemblance between him and them [the prophets]."[24]

And it is this that provided him with "a higher point of view than that of the Rabbis."[25]

Of the teachings themselves, Montefiore wrote:

> "If Mark had been the only Gospel preserved to us, how much teaching of value would there be added to our Jewish

store? How far could we speak of a *new* teaching? (i. 27.)
I do not think we could, but then as far as Judaism is
concerned, I hold that even when we add Matthew to
Mark and Luke to Matthew, we have supplementary teachings of value, but nothing fundamentally new. Nevertheless, some things which we find in Mark are of great value.
There is first of all the revival of the old prophetic teaching,
the application of it to the needs and circumstances of
another day. Here we can gain something from the Sabbath stories, but far more from the great saying, so new
and so illuminative, and so entirely in the spirit of the
Prophets, 'Whatever enters into a man from without cannot make him unclean.' Then we have the doctrine of
service wedded to the doctrine of humility. 'If any man
would desire to be first of all, let him be last of all and
servant to all.' To which we may add, 'Whoever shall
not receive the Kingdom of God as a little child, shall
not enter it.' Using the teaching of Jesus for the highest
earthly life rather than in its primary and directly intended sense, we may find sayings of value in 'If thine eye
cause thee to stumble, pluck it out,' or 'How hard it is
to enter the Kingdom of Heaven,' but above all, 'If any
man would be a true follower' (of Jesus, or as we should
say, of God) 'let him deny himself.' And again, 'Whoever would save his life shall lose it.' Then we find points
of value in the doctrine of Faith, in the saying, 'To him
who has shall be given,' in the teaching about Divorce,
and in the saying *reflecting the practice,* 'The strong need
not the physician, but the sick: I came not to call the
righteous, but the sinners.' All this teaching can well be
added on, and wedded to, the fundamental commands of
the Pentateuch and the great primary doctrines of the
Prophets."[26]

Without the necessity of examining all of the passages here
referred to, Montefiore's crucial interest may be discerned
from his discussion of Mark 7.1-23: "This section is of profound significance and value; it raises questions of the deepest

importance. Indeed, from the point of view of Liberal Judaism it might be said that this section is the most important section of Mark, and that its salient and outstanding feature is verse 15. For here Jesus enunciates a doctrine which appears not only to be new and emancipating, but which seems to constitute one of of the two chief justifications or reasons for the main way in which Liberal Judaism looks at the old ceremonial law."[27]

What Montefiore is seeking here is, as it were, support for his rejection of the dietary regimen of traditional Judaism; but he wants a particular kind of support. The prophets said—

> "The true service of God is not ceremonial but moral . . . Just as the prophets upset the old ideas about the service of God, so here Jesus upsets the old ideas about clean and unclean. As the prophets moralized and inwardized men's ideas about the service of God so Jesus moralizes and in- wardizes men's ideas about clean and unclean."[28]

The rejection of dietary proscriptions must be attached to the prophetic tradition as Montefiore understood it, and the only way to do that is to attach Jesus to the prophetic tradition and suggest that his statement: "Whatever enters a man from without cannot make him unclean," is of the same order and intent as prophetic attacks upon the cultus. Montefiore devotes thirty- seven pages to his discussion of the passages, suggesting as a most radical interpretation: " . . . it may, indeed be argued that in verse 15 Jesus virtually abrogates a most definite and elaborate Pentateuchal law . . . . " Then retreating: "It can- not be assumed offhand that Jesus himself transgressed the diet- ary laws of Leviticus and Deuteronomy or even that he would have approved of his disciples transgressing them." But then, quoting Carpenter: "15 cuts athwart the whole scheme of diet- ary laws; and this principle, together with that of man's lord- ship over the Sabbath, seems to me to amount to a complete breach with the law on its ritual and institutional side." Finally, he wrote: "But it does not follow that Jesus recognized this 'cut' himself, or realized the fullness of the 'breach'. His prac- tice may not have squared with his theory."[29] Which, I am afraid, is a way of having it both ways at once. In his detailed analysis of the passage, Montefiore was clearly influenced by the form-critical approach in his analysis of the passage and recognized its many problems, yet he wrote:

> "However all these critical problems may be decided, it is hard to believe that 15 is anything less than a genuine saying of the historic Jesus. It is true that we cannot argue from the greatness of a saying to its authenticity. Some of the biggest things in the prophets are not authentic. But verse 15 is in every way characteristic of Jesus and of his teaching. There is no reason why he should *not* have said it, and much reason why he should. To doubt its authenticity seems scepticism run wild. And Fascher has made me feel that some of Bultmann's scepticism may be rightly so characterized."[30]

But Bultmann is not sceptical of verse 15. It is, he wrote in *The History of The Synoptic Tradition* (p. 74), a *mashal* (a proverb) exhibiting Jesus as a teacher of wisdom (not a prophet). Vv. 18b and 19 are taken as a commentary on v. 15 which Bultmann accepts as probably an authentic saying, given the meaning that commends it to Montefiore, by the early church. ". . . it is obvious that the section comes from the Palestinian Church, for it was there that the problem of the relation of the παράδοσις to the law was a living issue. . . ."[31]

This whole discussion discloses quite clearly Montefiore's *Tendenz,* for he was, as indicated above, most appreciative of Bultmann's approach:

> "The detailed and elaborate work of Bultmann in this connection seems little known or appreciated so far in England [He is writing in the mid 20's], but his investigations, like those of his fellow *Formgeschichtler,* are ultimately bound to have their effect. We shall not be able to say: 'From Q or from Mark; therefore early; therefore authentic.' The laws or methods by which sayings were collected, added or grouped together and attributed to Jesus will have to be considered; the sayings which are

probably due to the community will have to be more carefully separated from those which are probably due to himself; others may have to be regarded as either older than
Jesus, but ascribed to him, or given a Christian adaptation.
What is of purely Palestinian origin will have to be distinguished from what comes from early, but yet Hellenistic
Jewish communities which had become Christian, and so
on. . . . All these and many other matters are discussed
in Bultmann's book, and though his conclusions, as regards
the authenticity and the 'historicity' of many stories and
sayings, is much overdone, it is (as it seems to me) very
improbable that his work will leave things as they were
and remain without influence or effect."[32]

Yet here, where the problem is not the authenticity of the sayings that is called into question, but their meaning and function
apart from those imposed upon them in a construction of the
early church, Montefiore, because of his theological tendency,
had to find Bultmann guilty of a scepticism he did not exhibit.

It is illuminating to note at this point that although Schweitzer's *The Quest of the Historical Jesus* appeared in 1906, Montefiore did not mention it in either the first or second editions.
The reason seems obvious. Commenting on Mark xiii, 1-37,
he wrote:

"This apocalyptic oration as a whole is certainly unauthentic. Much of it is built up upon the familiar lines of Jewish
apocalypses from Daniel (164 B.C.E.) onward. It has very
slight interest for us today and little or no religious value.
Judaism freed itself of apocalyptic dreamings sooner than
Christianity, but both religions have long advanced beyond
them now. We may indeed argue that there is no reason
why Jesus should not have conceived of the future upon
the ordinary lines of the prevailing Jewish apocalyptic
teaching. Because people today dislike the fantastic doctrines and conceptions of the apocalyptic writers, that is
no reason why Jesus should not have shared them."[33]

The eschatological understanding of Jesus Schweitzer proposed stood in complete contradiction to Montefiore's interpretation of Jesus as a moralist in what he understood to be the prophetic mode.

If these introductory paragraphs appear to be "a sharp criticism of the great man", it must be emphasized that their intention is no more than to underscore Montefiore's self-disclosed and self-confessed "peculiar point of view", so that the volume not be misused. It is the very personal statement of a theological point of view that has taken the form of a commentary as the *Synoptic Gospels,* because the writer's understanding of the Gospels suggested this as a congenial way of expounding that position. The reason that this appeared congenial to the author was his conviction that his point of view required the acquisition by his community of the Synoptic Gospels as he understood them, in order more fully and richly to play a role in its contemporary society. Montefiore was convinced, wrote Bentwich, "that many English Jews felt spiritually akin to their Christian environment, and that Jews must come to terms with the Gospels. If not, they would remain, 'a creed in a corner.' "[34]

That the work at hand is more than this, that it represents a rich yield of scholarship, careful reading will at once disclose. But it is not something other than this. It is not a Jewish *Strack-Billerbeck,* although it often brings rabbinical materials and the modern discussion and interpretation of them to bear on the subject at hand. It curries no favor with its Christian readers and often turns its back on their theological interests, in favor of its own. It points to the prejudices directed against and misunderstandings of Judaism on the part of scholars of many shades of opinion, withholding no judgment when its seems called for. Yet, at the end, it must be understood for what it is, a party document, that party being a party of one. It gave rise to no followers, no school. Subsequent Jewish scholarship as it has dealt with Christianity and its Scriptures, has eddied around it, diverted not at all from its course. Lindeskog in his final chapter, *Die Bedeutung Jesu für das moderne Judentum,* was hard-pressed to find companions for Montefiore. At most he could quote Klausner's encomium: "If ever the day should come and this ethical code be stripped of its wrappings of miracles and mysticism, the Book of the Ethics of Jesus will be one of the choicest treasures in the literature of Israel for all times"; and refer to some sermons of Emil G. Hirsch that, he rightly apprehended, were chiefly apologetic.[35]

The Hebrew author Achad Ha'am (Asher Ginzberg) in his sharp rejoinder to the first edition of the book, "Judaism and The Gospels," translated into English and printed in *The Jewish Review* (I, 3, Sept. 1910), summed up the whole problem of Jewish scholarship's approach to Christianity:

> "The author is doubtless correct in saying that a Jewish commentary on the New Testament is needed at the present time (Introduction, pp. xvii, xviii, ci). Living in a Christian environment, we imbibe a culture in which many Christian ideas and sentiments are inwoven, and it is therefore necessary for us to know their source, so as to be able to distinguish between them and the universal elements of culture. But this Jewish commentary must be far removed from any polemical propagandist intention on one side or the other. Its sole object must be to *understand* thoroughly the teaching of the Gospels, to define with scientific accuracy its character, the foundations on which it rests, and the differences which distinguish it from Judaism. What is needed is not the 'scientific accuracy' of the Christian commentators . . . who set out with the preconceived idea that the teaching of the Gospels is superior to that of Judaism and use their 'science' merely to find details in support of their general belief. When a writer claims to be 'scientific', we must recognize above all that in the field of religion and morality it is impossible to set up a universal scientific criterion, by which to measure the different teachings, and to pronounce one superior to another. In this sphere everything is relative, and the judge brings to his task a subjective standard of his own, determined by his temperament, his education and his environment. We

Jews, being everywhere a minority, are always subject to various influences, which counteract and weaken each other; and we, therefore are possibly better able than others to understand objectively ideas which are not our own. Hence, it was indeed right that there should be a Jewish Commentary (not a Jewish panegyric) on the New Testament. Such a commentary might perhaps have enabled Jews of our author's stamp to recognize that it is possible to treat with seriousness and justice a religion which is strange to us, without shutting our eyes to the gulf which separates it from ourselves."

Much has happened since Achad Ha'am wrote those words and New Testament scholarship has undergone that critical change Montefiore recognized as coming, in his appreciation of Bultmann's contributions. Perhaps the newer phase of the problem is thus summed up in Lindeskog's concluding words:

"Nochmals müss aber betont werden, dass nicht nur das, was sich liberales Judentum nennt, dem Urheber der christlichen Religion Verständnis und positive Einschätzung entgegenzubringen vermag. Denn die notwendige Voraussetzung hierfür: der in die Schule der historish-kritischen Forschung gegangene Religionsliberalismus greift weit über die Grenzen des liberalen Judentum hinaus."[36]

Which may mean that the time for a Jewish commentary has come and gone.

LOU H. SILBERMAN

[1] Arbeiten und Mitteilungen aus dem neutestamentlichen Seminar zu Uppsala herausgegben von Anton Fridrichsen, VIII, (Uppsala, 1938).

[2] Lucy Cohen, *Some Recollections of Claude Goldsmid Montefiore 1858-1938*, (London: Faber and Faber) p. 228.

[3] *Ibid.*, p.185.

[4] C. G. Montefiore and H. Loewe, *A Rabbinic Anthology* (Phila.: Jewish Publication Society of America, 1960).

[5] *Ibid.*, p. xix.

[6] Cohen, *op. cit.*, p. 230.

[7] *Ibid.*, pp. 25, 26, 37, 38, 42.

[8] Norman Bentwich, *Claude Montefiore and His Tutor in Rabbinics: Founders of Liberal and Conservative Judaism,* The Sixth Montefiore Memorial Lecture (The University of Southampton, 1966), p. 11.

[9] *Ibid.*, p.4.

[10] *Ibid.*, p.5.

[11] *Apud* Bentwich, p.5.

[12] *Op. cit.*, p. 3.

[13] *The Synoptic Gospels,* I, 1-2.

[14] *Ibid.*, I, ix.

[15] Cohen, *op. cit.*, p. 77.

[16] *Ibid.*, pp.171,173.

[17] *Op.cit.*, I, 143.

[18] *Op. cit.*, p. iv.

[19] *Op. cit.*, p. xxiv.

[20] *Ibid.*, p. xxv.

[21] *Ibid.*, p. xxvi.

[22] *Ibid.*, p. xxix.

[23] *Ibid.*, p. 306.

[24] *Ibid.*, p. 123.

[25] *Ibid.*, p. 42.

[26] *Ibid.*, pp. 305-306.

[27] *Ibid.*, p. 130.

[28] *Ibid.*, pp. 130, 131.

[29] *Ibid.*, pp. 146, 147.

[30] *Ibid.*, pp. 132-133.

[31] Rudolph Bultmann, *The History of the Synoptic Tradition,* trans. by John Marsh (New York and Evanston: Harper and Row, Publishers, 1963).

[32] *Op. cit.*, I, lvi-lvii.

[33] *Ibid.*, p. 296.

[34] *Op. cit.*, p. 11.

[35] *Op. cit.*, pp. 315-321.

[36] *Ibid.*, p. 321.

PREFACE

THE first edition of this Commentary was published in 1909, and it has been out of print for many years. The second edition has been carefully revised and considerably changed. I have omitted, on the one hand, and added, on the other. Much has been written about the Synoptic Gospels in the last seventeen years ; I have read, and profited by, a fair amount of this fresh material, and have made many quotations from books and articles by English, French, and German scholars. To find room for these, many of the quotations given in the first edition have been omitted. In my first edition these numerous quotations (from authorities who often differ widely from one another in their general conclusions and point of view, as also in their interpretations of particular passages) were criticised by some friends and reviewers, though praised by others. I have not seen my way to dispense with them, though perhaps they are now rather less numerous than before, and are drawn from a wider range of scholars. Most, but not all, of the French and German quotations have been translated into English.

In the earlier edition I printed a translation of each Gospel as a whole, repeating the translation piecemeal before each section of the Commentary. I have omitted the first translation in this edition, so that, although the Introduction and Commentary are somewhat extended, the total number of pages remains almost exactly the same. The character of the translation is set forth at the opening of § 2 of the Introduction. The text presupposed by the translation is usually the text which lies behind the R.V. : where that text has been departed from, it is indicated in the Commentary. I regret that I have been unable to say anything about textual history or criticism. My purpose was too restricted, the demands upon my space too great, and my own knowledge too meagre. But the student can easily obtain information on all textual problems, as on the history of the text, from many admirable works.

It was a very great disappointment to me (as I know it was also to many others) that the Additional Notes, some sixty in number, which my dear friend, the late Dr. Israel Abrahams, for many years Reader in Talmudic and Rabbinic Literature in the University of Cambridge, had intended to write, were never completed. These Notes were to have formed the third volume of the Commentary. I am well aware how many persons looked forward, very justifiably, to this volume as sure to prove much the most valuable section of the whole. For various reasons Dr. Abrahams found himself unable to write most of the notes ; some of them, with other important essays and material, were published separately as *Studies in Pharisaism and the Gospels* (First Series, 1917 ; Second Series, 1924), a work to which I constantly refer in the course of my Commentary. Dr. Abrahams knew how sad I felt that he was unavoidably prevented from carrying out his original intention, and in order that my second edition should, at all events, contain something from his pen, he wrote for me, when already ill, and at considerable sacrifice, an important essay upon that very obscure person, the ʿAm ha-ʾAreç. He gave me the MS. not many months before his death (October 1925), and he asked that I should return it to him for revision just before it was wanted for press. This essay, which is printed at the end of Vol. II., was therefore never revised by its author. Mr. Herbert Loewe, of St. Catharine's College, Cambridge, and Exeter College, Oxford, Lecturer in Rabbinic Hebrew, University of Oxford, has, at my request, most kindly looked through the MS., corrected any obvious slips or errors, and verified, and, where needful, corrected, all the references. He has also corrected the proof. I am deeply indebted to him for this labour, though I know that, because of his affection and admiration for Dr. Abrahams, it has been to him a labour of love.

I would like to mention the name of another great scholar who has died since the first edition of this book was published—Dr. Hastings Rashdall, late Dean of Carlisle. I had hoped to have thanked him in my Preface for the references to, and criticisms of, my work in his book entitled *Conscience and Christ*, and to have said how deeply I appreciated them, and how I had profited by them. How fair, how clear, how serene, those criticisms are ! I valued them the more as coming from one with whom, though far above me in learning and ability, I was, as regards general outlook and theological position, in such prevailing sympathy and agreement.

At an early stage of the first edition of my book, the Rev. Dr. Estlin Carpenter, for many years the Principal of Manchester College, Oxford, was good enough to read through a considerable portion of the Commentary. I owe a great deal to his suggestions, and I ventured to include (without asking his permission) some of the observations which he pencilled upon the margin of the paper into the body of my work. In most cases I have added his name.

My book does not pretend to learning. If it were not for my special point of view, I should have no justification to write upon the Gospels at all, and in any case I am keenly conscious of my own temerity and inadequacies. If it be asked : ' Why then do you venture to throw your work at the public ? ', I can only reply that the peculiar point of view to which I have alluded has, I hope, made my book of some interest and use to a few persons, both within and without my own religious community, and will, I hope, make it of some use and interest, in its new and revised form, to a few others.

This ' peculiar point of view ' is that of a Liberal Jew, who has not found his profound attachment to Liberal Judaism inconsistent either with a high appreciation of the lives and the teachings of many of the ancient Rabbis, on the one hand, or with a similar high appreciation of the character and teaching of Jesus, upon the other. It is also the point of one who, while well aware that he must often have fallen far below his ideal, has yet honestly striven to place himself ' above the facts ', and not to mind or care whether the most impartial study which he could give to those facts drove him to praise or criticise, admire or controvert, either the teaching of the Rabbis or that of, or ascribed to, Jesus. It is the point of view, as I hope, of reverence and freedom. And it is this combination of reverence and freedom which I owe to, and have learnt from, Liberal Judaism. For upon this combination it sets high store.

It hardly needs saying how dependent I am upon the labours and researches of the great scholars who have given their lives to Biblical or New Testament study. The names and the books of those to whom I have most frequently gone for help are mentioned in the Commentary or Introduction. In my first edition I quoted most often from Loisy, Wellhausen, and Johannes Weiss. In this new edition I still frequently quote from these distinguished scholars (two of whom have now passed away), but I also frequently quote from others whose books and articles have been published since

1908 or 1909. I would especially wish to mention the names of
Streeter, Burkitt, and Lake among English scholars, and of Bultmann from Germany. Canon Streeter's *Four Gospels*, on the one
side, and Bultmann's *Geschichte der synoptischen Tradition*, upon
the other, seem to me the two most important and valuable works
upon the Gospels which have appeared in the last seventeen years.
The conclusions of neither of these two scholars will, I should
imagine, in their totality, stand the test of time, but the work of
neither of them can rightly be neglected to-day. It is, I admit,
presumptuous of me to differ from so profound and brilliant a
scholar as Professor Burkitt, but I confess I can hardly share his
confidence that ' in another fifty years ' the critical study of the
Gospels ' will have reached its natural conclusion : we shall have
found out all that the documents can show us, we shall have learnt
with what precautions and what enrichments we should read the
Gospel according to St. Mark if we wish to gain an historical view.
The specialists, the antiquaries, will have done their work, and we
shall be able, to a certain extent, to know Christ after the flesh.'
(*An Outline of Christianity*, ed. Peake and Parsons, N.D., Vol. IV.
p. 342.) Besides other things, this apparently means that everybody will accept the general conclusions about Mark and the two
other Evangelists which Professor Burkitt and Canon Streeter put
forward so ably and eloquently to-day. Bultmann, Loisy, Dibelius,
or even Klostermann, will be relegated to the outer darkness and
forgotten. Well, another generation will see : for myself, I doubt it.

My manuscript was sent to the printers in June 1926, and several
books which have appeared since that date (*e.g.* Dr. Easton's *Gospel
according to St. Luke*, Mr. Gardner Smith's *The Narratives of the
Resurrection*, and Professor Bultmann's *Jesus*) I have been unable
to make use of. Not that by this remark I would imply that, up
to the date mentioned, I had read all that I might or should have
read bearing upon my subject. I was compelled, or deliberately
chose, to make a selection, and I must admit that I have chiefly
neglected the works of many scholars who champion an older, less
' critical,' and more orthodox point of view.

The Index in this second edition is the work of my old friend,
Mrs. McArthur. I owe her very cordial thanks.

C. G. M.

January 1927.

LIST OF BOOKS QUOTED FREQUENTLY OR BY ABBREVIATIONS

Abrahams (I.). Studies in Pharisaism and the Gospels. First Series (1917); Second Series (1924). Quoted as ' Abrahams, Studies, I.' or ' II.'

Allen (W. C.). A Critical and Exegetical Commentary on the Gospel according to S. Matthew. (1907.) Quoted as ' Allen.'

Bacon (Benjamin W.). (1) The Beginnings of Gospel Story. (1909.) Quoted as ' Gospel Story.' (2) The Gospel of Mark : its Composition and Date. (1925.)

Bartlet (J. Vernon). S. Mark, in ' Century Bible.' (1922.) Quoted as ' Bartlet.'

Beginnings of Christianity, The : Part I. The Acts of the Apostles: Vol. I. Prolegomena I. (1920); Vol. II. Prolegomena II. (1922), edited by F. J. Foakes-Jackson and Kirsopp Lake. Quoted as ' Beginnings.'

Bertram (G.). Die Leidensgeschichte Jesu und der Christuskult. (1922.) Quoted as ' Bertram.'

Bousset (Wilhelm). Kyrios Christos. 2nd ed. (1921.) Quoted as 'Bousset.'

Box (G. H.). S. Matthew, in ' Century Bible.' (1922.) Quoted as ' Box.'

Bultmann (Rudolf). Die Geschichte der synoptischen Tradition. (1921.) Quoted as ' Bultmann.'

Burkitt (F. Crawford). (1) The Gospel History and its Transmission. 4th impression. (1920.) Quoted as ' Burkitt, Gospel History.'
(2) Christian Beginnings. (1924.) Quoted as ' Burkitt, Beginnings,' or as ' Christian Beginnings.'

Burney (F. F.). The Poetry of our Lord. (1925.) Quoted as ' Burney.'

Cadman (W. H.). The Last Journey of Jesus to Jerusalem. (1923.) Quoted as ' Cadman.'

Carpenter (J. Estlin). The First Three Gospels ; their Origin and Relations. 4th ed. (1906.) Quoted as ' Carpenter.'

Clemen (Carl). Religionsgeschichtliche Erklärung des Neuen Testaments. 2nd ed. (1924.) Quoted as ' Clemen.'

Dalman (Gustaf). (1) Die Worte Jesu. (1898.) (The Words of Jesus, translated by D. M. Kay, 1902.)
(2) Jesu-Jeschua (1922).

Deissmann (Adolf). Licht vom Osten. 4th ed. (1923.) Quoted as ' Deissmann.'

Dibelius (Martin). (1) Die Formgeschichte des Evangeliums. (1919.) Quoted as ' Dibelius.'

(2) Die urchristliche Überlieferung von Johannes dem Täufer. (1911.)

Fiebig (Paul). (1) Jesu Bergpredigt. (1924.)

(2) Der Erzählungstil der Evangelien. (1925.)

(3) Die Gleichnisreden Jesu im Lichte der rabbinischen Gleichnisse des neutestamentlichen Zeitalters. (1912.)

(4) Jüdische Wundergeschichten des neutestamentlichen Zeitalters. (1911.)

von Gall (August). Basileia tou Theou : eine religionsgeschichtliche Studie zur vorkirchlichen Eschatologie. (1926.)

Goguel (M.). Introduction au Nouveau Testament. Vol. 1. Les Évangiles Synoptiques. (1923.) Quoted as ' Goguel.'

Gould (N.). A Critical and Exegetical Commentary on the Gospel according to S. Mark. (1901.) Quoted as ' Gould.'

Harnack (Adolf von). (1) Sprüche und Reden Jesu. (1907.) (The Sayings of Jesus, translated by J. R. Wilkinson, 1908.) Quoted as ' Harnack.'

(2) Die Entstehung des Neuen Testaments. (1914.)

(3) Neue Untersuchungen zur Apostelgeschichte und zur Abfassungs-zeit der synoptischen Evangelien. (1911.) (The Date of the Acts and of the Synoptic Gospels, translated by J. R. Wilkinson, 1911.)

(4) Lukas der Arzt. (1906.)

(5) Entstehung und Entwickelung der Kirchenverfassung und des Kirchenrechts in den zwei ersten Jahrhunderten. (1910.) (The Constitution and Law of the Church in the first two Centuries, translated by F. L. Pogson, 1910.)

(6) Erforschtes und Erlebtes. (1923.) (Many articles by Harnack are referred to under their full titles.)

Heinrici (C. F. Georg). Die Bergpredigt begriffsgeschichtlich untersucht, in Beiträge zur Geschichte und Erklärung des Neuen Testamentes. (1905.) Quoted as ' Heinrici.'

Holtzmann (H. J.). (1) Die Synoptiker, in the ' Hand-Commentar zum Neuen Testament. · 3rd ed. (1901.) Quoted as ' Holtzmann.'

(2) Neutestamentliche Theologie. 2nd ed. Vol. 1. (1911.)

Husband (R. W.). The Prosecution of Jesus : its Date, History, and Legality. (1916.) Quoted as ' Husband.'

Jülicher (Adolf). Einleitung in das Neue Testament. 5th ed. (1906.) Quoted as ' Jülicher.'.

Klausner (Joseph). Jesus of Nazareth: His Life, Times, and Teaching. Translated from the Hebrew by Herbert Danby. (1925.) Quoted as 'Klausner.'

Klostermann (Erich). Markus. 1st ed. (1907); 2nd ed. (1926); Matthäus (1909); Lukas (1919), in the 'Handbuch zum Neuen Testament.' Quoted as 'Klostermann' or as 'Kl.'

Knopf (Rudolf). Einführung in das Neue Testament. (1913.) Quoted as 'Knopf.'

Lake (Kirsopp). (1) Landmarks in the History of Early Christianity. (1920.)
    (2) The Stewardship of Faith. (1915.)
    (3) The Historical Evidence for the Resurrection of Jesus Christ. (1907.) Quoted as 'Lake.'

Loisy (Alfred). (1) Les Évangiles Synoptiques. (1907.) 2 vols. Quoted as E.S.
    (2) L'Évangile selon Marc. (1912.)
    (3) L'Évangile selon Luc. (1924.) Quoted as 'Luc.'

McNeile (Alan H.). The Gospel according to S. Matthew. (1915.) Quoted as 'McNeile.'

Marriott (Horace). The Sermon on the Mount. (1925.) Quoted as 'Marriott.'

Menzies (A.). The Earliest Gospel (A Commentary on Mark). (1901.) Quoted as 'Menzies.'

Merx (Adelbert). Die vier kanonischen Evangelien. (1902, 1905.) Quoted as 'Merx.'

Meyer (Eduard). Ursprung und Anfänge des Christentums. 3 vols. (1921.) Quoted as 'Meyer.' Where no vol. is mentioned, the reference is to Vol. 1.

Moffatt (James). (1) An Introduction to the Literature of the New Testament. 3rd ed. (1918.)
    (2) The New Testament: A New Translation. (1922.)

Norden (Eduard). (1) Agnostos Theos. (1913.) Quoted as 'Norden.'
    (2) Die Geburt des Kindes. (1924.)

Plummer (A.). A Critical and Exegetical Commentary on the Gospel according to S. Luke. 4th ed. (1901.) Quoted as 'Plummer.'

Ragg (Lonsdale). S. Luke. (1922.) Quoted as 'Ragg.'

Rashdall (Hastings). Conscience and Christ. (1916.)

Rawlinson (A. E. J.). S. Mark. (1925.) Quoted as 'Rawlinson.'

Reitzenstein (R.).   (1) Das iranische Erlösungsmysterium.   (1921.)

   (2) Das mandäische Buch des Herrn der Grösse und die Evangelien-überlieferung.   (1919.)

Schmidt (Karl Ludwig).   Der Rahmen der Geschichte Jesu.   (1919.)   Quoted as ' Schmidt.'

Strack (H.) und Billerbeck (P.).   Kommentar zum Neuen Testament aus Talmud und Midrasch.   Vol. I.   Matthäus.   (1922) ; Vol. II.   Markus, Lukas, etc.   (1924.)   Quoted as ' S.-B.'

Streeter (B. H.).   The Four Gospels : A Study of Origins.   (1924.)   Quoted as ' Streeter.'

Swete (H. B.).   The Gospel according to S. Mark.   2nd ed.   (1908.)   Quoted as ' Swete.'

Taylor (Vincent).   Behind the Third Gospel : A Study of the Proto-Luke Hypothesis.   (1926.)   Quoted as ' Taylor.'

Weiss (J.).   (1) Die Schriften des Neuen Testaments übersetzt und ... erklärt.   Vol. I.   Die drei älteren Evangelien.   3rd ed.   (1917.)   Quoted as ' J. Weiss.'

   (2) Das Urchristentum.   (1917.)

Wellhausen (Julius).   (1) Das Evangelium Marci.   1st ed. (1903), 2nd ed. (1909).

   (2) Das Evangelium Matthaei.   1st ed. (1904), 2nd ed. (1914).

   (3) Das Evangelium Lucae.   (1904.)

   (4) Einleitung in die drei ersten Evangelien.   1st ed. (1905), 2nd ed. (1911).   Quoted as ' Wellhausen ' or as ' W.'   ' Einleitung ' added where necessary.

Wendland (Paul).   Die hellenistisch-römische Kultur und die urchristlichen Literaturformen, in the ' Handbuch zum Neuen Testament.'   2nd ed. (1912.)   Quoted as ' Wendland.'

Werner (Martin).   Der Einfluss Paulinischer Theologie im Markusevangelium. (1923.)   Quoted as ' Werner.'

Wernle (Paul).   The Sources of our Knowledge of the Life of Jesus.   Translated by E. Lummis.   (1907.)   Quoted as ' Wernle.'

Weymouth (R. F.).   The New Testament in Modern Speech.   4th ed.   (1924.)

TABLE OF CONTENTS

VOL. I.

PROLEGOMENON (pp. 1-18).

INTRODUCTION (pp. xix—cxlvi).

COMMENTARY (WITH TRANSLATION) UPON THE GOSPEL ACCORDING
TO MARK (pp. 1—411).

INTRODUCTION

§ 1. *Character of the work : the Jews and the Gospels : the Jewish point of view.*

The task which I set before myself in this book is, I am fully aware, far too great for my narrow learning and capacities, yet it is one which so urgently needs doing that I have ventured to make a small beginning towards its accomplishment.

The book is fragmentary and tentative. A Jewish commentary to the entire New Testament is required, and here I have only given a commentary upon a portion. Moreover, it is fragmentary and tentative for other reasons as well. If I had waited for several more years I might have gained much fresh knowledge, and modified many opinions here expressed. But it seemed best to wait no longer. Life is uncertain, and other duties make the hours which can be given to study few, and sometimes even far between.

The book is also tentative because I am in many respects a pioneer. For of Jewish exposition of the Gospels there has been little. Endless Christian commentaries exist, written from many different points of view, with great learning and splendid patience, but Jewish commentaries can hardly be said to exist at all. Jewish scholars have usually taken up an attitude towards the New Testament, and more especially towards the Gospels, which does not lend itself to impartiality. It has not been a very fruitful and light-giving attitude. A main effort has been to show that to various admittedly admirable sayings of Jesus reported in the Gospels there are excellent parallels in the Old Testament or the Rabbinical writings. An atomistic treatment has usually been adopted. The teaching of Jesus has not been much discussed and appraised as a whole. And where it has been so discussed, the line has been rather to depreciate or to cheapen. Jewish writers have looked either for parallels or for defects. Considering what Judaism and the Jews have had to suffer at Christian hands, this Jewish treatment of the Gospels is not astonishing. No wonder that the Jews should show some injustice towards the literary origins of a religion from the adherents of which they have suffered such gross and terrible wrongs. No wonder that they should express some disdain at this supposed superior and superfine teaching of love which, so far as they are concerned, has so generally proved itself a religion of violence, cruelty, and hate. No wonder that they should desire to defend the excellence of their own religious writings and of their own religion, which have been so constantly depreciated and misunderstood by Christian writers. All this is quite human, quite natural.

It may be added that till recent times it was scarcely possible for Jews to dissociate the Christian claim that Jesus lived an exceptional life, and that his teaching was uniquely great and original, from the further Christian claim that he was divine, or indeed that he was God. It was the divinity of Jesus that was for Jews the true stumblingblock to any scientific estimate of his teaching. If all Christians had been Unitarians from the first, a drawing together and a good understanding between Jew and Christian as regards the place of Jesus in the history of Judaism and of religion would have been far easier. The objections to Jesus as a heretic, or as an iconoclast, or as a critic of the Law, would not have been so insuperably difficult. Moreover, for many centuries, to say publicly that Jesus was a good man and a fine teacher, but not divine, was exceedingly dangerous. It meant the stake or the sword. Hence to keep complete silence was much easier, and this negative attitude gradually became extremely general. And when the danger of speech was removed, the old objections and stumblingblocks were still in force.

Yet in England the time has come when it is right and possible for a Jew to look at the Gospels in a more historical, comprehensive, and impartial spirit. This at all events is my aim, and though I am very deficient in learning, the circumstances of my education, environment, and life, perhaps too the 'cross bench' cast of mind with which I chanced to be born, have given me some advantages for its partial attainment.

I do not want to depreciate the Rabbis or their teaching, but I have no desire unduly to exalt them. And at the same time I do not want to depreciate Jesus or unduly to exalt him. It may sometimes be necessary to indicate parallels or contrasts, but the object which I have set before myself is not to find either the one or the other. So far as I can, I am anxious to get at the facts, and to let them speak for themselves ; to look at things as they really are.

Yet I know that one cannot get rid of one's upbringing, one's origin, and one's own peculiar point of view. I have no doubt that a Buddhist or Mohammedan critic would be able to detect in my book many a prepossession and a prejudice. Yet that I shall seem to Jewish critics too Christian, and to Christian critics too Jewish is, I trust, likely, and is to me a source of some hope that now and then I may have said the truth.

I also realize that the scientific or historical character of the book is spoiled, as it were *ab initio*, by the fact that it has a by no means purely scientific object. The book has been mainly written for Jewish readers, though I fear it is not probable that many will read it. It has turned out somewhat too long and too dull. It is, however, mainly written for Jewish readers, though I hope that a few Christian readers may find some of its passages not without a certain interest.

It seems to me (for reasons into which I cannot here enter) that it is of great importance for Jews to understand and appreciate aright the life and teaching of Jesus. What should be the right relation of Judaism to that teaching? What place should Jesus and his teaching take or fill in the religion of ' his own people ' to-day? What should be the place of the New Testament in Jewish eyes and for the Jewish religion? To find the due and proper answer to these questions seems to me one of the most important duties which lie before modern, and especially before liberal, Judaism. Up to now, the work has been hardly tackled at all, at least not to any serious or profitable purpose. And this is another reason why my own book is tentative. For under such circumstances, when a man is not following in a well-beaten path, it is not likely that he, in his loneliness, will make much progress. I am not so conceited or silly as not to realize this. Not only is my own book but a commentary upon one small piece (though the most important piece) of the New Testament, but it is a mere temporary beginning, a provisional contribution. To find the long-delayed answers to so large a problem one man will not suffice, or one generation.

I shall be content if I have contributed a little material and a few unsystematic suggestions towards the right and final answer —if indeed a final answer there can ever be. This commentary upon the Synoptic Gospels does not contain (it is not its aim) any systematic presentation of the life and teaching of Jesus, or any systematic discussion of the relation of that life and teaching to modern Judaism. It deals with the various points as they arise in their place in the narrative, and it deals with them, moreover, very often in a somewhat halting and undecided way.

For this is one more reason why my book is tentative. To several of the problems connected with the life of Jesus, and to some connected with his teaching, I myself, with the material at our command, do not, so far, see my way to any clean-cut and decisive replies. Thus, when I do not feel sure, I prefer to express my uncertainty. I have freely quoted from the works of great scholars and distinguished authorities. The reader will, at all events, hear what *they* think, and perhaps he will judge between them more rapidly or confidently than I, so far, have been able to do. The quotations are almost all from the works of great Christian scholars, German, French, and English. Though I have, as it were, sat at the feet of these scholars, and learned from them a very great deal, I have not hesitated to point out where, from my Jewish point of view, they seem to me prejudiced and therefore inaccurate, or when they seem ignorant of matters about which a more intimate knowledge of Jewish thought, and a more intimate experience of Jewish life, can bring correction.

That my own book may be soon superseded by another book from a Jewish pen which will be more learned, more impartial, and more conclusive than mine, I earnestly hope. Meanwhile even provisional books and provisional suggestions may have their temporary uses. Such, I hope, may be the case with mine. If its readers will judge it as a whole, they will judge it as it asks to be judged.

§ 2. *Contents of the work : the Synoptic Gospels : origin and meaning of the word* synoptic.

My work consists of a translation of, and a commentary upon, the first three Gospels—Matthew, Mark, and Luke, or according to the order in which they are here placed—Mark, Matthew, and Luke. The translation is based upon the Authorized Version. I have, however, made many changes, mainly in order to obtain greater accuracy. Sometimes the variation is due to the fact that a better and earlier Greek text can now be obtained than was known to the translators of King James's Version or to their predecessors. Occasionally the changes are due to the omission of an archaism. (I fancy that many Jewish readers coming to the Authorized Version of the New Testament for the first time would suppose that John the Baptist's head was brought to Herod upon a horse.) I have, however, not sought to produce a consistently modern version, though I have derived help and benefit from a frequent consultation of Dr. Moffatt's and of Dr. Weymouth's interesting translations.

The first three Gospels are frequently called the Synoptic Gospels, because ' they are all constructed on a common plan, and from first to last, amid minor differences, the teaching and work of Jesus are presented from the same general point of view '

(Carpenter, *First Three Gospels*, p. 7). The use of the word Synoptic as applied to the first three Gospels is due to J. J. Griesbach, a German theologian of the eighteenth century. In 1774 he published the first part of a new edition of the ' historical books of the New Testament,' containing ' a *synopsis* of the Gospels of Matthew, Mark, and Luke.' In his preface (p. iv) he states that the ordinary editions of the Gospels are unsuited to students. ' For,' says he—and as not one person in a thousand is likely to look up Griesbach's book, his actual words (translated from the Latin) are worth quoting—' in the first place, if Matthew, Mark, and Luke are commented on one by one in the order in which they follow one another, the frequent repetitions of narratives recorded by two of them, or by all three, steal away too large a portion of our small span of time without any corresponding advantage. Hence it seemed worth while to construct a sort of *synopsis* of these three Gospels, in which the parts common to all three, or to two of them, should be put side by side in such a way that the interpretation of one Evangelist should serve to make the rest intelligible, or at least leave but a few points over for explanation. Indeed one may hope that a *synopsis* of this kind will contain several advantages.' There had been harmonies of the Gospels compiled before for apologetic purposes. Griesbach is careful to point out that his new *synopsis* is not one of these. Later commentators on the basis of what Griesbach had done, used the adjective *synoptic* to characterize those first three Gospels of which it was possible and useful to form a *synopsis*. I have not, however, discovered who was the first man to do this. Perhaps I should add for those of my readers who know no Greek that *sun* (σύν) in Greek means ' with ' and *opsis* (ὄψις) means ' look, appearance, sight.' Hence *sunopsis* (σύνοψις) means ' a seeing together, a general view.' The adjectives *sunoptos* (σύνοπτος), ' that can be seen at a glance,' and *sunoptikos* (συνοπτικός), ' seeing the whole together,' are both used by good Greek writers.

It will, therefore, be noticed that of the four Gospels this book only includes three. The fourth, the Gospel of John, is omitted. The reason is that, whilst the first three Gospels treat their subject from this common point of view and arrangement, the fourth is different in both. It has a different conception of Jesus, and tells in many respects a different history. The words which it puts into Jesus's mouth are peculiar and special. Moreover, this fourth Gospel is less historic than the first three ; it gives ' an *interpretation* of the person and work of Jesus rather than a record of his words and deeds ' (*First Three Gospels*, p. 9). Notable, great, and important as this Gospel is, it can—and indeed must—be studied by itself, and not together or in conjunction with the first, the allied, three. Therefore it forms no part of the present more limited undertaking. For that undertaking, though limited, is yet sufficiently, and more than sufficiently, arduous, intricate, and obscure.

§ 3. *Reasons for brevity of much of this Introduction.*

The questions connected with the origins, the form, the sources, and the dates of the Gospels are many and complicated. In Moffatt's *Introduction to the Literature of the New Testament* the sections dealing with the Synoptic Gospels take up some ninety-five closely printed pages. And yet Moffatt's book is only a summary : the ninety-five pages are just one bit of a much larger whole. On account of my special point of view I can be exceedingly brief. For many matters, which in themselves, as critical or literary problems, are delightfully interesting, are not for me of any great moment. For instance, whether the Gospel of Mark was written a little before A.D. 70 or ten or twelve years after ; whether it was written in one jet just as we have it now by one hand from i. 1 to xvi. 8, or whether it has suffered additions and interpolations ; whether its sources were written or only oral, or both written and oral ; whether the written sources, if any, were composed in Aramaic ; what sorts of compositions (in length, in character) these sources were : all this, though very interesting, and though, for the complete exposition of Mark and of ' the Synoptic problem,' very necessary to discuss, and, so far as one can, to settle, is not of first importance for me. I may even go further. A burning question as regards Mark is its relation to eyewitnesses of the life and ministry of Jesus, and more especially to one eyewitness, the apostle Simon Peter. Is Mark, or how far is Mark, the direct and immediate record of statements made by word of mouth to the writer by Peter and other contemporaries ? Even this question, which seems so vital and so overwhelmingly interesting and important, is not for my purpose *quite* so important and interesting as it seems.

For Jews—so long as they are and remain Jews (*i.e.* members of the Jewish faith)—the great interest or value of the Synoptic Gospels lies in the *teaching* ascribed to Jesus rather than in the personality or the life. We persist in separating the one from the other, whereas to Christians they form a unity, a whole. From his childhood upwards the Jew's highest conceptions of goodness and God have never been associated with Jesus. These conceptions may have been due to an idealization of O.T. teaching, or of Rabbinic teaching, or of both. Some might argue (whether wrongly or rightly) that they are partly due to an unconscious absorption and adoption of Christian and Gospel teaching. But, consciously and deliberately, his highest conceptions of goodness and God have been ever presented to the Jew, whether the orthodox or the liberal Jew, as wholly and characteristically Jewish. Moreover, he has had it ingrained into him that there need and can be nothing— no mediator, no divine man—between himself and God. The position of Jesus, the place he fills, even in Unitarian Christianity, is impossible for the Jew, for two reasons which, at first sight, may seem somewhat irreconcilable with each other. God is too ' far ' ; God is too ' near.' To make Jesus as ' divine ' as Christians make him seems to the Jew presumptuous and out of the question. Man is man, he says ; God is God. The best man is infinitely removed from the perfect goodness of God, and the fullness of the divine righteousness can be revealed in no man's life. On the other hand, God is so near that there is no *room*, as well as no *need*, for a *tertium quid* between man and God. The Jew, so long as he is and remains a Jew, simply cannot believe that any man was ever endowed with the fullness of every conceivable moral excel- lence—that any man was ever wholly sinless, and conscious of his sinlessness, the more perfect because of this consciousness, the acme and cream of goodness and love. The Jew simply cannot believe in such a being, on the one hand, and he has no room or place for him, upon the other. Jesus has not introduced the Jews to God in their childhood ; they do not require him in order to get to God in their manhood.

But the *teaching* of Jesus abides. The unprejudiced Jew, even remaining a Jew, can find bits of his teaching which go beyond O.T. teaching, or which, at any rate, bring out occasional utterances and teachings of the O.T. more clearly and fully. Jesus links on to the Prophets, and sometimes seems to go beyond them. Let us imagine that the writings of a new Hebrew prophet, a con- temporary, say, of Isaiah or Jeremiah, were brought to light. The Jewish position would not be changed, but Jews would be delighted to obtain some fresh teachings and sayings of beauty and value, and even of originality, to add to those which they already possess. So it is, or so it can be, as regards Jesus and the Gospel. But the Christian, even the Unitarian Christian, has received his highest conceptions of God and righteousness through Jesus. To the Christian, alike in his teaching and in his personality and life, Jesus reveals God. To the Christian, even to the Unitarian Christian, the N.T. is the book which tells him most truly and fully about goodness and God, and within the N.T. it is the Gospels which tell him best of all. He fits in Jesus with his purest thoughts of God ; Jesus brings God near to him. Whereas, to the Jews, Jesus—or any man—would be in their way in their relations with, and in their approaches to, God, to the Christian, even to the

Unitarian Christian, Jesus smooths the way to God and shortens it. He *is* the way. Without Jesus—if that fatality could for a moment be conceived—God, even to the Unitarian Christian, would be more distant and more dim ; without Jesus, God, to the Jew, would be no less near and no less bright.

Again, the value of the teaching in the Synoptic Gospels does not really depend on whether it was said by Jesus or not. No doubt, if you could *prove* that Peter told Mark in Aramaic every word of chapter vii., and that Mark wrote it all down in Greek, the likelihood that Mark vii. 15 was actually said by Jesus would be immensely increased. But the value or the truth of the saying would not be increased. It would remain as before. The magnificence of the teaching in Matt. xxv. 40 remains the same whether Jesus said it or did not ; the hatefulness of the teaching in Matt. xxv. 33, 41, 46 remains the same likewise. Moreover, in any case, Jesus gave the impetus for the teaching of the Gospel as a whole. It can now be *regarded* as a whole and assessed as a whole. We can just speak of its aroma, its spirit, whether Jesus said everything which is ascribed to him or not.

And there is something more. The exact truth, or exact measure of truth, in the stories about the life and death of Jesus does not, from one point of view, matter so much to us, or affect us so much, as it would have affected our ancestors. To them, whether Jew or Christian, it was often a question of *all* true or *all* false. To us there are degrees, and even kinds, of truth. I am thinking more especially of the miracles. We no longer believe in miracles in the old sense of the word. They do not worry us one way or the other. And several of the healing miracles of the Gospel story seem to us both non-miraculous and yet—in a greater or less degree—quite true. Again, we know how quickly miraculous stories get produced and circulated even in modern times. Thus, for us, it does not much matter whether the transfiguration, or the miraculous feeding, or the walking on the water, was reported by an eyewitness or no. We should not believe in the stories as records of objective facts any the more. Meyer, for example, in his *Ursprung und Anfang des Christentums*, regards much of Mark as the direct record of an eyewitness, including many of the miracles ; but he does not *believe* in the miracles (in the old-fashioned sense of the words ' believe ' and ' miracles ') any the more. He compares them with the miracles of the Mormons ! Thus whether—to put it concretely—Streeter is right in his believing conservatism, or Bultmann in his sceptical radicalism, is not, from my special point of view, of such overpowering importance. It *is* important, it *is* interesting ; but it is not of the *greatest* importance and interest of *all*. For what, for my present purpose and for my present book, is of the greatest interest and importance of all is the teaching. And the value of the teaching remains the same whether Bultmann and Dibelius are right or whether Streeter and Burkitt are right. The latter would not make it better ; the former would not make it worse.

§ 4. *General character of the Synoptic Gospels ; their dates and their sources : the Gospel of Mark.*

What sort of books are these first three Gospels ? More especially what sort of book is the earliest of them, the Gospel of Mark ? A good deal has been written on this subject in the last eight or ten years, but it still, I think, remains true that the Gospels, like the ' books ' of the Hebrew prophets, are hardly to be brought under any previously existing class or category of literature. In 1901 the distinguished theologian H. J. Holtzmann said of them : ' Both in form and in contents they are unique in ancient literature : they form a group by themselves, and they cannot be assigned to any of the traditional and then existing classes of literary composition —not even to the class of Jewish didactic stories which would seem otherwise to lie nearest at hand ' (*Hand-Commentar*, third edition, p. 36). Analogies can be found for them both in earlier and later literature ; partial parallels can be discovered for their component parts, for the sources from which they were put together, but as wholes, as they stand, they may still fitly be regarded as unique. So far as we know, and, even more, so far as we may justly surmise, Mark is not only the oldest Gospel, but the first Gospel. There were sources behind him, even written sources, but no continuous Gospel, no continuous account of the ministry of Jesus, even in the baldest form, from the beginning to the end. If that be so, (like every other statement about the Gospels and their hero, it is disputed), Mark, even though he be only a collector and editor of ' sources,' was yet one of the great originators in religious literature, perhaps one might even say, in biographical and historical literature. Though only a collector and an editor, he was a genius ; he was, at any rate, most happily inspired.

Yet Mark can hardly be said to have compiled a biography of Jesus : none of the Gospels is a biography in anything like our modern sense of the word, not even Luke. They were written for purposes of edification, for religious propaganda ; not as scientific history. Mark, at any rate, is not to be compared with familiar Greek names such as Thucydides or Xenophon or Plutarch. In an intensely interesting essay by K. L. Schmidt on *The Place of the Gospels in General Literature* (' Die Stellung der Evangelien in der allgemeinen Literaturgeschichte ') the author points out that Mark

and Matthew, and to a much lesser degree even Luke, belong not
to the class of literary historians (to *Hochliteratur* as he calls it),
but to the class of popular writings or compositions, to *Klein-
literatur*. They are folk writings, at least as far as the greater
portion of their contents are concerned. They are products of the
Christian community, its needs, its conversations, its disputes, its
memories, its yearnings, its hopes, and, not least, its worship.
Schmidt speaks of the Gospels as *Kultische Volksbücher*, or *volkstümliche Kultbücher*. They represent, they are from the beginning,
' nicht Hochliteratur, sondern Volksbuch, nicht Biographie, sondern
Kultlegende.' Mark tells of the ministry and of the martyrdom of
an actual historic person, who was put to death about forty, or,
at the most, fifty, years before he compiled his book, and yet that
historic person was to Mark already a divine being, and the subject
of a cult, a worship, and a myth. It is this very combination which
partly causes the uniqueness of his book. It enables it to contain
much history as well as much legend, much truth in detail as well
as an all-enveloping myth. The very nature of the subject as well
as the greatness of the subject make the three Gospels from Mark
to Luke so unlike other books of the world's literature, in spite of
many parallels and analogies (I leave out of account any Indian
books about Buddha).

Yet even though the Gospels are fitly described as 'community' or popular productions, they are, as they stand, the
works of single minds. Even Mark was probably written by one
man very much in the form in which we now possess it. The same
can be said of Matthew ; and, still more, of Luke. Here, again,
this combination of the Many and the One seems a special feature
of the Gospels. And, then, the Gospels, even Mark, the oldest of
them, are written in Greek. We may have to touch on the questions : what lies behind Mark, and when do we reach the vernacular ?
But it would appear probable that Mark, as we have it, is not a
mere translation from the Aramaic. There never existed an Aramaic
Mark, even though there did exist Aramaic written sources of Mark.
Mark, therefore, like the Wisdom of Solomon, like Philo, is the
work of a Jew writing in Greek ; the work of a partly Hellenized
Jew. Mark and Matthew, and still more Luke, are not purely
Hebraic books. So far as Mark presents to us a life of Jesus, he
probably does so in virtue of the Greek element in him, in so far
as, or because, he was a partly Hellenized Jew. Jesus was purely
Jewish : there was in him nothing of the Greek, and it is doubtful
whether he understood a word of Greek (in spite of Birt, *Alexander
der Grosse und das Weltgriechentum*, 1925, p. 496, and G. Kittel, *Die
Probleme des palästinischen Spätjudentums und das Urchristentum*,
1926, pp. 34–41) ; but without the Hellenistic element in Mark,

there would have been no Gospels. It is the combination of Hebrew and Greek, working upon the basis of a great historic figure and genius, of a religious enthusiasm and exaltation, and of growing needs and a growing worship, which produced the Gospels, even the Synoptic Gospels, even Mark. (For some admirably suggestive remarks as to the excellence of the Gospels and its causes one may still, with profit as well as for sheer pleasure, read Renan in *Les Évangiles*, chapters v. and vi.)

The first three Gospels tell of the life and death and alleged resurrection of Jesus of Nazareth. The word Gospel means ' good spel,' ' spel ' signifying ' speech ' or ' story.' It is thus intended to be a literal translation of the Greek word εὐαγγέλιον (*euangelion*) or ' good tidings.' We keep the Greek in the word ' evangelist,' but ' evangel ' for ' Gospel ' is rare. German and French both use the Greek form : *les évangiles, die Evangelien*. When we speak of the four Gospels, or of the Gospel according to Mark, we mean the particular books in which the preaching of the Good Tidings and the life of the preacher are recorded. Some remarks upon the original meaning of the word will be found in the note on Mark i. I.

A primary question which suggests itself to anybody to ask about the Gospels is, When were they written ? As to that question no complete agreement has yet been reached by scholars. But the limits of variation are not very wide. It is generally believed that the Gospel according to Mark, the oldest Gospel, and one main source of the other two, was in existence in the form in which we now possess it soon after, or even a little before, the destruction of the Temple in A.D. 70. Bacon would date it about A.D. 80. Matthew and Luke are later : we may roughly place them somewhere between A.D. 80 and 100. We have therefore to remember that the earliest Gospel was written not more than forty or fifty years after the death of Jesus. If a disciple of Jesus was thirty years old when his Master died, he was not much more than seventy or eighty years old when the Gospel of Mark saw the light. (There is only one O.T. book, Daniel, which we can date with anything like the exactitude that we can date the Gospels.) Thus there seems every reason why Mark should contain much true historical matter. For it was written when a few people who had actually known and talked to Jesus were still alive. Even if Mark was written as late as A.D. 80 (as Bacon thinks), men who were twenty years old in A.D. 30 would only be seventy in A.D. 80. If we did not remember how soon legends cluster round the most historical characters, often even in their lifetime, we might be surprised, not that Mark contains so much history, but that it also contains so much that the impartial critic, standing well above his subject, cannot regard as ' history,' but only as legend, theory, or myth.

Jesus himself, so far as we know, wrote nothing. He had, however, many disciples, and eastern disciples of an eastern Master have retentive memories. When he was put to death, there must have been a store of reminiscences of his words and deeds. When his disciples began to preach that he was the Messiah, they drew upon this store. They comforted themselves for the loss of the Master's presence by repeating his words and recalling his deeds. At first, for a few years after the crucifixion, the need for writing down these reminiscences may not have arisen ; all the more, as for these few years the disciples still expected that the End of the Age, or, as we may also call it, the End of the World, would soon ensue. But after a time the necessity for such written records would naturally make itself felt. The disciples and eyewitnesses became fewer and died ; there was a danger lest the words and deeds of the Master should be forgotten or wrongly told ; as the new religion—for this it soon became—was preached to ever wider circles, the need for written documents became greater. Thus in the most natural way collections of the Master's sayings, records of his doings, and of the miracles which he wrought, must gradually have been composed. Luke, writing about A.D. 90 to 100, speaks of many such narratives and collections as already in existence.

We naturally ask, What relation does our oldest Gospel bear to these oral traditions and reminiscences ? Have we in it the exact written precipitate or record of what contemporaries and disciples of Jesus saw and heard ?

This is a very difficult question. How we answer it partly depends upon our different points of view. What I mean will be made clear by an example. In the sixth chapter of Mark Jesus is reported to have made, through miraculous multiplication, five loaves and two fishes suffice for a good meal to five thousand men. He is also reported to have walked upon the sea. If we are willing to believe these miracles, we shall be inclined to say that these events were remembered and repeated by the disciples, and may easily enough have been reported to the author of the Gospel of Mark by a man, or by men, who actually saw them take place.

If, on the other hand, like the writer of this book, we do not believe that the miracles happened, then it seems tolerably certain that whatever substratum or residue of non-miraculous fact these stories may contain, they could not have been directly reported, in the form in which we now possess them, to the writer of the Gospel by actual eyewitnesses. We must, at any rate, assume that the eyewitnesses thought they saw a miracle when they did not see one, or that they exaggerated, or that their memories soon gave way. Or we must assume that, even before Mark or his sources were written, many of the eyewitnesses had died, or that the writer or writers drew rather from the general volume of popular oral tradition, as it had constituted itself in the Christian community, and as it was floating about in their environment, than from the direct reports and communications of the actual disciples or eyewitnesses of the Master's deeds and words. It is probable that for different stories and speeches one or other of all these various ' assumptions ' would have to be used. The facts require, or are the product of, all of them, though in various degrees.

How, it may justly be asked, is the date which we have given for Mark—round about A.D. 70—determined ? We may answer : partly by external and partly by internal evidence. Putting aside the external evidence, the internal evidence seems to show that the events which led up to, and culminated in, the destruction of the Temple were very recent. Much of Mark seems to posit the existence of the Temple. Some of its material seems to assume that the troubles which led up to the great catastrophe had begun, but that the catastrophe itself was still to come. Mark's twelfth and thirteenth chapters may imply that the destruction of state and temple had already taken place, but if so, the words used and the general tenour of the whole make it probable that it could only have happened a little while before. And the external evidence, including the use of Mark in Matthew and Luke, all points to the same conclusion.

If we now ask, ' What lies behind Mark ? ', we are immediately confronted with great difficulties. Omitting the external evidence from immediate consideration, we may, nevertheless, mention some of the theories to which the evidence as a whole has given rise.

First of all, there is the question as to whether Mark is a Unity. Was one hand responsible for the whole up at least to xvi. 8 ? (The last few verses are universally acknowledged to be a much later addition. The true end has been lost, though a few scholars have held that xvi. 8 is the true and original end.) On the whole, that is the view which is now, perhaps, the more popular, and by some English conservative scholars, such as Burkitt and Streeter, it is championed with almost passionate intensity. The phantom, *Urmarcus*, Streeter says, with impatience and scorn. Others suppose that Mark is the work of several hands. There was an original Mark or *Urmarcus*, and this Urmarcus was interpolated and added to by one or more editors or redactors. It does, indeed, seem hard to believe that any one and the same person could have written so oddly as some passages in Mark are written. There are such obvious breaks in continuity ; such plain additions ; such poor connections ; even some contradictions and some differences in points of view. And yet it is by no means impossible that one hand, working on and collecting various sources, and writing from another point of view than those sources, might have produced the book exactly, or very nearly, as it now stands. Any way, it is tolerably certain that Matthew and Luke used the same, or *very* nearly the same, Mark as we now possess. For the purposes of my book the question of an Urmarcus is of no very great importance, and need not be further discussed, though it is not hard (when the external evidence about Mark—who he was and how he wrote—has been stated) to see why to conservative critics it becomes very desirable that all Mark should have been produced by one particular person. The case for an Urmarcus is well put by Moffatt in his valuable Introduction, and to his book I would refer my readers.

Secondly, then, taking Mark as it stands, as a unity, though a very odd one, from what material did its author build it up ? There are a few great scholars who suppose that there is no written source whatever behind Mark. Mark, says Professor Burkitt, is 'not itself based on older literary sources.' The only possible exception allowed is that 'a written source may underlie the eschatological discourse in chapter xiii. 3–37' (*Gospel History*, p. 62). In other words, Mark is a collection of orally transmitted sayings and tales, and these saying and tales 'represent the way in which the disciples of the disciples of Jesus told to one another such stories of the earthly Ministry of their Lord as they remembered in the light of all that had happened during the momentous thirty or forty years which succeeded the Crucifixion.' It may be noted, however, that Professor Burkitt, who is so very much against the theory of an Urmarcus, and who also opposes the idea of any literary or written sources lying behind Mark, does not seem to believe in the statements of Papias, or that what we have in Mark is the direct record of what was said to him by Peter (see below). He speaks of stories told by 'the disciples of the disciples' to one another and he dates Mark between A.D. 70 and 80.

More probably, however, the more numerous scholars who believe that written sources lie behind and were used by Mark, though he may have used oral stories as well, are correct. It is exceedingly difficult to believe that not only parallel stories (doublets as they are usually called), but *groups* of parallel stories, *groups* of doublets such as we find in vi. 34–56, vii. 31–37, and viii. 1–26, can have any other than a literary or written origin. Nevertheless, it is the separate stories or sayings—stories which culminate in a saying, or sayings or parables which are independent of any story, or stories which report a healing or an exorcism or a quarrel or a dispute with antagonists—with which the written sources are now commonly supposed to have started, though we can hardly imagine that, almost from the very beginning of the writing stage, more than one such story or saying were not jotted down *together* and handed round. Yet the separate story, the separate saying, lies at the bottom of the Gospels, and scholars are now beginning to sort these stories or sayings into groups, to argue how they were put together, to discuss their analogies and parallels to other separate stories and sayings in other literatures or about other religious teachers, the inner laws, if any, of their composition, the degree of their credibility, and so on. If the separate stories have, in many cases, to be regarded with suspicion, still more have we to suspect their connections. For these are largely editorial and artificial ; *how* largely, however, is a matter of dispute and of separate discussion in each case. The literary sources of Mark were not merely a number of isolated, separately written, tales and sayings. One can hardly even imagine a number of separate ' broadsheets,' each containing one story, and, still less, one saying. Mark used some collections or groups of such tales and sayings. In fact, in the previously mentioned cases of vi. 34–56, vii. 31–37, and viii. 1–26, he used two collections in which the same incident, and even the same topographical statement (Jesus crossing the lake) are twice repeated, and yet in spite of the slightly different form of the incident in the two collections, it is obviously one and the same story which is in question, followed by one and the same journey. Some scholars think that Mark's sources went much further than such collections. Loisy, for instance, supposes that he used a narrative source which contained a collection of short stories, from the opening of the ministry to the resurrection, already arranged in rough chronological order. In addition, he used (according to the great French scholar) a somewhat later collection of stories mainly of a markedly miraculous character, and a collection of sayings and teachings, of which much more will have to be said presently. Thus the part of the editor himself—the part of Mark—is reduced to comparatively small dimensions : he is only responsible for certain later additions and accretions, as well as for the general style and character of the whole. Others suppose, I am now inclined to think with greater probability, that Mark found no such narrative source to his hand, except for the story of the Passion— the arrival at, and the teaching in, the capital, the arrest, the trial, the death, and the resurrection of Jesus—but that, for the order of the rest, he (Mark) is largely himself responsible.

In any case, the setting, framework, and order of the stories and sayings are, as I have said, less likely to be authentic—they go back less far—than the separate stories and sayings themselves. Some of the stories are quite possibly told in their wrong place : some of the connections of saying with saying, or of story with saying, or of story with story, are almost certainly artificial. The length of the ministry is not stated ; indeed the chronology is very meagre ; event is strung to event by an 'immediately' or an 'again' : only once up to the entry into Jerusalem are we told of any definite interval of time beyond ' on the morrow.' The public ministry according to Mark may have occupied about a year or a year and a half. It can to some extent be divided into sections : an early period of preaching and healing and collecting of disciples : a growing antagonism of the official teachers, following upon a series of disputes and arguments with them ; a period of wandering outside Galilee and the localities of the early portion of the ministry ; after a great and decisive scene with the apostles, in which the new Messiahship is assumed and explained, a journey to Jerusalem with events and teachings upon the way, and, then, the arrival at Jerusalem and the end.

There is at bottom little variety of opinion among scholars as to the accuracy of this very general outline, though the cause and the purpose, and the extent and even the fact, of the ' period of wandering outside Galilee' are disputed. But over and above this broad and somewhat obvious disposition of events, there are considerable differences, varying from much scepticism (*e.g.* Bultmann) and strong advocacy of correctness (*e.g.* Burkitt). The former scholar doubts the historic accuracy of a number of the incidents and a number of the editorial settings which the latter regards as in every way reasonable to believe. To some of these differences of opinion the commentary will allude. The truth probably lies—if I may venture to criticize two such distinguished, brilliant, and learned scholars—between the two extremes. Neither stories nor settings are so historic as Burkitt would have them, or so unauthentic as Bultmann. The cautious Schmidt or Klostermann is probably more right than either of the other two. But for our purpose the precise measure of ' historicity ' (ugly word) is of no very enormous importance. Whether, for instance, Jesus did or did not select precisely twelve inner disciples, whether he sent them out to preach and heal, whether at a particular point in the ministry he ceased teaching in the synagogues, whether fairly early he had to avoid being captured by Herod Antipas in league with the Scribes and Pharisees, the precise geographical course of his wanderings till the entry into Jerusalem,—all these questions do not greatly concern us. The growth of his ' Messianic ' consciousness, on the other hand, the meaning *for him* of the terms Son of man and Messiah, if he used the one and laid claim to the other, above all, the true nature of the disputes between himself and the Rabbis, and the measure of ' rightness ' on either side—these are questions which touch the scope and object of my work much more nearly.

I have already indicated the way in which a Jewish writer is obviously bound to regard the miracles. But I have also indicated that a miraculous story, or a story which the narrator and the editor regarded as miraculous, need not necessarily be unhistoric. Healings and exorcisms may be due to ' faith,' or to ' suggestion,' or to the influence of one mind and personality upon another. There are, however, limits to such possibilities, and some of Mark's miracles we must reject. Of such stories we shall never be able to tell their possible historic basis or their exact measure of historic truth. Nor will the degree of the miraculous be the only test for assessing and weighing the historic accuracy of a particular tale. There are others which will be used, of which one is the obvious desire of Mark and of the earlier narrators to make Jesus triumph in every dispute, and emerge triumphant from every verbal contest ; their perfectly natural wish to exhibit the moral nobleness and perfection of the hero and the moral obliquity and imperfection of his antagonists. Certain considerations, which chiefly affect the authenticity of the *sayings* of Jesus, will be mentioned in due course. Mark, and the Synoptic Gospels generally, are odd mixtures of *Tendenzschriften*, on the one hand, and of naïve folk-tales on the other : or, again, they are odd mixtures of unbelievable miracles and unhistoric sayings and statements, on the one hand, and of pretty obvious reminiscences of eyewitnesses and ear-witnesses upon the other. There is in them much which is historic-ally accurate and true, and much which is historically inaccurate and untrue.

If we take Mark from i. 16 to xii. 44 and analyse the contents, attempting to put these contents into classes and categories, we might put the sayings and the conversations in one class, and what we might fairly call the incidents in another. Of such incidents there are some thirty-one, and of these twelve are healings, six are miracles, and thirteen are neither one nor the other, though at least one is visionary or supernatural. Many of the twelve healings could not have happened exactly as they are reported ; two are doublets ; one or two are exceedingly doubtful. Of the six miracles none can be accepted as they stand. Of the thirteen other incidents, two are doublets ; four are dubious, seven are likely to be entirely authentic. We thus see how meagre and dubious are the materials for any connected story of the ministry of Jesus, from its opening with the call of Simon and Andrew to its close with the ' incident ' of the widow's mite.

§ 5. *Who was Mark ? The statements of Papias.*

Passing from such general considerations, drawn from the book itself, one asks more specifically, Is anything actually known as to

the origin of the oldest Gospel ?   Who was Mark ?   Is he the author
of the book which bears his name ?

There was a John Mark, a Jew by birth, of whom we hear several
times in various New Testament books.   His mother's name was
Mary, and she lived in Jerusalem and belonged to the Christian
community.   To her house Peter is said to have come when he
escaped from Herod's prison (Acts xii. 12).   He was the cousin of
Barnabas (Colossians iv. 10), and is said to have accompanied the
apostle Paul on some of his travels (Acts xii. 25, xiii. 13, xv. 37–39 ;
Philemon 24 ; 2 Tim. iv. 11).   Moreover, in Jerusalem Mark is
supposed to have become acquainted with, and a constant companion of, the apostle Peter.   In the first Epistle of Peter (v. 13)
he is spoken of as at Rome.   ' She (*i.e.* the Church) that is in
Babylon (*i.e.* Rome) salutes you, and so does Mark my son (*i.e.* my
spiritual son).'   Thus it is further supposed that Mark wrote his
Gospel in Rome.   And to Mark, the author of the Gospel, there is
supposed by some to be an allusion in the Gospel itself (see note
on xiv. 51, 52), and it is even conjectured that the place of the
Last Supper was the house of Mark's mother.   As to the value of
these traditions, so far as they bear upon the problem of the authorship of the second Gospel, something will be said later on.

The oldest reference to Mark as a writer comes from Papias,
Bishop of Hierapolis in Phrygia, who wrote about A.D. 140–150.
Excerpts of his work have been preserved by Eusebius, Bishop of
Cæsarea, A.D. 265–340.   Papias, then, is quoted by Eusebius as
having received information from ' John the Elder,' as follows :
' This also the Elder used to say : Mark, having become (or, who
had been) Peter's interpreter, wrote down, accurately, though not
in order, all which he (Mark) remembered (or all that he [Peter]
mentioned), that was said or done by the Christ.   For Mark had
neither heard the Lord nor followed him, but afterwards, as I have
said, followed Peter, who used to frame his teaching according to
the needs (of his hearers), but not as making a connected series
(σύνταξιν) of the Lord's discourses (or, without any attempt to
give the Lord's words systematically).   So Mark committed no
fault, in that he wrote down (or, as having written down) some
particulars (ἔνια) just as he remembered them (or, as he, Peter,
narrated them from memory).   For he took heed (but) to one thing,
to omit nothing (in the sayings or stories) which he had heard, and
to make no false statement in his account of them.'

In this quotation from Papias there are several words which are
a little uncertain, and as a whole it gives rise to a great deal of
doubt and discussion.

First, as to a few of the details.   Up to what point is Papias
quoting the Elder ?   Probably only up to the end of the first

sentence ('done by the Christ'). The rest is the commentary of Papias. Next, what is the meaning of 'interpreter' (ἑρμηνευτής)? Some think the word means that Mark merely became the interpreter of Peter by writing his Gospel. But this explanation is extremely unlikely. The word ἑρμηνευτής, 'interpreter,' must indicate a personal relationship. And the probable meaning is that Mark orally translated Peter's Aramaic discourses and preachings into Greek, and then carefully wrote down what Peter had orally said. Thirdly, as to the word ἐμνημόνευσεν. What is its exact meaning? Who is its subject? Some have rendered 'all that he (Peter) mentioned,' but more probably 'all that he (Mark) repeated (from memory)' is meant. The word may also mean 'remembered,' and in that case too either Peter or Mark may be its subject. The same doubt exists about ἀπεμνημόνευσεν a little farther down. That word is probably to be translated 'as he (Mark) exactly repeated them from memory.' Peter spoke in Aramaic; Mark translated orally, and then, later on, wrote down, as accurately as he could, the discourses which he remembered, and had himself verbally delivered. Another important detail is the phrase 'not, however, in order,' οὐ μέντοι τάξει. Does this refer to chronology? More probably it refers to good arrangement and sequence (in which chronology would, to some extent, be included). Moffatt says : ' By the time that Papias wrote, if not much earlier, difficulties were evidently felt about the differences in the four gospels, which implies that they had begun to be read together or, at any rate, laid side by side. The divergence, e.g., between Mark's τάξις and that of the Fourth Gospel seems to have occasioned surprise. Papias writes in an explanatory tone. He quotes the presbyter in order to defend Mark against a certain depreciation, and his defence presupposes that the authority of the Fourth Gospel was so strong in certain local circles that it served as a standard for estimating the style and shape of earlier [Gospels] (p. 187). 'Afterwards, as I have said, he followed Peter.' Some suppose that 'afterwards' means 'after the lifetime of Jesus'; others that as Papias had elsewhere remarked that Mark had 'followed' Paul, so now he tells us that 'later on' he became the follower and interpreter of Peter. Lastly, what is the meaning of 'some particulars, matters, or things' (ἔνια)? We must not apparently suppose that this word ἔνια (' some things ') implies that to Papias only a part of the Gospel of Mark goes back to Mark. Papias is alluding to our Gospel and not to a part of it. The ' some things ' simply refer to the separate particular teachings and preachings of Peter according as Mark remembered them.

The value of the statement of Papias would be increased if we knew more about Papias's authority, John the Elder. But from another fragment of Papias, quoted by Eusebius, it is practically certain that John the Elder was not the apostle John, and indeed was probably not an apostle at all or an immediate disciple of Jesus. ' If,' says Papias, ' anyone arrived who had followed the Men of Old Time (the Elders) (παρηκολουθηκώς τις τοῖς πρεσβυτέροις), I inquired as to their words : what Andrew or what Peter said or Philip or Thomas or James or John or Matthew or any other of the disciples of the Lord, or what Aristion or John the Elder [the disciples of the Lord] say.' Here clearly the apostle John and John the Elder are distinguished from each other, while the bracketed words are in all probability a gloss. It is not even certain that Papias had spoken directly with John the Elder : he may only have spoken with someone who had ' followed ' him. Under these circumstances the statement of Papias may simply come to this : that a disciple of the disciples told him a tradition about the origin and authorship of the Gospel of Mark. Thus Loisy observes that what Papias, on the authority of John the Elder, says of Mark and of Matthew, has not a strictly historical character, and one has even the right to ask if his statements are not semi-conjectures, ' complétant des demi-renseignements,' about books already in credit, which needed to be covered with an important name in order to maintain the authority they had acquired, at a time when nobody quite knew how they had acquired it (E. S. 1. p. 24). It is necessary to test the assertions of John the Elder by an examination of the Gospel itself and by such other evidence as may be available. The connection of Mark and Peter mentioned in the so-called first Epistle of Peter may be of little importance. The Epistle is in all probability not authentic, and was written after the Gospel. Perhaps even the very mention of Mark's name in that Epistle is not without connection with the attribution of the Gospel to a disciple of Peter. ' Ce serait une mention intéressée, comme le dire de Jean l'Ancien ' (E. S. 1. p. 113). But however this may be, most scholars believe that there was some real historic relation between the Gospel of Mark and Peter, the famous disciple ; in other words, that *some* of the material, at least, in Mark is derived, at first or second hand, from the orally delivered reminiscences of Peter.

§ 6. *Papias, Peter, and Mark.*

There are many other theories as regards the statement of Papias, ranging from full acceptance to denial. One is that the Gospel of Mark is a unity, all written by one hand, and that the writer was the Mark of the Acts, the companion of Paul and the interpreter of Peter. If Mark only used oral sources, many of his sources may have been the sayings and stories which he heard, or had heard, from Peter. The words of Papias do not necessarily mean that Mark wrote down the stories from Peter's mouth as Peter told them. He may have compiled his book after Peter's death, and one tradition, mentioned by Irenaeus, is that he did so. Again, Mark may have written down Petrine stories and sayings (as well as others) as a sort of first draft, and afterwards compiled his Gospel. Or, Mark may have written an Urmarcus, which was added to and revised by a later editor. Moffatt holds, *e.g.*, that there are 'insuperable difficulties in the way of rejecting the Papias tradition' altogether, or of identifying the work of which Papias speaks with our ' canonical ' Mark ; the solution he advocates is that *our* Mark is a later edition of the original Mark : *our* Mark, ' written shortly after 70, is based for the most part on Mark's draft of the Petrine reminiscences' (pp. 191, 192, 227). Indeed this theory can be put in such a form that it avoids any use of the Urmarcus, which is such a red rag to certain conservative scholars. We may say that the writer or compiler of our Mark employed several written sources, one of which was a collection of stories about Jesus written by Mark. Or we may give up Mark altogether, and simply say that Peter is the ultimate source for some of the stories, and that this fact, as well as the desire to obtain apostolic authority for this Gospel, suggested the tradition about Mark.

It may be noted here that some scholars have urged that Mark is himself the man with the pitcher of xiv. 13, that the last supper was held in the house of his mother, and that the young man of xiv. 51, 52 was also Mark. But all, and even the last of, these hypotheses are exceedingly doubtful. (*Cp.* Goguel, *L'Évangile de Marc* (1909), p. 272.)

Scholars still differ widely as to the amount of accuracy enshrined in the words of Papias, and as to the amount of the ' Petrine' material in our canonical Mark. For my own part, I am inclined to be somewhat sceptical on the first point, and to be reserved upon the second. Both for what Papias says about Mark and for what he says about Matthew I am disposed to agree with Wendland, whose fifteen pages about Mark seem to me most judicious and sensible (pp. 258–272). ' The oldest biographical tradition of the Christians is in exactly the same plight as that of the Greeks. Those statements of Papias lay themselves strongly open to the suspicion of being a " tendencious " construction which, in order to legitimize the Church-Gospels, wishes to establish a line of tradition going back to the apostles, so as to counter any gnostic appeal to secret apostolic traditions.' And it is, perhaps, safest to be content with the opinion that genuine traditions, not always exactly to be picked out from the whole, lie at the bottom of Mark's narrative. On the other hand, it is impressive that a great and unprejudiced historian —not a theologian—like Eduard Meyer, holds that the Papias statement rests on ' the very best tradition,' that internal evidence fully confirms it, so that Mark ' indeed, to a great extent, reproduces stories which he owes to Peter himself' (i. p. 158 *fin*.). Meyer's theory is that the stories in which Peter himself plays a part (they will be mentioned in most cases in the commentary) are directly due to him. Otherwise Mark is mainly composed of two written Aramaic sources, of which one is of *very* early date, written, indeed, ' in the first decades of Christianity.' ' It can be shown that for our knowledge of the history of Jesus we are by no means merely dependent on writings (*Aufzeichnungen*) of the second, post-apostolic generation, but are led far beyond it right into the first generation, which knew Jesus well personally, and still preserved a living memory. These oldest reminiscences we possess in several recensions. Thus there is no reason at all why we should not regard these oldest reminiscences as historically accurate both in the chronological arrangement of the history and in all essential matters ' (i. p. 146). The ' formegeschichtliche ' investigation of the Gospels gives a reply to Meyer's excessive confidence in the historic accuracy or authenticity of so many of Mark's stories and sayings. *Cp*. the references to his book in Schmidt's essay on ' Die Stellung ', etc., previously referred to.

In an interesting review of the first volume of Meyer's *Ursprung des Christentums* (in the *Deutsche Literaturzeitung*; I have, I am ashamed to say, mislaid the reference, and cannot give the exact date) Dibelius observes, 'Die Nachricht des Papias, dass Markus das aufgezeichnet habe, was Petrus in seinen Predigten von Worten und Taten Jesu mitzuteilen pflegte, drängt doch den Prozess der Literarisierung zu nahe an den ersten Verkünder heran. Sie gibt —ebenso wie die entsprechenden Nachrichten über die anderen Synoptiker—dem unliterarischen Zeugen aus dem Apostelkreis schon eine Art Sekretär an die Seite, der spätestens nach dem Tode des Petrus sich daran gemacht habe, dessen geistiges Erbe der Nachwelt aufzubewahren. Und sie vergreift sich dabei völlig in der sozialen Sphäre : so stellen sich Menschen der zweiten oder dritten Generation die Sache vor, die selbst schon mehr Fühlung mit dem literarischen Betrieb der Welt haben und, trotz der Hoffnung auf das Weltende, es wagen, wieder für eine Nachwelt zu arbeiten. Die literarische Art des Markusevangeliums weist keineswegs auf eine so individuelle Entstehung : das älteste Evangelienbuch scheint vielmehr von verbreiteten und natürlich anonymen Tra-ditionen verschiedener Art, verschiedenen Stils und (darum) verschiedenen Interesses abhängig zu sein. . . .

'Der Ausgangspunkt der gesammten alten Überlieferung von Jesus war die Missionspredigt, die einer fixierten Tradition als unentbehrlichen Hilfsmittels bedurfte.

'Das Fehlen persönlicher Einzelheiten erklärt sich aus der rein predigtmässig interessierten Art der Überlieferung: dann ist aber freilich die Formung der Tradition auf die Missionare und nicht auf die persönlich an den Dingen teilhabenden Zeugen zurückzuführen. Diese kommen zwar als die ersten und besten Gewährsmänner der sich bildenden Überlieferung in Betracht, sind aber nicht als deren eigentliche Bildner anzusehen.'

We may, perhaps, rest in the conclusion that some of Mark, or some of Mark's material, goes back to, or is based upon, the reminiscences and statements of Peter. Over and above the tradition to this effect, there are some positive arguments to be drawn from the Gospel itself. These will be noticed in their place. The opening scenes of the Galilæan ministry are located in Peter's home : the Gospel begins to be detailed where Peter had personal knowledge. The story of Peter's denial must, it is argued, be due to him and him alone : would tradition have invented a story so damaging to the reputation of the great apostle ?

Dr. Carpenter says, 'How Peter's reminiscences were shaped into our Mark we cannot tell.' But he thinks that 'at any rate it remains probable that the main facts of our second Gospel were derived from Peter ; the baptism, the ministry in Capernaum and on the lake, the choice of the disciples, the enlarging work, the opposition and the conflict, the confession of the Messiahship, the journey to Jerusalem, the entry into the capital, the last days of gathering danger, the fatal night of anguish and desertion—of all these he may have spoken. The leading outlines of the immortal story are drawn from the life. Here Jesus thinks, prays, speaks, feels, acts, as a man' (*First Three Gospels*, p. 231). The many graphic touches which we shall frequently notice in Mark bespeak, to many scholars, the eyewitness. Yet these very 'graphic touches' may, as Wendland thinks, only reveal 'the pleasure in relating,' ('die Freude am Erzählen') characteristic of 'volkstümliche Erzählungskunst' (p. 270). Bacon, Wellhausen and others depreciate the significance of the references to Peter and the deductions which can be made from them. Wellhausen, for example, observes that the traditional material which Mark reduces to writing is 'comparatively rich for Jerusalem, but poor for Galilee.' Would this be so if this tradition went back to the apostles ? 'It would rather seem as if the narrative tradition in Mark did not mainly proceed from the intimate friends of Jesus.' 'It has for the most part a somewhat rough popular manner. In the form in which we now possess it, this tradition must have passed through many people's mouths to have reached its present rather blunt and rough-hewn shape' (*Einleitung*, 2nd ed. p. 45).

The argument that many of the miraculous stories cannot rest upon the direct reminiscences of eyewitnesses is perhaps of not much value. It is rejected by Meyer (p. 159 n. 1), and long before him was rejected by Renan. The miracles, the 'materialistic thaumaturgy,' are, he thinks, quite in keeping with Peter's disposition. The Gospel of Mark is 'a credulously written biography.' The miracles are no proof of its unhistoric character. 'Things which upset us in the highest degree were matters of everyday occurrence to Jesus and his disciples. The Roman world even more than the Jewish world was a dupe to these illusions. The miracles wrought by Vespasian are of precisely the same type as those of Jesus in the Gospel of Mark. . . . But the characters in the legend, the vagueness of the circumstances, the indistinct softness of the outlines, are very noticeable in Matthew and in Luke. In Mark, on the other hand, everything is vivid and lifelike : we feel that we are in the presence of reminiscences' (*Les Évangiles*, p. 118). Moffatt sums up his conclusions thus : 'Notes of Peter's reminiscences written down by Mark (hence the Aramaic colouring and vivid detail of certain sections) were afterwards edited by a (Roman ?) Christian, who used not only the small apocalypse, but some other logia of Jesus (not necessarily Q). The gospel is not a gospel of Peter, but it contains a cycle of traditions for which Peter is the authority and in which he plays a prominent rôle. . . . The connection of the Urmarcus' (Moffatt is an impenitent believer in Urmarcus) 'with Peter accounts for the historical nucleus at the bottom of the Marcan stories. Several of the latter are more than circumstantial ; they reveal the man who was there. The secondary features of the gospel are adequately accounted for by the process of editing, which has left the gospel something very different from the naïve transcript of an eyewitness's reminiscences' (pp. 232, 233).

Certainly if we had to choose between accepting Papias's statement as applying to Mark in its present form or rejecting it altogether, we should have to reject it. For though 'the chronological sequence of the gospel is better marked in its large sections than in details' (Moffatt, p. 220), though the 'order' is often artificial, yet our Gospel of Mark is anything but a simple addition of story to story, without any *arrière pensée* or ulterior purpose. Mark is no mere collector. The author does not give a 'mere artless transcript of oral reminiscences' (Moffatt, p. 226). He is a theologian ; not a theologian like Paul or 'John,' but yet a theologian. He looks at the life and death of Jesus from a special point of view. He has his theories about them. His book contains stories which reflect the very lifetime of Jesus, but they are put in a setting which reflects the very rapid development of Christology made in the twenty or thirty years after the Crucifixion. And not only are they put in such a setting, but the stories themselves are often revised, modified, or expanded, in order to suit the theory. Jesus in the oldest stories is a teacher, a healer, a prophet (in the old sense), but yet a man : he is a man who cannot always succeed in his healings, who recognizes the vast difference between himself, a man, and God. But to the author of Mark he is the Son of God, a being semi-divine ; recognized as such by demons ; he is the Son of man who is more than man, and who is to sit at God's right hand after his death and resurrection, and to return to earth as the Heavenly Man, as God's viceregent, as the ultimate Judge. From the moment of his baptism, if not before, Jesus is filled with the divine spirit ; he knows who he is or what he has become ; he knows that he is the Messiah, the Son of God ; to him has been given the power, hitherto reserved by God to Himself, of the forgiveness of sin. He knows indeed that he has to suffer and to die, but he knows also that even his corpse will not remain long within the tomb ; it will be miraculously quickened, and he will rise to everlasting glory. Himself conscious, from his baptism, of his messiahship and sonship, he is to keep it hidden from all till the end is near. Such a theory, consistent, articulate, and resting upon developments which only took place after, even if soon after, the death of Jesus, are quite inconsistent with the conception of a book which is little more than a collection of the reminiscences of Peter, the eyewitness. The Gospel of Mark, say Lake and Foakes Jackson, ' was composed partly to show that the deeds of Jesus during his ministry prove that he was the Messiah, though he never made the claim, and partly to indicate why he abandoned the Synagogue, organized the Twelve, and began a more extensive mission. In common with the other evangelists, Mark desires to explain the reason for the breach between the Church and the Synagogue, tracing it back to the beginning, and showing that it was due, not to any schismatic conduct on the part of Jesus and his followers, but to the rejection by the Jews of the Messiah whom they ought to have recognized in him, as his disciples had done, on the ground, not of his own assertion, but of the sufficient testimony of miracles, of demons, and of the divine voice from Heaven.' ' The most probable view seems to be that the Gospel of Mark is in some way connected with a tradition which ultimately goes back to Peter, but it does not seem probable that the text of the Gospel is so directly connected with him as tradition suggests. It is difficult to think that any one who had actual intercourse with Peter could have been so ignorant of the meaning of Son of man as the editor who produced our Gospel must have been ' (*The Beginnings of Christianity*, Vol. I. p. 267).

Since the first revision of my Introduction was completed, Professor Bacon's important work, *The Gospel of Mark*, has appeared. It contains a very full and exhaustive analysis of Papias's famous statement. For Bacon, the Elder's testimony (his date ' must be placed approximately at the turn of the century ') (p. 39) ends at πραχθέντα ; 'Mark, who had been Peter's interpreter, wrote down carefully as much as he remembered ; (recording) both sayings and doings of Christ ; not, however, in order.' The Elder's testimony ' amounts to this ' : the reminiscences ' should be received as really representing the preaching of Peter. They may properly be regarded as Markan, given out in some sense under the hand or authority of Mark, who in his earlier life had indeed been associated with Peter, but later became a helper of Barnabas, and ultimately one of the leading lieutenants of Paul. The work shows the merits of careful compilation (ἀκριβῶς ἔγραψεν). But it consists of miscellaneous material arranged only in such order as the editor could command. The reserve of this commendation shows that to the Elder's mind the Gospel of Mark could not take the place of a full account in proper τάξις (whatever that might be) of the teachings and work of the Lord.'

Perhaps I am too inclined myself to be affected and influenced by the last book I have perused, but after reading Bacon's work carefully through, I feel that his elaborate arguments for the post-apostolic date of Mark are of very great strength. The historic Mark, for Bacon, is *not* the final author of the Gospel as we now possess it. Its ignorances and mistakes, what it omits as well as a good deal of what it includes, make that impossible (pp. 301–307). External and internal evidence all point to a date some ten years later than the fall of Jerusalem. I have no space to quote from the arguments. For our Gospel's ' combination of history and legend, realistic story and religious elaboration, there can be but one explanation. It is that afforded by documentary analysis. We are compelled to admit the justice of the primitive claim to Peter's testimony in this compilation. But we are equally compelled, by the very same evidence, to deny that this covers the whole. We have neither wish nor ground for rejecting the ancient witness for the authority of Mark as guaranteeing the general authenticity of this Gospel. But the phenomena we have just reviewed compel us to take the expression "according to" (κατά) in the looser sense. This Gospel represents the story of Peter, not as recorded, but *as it used to be preached*, by Mark ' (p. 306). The Gospel ' is an elaborate compilation from written sources originally Aramaic, by a compiler somewhat remote from the scenes, events, and persons described ' (p. 310). ' On the other hand individual traits in the composition are undoubtedly early. Some scenes bear the impress of first-hand report, in all probability that of Peter. But the Gospel consists of a compilation of earlier documents. Such is the most convincing result of the recent studies of its " translation Greek," to say nothing of previous source analysis. That some elements from oral or written tradition should retain an archaic character, however late the compilation as a whole, would be only what we should expect. It is the latest elements which determine the date ' (p. 311).

There are, indeed, two or three strands or elements in the Gospel of Mark as we now possess it. And it may be, and it has been argued, that the very co-existence of these different strands is a proof for the historical character of one of them. Mark has not produced a consistent picture of Jesus. All the more proof that some of the traits of this inconsistent picture were drawn or taken from the life. This seems a good argument up to a point. For if Mark's object is to show that Jesus is the divine Messiah, the Son of God, and if, in spite of this conception of his hero, a simpler, and more human figure can nevertheless well be discerned beneath all later theological overwrappings in the pages of Mark, are not many critics right in regarding this as a tremendously powerful argument for the accuracy and primitiveness of the tradition, which, in spite of the later accretions and developments, still keeps its original character ? Has not Mark reported many things faithfully ? And of these many things must not Peter be the ultimate source and authority ? So much, then, about Mark's relation to Peter. We have next to consider the inferences which may be drawn from his theology as to his possible relation to Paul.

§ 7. *Mark's Theology and Paul's.*

If Mark was in any sense the author of the Gospel which bears his name, this author was not only the ' interpreter ' of Peter, but also, at certain stages of the apostle's career, a companion, if not a disciple, of Paul. He is alluded to, as we have seen, in Acts xii. 12, 25, xiii. 5, 13, xv. 37–39, and in Colossians iv. 10, Philemon 24, and 2 Timothy iv. 11. Whether, however, the actual historic Mark was the writer or compiler of any portion of the Gospel or no is for us a subordinate question. Much more important is the question : Whoever the writer of the Gospel may be, how far do his theology and religious position tally with those of Paul ? Is he a Paulinist ?

To this the general, and more probably true, answer is that ' Mark ' is *not* a Paulinist, but that he has been influenced by Pauline teaching to some limited extent. We shall notice this influence in the course of the commentary. It is sufficient to state here that the theories expressed in iv. 10–12, in x. 45, in vii. 19, seem at least allied to those of Paul. The words used in the Last Supper xiv. 22, 24 also appear to many scholars as Pauline. But, on the other hand, recent investigation by Werner and others has proved considerable divergency of view and of terminology as well. The extent of Mark's Paulinism advocated, *e.g.*, by Loisy would seem to be exaggerated. (*Cp.* Moffatt, pp. 235, 236.) Moreover, we have to recognize that Christology had made advances among Hellenistic Christian converts independently of, or concurrently with, Paul. And the *special* theory of Mark—the hidden Messiahship, the veil of secrecy lifted miraculously from time to time, but when lifted, uncomprehended— is peculiar to himself and unknown to Paul. It is needless to set out that theory here ; it will be alluded to in the commentary. It is a wonderful thing how quickly the man Jesus grew into a divine being, but yet, when the Hellenistic influences are reckoned in, on the one hand, and certain Jewish conceptions, upon the other, according to which the Messiah was, or was to be, no longer the purely human hero and king of Isaiah xi., but a semi-divine being sent down from heaven—when, as I say, we remember all this, and add to it the mighty genius of Paul, the astonishing result becomes by no means inexplicable. Judaism went forward on its own narrowed and stricken way—a perpetual protest against any deflection from pure and unqualified Monotheism, against any dubious confusion between man and God, against any lowering of the standard of the Divine Unity.

The ' influences ' of Pauline teaching upon Mark, both direct and indirect, have been subjected to a fresh examination by Bacon, who alludes and replies to Werner's interesting study. Bacon seeks to show that while of direct borrowings there is little, and while there are (as Werner urges) many phraseological and doctrinal disagreements, yet Mark must be considered as later than, and, as a whole, inconceivable apart from, the teaching of Paul. Mark's book postulates Paul no less than it postulates Peter. It is ' the first attempt to give to the world a joint message from the martyred Peter and Paul ' (p. 332). On the one hand, as regards the actual writings of Paul, if Mark knew them, then the ' influence they have exerted upon him has reached his mind rather than his pen. The few cases of phraseology which might be designated Pauline are such as can be easily accounted for through the currency in oral and traditional teaching of certain half-stereotyped terms. But if the question be put in another form, less specific, but equally conclusive as regards the question of date and composition, the answer will be quite different. If it be asked " Can we imagine a gospel such as Mark taking form in a community ignorant of the teaching of Paul ? " the answer must be a decided No. The whole aim of the Gospel, its Christology and soteriology, its discourses and the framework of their composition, especially what we are able to trace out of its relation to earlier sources, make it impossible to account for such a composition as this without the life, the thought, and the teaching of Paul. Mark shows a direct, but not a literary, dependence on the teaching of the great Apostle to the Gentiles' (p. 271). There seems to be much force in the arguments on which these conclusions are based.

§ 8. *Mark and Q.*

We may assume that written (some of them probably Aramaic) sources lie behind Mark, though he used oral sources as well. Whether any one of these sources can be even as roughly ascertained as Loisy, in his edition of the Synoptic Gospels, sketched out the contents of his supposed narrative source, may well be doubted. Still more difficult is it to ascertain anything of a source for the sayings and parables. That there was such a source—some collection of Logia—would, however, seem to be most probable. Now over and above our Gospel of Mark which, as has been said, was one source for both Matthew and Luke—and, indeed, so far as their narratives are concerned, up to the Passion at any rate, by far their most important source—they both used another source which was specially devoted to sayings, teachings, and parables. For the sayings, teachings, and parables which they include often verbally tally and agree to such an extent and degree as to preclude any other hypothesis than that of a common and written source. (That Matthew borrowed from Luke or Luke from Matthew is now, for reasons into which I need not enter, almost universally rejected.) This source is generally known and designated under the title of Q (Q being the first letter of the German word *Quelle*, 'a well, a source'). This common material includes some most important sayings of Jesus ; for instance, it includes a large portion of the Sermon on the Mount, and such an immensely important saying as Matt. xi. 25–27 (Luke x. 21, 22). The date and origin of this source become, therefore, a matter of the first importance. The material common to both Matthew and Luke, which in all probability was drawn from this source, enables us to make some conjectures about its nature. It was mainly a collection of sayings of Jesus : it probably contained a few brief narratives, but these narratives were included as settings and occasions for sayings and discourses rather than for their own sake: it closed apparently before the story of the Passion.

I cannot enter into the theory relative to Q which is maintained by Bacon in his learned work, *The Gospel of Mark* (1925). To him, among the material which Mark employed there was a document which he would like to call the Second Source. This second source he considers to be improperly named Q. For while from the second source was derived most, though perhaps not all, of the 'double tradition material,' which is what should properly be called Q, the second source contained other material as well. Now though Q (in loose parlance) or the Second Source, ' may properly be recognized as predominating in discourse material,' yet ' this by no means implies that it was not a true gospel, mainly concerned (like all gospels) with the person, mission, and fate of Jesus as the Christ of God. Its Christology differs from the Markan in presenting Jesus as the supreme incarnation of the revealing and redemptive Wisdom of God. Because it conceives salvation much as it is conceived in James (an indwelling of the divine gift of " wisdom," a being " brought forth by the word of truth to be a kind of ' firstfruits ' of the creation ") the evangelist naturally places teaching in the foreground. Like " James," the author of the Q material is a Christian Wisdom writer. To him the message of Jesus is an " implanted word which is able to save men's souls." It is a " royal law," a " perfect law of liberty." Why should he not be anxious to tell this teaching of Jesus to the fullest possible extent ? And yet, the work and person of Jesus were central to the whole composition ' (p. 154).

Now though this hypothetical document Q contains much material which, common to both Matthew and Luke, is entirely wanting in Mark, it also contains material to which there are close parallels in Mark. In Luke we often find the same sayings recounted twice over, once, as it is fairly easy to judge, from Mark, and once, we may surmise, from the other extra source Q. Moreover, there are one or two incidents (*e.g.*, the Temptation) which appear in Matthew and Luke in a longer form than in Mark, and it can be argued, with *some* probability, at all events, that the shorter form appears to be a contraction of the longer form. If, then, for the comparatively few sayings, teachings, and parables (over and above the sayings embedded in the stories) recorded in Mark, Mark used a special written source, and if some of these sayings and parables are also found, though not always in the same places and connections, in Matthew and Luke, may it not be that the special extra source of Matthew and Luke (known as Q) was also one of the sources of Mark ?

This is a question of acute controversy which has aroused quite strong feelings among the theologians, and for a very good reason. If Q, the extra source of Matthew and Luke, is older than Mark, *its relatively early date is secured.* If Q is later than Mark—secondary as compared with Mark—then the authenticity of its material is *pro tanto* less probable. Let us suppose, however, that Mark did not know or use Q, and that his sayings and parables which are parallel with those of Q come from some other source, then it may be that his ignorance of Q did not result because Q was written after him, but because, though Q is earlier than he, he had not come across this particular source. In that case, Matthew and Luke use a source which is older than Mark, though Mark did not use it. And, in that case, the early date of Q is still secured, and the probable authenticity of its material unimpaired !

The question whether Mark used Q, and the exciting question whether Q is older or younger than Mark, are only to be decided by internal evidence. This evidence has led to opposite conclusions. Wellhausen (followed by Meyer) is a great champion of the priority of Mark ; he finds in Q constant traces of later and secondary traits, or of more ' developed ' points of view, when compared with Mark. Other scholars take an almost precisely opposite view. Wellhausen holds not only that Q is later than Mark, but that Q knew Mark and used him. The great theologian Harnack, who in 1907 published a small and valuable treatise on Q—the apostolic and early character of which he warmly defends—then held that the verbal parallels between Mark and Q were not due to either having borrowed from the other. Both he then held were independent of each other, though Q was older than Mark. The verbal parallels were due to common oral tradition. ' No proof can be given,' said the great Harnack in 1907, ' of any literary relationship between the two works. And this fact is an indication that we must not date Q all too early: for had Q been already long in circulation, we could neither understand that Mark did not know it nor that he did not make use of it, even though he wrote at a distance from Palestine' (*Sprüche und Reden Jesu*, p. 172). Later on Harnack admitted that ' at least Mark knew the circle in which Q, or large portions of it, existed orally, before it was committed to writing, and existed substantially in the same form.' (See Moffatt, p. 205.)

The hypothesis that Mark knew and used Q has been strongly maintained and upheld by a number of distinguished scholars, such as Loisy, Bacon, Bousset, and others. The first-named writer, in his edition of the Synoptic Gospels, published in 1908, was willing and ready to believe that for Q, no less than for Mark's narrative source, Peter was an ultimate authority. Like the narrative source, the ' sayings ' source was not formed without him. The date of both sources may be about the same ; their place of origin (Jerusalem), their original language (Aramaic), may also be the same. And the spirit of the two sources, ' so far as one can judge, was about the same. Both expressed the recollections and the faith of the earliest Christian community without any influence of Pauline theology : the Galilæan apostles appeared in both as the authorized witnesses of the life and the teaching of Christ' (*E. S.* i. p. 114).

Loisy suggests that the following bits of Mark may be due to Q :

(1) The summary of the preaching of John (i. 4, 7, 8).

(2) The stories about the Sabbath (ii. 23–28, iii. 1–6).

(3) The dispute about Beelzebul (iii. 22–30).

(4) The parables (iv. 1–34).

(5) The saying about Jesus eating with tax-collectors and sinners (ii. 17).

(6) The saying about fasting (ii. 19, 20).

(7) The saying about that which defiles a man (vii. 15).

(8) The answer to those who asked for a sign (viii. 12).

(9) The saying about the leaven of the Pharisees (viii. 15).

(10) The saying about renouncement (viii. 35).

(11) The teachings given at the last stay of Jesus at Capernaum (ix. 33–50).

(12) The saying about divorce (x. 1–12).

(13) The sayings about service (x. 42–45).

(14) The curt summary which is all that Mark gives of the discourse against the Pharisees (xii. 38–40).

(15) Certain bits in the apocalyptic discourse (xiii.).

Goguel (*Introduction*, pp. 250–267, 328–332) draws up a similar, but not identical, list of passages.

In my first edition I was inclined to believe that Loisy and the others were right, and that Mark both used and knew some form or recension of Q. But now I am much more doubtful. There seems a great deal to be said for the older view of Harnack, strongly urged by Moffatt, that Mark and Q are independent of each other. Why should not many sayings of Jesus have been reproduced in more than one collection and source ? ' Sayings of Jesus, such as come into question here, must have been circulating in many directions; it is contrary to all probabilities that they were drawn into the single channel or canal of Q, so that any other writer had to derive them from this source. In the nature of the case there must have been a considerable amount of material common to the Petrine tradition and the Matthæan Logia ; it is to adopt an ultra-literary method if we explain any parallels between the reproduction of the former in Mark and the latter by the hypothesis of borrowing, especially as Q itself must have gone back partially to the Petrine tradition of the sayings. No satisfactory explanation is offered why Mark made such scanty use of Q. Several of its sayings would have been perfectly relevant to his purpose ; we can hardly imagine a Christian evangelist ignoring words like those of Matt. xi. 27, or assuming that because his readers already possessed Q, it was superfluous to repeat its contents, and even the hypothesis that he only knew a shorter form of Q fails to meet this objection. In no instance is it absolutely necessary, either on the score of substance or of style, to assume that Mark borrowed from Q ' (p. 205). ' The abstract possibility must indeed be left open, that the author of Mark (though not the Ur-Marcus) was acquainted with some form of Q ; he could hardly fail to be.' ' The later Mark is dated, especially as the edition of an Ur-Marcus, the more difficult it is to deny the possibility, and even the probability, that the writer knew Q, and to explain how it could be merely a subsidiary source ' (p. 206). A good deal depends upon whether we are to assume that Mark wished, or intended, to include everything that he knew about Jesus, or whether his object was to present a record of his ministry and death, and to set forth and prove a certain theory about him— his Messiahship, his divine Sonship, why he was rejected by the Jews, etc.—but not to include all he knew or had read of his teaching, only to give a few specimens and illustrations of it. Of these two different conceptions of Mark's purposes something will be said in the next section.

Bacon, in his latest work, still maintains that Mark used ' the second source.' It is ' not conceivable that the evangelist was ignorant of those important elements of the teaching of Jesus which he frequently refers to, but does not give *in extenso*.' ' The exclusions of Mark are deliberate. He has exercised a selective choice in his material, preferring that which appeals to the eye as compared with what was addressed to the ear. But his reason for this cannot have been merely literary. His purpose was nothing less than a declaration to the reader of the Way of Eternal Life as understood by Christians. If, then, we find greater emphasis on " things done " rather than " things spoken " in this Gospel, we are entitled to conclude that the evangelist conceived " the Gospel " in these terms. Now Mark has only one parallel in the primitive age for such a conception, a parallel which goes far beyond it. Paul's example in treating " the Gospel " as concerned primarily with the work of God in Christ is carried to an extent which no later evangelist would dare to emulate ; hence the extent to which Mark has carried this relative neglect of the teaching of Jesus may be reckoned in a broad sense among the evidences of " influence from Paul." The paucity of teaching material, reckoned as a defect by later evangelists, is really an evidence for the early date of Mark ' (p. 138). ' In the Second Source (really older than Mark and in several respects better informed) the main interest had been the " sayings " rather than the " doings." Perhaps because of its arrangement of the material in the form of brief anecdotes intro-

ducing discourses in which the " sayings " had already extended
into the form of didactic discourses, perhaps because it lacked the
prestige attaching to Mark as directly representing Peter, the
original order of Q has not survived.   Both later Synoptists use
the order of Mark in preference to that of the Second Source, if
indeed the original order and literary structure of the Second
Source had not by their time already been largely modified by
revision and accretion.   Our study confirms the generally accepted
verdict of criticism that the Gospel of Mark is based on written
sources, among which must be included some form of the Second
Source, though for reasons of his own Mark has used Q in only a
sparing way, and with the primary object of obtaining from it data
bearing on his own account of the career and person of Jesus.
Certainly when employed in common by Matthew and Luke, and
probably when employed by Mark, the Second Source had already
been translated into Greek from its original Aramaic ' (p. 317).

§ 9. *Wellhausen and others on Mark and Q.*

The reasons which induced Wellhausen to hold that Q is everywhere later than Mark are largely, though not exclusively, due to
a comparison of the form and the environment of certain passages
in Mark, parallels to which are also found in Matthew and Luke
and were presumably borrowed from Q, with their environment
and form in Luke and Matthew.   In every case he finds reasons
for thinking that form and environment in Q suggest a later date
for Q.   Thus there are some nine verses in Mark which are parallel
to some nine verses in Matthew's Sermon on the Mount (which
occupies 107 verses in all).   Wellhausen holds that the originality
in the case of each of these nine verses is on the side of Mark.
And so on.   We shall have occasion to notice some of Wellhausen's
arguments about such parallel passages, together with those of his
opponents, in the course of the commentary.   But in addition to
these comparisons Wellhausen has general reasons as well.   He
holds, for instance, that the general religious point of view of Q is
later than that of Mark.   Into this delicate and difficult point I
cannot enter here : it will be incidentally alluded to more than
once in the commentary upon Matthew.   But there is a further
argument which more especially concerns Mark.   It is this.   The
Gospel according to Mark is much the shortest of the Synoptics.
Luke is a little longer than Matthew, and Mark stands to Matthew
in the proportion of two to three.   Mark consists of stories and
incidents in the life of Jesus, together with some specimens of
his oral teaching.   But the stories occupy a far bigger space than
the words.   Of speeches which occupy more than two or three

continuous verses, or which do not, as it were, form part of the
narratives and stories, there are very few.   They certainly do not
occupy more than one-fifth of the first twelve chapters.   Hence, as
I have already indicated, the question arises : Did the author of the
Gospel of Mark absorb and reproduce *all* that he had heard, and *all*
that he had read (if written sources were known to him), about the
life and teaching of Jesus ?   It is not so much in connection with
incidents and stories in Jesus's life that this question is important ;
its main importance lies in connection with what Jesus *said*, with his
speeches, parables, and oral teaching.   Of these there is a great
deal in Matthew and Luke which is not found in Mark.   Did Mark
know of the existence of all these extra speeches, or did he not ?
If many of them existed in Q, and if Mark knew and used Q, why
did he omit them from his book ?   On the fact of this omission,
which one must agree with Jülicher in regarding as very remarkable
(*im höchsten Grade merkwürdig*), Wellhausen naturally lays stress.
For he holds that there is no reason to believe that Mark deliberately
omitted from his Gospel many sayings and words of Jesus which
nevertheless were known to him.

'Attempts have been made to lessen the importance of literary
scrutiny by the contention that oral tradition is older than its
written sediment, and that the former must have contained more
than the latter.   This consideration is in itself justified, and may
be of practical moment in some cases.   But it must not, indeed,
be overlooked that in the course of time the primary tradition
decreased and the secondary tradition increased.   Without doubt
Mark intended to write down the whole tradition : the sayings of
Jesus together with the stories about him.   It is impossible to
allow that he did not put in everything he could procure, that he
left out what had been written down already.   He is by no means
merely a filler-in of gaps.   If unintentionally, or against his intentions, this thing or that escaped his notice, the gleanings of old and
genuine material which he left to the others cannot have been
immeasurably richer than his harvest.   The Sermon on the Mount,
the absence of which has been much noticed in Mark, and which
formerly some wished to ascribe to him, is not only unknown to
him, but entirely contradicts his presentation of the Galilæan
activity of Jesus.   The same thing is true of the Lord's prayer.   In
Mark (xi. 22–25) Jesus also exhorts his disciples to pray, and at the
same time impresses upon them, 'As we forgive our debtors,' but
he does not give them the formula of a community prayer because,
so far, they are not a community.   As B. Weiss has realized, the
Lord's prayer in Matthew is only an addendum.   According to
Luke it was given to the disciples so that they should not lag
behind the disciples of John, who were organized as a community

before the disciples of Jesus. Probably it originated at a time—as did also fasting and baptism—when Christian worship became actually established, *i.e.* after the death of Jesus' (*Einleitung*, p. 77).

The Christian community, W. urges, is in Q already formed. It has undergone persecutions. The new era has appeared. John the Baptist belongs to the old era which has passed. The Kingdom of God has begun. To Mark, Jesus, it is true, is already in his own mind Son of God and Messiah from the baptism, but a theory is needed to explain why he does not *teach* that he is that: for in historic reality he did not do so. But in Q the deep division between after and before the scene at Cæsarea Philippi is not recognized, and in any case the Messianic or Sonship consciousness of Jesus is expressed by Q in more exalted terms than in Mark, and in sayings and scenes which are supposed to take place before the confession of Peter. (Matt. xi. 26, which most great scholars allow to be unauthentic, shows a very developed Christology.) Jesus doubtless made many long speeches and 'sermons,' but these would not be remembered as they were spoken. The speeches and sermons of Matthew or even of Q are expansions and bringings together of shorter sayings such as we find in Mark. The parallel sayings in Mark are not bits of speeches which Mark has taken from their settings and scattered here and there in his book. Moreover, Wellhausen denies that Mark and Q can be regarded as independent of one another. 'Gospel literature took its rise in the Jerusalem community, and its beginnings, which did not become at once very large, must [all] have been known within this limited and closely-related circle. It is especially difficult to imagine that among the authors themselves the predecessor could have escaped the notice of the follower' (p. 157).

It cannot be denied that there is some force in Wellhausen's contentions. Jülicher, who, as I have said, admits that the fact of the omissions is remarkable, also attempts to explain it. And doubtless his explanations, if we hold that the arguments which go to prove Mark's use of Q are too strong to be rejected, must be accepted for lack of better. He (like other scholars) thinks that we must take into grave account the nature and object of Mark's work and book. Mark's great object was to show that Jesus was the Messiah, the Son of God. Hence, like Paul, he does not care so much for Jesus's sayings as for his person, his Messiahship, his relation to God. He desired to depict the life and Messianic character of Jesus rather than his teaching. His Gospel was intended for the use of missionaries and preachers. To convert the heathen, it was useful that the proof of the Messiahship and the superhuman character of Jesus, with a description of his many miracles, and of his Passion and death, should be in the hands of the preacher. ' On the other hand, the precepts which Jesus had given, his teachings about prayer, trust in God, forgiveness of sin and so on—these were reserved for those who had already accepted the new faith' (*Einleitung*, p. 286). In another connection the same author observes that perhaps Mark (in obedience to the maxim contained in Matt. vii. 6) was anxious to entrust only so much of the holy words of the Master to the publicity of a Hellenistic world as it must needs know in order to realize his greatness. We can scarcely attach much cogency to this suggestion : perhaps we may rather accept his other observation that the only tolerable explanation which he can think of for the smallness of space given in Mark to Jesus's words is that a collection of that kind (*i.e.* Q) was already in the hands of believers. The oldest edition of Q is thus known to Mark, but because it exists, he does not think it necessary to make use of it in his own work. So too thought Renan, who further supposed that the spirit of Peter, ' somewhat narrow and unimaginative,' was perhaps the cause ' of such a suppression.'

But, perhaps, on the whole, the least unsatisfactory explanation (for one can hardly call it more) of the difficulty is that the Q which was known to Luke and Matthew was other and bigger than the Q which was known to Mark. In other words, as was implied in the preceding paragraph, Q went through several expansions and editions : it grew, and was added to from time to time. We may perhaps assume, in the words of Jülicher, ' a gradual expansion and growth of Q from some isolated series of sentences to that sort of half-Gospel, in which we can first trace its existence in history ' (' Ein allmähliches Anwachsen von Q aus losen Spruchreihen zu dem Halbevangelium als dass es dann in der Literaturgeschichte auf uns stösst '). ' Its beginnings would go back to a very early period, long before Mark : while later on, under the influence of Mark, it would have become more and more rounded off and completed ' (*Einleitung*, p. 322). It is difficult to believe that if Mark had known of such a saying as Matt. xi. 27, he would not have taken care to include it in his book. What more significant evidence and proof of the unique relation of Jesus to God ?

In spite of the many distinguished scholars who maintain either that Mark knew and used Q, or that, at any rate, Q is as early as, or earlier than, Mark, it seemed desirable to repeat these paragraphs from my first edition as they stood. Nor can it, I think, be denied that the passages in Matthew and Luke which verbally correspond most closely together, and are therefore most surely to be ascribed to Q, are by no means all of equally probable authenticity. Nor because a given saying or paragraph is beautiful, original or important is it necessarily authentic. Wellhausen utters a maxim which I have quoted, or shall quote, more than once. ' Truth only testifies to itself and not to its author.' ' Die Wahrheit bezeugt nur sich selber und nicht ihren Autor.' Moreover, the spirit of Jesus continued to live in the community which his life and his death brought into being, and words in which his spirit was expressed seemed, with some inner justification, worthy to be reckoned as his ; it was what he would have said in the given circumstances. His ethical teaching was developed upon the basis which he had created. Written in more sarcastic manner is Wellhausen's remark in the second edition of his *Einleitung* : ' If the essential value of a given saying is to be regarded as any proof of its age and authenticity, such a test would remind one of the fabulous archæologist who recognized the genuineness of an antique because the look of it made him cry. If that which moves us, elevates us, and goes to our heart is therefore genuine, all exegetic and historic and literary investigation becomes superfluous ' (p. 159).

On the other hand, if, as Bacon urges, we need not assume that Mark wanted to include all the words and teachings of Jesus within the compass of his book, or if again there may have been many authentic sayings of Jesus of which he had never heard, and the records of which he had never seen, we have no reason to bother with regard to the omissions from his Gospel of what we may conjecturally assign to Q. And then Q may be as old as Mark, or, in parts, even older. The arguments by which Wellhausen would prove the secondary character of Q as compared with Mark, more especially in those passages where there is a parallelism between them (where both record the same saying or incident) are, it must be allowed, and as will be noticed in the commentary, traversed by other scholars in almost every case.

Meyer, while agreeing with Wellhausen that Mark did not use Q, yet assigns to Q a very high authority and a comparatively early date. Both Mark and Q are ' products (*Brechungen*) of one and the same tradition. Beide gehen auf die älteste Phase des Christentums zurück, die noch ganz im Judentum wurzelt, und auf semitischem Boden sich abspielt; die Übertragung ins Griechische ist erst später hinzugekommen ' (I. p. 226). (I should not be able to allow that Matthew xi. 25–27 is ' rooted in Judaism '). Meanwhile, it is possible that the quarrel between Wellhausen and his opponents about Mark and Q may before long become of minor importance. For if, in each particular saying or sentence, we have to weigh its origin and nature quite apart from its *provenance*, apart from the mere fact of its being found in Mark or in Q, if we have to judge its authenticity from itself or from its immediate setting, then the catchword ' Mark ' or ' Q ' becomes, it would seem, of secondary value. The detailed and elaborate work

of Bultmann in this connection seems little known or appreciated
so far (1926) in England, but his investigations, like those of his
fellow *Formgeschichtler*, are ultimately bound to have their effect.
We shall no longer be able to say : ' From Q or from Mark ; therefore
early ; therefore authentic.' The laws or methods by which sayings
were collected, added or grouped together, and attributed to Jesus
will have to be considered : the sayings which are probably due to
the community will have to be more carefully separated from those
which are probably due to himself ; others may have to be regarded
as even older than Jesus, but ascribed to him, or given a Christian
adaptation. What is of purely Palestinian origin will have to be
distinguished from what comes from early, but yet Hellenistic,
Jewish communities which had become Christian, and so on. For
even Q, though originally composed in Aramaic, and giving a
picture of Jesus from the basis of Palestinian tradition, was probably
soon translated into more than one Greek version, and received
additions from early Hellenistic Christian sources. All these and
many other matters are discussed in Bultmann's book, and though
his conclusions may often need modification, and though his scepticism, as regards the authenticity and the 'historicity' of many stories
and sayings, is probably much overdone, it is (as it seems to me) very
improbable that his work will leave things as they were and remain
without influence or effect.

Canon Streeter, in his learned book on the Four Gospels, never
mentions or alludes to any of the *Formgeschichtler*. Dibelius,
Schmidt (K. L.), Bultmann, are absent from his index. His own
conclusions, as my commentary will show, are highly conservative,
but they are none the more negligible on that account. As regards
Mark and Q, he now comes out strongly for the opinion that ' the
evidence is decidedly against the view that Mark used Q.' His
main argument is that in the more prominent cases where Mark and
Q ' overlap,' it is practically impossible to believe that Mark could
have had Q before him. ' If Mark did use Q, he must have trusted
to memory, and never once have referred to the written source.'
But yet Streeter holds that Q's version of common material is often
more authentic than Mark's. So ' the general, though not invariable, superiority of the Q version remains to be accounted for. This
can only be done if we suppose that Q was a document of very early
date and represents a peculiarly authentic tradition' (p. 191).
Thus, while Streeter and Wellhausen both agree that Mark did not
use Q, the latter seeks to show that Mark is everywhere earlier and
more primary than Q, whereas Streeter argues that Q is earlier, and
often better informed, than Mark.

§ 10. *Date of Mark.*

The Gospel of Mark was written either in one jet, or ' edited ' throughout on the basis of an older form of it ; in either case, it was written on the basis of older sources, somewhere, perhaps, about A.D. 70.   It is generally agreed that it was written outside Palestine, and for Gentile readers.   Moffatt justly observes, ' That the gospel, in its present form, was intended for an audience outside Palestine is plain not only from Mark's omission of much Jewish detail that is preserved in the ordinary synoptic tradition, but from his careful explanations of customs, phrases, and names which would be unfamiliar to Christians of Gentile birth throughout the empire ' (p. 236).   Some authorities plead strongly for its origin in Rome and for the use of the Roman church.   Its occasional Latinisms would favour this view.   Loisy observes that ' it seems impossible that the author of Mark should have written his work in Palestine or in a locality where ' the tradition of the first apostles and the immediate disciples of Jesus must have been widely represented.'   ' This circumstance does not exclude Rome, but does not decisively recommend it ; nevertheless the presentation of Mark by the side of more complete Gospels, or the probability that it was compiled in a country of Latin speech (though its use of Latin words is not a decisive argument seeing that Roman rule had necessarily introduced many Latin words even in the East) can be invoked in support of the more or less traditional hypothesis.   Perhaps even it is due to its character as an old *Roman* Gospel, rather than to the origin of one of its sources, that the book owes its attribution to a disciple of Peter ' (*E. S.* I. p. 119).   Canon Streeter is much more definite. ' The tradition connecting the Gospels of Mark and John with Rome and Ephesus is so early and fits in so well with other pieces of evidence that it may safely be accepted.   In particular, the view that Mark was the old Gospel of the all-important Church of Rome would completely account for its inclusion in the Canon ' (p. 12).   He accepts unhesitatingly the tradition about Mark and Peter, and Mark, moreover (as an Urmarcus is a mere phantom), is the author of the whole Gospel as we have it now.   He is quite angry with, or contemptuous of, those who would reject tradition in this regard (p. 562).   Yet how differently other scholars, no less capable of judging than he, assess the same evidence.   ' By far our best source as to the history of Jesus is the Gospel according to Mark, but it is strange how little we know of its origin.   Papias and Irenaeus are our only early informants, but, except for a vague tradition that the Gospel is connected with Peter, they tell us nothing ' (*Beginnings*, I. p. 267).   As to Mark's date, Streeter assigns it to about A.D. 65 (so also Meyer, I. p. 237), for Mark xiii. 14, rightly interpreted,

does not imply that the Temple had fallen, but more probably the
reverse. The Church had begun to think less of a near End. It
found it ' necessary to look backward. The Church of Rome
becomes interested in history ; it demands at least a record of the
Founder's life. The Gospel of Mark is the response to that demand.
The story told by Clement of Alexandria (ap. Eus. *H. E.* vi. 14),
how the Roman Christians besought Mark, as the disciple of Peter,
to produce such an account, may be only a conjecture. But since
Mark seems to have been in Rome about this time (2 Tim. iv. 11), it
is exactly what we should have expected to occur, though we need
not, like Clement, suppose that everything in Mark's Gospel was
derived from Peter. Once a Gospel like that of Mark had been
composed, its utility and interest—more than that, its indispens-
ability—would have been obvious to all. Christians would have
wondered, just as we to-day wonder, how the churches had managed
to get along at all without some such work. Everywhere, throughout the Empire, a Life of Christ by a disciple of Peter would have
been hailed as the satisfaction of what had been for long a half-
conscious need ' (p. 497). It is intensely interesting that we get
distinguished scholars such as Streeter and Bultmann, who have
both devoted so much time and thought to these questions, coming,
even to-day, on the basis of all that has been written on the matter,
to such very different results. Yet as to the *date* of Mark there is,
after all, not so much difference between them. Both would agree
that it was written between about A.D. 65–75. A limit of ten years
unites them. But one feels that, whereas to the one, Mark and Peter
together may justly allow one to believe that most of the stories
told in the second Gospel about Jesus happened just as they are
repeated to us, and that most of the words put into the mouth of
Jesus were actually uttered by him, to the other, Mark and Peter,
in the last resort, have little to do with the book as we have it before
us, and many of the stories and many of the sayings are probably
unauthentic and unhistoric. Happily there are various resting-
places between Streeter and Burkitt, on the one hand, and Loisy
and Bultmann, on the other. Moffatt, Klostermann, and other great
scholars would, I believe, still sanction the view that the main
historic outlines of the brief public career of Jesus and of the circumstances of his death are to be *really* found in Mark and are *only*
to be found there. Problems indeed there are which the Gospel
suggests and raises in plenty. They will meet us in the course of the
commentary. But, in spite of them, we are enabled to get from
Mark an insight into the general course of that last fateful year or
eighteen months of Jesus's life, and also into some main elements
of his teaching and character. We cannot be grateful enough to
the author of this Gospel. We may still retain our gratitude even

though Mark does not provide us with ' a history of Jesus told for its own sake,' but rather ' with an early and authoritative statement of the evidence by which the first Greek-speaking Christians justified their own position,' so that Mark ' is far more a primary authority for the thought of the Apostolic Age than for the life of Jesus ' (*Beginnings*, I. p. 268). Even so, the historic Jesus is, at least partially, revealed to us in Mark.

Bacon, as we have seen, advocates a date not earlier than A.D. 80. The Christian community has already known persecution of various kinds. ' Like all the Gospels, that of Mark, their prototype, rested primarily on the accumulated teaching material of some local community. It circulated at first only in the region of its birth. Probably it passed through several phases of enlargement before it found wider acceptance.' Bacon, too, accepts the Roman *provenance*. ' The situation which would best account for its militant tone is one which calls for the same heroic stand on the part of the world-wide brotherhood in imitation of the martyr death of the Servant as that to which the writers of Hebrews and First Peter summon their readers. The social character of Mark is that of a community product. But its community is no narrow one. The believer who in imitation of the Lord forsakes all, incurring the enmity of those of his own household, being delivered up to death by parents, children, brothers, hated of all men for Christ's sake, will find his reward not only in the eternal life of heavenly glory, but also in the present age. The love is as wide-spread as the hatred. Many of those to whom this Gospel was first given had already suffered the spoiling of their goods. They could find comfort in Jesus's answer to Peter and the Twelve when these began to say, " Lo, we have left all and followed thee." Jesus had promised that such sufferers should "receive a hundredfold now in this time, houses and brethren and sisters and mothers and children and lands, with persecutions." Mark and First Peter have readers who know what it is both to " suffer for the name " and to receive kindnesses "in name that ye are Christ's." It is in this deutero-Petrine age of world-wide suffering under persecution, offset by a world-wide drawing together of the Church, that we must find the true environment of the first attempt (or at least the first surviving attempt) to bind together the scattered anecdotes of the apostolic preaching into a story of the ministry and martyrdom of Jesus ' (p. 324). We have in Mark stories and sayings which we may regard as due to men who heard and saw Jesus do some of the things and say some of the words which are attributed to him. Perhaps we have, in edited form, reminiscences of Peter himself. But we have also the echoes of early reflection upon these doings and sayings, echoes of the fortunes of the early community, of their hopes and fears, their troubles and sorrows, their enthusiasm and their faith. Mark is a wonderful amalgam, but the strands are partially recoverable by patient and impartial investigation into those far-off days.

§ 11. *The Gospel of Matthew : its relation to Mark.*

It has already been said that almost the whole of Mark is incorporated in Matthew, who also to a very considerable extent follows the order of Mark's narrative, both as to the sequence of the stories which Mark relates, as well as, naturally, in the general outline of the life. In Matthew, as in Mark, we find Jesus first teaching in Galilee, passing for a brief space northwards, out of Galilee, on to heathen soil, and then turning again southwards and moving towards Jerusalem. But Matthew is much longer than Mark. As regards the last days of Jesus's life, the arrest, the trial, and the crucifixion, there is no great difference between them—136 verses in Matthew and 119 verses in Mark. But Matthew opens his book with a long genealogy and with an account of Jesus's birth and infancy, which are wanting in Mark. These occupy forty-eight verses. From the opening of his book to the beginning of the events of the Passion, Mark has thirteen chapters and 539 verses. From the point where Mark begins to the same place in the narrative, Matthew has twenty-three chapters and 863 verses, that is, 324 verses more than Mark, or just three-fifths as much again. Of this large amount of extra material a very considerable proportion consists of speeches—reports of words said by Jesus rather than of things done by him.

But in reality the extra material of sayings is still larger. For many narratives in Mark are considerably curtailed in Matthew, and there are a few things in Mark which do not appear in Matthew at all. Roughly speaking there are some 410 verses in Matthew which contain sayings of Jesus which are not found in Mark, and of these 410 verses we may take it that some 230 have more or less close parallels in Luke, while some 180 verses are peculiar to Matthew. Thus Matthew (like Luke) is composed of three parts : material common to him and Mark, material common to him and Luke, material found only in him. (It should, of course, be remembered that much of the Mark material which is reproduced in Matthew is also reproduced in Luke.)

§ 12. *The relation of Matthew and Luke to Q.*

Of those portions of Matthew which have no parallel in Mark, and which, as we have seen, as regards the sayings of Jesus, amount to about 180 verses for what is peculiar to Matthew, and about 230 verses for what he shares with Luke, the portion which is common, more or less completely and verbally, to the first and the third Evangelists, is supposed by most great scholars not to have been borrowed by Matthew from Luke, or by Luke from Matthew, but to have been taken by both Matthew and Luke from a common source, now generally spoken of as Q. It will be convenient to adopt this same nomenclature here.

Some remarks about Q have already been made in the preceding section. The range, character, and origin of the document are still in dispute. It probably began with the baptism of Jesus, and thus, like Mark, regarded Jesus as entering upon his Messianic office from that moment. It included the temptation, but most scholars hold that it did not include any account of the Passion or resurrection. It was essentially a collection of the sayings and speeches of Jesus, and where it incorporated any story, it did so in order to give the occasion and background of a saying or a speech. I have already mentioned Harnack's book on the subject of Q, in which the great theologian earnestly and even vehemently pleads for Q's primitive character, authenticity, and early date. I have also mentioned how Wellhausen maintained a contrary hypothesis, arguing that Q is later than Mark, and that the words which Q puts into the mouth of Jesus must always be regarded with more suspicion than those which are assigned to him by Mark. Not that Wellhausen would by any means wish to controvert the authenticity of *all* the Q material. But he held a much smaller proportion to be genuine than Harnack, who practically accepts the whole.

How much of what we now find in Matthew and Luke may be assigned to Q ? This is a still disputed question, and can never be ascertained with certainty. Harnack is very cautious. His estimate of Q comes only to about 202 verses, while some 28 verses more are regarded as doubtful. Loisy assigns to the source a very much larger quantity of verses. For example, many of the parables which are *only* found in Matthew or are *only* found in Luke, Loisy assigns to Q. Wellhausen thought it doubtful whether all those passages which are common to Luke and Matthew may with some assurance be always assigned to one source only. And the same doubts are virtually expressed by Moffatt as well. ' Some of Q's logia were in circulation in other forms.' The material in Matthew and Luke which, at the first glance, appears to be drawn from a common source is by no means always verbally identical. It varies from practical identity to very considerable divergence. As to the bits which are verbally or practically identical, there can be very little hesitation in assigning them to Q—in assigning them, that is, to a single written, if hypothetical, document used by both

Matthew and Luke. The doubts and the needful fresh explanations begin when we come to the passages which differ in their wording more or less considerably in the first and third Gospels, and yet show that they are fundamentally the same saying, discourse, or parable. How are the differences to be accounted for ? That the changes are merely due to Matthew and Luke themselves, that is, to the two men who used Q, and that they edited Q, each one in his own way, will not explain the differences adequately, or explain why so often there are no differences or virtually none. Hence it has been held that, even though Q was a written document, it circulated in more than one form, even before its translation into Greek. But it was translated (so many scholars believe, on the basis of a second famous Papias passage, see below), into more than one Greek version by different hands, and these translations naturally varied. Or one translation may have had several ' recensions,' and some things were added to the Greek which had never existed, or had never been written down, in Aramaic. Matthew used one of these recensions, Luke used another. So Q in this way becomes a very elastic sort of document ! Some things in it may be much older (so far as writing down is concerned) than other things ; many passages of Aramaic origin are not merely Palestinian, but very ' Jewish,' though also very probably authentic ; others may be of Hellenistic-Christian origin, were, perhaps, written in Greek from the start, and are more doubtfully authentic. There is one most famous saying which appeared early in Q, since it is verbally the same both in Matthew and Luke, and which, nevertheless, seems of Hellenistic-Christian origin and not authentic. (See the commentary on Matt. xi. 25–27.) This theory of (a) an expanding Q, a Q with accretions, (b) a Q of different recensions, altered in translation, and ' worked over ' (Moffatt, p. 196) in different ways by the two evangelists concerned, might be, and has actually been, used to explain why some of the Q passages in Matthew and Luke seem older, and to reflect a more primitive point of view, than Mark, while other passages seem later, and appear to reflect a more ' developed ' point of view. In this way the views of Wellhausen, put with such great force and brilliancy in his Introduction and commentaries, and the views of, say, Harnack, Loisy and others, may be capable of partial reconcilement. It is in this way that Jülicher attempted to reconcile them.

§ 13. Streeter on Q and on M.

An entirely different explanation of the differences between Matthew and Luke in some of the supposed Q material has been put forward, with great force, learning, insight, originality, and clearness, by Streeter. For reasons which I have no space to reproduce here, he dismisses the hypothesis of different recensions or editions of Q, and he supposes that (a) the discourse and parable passages in Matthew and Luke which, though showing fundamental agreements, show also large verbal differences, and (b) the discourse and parable passages which are peculiar to Matthew or peculiar to Luke, come from two other old and valuable sources which he styles respectively M and L. Thus there are four very ancient sources for the life and the words of Jesus—Mark, Q, M, and L. Q is dated at about A.D. 50, L and Mark at 60, M at 65. They come from different churches and localities ; L (the author of which was no less Luke than the final editor of the entire Gospel) from Cæsarea, Mark from Rome, Q from Antioch, and M from Jerusalem. Matthew, there-fore (over and above oral tradition), has three main sources, Mark, Q, and M. What is peculiar to Matthew, and what, while parallel with Luke passages which come from Q, is so different from Q that it cannot be rightly regarded as coming from Q, was drawn from M. Streeter admits that he cannot *prove* that all the material which is peculiar to Matthew came from a single source. ' All that we can say is that, while only a few passages are Judaistic in the party sense, the whole of it is redolent of the soil of Judaea ; that it is the kind of collection we should expect to emanate from Jerusalem ; and, lastly, that it is hard to account for the fact that so very little tradition of any value has survived outside the Four Gospels, unless we suppose that the tradition of the Church of Jerusalem, which we should expect to be quite exceptionally rich, is incorporated in one or other of those Gospels. That Matthew made use of a source or sources which were in some respects parallel to Q and L, I regard as proved ; that this material, along with, at any rate, the bulk of his peculiar matter, was the cycle of tradition of the Church of Jerusalem, is in no sense proved ; but it seems more probable than any alternative suggestion ' (p. 261). M, then, was Judæo-Christian. ' The material peculiar to Matthew, in sharp contrast to Luke's, is characterized by a conspicuously Jewish atmosphere ; and, though rich in anti-Pharisaic polemic, it asserts the obligation of obeying not only the Law but " the tradition of the scribes," and it has a distinctly anti-Gentile bias. It reflects the spirit and outlook with which in the New Testament the name of James is associated ; though James himself, like most leaders, was doubtless far less extreme than his professed followers. The source M will naturally be connected with Jerusalem, the head-quarters of the James party ' (p. 232). ' Judaistic sayings in Matthew only occur in contexts which on other grounds we should refer to M, or where there is evidence of conflation between Q and another source. In all these Judaistic passages it is difficult not to suspect the influence of the desire of the followers of James to find a justification for their disapprobation of the attitude of Paul, by inventing sayings of Christ, or misquoting sayings which, even if authentic, must originally have been spoken in view of entirely different circumstances. The sayings of every great leader have always been quoted by his followers in the next generation to justify their own attitude in circumstances quite different from his ; and where there exists no written or printed record to check their original form it is easy for the actual wording, as well as the application, of the sayings to become changed ' (p. 256). Q, on the other hand, is pro-Gentile. It comes from Galilee and Antioch. Q is ' a Greek document which the authors of the First and Third Gospels had in common, and the fact that this Greek document was known to the authors of both these Gospels means that it probably came to them with the backing of the Church of some important Greek city. But that is no reason why it may not have been a translation of an Aramaic work by Matthew—possibly with some amplification from local tradition. What became of the Twelve Apostles is one of the mysteries of history. The resident head of the Jerusalem Church was, not one of the Twelve, but James the brother of the Lord. From Galatians and Acts we should gather that to Peter and the sons of Zebedee Jerusalem was for a time a kind of headquarters. But in regard to the rest there is no tradition which, either from its early date or its intrinsic probability, deserves credence. But we know from the Rabbis that for many centuries Capernaum was a great centre for " Minim " or Christians, so that it is probable that others of the Twelve made that city their headquarters. Geographically Capernaum is between Antioch and Jerusalem, and some Christian trader from Antioch having business at Capernaum, or in some city of Decapolis, may well have come across a collection of sayings made by Matthew and brought it home. The hypothesis that Q emanated from the (perhaps, freer) atmosphere of Galilee and became the primitive " gospel " of a Gentile Church, like Antioch, accounts for its inclusion of the saying (Luke xvi. 16, Matt. xi. 13), " The law and the prophets were until John." It also explains at once the puzzling fact that in a document, otherwise apparently entirely confined to discourse, there should have stood the one single narrative of the centurion's servant. That story leads up to, and gives the facts that called forth from Christ the saying, " I have not found so great faith, no, not in Israel." At a time when the Judaizing section of the Church wished to give the uncircumcised an inferior status, that story was in itself a charter of Gentile liberty. The Greek translation of Q, at any rate, must have been made for the use of a Greek Church, and since, if we regard the material peculiar to Luke as representing the tradition of Cæsarea,

that city is ruled out, Antioch, the first capital of Gentile Christianity, is the most likely place of origin ' (pp. 232, 233).   If it be
argued that it is needless to regard the pro-Gentile and the anti-
Gentile passages as coming from two different documents, for, as in
Matthew the two kinds of sayings occur side by side, the same thing
may have happened in Q, Streeter replies that ' it is not very likely
that the author of a primitive document would put side by side
sayings implying contrary rulings on what at the time he wrote was
a highly controversial issue ; it is quite another matter for a later
writer, very conservative as Matthew is in his use of his sources, to
include contrary sayings found in two different ancient documents,
especially as the controversy in question had by that time largely
died down ' (p. 256).   Streeter suggests (again from reasons which
I cannot give) that ' the passages of Luke that we can identify as
Q represent that document, not only approximately in its original
order, but very nearly in its original extent.   And seeing that
Matthew's method of rearranging sources led necessarily to considerable verbal modification, it is probable that, allowance being
made for a slight polishing of the Greek, the form in which the
sayings appear in Luke is also on the whole more original ' (p. 291).
Here I may add that the question of the greater ' originality ' of Q
in Matthew or in Luke, and the question of Q's original order and
grouping as compared with the order and grouping of the excerpts
from it in Matthew and Luke, are old and very disputed problems.
The first is still more important for those who regard the passages
where Matthew and Luke differ considerably in the wording as yet
both coming from Q.

   Streeter draws up a list of his supposed Q passages.   ' Brackets
signify considerable doubt : Luke iii. 2–9, (10–14), 16–17, 21–22 ;
iv. 1–16a, vi. 20–vii. 10 ; vii. 18–35 ; ix. (51–56), 57–60 (61–62) ;
x. 2–16 (17–20), 21–24 ; xi. 9–52 ; xii. 1a–12, 22–59 ; xiii. 18–35 ;
xiv. 11, 26–27, 34–35 ; xvi. 13, 16–18 ; xvii. 1–6, 20–37 ; xix. 11–27.
Unbracketed verses = 272.   As thus reconstructed, Q is a document
the purpose and character of which are perfectly intelligible.   It
is comparable to an Old Testament prophetic book like Jeremiah,
consisting principally of discourse, but with an occasional narrative
to explain some piece of teaching.   The Baptism and Temptation
are described because the author regarded these as virtually the
" call " to the Messianic office.   The author would regard them,
like the " call " of the Prophet so often given in the Old Testament,
as of great apologetic value as evidence of the Divine authorization
of our Lord's mission.   The relatively large amount of space given
to John the Baptist, and the emphasis on his relations with our
Lord, suggest that Q was composed at a time and place where the
prestige of John was very considerable.   There is here a contrast

between Mark and Q. In Q John's testimony to Christ is appealed to, because among those for whom it was written " all held John to be a prophet." In Mark the apologetic motive for mentioning John is that he fulfilled the prophecy of the forerunner ; that is to say, it is not John's personal prestige which is appealed to, but the fact that his coming at all was part of that "programme," so to speak, of events, anciently foretold and in the career of our Lord recently fulfilled, which was the main plank of early Christian apologetic. It is the difference between the point of view of Rome *c.* A.D. 65 and Syria (where John's name and following were great) fifteen or twenty years earlier ' (pp. 291, 292). It may be noted that this explanation concerning the differences between Mark and Q about John the Baptist is disputable. A very different explanation is given by other scholars, and is referred to in the commentary.

Hardly any of the parables come from Streeter's Q. Hence ' a large part of the most obviously genuine, original, and characteristic teaching of our Lord is derived, not from Q, but from sources peculiar to Matthew or Luke. The Good Samaritan, the Prodigal Son, the Pharisee and the Publican, are peculiar to Luke ; the Labourers in the Vineyard, the Pearl of Great Price, are given by Matthew alone. There cannot be the slightest presumption that a source which lacked such material as this is a more reliable authority than those which contained it. Some scholars, indeed, have been so far hypnotized by the prestige of Q that, from the possible absence from Q of the longer narrative parables, they have drawn the conclusion that such parables formed no part of the original teaching of our Lord, but are developments in later tradition, though probably in some cases being expansions of shorter authentic sayings. Nothing could be more absurd. Our Lord was above all a popular teacher ; it was the common people who heard Him gladly. But everybody knows that a story told vividly and in detail is the one thing most likely to attract the attention and to remain in the memory of a popular audience. A friend once said to me, "You can preach the same sermon as often as you like, provided you don't repeat your illustrations ; but tell the same story twice, and even if the rest of your sermon is on a totally different topic, people will say that you repeat yourself." If one considers the teaching of Christ from the standpoint of the psychology of everyday life and not of academic theory, it is obvious that the parables, and that in their most graphic and least curtailed form, such as we find in Luke, are just the element most likely to belong to the earliest stratum of tradition. Why the author of Q included so few (or, possibly, none at all) of them, we cannot say, any more than we can say for certain why he did not include an account of the Passion.

Probably the reason for both omissions was the same. He wrote to supplement, not to supersede, a living oral tradition. Both the longer parables and the Passion story were easy to remember, and everyone knew them ; and what he was most concerned to write down was something which was either less well known or easier to forget ' (pp. 228, 229). Here, again, the arguments about the authenticity of all the parables, though forcible and ingenious, are disputable and disputed.

Harnack assigned about 202 verses from Matthew to Q. These 202 verses appear to have about 185 parallel verses in Luke. It should be observed that sometimes for two verses in Matthew there is only one verse in Luke. Of these 185 verses Streeter includes all but twelve (Luke ix. 2, 3, xi. 2–4, xv. 4–7, xxii. 28–30) in his reconstructed Q, but in addition to the 173, he has some 100 verses which Harnack has not. These are largely made up of verses completing sections or paragraphs, out of which only certain verses have more or less close parallels in Matthew. Streeter's M is not much smaller in extent than his Q, and it includes (as we shall see in the commentary) many famous passages in the Sermon on the Mount, including the ' Lord's Prayer ' Streeter's theory as to M is, to a considerable extent, the same as that of Allen and Burton's, to which I alluded in my first edition. A difficulty in regard to Allen's theory which I then mentioned applies partially to Streeter's ; it is that M will include passages which seem comparatively late. For Streeter would include in M xiii. 24–30 and (I think) xxv. 31–46. As to xvi. 17–19, it comes ' not from M, but from the local traditions of Antioch—the headquarters of this intermediate party. But we shall refer to M the doublet of this saying, Matt. xviii. 17, which confers the power " to bind and loose " upon the Ecclesia, that is, on the righteous remnant of the People of God, of which the Jerusalem Church was the natural headquarters and shepherd ' (p. 259).

§ 14. *The parallels of Q with Mark.*

It may be convenient to mention here some of the not very numerous parallels in Q to passages in Mark. The Q assumed here is Harnack's Q, not Streeter's. I have already indicated that some of these will come up for discussion in the commentary. There are three possible explanations: Mark borrowed them from Q; Q borrowed them from Mark ; both Mark and Q knew them independently from a common oral tradition. The first and third, or the second and third of these explanations may both be used for different passages.

(1) To four verses in that portion of Matthew's Sermon on the

Mount which Harnack assigns to Q there are four isolated parallels in Mark. (I do not here give the parallels in Luke.)

Thus Matt. v. 13 corresponds with Mark ix. 50.
,, v. 15 ,, ,, iv. 21.
,, v. 32 ,, ,, x. 11.
,, vii. 1 ,, ,, iv. 24.

(2) Again, in those verses which Harnack assigns to Q from the long oration in Matthew when Jesus sends out the apostles, there are seven parallels, namely,

Matt. x. 10 corresponds with Mark vi. 8.
,, x. 14 ,, ,, vi. 11.
,, x. 26 ,, ,, iv. 22.
,, x. 33 ,, ,, viii. 38.
,, x. 38 ,, ,, viii. 34.
,, x. 39 ,, ,, viii. 35.
,, x. 40 ,, ,, ix. 37.

(As to the inclusion of Matt. x. 40 in Q, Harnack declares himself very dubious.)

(3) Again, in Matthew's chapter about Beelzebul and Jesus's defence against the Pharisees, there are three important parallels :

Matt. xii. 25 corresponds with Mark iii. 24.
,, xii. 32 ,, ,, iii. 29.
,, xii. 39 ,, ,, viii. 12.

In addition to these we have (4) the parallel between Matt. xvii. 20 and Mark xi. 23, and (5) the parable of the mustard seed, which in Matthew and Luke Harnack holds was taken from Q and not from Mark (Matt. xiii. 31, 32 ; Mark iv. 31, 32). There are some other parallels than these which will be noticed in the commentary. If these parallels of Mark with Q, or the parallels of Mark with Streeter's L and M, mean also that Mark, on the one hand, and Q, L, and M, on the other, never drew from the same written source, just as even their oral sources could not have been *primarily* the same, then these parallels become ' doubly attested.' In this double attestation Burkitt finds for these sayings of Jesus a ' general assurance ' that they are really derived from Jesus himself and are not the ' half-conscious product ' of his followers. ' Where Q and Mark appear to report the same saying, we have the nearest approach that we can hope to get to the common tradition of the earliest Christian society about our Lord's words. What we glean in this way will indicate the general impression His teaching made upon his disciples ' (*Gospel History*, p. 147).

Burkitt draws up a list of 31 of these sayings; they will most of them be noticed in the commentary. The validity of the argument becomes impaired for those who believe that Mark drew upon, or had read, Q.

§ 15. *Authorship, date and character of Q.*

Something has already been said incidentally about all these matters. In its oldest form Q may conceivably go back to a very early date, say between A.D. 50 to 60. Is anything more known, or to be inferred, as to its author? Here too some weight may be assigned to a statement of Papias. He says (whether on the authority of John the Elder or no is uncertain), ' Matthew wrote the sayings (of Jesus) in the Hebrew language, and each one interpreted them as he was able' (Ματθαῖος μὲν οὖν ῾Εβραΐδι διαλέκτῳ τὰ λόγια συνεγρά-ψατο, ἡρμήνευσε δ᾽ αὐτά, ὡς ἦν δυνατὸς ἕκαστος). There have been tremendous discussions as to what this statement means. What are τὰ λόγια? Are they sayings in the strict sense of the word? Probably, yes, though ' the sayings must have often included a piece of narrative,' for some of Jesus's ' most striking words were associated with some event or incident.' (Moffatt, p. 189. *Cp.* Meyer I. pp. 245–251.) ' Mark's gospel was evidently felt by many to be incomplete, as compared with Matthew, besides being disorderly, as compared with John. The presbyter explains the reason of the former defect. The exigencies of its composition prevented Mark's gospel from giving a σύνταξις of the Lord's utterances; Mark was not able to provide this. But it was furnished by Matthew, a hearer and follower of the Lord. He composed or compiled τὰ λόγια, and his account, it is implied, was adequate, so far as contents went. This distinction, together with that of the language, may be regarded as uppermost in the Papias - traditions' (Moffatt, pp. 189, 190). Whether the statement about Matthew being the author of the sayings is true or no is disputed. In any case, as it is certain that Matthew was not the author of the Gospel which bears his name, the suggestion which has found favour with a large number of scholars is that the Logia, or sayings, which the apostle Matthew really drew up, was that source of the first Gospel which now is known as Q. Harnack calls this suggestion ' overwhelmingly probable'; Loisy, on the other hand, is very much more sceptical. How did Q get lost? Would a book, properly guaranteed as an apostolic work, and presented as such to the earliest Christian communities, have so easily disappeared? The matter can never be now ascertained. Meyer is quite ready to accept the Papias statement. He says: ' Thus Q, or the essential part of this work, which later on continuously received accretions, does really represent the Matthew-logia of

Papias; and there is nothing against the supposition that Q, in Hebrew or in Aramaic was the text or document (*Aufzeichnung*) which the apostle Matthew either made for himself, or at least used for his sermons' (p. 250). Goguel is more cautious: 'As to the place of composition, it would seem probable that the collection of the Logia originated in Palestine. According to Papias the apostle Matthew was the author. In any case, this statement can only be accepted with regard to the first core (*le noyau primitif*) of the collection, but it is also possible that the statement is only a conjecture of Papias or of his informant. Nevertheless, if tradition wanted to procure for the Logia a recognized author, it could have found a less hazy (*effacé*) person than Matthew. It is possible, therefore, that there was some real reason for choosing him' (p. 271). Streeter's view has been quoted already. What to me would seem highly probable is that, as Goguel says, Q is not a homogeneous document, but a collection 'which was in a frequent state of being added to' (p. 269). Some of the sayings may be, therefore, very old and very authentic and of Aramaic origin; others, like Matt. xi. 26, unauthentic, and written from the first in Greek. If the reference in Matt. xxiii. 35 were certain, one might say something more definite as to date, but it is disputed. Moffatt says: 'When the Matthæan Logia are identified with Q, the date of the latter (at any rate in its original form) is not later than the seventh decade of the first century; so far as the internal evidence goes, it may even fall within the sixth. It is thus an apostolic Aramaic treatise which has every likelihood of having been composed prior not only to Mark, but to the Ur-Marcus; it reflects the faith, mission, and sufferings of the primitive Jewish Christian church of Palestine, long before the crisis of A.D. 70 began to loom on the horizon' (p. 203). Wellhausen's view that Q is everywhere later than, and dependent on, Mark may be regarded, on the whole, as erroneous. Some words and passages of Q may be older than Mark, and some may be later. One has to consider each passage by itself. In spite of its accretions, Q undoubtedly remains a most valuable and ancient authority for the utterances of Jesus and for his conceptions of religion and morality, if not also for his conception of his own person and of his relation to God.

In contradiction with much that has been said above, Bacon, in his last work (*The Gospel of Mark*), elaborately argues that Papias means by the λόγια (the 'oracles' or 'sayings') nothing more nor less than our Gospel of Matthew. When Papias wrote (about A.D. 140–150), Matthew was regarded as a most authoritative work. Especially was it supposed to be 'an authoritative compend (σύνταξις) of the Lord's precepts.' Papias means that though Matthew, as apostolic, is 'entirely trustworthy as to order and completeness, nevertheless it exists only in translation, and unauthorized translation at that.' And though 'Matthew' was 'not written by Matthew,' and though 'modern critics have convincing reasons for their disbelief in the apostolic authorship of this comparatively late transcript of Mark, that does not alter the fact that in Papias' time such *was* the belief.' 'All attempts to read into the simple language of Papias about the Gospel of Matthew some obscure and recondite allusion to a document unheard of until the nineteenth century fall completely to the ground. Critics may have proto-Matthews and proto-Marks to their hearts' content. But to find them *in the language of Papias* is mere self-delusion. Papias gives no *tradition* concerning the origin of Matthew, but simply the *statement* whose bearing we have explained. He does not explain or defend his resort to Matthew for the precepts (λόγια) which he proposed to interpret. The reason is simple. No tradition was called for. His recourse to the standard 'compend' could be taken for granted. We do not find, therefore, that Papias cites any ancient tradition regarding the Gospel according to Matthew. We only learn that in 140–150 it already bore the same title as now ' (p. 26). *Cp.* pp. 40–49. The order of events in Matthew's Gospel as well as the order of the discourses was for Papias 'true and apostolic.' The Elder himself 'does not appear to be commending some other document in place of Mark as containing a better " order." He is merely entering a general caution' (p. 46). And, indeed, 'Mark has neither the τάξις [the *logical* order of the discourses] of Matthew nor the τάξις [the chronological order] of Luke, though it has attempts at both.' The Elder 'gives us no ground for supposing that he had knowledge of either Luke or Matthew' (p. 47). I cannot reproduce the wealth of argument by which Bacon seeks to substantiate these contentions.

I do not propose to deal here with the order of the Q passages as they appear in Matthew and in Luke, or with the question how far there already existed in Q regular orations and speeches such as we find in Matthew. Something may be said about these matters in the commentary. It is probable that the combination of sayings into long and formal speeches which we find in Matthew existed already in Q, though not to the same extent. But there may, perhaps, have already existed in Q portions of the Sermon on the Mount, an oration to the apostles on their being sent upon their missionary journey, a speech about John the Baptist, a diatribe against the Pharisees, and a speech about the Parousia and the ' last things.' Harnack is of opinion that, on the whole, Matthew has preserved the order of Q better than Luke. Other scholars present different views. We need not pursue them further in this place, or deal here with Matthew's method (on which Streeter speaks so fully) of ' conflating ' Q and Mark, and on Luke's method of giving separate

and distinct ' blocks ' of these two sources. Moffatt holds that Q
was not a ' heterogeneous mass of logia, but a collection moulded by
catechetical and homiletical processes, with sayings on the Kingdom
grouped together for the purposes of edification and apologetic,
strongly marked by eschatological traits, and shaped, more than
once, by polemical interests. The outstanding features are the
grouping of the sayings and the emphatically Jewish-Christian cast
of some sections ' (p. 197). This opinion must be modified if
Streeter's theories about Q and M are accepted.

I am not able to deal with the ' Case against Q '—the arguments
against such a document ever having existed—which have been
put forward by Dr. Lummes in the *Hibbert Journal*, July 1926,
and elsewhere.

§ 16. *The Gospel of Matthew : its character as a whole.*

' Matthew ' is a compilation, but it is something more. Its
main sources are Mark and Q, and, if Streeter's theory be accepted,
M. Even if that theory does not stand the test of the minute
and searching criticism which, I imagine, it will receive, it will
still remain true that by far the largest portion of Matthew depends
upon, and is taken from, written documents which the evangelist
found and used. This is even true for the largest portion of
Matthew's *Sondergut*—that part of his book which does not occur
in Mark or Luke. There are, however, a considerable number of
editorial changes, additions, and modifications—little touches of his
own—both in the narrative and in the sayings. The narrative is
enlarged here and there by accretions of a legendary kind. The
total result is that Matthew no less than Mark and Luke has a
special character of his own. One can justly speak of his theological position, of his religious and literary characteristics, of his
peculiar point of view, as well as of his peculiar methods of dealing
with his sources. A great deal has been written about all these
things. I can well be brief, for my main purpose is to explain and
discuss the actual words of his Gospel rather than to talk about it
as a whole.

In apparent opposition to the statement that Matthew has a
point of view and a theological position of his own, is the fact
that the Gospel seems to contain so many contradictions, and to
wear a double face. It is at once ' Jewish ' and anti-Jewish, ' legal '
and anti-legal, narrow and anti-Gentile and also catholic and
universalist. It includes indeed a curious mixture of ' particularist '
and ' universalist ' sayings. It is in places intensely anti-Pharisaic ;
in others it seems, on the contrary, to ascribe great validity and
honour to the Law and even to the official exposition of the Law.

These contrasts have been variously explained. It seems safest to assume that, for the most part, the particularist or 'legal' passages are quotations, and that to Matthew they no longer mean what they originally meant. They are spiritually interpreted, or again they are intended to press the authority of the Old Testament as a whole against certain extreme, though Christian, teachers who sought to depress its divinity and excellence. Some have seen in these particularist and legal sayings the opposition of the Jewish-Christian author to the Paulinists. But this view is very much more doubtful. Yet Professor Burkitt is probably quite right in saying that 'no book of the New Testament is so full of thoughts and expressions which have a real parallel in Rabbinical literature. The Evangelist is, so to speak, a Christian Rabbi, though no doubt he would have disclaimed the title. If the Gospel of Mark is most closely in touch with History, the Gospel of Matthew is most closely in touch with the Talmud. Like the other Gospels it is in form a narrative of the earthly life of Jesus Christ, but it sets forth that life with reference to the questions that most nearly concerned a Church composed of Palestinian Christians. No doubt the Evangelist felt himself and his brethren separated from the mass of his unbelieving fellow-countrymen. The Christians form an Ecclesia, a Society, of their own (xviii. 17), distinct from ordinary Jews. . . . But even so, the unbelieving Jew is nearer than the Gentile and the tax-gatherer ; he that is outcast to the Jew is outcast also to the Evangelist' (Burkitt, p. 191).

Or, again, even if these contradictions are to be explained by most of the Jewish, legal, anti-Gentile passages having been borrowed from one particular source (Streeter's M), yet it is Matthew, the compiler, who used them, adopted them, and fitted them into his book. They did not, perhaps, seem to him so one-sided and so strongly marked as they seem to us ; yet he must have been conscious of their character to *some* extent ; he must have included them with deliberation and intent. His Gospel must be a conscious reinterpretation of these special sayings. They were true, they were authentic : but they had been (so he thought) fulfilled and transcended ; they had received a new and a larger meaning. The new universal church had taken the place of the old national synagogue. The Jews rejected Jesus, the divine Messiah ; the Gentiles had accepted, and were accepting, him. They had stepped, and were more and more stepping, into the shoes of Israel. Or, again, the Gospel is a deliberate compromise, as is elaborately set forth by Streeter. Matthew comes from Antioch, and 'an Antiochene origin would account for the extraordinary interest shown by its author in the doings and in the primacy of Peter, who is far more prominent in this Gospel than in Mark, although that was written by his own disciple. Antioch follows Peter and stands for the *via media* between the Judaistic intolerance of those who called James master and the all but antinomian liberty claimed by some of the followers of Paul. Lastly, in the Church of Antioch, a city with an enormous Jewish population, we seem to have just the atmosphere of the Gospel of Matthew, which, though frankly recognizing that Christianity is for all nations, is yet saturated with Jewish feeling, preserves so many sayings of a particularist Jewish - Christian character, and altogether is less touched by the spirit of Paul than any other book in the New Testament. For Matthew Christianity is the new Law ' (p. 504 and see also pp. 511–524). Streeter supposes that Q, ' admittedly older, probably a good deal older than Mark,' had reached Antioch at ' a very early date.' Then Christian refugees from Jerusalem, fleeing from Jewish persecutions and the Jewish uprising against the Romans, arrived in Antioch with oral traditions or ' written summaries ' of the teachings of Jesus. These traditions and summaries would have seemed to the ' elders at Antioch far too precious not to be rendered into Greek and set down in writing without more delay. But this tradition, corresponding to that element in Matthew which we have styled M, included sayings of a strongly Judaistic character. The fact is one which has often been misconceived. It cannot be too emphatically insisted that this element in Matthew reflects, not primitive Jewish Christianity, but a later Judaistic reaction against the Petro-Pauline liberalism in the matter of the Gentile Mission and the observance of the Law ' (p. 512). About the same time (A.D. 65–70) Mark arrived too, and this Gospel would ' be hailed at once by the more liberal and pro-Gentile party as the Gospel of Antioch's own Apostle,' Peter (p. 513). For various reasons, however, a compromise was effected. ' Neither side could abandon accepted records of the teaching of Christ ; but the possibility that there had been some misinterpretation of the sayings most used in controversy could be explored. Perhaps another meaning could be found for those apparently Judaistic words of Christ which the James party were always quoting. By the time that Matthew wrote, a new exegesis which could reconcile the parties had been evolved. It was admitted on the one hand that the Master had said, " I was not sent but unto the lost sheep of the house of Israel " ; that He regarded the healing of a Syro-Phœnician as an exception, and that He had not Himself (as Mark's story would imply), even on that occasion, stepped outside the sacred soil of Palestine—for the woman had come across the border to Him (Matt. xv. 22). It was conceded also by the liberal party that in His first Mission Charge He had forbidden the Twelve to go into any way of the Gentiles or any city of the Samaritans (Matt. x. 6) ; in return, the other side admitted that this limitation was only intended for the time during which He walked the earth ; after His Resurrection He had on the contrary bade them " go and make disciples of all the nations " (xxviii. 19). Again, as the context (Matt. viii. 11) in which the prophecy is placed makes clear (quite a different one from that which, from its position in Luke (xiii. 28), we may conclude was original in Q), it was now agreed that Christ was referring to Gentiles, not Jews of the Dispersion, when He said, " Many shall come from the east and the west, and shall sit down with Abraham, Isaac, and Jacob in the kingdom of heaven : but the sons of the kingdom shall be cast forth into outer darkness." Finally, the fear —a very practical one—of antinomianism is met by a presentation of Christ's teaching as the New Law : the Sermon on the Mount is a counterpart to Sinai, and the five Great Discourses are, as it were, " the five books " of His " law of liberty." Thus complete reconciliation of the two parties of the James and Paul tradition, once hardly even artificially held together by Peter as a middle term, is now effected. That is much the most probable explanation of the famous saying, " Thou art Peter, on this rock I will build my Church." How far the words of this highly controverted saying as preserved in the First Gospel were actually uttered by Christ, and, if so, with what exact significance, it would be profitless to inquire. The form in which we have it is the version as remembered, repeated, and in repetition doubtless not a little modified, by those who disapproved alike of the undue conservatism of James and of Paul's too liberal attitude towards the Law, but were content to accept the *via media* of Peter. At Antioch all could rally round the name of Peter. He is the supreme Rabbi in whom resides the final interpretation (the power " to bind and to loose ") of the New Law given to the New Israel (" my (*i.e.* the Messiah's) Church ") by Christ ' (p. 514). All this is sheer hypothesis, but it seems, at any rate, to be *ben trovato*. We, perhaps, need *some such* hypothesis to account for Matthew's many-sidedness and peculiar character. Whether, however, the implication that all the ' narrow ' sayings in Matthew, as belonging to M, are *comparatively* late and unauthentic is, I think, somewhat dubious. The intention, albeit unconscious, seems always the same. We may observe it in so many different writers. All sayings which we moderns regard as fine and noble and broad are authentic ; all sayings which *we* consider to be narrow and cruel are not. But the historic Jesus did not regard himself as an apostle or prophet to the Gentiles, and therefore some of the ' narrow ' sayings may well be authentic. On the other hand, it is also possible that there was no need for Jesus to give vent to narrow utterances, in as much as the question of his followers directly converting the Gentiles had not arisen in his day.

Jesus believed (just as the old prophets believed) that many Gentiles would, of their own accord, accept the faith of Israel, but it would seem very doubtful whether he charged his disciples with a direct mission to bring the Gentiles within the fold. Similarly, however, it may be argued that he had no need specially to tell his disciples to restrict their activities to Israel.

Matthew compiled his Gospel some twenty years after the fall of Jerusalem. An appalling divine punishment had been inflicted upon the Jews for their rejection of the divine Messiah, the Son of God. Matthew was a Greek-speaking Jew, who, writing in Greek, composed his Gospel for the benefit of his fellow Christians of Jewish origin, and doubtless also for purposes of apologetic and propaganda. The great incidents in the life of Jesus, more especially his sufferings and his violent end, were—so Matthew desired to prove—preordained by God, and predicted in the Scriptures. To point out how Scriptural prophecies and statements were fulfilled in Jesus and by Jesus is a special feature and purpose of his book. Hence it is in Matthew that we have the largest number of Old Testament quotations. ' Matthew ' wrote in Greek, and many of his quotations are taken from the Septuagint. But others seem translated direct from the Hebrew—a fact which has been variously explained. It may be that the author understood Hebrew and made these translations himself ; it may be that in these instances he is merely borrowing from a source which already contained them. To him Christianity— for by his time one can speak of the new religion as distinct from the old—was the true development of Judaism, the fulfilment and consummation of the Law and the Prophets. ' The disciples are a new legitimate Israel, and bound together by a New Law which takes the place of the Old. The keynote of the work is not the opposition of Law and Grace, as in St. Paul, but the opposition of the Old Law and the New ' (Burkitt, p. 188). In one sense Matthew is less theological and dogmatic than Mark, but his Christology, though more simple, is more developed. Jesus is the Son of God from his birth : the story of the Virgin Birth is probably an integral part, not only of the first two chapters, but of the whole book. It was, in other words, known to, and accepted by, the Evangelist himself. The Messiahship is not concealed from the beginning of the ministry of Jesus till the revelation at Cæsarea Philippi. It is admitted and proclaimed from the first. Some care is taken, as will be pointed out in the commentary, to eliminate the human limitations which are still allowed to peep out of the narratives in Mark. Matthew's conception of the divine Sonship takes Jesus a step further away from the status of ordinary men, however good, and a step nearer to sheer divinity.

In Matthew, Israel according to the flesh having been rejected

by God, the Christian community takes Israel's place. The Church,
the Ecclesia, is a specially Matthæan conception. It is formed
both of converted Jews and of Gentiles: in spite of the 'narrow'
sayings being retained, the old oppositions are transcended and
overcome. And the Kingdom of God is already being partially
realised on earth in the Church. Yet the Church is by no means
perfect. It contains both good Christians and bad ones. It is to
Matthew's credit that he does not recommend any violent processes
of exclusion against the unworthy members of God's community
and Christ's. They are to be left to the final judgement, when,
however, the measures to be taken against them will be severe
enough! It is an imperfect toleration, but far better than nothing.
It is imperfect, because it is confidently predicted and expected that,
at the Judgement, the sinners will be, not converted or redeemed,
but destroyed, and this destruction is expected soon. Streeter has
attempted to explain why the fall of Jerusalem and the ruin of the
Temple had brought about a revival of Apocalyptic expectations and
interest. These awful 'things had come to pass—and still the Lord
did not return. To such a crisis different minds would react differently. To some it would induce an intensification of Apocalyptic
expectation and a more fanatic conviction of the immediacy of the
End. Others would slowly awake from Apocalyptic dreams and
see the necessity, before it was too late, of collecting and preserving
the surviving records of the mighty past. In the Gospel of Matthew
both these tendencies are seen reflected' (p. 517). 'No Gospel
makes so much as does Matthew of the expectation that the visible
Return of Christ will be within the lifetime of those who saw and
heard Him' (p. 520). 'Urgency is the note all through Matthew's
Gospel, though his Apocalyptic is subservient to a moral purpose'
(p. 522). The imminent End was regularly used by Jewish preachers
as a lever wherewith to urge men to repent of their sins: for when
the Judgement began—such was the gloomy belief of Jews and
Christians alike—there would be no opportunity for repentance any
more.

§ 17. *Wellhausen and Burkitt on Matthew.*

The second edition of Wellhausen's brilliant Introduction is
already (1926) fifteen years old, and, in spite of the great scholar's
confident belief that on the question of the priority of Mark to Q
criticism would ultimately have to come over to his view, as, in the
Pentateuch question, criticism, after long delay, came over to
Vatke—'this justifies the expectation that also my criticism of
Q, when once it has been long enough refuted by the accredited
experts, will ultimately prevail!' (p. 168)—it seems probable that,
in various particulars, Wellhausen will become obsolete or be super-

seded. Both on the conservative and on the radical side criticism
seems to have advanced to a fresh stage. Streeter and Burkitt,
Dibelius and Bultmann, seem, in some respects, to have moved
beyond Wellhausen. Nevertheless, on many points, by the very
brilliancy and incisiveness of his arguments and his language, he is
still well worth hearing. On Matthew's special parables he observes :
' They are the elaborately worked out products of careful deliberation ; they are not the creations of the particular moment, but (from
the standpoint of Jesus) they refer to the future. All of them deal
with the Kingdom of Heaven, regarding it as a sown field, or as a
vineyard, or as the earthly sphere of labour of the household servants
of God ; he as king, or master, or landlord, on the one side, is
opposed to the slaves or the sons (it comes to the same thing) of his
household on the other ; they work together on his property, and
among each other they are marked off by unimportant outward, and
also by important inward, differences. At the last, they receive their
reward, in that, distinguished now by the inward worth of their
service, some of them are received into the kingdom of glory, while
others are rejected ' (*Einleitung*, p. 60). But these assertions must
be tested in each individual case, and especially as regards the meaning which may have been originally intended in, and the meaning
which Matthew would have us give to, each particular parable of the
seven. So regarded Loisy may be right in thinking that the parables
of the treasure and the pearl and the net (xiii. 44–50), the parables of
the wicked servant and of the workers in the vineyard (xviii. 23–
35, xx. 1–16), and the parable of the two sons (xxi. 28–31), may
without much hesitation be assigned to Q and be authentic, while we
may hesitate more as to the origin of the parable of the wise and
foolish virgins (xxv. 1–13), and perhaps still more about the parable
of the tares (xiii. 24–30). Wellhausen is inclined to press the
Judæo-Christian character of Matthew somewhat emphatically,
perhaps too emphatically. ' Matthew is often thinking of the
Church even where he does not mention it by name, for example,
in his parables about the Kingdom. The Church comprises—in
true " Catholic " manner—both worthy and unworthy members :
the separation between them is left to God, and is only to take place
at the Judgement, when the Kingdom passes from its temporary
into its permanent and final phase. An erring member of the Church
is to be brought back to the fold by every possible means : only in
the last resort may excommunication be pronounced. The teachers
are the leaders : at their head is Peter. As the administrator of the
Kingdom, *i.e.* the Christian community, he bears the keys, the
mark of the majordomo. . . . Matthew has the primitive Christian
community of Jerusalem present before him, which, in spite of everything, yet sought to hold fast to Judaism. The Christian hostility

to the official representatives of the Law is nowhere expressed more bitterly than by him : only by him are they stigmatized absolutely and without qualification as hypocrites, who in truth are not what they seem, and are called upon to be. But this enmity is at the same time a rivalry for the same goal—for the fulfilment of the Law, for righteousness. The goal for Christians is set on a much greater height than for the Jews, but for that very reason they claim to be the true representatives of Judaism, and refuse to allow the false representatives (*i.e.* the Jews) to drive them out. They still take part in the Temple service in Jerusalem (v. 23–25) ; they pay the Temple tax and the tithes (xvii. 24, xxiii. 23) ; when no higher duty conflicts, they observe the Sabbath strictly (xxiv. 20). Fasting, praying, and almsgiving remain for them also important exercises in righteousness. Outside Jerusalem they restrict their missionary activity to Jews, they exclude heathen and Samaritans, and refuse to throw their sacred pearls before swine (vii. 6, x. 5). In spite of his keen opposition to the official and aristocratic elements in Jewry which were hostile to Christianity, Matthew is still very anxious to maintain the connection of the humble Christian community, who were drawn from the lower strata of the population, with their Jewish roots and soil : in language and manner he is a Rabbi who believes in Jesus the Messiah. But he is not entirely consistent : in some passages, differing from Mark, a universalistic tendency is developed, according to which Jesus had already before his mind and eye the passing of the Gospel from the Jews to the heathen ' (pp. 61–63). (Streeter's hypothesis would explain this apparent inconsistency.)

Again, Wellhausen observes that, in Matthew, the Kingdom, regarded as present, was founded by Jesus : he is its necessary condition. ' It was his purpose to found it, and for that very object does he appear, from the beginning of his ministry, openly as the Messiah. From the beginning too his teaching is specially directed to his disciples, in order to explain to them how his community is to be constituted, and what is to befall it in the future. He no longer (as in Mark) scatters his teaching seed upon the ground, careless of the result, but through his teaching about the Kingdom he sows the Kingdom itself, which is compared with the sown field or with the plant in the same way as with the vineyard. That by the Kingdom he means the Church (the ἐκκλησία) cannot be mistaken, though from reasons of historic propriety Matthew usually avoids the name. His true meaning is specially clear when he talks of scribes and stewards, of older and younger elements, of worthy and unworthy members, of the Kingdom of God ; or again when he says that John the Baptist, though the greatest Jew, is yet smaller than the lowliest member of the Kingdom. This equivalence of Kingdom and Church is perfectly intelligible ; for the community was the product of Jesus's activity, and was regarded as the preparatory stage for heaven (*die Vorstufe des Himmels*). But, nevertheless, this identification of Kingdom with Church is entirely Christian ; it cannot have been accomplished by Jesus, or, still less, have been assumed by him. And yet in Matthew he *does* assume it, without regarding any explanation of it as necessary. He speaks to his disciples as if they were already his community and organized as such : he projects himself into a future situation as if it were already present ' (*Einleitung*, p. 94). Nevertheless, Wellhausen, in spite of his own scepticism, and though, like other scholars, he holds that Matthew as a whole was written after the fall of Jerusalem, is yet obliged to point out that the background of the early Christian community at Jerusalem is very often clearly discernible even in those passages which are not derived either from Q or Mark. ' Some of them, as for example Matt. xvii. 24-27, must be drawn from a relatively old tradition. In the case of others we may help ourselves by the hypothesis that a Christian community existed in Jerusalem even after the destruction of the city, and that it continued to move on the old lines. But we must also reckon with the possibility that Matthew kept to the *form* of the tradition of the community of Jerusalem of set purpose, even though he occasionally violated it ' (*Einleitung*, p. 79). Thus Wellhausen's scepticism leads him to more than one dubious hypothesis. And, indeed, in all those sayings of Jesus in Matthew upon the basis of which Wellhausen constructs his opinion, it is necessary to ask how far they may not owe this later aspect to the editor, and how far, divested of setting and editorial modifications, they may not be genuine products (borrowed from some source) of the teaching of Jesus. Professor Burkitt, while admitting that Wellhausen's statements about Matthew contain ' a great deal that is undeniably true,' yet pleads most earnestly for the historical and authentic character of much which Matthew puts into the mouth of Jesus. At the worst the sayings of Jesus in Matthew (peculiar to that Gospel) are to be considered ' rather as adaptations of what the disciples had remembered of their Master's teaching than as new inventions made for the purpose.... The greater part of the substance of the teaching, and all that is most fresh and picturesque in its expression, come from historical reminiscence of the Master's words.... Nowhere in early Christian literature, except in the three Synoptic Gospels, do we find that picturesque outlook on men and nature that finds expression in the Parables of Jesus' (*op. cit.* pp. 195, 199). ' The important thing is not whether the parable of the sheep and the goats in Matt. xxv. is a literal translation of words once spoken by Jesus, or to discover the real time and place where they were first uttered. The important thing is to recognize that this is the kind of teaching which the Evangelist thought worthy to put in his Lord's mouth, and which the Church accepted as worthy. At the same time, the more we study the special aims and tendencies of the Synoptic Evangelists, the greater the gap appears between the theories which they themselves elaborate and the circle of ideas in which the Sayings of Jesus move. Again and again we find ourselves in the presence of something which may or may not be authentic historical reminiscence, but is in any case totally unlike the other remains of early Christian literature. We cannot tell whether the tale be well remembered, or how many steps there may have been in its transmission, but the difference of spirit is unmistakable, and we take knowledge of the Evangelists that they have been with Jesus ' (p. 206).

§ 18. *Loisy on Matthew.*

As distinguished from the sayings, the narratives which are peculiar to Matthew have rarely, if ever, any historical value. Unlike Luke, Matthew appears to have had ' no independent chronological tradition or information to guide him in placing either sayings or incidents. His choice and disposition of materials becomes less and less reliable, from a historical standpoint, when he leaves the Marcan record ; the Palestinian anecdotes which belong to his *Sondergut* rarely rise above the level of edifying stories to that of historicity. Matthew's corrections of Mark are not those of an eyewitness, or of one who had access to special, first-hand sources of information. Their origin is almost entirely topical ' (Moffatt, *Introduction*, p. 247). As Loisy remarks of them : ' They have rather the character of legendary developments than of truly traditional recollections.' The desire to find fulfilments of O.T. predictions or allusions in the life of Jesus has led to the creation of incidents of which it is ' unnecessary to observe that the historic value is nil.' Especially in the chapters which deal with the birth of Jesus is the influence of O.T. prophecies most noticeable. ' It does not seem that these stories have the slightest historical basis.' Loisy regards it as probable that the wide deflection of the birth and infancy narratives from historic reality and probability makes it likely that they and the Gospel of which they form part, ' acquired their essential traits outside Palestine and the Jewish-Christian communities of that country, in a land where, and at a time when, no eyewitness of, or even well-informed person about, the life of Jesus existed ' (*E. S.* i. pp. 140, 141). The author ' knew Hebrew, but had in view readers who did not. He was probably born a Jew, but he was not of Palestine : he wrote in the East, perhaps in Asia

Minor, or rather in Syria : by origin Jewish-Christian, he has a universalist spirit, though without polemical *arrière-pensée* in favour of Paul or against the Galilæan apostles : he unifies the apostolic tradition and regards the apostles as a sacred group of whom Peter is in some sort the representative ; he neutralizes the effect of the Judaizing sayings he quotes by a symbolic interpretation of them. To those who wished to advocate Jewish observances and live without rules he opposed the perfection of the Christian Law. A man of tradition, one might even say a man of the Church, he wrote a Gospel truly churchly and catholic : one might be almost tempted to see in him, if not one of the first bishops, at least one of those venerable personages who as elders or overseers governed those communities in which germinated the institution of that monarchic episcopacy which was the heir and successor of its apostolic forerunner ' (*E. S.* i. p. 143).

§ 19. *Renan on Matthew.*

Those who do not know them already may be strongly recommended to read Chapters x. and xi. of Renan's *Les Évangiles*, in which there are a number of remarks about Matthew, his relation to Mark, and the comparative authenticity of the sayings which he attributes to Jesus, full of suggestiveness and expressed in the most delightful and exquisite of styles. What can be better than this about the double character of Matthew, his combination of opposites ? ' The Gospel of St. Matthew, like nearly all good compositions, was the work of a mind " en quelque sorte double." The author is both Jew and Christian at the same time ; his new faith has not killed the old one, and has taken away from it nothing of its poetry. He loves two things at the same time. Does the Law hold good ? Yes and no. Jesus destroys it and fulfils it. The Sabbath ? He suppresses and maintains it. Jewish ceremonies ? He observes them and condemns their observation ' (pp. 209, 210). Or this about the difficulty of saying which of the speeches and parables were really said by Jesus and which were not. ' The life of Jesus and the history of the redaction of the Gospels are two subjects which interpenetrate one another in such a way that it is imperative to avoid defining their precise limits, even if one seems to contradict oneself. In reality this contradiction is of little consequence. Jesus is the real creator of the Gospel ; Jesus performed all things, even those which have been merely assigned to him ; he and his legend are inseparable. He was identified with his idea to such an extent that it became himself, absorbed him, and made of his biography that which it was to be ' (p. 204). And so on with much more of admirable mingling together of paradox and truth, or rather of truth made more visible by the paradox of its form. Or lastly, what can be more suggestive or thought-provoking than the sentences about the impression made upon us by the book as a whole ? ' The general effect is like a fairy palace built entirely of luminous stones ' (p. 198). Loisy is, I think, too depreciative in his estimate of Matthew's style and manner and power of story-telling (*E. S.* 1. p. 259), while Burkitt's ascription to him of ' great literary skill and dignity ' scarcely seems to hit the nail precisely on the head. Is not Renan perhaps nearer doing so when he calls Matthew's Gospel ' a masterpiece of a popular writer ? ...An airy genius whom we touch and embrace, but whose feet never rest on solid earth, speaks to us and enchants us. He doubts nothing and knows nothing. We are charmed as by the positiveness of a woman, who makes us smile, but captivates us ' (p. 198).

§ 20. *Some further remarks on Matthew.*

It is, as I have said, needless for the purposes of this book, to enter into any detail as to Matthew's literary methods, or as to the manner in which he uses and conflates Mark and Q (and M). If Q began to put together and group (more than Mark) the isolated sayings of Jesus, Matthew does so to a considerably greater degree. He builds up, or brings together, big blocks of sayings ; he collects in groups parables and miracles. It is through this collecting and grouping tendency that we get the noble Sermon on the Mount, placed significantly, as the summary and essence of the teaching of Jesus, at the very opening of his ministry. It has even some-times been thought that the whole Gospel may be divided into five intended sections : the new law as against the old. This is doubtful, though, anyway, Matthew shows a fondness for the numbers of three, five, and seven, and makes collections of three's, of five's, and of seven's. It is remarkable how little of Mark he leaves out ; on the whole he follows Mark's order ; into the reasons for his occasional changes and divergencies I cannot enter here.

It is, perhaps, the very disposition of his book—the great Sermon, the other set discourses, the collection of parables—which has given it its immense popularity. Renan calls it ' the most important book which has ever been written.' Bacon, it is true, demurs to the statement. ' Not Matthew, as Renan said, mistaking a mere transcript for the original, is the most influential book ever written, but Mark ' (*The Gospel of Mark*, p. 334). Nevertheless, though Mark gave the impulse, and but for Mark, Matthew would never have been composed, yet Matthew soon superseded Mark in its influence and in the affection which it inspired. That Mark was its predecessor, that Mark provided it with its narrative and its facts, was soon forgotten. Its calm confident catholicity also helped it. ' It is a catholic Gospel, and its genuinely catholic sentiment and tone have won for it its place among the four' (Jülicher, *Einleitung*, p. 265). Matthew ' voices the catholic and apostolic consciousness of the early church, which saw in its universal mission to the world a commission of Jesus to his disciples, and in its faith a new and final law of God's Messiah' (Moffatt, p. 256). Perhaps—a less pleasing reason—its markedly anti-Jewish character, its invectives against the Jews, its contrasts between Old and New (' ye have heard how it was said, but *I* say unto you '), may also have contributed to its success. It is, moreover, very sublime, and yet very simple. And while it shows how the Old Law has been superseded by the New Law, it yet satisfies a permanent need of human nature in that it still tells men what they are to do and from what they are to refrain. Outside the great Sermon, its *Sondergut* includes such notable passages as xi. 28–30 (' Come unto me, ye weary ones '), xvi. 18 (Peter and the rock) and xxv. 31–46 (the picture of the last assize). It also includes some striking parables such as those of the Buried Treasure, the Pearl, the Unmerciful Servant, the Two Sons, the Wise and Foolish Virgins, and the Labourers in the Vineyard. But, above all, the Gospel of Matthew is the Gospel of the Sermon on the Mount. Though a considerable portion of that Sermon is found in Luke, it is not massed together, but put in different places and connections, so that the effect is somewhat diminished. Moreover, portions of the Sermon, including the famous antitheses, the examples of the New Law, the supposed ' new ' principles of prayer, almsgiving, and fasting, are peculiar to Matthew. And it is Matthew who gives the Beatitudes and the Lord's Prayer in their fuller form. So, perhaps, it is the fact that Matthew is the home of the complete Sermon on the Mount, which has most of all helped to secure and retain for it its place of honour among the books of the New Testament and in the hearts of men.

As for its date, the obvious *terminus a quo* is that Matthew refers distinctly to the fall of Jerusalem, and uses Mark. For the *terminus ad quem* some scholars suggest 90, others 100 or even 110. We can hardly go wrong if we assume a date between A.D. 90 and 100, and we may well be content if any ancient writing can be dated within such brief and narrow limits. I may add here some words of Bacon which, if not entirely true, yet deserve quotation (*The Gospel of Mark*). ' The relation of our first Gospel to our second is anything but that of a hasty revision under pressure of such circumstances as those of Judæa in 66–70. Matthew is a work of the utmost care and attention.

It combines Mark and the Second Source with elaborate skill, weaving in certain minor factors to make a literary product such as only years of thought and labor could achieve. Both it and Luke must stand at no little remove from their common narrative source, if only to allow time for Mark to achieve its unrivalled pre-eminence in their estimation ' (pp. 104, 105).

§ 21. *The Gospel of Luke.*

The Gospel of Luke is the longest of the three Synoptics. It contains some 1146 verses, whereas Matthew contains about 1071. It has also the largest amount of matter peculiar to itself. Among this matter are several of the most beautiful of the parables. Some of these parables seem not merely very worthy of Jesus, which is not altogether a safe criterion, but on general grounds likely to belong to him. For many reasons we must not be too hasty in assuming that what is peculiar to Luke cannot have been said by Jesus.

Luke opens with a short, but highly interesting preface, in which the author speaks of his own position and object. He was no eyewitness or apostle ; he writes upon the basis, and with the help, of several writers who have preceded him. Thus he, too, wrote at a period when several written sources existed, though in his case, as in Matthew's, the two most important of those sources were probably Mark and Q. Still, we must assume that his peculiar matter is not mainly his own composition, but usually rests upon sources, the exact number and nature of which can no longer be convincingly ascertained.

' Luke's method,' says Moffatt, ' is historical, but his object, like that of John, is religious. He makes no claim, however, to be an eyewitness. All he professes is to write a correct, complete, and chronological (in the sense of well-arranged, or logical) account of the primitive παράδοσις as received from the first generation of disciples. This attempt was neither new nor superfluous. Luke had numerous predecessors in the enterprise, but their work did not satisfy his purpose, and he resolved to make a fresh essay. He makes no claim to be inspired ; his qualifications are simply the pains he had taken to acquaint himself with the contents of the παράδοσις (tradition). Luke did not rest his narrative on unsifted traditions ' (p. 263).

In contrast with Mark and Matthew the author of ' Luke ' is not a Jew, but a converted Gentile, and it is for Gentile Christians, or for Gentiles whom he hopes may become Christians, that he writes. His Gospel is the most ' universalist ' of the three. The universalism is not a matter of contention and argument : it is assumed. The Gentiles have entered into the inheritance of Israel, who have been punished by God because of their unbelief.

Thus Luke's universalism has no polemic tinge. He has not to combat any specifically Judæo-Christian view. He is a 'universalist' in a quite simple sense, as to the manner born. Though Luke preserves from his source sentences which might seem to show the contrary, he himself has apparently little knowledge of, interest in, or sympathy for, specifically Jewish considerations. Jesus sends his seventy disciples directly and emphatically to the Gentiles. The twelve apostles symbolize the twelve tribes of Israel, but the seventy correspond with and symbolize the Jewish idea of the seventy nations of the world. A further noticeable feature of Luke's Gospel is his marked sympathy for that side of the teaching and life of Jesus which had to do with sinners and the poor. A 'tinge of asceticism' (Burkitt, p. 214) pervades his Gospel. For the repentant sinner he has profound pity. Some of the finest stories, parables, and sayings which illustrate the compassion and love which Jesus showed, and which God feels, for the sinner who repents, are peculiar to Luke. Peculiar also to him are his sympathy for the poor and needy, and his somewhat accentuated antagonism to the rich. (This is, I think, true in spite of Goguel's protest, p. 503.) He has, as Loisy observes, ' a certain psychological note, a profound sense of the things of the soul, a penetrating tone, that indefinable quality which comes from the heart and goes to the heart ' (*E. S.* i. p. 260).

Luke, Renan has said, is pre-eminently the Gospel of forgiveness. Conversion is possible for all. It is also pre-eminently the Gospel of humility. And the greatest of the virtues is almsgiving. Not, however, in a Pauline sense is Renan justified in calling Luke the Gospel of pardon obtained by faith. Harnack points out the grave difference, in spite of his insistence upon the accuracy of the traditional authorship. Luke's 'faith' is less dogmatic and profound than Paul's, and his philanthropy is less limited and reserved (*Lukas der Arzt*, p. 100). The point of view is late and developed, but yet not so theological as that of Mark. The Jewish Law does not specially interest Luke or his readers : such questions as those discussed in Mark's great seventh chapter are omitted. The burning quarrels of Paul with the Judaizers have passed away. Luke's tendency is eirenic (Moffatt, p. 280), but perhaps it should rather be said that for the circles among whom he lived as well as for his own mind a peaceful stage had been attained. As to the divinity of Jesus there is no question or doubt. He is the Lord ; he is the Son of God in a unique sense ; nevertheless, the virgin birth is probably not an integral feature of his infancy narratives, but may have been super-added to them. In each of the three Gospels we see different conceptions of Jesus as regards his relations to God ; each of them is on the road to the full assimilation of Jesus with God, none of them has reached the full conclusion : each of them, but Mark by far the most clearly, shows how Jesus started, so to speak, as a man both in his own eyes and in the eyes of his followers, and how the fatal descent began (as Jews would say), from pure Jewish monotheism to the doctrine of the Athanasian Creed, or, as Christians would say, how the upward journey began from rigid, barren, abstract, untenable Jewish monotheism to the rich, true, and complete trinitarian monotheism of developed Christianity.

The ' author ' of the third Gospel is also the ' author ' of Acts, and the question of the authorship of ' Luke ' cannot be fully and properly discussed without bringing in the authorship of ' Acts.' Hence it is impossible for me adequately to discuss the matter in this place. The traditional view is that the author of both books is Luke the ' beloved physician ' mentioned in Colossians iv. 14, in Philemon 24 and in Timothy iv. 11. *That* Luke was the companion of Paul. It is, however, generally agreed that Luke was not a Paulinist in the sense of a man devoted to, or keenly interested in, the special doctrines and theories of Paul. The third Gospel is in some respects less Paulinist than Mark. There is little distinctive Paulinism in it, just as there is no marked antagonism to the Law. Thus Loisy justly remarks of the author of the third Gospel : ' he is not interested in the essential theology of Paul ; one might almost say that he ignores it ; he is not anxious, like the redactor of Mark, to defend the person of the great apostle and to make his ideas prevail in the gospel tradition ; in certain very characteristic passages (notably in xxii. 24–27) he neglects the Pauline additions of Mark and keeps to the primitive statements ' (*E. S.* i. p. 173). ' Really and truly,' says Jülicher, ' Luke did not take over from Paul more than that which the Church as a whole took over from him, to wit, the idea of the universality of salvation, and the conception of the boundlessness of the divine grace ' (*Einleitung*, p. 292). (*Cp.* on Luke's position Moffatt, pp. 301, 302, who accepts the traditional view as to the identity of the evangelist with the companion of Paul.) The question of authorship is, on the whole, of somewhat less importance in the Gospel than in the Acts, because it would be allowed on all hands that the authenticity and trust-worthiness of the sayings, parables, and narratives peculiar to the third Gospel depend mainly upon the character of its special sources. It is *their* trustworthiness rather than the editor's which has to be doubted or affirmed. It may be, as Loisy thinks (see below), that the real Luke is present both in the Gospel and in the

Acts, but that his work has been re-edited and enlarged by a later compiler.

For the special point of view of this book the grave differences between Loisy and Streeter as regards the third Gospel are of comparatively minor importance. For, first, the narratives, so far as they differ from Mark, whether by way of addition or change, are not necessarily accurate or historical, even if Luke's source or sources are very early, and even if the editor of *all* the Gospel, as we have it now, be the companion of Paul, the beloved physician. This remark is especially relevant to the miraculous portions of the narratives. As Moffatt says, ' the presence of miraculous anecdotes is no proof that they are unprimitive. A comparison, *e.g.*, of the historical traditions gathering round figures like St. Patrick or even Thomas à Becket will show that it is the most natural thing in the world for such stories to spring up within a man's lifetime, and the mushroom of legend appeared under certain conditions as rapidly in the East as in the West. This applies in some degree to the miracles in Acts as well as to those in the Gospels. On the other hand, their presence in Acts is no disproof of Luke's authorship ' (p. 302). In the second place, the additional sayings and parables peculiar to Luke are also not all necessarily authentic, even if Luke's sources are early, and even if Paul's Luke be throughout the author or editor of the Gospel. Doubtless the earliness of the source, if really it *could* be proved, is an argument in favour of the authenticity of the ' special ' sayings and parables. But it is not an absolutely final argument. For we have to remember, first, that from a very early date sayings and parables may have been attributed to Jesus which were not really spoken by him, and second, that internal marks of unauthenticity may compel us to revise our views as to the early date of any particular saying or parable.

Again, from the point of view or purpose of my book, the important point is not the authorship of any given saying or parable, but its doctrine. If an absolutely irrefutable proof were given that a particular saying was spoken by Jesus, that would (for Jews) be no extra evidence of its excellence. And if an absolutely irrefutable proof were given that the saying was composed in A.D. 35, that would be no evidence against its value. Some of the very greatest things in Isaiah i.–xxxix. were not said by Isaiah. Precisely the same may it be with some of the very greatest things in the Gospel. Yet these Gospel sayings, even though unauthentic, may, nevertheless, be due to the fertile and original spirit of Jesus which suggested them.

Looked at in the light of internal probability alone, quite apart from their source, and quite apart from the question whether their

' editor' (even though not their ' author ') be the true Luke or no,
many of Luke's peculiar stories and statements (at least up to the
Passion narrative, where Luke seems to draw upon a special and
more historical source) appear of highly doubtful character. This
will be often indicated in the commentary. Such, for instance, are
the stories or statements in iv. 16–30, in v. 1–11, in vii. 11–17, in
xvii. 11–19, in xix. 41–44. Not so very much better, from the
point of view of likely ' historicity,' are vii. 36–50, ix. 51–56, xi. 27,
28, xi. 37–39, xiii. 10–17, xiv. 1–6, xix. 1–10. Depending upon
good tradition may be viii. 1–3, x. 38–42, xii. 13, 14, xiii. 1–5, xiv. 31.
But even some of these seem to show qualities characteristic of the
editor (or of one of his sources) rather than of the historical Jesus.
Loisy may press the symbolism of certain passages too much.
Still such a narrative as v. 1–11 seems almost obviously symbolic.
(The fish are the heathen.) Again, why this very marked prominence of women in Luke ; why this tenderness towards, or interest in,
the Samaritans ? How is it Luke knows more about the truth here
—what Jesus actually said and did—than Mark ? That the
dispatch of the Seventy is unhistoric and symbolic is, I suppose, universally conceded. It seems more than doubtful whether the famous
story in Luke vii. 36–50 can be kept for the historic Jesus. Mark's
story (xiv. 3–9) is suspicious, but Luke's far more so. ' It is highly
significant that with him the anointing woman has become a harlot '
(Wellhausen, *Einleitung*, p. 61). While I cannot share Streeter's
contempt for those who question the authenticity of the parables,
they do seem to be the more probably authentic portion of Luke's
Sondergut. Yet even here some doubts arise. Moffatt speaks of
Luke's ' heightening of the authority and also of the tenderness of
Jesus, the place he assigns to women, his love of antitheses between
different types of character, the prominence given to prayer, to
the holy Spirit, and to thanksgiving ' (p. 280). This is true, but
one at least of these characteristics (the love of antitheses in pairs
of characters) is revealed in, and deduced from, his special parables,
e.g. the Pharisee and the Publican, Lazarus and the Rich Man, the
' good ' son and the Prodigal Son. (In the stories we have Martha
and Mary, the repentant and the unrepentant thief.) Again, it is
also true, but partly deduced from the parables, as Wellhausen says :
' The main type and antitype which these pairs provide is that of the
self-conscious righteous and the humble sinner, and the favourite
theme is that repentance is possible for all, whatever their situation
and circumstances, that it is necessary for everyone, and that it is
easier for the ne'er-do-well than for the virtuous. Luke has a
marked affection not merely for the despised and degraded " crowd,"
but also for outcast individuals. He presses the saying that the
sick, not the healthy, need the doctor.' The examples, adds

Wellhausen, in which Luke illustrates his favourite themes have a certain family likeness to each other, and also to the additions made to, or to the changes made in, the narratives of Mark. 'A somewhat sentimental trait and a similarity of literary touch extend through Luke's special contributions ; the artistic working out of the situation and the violent contrasts of the colours are noticeable. Their value may be as great as you please, nevertheless these special portions (*diese Novellen*) of Luke cannot be put on the same level (of authenticity) as the products of the old tradition' (*Einleitung*, p. 61). Thus it cannot be ascribed to mere ignorance or stupidity, a wanton desire to doubt, which makes some scholars hesitate to accept the authenticity of all Luke's *Sondergut*, even when the very parables themselves are in question. We can, if we please, suppose that there was one particular source in which some particular aspects of Jesus's teaching were specially emphasized, which in other sources (*e.g.* Mark and Q) had, to some extent, been neglected. This source may have collected many authentic sayings and parables, and may truly, if deliberately, reflect those particular aspects of the Master's teaching on which it likes to lay peculiar stress. Thus that aspect of Jesus in which he appears as the friend of tax-collectors and sinners is prominent in Luke, and this prominence may be due to a special source and may yet be historic. This hypothesis is strongly pressed by Bacon. It is the 'special source of Luke' which gives us a 'constant' (yet historic) 'depiction of Jesus as the champion of the " little ones," the unrecognized " sons " or "daughters of Abraham," the spiritually disinherited masses, publicans, women, Samaritans, outcasts from the Synagogue, scattered sheep, lost sons' (*Gospel Story*, p. xxxvii). There may be a good deal of truth in this, though whether there existed anything resembling 'spiritually disinherited *masses*' is open to the gravest doubt. On this point Bacon is still under the spell of old authorities and old ideas. But apart from this special point, we may, if we please, hold to a good deal of what is said by the American professor.

The date of Luke is assigned by most scholars to about the same period as Matthew, namely, A.D. 90–100. It has been supposed by some that Matthew knew Luke's Gospel, by others that Luke knew Matthew's. It seems more probable that neither knew of the other's. Which is earlier ? As to this point, too, opinions vary, and this is not wonderful, for the evidence is conflicting. For instance, the bits taken by both Evangelists from Q sometimes appear in an earlier form in Luke and sometimes in Matthew. The additions and accretions to them seem sometimes more developed and significant in Luke, and sometimes in Matthew. As regards the use which the third Evangelist made of the second, we may observe one highly curious and notable feature. He follows Mark in his order of events fairly closely up to the end of Mark's ninth chapter. In spite of various insertions from Q or other sources, he never leaves Mark for long together. But at this point he makes a huge intercalation, and leaves Mark altogether for several chapters, namely from ix. 51 to xviii. 14. Jesus during this intercalation is supposed to be journeying from Galilee to Jerusalem. At xviii. 15 Luke resumes his excerpts from Mark, very nearly where he had left them off. In this huge intercalation he places much of the matter which is peculiar to himself. And he has a peculiar view of how Jesus journeyed to Jerusalem. Mark makes him go through Peræa on the ' other side ' of Jordan ; Luke makes him pass through Samaria. Some few words about the great intercalation will be read in the commentary. The cause and meaning of it are obscure, and no satisfactory explanation has, so far, been given. It is perhaps the simplest hypothesis to suppose that Luke put in his big insertion the majority of those sayings, parables, and anecdotes for which his sources afforded him no indication of place or time. Almost all the sayings and parables peculiar to him are to be found in the insertion, together also with a certain amount of Q material common to him and to Matthew, which Matthew has placed and grouped in other connections. Dr. Carpenter writes cautiously : ' Matthew *in its present contents* is presumably the latest of the three.' Wellhausen, on the other hand, takes with his usual confidence the opposite view. In many incidents and conceptions he thinks that Luke shows a later stage of development than Matthew. So, too, Wellhausen also notes a certain ' inwardness ' and individualization in Luke, which, with other things, points forward to the still later author of the Fourth Gospel. In the story of the Passion, with certain elements that seem older or more historic than anything in Mark, there are others which point to a later stage than Matthew. So too in the story of the resurrection. On the traditional view of the authorship of all ' Luke ' and all Acts by the companion of Paul, the beloved physician, the Gospel might have been written about A.D. 80. This is the opinion of the great theologian Harnack, who has written a book to prove that Luke was the author of both the Gospel and the Acts. In this conclusion Harnack adopts the view of most English conservative theologians, and especially it may be noted that he too maintains that there is linguistic evidence to show that the author was a physician. Moffatt agrees with this contention ; Wendland (no mean authority) holds that this ' medical ' evidence is worth little. Some consider that A.D. 80 is somewhat too early a date for Acts as well as for Luke. It is just possible that if Luke was born about 30, he could have written his two books as late as 100. This is the view of Professor Burkitt, who believes in the traditional authorship, but holds that Luke had read and used Josephus, and that his Gospel and Acts were written about A.D. 100. As the date is in any case much the same, the question of the authorship is for our purposes of very secondary importance. The likelihood of the authenticity of its special material is neither much increased nor much diminished. And the importance and beauty of the third Evangelist's book are largely independent of its date. A distinguished classical scholar once observed to me that of the three Synoptists Luke seemed to him to have the ' keenest and deepest appreciation of both the humanity and the divinity of Jesus.' (The speaker did not mean divinity in the sense of deity.) This may be rightly said and finely observed, and even if Luke's *Novellen* are not authentic, they may nevertheless be truly illustrative of the genuine spirit of the Galilæan teacher.

Each of the first three Gospels has thus its own specific interest and importance.

§ 22. *Streeter and Loisy on Luke.*

Canon Streeter's hypothesis about Luke must be studied in his great book, *The Four Gospels*. He most strongly upholds the integrity and the traditional authorship for both the Gospel and the Acts, and, in addition, he has a special theory of his own as regards the Gospel. The Gospel, he considers, as we now possess it, was compiled by Luke on the basis of two main sources, Mark and Proto-Luke, or rather Proto-Luke and Mark, for Proto-Luke was the framework into which Luke, at convenient places, inserted extracts from Mark (p. 208). What is Proto-Luke ? It is a written document composed many years before our third Gospel by Luke himself : it consists of two documents, one of which is our old friend Q. ' Luke, during the two years he was at Cæsarea in the company of Paul, made good use of his opportunities of collecting information and made copious notes. Later on, probably not till after the death of Paul, a copy of Q came his way, and on the basis of this and his own notes he composed Proto-Luke as a Gospel for the use of the Church in the place where he was then living. Still later a copy of Mark came his way, and he then produced the second and enlarged edition of his Gospel that has come down to us ' (p. 218). The copious notes which Luke made (about 60) formed the document L, and Proto-Luke may be described as Q + L, though in the formation of Proto-Luke, not all of L may have been incorporated into Proto-Luke. Streeter calls Proto-Luke, the existence of which he considers ' a scientific hypothesis capable, to a considerable extent, of verification ' (p. 218), ' a kind of half-way house between collections of sayings, like Q, and the biographical type of Gospel of which Mark was the originator ' (p. 214). He assigns to Proto-Luke

practically all the special material of the third Gospel up to the
Passion narrative, more especially iii. 1-iv. 30, v. 1-11, vi. 14-16,
gives a 20-49, vii., viii. 1-3, ix. 51-xviii. 14, xix. 1-27, 37-44. As
he also tells us the verses which, more or less assuredly, may be
assigned to Q, if we deduct these from the Proto-Luke mass, we get
what Luke in his early days put down in his notes. We get to L.
L includes iii. 1, 15, 18-20, 23-38, iv. 16-30, v. 1-11, vi. 14-16, vii.
11-17, 36-50, viii. 1-3, x. 1, 23-42, xi. 1-8, 53, 54, xii. 13-21, xiii.
1-17, xiv. 1-10, 12-25, 28-33, xv., xvi., 1-12, 14, 15, 19-31, xvii.
7-19, xviii. 1-14, xix. 1-10, 37-44. We may note that L contains,
on the one hand, all the special Lucan parables ; on the other hand,
such highly miraculous and unhistorical or symbolic stories as the
young man of Nain and Peter's wonderful fishing. It also contains
the early rejection at Nazareth, the leprous Samaritan, Simon and
the harlot. Can many of these tales be so early as Streeter would
have them to be, in spite of the canon that the primitive is not necessarily unmiraculous ? Streeter observes (it is one argument for
Luke and Proto-Luke being by the same hand) that ' what to the
historian is one of the weak points of Luke, his preferring the more
to the less miraculous of the two versions of a story laid before him,
is characteristic both of the editor and his sources ' (p. 220).
Nevertheless, it is said : ' Neither Mark nor Proto-Luke are infal-
lible ; but as historical authorities they should probably be regarded
as on the whole of approximately equal value. But, if so, this
means that far more weight will have to be given by the historian
in the future to the third Gospel, and in particular to those portions
of it which are peculiar to itself ' (p. 222). But can this view really
be maintained ? Surely the special tales of Proto-Luke, such as
the young man of Nain, are much less probably historic than the
stories in Mark. In the Passion narrative Luke seems to depend
on a special source or on special sources, and every now and then
his narrative seems to be more historical than that of Mark (where
it differs from Mark). But can any such historical superiority be
ascribed to any narrative deviating from Mark before chapter xxii. ?
Proto-Luke, if one reads through connectedly the passages of which
it is said to be made up, seems a very odd sort of ' Gospel ' : it is,
indeed, ' a half-way house,' and a very queer one. One wonders if
it really ever did exist. There seems also some reason to doubt
whether Luke did not finally use more ' sources ' than Streeter's
hypothesis would allow, i.e. Mark, Q, and his own early ' notes ' (L).
It is said that ' the disentanglement of the elements derived from
Mark and from Proto-Luke respectively in the section xxii. 14 to
the end of the Gospel is in points of detail highly speculative.' ' But,
if the general position that Luke preferred Proto-Luke to Mark is
correct, we are entitled to approach the question with the preliminary

assumption that everything after Lk. xxii. 14 is derived from Proto-Luke, except those verses which there are special reasons for assigning to Mark on account of their close verbal resemblance to Mark and the possibility of their being detached from the context without spoiling the general sense ' (p. 216). Can we, however, be so sure (a) that the special Lucan material in the Passion narrative comes from the same source that gave us Nain and Peter's fishing, or (b) that it is all from *one* source ? Criticism will have, I suspect, a good deal still to say about Streeter's hypothesis.

It should be added that Streeter also holds that Luke expanded his own earlier work, not only by ' inserting extracts from Mark,' but also ' by prefixing the stories of the Infancy ' (i., ii.). He ' derived these chapters from a written Hebrew source ' (p. 267).

As to the date of the Gospel as a whole, it was written after A.D. 70, for ' what in Mark xiii. is a prophecy of the appearance of the Anti-Christ in the Temple becomes, in Luke's version, a prophecy of the destruction of Jerusalem and of the enslavement of its population. Now, seeing that in A.D. 70 the appearance of the Anti-Christ did *not* take place, but the things which Luke mentions *did*, the alteration is most reasonably explained as due to the author's knowledge of these facts.' On the other hand, as a ' date later than 90 is not very likely for Acts,' and as the Gospel was written first, A.D. 85 is a probable limit. Or if the ' Gospel was written some years before the Acts, before Luke returned to Rome and as soon as he came across a copy of Mark, a date like A.D. 80 seems more likely ' (p. 540).

What a remarkable contrast to the views of Streeter about Luke are those of Loisy ! The two books (*The Four Gospels, L'Évangile de Luc*), both published in the same year, 1924, show us scholarly conservatism on the one hand, and learned scepticism on the other. Loisy no less than Streeter believes in Luke, Paul's Luke, being the author of the prologue, but his work, both in the Gospel and in Acts, has been subjected to a very thorough ' remaniement,' to a process of adding, alteration, and editing, which has given it, to a very large extent, the character and special material which we now associate with it. Most of what Streeter assigns to his L, Loisy assigns to his redactor, a personage who lived probably in the reign of Trajan (A.D. 98–117), who knew Matthew and even John. This redactor introduces ' fictitious and symbolical scenes, doublets of early statements, daring transpositions and interpolations, equivalent to inventions ' (p. 51). From beginning to end there is much symbolism, from Peter's wonderful fishing to the two thieves who represent respectively Jewish incredulity and ' the sinful world which was converted to the faith of Christ ' (p. 59). This redactor ' would be glad to persuade his non-Christian readers, if any are to be found, that neither Jesus nor his adherents ever entertained thoughts which were unfavourable to Roman authority, and that notable personalities of the time could not help recognizing this ' (p. 58). If the real Luke drew his matter from several sources, no less so did the redactor. ' Everything that the critics place so readily in one source peculiar to Luke, from which was drawn all that did not come from Mark and Q, seems to have many different origins, and not to have been taken *en bloc* from any one book. It is deceiving oneself to pretend that one can assign to each anecdote and to each sentence in the Gospels a particular source and date. These, looked at in detail, and in final analysis, are not a matter of certain historic tradition, and lend themselves solely to more or less probable conjecture ' (p. 54). ' The third Gospel is, like the others, a kind of Christian catechism, and still more a manual of the Christian cult, the manual of the good tidings, of the salvation specially commemorated on the day of the Lord and intensively dramatized in the paschal solemnity. Sacred teaching, but also, and above all, sacred drama, a fact which explains the particular character of the stories. Nowhere is that character that of simple doctrine taken in by an attentive listener, of simple fact looked at by a curious spectator ; it is that of a belief which is affirmed and defended, defined and pictured liturgically, which finds its own realization in the creations that it animates with its spirit ' (p. 62). But Loisy carries his scepticism still further : he rivals Bultmann. Even Luke's own book, yet untouched by the redactor, ' was, in a word, nothing but a sacred legend, a " cult " legend, in large measure the product, and not the reminiscence, of the apostolic tradition invoked by the author of the prologue. The source of Mark, which is also at the same time the principal source of Luke as regards the facts, was nothing else. And the other source of Mark and of Luke, the collection of sayings, Q, is also, on the whole, a product of primitive tradition, of the apostolic tradition in its prophetic and didactic character. Doubtless it could not help being so ; but it is so because the simple fact of Jesus was so quickly transfigured into a belief in the Immortal Christ. We may believe that Luke in all sincerity presented to Theophilus as " accomplished facts " the first acquisitions, we may say the first visions, of the Faith concerning its crucified hero. The personal action of Jesus called forth (*déclenché*) the Faith ; but this beginning was never related independently of the faith which it awakened ' (p. 55). I doubt whether Streeter's conservatism will be retainable ; I doubt whether much which scholars such as he regard as history can rightly be so regarded. But no less do I doubt whether there is so little history in Mark and Luke as Loisy would now maintain. Nevertheless, just as Streeter's arguments must be examined without passion or prejudice, so also must Loisy's. The truth will probably be found to lie between the conclusions of these two great scholars, so that, in spite of their non-historical purposes, their ready acceptance of miracles, their ' tendenciousnesses ' and their symbolisms, the Synoptic Gospels will yet be held to include a good deal which was actually done and experienced and said by the historic Jesus.

§ 23. Date and Authenticity.

It may be observed here that the authenticity of a given saying of Jesus or of a particular incident about his ministry is not to be merely measured, or always chiefly measured, by the supposed date of the ' source ' which records it. Here one must bear in mind those considerations to which Jülicher in his *Neue Linien* again rightly called attention. It does not follow, he argued, that a given passage is authentic in direct proportion to its age. Even if, for example, Q, or ' the special source ' of Luke, were always younger than Mark, it would not necessarily follow that some parts of Q, or of the special source of Luke, might not be more authentic than some parts of Mark. The point is : where would tradition remember truly, and where would it, unconsciously or consciously, add, alter, and embroider ? Is not Jülicher right when he says that what must be looked at with most suspicion should be ' those sections of the Gospels which deal with the appraisement of the person of Jesus and with the representation of his self-consciousness ' ? (' die direkt auf die Schätzung der Person Jesu und die Darstellung seines Selbstbewusstseins bezüglichen Partien ') (p. 73). If this be so, we shall be disposed to regard as more presumably authentic those words of Jesus in which he does not speak of his own powers, or of himself, or of his future. We shall be disposed to regard those doings of Jesus as more presumably authentic which are not specially Messianic or specially in accordance with the later beliefs of the Christian disciples, as they were rapidly formed between A.D. 30 and 60. Over the Messianic consciousness of Jesus, and over those words and deeds of his which betray it, a dark shadow of doubt must continue to hover. We cannot get beyond the Jesus ' des ältesten Gemeindeglaubens '—the Jesus as the faith of the earliest community conceived him. Old history and new faith are fused together ; the picture of Jesus, which the Synoptics show, has not only many painful gaps, but is throughout covered with a varnish which here and there does not allow anything of the original to shine through (*Neue Linien in der Kritik der evangelischen Uberlieferung* (1906), p. 71). Just where we most want to know, we must always be content to conjecture.

But let me again press the point that the importance of the

Gospels for modern Judaism does not by any means merely hinge upon the question of authenticity. From one point of view the question of authenticity does not greatly matter.

The excellence of the Sermon on the Mount is neither impaired nor increased if Jesus said all of it or much the greater part of it, or if he did not. Modern Judaism must study the words ascribed to Jesus and take up an attitude towards them, whether Jesus spoke them or not. Yet, historically or biographically, the question whether all the Sermon on the Mount, or whether Matt. xi. 25–27, is authentic or not, remains very important and interesting. Though these authenticity problems can never be definitely resolved, they are bound to retain their fascination and attractiveness.

I should like to refer again to the old argument, used to much effect by Seeley in his *Ecce Homo*, that the greatest, most striking, most original things in the Gospels must be authentic because only Jesus could have thought of them. It can be shown, it is said, that his disciples or reporters were mediocre men for the most part, who often misunderstood their Master, and were certainly not capable of creative and original thought. On the contrary, we find instances in which a too daring utterance of the Master has been subjected to compromise and commonplace by addition or qualification. I had never been quite persuaded by this argument. Each case must be dealt with on its merits, and when so dealt with, the argument does not always seem to hold. For instance, one of the noblest sayings in the Gospels is surely : ' Father, forgive them, for they know not what they do ' (Luke xxiii. 34). But this verse is very possibly not authentic. Again, take such a passage as Matt. xxv. 35–40. Can anything be imagined more superb? Anything which, given and assuming the point of view of the writer, is more redolent of true inspiration ? But is it not more than probable that this passage was not spoken by, and is later than, Jesus ?

Wellhausen, perhaps, presses too greatly the canon that as the measure for the authenticity of the words assigned to Jesus we have first and foremost to take the degree of literary testimony. Thus in the first degree of value would come, according to him, what is said by Jesus in Mark, next what is said by him both in Matthew and Luke (Q), and lastly, what is said by him only in Matthew or only in Luke. Wellhausen admits that the oral tradition is older than its written precipitate, and not only older, but larger. But he urges that in the course of time (and of a comparatively short time) the primary authentic tradition diminished, and the secondary unauthentic tradition increased. And in opposition to the current opinion he holds ' that the oral tradition of the sayings and speeches gradually increased and developed in much greater bulk than the

tradition of what Jesus did and what befell him ' (' dass die Überlieferung des Redestoffs sich im Lauf der Zeit viel stärker entwickelt
und vermehrt hat als die des erzählenden Stoffs') (*Einleitung*,
p. 76, 2nd ed.).

On the other side, we have to remember that Jesus may, or even
must, have repeated some of his sayings, parables, and teachings
again and again, and that the memories of orientals who write little,
and use no note-books, are very retentive. After his death the
words of Jesus will have been constantly recounted to fresh disciples ;
they will have been treasured up and pondered over. Hence it may
be argued that, if there are not definite internal reasons which plead
for a later date, we may fairly confidently assign to Jesus the words
ascribed to him by Matthew only and by Luke only, if they are
words which seem to harmonize with his character and teaching as
we can gather and infer them from the pages of Mark and (as most
scholars, in spite of Wellhausen, would add) of Q.

It may be noted that in the important and striking section (19)
in which, in the second edition of his *Introduction*, Wellhausen again
states and defends his theory about Mark and Q, he observes that
for connected discourses the memory of orientals was no stronger
than our own. He illustrates this dictum by the Hadith, that is,
the record of the oral tradition of those sayings of Mahommed which
were not written down in the Koran : it is, he declares, very untrustworthy (p. 161, n. 1).

Yet, when all has been said, and when criticism has done its
worst, it will probably remain true that it is, in large measure, the
words ascribed to Jesus in the Synoptic Gospels which argue for the
historical character of the man and of his life. I would like to
quote here the measured statement of the great philosopher Wundt,
which I happened to come across in turning over the leaves of his
huge *Völkerpsychologie* (Zweiter Band, ' Mythus und Religion,'
Dritter Teil, 1909, p. 528) : ' No unprejudiced person, who is only
tolerably familiar with the ways in which myths are formed, and
who has also fairly followed the growing discovery and elucidation
of the sources of old oriental legends, can to-day any longer doubt
that with the exception of a few incidents in the narrative of the
Passion, which probably possess an adequate historic attestation,
the outward life of Jesus is a tissue of legends. But that which these
legends leave untouched, and that which is never found in their
mythological counterparts and predecessors, is the series of sayings
and speeches of Jesus, as they have been handed down to us in the
Synoptic Gospels.'

§ 24. *The condition of the Jews during the age of Jesus.*

Jesus was born in the year 4 B.C. or perhaps a year or two earlier. He died probably in A.D. 29 or 30. The Gospels of Mark, Matthew, and Luke were compiled, as we have seen, between the years A.D. 70 and 100. It is, therefore, desirable for those who read these books to know something about the history of the Jews during that period of 100 years. Something ought to be known of the external history ; something of the internal condition. But this knowledge cannot be given here ; it must be sought elsewhere.

Jesus's birth falls in the last years or even year of the reign of Herod the Great. The fortunes and deeds of this remarkable man should be read in Josephus. He exercised, we have to remember, a kind of quasi-independent rule under the overlordship of Rome. When he died his territories were divided. His son Archelaus received, and was confirmed by Augustus in the possession of, Judæa, Idumæa, and Samaria. He was not called king, but ethnarch. A second son, Antipas or Herod Antipas, often merely called Herod in the Gospels, was given Galilee and Peræa. His title was that of tetrarch, ' a title which was often used for rulers of a divided kingdom without reference to its precise etymology.' In the Gospels he is sometimes called king, but this is technically an error. Another son of Herod called Philip received some more north-eastern portions of Palestine, which had been attached to Herod's dominions by Augustus. The town of Cæsarea Philippi was in the territory of Philip.

The reign of Archelaus did not last long. He seems to have ruled with harshness and cruelty, and not to have possessed his father's ability for extracting himself from a difficult situation. So when the Jews complained of him to Augustus, and he had to appear at Rome, his defence was not accepted, and he was deposed and banished (A.D. 6). Henceforth, with one brief interval, Judæa and Samaria were directly administered by Rome. There was a Roman Procurator whose headquarters were usually at Cæsarea. Above him in rank and authority was the Legate or Governor of the province of Syria ; he was of senatorial rank, whereas the Procurator was only a ' knight.' Thus Judæa during the life of Jesus was under the direct authority of Rome, although a certain measure of home rule was still allowed. The Sanhedrin was apparently not only the highest legal court, but the high priest's council of government. The high priest presided ; his influence was predominant. But the power to inflict and carry out the death sentence had been removed from this native court by the Romans. In Galilee, on the other hand, Herod Antipas occupied the place of the Roman administrator in Judæa. His reign continued till after the death of Jesus. Ultimately (A.D. 39) he too was bereft by Caligula of his tetrarchy and banished to Lyons.

§ 25. *The Law and the State: classes of the people: Rabbis and Pharisees.*

It is very difficult to form any adequate or accurate picture of Jewish life in the first half of the first century A.D. A condition of things existed which in many respects was very different from anything which has existed since. Moreover, there was less homogeneity of conditions then than afterwards. There must have been a considerable diversity of life, of manners, of opinions.

The history of the Jews from the Maccabean revolt till the crucifixion of Jesus and the destruction of the Temple is a curious one. It seems to show that the domination of the Law was unsuited for national independence. On the whole, it must be said that the supremacy of the Law in political affairs bred a good deal of fanaticism and tended to produce a certain amount of violence. On the other hand, it made heroes and martyrs, and taught men how to die unflinchingly for their ancestral religion.

It is hard to think of the Jews as independent or as persecuting; one can but think of them as persecuted. For over 1800 years persecutions in one form or another, and in one degree or another, have been their recurring lot. After the fall of their State and the horrors of the Hadrianic war, they formed separate and alien religious communities in a hostile environment; they were despised, ill-treated, mocked at, and abused. Intervals and breathing spaces there are, but this is the general story. Their virtues have been those of hidden lives and of obscure communities. But their beloved Law becomes more supreme than ever. It constitutes their manhood. It trains their intellect. It is their recreation, their joy, and their solace. It is their treasure and their guide. There are practically no parties; who would remain a Jew, if he did not love the Law? And the love of the Law expresses itself on the same lines: he who loves the Law fulfils, or seeks to fulfil, its enactments. Rome and the Church oppress, degrade, torture, and kill; the Law brings poetry, and hope, and idealism, and God.

Under Herod the Great and Antipas and the Procurators too, the Law doubtless to some extent brought these blessings. In Judæa and in Galilee during the years A.D. 1–30 there must have been many retired, quiet men and women who lived pious lives according to the Law and did not concern themselves with politics. But there was also much more. There were several other types and classes.

For though the Romans are the ultimate rulers and arbiters,

a Jewish State is in existence. An ecclesiastical State in some measure; for though Herod is anything rather than a servant of priests, and Antipas is not the servant of Rabbis, still the Pentateuch and its developments are yet in large measure the Law of the State. Certainly the connection of Church and State was not a happy one in Judæa, and produced some unpleasing results and characters. We have, then, to do with a State. Even when Archelaus is deposed, and Judæa is under the administration of the Roman Procurator, we may, nevertheless, still in a certain sense speak of a continuing Jewish State. And, like every other State, this one too has its various parties and classes, many of whom largely disappear after its destruction. It has soldiers and politicians; it has nobles and priests and rulers. It has schemers and agitators. It has all these and more, and all of them either feel religiously—whether according to a pure religion or no, an outward or an inward one, need not here be considered—or use religion for their own purpose. The national and political life was mixed up with religion in a peculiar way, not wholly to the advantage either of the one or of the other.

And with this variety of classes and persons there existed, as I have already indicated, a variety of thought. The distinctions of Pharisees, Sadducees, and Essenes are familiar to most people, yet they hardly represent with accuracy what actually existed. They are not very informing. The ruling priests at Jerusalem seem to have constituted the mainstay and chief element of the Sadducees. They were in a sense conservative. The letter of the Law was enough for them; they did not want the developments of the Rabbis. In doctrine too they were against innovation. Thus we hear that while they did not, apparently, deny Immortality, they would have nothing to say to the doctrine of the Resurrection, in which we may nevertheless assert with confidence that eleven-twelfths of the nation already firmly believed. Many of these priests, and many of the nobles and 'rulers,' possessed, I should think, but a very formal and outward religion. We may compare them with many of the bishops, barons, and rulers of the middle ages.

In spite of the intense devotion of the Jews to the Temple, the religious teachers of the people were not the priests. The Temple was the mark of the national life as well as the public expression of its religion. Unlike any other nation, the Jews offered sacrifices at one spot only, and upon this single Temple were concentrated all the glory and pride which among any other people were distributed over a hundred different fanes. Yet in spite of this adoration of the Temple—to thousands a distant Temple which they rarely saw—the Judaism of the day was not a priestly religion, though priestly ideas of cleanness and uncleanness filled an important part of it. The Synagogue and the Rabbi overshadowed the Temple and the priest.

The Rabbis and their followers constituted the Pharisees. It is probably no exaggeration to say that five-sixths of the nation were Pharisaic more or less, though where and how the limits ran it is hard to say. The Rabbis of A.D. 30 were not quite identical with the Rabbis of A.D. 300. For among them too there must have been many types and kinds. Some combined politics with religion ; others kept themselves aloof from the governing and political world.

§ 26. *The Law and the infant Church: persecution and intolerance.*

The rule of the Law had only gradually asserted itself after Ezra. It was growing during the Persian period (450–330 B.C.), and during the Greek period after Alexander. But the stages of its growth can no longer be traced. It was subjected to a counter current and a cross influence by the introduction and development of Hellenism. Then came the persecution of Antiochus Epiphanes, the Maccabean revolt, the restored national independence and the heightened national consciousness. The Law begins to rule not merely the actions of private life, but the public working of the State. And, as is so often the case, fanaticism and intolerance go hand in hand with, or follow hard upon, heroism and martyrdom. The same temper which breeds the martyr breeds the fanatic. The Maccabean heroes kill the recusants or the lax to-day ; they are ready to be killed themselves to-morrow. And when seated in the saddle of power, they impose the Law upon others by sheer force. Militant Judaism extends its borders, and whole territories must submit to compulsory circumcision.

This is not the place in which to speak of the history of the infant Church from the death of Jesus to the end of the century. But the readers of the Synoptics must be prepared, both in the words ascribed to Jesus and outside them, to find a reflection of circumstances and moods which fall within those seventy years. And prominent among those circumstances will be this, that the young Christian community suffered persecution from the Synagogue. Even while the early Christians of the Jerusalem community observed the ceremonial enactments of the Law. there was still enough difference to make occasional persecution highly probable. It must, moreover, be remembered that the first Christians were Jews, and while they claimed or desired to remain within the Synagogue, they must have been a constant source of irritation.

A family quarrel is often the bitterest of quarrels. That the new community believed that the Messiah had already appeared was in itself a serious point of difference. A lax attitude toward the Law was soon to follow. The Christians had their own organization, their own meetings, their own expectations. Worst of all, the Christians soon began to assert that the Founder of their faith was a divine being, a very incarnation of God. He became the object of worship. This to the Jews seemed rank idolatry. The dominant Pharisaic religion could not brook or tolerate so marked and serious a dissidence. Renan is possibly right in saying that but for the Roman overlordship, and the difficulties put in the way of Jews exercising the right of life and death, the persecution would have been more grave and more extensive. The historian has to record what he finds. He may interpret the facts, but he cannot conceal or alter them. It can hardly be denied that the secular persecution of the Jews by Christian authorities may be regarded as the abiding and multiplied revenge of the brief persecution of the Christians by the Jews. ' Persecute your enemies even unto the hundredth generation ' has been the principle according to which the Church has exercised an awful punishment upon the primary offending of the Synagogue. Such persecution as Jews inflicted upon Christians must be regarded as due to a determination to defend Judaism against what seemed erroneous and defiling opinions. The first Christian missionary efforts were made in the synagogues, and this it was which largely aroused Jewish opposition. When the Church became quite distinct from the Synagogue, and when its adherents were pagans, Jewish opposition died away. The alien religion could go its own way. (See for all this Abrahams, *Studies*, 2nd Series, pp. 56–71.)

Judaism, like Christianity, could in those days be hardly other than intolerant. Like Christianity it was better and more attractive in low places than in high ones. For the Jews, like the Christians, believed in the exclusive rightness of their own faith as well as in the soleness and exclusive sovereignty of their own God. To believe correctly was a virtue ; to believe otherwise a moral defect, a social injury. Toleration combined with such a faith was at that time impossible, whether for Christian or for Jew.

Successful fanaticism grows by what it feeds on. Yet it may also be said that it grows by persecution. Still though stimulated by persecution as well as by success, fanaticism, when persecuted, is generally unable to issue in act. And its effect upon character is partly checked and hindered by other influences and agencies. The men who breathe wild imprecations upon their persecutors are often within their own community models of gentleness, piety, and love. But successful and active fanaticism tends, as it would seem, to harden and dry up man's soul. Hence we notice, from the Maccabean revolt to the destruction of the State, a certain fierce and arid temper of mind and type of religion which are unpleasing to our modern ideas.

On the other hand, it must be said that the political domination of a national religious Law never got a really fair chance. The Maccabean rulers never properly and completely freed themselves from trouble and turmoil with the Hellenistic Syrian power. Under Simon's son, John Hyrkanus (135–104 B.C.), the height of Maccabean power is reached ; yet towards the close of his reign Josephus records that the seeds of future trouble were sown by John's quarrelling with the Pharisees, or national party, and 'joining the Sadducees.' His son Alexander Janneus, who succeeded him after a year of bloodshed and confusion, passed much of his reign in wars, both external and civil. The Pharisees are his declared and lifelong enemies. He slays, according to Josephus, no fewer than fifty thousand of his own people. Upon his death-bed he recommends his wife Alexandra to be reconciled with and to obey the Pharisees ; his advice is followed for nine years (76–67). The violent feud between her two sons, which breaks out after her death, leads to the introduction of Pompey and the overlordship of Rome (63).

There followed twenty-three troubled years till the accession of Herod the Great. It was thus partly due to the native rulers, and partly to the Roman Governors and administrators, that the land was never happy and at ease. Intrigue and oppression, corruption and cruelty, often or usually prevailed. In addition to this there was in the Roman period a frequent violation of Jewish suscepti- bilities. Herod wanted to play the Hellenistic and cultivated king. His baths, gymnasia, and temples grossly offended the intense religious feeling of the people. The Roman governors were avaricious and imprudent. The last and the worst of them, Gessius Florus, aimed directly at stirring up insurrection and war. Thus the people were constantly kept in unrest, excitement, and wretchedness. There was every opportunity given for hatred and religious bitterness. The 'zealots' and ultra-nationalists, who finally got supreme control, were the natural product of the events and policy pursued by the rulers. Fanaticism was, as it were, artificially fed and stimulated. The religion of the day was exclusive, anti-heathen, and rigorous : the Law breathes a spirit of hostility and antagonism and ruthless severity to all idolatry, idolaters, and image worship. But the fierce passions of men could have been tolerably easily kept in check and abeyance by scrupulous respect for national and religious susceptibilities : instead of which they were constantly ruffled and violated.

§ 27. *The Messianic hope.   Did all classes observe the Law ?*

Under these circumstances it is not surprising that the Messianic hope should have revived.   We do not hear much about it in Josephus, but there were special reasons why he desired to keep it dark.   The blacker the actual condition of things was, the more men hoped for the coming of the Golden Age, when Israel should be prosperous, powerful and free, and when righteousness and peace should reign supreme.   With the invariable optimism of the Jews—without which they could hardly have survived their age-continued miseries—the final crisis, the breaking of the dawn, were not merely longed for, but expected in the near future.   The end would come soon.

Dr. Abrahams reminded me that we have no conclusive evidence that this belief was actually held, but it seems necessary to assume it in order to explain the course of events.   Gradually the Jews must have thrown the hope of the end more forward into a remote future.   But, in the first century, there must have been some, or even many, who, like Jesus, thought of the change as one which the morrow would suddenly witness.   The old order would soon close for ever : the new order was about to begin.   The Kingdom of God was surely at hand.   These hopes and beliefs were combined with the now almost universally accepted doctrine of the Resurrection of the dead.   They were often, but not necessarily, associated with the figure and expectation of the Deliverer-King, the Messiah-Prince, of whom some of the prophets, and notably Isaiah, had spoken. It is these hopes and expectations which form the background, and explain the appearance, of John the Baptist and his preaching.

It is, however, to be remembered that we are dealing with a society which is not homogeneous.   It may be called, with perhaps as much right as any other, transitional.   I have spoken of the domination of the Law, and of a certain fanatical temper.   But the domination of the Law was not quite complete.   The legalism of A.D. 300 embraced the entire body of Jews more equably and with fewer exceptions than the legalism of 30.   It was more all-pervading, yet, what to many will seem odd, there is some evidence and reason to think that this more all-penetrating legalism of 300 was sweeter, more spiritual, and more inward than was the legalism of 30.   It was more religious, less national.   It had become more assimilated with, more part and parcel of, the entire life of every individual Jew.   The legalism of 30 seems to have left a certain section of the people outside its influence.   It had not absorbed everybody.   Some there were who, for one reason or another (and the reasons are obscure), did not live according to the Law.   They have either fallen out of the ranks of the legal army or they have never entered them. There were nobles and rich landowners who were above the Law, there were unfortunates who were below it. There were occupations, such as that of tax-collectors, soldiers, and others, upon which the Rabbis and Pharisees, for one reason or other, looked with suspicion. Either the occupation prevented those who followed it from obeying the ritual enactments of the Law or it made them likely to disobey its ethical commands. Those once outside the legal ranks the Rabbis and Pharisees seem to have made little or no effort to reclaim or convert. They were left severely to themselves. Yet these classes could not have been very large.

It must, however, be frankly stated that the foregoing remarks are really based upon inferences from the Gospel narratives themselves and upon little more. They therefore rest upon dubious evidence. For what the Evangelists say, and what Jesus is made to say, about the Pharisees, the Rabbis, and the Jews generally is naturally to be taken with the greatest caution and suspicion. What Catholics say about Protestants, or Protestants about Catholics, or Jews about Christians (I quite admit that this hits me), or Christians about Jews, must always be *very* critically regarded. But the evidence of the Gospels comes very much under this category. It was inevitable that the Pharisees and the Rabbis should be presented as worse than they really were. And similarly it was inevitable, if there existed a small section of persons who were outside the ranks of the ' respectable ' classes that observed the Law, that this section should be represented as larger and more important than it really was.

The unfortunate thing is that in the Rabbinical literature we get no clear and undisputed evidence which substantiates the Gospels. To begin with, that literature is almost all of it very much later than the first century after Christ.

And not only was it written later, but the Rabbis whose utterances and stories it reports and chronicles, the circumstances it reflects and tells of, were almost all later than Jesus, later than the fall of the State, later than the Hadrianic revolt. If you cannot argue on the good side from the Talmud, you cannot argue on the evil. The evils and the excellences of the Talmudic periods are not necessarily the same as those of the period of Jesus.

§ 28. *The 'Am ha-'Areç' and the neglected ' multitudes.'*

The Rabbinic literature does indeed contain various statements and sayings—more especially sayings and statements about certain people, or a certain class of people, called 'people of the land,' 'Am ha-'Areç—which have been much used in supposed substantiation of the Gospel narratives about 'sinners' or about what Matthew makes Jesus say respecting the multitude who were harassed and prostrate like sheep without shepherds. It has been freely supposed that the sinners and neglected multitude of the Gospels and the 'Am ha-'Areç of the Talmud are one and the same.

But this identification is precarious. The Talmudic passages about the 'Am ha-'Areç are obscure, and their meaning is disputed, They were written down long after the age of Jesus and many of them seem to refer to a period after his death. The features which characterize the Talmudic 'Am ha-'Areç do not appear to be the same as those which characterize the Gospel 'sinners' or 'multitudes.' It is therefore unsafe to use the passages in the Talmud in illustration or confirmation of the passages in the Gospels. The researches of Dr. Büchler have even made it possible that the Talmudic 'Am ha-'Areç did not belong to the 'multitude' at all, that they were not poor and unhappy and degraded, but rich and comfortable and prosperous. Many of the Rabbis, at any rate, were drawn from the people, and were emphatically of the people. Some of them were extremely poor ; working with their hands in the day-time, studying, discussing, and teaching in the evenings and on Sabbaths and festivals. An habitual antagonism between them and the 'multitude' is out of the question. And thus though it would be unsafe to aver that the Gospel narratives are totally inaccurate, it would be equally unsafe to regard them as more than exaggerated representations of the facts. Dr. Büchler holds that there is no Rabbinic evidence that any portion of the population, whether in Judæa or in Galilee, consisted of poor, despised persons who did not observe the ritual Law, and had 'fallen out of the legal ranks.' The people who did not observe the Law were the rich rather than the poor : the 'tax-gatherers' were rich, as even the Gospels allow, and so in all probability were the 'sinners.' The 'Am ha-'Areç are especially held up to reprobation in Rabbinic literature, because they did not carefully tithe their land. Therefore they were possessors of property, with whom a 'submerged tenth' is not usually identified ! We thus see how doubtful and obscure all the Gospel allusions to poor, neglected, or spiritually unhappy people really are.

In spite of John vii. 47, 48, contrasting rulers and Pharisees with 'this populace who know not the law' (a favourite passage with the ordinary Christian commentator), it is improbable that there was an *unobservant* populace, on the one side, an observant small minority of Scribes and Pharisees on the other. It is true that the great majority could not be *learned*, but it does not follow that they could not be *observant*. For, it is, I think, inaccurate when Lake and

Jackson say (*Beginnings,* I. p. 125) 'To observe the Law a profound knowledge of its requirements was needed, demanding long
and arduous study.' That is certainly untrue of orthodox Rabbinic
Judaism to-day, and it was, I think, probably untrue of Rabbinic
Judaism in the days of Jesus. It is not so difficult to know enough
to be exceedingly ' pious ' in the outward sense to-day : heaps of
Jewish families are so, but they are not learned, and have no learned
man among them. A special doubtful problem can be easily settled
by reference to a Rabbi. It was not, I fancy, so very different in
the days of Jesus. It would almost seem that there was a class of
people who did not *care* to observe, who did not give themselves
the trouble ; they could have observed enough for all practical
purposes not to have drawn upon themselves the anger of the Rabbis.
They did not care to. But most of them, I suspect, were not in our
sense of the word ' outcasts.'

If there really *did* exist a ' submerged tenth,' who neglected the
Law, disliked the Rabbinic teachers, and were disliked by them
in return, we may feel fairly sure that it was a *small* tenth and no
more. The mass of the nation at any rate, both women and men,
held with keenness and affection to the Rabbinical religion, and the
leaders of the Pharisees were the leaders of the people. Josephus
is not likely to be wrong when he emphasizes over and over again
that the Pharisees had ' the multitude ' on their side. Those who
hated the Scribes and Rabbis must have been few. Yet we may,
perhaps, assume that between them and those who followed whole-
heartedly the Pharisaic faith and the enactments of the Law, there
were some who admired, but followed at a distance, or who followed
only partially, or who followed with discontent, reluctance, weari-
ness, or dissatisfaction. To a few the Law did, perhaps, present
itself rather as a burden than a grace, as a worry and a bondage
rather than as a distinction and a joy. The Law of 30 was not the
Law of 300. It had not yet become the solace, poetry, and pride
of a hunted and despised people. In 30 it produced, we may,
perhaps, believe, more failures, less happiness, less spiritual satisfaction and well-being. The degrees between joyful observance and
full content on the one hand, and complete neglect or ' outsidedness '
on the other, were perhaps very many. There were many degrees
and shades of observance and neglect. Such outsiders, who were,
perhaps, more numerous in Galilee than in Judæa, were attracted
by the teaching and personality of Jesus, and to such persons (the
' sick ' and ill at ease) did he deliberately and with compassion turn
and minister. He cheered them and brought to them a new hope,
a new light. He led them to God.

With the addition of the third paragraph, I have left this section
exactly as it stood in my first edition. But Dr. Abrahams not long

before his death wrote specially for my present second edition a most valuable note on the 'Am ha-'Areç which, I fancy, gives more trustworthy information than can be found in any other book. The reader is recommended to study this note of the distinguished scholar with much care.

§ 29. *The various classes of people with whom Jesus came in contact : formalists and outcasts ; liberals and apocalyptists. The Essenes.*

We may, then, suppose that in Galilee Jesus had come into more or less close personal contact with various classes of persons before his ministry began. First and foremost there were the Pharisees and the Rabbis—the great majority of the total population. These we may describe as the conforming members of the established Church with their leaders and teachers. The measure of their conformity or their enthusiasm doubtless varied among the adherents of that ' church,' as it varies among the adherents of any existing ' church ' to-day. But yet we may call them roughly and rightly the party of the Pharisees. There can be little doubt that the parents of Jesus belonged to this ' party,' and that he was brought up to obey the enactments both of the Written and of the Oral Law, so far as that second or Oral Law had been yet developed or was generally observed among ordinary persons. Jesus, then, knows the Pharisees ; he also knows the prosperous rich, the landowners and nobles, neither whose moral nor whose ceremonial standard of living comes up in many instances to a high level. And again he knows others, such as merchants, shepherds, tax-collectors, soldiers, who are looked upon with grave suspicion by the Pharisees because their occupations and way of life either rendered it difficult for them to observe the ceremonial law, or subjected them to moral temptations from which they were commonly thought not to escape unscathed. And then again he perhaps knew a few others, poor, despised, unfortunate, degraded—not many in number, but in quality and circumstance interesting and important—who also were not supposed to belong to respectable society, and from whom most Pharisees and Rabbis kept aloof. For all such outcasts, whether rich or poor, Jesus felt much concern. For sinners and for unfortunate persons, for the spiritually destitute, for the physically afflicted, for the unhappy of all kinds, he had an open ear and a loving heart. He observed that few official teachers or Rabbis sought them out : yet they were children of Israel all, and if the call to repentance arose, surely they should not be left outside. Beneath their wayward and sinful and afflicted lives he could discern hearts which were susceptible to stirring appeal or personal affection.

But in addition to these, there were other classes in Israel as well. The tendency of the Pharisees and Rabbis was to interpret the Law more and more strictly, and to increase the wall of legal severance which separated the Jew from the Gentile. It would be unfair to say that the Rabbis deliberately extended the ceremonial at the expense of the moral Law, but it is true to say that their devotion to the non-moral side of the Law did occasionally produce evil results on the moral and spiritual side both in themselves and in their followers. In a master spirit like Hillel the moral and ceremonial side of Judaism were combined into a beautiful and harmonious whole. The same is true of R. Jochanan ben Zakkai, and of many others both of the first century and later. But in the case of many smaller and weaker men this harmony was, perhaps, absent, and the evil results of legalism may have shown themselves in the ways which Jesus so powerfully exposes and castigates. The 'good' and the 'bad' Roman Catholic can be profitably compared. Moreover it is a true paradox that the more universal, everyday, and obvious the dominion of the ceremonial Law became, the less also in some important respects grew its moral and spiritual dangers. When everybody strictly observes the Sabbath, and when nobody eats milk and meat together, the fulfilment of such ceremonial enactments gives no distinction. They have almost become customs of propriety, the neglect of which would indeed be outrageous, but the observance of which is nothing to boast of. Distinctions, differences, and 'merits' had once more to become concentrated upon the moral laws, which, by the very constitution of human nature, are by some obeyed well, by others feebly, and by yet others transgressed. But in the days of Jesus the domination of the ceremonial Law, as interpreted by the Rabbis, was not yet, as we have seen, coterminous with the whole population.

It may also be observed that Judaism was not wholly wanting in liberal tendencies in those days, 'and men of such tendencies were probably not only to be found outside of Palestine. There were those who held and believed that the true circumcision was of the heart rather than of the flesh, and who were willing to argue that, for the proselyte at least, such spiritual circumcision was all that God required or that man should ask. They were anxious to throw the moral laws of the Pentateuch into strong relief, so that the dangerous multiplication of ritual and ceremonial enactments might be counteracted. Ceremonial laws were symbols, perhaps allegories, of spiritual and ethical realities. Whether Jesus was influenced by any such persons it is impossible to say. It is not inconceivable.

Others there were who studied deeply the prophets rather than the Law. They fed their hopes upon the Messianic utterances of the book of Daniel, and, following in the wake of the writer of that book, they dreamed visions and wrote them down. The apocalyptic writers are by no means to be identified with the liberals, but yet they stand off the line of the regular and orthodox Rabbis. They and their disciples were the most ardent believers in the near coming of the crisis, the *dénouement*, the Judgment. But, on the whole, they were less spiritual than the Rabbis, who, by the way, came to regard it as a sin to calculate the advent of the Messiah. The Judgment to the apocalyptists was inclined to become all too exclusively a judgment upon Israel's foes. That Jesus was influenced by them seems likely. At all events we know that he began his short ministry because he believed that the End was at hand, and that he must proclaim its coming. But he markedly differed from the apocalyptic seers in keeping more closely than they to the teaching of the oldest and the greatest of the prophets. Sin would be struck down within Israel as well as without it. John the Baptist struck a similar note : indeed from him it was that Jesus heard it and passed it on.

The religious ferment and variety of the age of Jesus are also illustrated by the brotherhood of the Essenes. It is still a disputed point among scholars whether their customs, doctrines, and rites as described by Josephus and others were due to any extent to foreign influences, and if so what these foreign influences were. In some respects they exaggerated certain rules and habits which prevailed among the stricter Pharisees. Thus they laid great stress upon bodily purifications and purity, and upon the observance of the Sabbath. But in other matters they broke new ground. They formed a communistic brotherhood, and for the most part remained through life unmarried. Those who read Josephus' account of them in the eighth chapter of the Second Book of the *War* will be reminded of some things in the Gospels and in the teaching of Jesus. Such points are the stress laid upon continence, the objection to money, the habits in travel, the dislike to oaths, perhaps, too, the communistic brotherhood. But in other respects there is the strongest unlikeness. Jesus, as we shall see, laid no stress upon outward purity, he was probably not over particular about dietary laws, he was not intensely strict in Sabbath observance ; above all he did not ' keep himself to himself ' ; he moved freely among ' unclean ' and outcast persons; he sought these out, and did not avoid them. In the Pharisaic and Essenic sense he did not ' hate the wicked and help the righteous.' Thus Jesus was certainly not an Essene, though he may have been attracted and influenced by certain points of their doctrine. Whether John the Baptist had closer relations with them is not so clear, but it is not very likely.

§ 30. *The contradictions of Judaism : the one God
and the national cult.*

The existence of these various types and classes shows that the
Judaism of the first century was not only full of variety, but that
it might also be said to be full of contradictions. To a certain
extent these contradictions have not been overcome in Judaism
even to-day. These contradictions were and are largely due to the
fact that a pure monotheistic doctrine was wedded to a national
ritual. Tribal customs formed the outer expression of what was,
in its fundamental tenet, a universal creed. The result was confusion. It was the more noticeable before the Temple fell because
of the incongruous mixture of nationality and religion. The laws
of the nation were also its religious doctrines and its ceremonial
rites. Politics and religion were closely blended. The greatest
religious hope was also the greatest political hope, the greatest
national hope. This tended to obscure the purity of religion. It
is one of the remarkable points about Jesus that he is apparently
interested only in the individual and in religion. He does not
seemingly concern himself with politics or with the national life.
An apparent effect of this peculiarity upon his conception of the
Messiah and his office will be often alluded to in the notes. Paul
consciously freed himself and his religion from national contradictions and confusion by means of a theory. Jesus freed himself
of them unconsciously by his pure religious genius. They dropped
away from him, neglected and unnoticed. It may be observed that
I have, to some extent, qualified these statements by the use of
words such as ' seemingly ' and ' apparently.' I have done this
because we cannot be entirely sure how far this neglect of, or
indifference to, the national life on the part of Jesus is in perfect
accordance with historic fact. When the Gospels were compiled,
the Temple had fallen, and the Christians were separated, or were
fast separating themselves, from the Jews. The Evangelists would
not have wished that any trace of Jewish patriotism should have
been visible in their Master's teaching. If there were any such
traces in the sources upon which they drew, whether written or
oral, they would have deliberately omitted them. Thus we cannot
be quite sure that the picture which they draw is entirely true to
life. We may also observe that by the irony of history the
Christian community was destined to reintroduce the association
of religion and politics upon an enormous scale. And this association
it was which ultimately led to much disturbance in the national life
of Europe. It would almost seem as if the association of Church
and State were inherently liable to injure both.

One of the contradictions in Judaism to which I have referred would not have arisen in an ordinary heathen religion, or even in one where only one god was worshipped, but that god merely and solely the god of the nation. For a national cult and national religious laws would harmoniously fit a national god. But though the God whom the Jews worshipped was in a special sense *their* God, their national God, he was also much more. He was the only God ; the one and unique God ; the God of the whole world. But such a universal God required a universal cult. A national worship does not fit him. Hence some of the confusions to which I have alluded. They are illustrated in the attitude of the Jews towards proselytism. I have already referred to the existence of a liberal school of thought among the Jews, and to the view, expressed by one Rabbi (and perhaps shared by others), that circumcision of the flesh was unnecessary for the new-comer. There is evidence that outside Palestine, and to some extent also within it, there was a considerable amount of propagandist fervour, crowned with a considerable amount of success. This is not the place in which to speak at length about a most intensely interesting chapter of Jewish history. But that Judaism for various reasons exercised a great fascination upon the heathen in the first century before and after Christ is undoubted. It is also certain that there was, in one way and another, a good deal of effort expended in order to obtain proselytes. (I am not merely alluding to the compulsory proselytization and circumcision of adjacent tribes between the times of Judas Maccabæus and Herod the Great.) Yet there was always a certain difficulty about proselytes, and a school of thought existed which was opposed to them, for the convert had not only to adopt a new religion, but a new nationality.

The Jews were proud of their monotheistic religion. In a sense they were keen to push it and to proclaim its merits, but they were hampered by their nationalist Law. They wanted to stand high in the opinion of outsiders, but their Law to a considerable degree made them hostile to foreigners, and unable and unwilling to associate with them. To this Josephus bears abundant witness. The proselytism which many of them attempted was sometimes, as it would seem, undertaken less for the benefit of the heathen than for the glory of their nation or the glorification of their creed and Law. Jewish proselytes, we may well believe, were readily influenced by the preaching of Paul. For here, amid some blurring of monotheistic purity, and in spite of infractions, through alien conceptions, of the ethical and religious teaching of the prophets and of Jesus, is at last reached a religion where doctrine and cult are homogeneous and equally universalist, a religion a central feature of which is that, before a common allegiance, there is no difference between Jew and Gentile, and no profit in circumcision or uncircumcision.

Yet here again, when, later on, a declared belief in a particular set of dogmas became the only way of admission into its fold, the religion tended to lose its purely universalist character, while the intrusion of heresies weakened its homogeneousness.

§ 31. *Were the Jews and the Rabbis of* A.D. 30 *religiously inferior to those of* A.D. 300 *and* 600 ?

A theory has been started, to which allusion will be made in the notes, that the religious condition of the Jews in the age of Christ was much inferior to what it became after the awful purgation of the war, the destruction of the State, and the Hadrianic revolt. This theory has been partially accepted in the foregoing remarks, but only in a very modified form. The legalism of 300 and 600 was probably superior to the legalism of 30. There were unpleasing elements in the very varied religious phenomena of 30, from which the more restricted and homogeneous religious phenomena of 300 and 600 were free. The aristocratic priesthood and the political Pharisees, with their externalism and selfish interests, disappear. The 'outcasts' and 'submerged tenth' at the opposite end of the scale disappear also. All become nearer, and conform more closely, to a single type, and find in conformity to one ideal their satisfaction and highest good. The others disappear or become Christians. Less extremes and less variety existed in 300 or 600 than in 30. There was less breadth and less liberalism on the one hand, but also less apathy, aridity, and political externalism.

It is a different question whether the average and ordinary Rabbi of 30 was inferior in moral and religious worth to the average and ordinary Rabbi of 300 or 600, or whether the religion which he taught in 30 was inferior to the religion taught by his successor in 300 or 600. The theory of improvement was invented, not as a result of an examination of the evidence, but in order to save the accuracy of Jesus's sweeping indictments against the teachers of his time in certain portions of the Synoptic Gospels. It is more probable that this difference between the average Rabbi of 30 and the average Rabbi of 300 or 600 is largely imaginary, and that the denunciations put into Jesus's mouth are too sweeping and generalized. Of this there will be something to say in the notes. Probably Jesus did not condemn so profusely as his reporters—with whom the great conflict between Jew and Christian had begun—make out. Probably they darken the shadows to increase the light. Probably too Jesus himself, like Jeremiah and the prophets and every other religious reformer, exaggerated. He too tended to think that those who differed from him must be bad, and he failed to realize that minute ritual observance may lead up to God as well as away from Him. In this failure he is followed by several of even the most impartial theological historians at the present day, who think that ' legal ' and ' spiritual ' are necessarily antithetic or opposed to each other. Both in 30 and in 300 there were doubtless good Rabbis and bad Rabbis, and both in 30 and 300 a distinctively legal religion had the defects of its qualities. Formalism and externalism, self-righteousness and hypocrisy, were its faults in 300 as well as in 30, but we may well believe that, especially in middle-class society, these faults were in 30 no less than in 300 the exception and not the rule.

§ 32. *The condition of Galilee in the age of Jesus.*

In any appreciation of the character and teaching of Jesus it would have to be borne in mind that he was a native of Galilee. And it remains to be asked whether the somewhat general and vague conclusions which have been reached as to the religious condition of the Jews in the first century after Christ need special modification or emphasis in any particular direction for the case of Galilee. Its population at that period was predominantly, though not exclusively, Jewish. It was fertile, and thickly populated. It has been supposed that the number of ' outcasts and sinners,' or, in other words, of persons who did not scrupulously observe the ceremonial Law, and were despised and condemned by orthodox Rabbis and Pharisees, was proportionately greater in Galilee than in Judæa. This, however, is by no means certain. Nor does much good evidence exist for what Professor Cheyne has called their imperfect legal orthodoxy. In fact, another scholar observes that ' upon the whole they are said to have been strict in their religious observances.' It has also been supposed that the number of Rabbis who taught and argued in Galilee was far smaller in proportion to its population than in Judæa. From the Gospels it has been inferred that ' the Messianic hope burned more brightly in Galilee than anywhere else in Palestine ' ; ' Galilee,' say Jackson and Lake, ' was essentially patriotic, far more so than Judæa, which in the time of Jesus was still under the influence of the Scribes and priests, whose resistance to Rome was essentially passive ' (i. p. 290). It is not clear that these statements have very much to back them up outside the Gospel narratives. That the land was far from the capital must count for something. It will have contained many pious families who lived quiet and simple lives, and did not meddle with politics. In such a family it may be that Jesus of Nazareth was born.

§ 33. *The 'prophetic' character and mission of Jesus: the 'lost sheep': the Kingdom of God: Jesus and the Law.*

It is not within the scope or purpose of this Introduction to give any account of the career and the teaching of Jesus even upon the smallest scale; but I would like to indicate very briefly some of the points or problems as regards the teaching, at any rate, to which the reader's attention must be called.

Jesus is often described (especially in Luke) as a prophet. And it is from the prophetic point of view that his teaching, with the conflicts which it brought about, must primarily be regarded. This does not mean that Jesus was specially a foreteller of future events. It means that Jesus seems in many respects to take up the *rôle*, and to continue the teaching, of the eighth and seventh century prophets, of Amos, Isaiah, Jeremiah, and Ezekiel.

Like the prophets he announces a doom—a doom upon the unrepentant, upon sinners. It is true that the Judgment, the *dénouement*, the crisis, which is imminent, will affect the Gentile as well as the Jew. But Jesus—so far at least as we may gather from the fragments of his teaching which have been preserved to us—was mainly concerned to emphasize the doctrine that Israel, just because of its 'sonship,' would not be exempt from punishment. There are many sinners in Israel; sinners in high places as well as in low. And many who proudly think themselves secure will, unless their hearts are changed, be swept away in the coming storm. We may conceive that Jesus would have heartily concurred in the famous words of Amos : ' You only have I known of all the families of the earth ; therefore will I visit upon you all your iniquities.' It is not improbable, therefore, that Jesus may have predicted the fall of the Temple, even as we find it stated in Mark (xiii. 1, 2).

But Jesus was not merely the prophet of collective or general doom. He is much more the teacher of the individual than was Amos or Isaiah. By his time religion was individualized : the process which had begun with Ezekiel was continued, or, shall we say, completed, by him. Jesus, like Ezekiel, is the watchman : he is to warn the wicked and to turn him from his evil way.

He is sent, as he himself says, to the lost sheep, to the sinners. But to them, as we have seen and shall abundantly see, his message is not merely one of denouncement. He goes among them and eats with them. He will touch their heart in a number of different ways : he will touch it by arousing admiration, hope, and love, by encouragement and consolation, by powerful suggestion that the bonds of sin can be, or have been broken, and that a new life can be, or has been begun. Like the God of whom Ezekiel teaches,

Jesus has ' no pleasure in the death of the wicked,' he is desirous ' that the wicked turn from his evil way and live ' ; and so he goes about, intentionally and directly, ' to seek that which was lost and to bring again that which was driven away ' (perhaps driven away by the false severity, or pride, or carelessness of man). He will ' bind up that which is broken and strengthen that which is sick.'

This we may regard as a new, original, and historic feature in his teaching. And it is just here that opposition comes in and begins. To call sinners to repentance, to denounce vice generally, is one thing. To have intercourse with sinners and seek their conversion by seeming to countenance them and by comforting them—that is quite another thing. Did not all respectable persons pray and resolve ' to keep far from bad companions,' to avoid the dwelling-place of the wicked ? How can one keep the Law of God if one associates with sinners ?

In the next place Jesus's teaching was prophetic because he announced the coming of the Kingdom of God. The Judgment is to culminate in the Kingdom. Indeed the real importance, so to speak, of the Judgment is that it must herald and usher in the new order. The Kingdom of God seems to have been the central feature in the teaching of Jesus, and to his conception of it attention must constantly be directed. To enable as many to enter the Kingdom as the conditions would allow, and to enunciate and explain what these conditions are, occupied much of his time and care. Many who thought that they would infallibly enter it would, he held, be excluded. Many whom others thought would be excluded he, Jesus, would cause to enter. So far as it was supposed that, if the Kingdom were soon to come, all Jews would enter it from the mere fact of their birth, Jesus, we may be sure, like the true prophet that he was, combated a confidence so erroneous and irreligious ; whether, however, he went further, and, building upon and developing certain well-known prophetical utterances, declared that the inmates of the Kingdom would be rather Gentiles than Jews, is a point upon which opinion is still divided. Two things, at any rate, seem clear. First, that Jesus himself never dreamed of any preaching outside Israel (either directly or by his disciples). Secondly, that no universalist element in his teaching constituted any part of the conflict between himself and the Jewish authorities, whether Sadducean or Pharisaic.

The Kingdom would appear to have been the starting-point and the goal of Jesus's teaching. But much lies in between. A large proportion indeed of his entire religious and moral teaching lies in between : most of that for which his teaching is cared for and admired to-day.

And here we once more see in him the prophet. What are the

conditions of entry into the divine Kingdom? Like Ezekiel, Jesus represents the entry both as a grace and as a guerdon. 'God will give you a new heart: make you a new heart,' says Ezekiel. And Jesus says : ' God will choose those who are to enter the Kingdom, God will bring them in ; strive to enter the Kingdom, and this is how you should set about it.' The demands of the prophets are the demands of Jesus. Justice, charity and pity towards man, humility and love towards God ; the prophets had inculcated these, and Jesus inculcated them again.

But the great point of resemblance was this. The prophets had said outward worship, sacrifices, ceremonial religion, are of little good and little avail. Inwardness, moral goodness—these are the essentials. Jesus took up this teaching. And as sacrifices played a far less important part than heretofore in Jewish life—at any rate outside Jerusalem—as quite other outward forms and ceremonies were now predominant, it is these which he depreciates, and in the heat of argument is even led on to attack. It is the laws about the Sabbath, or about food, the rules about clean and unclean, which he criticizes and arraigns.

Jesus resumes the *rôle* of the prophets, but since Amos and even since Jeremiah spoke, how immeasurably great was the difference ! For Amos and Jeremiah spoke when there was no universally accepted code, no Mosaic Law, regarded on all hands as perfect, authoritative, and divine.

Thus Jesus, with his clear prophetic insight, his pure religious spirit, is brought up sharp against a tremendous obstacle. The Law does not indeed say that it is more important to observe the Sabbath than to ' love mercy ' : it does not indeed say that not to eat rabbits is of greater consequence than to ' walk humbly with God.' But it does say that all its ritual and ceremonial commands are the direct ordainment of the perfect God, and that they were to be perpetually observed throughout all the generations of Israel. Was then the Law not divine ? Or had Jesus power to abrogate it ? Here comes in the tragedy ; here is the great dividing line between the new Master and the old teachers. Here is where the conflict begins. What was the attitude of Jesus towards the Law ? How is it that the Law is to be both disobeyed and obeyed ? To be honoured in its breach as well as in its observance ? We can now see that to the mind of Jesus there was, as it were, set an impossible task. It was impossible for him to be wholly consistent; impossible for him to formulate any consistent theory. Upon the rock of the Law the new prophet was bound to stumble. To this point, then, to the relation of Jesus to the Law, to his criticisms of various legal enactments, to his conflicts with his opponents, and to their criticisms of him, the attention of the reader will have constantly to be called.

Jesus and the Law—this is one of the great problems of his life ; and it is a problem in which we have to try our utmost to understand his opponents and our utmost to understand him.

An essential feature of the prophet is the sense of commission and vocation. He is called by God to deliver a message, and thus stands towards God in a certain special relation. What he speaks he speaks in God's name, and he believes that it is the divine spirit which impels him to his work and directs his words. Jesus does not preface his speeches with ' Thus saith the Lord,' but in the conviction of inspiration, in the assurance that he too was called and chosen by God to do a certain work, he entirely resembles Amos, Isaiah, and Ezekiel. And herein lies his originality. It is hardly possible to say with any certainty how far, in the best O.T. sense of the word, we may suppose that John the Baptist was a prophet. We do not really know enough about his teaching or about his attitude to the Law to say this. But we do, I think, know enough about the great Rabbis of the first century A.D. to say that, however fine and noble their teaching may have been or was, it cannot properly be called prophetic. They were not called prophets, and they could not properly have been called so. However much they may have recognized that, at bottom, the Pentateuchal laws of morality were greater than its laws about sacrifice or 'clean and unclean,' they could not, they did not, deal with the subject in the same way and spirit as Jesus. Hillel was ever the servant of the Law, and never its Judge. In a sense he was more consistent than Jesus ; but for that very reason he was less prophetic. Sabbath conflicts, such as happened to Jesus, could not have happened to him. That is why, or that is one ' why,' the production of parallels from the teaching of Hillel with the teaching of Jesus is mostly futile. The spirit is different. The prophetic touch is present in the one case and absent in the other, and it is the prophetic touch which makes the difference. It is true that Jesus was called a prophet mainly because, as we have just seen, he announced with the assurance of conviction, with inspiration and therefore with authority, the imminence of the Judgment and of the Kingdom. In this, too, he resembles the ancient prophets, and he may indeed be said to have combined the parts of Amos and of the Second Isaiah. He announces doom to the unrepentant and the wicked : he comforts the repentant and the seekers ; the afflicted and the poor ; the humble and the yearning. And in this more primary sense of the word he was, if not so original as in the other, yet also unlike his Rabbinic contemporaries. The combination at least was new : Jesus was teacher, pastor, and prophet in one, and in this combination too lies something of his originality.

§ 34. *Jesus as healer : the forgiveness of sins.*

Different times require different kinds of prophetic manifestation. Jesus not only speaks, but also acts. He heals. He heals both the afflicted body and the afflicted minds. And in his healings he sees of necessity the most evident proof of his divine mission. The healings would not of themselves have produced a conflict, but if the healer was suspected and criticized on other grounds, then it was almost necessary to urge that the healings were due not to divine agency, but to a power of evil. Neither friend nor foe had any other explanation than these to offer. If Jesus, because he attacked the Law, was no messenger of God, then his very healings proved him to be the messenger of the Devil. They proved that his powers came from demons, not from ' on high.' His healings were ' supernatural,' but supernatural in an evil sense. This logic was irresistible, and the conflict was sharpened at this point.

Jesus called men to repentance : and with the call there went not merely denunciation, but comfort, consolation, encouragement. He sought to open the eyes of the blind, to lead the prisoners from the prison. An older prophet had begun his message with the assertion that the iniquity of Jerusalem had been pardoned. Jesus dealt with individuals rather than with the community as a whole, but he too seems to have felt that part of his message was to announce to this person and to that an emancipation from the bondage of sin. Strange results ensued from his activities. Bodily ailments, in which, with the majority of his contemporaries, he often saw a punishment for sin, were healed by him : some who had hitherto led a sinful or dubious life were converted by his word. Had not then God given to him the power to cancel the punishment of sin and to turn the sinner from his iniquity ? Was he not, now and again, impelled as God's messenger, to say to this or that individual on whom the effects of sin lay heavy, and in whom he saw the possibilities of a better life, ' thy sins are forgiven ' ? Upon this feature of the activity of Jesus we shall have to dwell early in the commentary upon Mark. It may have been emphasized too strongly by the Evangelist, but it was probably historic, and it may also have constituted, as Mark's narrative declares that it did, one cause of the conflict between Jesus and the Rabbis. Did he ascribe to himself a power which belonged only to God ? Misconception on such a delicate subject was only too likely to arise.

§ 35. *Jesus and the claim to Messiahship.*

But Jesus did not—so the gospel story would have us believe— merely regard himself as the chosen prophet of God, invested, as the other prophets before him, with a divine message and with God-given powers. At some period of his career the conviction seems to have come to him that he was yet more than a prophet, that he was in fact none other than he of whom prophets had spoken and for whose coming so many generations had yearned, the Anointed One, the Messiah. In what sense did Jesus believe himself (if indeed he did so believe at all) to be the Messiah ? Here we touch upon the biggest problem of the gospel story. Was his Messiahship effective during his life or only latent ? Was he only the Messiah to be, and when would he be invested with his kingly office ? And what sort of office was it to be ? A king, such as Isaiah of Jerusalem conceived him, ruling in righteousness over a liberated people, a powerful monarch, just and good and kind, but yet a real monarch, such as other monarchs are, though ruling for his people's good and not for his own ? Or was his kingship merely spiritual ? Was he to rule only over men's hearts and minds as the revealer of a new and higher conception of life, of goodness, and of love ? Was the scene of his kingship to be Palestine ? Or was there to be a new heaven and a new earth, and was the Kingdom of God, in which he, the Messiah, should rule, to be that semi-material realm to which the quickened dead should rise again ? And was this kingship with which he was to be invested to come to him during his lifetime, while he was still clothed with ordinary flesh and blood, or must he first pass through some great change, undergo perchance suffering and death, and only through these attain unto his glory ? Was the Messiah, in whom and in whose coming he believed, and with whom he identified himself, just a man, as the author of Isaiah xi. conceived him, or was he more than man, as some seers and dreamers at that time conceived him, a sort of heavenly man, pre-existent in heaven, but to come down from heaven when his appointed time had arrived ? Had he (the Messiah) ' come down ' unknown to all, had he been born of a human mother and a human father, born of Mary, begotten of Joseph, the carpenter of Nazareth ? Was he, Jesus, that heavenly man, to be revealed as such, to return to heaven, and then to descend again in glory ? And, again, was the Messiah, for that very reason, not to be, as of old men thought, as many still thought, a descendant of David, but something far higher, because more divine, a man chosen by the Lord, filled with the divine spirit, the Son of God ? And was this Man, greater than all, yet to serve all ? Was *this* his destiny, was *this* his function, not to conquer and rule by arm of flesh, but to serve and suffer and redeem, and then to rule un-questioned and supreme ? Were the Messiah and the Suffering Servant one and the same ? All these are questions to which various answers can be, and have been, given, some of which, with the arguments on this side and on that, will be submitted to the reader's judgment in the course of the commentary.

If Jesus in any of these senses claimed to be the Messiah, or if his disciples claimed the Messiahship for him, this claim would have been the greatest and the sorest source of conflict with all the Jewish authorities. So far as the Sadducean priesthood is concerned, for the obvious reason that a claimant to the Messiahship meant the displacement of their régime, popular disturbance, and war with Rome. So far as the Pharisees and Rabbis were concerned, for one main reason, and perhaps for another. That a prophet and teacher who had dared to criticize the Law and had denounced the official exposition of it, should then claim to be Messiah, was an insufferable pretension and arrogance. And very possibly, the Messiah whom Jesus claimed to be, or to become, was not, in the opinion of the Rabbis (whatever else he was), the Messiah whom older prophecy had described and foretold. Not so would the Son of David appear to claim his own.

§ 36. *The relation of Jesus to God.*

Some of the questions stated in the preceding paragraph lead on to the problem which is to be mentioned (but not discussed) in this one. Did Jesus, just because, or partly because, he felt himself to be Messiah, feel himself to be more than ' a mere man,' feel himself in some special relation to the Divine Father ? For was not the Messiah the Son of God ? As I have said, some Jewish thought had not remained content with the purely human conception of Messiah contained in Isaiah xi. A few thinkers and dreamers had, perhaps, come to picture the Messiah as a semi-divine being, pre-existent, already and for long ages back living with God in heaven till the fated moment of his descent upon earth should arrive. If Jesus came to the conclusion that he was Messiah, did he therefore also believe that he was nearer and more akin to God than all other men—if not less human, yet certainly more divine ? Or was the process just the reverse ? Was it his purely religious conception of sonship which led him on to the belief in his Messianic vocation ? Did he hold that none had felt God to be their Father with the same intensity that he felt it ? Did he believe that, just because he was God's son as no man before him had ever been, therefore he was, or would be, God's anointed ? These questions too will be alluded to in the notes. Their immense importance needs no proving. And if Jesus put forward any such personal claim, if he ascribed to himself any semi-divine powers or nature, the opposition of Jewish teachers would be increased tenfold. For even though some thinkers and dreamers might hold that Messiah was, or would be, more than man, such a theory was very different from a regular claim made by a particular living individual, whose ' mere humanity ' seemed obvious to every eye. Such a claim from such a person was almost blasphemy : no man might venture to arrogate unto himself the qualities and the nature of the divine.

Such, then, are some of the main features in the teaching and the position of Jesus which present problems for discussion and for doubt. Such, too, are the main features which seem to have brought about his conflicts with the Rabbis and the priests, and ultimately to have caused his death.

And all these features became intensified or exaggerated after the crucifixion and in the later reports of his life and teaching. The question which constantly presents itself to us is : how far did these features actually appear in his lifetime and in his actual, historic ministry ?

§ 37. Changes made in the teaching of Jesus after his death : (a) Israel and the Gentiles ; the Pharisees and the Law.

For with his death the whole perspective changed. It really speaks exceedingly well for the accuracy and honesty of the oldest sources that we can discern as much history in the Gospels as (in the opinion of most critics) we actually can—that we can discern through theory, exaggeration, legend, and even myth, the true lineaments of the historic Jesus.

If Jesus preached the Kingdom, his followers preached *him*. As Loisy says : ' What the apostles began to preach was not the story of the Christ, still less a system of doctrine, a scheme of teaching drawn up and fixed by him, nor was it the proclamation of the Kingdom of Heaven as Jesus himself had formulated it up to the very day before his death. The unexpected death of the preacher, ignominious and terrifying as it was, had deranged the equilibrium of their faith ; and when this faith found once more a firm basis (*assiette*) in the belief of the Resurrection, it had already advanced a large step beyond the limits within which the teaching of Jesus had been confined. For now, in order to diffuse itself, that faith had not to speak directly of the Kingdom, but of the Christ, whose manifestation had to be shown as certain, although retarded (*dont il fallait que la manifestation parût acquise, bien qu'elle fût retardée*). Instead of first of all believing in the Kingdom which had not yet come, one had to believe in the Messiah who *had* come. To prove to the Jews that Jesus, though he died on the cross, was none the less the Messiah,—this was the task which was now imposed

upon his disciples. For its fulfilment it was not sufficient for them
to use their memories ; they had to find new arguments for the
support of their faith ' (*E. S.* 1. p. 176).

A crucified Messiah, and a Messiah whose history should consist
of two parts—the first part an ordinary, human life ending in a
shameful death ; the second, a later, not yet fulfilled, appearance
in heavenly glory (the one a conception unknown to, and unthought
of by, all Jews, the other a conception thought of, or imagined, by
only a few)—had now to be championed and maintained. And
with this huge change other changes came as well. The breach
with the Synagogue gradually widened. The Law was more and
more neglected and violated—at least by many of the new-comers
and under the influence of Paul. The new religion began to be
preached, and to find its warmest and best adherents, among the
Gentile world. These very changes brought about an inevitable
exaggeration of the original points and features of conflict.

First, as regards doctrine, apart from the personality, nature,
and office of the Master himself.

Jesus had undoubtedly, prophet-wise, denounced the sinners
in Israel, and possibly he had even foretold, like Jeremiah, the
destruction of the Temple. These historic sayings become,
after his death, unconsciously exaggerated. The privileges of
Israel are to be taken away ; the holy city is to be destroyed (as
the disciples of the disciples themselves witnessed) ; no longer
unbelieving Israel, but the new Israel, the community of Christian
believers, is to inherit the ancient promises and to enter into the
Kingdom of Heaven. For those Israelites who refuse to accept
Jesus as the Messiah the doom is Hell, with its everlasting punishment, with its wailing and gnashing of teeth unto the end of time.

Jesus in his lifetime had conflicts and differences of opinion with
the Pharisaic champions of the Law, with the Rabbis of Galilee and
of Judæa. Though his death was primarily caused by the priests
and the Romans, yet doubtless some of the Rabbis in Jerusalem were
also privy to his arrest and assented to his condemnation. This
conflict becomes exaggerated. From the beginning the Pharisees
and Scribes are his enemies ; they denounce him ; he denounces
them. They are all bad ; they are full of sins and corruption ; they
long to compass his destruction and his death.

In respect to the teaching of Jesus about the Law, as in respect
to his teaching about the Gentiles, the tendency to emphasize and
exaggerate was checked by a cross-current. For one section of the
earliest Christians still cared for and observed the Law. Jesus had
not attacked and violated the Law to such an extent as to make this
legal position untenable for any of his adherents. He had adopted
a prophetic attitude towards the Law. The Inward rather than

the Outward ; love rather than sacrifice ; this was his position. Whether he had formulated any more theoretic point of view may well be doubted. Thus we find in the Gospels exaggerations of both kinds. ' Not one jot or tittle of the Law shall ever pass away till all is fulfilled.' On the other hand, we find the conception that at least one Mosaic ordinance was given to the Israelites because of the hardness of their hearts. We find a theory announced that Jesus came to ' complete ' the Law, not to ' destroy ' it, but this completion, in regard to such an important element of the Law as the dietary injunctions, comes upon occasion to something not remotely resembling abrogation. Here in each case the question as to historical accuracy needs careful weighing. Have the reporters exaggerated the hostility of Jesus to the Law, have they exaggerated his esteem for it ? Have they, rather than *he*, formulated his theoretic attitude towards it ?

And so as to the Gentiles. Did Jesus contemplate, again prophet-wise, the inclusion of the Gentile world in the community which he sought to found ? Did he bid his disciples preach the gospel to all nations, or did he bid them carefully avoid those who were not of Israelite blood ? What was his own attitude towards the heathen ? Did he share ' Jewish particularism,' or had he consciously and deliberately overcome it ? The double tendency in the Gospels makes the answer the more difficult and uncertain.

§ 38. (b) *The Messiahship and the relation to God.*

But exaggeration was naturally most rampant in all that had to do with the person and office of the Master.

In some manner about which believers and unbelievers, Jews and Christians, are bound to dispute, the disciples of Jesus, beginning from Peter, began to be convinced that the same fortune which befalls other men after death had not befallen Jesus. A special lot had befallen him. He had been seen again. In some way or other, in some form or other, he had risen from his tomb, and ascended into heaven. Whether the visions of the risen Jesus, which we may all believe that Peter and other disciples saw, were purely ' subjective '—even as men may ' see ' a ' vision ' to-day—or whether such an hypothesis does not adequately explain them (because Peter did not expect a vision, but on the contrary believed that the cause of Jesus had failed, and that his faith in Jesus had been doomed to disappointment), cannot here be discussed. Somehow or other, the belief arose. The Master had risen. His Messiahship was thereby proved ; his uniqueness more than ever assured. Every side and aspect of his teaching and his mission, of his life and of his death, were, therefore, liable to speedy exaltation. And speedily did they receive it.

Thus, for example, Jesus had undoubtedly performed some striking wonders of ' healing.' These are made more wonderful still. Fresh miracles are invented ; ordinary events are turned into miracles. The ministry of Jesus becomes one long exhibition of divine power fighting the powers of darkness. Jesus is always in the right ; his opponents are always in the wrong. He reads men's thoughts and hearts. He, not so much as God's prophet, but in virtue of his own personality and authority, announces and grants the forgiveness of sin. He is the Messiah, and God proclaimed his Messiahship to him at the very beginning of his ministry. If, for certain reasons of his own, he concealed that Messiahship for a while, the powers of darkness at any rate always knew him for what he was. He foreknew and foretold the sequence of his life and death : all was prearranged, foreordained. He predicted his arrest, his Passion, his resurrection ' on the third day.' His life becomes a divine drama ; even his teaching becomes a mystery, which was intended to darken the minds of all except the Elect. Jesus foresaw the persecutions of his disciples from the hands of Jews and Gentiles. He told them how they were to behave under these persecutions : he gave rules for the new community and its government. The cross upon which he died becomes an emblem of his teaching. Those who would be his disciples must be prepared to die even as he died, nay even to bear their cross daily in a life of hardship, self-denial, and renunciation. If Jesus the Messiah suffered at his death, the suffering tends to be regarded as even anticipated in his life : he is, at least, a homeless wanderer who has nowhere to lay his head in safety and repose.

Jesus, the Messiah, had ' risen ' after his death to immortal life. This too he predicted and foreknew. Did the historic Jesus foresee his death ? Did he go to Jerusalem to conquer or to die ? Had he at any rate a vague presentiment—anticipations of disaster to himself, though not to the Kingdom ? Did he think that the service he had to render to the coming and imminent Kingdom might even demand his own death ? In that case he might also have held that if he had to die before the Kingdom came, he would rise again soon in order to share in it or to become its chief. All these are questions which the Gospel narratives insistently demand of us. The ' line of exaggeration ' it is not difficult to see. Jesus knows exactly all that is to happen. First his death, then his resurrection, then (after an interval) his reappearance on the clouds in glory as openly manifested Messiah. To the Death succeeds Resurrection ; to the Resurrection succeeds a triumphant Parousia. Then will the drama of Israel and the world conclude : the Messiah will be also the judge

—the heavenly judge who shall assign to all then alive and to the risen dead their portions of gladness or of misery for ever and ever. Amid all this development and ' exaggeration ' how are we to discover the sense in which the historic Jesus accepted the Messiahship for himself, what he meant by it, and what he anticipated would be the manner of its manifestation ?

The Messiah was God's son. Had not the Psalmist made God say of him : ' Thou art my son : this day have I begotten thee ' ? Both in this Messianic sense, and in a spiritual sense, Jesus may well have felt and held himself to be the Son of God. Here too the Gospel ' exaggerates ' upon a historic basis. It pushes the date of his sonship backwards : it hardens the meaning of it, separating Jesus ever more and more from other men, increasing his measure of divinity, magnifying his conception of it, till finally we get the stories of the infancy, the annunciation, and the miraculous birth. Jesus becomes the Son of God not merely as the Messiah, but as metaphysically related to the Godhead. He becomes not merely a divine being, but himself a part of God, with powers hardly inferior to those of his Father. And with these exalted powers there comes an increased and deadly particularism. If Jesus, like all passionate reformers, could not imagine that there could be any right which was not on his own side, his disciples soon came to believe that none could know God and love him well unless they believed in Jesus and his divinity. It was a very early ' exaggeration ' of his prophetic self-assurance which induced them to make Jesus say : ' All things have been delivered unto me by my Father ; and no one knoweth the Son, save the Father ; neither doth any know the Father, save the Son, and he to whomsoever the Son willeth to reveal him.' Or is this famous passage authentic ? Did Jesus carry his claims so far ? Did his conception of God, and of his own sonship, and of their relations to each other, amount even unto this ? Here we have the problem of authenticity at its acutest and most important point.

However this special question may be determined, it is, at any rate, at these very points, where conflicts soon arose between the Christian and the Jew, and where the centre of gravity of the new religion lies, that the records of the Gospels are to be most critically examined. And this whether they deal with incident or with teaching. But a large part of the teaching, including the famous paradoxes of the Sermon on the Mount, lies outside. And just as it is quite certain that, however much (if such be our judgment) this teaching transcended or even contradicted the teaching of contemporary Rabbi and Scribe, Jesus could, nevertheless, have gone on inculcating it for ever without coming to an evil end, so also is it here that we may look for the greatest accuracy in the record and the greatest measure of authenticity. Wellhausen's caution as regards the tradition of the teaching and the sayings may well be borne in mind, but it has, I venture to think, to be checked by this other principle or test which has just been laid down.

§ 39. *The various problems raised by the life of Jesus.*

A commentary upon the Gospels is in any case not also a ' Life of Christ.' Whether the material for such a Life exists may well be doubted. And the Introduction to such a tentative commentary as this is still less the place in which to attempt it. Only incidentally, and as occasion rises, will the commentary discuss questions relating to the character of Jesus, the nature and development of his teaching, the manner of his life and death. It will also occasionally consider how far the Gospel narratives can be regarded as historic, and how far the Jesus of actual fact must be conjecturally supposed to have differed here and there from Jesus as Mark, Matthew, and Luke portray him.

Perhaps, however, before bringing these few introductory pages to a close it may be desirable to call attention once more in yet another way to those problems to which, in the notes, the reader's attention will more frequently be directed.

The exact years of the birth and death of Jesus may still be in dispute, but that he was born about 4 B.C. and died about A.D. 30 seems fairly certain. And what appears equally sure is that the length of his ministry did not extend over more than a year and a quarter, or a year and a half. Hence it follows that all the problems about Jesus to which any answer is possible are concentrated about the last two years of his life. How he lived, what he did and how he developed, from infancy till he was about thirty-two, we cannot say.

The short last section of his life of which the Synoptic Gospels tell may be roughly divided into two portions of unequal length. The first of these is the Galilæan period ; the second the journey to Jerusalem, and its results. It may be said that the main problem of his life is contained in the question, How did he come to die ? Or, again, the question may be put thus : To what end did he go to Jerusalem ?

Among other difficult matters which this question involves is the fundamental problem as to what Jesus thought of himself. This problem has been touched upon already. Did Jesus suppose himself to be the Messiah, and, if so, in what sense ? Did he start the Galilæan ministry with this idea, or did the idea only assume definite shape and conviction towards its close ? We shall see that while Jesus from first to last seems to have believed in the imminent end of the world, or of the Existing Order, he did not, probably, for a while, regard himself as the Messiah. He felt himself to be divinely sent, a prophet like the prophets of old, but not at once, or very soon, the Messiah.

Some scholars, we shall hear, think that Jesus never claimed to be the Messiah at all. This we shall consider a less probable hypothesis. But if he claimed to be the Messiah, what sort of Messiah did he conceive himself to be ? Was it completely new wine which he poured into that old bottle ? Here we shall see that no final and satisfactory result has been, or probably can ever be, attained.

Did he call himself the Son of Man, and, if so, with what intention, and with what relation to the Messianic title, to the ordinary Messianic conception, or to his own Messianic claim ? Many theories can be drawn up ; many varying answers can be given. Some fit some of the facts and statements ; others fit others. None, perhaps, fit all. Hence the difficulty of coming (with such meagre and in parts untrustworthy material) to any confident and certain result.

Among the minor questions which the fundamental question includes are these : What was the view of Jesus concerning the rule and overlordship of the Romans ? And upon what charge or charges—whether false or true—was he condemned to die by the Jewish authorities and by the Roman governor ? Who is responsible for his death ? Even here, too, the answers that may be given, with fair arguments and show of reason, are different, and even here, while we shall see that one answer is more probable than another, definite certainty cannot be arrived at.

As regards the teaching of Jesus, if the question be asked, What was its special character or nature, the answer is partly dependent upon the answer to that other question, What did Jesus think and teach about himself ? But we shall see that it is only partly so dependent. It is, moreover, only partly dependent upon, or connected with, Jesus's belief in the imminent End of the Age. We shall observe that Jesus was not always thinking of that great event. It formed, doubtless, the background for all his teaching, but much of that teaching was spoken as if no such terrific change was at hand ; or, at any rate, much of it was applicable to, and was even intended for, ordinary conditions of existence, such as they were when his words were said, and in some respects, at least, such as they are even to-day. Whether there was any change or development in the religious and ethical teaching of Jesus, whether the demands he made upon those who would be his true disciples were increased, whether his teaching was at first less ' apocalyptic ' and became more so, are also questions which will be noticed as they arise. This last question is to some extent connected with the meaning to be assigned to that term frequently upon Jesus's lips— the term with which his ministry opens—but of which the precise signification is still often doubtful and disputed—namely, the famous ' Rule, Dominion, or Kingdom of God,' or, as Matthew calls it, the ' Kingdom of Heaven.'

§ 40. *The Jewish conception of the Messiah and the conception formed by Jesus.*

The various theories about Jesus and the ultimate objects of his brief career often rest upon fragile bases. Many of them seem to do violence to some part or other of the Gospel evidence or to the evidence of the Rabbinical literature. Or, if they do not do violence to what the Gospels say, they seem, if I may put it thus oddly, to do violence to what they do not say.

Take, for instance, the question as to whether Jesus thought himself to be the Messiah, and if so, what sort of Messiah he thought himself, or wanted, to be. The hypothesis that he never identified himself with the Messiah at all cuts the Gordian knot too crudely. It explains some facts, but it leaves others—and more important and crucial ones—unexplained. It is not merely that various stories recorded in the Synoptics must then be regarded as unhistorical, but the very career of Jesus, with its crisis and its end, become vague and difficult to understand.

Yet not much less difficult is the conception, repeated in a hundred different forms and shades, that Jesus did indeed claim to be the Messiah, but such a Messiah as had never before been thought of, above all things not a Jewish Messiah. He allowed his disciples to regard him as the Messiah ; he had no better name to invent ; but it was a mere shell, a mere name, for something totally different from the ordinary Jewish conception. In the course of the commentary this hypothesis will crop up more than once, and we shall see how difficult it is.

What is usually meant by the ' ordinary Jewish conception of the Messiah ' ? The answer must be : something extremely disagreeable. Indeed the ' ordinary Jewish conception of the Messiah,' created by Christian theologians as a foil to the ' pure spiritual ' conception of Jesus, is an eviscerated conception in which all the cheap things are left in (and exaggerated) and all the valuable things are left out.

The ' ordinary Jewish conception of the Messiah ' means, so far as I can gather, that of an intensely ' national ' and ' legal ' king, under whose warlike and bloody rule the Jews avenge themselves upon their enemies, kill the majority, enslave the rest, and live in gorgeous, outward, material prosperity for ever and ever. Now this is a caricature for many reasons. It is a half truth, and we know what half truths are.

The desire for prosperity, for freedom, for 'imperial' rule in the place of cruel subjection, was doubtless strong in the popular mind, and the desire for revenge—especially after Titus—was not especially absent even from all the Rabbis. But the essential feature of the ordinary conception of the Messiah was that of a *righteous* king ruling over a righteous people; the Messianic era was indeed one of prosperity, but far more was it one of peace and goodness and the knowledge of God. So far as it was this, why should not Jesus have wished to be the Jewish Messiah? What is there so very dreadful and immoral and unspiritual in the conception of Isaiah xi.—of a righteous king and a God-fearing and righteous nation?

But then, there comes another difficulty. We talk of the 'ordinary Jewish conception of the Messiah.' But what *was* ' the ordinary Jewish conception of the Messiah' in the age of Jesus? And was there one prevailing conception at all? We do not really and certainly know. The idea of the warlike king seems to have been on the wane. God would accomplish the redemption and establish the Kingdom at his own time and in his own way. May we go so far as to say that the king would rather teach than fight? Might he be discovered, perchance, healing the sick, and only ascend his 'throne' when all 'enemies' had been destroyed or been converted?

So although Jesus did not—and this is certain—conceive that the assumption of his throne and the establishment of the Kingdom would involve his own appearance at the head of an army, nevertheless he would not, for *this* reason, have formed a conception which was un-Jewish and unfamiliar.

If he had formed a conception of his Messianic office which was wholly unlike that of most of his contemporaries, why did he choose and allow the name? Why did he not reject it? Why did he not more clearly explain : ' Though I do not object to your thinking me the Messiah, and though I shall die as King of the Jews, yet you must understand that my Messiahship, even after my resurrection, will never remotely resemble the ordinary Jewish conception of the Messiah'? Why was it left to the author of the Fourth Gospel to make him say that?

We shall be inclined to believe that most facts (though not necessarily all the facts) will be accounted for if we suppose that Jesus did believe that, either at a *dénouement* before his death or at the Parousia after his death, he would 'rule' over a righteous people. We have no means of deciding what he thought would be the fate of the huge Gentile world. Perhaps he thought (with the best utterances of the older prophets) that they would all be 'converted' and become voluntary subjects of his Kingdom—all of them, at least, who had escaped the Judgment. For Jesus, like his contemporaries, undoubtedly believed in a Judgment, and moreover he seems to have believed that the number who would be 'lost' in the Judgment would be (to our ideas) painfully large. Among those victims of the Judgment there would doubtless be, in his opinion, a number of Gentiles as well as a very large quantity of Jews. Those who remained over, whether Jewish or pagan by birth, would now become pure worshippers of the One God and loyal subjects of the Messianic King.

§ 41. *Jesus and the 'masses.'*

It has been supposed by Prof. Bacon that Jesus regarded himself as the Messiah, or was willing to let others so regard him, only in so far as he stood forth 'as the leader, champion, and vindicator of the disinherited sons.' The Messiah to Jesus had no 'theocratic connotations'; it meant merely 'He who brings Israel into its predestined relation of sonship to God.' Over and over again does Prof. Bacon speak of the 'masses' and of Jesus as their champion. The 'masses' are apparently put on one side : a few Rabbis, Pharisees, and priests on the other. He speaks of the 'narrow cliques of scribes and Pharisees,' 'the *chaberim* of synagogue orthodoxy on one side, the *'Am ha-'Arec*, the masses of the people on the other.' These masses are 'spiritually disinherited.' This is probably the weakest theory of all, so far as the facts are concerned. Prof. Bacon allows that Jesus '*did* follow a rôle that led to his execution by Pilate as a *political* agitator' (*Gospel Story*, p. 106). Nevertheless all that he will allow as to the Messiahship is this championship of the 'disinherited masses'; only thus may Jesus have 'regarded his calling as in some remote sense Messianic.'

But there is little evidence of disinherited masses, even within the Gospels. Even the Gospels scarcely imply that the *masses* had no religion which they cared for or brought them comfort, or that the Rabbis were not their teachers or their friends. And outside the Gospels the evidence is the other way. The Pharisees, as Josephus tells us, formed the popular party. They have the people on their side. And if ever there was a teaching class drawn from the people, it was the Jewish Rabbis of old—men who took no pay for their studies and services, and in many cases earned

their living by their hands. As I have already mentioned the
'Am ha-'Areç may possibly be not poor folk, but rich folk. In any
case they are not the *people*—a more dubious identification was
never made. There were doubtless many bad Rabbis in those
days as later; the Talmud itself castigates such, but the greater
number of Rabbis, even as they sprang from the people, loved the
people, taught the people, and had the people at their back. The
masses were *not* disinherited : the martyr race *par excellence* found,
and continued for long ages to find, its best happiness in the practice
of its religion. There was no need for Jesus to teach them that
God was their Father; they knew it all along. They knew it then ;
they continued to know it; they know it now. If they *had* not
known it, they would not have died in thousands for their faith :
if they *did* not know it, they would not be suffering now. With
the leading priests at Jerusalem the case is different, but even there,
and in spite of the oppression and dishonesty which undoubtedly
were practised by many, we must not suppose that either Rabbi or
people was not attached to the Temple and its services. We must
not measure the men of ancient time by modern standards.

§ 42. *Jesus as prophet : did he intend to found a new religion ?*

It does not, however, follow from what has just been said that
the teaching of Jesus was not greater or more original than that of
the ordinary teacher of his day. It undoubtedly was. And there
is a further point still.

That the teaching of Jesus was in important points opposed to
the teaching of the contemporary Rabbis seems certain. I have
ventured to say that Jesus, at any rate in his earlier ministry,
seems most aptly to be described as a true successor to the old, and
especially to the great pre-Exilic, prophets, Amos, Hosea, Isaiah.
And this is the impression which he made upon his contemporaries.
They, too, found his teaching new, inspired, prophetic. The
difficulties which such teaching brought to its author, and the
honest opposition which it encountered, were due to the profoundly
important fact that when Amos and Isaiah spoke there was no
authoritative, divine, ' Mosaic ' Law in existence, and when Jesus
spoke there was. Of the relation, partly conscious and partly, as
it were, unconscious, in which Jesus stood to the Law there will be
much to say in the notes. Jesus, as I have said, had to hark back
from the Law to the prophets. His teaching is a revival of prophetic
Judaism, and in some respects points forward to the Liberal Judaism
of to-day.

If we ask wherein his hearers found the teaching of Jesus ' new, inspired, prophetic,' to use the words of the preceding paragraph, it is not quite easy to reply. For, except as regards the Law, one can probably discover parallels in the Rabbinic literature to every portion of his teaching. But the words ' new, inspired, prophetic ' are, nevertheless, not rashly or falsely chosen. It is the spirit of the teaching, its unity, its fervour, its intensity, its enthusiasm, which were new, inspired, prophetic, rather than any one particular part of it. Pity, faith, love, trust—contemporary Rabbis spoke of all these things, but they did not, perhaps, speak of them with the same intensity and genius. They did not, perhaps, quite in the same way, demand All for the Highest. They did not preach the same impassioned doctrine of sacrifice. They did not show the same yearning to save the sinner from the fastnesses and the morasses of sin, or from the physical and mental evils which in those days were so closely associated with sin. It was in these more indefinable and subtler ways that the teaching, like the bearing, of Jesus was new, inspired, prophetic, rather than in any novelty of doctrine in any one definite particular.

The important points in which the teaching of Jesus was opposed to the teaching of the Rabbis are all connected with the Law. His teaching about divorce, about the Sabbath, about clean and unclean, was in the spirit of the Prophets, but not in strict accordance with the letter of the Law. His conflict with the Rabbis did not come because he went beyond their teaching about loving one's enemies, or about the deep value of inward purity in itself, or of every sort of moral inwardness in itself ; the conflict came because Jesus drew certain practical conclusions in respect of Inwardness, and these conclusions led logically to a transgression of the Law. The doctrine of the divine Law put both ceremonial and moral injunctions upon an equal footing, and never contemplated any conflict between them. It gave no clear guide for action should such conflict ever arise. This doctrine of the divine law, with divinity extending to the ceremonial as well as to the moral, placed both Jesus and the Rabbis in a very difficult position. For Jesus, too, though less fervently than his Rabbinical opponents, professed to believe, and did actually believe, in the divineness of the Law. But his impassioned prophetic attitude drove him on to action and to teaching which were in violation of the Law, while the Rabbis, in their profound veneration and adoration of the God-given and perfect Law, could not look at the relation of morality to ceremonial, of the Inward to the Outward, from a purely prophetic point of view. The conflict between Jesus and the Rabbis was thus inevitable and had all the elements of tragedy. It was ' tragic,' and produced a tragedy.

Another gravely important question which may be asked about the teaching of Jesus is : Did he intend to found a new religion ? This question is distinct from the other one as to whether his teaching is sufficiently novel, distinctive, and comprehensive as to justify a separate religion with a separate name being founded upon it, even apart from any doctrine as to his Messiahship or divinity. Such might be the position of much modern Unitarianism, for which doubtless its advocates can find much to say. Whether Jesus himself intended to found, or foresaw the founding, of a new religion apart and distinct from Judaism, is, however, another question. It is, in part, clearly dependent upon the views which Jesus held as to the end of the world. If he thought that that end was near, he can hardly have also intended to found a new religion and a new religious community. Taken all in all, it seems probable that Jesus was *not* the conscious founder of the Christian Church. He was, and meant to remain, a Jew. Or rather the question of separating from the Synagogue never presented itself to his mind. He wanted to purify, to quicken, to amend, but not to break away and make a fresh beginning. He continued the work of Amos, Hosea, and Isaiah. His Kingdom of God, from one point of view, was a reformed Judaism. And possibly it may come to pass that in his teaching there may be found a reconciliation or meeting-point between a Reformed or Liberal Judaism and a frankly Unitarian Christianity of the distant future. *That* Judaism and *that* Christianity may find that they differ in name, in accent, and in memories, rather than essentially or dogmatically. *That* Judaism and *that* Christianity may both claim Jesus as their own.

§ 43. *The Gospels, the New Testament, and the Jews.*

It might be asked : What is, or what should be, the Jewish interest in the New Testament, in the Synoptic Gospels, or in the life and character of Jesus ? To these questions, too, the commentary will supply some incidental answers. The origin of a great religion, which has filled so immense a place in the history of the world, must surely be of interest to every cultivated person. To know something about a Book and a Person that have been of such huge and amazing importance, and that are of such great importance still, is a right and reasonable thing—a desirable part of knowledge. But the European Jew lives in a Christian environment, a Christian civilization. He has absorbed much of this civilization himself ; he breathes it in ; it is part of him. He reads the history of the country of which he is a citizen. This civilization and this history are all unintelligible without Christianity. They rest upon the New Testament and the Gospels. The book which has had the greatest influence upon European history and European civilization is the Bible. The Jew does not mind saying and repeating this. But he too often forgets that the Bible which has had this influence is not merely the Old Testament. It is the Old Testament and the New Testament combined. And of the two, it is the New Testament which has undoubtedly had the greater influence and has been of the greater importance. It is the Gospels and the life of Christ which have most markedly determined European history and most influenced for good or evil many millions of lives. If it is an improper ignorance not to have read some portions of Shakespeare or Milton, it is, I am inclined to think, a much more improper ignorance not to have read the Gospels.

The curiosity of the Jew as regards these writings might also be legitimately aroused when he reflects that the Gospel hero was a Jew, and that the books of the New Testament were mainly written by Jews. Jewish ignorance of the Gospels is indeed not unnatural. It has many causes which I will not here enumerate. It needs, even to-day perhaps, some detachment of mind to say : ' I will read and study the book upon which is based the religion which has inflicted upon my ancestors such incalculable cruelty and wrong. I will read and study the book from which comes the religion which vaunts itself to be a religion of love, but which, so far as my race is concerned, has usually been a religion of hate. I will read and study the book from which proceeds a monotheism less pure and lofty than my own, a monotheism, if it can be called such, which has deified a man and invented the Trinity. I will read and study the book from which was evolved the religion which pretends to have superseded and to be superior to my own —to be purer and better than my religion, of which the cardinal doctrines are contained in such words as : Hear, O Israel, the Lord thy God the Lord is One. Thou shalt love the Lord thy God with all thy heart. Thou shalt love thy neighbour as thyself. What does the Lord require of thee, but to do justly, and to love mercy, and to walk humbly with thy God ? '

Yet this detachment of mind must now be demanded. Judaism, and therefore the Jews or some Jews, must answer the questions, and answer them better and more impartially than they have yet been faced and answered : What is the right Jewish attitude towards the New Testament ? What are we to think about the Gospels and the Gospels' hero ? I cannot believe that the best and final answers will be merely negative. They will not be framed upon the familiar lines that what is new in the Gospels is not true, and what is true is not new. Does Judaism really expect that in the future—even the distant future—the Old Testament will be 'accepted' and the New Testament 'rejected'? Does Judaism really expect that the Bible, for the Europe of the 'Messianic' age, will be a smaller Bible than the European Bible to-day? Will it include the Old Testament only? But if such an idea is inconceivable, if the Bible for Europe has been constituted once and for all—whatever men may think of its theologies—should not Judaism take up some more reasoned and studied attitude towards so permanent a part of the religious literature and religious consciousness of the Western world?

One view which will be incidentally maintained and supported in this commentary is that Judaism has something to gain and absorb from the New Testament. There are teachings in the New Testament, and above all in the Gospels, which supplement and carry forward some essential teachings in the Old Testament. It seems true to say that in respect of moral and religious value we can dispense neither with the Old Testament nor with the New Testament. I will not attempt to sum up here the special excellences and values of either. So far as the Gospels are concerned, these excellences will be alluded to in the commentary. But over and above the excellences in detail, there is the spirit or impression of the whole. So too with the Old Testament, the Hebrew Bible. The strong, virile, healthy tone of the Old Testament religious teaching is sometimes contrasted with a certain sentimentality and introspectiveness in the New. Its vigorous social and 'collective' morality—its insistence upon justice and righteousness in society and the State—are also sometimes contrasted with a certain marked individualism in the New. Contrasts proverbially exaggerate, yet there may be something not wholly false in this contrast as in others. Meanwhile we need both the Old Testament's imperative demand for a righteous nation, and the New Testament's insistent emphasis upon the value of the individual soul; we need both the severity of justice and the tenderness of love. As regards the latter pair of apparent opposites they are both present in both Testaments, but in different ways. And these different ways could themselves be made to form one illustration the more for my contention that an Englishman, a German, or a Frenchman, be he Christian or be he Jew, has something to gain, something of moral or religious value to absorb, both from the New Testament and the Old, or, if the collocation be more emphatic, both from the Gospel and the Law.

§ 44. *Parallel passages to the Gospels in Rabbinic literature.*

Something will be said about parallel passages in the next section also. I have myself quoted very few of these passages in my commentary : I had not the space. Moreover, they have been collected, and are available, in many different books, notably in S.-B.'s huge volumes, and, for the Sermon on the Mount, in Fiebig's and in G. Kittel's useful little pamphlets. Parallels are rather dangerous things. They can be used critically and uncritically. In the case of the Gospels and the Rabbinic literature both Jews and Christians often use them (as I think) uncritically. I have spoken more at length about this matter elsewhere. In addition to what is said in the next section, the following consideration is, I think, of much importance. What we are concerned to know is this : what is really character- istic of the Rabbinic religion and what is not ? To know this needs, doubtless, familiarity with the subject, but it needs also impartiality and a certain tact or *flair*. A saying may be fished up from the sea of the Talmud which may be a close parallel to a saying in the Gospels. Now the date of the Talmudic saying is, to my mind, of very secondary importance. It is pretty sure to be much later than Jesus. But what really matters is this : Is the saying *characteristic* or not ? Or is it quite isolated and exceptional ? It may be char- acteristic, even if in the whole Rabbinic literature you cannot find another exact parallel to it. Or it may not. In the first case it is a good parallel to the Gospel saying ; in the second case, it is not. One thing is, to my mind, sure : Rabbinic religion and Rabbinic morality developed in their own way : they were wholly unaffected by the teaching of Jesus. Any excellence they have is their own ; it is borrowed neither consciously nor unconsciously. The origin- ality of any given teaching or saying of Jesus, on the other hand (apart from the originality of his teaching as a whole), cannot be tested off-hand by the production of, or even the failure to produce, an exact Rabbinic parallel. And this again has nothing to do with dates. It is quite another originality, a higher originality, than the originality of time that I am thinking of. For instance, Jesus says in Luke xv. 7, " There will be more rejoicing in heaven over one repentant sinner than over ninety-nine righteous persons who have no need of repentance.' Now, it does not matter two pins whether you can produce an exact verbal parallel to this saying or not. And if you do produce it, its date is of no significance either. Those who have the *flair* I speak of even to a slight degree will immediately say : There is nothing original in this saying of Jesus at all. It is essentially Rabbinic. No Pharisaic or Rabbinic audience or Scribe would have turned a hair at it. Paradoxes of that kind about the sovereign glory of Repentance were quite familiar to them. Some Rabbis might, perhaps, have thought and smiled, ' That is rather stiff,' but hardly more. On the other hand, Jesus is reported to have said (Mark vii. 15) : ' There is nothing outside a man which, entering into him, can make him unclean ; but it is the things which come out of a man that make him unclean.' Now you might conceivably find a parallel to this utterance in the vast Rabbinic literature, and it *might* even be a real parallel : I mean, it is conceivable that some one Rabbi did once make an audacious remark of this kind, and that it was remembered and recorded. That would be doubtless interesting, and we should all now like, as it were, to take off our hats to this Rabbi, and thank him. And the parallel would be a true parallel. But yet, in the higher, historic sense, it would be no parallel at all ; or, at any rate, a parallel without value or significance. For the saying of Jesus, even though there *were* a perfect Rabbinic parallel to it, is both original and characteristic : the Rabbinic parallel would be entirely uncharacteristic of Rabbinic teaching, and would be, therefore, no true parallel at all. Now Luke xv. 7 and Mark vii. 15 are extreme instances and very easy instances. In many cases decisions may be far more difficult. But the real test is in every instance the same. Presence or absence of verbal parallels is of minor or no importance. The only truly dominant and pertinent question is : characteristic or uncharacteristic ? Characteristic or uncharacteristic of the Rabbinic religion at its purest, fullest, and best, characteristic of it at A.D. 300, 400, 500, quite as much as, or even more than, characteristic of it in 1 or 30 or 100. And to answer this question you may have read the whole Rabbinic literature four times through, and yet make false answers. For though you need (1) knowledge and lots of it, you need also, and still more, (2) complete indifference as to whether, in any single case, the answer is Yes or No, and (3) the *flair*. Almost all of us, whether we be Jews or Christians, would sometimes fail in one or other of these three tests : *e.g.*, I should fail in (1) for certain ; sometimes also in (3), and, perhaps also, unconsciously to myself, now and again in (2).

§ 45. *The Gospels, the Rabbinical literature, and Judaism.*

If it be said that the Jew is not confined to the Old Testament, but that he has also the Rabbinical literature, and that therefore he need not study the New Testament, there are several rejoinders. First, there are things of value in the New Testament which are not to be found in the Rabbinical literature. Secondly, whereas in the Rabbinical literature the great things are scattered around and among a huge mass of third and fourth rate material, in the New Testament they are found knit together in a small compass, emphasized, concentrated, and condensed. Thirdly, the great things in the Rabbinical literature are often the casual utterances of a hundred different authors, whereas, in the New Testament,

they to a great extent form an essential part of the teaching of one
or two great minds, and they are strikingly and splendidly expressed.
Fourthly, the Rabbinical literature is unwieldy, huge, and suited
for the specialist only ; whereas the New Testament is small and
short, instinct with genius, first-class literature, and, as regards the
Gospels, quite suited for modern readers. Being first-class, it bears
translation. Being the work of genius, it is a book not for one age,
but practically, like Shakespeare or Homer, for all time. Fifthly,
the average Jew is not acquainted with the Rabbinical literature,
even if it could supply the place, which it cannot, of the New
Testament and the Gospels. Except the Liturgy, which, as it
includes the Sayings of the Fathers, is, I admit, a very important
exception, he knows the Old Testament only. Sixthly (and this
is perhaps the most important point of all), the religious value of the
teaching of the Synoptic Gospels for the modern Jew is not to be
measured by the presence or absence of parallels to the various
sayings of Jesus in the later Rabbinical literature. I do not
merely refer to the fact that almost all the parallels are later in
date. I am not thinking of the question, Upon which side is
the originality ? When Talmud and Gospels are compared, the
originality is almost always on the side of the Gospels. But this is
not my present point, which is the following. Jewish apologists
have a habit of breaking up the Gospels into fragments. They
are somewhat inclined to do the same with their own literature.
But a great book is more than its own sentences taken singly or
disjointedly. A great personality is more than the record of its
teaching, and the teaching is more than the bits of it taken one by
one. It must be viewed as a whole. It must be judged as a whole—
so far, at least, as this is possible. It has a spirit, an aroma, which
evaporates when its elements or fragments are looked at separately.
This piecemeal way of looking at a book, a teaching, a person, is,
perhaps, one of the evil results of Jewish legalism. Virtue, as Plato
would say, is cut up into pieces and made into mincemeat. It
suffers in this process. Virtue is more than a parcel of virtues ;
character is more than its elements. A man is more than the sum
of this and that and the other. Righteousness is more and other
than a number of excellent positive commands and excellent negative
ones.

There is a certain spirit and glow about the teaching of Jesus
which you either appreciate or fail to appreciate. You cannot
recognize or do justice to it by saying, ' The teaching of Jesus
comprises the following maxims and injunctions. Of these some
are borrowed from the Old Testament, some are paralleled by the
Talmud, and a few are impracticable.' The teaching of Jesus,
which has had such gigantic effects upon the world, is more and

other than a dissected list of injunctions. It is not merely the sum of its parts ; it is a whole, a spirit.

That spirit has the characteristics of genius. It is great, stimulating, heroic. One may not always agree with it, it may not always be ' practical,' but it is always, or nearly always, big and grand. Even if you could find separate close parallels for 970 out of, say, the 1000 verses in the Gospel in which Jesus is the speaker, and even if you put them together and made a nice little book of them, you would not have produced a substitute of equal religious value. The unity, the aroma, the spirit, the genius, would all have fled. Or, rather, you could not infuse *them* into your elegant collection of fragments and tit-bits. *Morceaux choisis* remain just *morceaux choisis*.

This is by no means to say that a good compendium of Rabbinic ethics and religion would not be very valuable and helpful for our religious life. We should be the better for it. We need both the Rabbinic compendium *and* the Gospels. For the life of every day we need both. The great, heroic teaching, and the detailed and more average teaching. We want them both. The teaching which demands the most complete self-sacrifice, which is inspired by the most thoroughgoing idealism, and the teaching which is not so far removed from, and addresses itself more directly to, the average righteousness and the average wickedness of ordinary and everyday life. As the right condition of the elementary school depends ultimately upon the University, so average, ordinary, humdrum life needs—to keep it as stretched as may be—the idealisms of ethics and religion which are so much above its level. In hours of comfort and peace these idealisms are needed all the more. Persecution and misery supply to a great extent their own idealisms ; they transfigure the ordinary into the heroic. The religious and ethical teaching of Rabbinic literature is above the level of Proverbs and Ecclesiasticus (and these too have their place and value), but it deals perhaps somewhat too often in rather small coin. I am speaking of the general mass, and of the spirit of the whole. A few individual sentences which will be quoted against me cannot suffice to prove the contrary. Just ordinary people need, in addition to the admirable sayings and exhortations of the Rabbis, the ideal and heroic spirit which inspires the teaching of the Synoptic Gospels. ' A man's reach must exceed his grasp '—just upon earth must it do so, even for the non-angelic beings that we are. We know that ' little deeds of kindness and charity, well within our power,' make the wheels of life run more smoothly. But the little deeds are not enough. We must not be satisfied with them. Or, rather, to keep them sweet and clean, to multiply them and preserve them, one needs the great deeds too. Or, at least, the desire for them, the appreciation of them. We require the heroic teaching and the example of heroes to stimulate and call out our own poor powers to the full. We require them to make us conscious of our own failures, to destroy conceit and self-righteousness, to purge us of anything like moral Philistinism or religious snobbery. Religious and ethical teaching must produce not merely right and excellent actions, but also (and above all) noble characters. I will not emphasize the distinction between the commands, ' Do this ' and ' Be this,' or urge that, upon the whole, the Rabbinic teaching tends to the former type, and the Gospel teaching to the latter. Something too much, perhaps, has been made of the difference, though a philosopher so removed from the orthodox Christian standpoint as Leslie Stephen seems to press it. But it is, at any rate, not *wholly* unimportant and unreal, and its application to Talmudic and Gospel teaching not *wholly* inaccurate. It is in a country like England, where the Jews have full rights and complete liberty, that the large demands and the heroic stature of the Synoptic teaching would be of advantage for the production of noble and ideal personalities, for the production of people who grandly are, as well as of those who only rightly do.

It may be said that there is much in the Gospels and in the other books of the New Testament to which the Jew will always take exception, and which he will always regard as false and erroneous. This is so, and therefore at this time of day it is impossible for the Jew to make his Bible include the New Testament. To what I said about this matter in Vol. II. of my *Bible for Home Reading*, pp. 779 and 780, I myself still adhere. But the Liberal Jew at any rate will not be deterred from gaining all the good he can from the Gospels (or from the rest of the New Testament) because there are many things in it which he holds to be erroneous. The Pentateuch also contains things which he holds to be erroneous, it also contains a lower and a higher. So too the Prophets. But he does not therefore reject them. He regards them historically, and gratefully accepts and ardently treasures whatever there is in them which is true and good and great. He perceives that each section of the Old Testament has in it something special, invaluable, unique. He would not dispense with the Law because he has the Prophets, or with the Wisdom literature because he has the Prophets and the Law. Even within the Prophets themselves, he would not dispense with Jeremiah because he has Isaiah, or with the ' minor ' prophets because he has Isaiah, Jeremiah, and Ezekiel. In the same way, he will, I believe, be glad to study and absorb (even though they are not a portion of his ' Bible ') the Gospels and the other books of the New Testament. They too are *sui generis* ; they too can add something of value and power, something fresh and distinguished, to his total religious store.

These remarks are general and tentative. They make no attempt to estimate the teaching of Jesus as a whole, or its right place in modern Judaism, or its measure of novelty and truth. And if they do not attempt this, the commentary will not do so either. It will give a few suggestions and incidental appreciations ; nothing more. The same limitation holds for the question as to the attitude which Judaism is to take up towards the Gospel hero himself. For the teaching of Jesus is not put forward in the Gospels as a philosopher puts forward his teaching impersonally in a book. It is bound up with a certain life and character. This question has also been alluded to in previous sections of this Introduction, and a few hints have been given as to the sort of solution in which the present writer is himself inclined to believe. Let me add this one further remark. Whether the life and character of Jesus, as they can be inferred from the Synoptic Gospels, or as they are presented to us in those writings, are completely historic or no is undoubtedly a question of the gravest moment. But it does not follow that this life and character are of no value, because we can never determine their precise proportions of truth and error. We can derive some help from the life of Moses as presented to us in the Pentateuch, even though we are aware that that life as thus presented is by no means historic. Such a use of such an ' ideal ' biography is not to be deprecated. A similar use has been and can be made of the life of Jesus as presented to us in the Synoptic Gospels. That life, too, is partly ' ideal,' but it may be a great and inspiring ideal none the less. In such a light it may be possible for the Liberal Jew, at any rate, to regard it, and it may become for him a great and valuable religious asset. Especially for those who feel that Liberal Judaism is largely prophetic Judaism, will the prophet of Nazareth—as his contemporaries with true instinct entitled him—be cherished and admired. Perhaps in the future Christianity and Judaism will be able to shake hands over the Sermon on the Mount and the fundamental elements in the moral and religious doctrine of Jesus. They will perhaps allow the vexed question of originality to slumber. A great Christian scholar has said (Paul Wernle, *The Sources of our Knowledge of the Life of Jesus*, E. T., pp. 162, 163), ' What is crucial ' in the words of Jesus is ' trust in God, purity of heart, compassion, humility, forgiveness, aspiration —this and nothing else. This is the will of God, as epitomized in the Sermon on the Mount ; he who does it is Jesus' mother and sister and brother.' Assuredly, if this be so, there have been very many Jewish mothers and sisters and brothers of Jesus all these long years from Jesus until now. For Jewish teachers have never ceased to say that these things were the essential will of God, and many Jews and Jewesses have never ceased to practise them. And lastly, may I venture to hint at one reason why it is that, in the words of this great scholar, ' what the Master desired first and before all things shines forth upon us out of the Gospel to-day ' so brightly and wonderfully, and why it seems to be so much more a discovery to him than to his Jewish reader ? Is it not because, to quote his own words again, he and those who feel with him ' have been satiated with Christology even to nausea,' and therefore doubtless ' long for God ' ? The Jew, on the other hand, has always rejected all Christology, and has ever found his way, direct and without a mediator, to the Divine Father.

[Both in the Introduction and in the Notes I have, perhaps, not adequately distinguished between the ' Days of the Messiah ' (or the Messianic Age) and ' the world to come.' The Rabbis, according to their more systematic reckoning, divided the Future, for which they prayed, and in the advent of which they believed, into two portions of very unequal length. (1) First would come the appearance of the Messiah (with whatever happenings his manifestation might be preceded and accompanied) and his long rule and reign. (2) This reign would not, however, be eternal, nor would the Messiah live for ever. At its close, and after the death of the Messiah, there would take place the Resurrection of the Dead, the Last Judgment, and the Age of everlasting felicity for the righteous (with either annihilation or temporary or everlasting punishment for the wicked). This Age it is which is the true ' World to Come,' and not the days of the Messiah. (What part the Messiah, who, I suppose, would be resurrected with the rest, would play in the World to Come does not seem very clear. Apparently his office and duties extended only to his own special era). But in common speech, and in ordinary teaching, the two divisions of the Future tended to become confused with one another. The expressions, ' the world to come,' or ' the time to come,' were often inexactly and loosely used to designate the days of the Messiah. Both ' the days of the Messiah ' and ' the world to come,' in the stricter sense, were in the future ; both were eras of happiness, in marked contrast with the present. One can easily see how the two periods could be somewhat confused together, and loosely referred to by one single term. Moreover, there was a further confusion, inasmuch as the World to Come was often thought of, not as something far distant, which the righteous would not attain till the resurrection, but as something which would befall them immediately after death. (Even as we to-day speak of the Future Life as a blissful condition, for which we have not to wait after our death, but which we begin directly we have died.) The expression 'Kingdom of Heaven' could apparently be used to signify both the Days of the Messiah and the World to Come (in the stricter sense of the words).

In the Synoptic Gospels, Jesus does not seem to distinguish between the Days of the Messiah and the World to Come. He seems to run the two together. He does not seem to imply that the new Age, which was about to dawn, would be separated in time from the Judgment and the Resurrection of the Dead by a long interval. There would not be, first, a long Messianic era, and then the Resurrection and the Judgment. But the new Age would mean the Resurrection and the Judgment straightway, and those who were yet alive when the new Age appeared would not need to die. The Kingdom of God means with him, not the temporary Messianic Age, but the everlasting World to Come. Whether this view of the future is due to his rejection of the ordinary 'Messiah' conception and doctrine, and his acceptance of the Son of man conception and doctrine (as v. Gall, for example, would hold), is another question. Moreover, in addition to his doctrine of the future Kingdom and of the Resurrection and the Judgment, Jesus also taught occasionally that the righteous, at their death, pass immediately into Paradise (that is, they attain the world to come straightway). The same confusion which is met with in the Rabbinical literature is also met with in the Gospels.]

MARK

CHAPTER I

1–8. JOHN THE BAPTIST

(*Cp.* Matt. iii. 1–6, 11, 12 ; Luke iii. 1–6, 15–18)

1 The beginning of the gospel concerning Jesus Christ, the Son of
2 God. As it is written in Isaiah the prophet, ' Behold, I send my
3 messenger before thee, who shall prepare the way for thee. The
   voice of one crying in the wilderness, Prepare ye the way of the
4 Lord, make his paths straight.' So John the Baptist appeared in
   the wilderness, proclaiming the baptism of repentance for the
5 forgiveness of sins. And there went out unto him all the land of
   Judaea, and all the inhabitants of Jerusalem, and they were bap-
6 tized by him in the river of Jordan, confessing their sins. And John's
   clothing was of camel's hair, and he had a leathern girdle about his
7 loins ; and he ate locusts and wild honey. And he proclaimed,
   saying, ' After me comes one who is mightier than I, the latchet
8 of whose shoes I am not worthy to stoop down and unloose. I have
   baptized you with water : but he will baptize you with the Holy
   Spirit.'

The object of these notes is by no means to make another commentary superfluous even for a Jewish reader. There are many
points and difficulties in the Gospels about which my notes will
give no explanation, or very little, or which I shall discuss inadequately—and this partly from lack of space, largely from lack of
learning, and largely from deliberate intention.

My main purpose has been to concentrate attention upon those
passages in the Gospels which have religious value or interest for
Jewish readers at the present time. Passages which do not possess

this interest or value I have dealt with very cursorily. It is not
implied that such passages do not possess other kinds of interest,
historical or theological, even for Jewish readers. They may also
be of great importance for the full comprehension of the Gospels as
a whole. They may possess great religious interest for the student
of religion, to whatever creed he belongs, and great religious value
to the Christian believer. All I mean is that they have comparatively little interest or value to Jewish readers from a purely religious
point of view.

Among the inadequately discussed passages are some which have
special relation to Christian dogma and belief concerning the person
and Messianic consciousness of Jesus. Moreover, so far as these are
touched upon at all, they are treated from a purely historical point
of view. No attempt is made to discuss how far Jesus was right or
wrong in any claim he may have made, or in any consciousness that
he may have had, that he stood nearer to God than any other member
of the human race. My point of view is frankly that of a Jew, that is
of some one who stands outside every form and phase of Christianity.
I try to write about Jesus as an impartial but sympathetic, critical
but appreciative, Christian believer might write about Mahommed
or Buddha. That Jesus did not literally fulfil the Old Testament
conditions and characteristics of the ' Messiah ' is obvious. Whether
he fulfilled them in some higher and spiritual sense I have not
discussed. Jesus is not ' our Lord ' to the Jewish reader, and can
never become so. Our interest in him, from the purely religious
point of view, is limited to his contributions to religious teaching.
That the love of him and the service of him have been, and are,
noble life-motives for Christians of all sorts and shades, no one can
deny ; such love and service can with Jews be felt and rendered
only to God. Thus, whether Jesus claimed to be the Messiah, and
in what sense and at what stage of his life ; whether he thought
himself nearer to God than all other men ; whether, and in what
sense, he believed himself to be the Son of God—all these to
Jewish readers are questions of a purely historical interest. We
shall not admire his moral and religious teaching either more or
less because he believed himself, or did not believe himself, to
be the Messiah ; we shall not admire his character more if he
thought himself the ' Son of God ' in a special sense ; we shall
assuredly not admire it less if he did not. Again, as these very
questions have for Jews an historic interest only, and not a
religious interest, they can and ought to be, dealt with briefly and
inadequately in these notes. It may be tempting to discuss them,
but the temptation must be resisted.

Mark has a very brief introduction before coming to close grips

with his subject—the life and the death of the Messiah.   A few
necessary lines about John the Baptist lead on to the baptism of
Jesus, and then to the beginnings of his ministry.   Mark, perhaps,
knew no details of his ancestry, or of his childhood or birth.   He
passes over the baptism, the return to Galilee and the first preaching there, with a few short and rapid strokes, so that one can regard
the introduction as extending to 15 with as much justification
as confining it to 1–8.   Mark starts the details of his story with the
coming of the new Preacher to the Lake of Galilee and to Capernaum.
Of what happened before that he seems to know no more than the
barest outline as regards the baptism (9–11), the temptation (12–13),
and the earliest preaching in Galilee (14–15).   It has been argued
that Peter's recollections, of which, as some believe, Mark made
use, could naturally go no further back than the incidents which
come before us in 16–20 and after.

1.   Following Wellhausen's rendering, I have put a full stop at
the end of the verse after the words ' Son of God,' and translated
' Beginning of the Gospel about Jesus Christ, the Son of God.'   The
words are the title for the whole book.   So too Moffatt (pp. 229–231).
They mean :   The beginning of the story of Jesus Christ (cp. Streeter,
p. 498).   Harnack, however, combats this view.   He thinks that
the Gospel means throughout that which Jesus proclaimed about
the nearness of the Kingdom.   ' Beginning of the Gospel of Jesus
Christ' means, according to Harnack, 'Here begins the glad tidings
proclaimed by Jesus Christ of the nearness of the Kingdom.'
(Harnack, *The Constitution and Law of the Church in the First Two
Centuries.*   E. T. 1910.   Appendix III., Gospel, p. 284.)   Menzies
says :   ' In the apostolic age the word " gospel " does not denote a
book, but a spoken proclamation.   Only in the second century did
the Lives of Christ begin to be called Gospels.   The original gospel
was a spoken proclamation of the great Christian facts, the Messiahship of Jesus and the fulfilment of the prophecies in Him ' (*The
Earliest Gospel,* p. 56).   The earthly life of Jesus was only the
beginning of this proclamation.   The more important part was that
which came after his death and was even still to come.   Professor
Turner, in his essay on Parenthetical Clauses in Mark, has a new
and very ingenious explanation of verse one.   He holds (following
some ancient Fathers) that there should be a bracket after θεοῦ
and before ἐγένετο.   We then get :   ' The beginning of the proclamation of good news about Jesus as Messiah and Son of God
was John the Baptizer's preaching in the wilderness of a baptism
of repentance for remission of sins ' (*J. T. S.,* Vol. XXVI., 1925, p.
146).   The same view is also taken by Rawlinson.   He thinks that
the quotation from Malachi has been inserted into the text by

'a very early copyist, who was more interested in fulfilments of
Scriptural prophecy than the Evangelist himself was, and who
derived it from Matt. xi. 10.' Rawlinson (p. 251) also strongly
combats Harnack's interpretation of the 'Gospel' or Good Tidings.
Klostermann thinks that verse 1 is an introductory sentence
without a verb, like xiii. 8, and means: 'The Sacred Tidings
(*Heilsbotschaft*) about Jesus Christ, the Son of God, begin with what
is in accordance with that which is written in Isaiah, namely, with
John the Baptist proclaiming in the wilderness,' etc. And this
interpretation is, after all, perhaps the safest.

The origin of the technical meaning of the word 'evangelion'
(εὐαγγέλιον), 'good tidings' or 'gospel,' is apparently to be found
partly in the use of the verb (εὐαγγελίζω) in the Greek version of
the later chapters of Isaiah, partly in the already current Greek
use of the noun to signify 'good tidings.' The noun, εὐαγγέλιον,
occurs in the Greek translation of the Old Testament (Septuagint)
two or three times, and also another form, εὐαγγελία. The verb
εὐαγγελίζειν occurs some twenty times. The passages in Isaiah
xl. 9, lii. 7, lx. 6, lxi. 1, are worth looking up. So, too, Psalms xl. 9,
lxviii. 11, and xcvi. 2. The word has also been found in inscriptions
in connection with the worship of the Emperors. It occurs in a
famous inscription found at Priene in a passage about the birthday
of the divine Augustus (the date is about 9 B.C.). '[The birthday]
of the god was for the world the beginning of good tidings on account
of him' (see Deissmann, *Licht vom Osten*, 4th edition, p. 313, who
has adopted a somewhat different translation). It seems almost a
pity that we have not adopted an identical rendering in English
(*i.e.* 'evangel' instead of 'gospel'), like the German 'das
Evangelium.'

The oldest use of the word in Christian literature is reflected in
Mark. In this, its special Christian sense, the word, W. thinks,
could not have been used by Jesus. For, in Mark, Jesus himself is,
almost always, the content of the gospel. He is the good tidings.
He is the gospel. In this sense too is the word employed by Paul.
Mark's whole book is to be the story of the ministry and death and
resurrection of Jesus the Messiah. Hence his book is the gospel of
Jesus. Jesus in Mark is made to follow and adopt this usage. Out
of seven times in which the word is used, five occur in speeches of
Jesus. (The other two places are i. 1 and i. 14.) He speaks of *the*
gospel, meaning not what he has to say and teach about religion,
morality and the Kingdom, but practically himself. 'For my sake
and for the gospel's' are close synonyms. 'For the sake of the
gospel' means for the sake of making known the tidings about
Jesus. 'The gospel is to be preached unto all the nations' means
that Jesus Christ and his life and death are to be preached. The

one exception to this usage in Mark seems to be i. 14, 15, where, however, in truth the meaning is still the same, however inappropriately put into the mouth of Jesus. Jesus could only have said ' Repent, for the Kingdom is near '; the words ' Believe in the gospel ' would have had no meaning to his contemporaries at the outset of his ministry. Jesus is thus made to use the word in a proleptic or anticipatory sense. (Cp. Klostermann, ed. 2, pp. 4 and 5.)

In Matthew, and in Luke (who only employs the verb and not the noun, whereas Mark and Matthew employ only the noun and not the verb, except Matt. xi. 5), the usage is somewhat different. To them the gospel includes the contents of Jesus's teaching. The gospel of the Kingdom means the tidings and teaching about the Kingdom. Jesus proclaims that with him the Kingdom has appeared upon earth, and this proclamation is the gospel. But this use of the word is not earlier than its use in Mark, but later, just as the Kingdom as present is later than the Kingdom as future. Streeter urges that ' the world-wide circulation of Mark affords an easy and natural explanation of what, from the purely linguistic point of view, is the rather curious usage by which the word " Gospel " became the technical name for a biography of Christ. The Greek word *evangelion* means simply " good news," and in the New Testament it is always used in its original sense of the good news of the Christian message. Commentators have tried elaborately to trace a gradual evolution in the meaning of the word until it acquired this new usage. No such gradual evolution is necessary, or even probable. Among the Jews it was a regular practice to refer to books, or sections of books, by a striking word which occurred in the opening sentence. That is how Genesis and Exodus derived the titles by which they are known in the Hebrew Bible, *i.e.* " In the Beginning " and " (these are the) Names." As soon as portions of Mark were read in the services of the Church—and that would be at once—it would be necessary to have a name to distinguish this reading from that of an Old Testament book. Mark opens with the words ἀρχὴ τοῦ εὐαγγελίου, " The beginning of the Gospel." ἀρχή would be too like the Hebrew name for Genesis, so εὐαγγέλιον (nom.) would be an obvious title. When, fifteen or twenty years later, other Lives of Christ came into existence, this use of " Gospel " as a title would be an old-fashioned custom and would be applied to them also. Then it would become necessary to distinguish these " Gospels " from one another—hence the usage τὸ εὐαγγέλιον κατὰ Μάρκον, κατὰ Λουκᾶν, the Gospel, *according to* Mark, to Luke, etc.' (p. 497).

It is disputed whether the oldest reading had ' Son of God ' after the words ' Jesus Christ.' If it had, the phrase must be

understood either in the same sense as in iii. 11, or in the sense of
a heavenly being, of divine nature, though distinct from, and
subordinate to, God. The deification of Jesus began early, and it
was helped forward by the fact that to a certain school of Jewish
thought in the first century the Messiah was a pre-existent heavenly
being, and not a 'mere man.' It is worth while to read the careful
and up-to-date summary of the discussions about the origin of the
term 'Son of God' as applied to Jesus in Clemen, *Religionsgeschichtliche Erklärung des neuen Testaments*, 2nd ed., 1924, pp.
76–81. Clemen's conclusion is that the term 'Son of God' was not
uncommon in Syria, and was first applied to Jesus in that district.
Cp. Bousset, *Kurios Christos*, 2nd ed., pp. 151, 152.

'Jesus Christ.' The wording was originally 'Jesus the Christ';
'Jesus the Anointed'; 'Jesus the Messiah.' But here 'Christ'
has already become a proper name, a surname for Jesus; therefore
it has lost the article. This is a rare use. In Mark it is only found
again in ix. 41. For the Rabbinic use of the word 'Christ' or
'Messiah,' as a personal name, see Abrahams, *Studies*, 1. chapter
xviii.

2, 3. Some regard the quotations as an early interpolation.
Moffatt (p. 230) thinks that καθώς as introducing a quotation is very
unusual and abnormal here, and he regards the quotations as due
to an editorial hand, inserted from some book of testimonia or
florilegia (p. 24). Goguel, on the contrary, believes that Mark
(and no editor) wrote what we now have, except that the
Malachi quotation is 'a later, though hardly happy, interpolation,
based on Matt. xi. 10' (p. 257, n. 1). Elsewhere Mark, as editor,
never quotes the Old Testament. There are other difficulties.
The quotations are made up of Malachi iii. 1 and Isaiah xl. 3. Was
the Malachi passage erroneously supposed to come from Isaiah?
Or is the Isaiah quotation original to the writer of verse 1, and was
the Malachi passage prefixed later? The latter is more probable.
The Malachi quotation follows the Hebrew rather than the
Septuagint, which is another reason why it may be regarded as not
having been inserted at the same time as the Isaiah quotation,
which follows the Septuagint. But the Malachi quotation makes an
important change from the Hebrew to render it suitable for the
context. The Hebrew has: 'Behold I send my messenger, and he
shall prepare a way before *me*.' Whereas Mark has: 'My messenger
before *thy* face, who shall prepare *thy* way,' that is, before the face
of Jesus. The way which John prepared may be taken to mean
his preaching of repentance. There is also a notable change in
the quotation from Isaiah (which otherwise follows the Septuagint,
and erroneously adds 'in the wilderness' to 'a voice that cries,'

instead of to ' prepare ye ' : see Revised Version). Septuagint and Hebrew read alike : ' Make straight in the desert a highway for our God.' But in lieu of ' a highway for our God ' Mark puts ' his paths.' The object of this seemingly small change was to make ' the Lord ' of the first clause a synonym, not for God, but for the Messiah—a complete violation of the original. Evangelists and Rabbis were both frequently guilty of forced and strained interpolations of the text. Here we have a misrendering or alteration for religious purposes. It may, however, not be deliberate. It may be unconscious ; under the influence of preconceived ideas, writers sometimes misquoted from memory to suit their own views.

4. Without the quotations the order would be clearer. ' Beginning of the Gospel. John was in the desert, preaching,' etc. The wording is notable : ' A baptism of repentance for the forgiveness of sins.'

We need not assume that the baptism is regarded as a sort of magical or sacramental prophylactic or safeguard. Those who did not repent could not be saved at the Judgment, whether they had been baptized or not.

The baptism is to be the outward sign of an inward repentance, and this repentance is to lead to the forgiveness of sins. It was in view of the coming Kingdom that the remission of sins was urgent. The confession is to be understood as a free, public confession and of a general character.

The great method to obtain forgiveness, according to Rabbinic doctrine, was through repentance. For the Rabbinic doctrine of repentance, see my article on ' Rabbinic Conceptions of Repentance,' *J. Q. R.*, Vol. xvi., January 1904.

For the Jewish reference to John and for the Rabbinic practice and theory of baptism, see Abrahams, *Studies*, i., chapters iii. and iv.

The best translation seems to be : ' John the Baptizer appeared in the wilderness and preached,' etc.

The wilderness is the low country by the Jordan, called the Araba (desert or steppe) in the Old Testament. See 2 Sam. ii. 29, etc.

5. The concourse of people must be exaggerated.

The immersion was the worshipper's own act. ' Baptized by John ' would mean ' under his influence and by his instigation and sanction.'

6. His dress is reminiscent of 2 Kings i. 8 and Zech. xiii. 4. His food indicates the ascetic.

7. John proclaims himself to be the forerunner of one mightier than he. It is notable that Mark, unlike Matthew and Luke, does not represent John as proclaiming that this mightier one will also hold the Final Judgment. Yet Mark must mean that John is the forerunner of the Messiah. John proclaims the advent of the Messiah, without knowing who he is. If he did announce the Messiah's near advent, he did not refer to Jesus in particular. To the Evangelists, however, Jesus *is* the Messiah, and thus John, as the forerunner of Jesus, is the forerunner of the Messiah. Indeed, the urgency of the call to repentance by John must be (as in the case of Jesus in verse 15) because the time is soon at hand when repentance will be impossible. For repentance belongs to, and is only possible within, the old era. The new era will show the results of repentance or the results of obstinate sin.

' Mightier than I.' In what respect ? Either generally more potent, invested by God with greater authority (shown in his healings, teachings, miracles, etc.), or specifically in the higher mode of his baptism.

There is some reason to believe that John did not proclaim the coming of the Messiah. The story in Mark is coloured by later Christian reflection. In any case John did not recognize in Jesus the Messiah : Jesus was to him merely one among the many who sought baptism, and was not in any way distinguished from the rest by a supernatural revelation or by an unaccountable intuition.

8. The giving of the spirit is a substitution for the baptism by water, and excludes it. But afterwards the Christians adopted a baptism by water for their proselytes just like the Jews. Baptizing with the spirit is a metaphorical baptism, the reception of a precious and divine gift. The meaning would be cognate to that of Isaiah xliv. 3, Joel ii. 28. In the Messianic age—in the Kingdom—the Spirit of God was to be poured out over all who were worthy or chosen to enjoy the beatitudes of the new era. The possession of the Spirit meant a higher enlightenment, a fuller knowledge of God, a more perfect accomplishment of His will. On the other hand, the extra source of Matthew and Luke (Q) spoke of a baptism with ' Holy Spirit and fire ' (Matt. iii. 12, Luke iii. 16). But some think that ' Holy Spirit ' has been inserted from Mark, and that what Q had was only ' with fire.' This would mean a baptism in an evil or ironic sense—a baptism of punishment. It would refer to the consuming fire of the Final Judgment. *Cp.* Amos vii. 4, Mal. iii. 2. And it may be urged that this is the more original version, and that it is more in character with what John is likely to have said. Mark made a ' Christian ' change, substituting ' spirit ' for ' fire ' ; Matthew and Luke combined his reading with the reading

of the source. And originally, doubtless, what John said was more different still. For he who gives the fire baptism to sinners is not the Messiah, but God. For the entire relations of John and Jesus with each other the student should read Dibelius, *Die urchristliche Überlieferung von Johannes dem Taufer* (1911). *Cp.* also *Beginnings of Christianity*, pp. 101–109, Burkitt, *Christian Beginnings*, pp. 13–22 (1924), and especially Meyer, Vol. I. (pp. 82–94). The most probable view is, I think, that John never knew or heard anything about Jesus, but that Jesus knew about, was even perhaps baptized by, John. 'John most likely knew nothing of Jesus ; if he *did* baptize him, he was only one of the many who thronged to be baptized' (Meyer, p. 84). For various reasons it was almost inevitable that the two teachers should be brought into close and closer contact with each other, and that John should be made to recognize his own inferiority to Jesus, and to state openly that he was a mere 'forerunner.' We can trace various stages in this process within the Gospels themselves.

The difference of view as to the origin of Mark is illustrated rather strikingly by Goguel's and Moffatt's judgments about Mark i. 1–8. The French scholar sees in this section a sure proof that Mark used Q in one or other of its forms. For it is acknowledged that Matthew's and Luke's account of John the Baptist depend on Q. Now Matthew and Luke put the quotation from Isaiah after the introduction of John himself ; this is much more natural than Mark, who places the quotation at the head of his narrative in order to start with a passage from Scripture. Again, the Messiah of whom Matthew and Luke make John speak is 'an apocalyptic Messiah,' and the baptism is an apocalyptic baptism or judgment. In Mark, the Messiah is the historic Jesus who brings a Christian baptism. Therefore Matthew and Luke's version is taken from an older source than Mark, and Mark knew and used and christianized that version. Moffatt, on the other hand, thinks that Mark did not use Q, any more than Q used Mark. 'Throughout the whole section one has the impression of a writer who is outlining rapidly a familiar story in order to reach the point at which either his characteristic contribution or more probably the source before him first begins. There is no reason why the facts of i. 1–13 (15) should have been only accessible in Q or in any other document. In that primitive Christian world even Q had no monopoly of such traditions ; and although Q were prior to Mark, there would not be the slightest necessity to postulate any documentary source from which the latter must have drawn the contents or even the form of the summary in i. 1–13' (p. 221). With the words in i. 13, compare 'Testament of Naphtali : ὁ διάβολος φεύξεται ἀφ' ὑμῶν, καὶ τὰ θηρία φοβηθήσονται ὑμᾶς, καὶ οἱ ἄγγελοι ἀνθέξονται ὑμᾶς.

The words of John about Jesus must be regarded as without any historic basis. Völter's attempt to detect historical elements in them by theories of interpolation can hardly be regarded as successful. See notes on Matthew. Meyer says not without good reason : ' Die Geschichtlichkeit der Taufe Jesu muss ich mindestens für problematisch halten : der Bericht darüber, der mit der Versuchung aufs engste zusammenhängt, gehört dem mythischen, nicht dem geschichtlichen Bestandteil des Evangeliums an ' (ii. p. 406, n. 3). See further Klostermann's excellent and informing note on 9–11 in his ed. 2.

9–11. THE BAPTISM OF JESUS

(Cp. Matt. iii. 13–17 ; Luke iii. 21, 22)

9   And it came to pass in those days, that Jesus came from Nazareth
10 in Galilee, and was baptized by John in the Jordan. And straightway as he came up out of the water, he saw how the heavens parted,
11 and the Spirit like a dove descended into him. And a voice from heaven said, ' Thou art my beloved Son ; in thee I am well pleased.'

A complete commentary upon the Gospels must devote pages to this tiny section, but I can be exceedingly brief.

The religious value of the Gospels for Jewish readers to-day has nothing to do with the story of the baptism. Nevertheless, that Jesus was baptized by John may be regarded as historic. It was, moreover, in all probability a turning-point in his life—the near antecedent of his taking up John's task and continuing John's message, though on other lines. We cannot tell whether Jesus thought he saw, and fancied he heard, strange sights and sounds on that occasion. No critical reader to-day can believe, I suppose, in the literal truth of 10 and 11. For him the question needs no discussion. Jesus, we may assume, comes, as Matthew says, with the express purpose of being baptized. He wants to hear and see the new prophet. What he has been told of him may fit in with the aspirations and presentiments of his own soul. It may be, and has been, asked : Was he conscious of special sins because he sought the baptism ? It is not necessary to believe this. Doubtless, if the story is historic, Jesus too felt the general need of repentance which John demanded.

10, 11. Professor Turner in a learned and interesting article in *J. T. S.* (January 1926, pp. 113–129) seeks to prove that ἀγαπητός must be rendered here, as in ix. 7 and xii. 6, not ' beloved ' but ' only,' *i.e.* ' Thou art my only son.' The deductions which he would draw from this very possibly correct translation are a very different matter !

What may be the historic, or rather the inward, psychological fact at the basis of the stories of the baptism and the temptation it is impossible to say.   Yet it is possible that the baptism did mark a decisive epoch in the views and feelings of Jesus as to his mission, and that it was succeeded by no less important internal developments in some lonely wanderings in the desert.   Klausner strongly urges the importance of the Baptism.   ' Jesus's baptism in the presence of John was the most decisive event in his life.'   Klausner even ventures on a little ' rationalizing' (in which, it must be admitted, he rarely indulges).   ' Dazzled by the blinding light of the Judæan sun, it seemed as though the heavens were opened and that the Shekinah shed its light upon him.'   ' Suddenly there flashed through Jesus's mind, like blinding lightning, the idea that *he* was the hoped-for Messiah.   This was the voice which he heard within him and for which he had been prepared by his thirty years of rich, cloistered, inner life at Nazareth.   His dream acquired its utmost realization at this great moment in his life, the solemn moment of his baptism ' (pp. 251, 252).

According to Mark, Jesus alone sees and hears.   The baptism is the equivalent of anointment.   The words uttered by the voice from heaven are a reminiscence of Isaiah xlii. 1, ' Behold my servant whom I uphold ; my chosen, in whom my soul delighteth,' and Psalm ii. 7, ' Thou art my son ; this day I have begotten thee.' Jesus, in his own consciousness, is now supposed by Mark to know himself to be the Messiah.   He enters the water as an ordinary individual ; he comes out of it as the Son of God, the Messiah. Thus, according to Mark, Jesus *became* the Son of God at his baptism. He is not the Son of God through his birth.   At the baptism he receives the Divine Spirit and becomes thereby a superhuman being, an instrument of the Spirit, as he shows by his miracles.   The immediate effect of the Spirit is that it drives him forth into the wilderness.   But ' Son of God ' did not to Mark mean that Jesus was, or would ever become, an integral part of Deity.   He was more than ' mere ' man, but he was also distinct from, and subordinate to, God, both in his earthly life and in the heavenly life which succeeded the earthly life.

Another view is that *to Mark* Jesus was the Son of God from his birth, as he was to Paul—and this quite independently of any virgin birth.   The oldest form of the heavenly voice was, perhaps, ' Thou art my Son, to-day I have begotten thee ' (*i.e.* Psalm ii. without Isaiah).   This is found in one important reading in the story of the baptism in Luke.   This form Mark avoided in order *not* to make the Sonship begin at the baptism.   What the baptism did was to make Jesus *realize* his Sonship.   He realizes that he is the heavenly commissioned and appointed Messiah, and his earthly work has now to begin.   *Cp.* the notes on Luke iii. 22.

It is perhaps important that the words of the voice are partly made up from Isaiah xlii. 1.   ' The servant of the Lord ' was identified with the Messiah.   And in Greek παῖς, the rendering of the Hebrew *ebed*, means both ' servant ' and ' child.'   If one could show that Jesus himself thought that he was the ' servant,' and that he fulfilled the servant's *rôle*, if one could show that he believed that the ' servant ' was the true Messiah rather than, or as well as, the king predicted in Isaiah xi. (and a far higher and better Messiah too), or that he accepted the one sort of Messiahship and rejected the other, many difficulties would be solved.   But it is extremely difficult, if not impossible, to show this.   In the Synoptic Gospels Jesus is hardly ever made to allude to the Servant passages in Isaiah, and he never makes any definite pronouncement that his idea of Messiahship is the Servant of Deutero-Isaiah.   Thus how far Jesus was influenced in his career and thought by the ' Servant ' passages of Isaiah xlii. and liii. it is impossible to say.   The references to the Servant passages belong to Matthew and Luke rather than to Mark. See Matt. viii. 17, xii. 17–21 ; Luke iv. 18, xxii. 37.   The idea of a suffering Messiah was not, so far as we can gather, suggested to Jesus by Isaiah liii.   Nevertheless, Dr. Carpenter (*First Three Gospels*, p. 92) pleads that ' the presence in the Gospels of the " Servant " aspect of the Messiah's work is palpable.   We may not always be able to accept as genuine the incidents or sayings through which it is expressed.   But when we try to trace it back to its source, shall we be wrong if we ascribe it, at least provisionally, to Jesus himself ? ' But this seems to be risky.   We do not even know whether he thought the king Messiah of Isaiah xi. a mistaken conception or not.   If the account of his entry into Jerusalem is historic, he can hardly have done so wholly.   Yet he never alludes to Isaiah xi., and though to him the Messiah was undoubtedly a king in a *certain* sense, he was probably more and other than the righteous ruler of that famous chapter.   It is impossible ever to know how Jesus interpreted the great Messianic utterances of the prophets.   He may likely enough have formed no consistent theory about them.   In the Targum (*i.e.* the Jewish Aramaic translation of the Old Testament), Isaiah xlii. 1 reads : ' Behold my Servant, the Messiah.'   And the Servant of Isaiah lii. 13–liii. is also specifically called the Messiah. Yet the very same writer who thought that the ' Servant ' was the Messiah probably also thought that the king of Isaiah xi. was also the Messiah !   In matters of religion the human consciousness is often unaware of the oddest inconsistencies.   The religious mind, guided mainly by feeling and desire, makes up its own conceptions and interpretations ; it takes and leaves and combines ; exegesis, consistency, historic interpretation, are remote and indifferent to it.

Let me, however, attempt to say a very few words as regards the vexed question of the Messianic consciousness of Jesus. And first as to the character of the problem, the sources for its solution, and the answers which have been given. The only material available with which to answer the question is contained in the three Synoptic Gospels. Yet here the evidence is so small, so fragmentary, so dubious, and even so contradictory, that learned scholars have disputed over it for generations, and dispute over it still. Some think that Jesus did not believe himself to be the Messiah ; others— most others—that he did. Of the second class, some think that he only very gradually came to the conviction that he was the Messiah ; others, that he believed himself to be so from the beginning of his ministry. But even if we neglect the view that Jesus did not believe himself to be the Messiah, the doubts and divergencies are by no means over. For supposing that he held himself to be the Messiah, what sort of Messiah did he think that he was ? What was his conception of the Messiah ? And did that conception change in the course of his ministry ? What was his conception of the Messianic office, of the work which the Messiah had to do ? What part had the Messiah to play at the end of the existing order and in ushering in the new order ?

Now the answers to these questions not only are dependent upon, and suffer from, all the uncertainties due to the fragmentary, dubious, and often legendary and miraculous character of the Synoptic material, but they also suffer from a further uncertainty, which to an uninformed Jewish reader of the present day is at first surprising.

The ordinary, uninformed Jew to-day thinks of the Messiah partly in terms of one or two salient passages of Isaiah, and partly in terms of late Jewish theology. To him the Messiah is essentially the figure described in Isaiah xi.—a righteous ruler, wholly human, who restores the Jews to their own land from their exile, and inaugurates a lasting reign upon earth of peace and goodness and the knowledge of God. The Messiah, in fact, ushers in the earthly Kingdom of God. Nothing is more inaccurate than the assertion that the Jewish conception of the Messiah is merely material, and merely political, and merely national. It is, doubtless, all three. It involves, precisely like the new era in the Gospels, a destruction of enemies, but its most essential feature is the coming of righteousness and peace. When the Messiah has done his work, men ' shall beat their swords into ploughshares and their spears into pruning-hooks ; nation shall not lift up sword against nation, neither shall they learn war any more.' When the Messiah has done his work, God ' will turn to the people a pure language, that they may call upon the name of the Lord, to serve him with one consent.' ' And the Lord shall be king over all the earth ; in that day shall the Lord be One, and his name One.' This is what the ordinary, uninformed Jewish reader thinks of the Messiah and of the Messiah's work and its result.

But it does not follow that what the ordinary Jewish reader thinks to-day is what was thought by all the contemporaries of Jesus 1900 years ago. And this is the further uncertainty alluded to just now. We do not exactly know what was the prevailing conception, or what were the various conceptions, of the Messiah and of his office in the days of Jesus.

We have some evidence which is earlier ; we have much evidence which is later. We have little which is contemporary. But we know from the apocalyptic literature that the old conception of the Messiah had been modified considerably. To begin with, the Messiah was not to all Jews of that age so purely human, so merely ' a man,' as he was to the author of Isaiah xi., as he is to the ordinary Jewish reader of to-day. He had become to some circles, to some thinkers, a more or less divine or supernatural being. He had, perhaps, been combined with other conceptions, as, for instance, it may be, with the archetypal Man, who was not mere man, but ' superman,' pre-existent and heavenly. This was one change, and that a great one.

Another was that, to some thinkers, the Messiah was not the warrior who fights against Israel's foes, and then inaugurates an earthly era of righteousness and peace. The doctrine of the resurrection of the dead had profoundly modified and enlarged the conception of the whole Messianic age. Doubtless Israel was still to be freed from its oppressors ; it was to live in its own land, happy, triumphant, prosperous, and peaceful. But the whole *dénouement* and transformation, culminating in the Resurrection of the Dead and the Last Judgment, was to be brought about by the more direct and sudden interposition and intervention of God. The successful and righteous warrior, the virtuous and prosperous ruler, made way, among some groups and persons, for a more mysterious, semi-divine, semi-human Figure, who should preside over the rapidly changing scenes of a vaster and grander drama.

Men's conception of the nature and office of the Messiah may perhaps, in the age of Jesus, have ranged from the old conception (which is also the modern Jewish conception) to the other conception which has just been sketched. Between the two extremes there would be room for many combinations and degrees, which might be held by different persons, more or less distinctly, at the same period. What, however, was the Messianic conception in Nazareth and Capernaum, what in Jericho and Jerusalem, in the age of Jesus it is scarcely possible to say with precision. Did Galilee differ from Judæa ? Do the more supernatural and enlarged conceptions of the apocalyptic writers imply that such conceptions were widely spread among the common people, or were they rather the possession and the dream of but a few ? Did the ordinary Rabbi, the official teacher, as well as the populace, ignore them and pass them by ? Or was the entire conception of the Messiah little thought of and little prominent in those days ? All these questions are only to be conjecturally answered. Adequate material for an adequate answer is, unfortunately, lacking.

One therefore comes back to the question, What sort of Messiah did Jesus suppose himself to be—if he supposed himself to be the Messiah at all—with added uncertainty. Still a few points emerge. It would seem that Jesus was affected to a considerable extent by the great developments of the Messianic conception to which allusion has been made. The dreams of the apocalyptic writers can hardly have escaped his notice entirely. He was not unfamiliar with them. Hence we may assume that the Messiah to him was something more and other than the Messiah of Isaiah xi. He was a being who was to take a leading part in a greater drama. And that greater drama, the coming of the Kingdom, with all that this involved, including, perhaps, the Final Judgment, at first overshadowed the personal or individual element. (Jesus starts by preaching the Kingdom ; not the Messiah or himself.) God was going to make an end of the old order ; there was no need for man to fight ; the Roman dominion would presumably fall to pieces of itself, or through divine agency, when the new order and the divine Kingdom were established. In this sense, then, the Messiah to Jesus was not a ' political ' personage ; not a warrior ; not an ' earthly ' prince ; not a ' merely Jewish ' monarch. In this sense he was to Jesus probably more like the Messiah of apocalyptic dreamers. Nor is it improbable that many Rabbis and Pharisees, who were not apocalyptists, shared these opinions. To many of them it was only God, and not the Messiah, who would destroy the power of Rome.

But this newer Messiah, because a bigger, less purely human, or if you will, less purely *Jewish*, personage, was not, therefore, *necessarily*, more virtuous, more spiritual, less prejudiced. What is Jewish and national may yet be ethical ; what is superhuman and mysterious may be unethical. To Isaiah and to those Jews who thought on these political and ' national ' lines, the Messiah meant the triumph of righteousness and the destruction of wickedness ; to the apocalyptic dreamers he did not mean anything better ; perhaps the stress upon righteousness was, indeed, lessened. It is even doubtful whether the nationalism of the apocalyptic dreamers was less intense than the nationalism of those who rejected these apocalyptic visions and stuck to the prophets and to Isaiah xi. And we have no clear evidence that Jesus thought of the Kingdom, and of the Messiah's work in connection with that Kingdom, upon *deliberately unnational* lines. There is no clear evidence that he rejected the primacy of Israel, or its continuance as a nation, in the new order and in the Kingdom. There is no special advance to be noted here, *just because*, or *as a result*, of the fact that the Kingdom was to be established by direct divine intervention, and the Messiah was not to be a successful warrior and mere earthly king. It is not here that the advance of Jesus, if indeed in *this* province of thought he made an advance, can be found to lie. But it does seem as if *other* elements of his teaching and character had their reflex influence upon his conception of the Messiah.

For we may reasonably argue that Jesus, as a great and original religious and ethical teacher and thinker, could hardly not have allowed his religious and ethical views to affect his conception of the Messiah. It is not right to call his ethical doctrine a mere ' Interims-Ethik.' Righteousness was to be the keynote of the new Kingdom, as well as the passport of admission within its gates. Like many another religious teacher, Jesus did not ask himself the question how far the virtues upon which he laid such great stress would be needless, or incapable of being realized and practised, in the renovated world. He was keen about them for their own sake, apart from their immediate effects. He did not consider the difficulty that their effects would (partially, at any rate) hinder their continuance.

And among those virtues upon which he laid stress may we not safely assume that the virtue of self-sacrifice, of service for the sake of others, was undoubtedly one ? Is it not reasonable, then, to suppose that he looked upon his own life as a service, and that this thought may even have developed into the idea that he might have to die in order to complete his service ? Death would not be the end; death was to no man the end; certainly not to the righteous ; least of all to the Messiah. Was the glory and was the triumph perhaps only to come *after* the life of service had been ended by a death of sacrifice ? If the principle of non-resistance was adopted by him in his ethics for daily life, it is not unnatural that it should have been adopted by him as regards his own special life and his position as Messiah. Hence we see how it may have come about that his conception of the Messiah may have been modified. The Messiah was no more the conqueror and the warrior-prince : what destruction there was to do would be done by God. The Messiah would, indeed, rule in the perfected Kingdom, but this rule was hardly looked upon in the ordinary way, and the stress was not habitually laid upon it. The stress was rather laid upon the Messiah's work in the present and the near future, a work of service, even of lowly service, and a work which was, perhaps, to culminate in death. This, then, may have been the special development made by Jesus to the conception of the Messiah ; and such a view would fit in with the supposition that Jesus identified the Messiah with the mysterious Man (Daniel vii. 13) who was sent by God at the great crisis to superintend the final consummation, and that he believed that this Man was himself—himself as he was to be in his glory, rather than himself as he then was.

It does seem a fact that Jesus showed a curiously negative attitude towards national and political questions. It remains true that, as I have said, there is no clear evidence that Jesus rejected the primacy of Israel, or its continuance as a nation, in the new order and in the Messianic Kingdom. One passage which would imply this may have been written and composed many years after his death. But it also seems to be true that the nation as such never appears to interest him at all. Instead of the nation, he is always concerned with individuals. A man's qualifications for the Kingdom are not decided by birth, but rigidly and exclusively by character. ' The hopes of Jesus were absolutely neutral as regards the opposition of Israel and the Roman dominion. Who would give a thought to the fall of the Roman Empire, when he looks forward to the overturning of heaven and earth? It is not as if we found any sympathy with the national enmity to the Romans. But we find rather a clearly expressed indifference. It is just in this point that Jesus plainly stands apart from the most exalted passages in the Psalms of Solomon. His attitude is in extreme opposition to that of the party of the Zealots. So far is he from revolutionary thoughts that the whole question seems to fail to interest him. It is impossible too that he should have adopted this position only in the later period of his life, it was clear from the beginning of his career ' (Wrede, ' Die Predigt Jesu vom Reiche Gottes,' in *Studien und Vorträgen*, p. 116). On the other hand it is exaggeration to say that he saw in the political rule of the Romans no diminution of the Kingdom of God, or that the rule of God was not going to remove the rule of strangers over the nation, but all powers hostile to God in the soul of man (Dalman), or again that Jesus's conception of the Kingdom of the Messiah was quite consistent with the maintenance of the Roman Empire (Gardner). It would probably be far nearer the truth to say that though the work of Jesus had nothing in common with that of a Judas Maccabæus, yet ' the chosen of the Kingdom will be dependent on no human power ; the servitude under which Israel labours will be destroyed ; there will remain no place for the authority of Cæsar in the city of

God: but God Himself, and not man, will substitute His rule for that of men. In his reply to the tribute question (Mark xii. 13-17) the respect which Jesus shows for the constituted authorities is quite negative. He in no wise intended to sanction the right of the Emperor as a principle of the society which was to come. The Emperor belongs to the providential order of this world, like Sennacherib or Nebuchadnezzar: he does not belong to the definite order of the Kingdom, and his power will fall, as is befitting, with the power of Satan, of whom he is, in certain respects, the representative' (Loisy, *E. S.*, i. p. 231).

The student must certainly read the valuable pages in *Beginnings of Christianity* on the Baptism passage (i. pp. 397-400). It may truly be said that almost every word in Mark i. 9-11 contains a puzzle. Are we to suppose that Mark thought that the voice from heaven was quoting Psalm ii. or not? And did he think that 'Son' was equivalent to Messiah? It is not easy (as the editors of *Beginnings* show) to give any definite or certain answer to these questions. Again, what exactly is the exact meaning of εὐδόκησα, 'in thee I am well pleased'? It would appear that εὐδοκία includes some reference to choice. Hence the voice means something like an appointment, or choosing at the moment, of some one to be a Son who had not been son before. Bacon renders: 'I elected thee' (*Gospel of Mark*, p. 251).

The question is also discussed whether the voice at the Baptism (like the Temptation) has any historical basis whatsoever. In Mark it is only Jesus who sees and hears. Hence we may suppose that what is recorded is a vision. Now it is ably argued by J. Weiss (*Schriften*, 3rd ed.) that some inner event, some spiritual upheaval, must have taken place in the soul of Jesus in order to account (*a*) for the opening of the ministry, for his undertaking of his office and mission, and (*b*) for the form which that ministry and office assumed. And the Voice and the Temptation are the reflection, the popular expression, of these inward experiences and agitations. The Prophets too started on their ministry, and were impelled to it, by a vision. On the other hand, we have the difficulty (though Burkitt, *Beginnings*, p. 23, does not find it so) that if these events had any historical background even as inward experiences, Jesus must have said something about them to the disciples. Is this probable? Secondly, there are the mythical parallels which lead to the argument that we have both in the Voice story and in the Temptation pure legends with no historical basis at all. Those who would wish to pursue the subject further can read Bultmann, pp. 151-156 (with the references there given), and the criticism of Bultmann in Fascher, pp. 132, 133. See also Leisegang, *Pneuma Hagion*, pp. 80-95 (1922), criticized unfavourably by Bultmann in the

Theologische Literaturzeitung, 1922, p. 426. I am rather impressed that Meyer, I. pp. 94, 95, also regards both the Voice and the Temptation as purely mythical. For if, on the one hand, one must give weight to what this distinguished and practised historian says as to the authenticity of large portions of Mark, as to the entire reasonableness of the ' Petrine recollections,' so, on the other hand, must we, I think, give some weight to his views when he is sceptical.

Some scholars think—and this view is, on the whole, to my mind, the more probable—that Jesus, though he may have felt at the Baptism some call to be a Teacher and a Prophet, did not believe himself to be the Messiah or Son of man till a later period in the Ministry. His ' Messianic consciousness ' was the product of his ministry : he did not start with it. Thinkers as far apart as Loisy and Peake both combat this view. Peake holds that at the Baptism Jesus obtained the assurance of a unique Sonship, which probably included the conviction of Messiahship as well. He says : ' The probabilities of the case speak strongly for the view that at the Baptism Jesus attained the consciousness of Divine-Sonship. The definite conviction of a Divine call to a special mission could alone have justified to Him the acceptance of His vocation and the entry on His public ministry. The experience in the wilderness follows naturally, one might almost say inevitably, upon this. And Q's story of the Temptation, if authentic, guarantees the story that in the Baptism Jesus attained the conviction of His Sonship. The denial of the experience on the banks of the Jordan logically carries with it the rejection of the triple temptation, which would then lose its occasion and starting-point, and this one act of critical violence logically leads on to another. In view of all these considerations, we may with some confidence accept the representation of our sources that with the submission to John's Baptism there was linked the consciousness of Divine Sonship ; that its sequel was retirement into the wilderness and temptation there ; and that this temptation took the form which it received in Matthew and Luke, who at this point were drawing upon Q. The consciousness which Jesus attained in His Baptism was not of a Sonship shared by others, for this had all along been central in His religious life, but of a Sonship which was unique. It probably included the conviction that He was the Messiah, for this seems to be implied in the third temptation ; but it need not have been exhausted by this.' (*The Messiah or the Son of Man,* p. 9). All this seems to me very doubtful.

For the Spirit assuming the form of a dove, see Abrahams, *Studies,* I. chap. v.

12, 13. THE TEMPTATION

(*Cp.* Matt. iv. 1–11 ; Luke iv. 1–13)

12 And immediately the Spirit drove him into the wilderness. And
13 he was in the wilderness forty days, being tempted of Satan ; and
he was with the wild beasts, and the angels ministered unto him.

Though Mark's account may be the older, it will be better to
reserve the little that it is necessary to say about the Temptation
for the notes on Matthew. It is possible that Mark followed a
different version of the Temptation legend from that given in Q.
In it, perhaps, Jesus did not fast, but was fed by the angels. Both
in Mark and in Q the temptation is ' Messianic ' : *i.e.* it is the
temptation of the Messiah, not of an ordinary individual. The
victory of Jesus over Satan is not mentioned ; it is assumed. ' He
was with the wild beasts.' The meaning is not quite clear. This
touch is found in Mark only. The animals may be mere ' scaffolding ',
as some think ; they heighten the desolateness of the wilderness.
Cp. Isaiah xiii. 21 ; 2 Macc. v. 27. They may also be interpreted
messianically. *Cp.* Job v. 23 ; Ez. xxxiv. 25 ; Ps. xc. 13. The
wild beasts cannot hurt the Son of God. Others think that all
three Evangelists drew from a common source, which Mark curtailed
and altered. But this is unlikely. The true view is more probably
that Mark and Q are independent of one another. See Streeter,
p. 188 : ' In Mark's account of the Temptation there is no mention
of the fast. Indeed, if we did not unwittingly read into Mark's
account what is so familiar to us from the other two Gospels, we
should naturally interpret the imperfect tense of the verb in the
phrase " the angels ministered to him " as meaning that Jesus was
continuously fed by angels, as once Elijah was by ravens. Again,
while in Matthew and Luke the emphasis is on the internal content
of the various temptations of our Lord to a misuse of His lately
realized Messianic powers, in Mark it is on the external fact that
" he was with the wild beasts," which is not even mentioned in the
other accounts. Mark's representation of this incident is so wholly
different from that in Q that, if we were compelled to assume that
he could have derived it from no other source, we must say that he
had read Q long enough ago to have had time to forget it.'
I can only briefly refer here to Bacon's theories as regards the
Christology of the Synoptics, and especially of Mark and of its relation
to Paul. The student will have to peruse carefully chapters XVII.–
XIX. of *The Gospel of Mark*. The Baptism and Temptation stories
in Mark rest, according to Bacon, upon Q material, embodying
' Servant ' Christology, which is distinct both from the ' Son of

man' Christology and from the 'Son of David' Christology (the last alluded to, but rejected, both by Paul and Mark). In the Q material, Jesus is the Servant, 'chosen of God, the Beloved whom He elected from eternity. God has put His Spirit upon him, that he may carry out His purpose of redemption for the lowly and broken people. Though inconspicuous and unknown he will bring true religion to its triumph in the world, and even the Gentiles will find the goal of their hopes in him' (pp. 250, 251). But in Q he is not *called* Servant. He is the 'agent of the revealing, redeeming Wisdom of God, who makes known His judgments to the lowly, and wins her victories in quietness among these her children. Only (as often in Wisdom of Solomon), the title employed is not Servant, but Son (υἱός) of God. The Servant Christology is here basic, but developed as in the Wisdom writings' (p. 251). This Christology culminates in the great passage Matt. xi. 25–30. Bacon thinks that Mark alludes to, but does not himself really adopt or make his own, the Servant Christology, though it is referred to in such passages as Mark ix. 12 or x. 45 or xiv. 24. 'Mark's own Christology is the doctrine that Jesus is a (? for 'a' put 'the') Son of God' (p. 149). He was made Son of God at the Baptism. The Transfiguration story 'teaches a messiahship by apotheosis. It is nearer to the Son of Man than to the Servant Christology' (p. 253). It is 'apocalyptic in type, aiming to set forth a Son of Man Christology, and (if we may judge from the quotation of Dt. xviii. 15 in the heavenly Voice) embodying a soteriology based on the conception of the Prophet, the Second Moses. Obedience to him is the pathway of salvation and eternal life. Verbally we have traces of the Servant Christology. The Voice proclaims Jesus "the Beloved Son" (in Luke "the Elect"), and the whole scene seems to be almost a replica of the Vision at the Baptism. But surely the conception of salvation is quite different, whether as regards method or result. As a preface to the Passion and Resurrection gospel this midrash serves very well the purpose of Mark. It contrasts the Son of David ideal with that of the Son of Man, making the doctrine of the cross central and indispensable. But there is no hint of the Servant doctrine, and none whatever of the Wisdom Christology' (p. 256). Mark 'has no use for Q Christology, the doctrine of the incarnation of the Wisdom of God in the Servant. This constitutes his widest divergence from Paul' (p. 253). As to the vexed 'Son of Man' title it appears in 'Mark as a totally undigested foreign element. The reader receives no explanation whatever. He is expected to know why Jesus speaks of himself as the Son of Man (ii. 10, 28, etc.), just as he is expected to know without explanation why the multitude call him Son of David. The evangelist is probably not conscious that he has given none; but this only makes it the more certain that the doctrine *is* presupposed, and of no recent growth. Were it recent the necessity of explanation would be felt ' (p. 226). Son of man is used in Q, but not in any old apocalyptic sense. For the ' Christology of Q is a Servant Christology in Wisdom development. The Works of the Christ are such as proclaim him the Servant. But just as in Wisdom of Solomon the Servant is an incarnation of God's Wisdom. As endowed with the true *gnosis* Jesus is the " Son " who reveals the unknown Father. But not even in Q is Jesus ever *spoken of* as the Servant. The baptismal Voice from heaven itself changes the phraseology of Is. xlii. 1–3 in order to substitute Son for Servant, and the Temptations interpret the title Son ' (p. 227). ' A large part of the Q material conspicuously displays this Christology of the Isaian Servant-prophecies. We may even say that in such passages as the Temptation it is definitely set over against the Son of David Christology, and in others, such as the Parables of the Kingdom (Mk. iv. 1–34) and Works of the Christ (Matt. xi. 2–19 = Luke vii. 18–35), it is differentiated from the Son of Man Christology also ' (p. 223). The Temptation story, the rebuke to Peter (Mark viii. 33), the story ' Whose son is the Messiah ? ' (Mark xii. 35), are all attacks upon the Son of David Christology (p. 225), which, therefore, like the Son of man Christology is also known to Q. Q's own Christology is not an apotheosis doctrine like Mark's, but an ' incarnation doctrine.' Jesus is ' an incarnation of the revealing and redeeming Wisdom of God ' (p. 227). I cannot discuss all this. But it seems to me doubtful whether such a passage as Luke xxi. 27, or even Mark x. 45, in its root idea, implies a Christology, or an application of Isaiah liii. The historic Jesus may have conceived that his office as Messiah lay in service, and this conception may have constituted its originality. Whether this idea of service went also so far as service in and through death seems to be a distinct question. It might have possibly have done the one and not the other.

As to the relation of Mark to Paul, Bacon's views deserve most careful consideration. *Cp.* Introduction, § 7. They are complementary to, and corrective of, the views of Werner, and show a deeper appreciation of the problem. It is not unlikely, it seems to me, that they may, on the whole, be approved by the next generation of scholars.

14, 15. THE MISSION IN GALILEE
(*Cp.* Matt. iv. 12–17 ; Luke iv. 14, 15)

14 Now after John was thrown into prison, Jesus came into Galilee,
15 and proclaimed the good tidings of God, saying, ' The time is fulfilled, and the kingdom of God has drawn nigh ; repent ye, and believe in the good tidings.'

Mark seems to wish to give here a sort of summary of the entire purpose and scope of the ministry of Jesus. Or, at all events, he wishes to show why he began to preach, and what was the content of his first preaching.

14. 'Gospel of God.' Apparently a Pauline expression. *Cp.* Romans i. 1, xv. 16; 2 Cor. xi. 7; 1 Thess. ii. 2, 8, 9. 'The Gospel of God was an expression first popularized, if not coined, by Paul, so far as we know' (Moffatt, p. 233, n. 1). For 'the time is fulfilled' we may also compare Gal. iv. 4. The two verses 14, 15 'are a summary (*Sammelbericht*) which it is best to ascribe to the evangelist. He has given this summary in order to make a transition or introduction to the individual scenes which follow' (Schmidt, p. 33). If that be so, we must not, perhaps, lay much stress upon their historic accuracy. Nevertheless, the joyful and the solemn side of the Preaching, and the essence of it, are, perhaps, accurately given. The Kingdom is at hand; for the repentant it will be bliss; for the wicked, darkness and pain.

15. 'The kingdom of God was at hand.' In other words, Jesus believed that the great world crisis was about to begin. We know that a similar belief was not uncommon at this period. It apparently had been proclaimed by John the Baptist. It was the old belief of the Jewish prophets. 'The day of the Lord is at hand.' Was the announcement one of doom or of joy or of both? The summons to repentance shows that there was in it in any case an element of doom. Men must repent in order to avoid condemnation. Evil doers must repent and amend their ways, so would they not perish in the judgment. For though no word is said of judgment, and only the Kingdom is mentioned, yet the coming of the Kingdom, or rather the dominion and rule of God, implied a judgment. The rule of God meant that the wicked would be punished, and perhaps done away with for good and all; the good, who are so often oppressed and unhappy, would triumph and be rewarded. To enter into the Kingdom, to enjoy the rule of God, let the wicked repent. Then, perhaps, they would be forgiven. At the time when Jesus lived, the ideas about the Kingdom of God were by no means clear and all of a piece. They were based upon the teachings of the O.T. prophets, but many developments had taken place. To Amos the day of the Lord had meant a judgment upon wicked Israel, but to the later prophets the Day had meant (as in preprophetic times) a judgment upon Israel's foes, and a deliverance of Israel. The scene of the judgment was earth: nothing was known of a resurrection. When Jesus lived, there was still the idea of a deliverance: Roman dominion would be destroyed; the oppressor overthrown. But combined with this went the idea of an internal purgation as well. Jewish

sinners would be punished as well as foreign tyrants. The whole conception had been enormously widened by the doctrines of the resurrection and of the after life which were held in a variety of forms, by no means always consistent with each other. It is needless to give a full account of them in this place. The only question of interest for us here is how far did Jesus share the ordinary ideas of his time about the Future, the Judgment, the Kingdom of God ; how far did he deviate from them ? How far did he teach something more spiritual, more ethical, of value for our time as well as for his ? This is a most difficult and puzzling question, and will come before us again. In these verses of Mark, the Kingdom has primarily a severe side, a side of doom, for persons then alive. Except by the use of the word ' evangelion ', it is not distinctly stated that it has also a good side, a side of deliverance and joy, for the good and the oppressed, but this is doubtless implied. Nor is there any distinct reference to the life after death. It is not stated whether, after the advent of the Kingdom, the good will live for ever upon a renovated and regenerated earth, or whether they will live in heaven, or whether the bad will be punished in pain, and, if so, where, or whether they will be annihilated. It is not stated whether, after the good have lived for a time upon a regenerated earth, there will be a second or final judgment. Quite probably the ideas of Jesus upon all these matters were themselves not always clear and consistent. He certainly believed that the bad would be punished and the good rewarded, and this was the main or fundamental portion of his teaching upon this subject. What part he would himself play in the judgment or in the Kingdom is not here stated. That will be mentioned further on.

What is curious, however, is this. The particular belief which caused Jesus to become a public preacher—for we are not given to understand that he had preached and taught before John was imprisoned — which started him on his brief ministry (probably not much more than one year in duration), was his belief that a great crisis—the end of the old World Order—was at hand. For this is what the Kingdom meant to him as to all Jews : the end of the old World Order : the opening of a totally different Divine Order. It also meant the definite and final overthrow of the wicked : the definite and final establishment of the good in happiness and spiritual bliss. Now in this belief he, like all the teachers who had preceded him, was wrong. The old order did not cease ; the new order did not begin, and has never begun. Moreover, all the teaching of Jesus about the New Order, or, rather, perhaps, I should say, all the teaching of Jesus about the divine judgment, and as to what will befall men after death, or at, and after, the judgment, or at, and after, the resurrection, or about ' Heaven ' and ' Hell,' or Paradise

and Gehenna, is for us the least valuable and interesting and original
and permanent part of his entire teaching.   For Jesus knew no more
about what will happen to us after death than we do ourselves.   He
knew no more about the divine judgment than we.   We too may
believe that the bad will be punished, the good rewarded ; though we
should say (for herein we see, I think, more clearly than he), that the
bad will be disciplined and purified, and the good will be purified and
satisfied (or whatever words seem to us less gross than ' rewarded '),
but beyond this simple doctrine or faith we know no more than he,
and he knew no more than we.   ' The secret things belong unto the
Lord our God.'   Yet started, called into being, by this teaching as
to which, on the one hand, he was mistaken, and about which, on
the other hand, he knew, and could know, no more than we, came
all those portions of his teaching in which he was really great and
new, in which he said things that remain of value for our own time,
and are likely to remain of value for all the generations of man.   He
could not see further than his contemporaries about the judgment,
or the New Order, or the life after death, but he did see further than
they about goodness and the relations of man with God.   His true
greatness was revealed in teaching which, in a sense, was subordinate
to, or dependent upon, or was, at any rate, evoked by, teaching which
was ephemeral and traditional.   And this statement is, I think,
true, even if (which is by no means sure) there are elements in his
teaching about the Kingdom or dominion of God which were original
and new.   So strange are the ways of God ; so mysterious the
methods of his inspiration and of his rule.

And though the more original and beautiful parts of the teaching
of Jesus are, as it were, set in the framework of the conception
of the coming Messianic era, and were partly produced by this
dominant idea, they are yet independent of the framework, and they
can be detached from it and can survive it.

Doubtless the teaching of Jesus is partly to be estimated and
described by whatever conclusions we come to about his view of his
Messiahship and office.   Yet it is an important fact, and one of
which we must take adequate note, that there is a good deal of his
religious and ethical teaching which was not directly related to, or
dependent upon, any eschatological conceptions, any belief in the
nearing end of the world.   Or, if this goes too far, it is at least right
to urge that there is a good deal in his finest religious and ethical
teaching which can survive such conceptions and be easily detached
from them.   For example, the ' inwardness ' of his teaching, his
spiritualization, or screwing up the standard, of human righteousness and human religion ; his estimate of ceremonial observances
and ritual uncleanness ; his heroic paradoxes concerning the love
of one's enemies ; his looking at morality and religion in the light

of a few great illuminating and unifying principles, such as the love
of God and the love of man; his doctrine of a needful childlike
attitude of mind; his doctrine of faith; his attack upon certain
aspects of the doctrine of proportionate retribution and reward;
his insistence upon eager service, upon lowliness in service, and upon
the nature of true greatness or superiority; his doctrine of actively
seeking out the sinner and the outcast in order to redeem them;
his doctrine of self-sacrifice. Here are large and important teachings, either quite independent of, or easily detachable from, any
eschatological opinions.

A good deal of controversy still continues as to the sense or
senses in which Jesus used the expression 'the Kingdom of God.'
There is no doubt that he often meant by it the new era, the
Messianic age, the earth as it would be when ruled wholly by God
and responsive to his rule. The Kingdom of God would exist upon
earth when the dominion of Satan was wholly destroyed, or when
sin and iniquity were no more. This Kingdom was future, but
at the same time it was near at hand. Only those who made
much sacrifice in the right spirit would enter the Kingdom.
And, on the other hand, the Kingdom would come as a gift.
It would be given as a gift to those who were by nature and
grace fitted to receive it. The childlike in heart alone could enter
the Kingdom. So far all is pretty clear and pretty uncontestable.
But some think that Jesus did not only use the phrase in this
single sense. (1) The Kingdom is not, apparently, on all occasions
to be located upon earth. It is, apparently, also used as a synonym
for what we call 'heaven': *i.e.* Jesus sometimes speaks as a modern
preacher might, who tells us that when the 'righteous' and the
'elect' die, they enter upon a heavenly life, the real and true life
of the soul. The Kingdom seems sometimes to mean this heavenly
life. (2) The Kingdom is also sometimes, but rarely, said or
implied to be already present. This may have several meanings,
of which one is easy, the others more hard. The easy meaning (*a*) is
that the Kingdom has practically begun with the appearance and
preaching of Jesus. The decisive moments are near at hand. Under
these circumstances, it has been argued that it was as natural for
Jesus sometimes to say the Kingdom is already present, and has
begun, and sometimes to say the Kingdom will come, as it is natural
for us when dark clouds are rolling up and the lightning flashes on
the horizon to say either 'a storm is coming' or 'there is a storm.'
But (*b*) the Kingdom as present *seems* also to be used in other senses
still. For—

(*a*) It seems sometimes to be considered as a process which
would not come suddenly by divine interposition, but gradually

by the inward working and ferment of the teaching of Jesus upon and within the hearts of men. And again,

(β) It seems sometimes to be used in an ideal way of the true disciples or of the true Church, as if the company of those who had the right faith in God and in the tidings did actually constitute the Kingdom in its present, though not completed, realization.

And (γ) it seems also to be used as if the Kingdom were what Dr. Carpenter calls a 'spiritual fact,' 'a symbol of living spiritual relations,' as a principle living and working in the hearts of men, as if it were something not visible or concrete, not to be realized by a divine revolution, no Kingdom to be created upon a regenerate earth, but something invisible, spiritual, and inward. You enter this Kingdom, only in so far as this Kingdom enters you. If you are spiritual, 'righteous' in the higher and newer sense, then you are already in the Kingdom, for the Kingdom is in you, and so far as the Kingdom has a collective signification, it is made up of those spiritual men and women in whose souls the Kingdom already is.

In which sense the Kingdom is used, and whether it is really ever definitely used in any of the last three senses, must be determined on each particular occasion by the context and meaning of each individual passage.

Meanwhile it may be said that it seems most probable that for both the historic Jesus and the Jesus of Mark the Kingdom had nearly always, at bottom, its eschatological signification. It is the Messianic Kingdom of the near future. In Matthew the Kingdom in the sense of the Church as already existent, the fellowship of believers, comes also to the fore. How far it is ever a 'process' or an 'inward spiritual fact' is very much more doubtful.

Jesus only began his public ministry after the imprisonment of John. That John could not continue his work may perhaps have impelled Jesus to take it up.

'The time is fulfilled,' i.e. the great change is at hand; the Old Order is coming to an end ; the New Order is about to begin. Whether Jesus used these words or no, there is no reason to doubt that their sentiment was his.

'Believe in the good tidings.' If Jesus used the words, they must mean, 'Believe in the good news that the Kingdom of God is at hand.' But 'repent and believe in *good* news' is an odd combination : 'repent and believe in solemn news' is a more suitable collocation. 'Repent, for the Day of the Lord is at hand' is what Jesus more probably said, as in Matt. iv. 17. Jesus began like the prophets of old. Only after Jesus had passed away could the saying 'repent' be regarded as a *good* tidings. It then came to mean : 'believe in Jesus as the Messiah, join the Christian community.' This could be pretty easily done. Hence in such circumstances 'repent, for the day of the Lord is at hand,' became a tidings not of severity, but of gladness. Harnack (*Constitution and Law of the Church*, E. T., p. 279) denies the validity of the argument. The near advent of the Kingdom was good tidings to the poor and the repentant. Jesus himself did not put it so summarily as the Evangelist : ' Repent and believe in the good tidings.' But he could nevertheless have spoken of good tidings, for the message of the Kingdom was not only one of Judgment, but more essentially one of deliverance and of joy.

Jesus is not reported to have said at the opening of his ministry that the Messiah had come, or that he was the Messiah. Perhaps he did not yet believe that he was the Messiah ? Perhaps when the idea came to him, he desired to keep his Messiahship dark ? Here we touch upon one of the fundamental questions and problems of the Gospels and of the life of Jesus, about which it would be tempting to discourse at great length, but which, for the reasons already given, I can only touch upon here and there in the briefest possible way. On the whole, I am inclined to believe that if Jesus held that he was the Messiah, and allowed, helped, or taught other people to think so too (and his death and some features in his life cannot be satisfactorily accounted for upon any other hypothesis), he did not start with this belief at the very opening of his ministry, but yet reached it fairly soon after he had entered upon his brief career.

16–20. The Call of Simon, Andrew, James and John
(*Cp.* Matt. iv. 18–22 ; Luke v. 1–11)

16 Now as he walked along the lake of Galilee, he saw Simon and Andrew his brother casting a net into the lake : for they were 17 fishermen. And Jesus said unto them, ' Come ye after me, and I 18 will make you become fishers of men.' And straightway they left 19 their nets, and followed him. And when he had gone a little further, he saw James the son of Zebedee, and John his brother, who were 20 also in a boat, mending their nets. And straightway he called them : and they left their father Zebedee in the boat with the hired servants, and went after him.

On returning to Galilee, Jesus either did not go back to his own home in Nazareth, or he went there first and then went on to

Capernaum (so Matthew).   Why he went to Capernaum and the
lake is not stated.   Perhaps Meyer is right in holding that the
adverse attitude of his family and home environment induced him
to seek another locality for his preaching and ministry (I. p. 99).

Here we have the first story which Mark has to tell about the
preaching of Jesus.   Mark gives us no real biography of Jesus ;
what we find is a series of tales and sayings only partially arranged
from a chronological point of view.   The first thing he could
discover about Jesus's missionary career in Galilee was the call of
the four chief or earliest apostles.   Of the effect of the general
proclamation given in i. 14, 15, he tells us nothing.   In fact, it
seems to be forgotten, or to have no definite result.   The reputation
which Jesus acquires in Galilee (i. 28) seems to rest on different
grounds.   But directly one begins to read the Gospel one enters on
a land of half-lights and shadows, a land of puzzles and problems,
though also a land of beauty and distinction.

In this story we have not yet arrived at anything which is of
value for ourselves.   But we get something which is new.   It is
the implication in the phrase, ' fishers of men ' (cp. Jer. xvi. 16
for the wording).   For here we have the first indication that one
object of the ministry of Jesus was to save, to redeem ; not to
study, not even to teach those who chose to come and hear him
within the Synagogue or within the walls of the House of Learning,
but to go forth and actively seek out those who were in spiritual
sickness or need, and to help and to cure them.   Perhaps Ezekiel's
career was the prototype for such a ministry, but it was not, I
think, the usual Rabbinic method.   The Rabbis did not teach in
that way.   They 'studied.'   But Jesus in his ministry does not
' study.'   His time is otherwise occupied.   He seeks to convert and
save, some here and some there.   He would be a shepherd of souls,
and bring men into the Kingdom.   Whether these four men were
really ' called ' by Jesus in this particular dramatic way is another
matter.   It may have been less sudden and absolute.   But that
there was a call, and even that the story goes back to Peter's own
recollections and statements, many commentators and critics
believe.   To Mark, the Messiah's call could only have seemed
absolute, imperative, and complete.   By the men called, Jesus was
not acknowledged or recognized as the Messiah, but as a teacher, or
(at most) as a prophet.   ' In reality the affair probably happened
somewhat differently ' (Wellhausen).   ' Obviously this first day at
Capernaum cannot be the beginning of Jesus's activity, for the
" call " of the first disciples shows that these people who are going
to leave everything know who Jesus is, and why he calls on them
to follow him.'   ' It is impossible that the section i. 16–20 reports
the first meeting between Jesus and the Galilæan fishermen : the

" call " which Jesus addresses to them is not explicit enough for
us to comprehend the decision which they make on hearing it,
unless they had been previously informed with regard to the plans
of Jesus, to his purposes, and to the work which he sought to
accomplish and for which he needed their help ' (Goguel, I. pp.
316, 334). We are not told how much preaching Jesus had already
done, nor for how long, nor whence he had come to the lake. The
' separate story ' is just hooked on to the editorial summary in 14,
15 (Schmidt, p. 43).

It is not of importance to us Jewish readers to-day whether this
first story in Mark, or whether many other of his stories, are wholly
true or wholly imaginary, or partly true and partly imaginary.
For Liberal Jews more especially, this indifference is very pronounced. For Orthodox Judaism there would be a certain importance or even value, if it could be proved that many of the stories
were inaccurate, exaggerated, or even imaginary. For all Christians
there is a certain importance and interest, one would imagine, if it
could be proved that the stories are entirely historical and accurate.
After all, it would be, one would suppose, rather disconcerting to
regard *him* as your Master and Lord the stories of whose life were
dubious or unhistorical. And how can one say that Jesus had a
perfect character or possessed a unique personality, if two-thirds,
let us say, of the very meagre number of stories about his exceedingly
brief career could be proved to be either altogether unhistorical, or,
at all events, so mixed up with accessory inaccuracies and legends,
that one can hardly distinguish the false from the true ? But to
Liberal Judaism it does not really matter one way or the other.
Our religion remains the same whether, *e.g.*, Jesus ' called ' these
four men in the manner described, or whether he did not. I do
not here refer to the actual miracles, or to the supernatural revelations. Doubtless no one could believe all of these, and remain a
Jew, whether Orthodox or Liberal. But, nowadays, there are
many sincere and ardent Christians who do not believe them,
and from the point of view from which my whole book is written
it is unnecessary to pursue the subject further. In the literal truth
of such stories as Mark i. 11 or v. 40 or vi. 48 or ix. 7 we no more
believe than in the literal truth of corresponding stories in the Old
Testament.

As an example of Meyer's line of criticism I will quote what
he says about the call of the first four apostles (I. pp. 98, 99) :
' Concerning the previous history of Jesus historical tradition knows
nothing ; its accounts begin with his appearance as a teacher in
Galilee, and bound up with this are the disciples, his constant
followers. The two pairs of brothers, Simon (Peter) and Andrew,
and James and John, the sons of Zebedee—the only four disciples

who play any part in the tradition—are inseparable from him. That is the reason why their " call " has been placed at the beginning. An exact historical narrative does not exist even about the call. The story already presupposes the authority of Jesus which, in reality, he had first to substantiate: the two men follow his command without hesitation. To Peter and Andrew Jesus says that they are in future to be fishers of men. James and John left their father in the ship with his hired servants, and straightway followed him. Therefore Zebedee must have been a comparatively wealthy man. In itself, it seems hardly likely that Jesus would have won over the two pairs of brothers practically at the same time. Among the four, Andrew stands quite in the background. There is nothing to be related about him. Unlike the other three, he is never mentioned in the history of the primitive community at Jerusalem : may one conclude that he died early ? Thus for us he is nothing but a name. Peter, on the other hand, appears all the more prominently : the first stories of the activity of Jesus are nearly all located in Capernaum where Peter lives with his mother-in-law. Amongst the Jews (*cp*. Gen. ii. 24)—as at the present time in Italy—it was not unusual for the young married man to live in the house of his parents-in-law. The healing of this mother-in-law is Jesus's second miracle. Thus we see quite clearly that the foundation (*Grundstock*) of our tradition goes back to Peter ; tradition knows nothing of what Jesus may have experienced or done prior to the call of Peter; it starts with the connection between Jesus and him.' Again, ' It is quite understandable that Peter did not relate anything concerning his relations with Jesus before the " call " ; for these simple souls the religious experience which forms the turning-point of their whole life is the main thing ; behind it everything else disappears. Thus it is quite sufficient for him to relate that, when he was sitting in the fishing-boat with his brother, Jesus stepped up and summoned them to follow him. What relations existed between them previously, what was the inner preparation for the " call "—all this has no longer any importance for Peter ' (p. 160). This would certainly seem to imply that the ' call of Peter ' as told by Mark is historic. Yet elsewhere Meyer says : ' We learn nothing about the " call " of Peter that can be regarded as historic ' (p. 147).

21–28. JESUS IN THE SYNAGOGUE AT CAPERNAUM—THE UNCLEAN SPIRIT

(*Cp*. Luke iv. 31–37)

21 And they went into Capernaum ; and straightway on the
22 Sabbath day he entered into the synagogue, and taught. And

they were amazed at his teaching, for he taught them as one having
authority, and not as the scribes.

23   And straightway there was in their synagogue a man with an
24 unclean spirit ; and he cried out, saying, ' What have we to do with
25 thee, Jesus of Nazareth ?   Art thou come to destroy us ?   I know
    thee who thou art, the Holy One of God.'   And Jesus rebuked it,
26 saying, ' Hold thy peace, and come out of him.'   And the unclean
    spirit tore him, and cried with a loud voice, and came out of him.
27 And they all marvelled, so that they discussed among themselves,
    saying, ' What is this ? a new teaching with authority !   And he
28 commands the unclean spirits, and they obey him.'   And im-
    mediately his fame spread abroad throughout all the region of
    Galilee.

21. This verse and 22 give a brief picture of how Jesus taught
in the synagogue.   Mark's favourite $\epsilon\dot{v}\theta\dot{v}s$ has little value or
meaning here.   There is an obvious gap between 20 and 21.   The
scene in 16-20 could not have taken place on a Saturday (Schmidt,
pp. 48-51).   But 21-39 appear to belong together and to form a
whole already available for the Evangelist (p. 67), even including
28, though what we are told in 28 was the result of more than
one day's preaching (p. 51).   In 20-28 Mark seeks to put at once
before his readers the two main sides of the activity of Jesus,
which brought him disciples, reputation, and (ultimately) difficulty
and opposition.   The first was his teaching ;   the second, his
miraculous cures.

As regards the first, the teaching, though no examples are here
given of it, was not by Mark supposed to have been limited to
what was summarized in i. 15.   Though the coming of the New
Order and the end of the Old Order were motive and background,
the teaching ranged doubtless, even as we find it in Matthew and
Luke to range, over a wide religious and ethical field.   And Mark
would have meant us to understand this.

There was much less formality in the synagogues then than now.
Any new teacher would be asked, or could ask, to speak.   See
Abrahams, *Studies*, i. chap. i.   But the teaching of Jesus is described
as unusual and novel.   ' He taught as one having authority and
not as the scribes.'   The same words are found also in Matthew
at the end of the Sermon on the Mount.   This famous phrase does
not tell us anything about the teaching of Jesus which is valuable
for us to-day, but it excites our curiosity, and inclines us to believe
that we shall hear something which, in relation to all Jewish teaching
that had preceded it, or, at all events, to all contemporary
Jewish teaching, was new and original.   The words ' as one having

authority' apparently mean that the teaching of Jesus was not deduced from passages in the Law. It did not refer to the sayings of older teachers. It seemed charged with power. It was independent. There seemed nothing between it and God, by whom it was inspired. In this it resembled the teaching of the prophets, and seemed different from the method and form of the teaching of the ordinary Rabbi, just as it was often very different in matter. So we may, perhaps, draw out the meaning of the phrase with tolerable accuracy. The main connotation of ' authority ' to the Evangelist seems to be that of inspiration. Jesus seemed to be possessed, or fired, by the spirit of God. There was a freshness and immediacy about his teaching, and also a personal note in it, which appeared lacking in the teaching of the ordinary Rabbi. But see also what Dr. Abrahams says on the subject in the opening chapter of his *Studies* (I.). One must be cautious in this matter, and not assume too quickly that the difference between Jesus and all the Rabbis of his age was as great or as immediately noticeable as Mark would wish us to believe.

We may, therefore, ask whether this statement of Mark does really reproduce what was actually felt at the moment by those who heard Jesus for the first time. I am inclined to think that it does in this : the teaching of Jesus is markedly prophetic ; it has the temper and tone, and some of the very content, of the teaching of men like Amos and Isaiah. We can hardly say that even the teaching of the great Rabbis like Hillel and Akiba gives this impression. There was also something about the teaching of Jesus which is unlike that of the teaching of the prophets, but which makes the ascription of ' authority ' still more understandable. Jesus did apparently put forward his own personality (apart from the question of the Messiahship) in a way which the prophets did not. The prophets declared : ' Thus says Yahweh,' or ' Thus says the God of Israel.' Jesus, if not in so many words, yet implicitly, declared : ' Thus and thus say *I*.' So he asked disciples to ' *follow* ' him. Doubtless, by ' thus and thus say I,' he meant, ' thus and thus say I, who am inspired by my heavenly Father.' But he does seem to have put his own personality more into the forefront than did the prophets. And this personality of his, this personal note, seemed both to claim, and to possess, authority.

23-28. We are now given a first and typical example of the wonderful cures which Jesus effected. Many of these cures take the form of an expulsion of demons. All of them appeared miraculous to Mark, and we may add that, so far as these cures are historic, they appeared miraculous to the patients and to the onlookers. There are many parallels to them in Rabbinic literature. See

Fiebig's *Jüdische Wundergeschichten des neutestamentlichen Zeitalters* (1911).

To Mark, Jesus was the Messiah. That he was the Messiah was known, to himself at least, from his baptism. It must also have been known to supernatural powers all along. Hence the demons must have recognized him for what he was. They recognized their master, who was to put an end to their rule.

On the other hand, Mark has a tradition (which we may assume to be in accordance with actual history) that Jesus did not openly claim to be the Messiah till later in his career. Hence the demons must have been told to hold their tongue upon the subject. The Messiahship was proved by the wonders Jesus performed; it was stupid, hard-hearted, obtuse of people and of disciples not to understand that Jesus was the Messiah; and yet it was intended that even the disciples were not for some while to recognize his Messiahship.

Thus Mark is involved in contradictions. The Messiah is, and is not, recognized. He should, and he should not, be acknowledged. His Messiahship is constantly revealing itself and as constantly ignored—both by wicked opponents and even by dull disciples. How much theology and how little history there must be in all this is very apparent.

24. The demon in the man speaks in the name of his class. Hence his use of the plural ' we.' ' The Holy One of God ' the demon calls Jesus—*i.e.* the Messiah. Israel is also the Holy One of God, just as he is God's Son. The epithets of Israel were transferred to the Messiah. But this, with the parallel in Luke iv. 34, is the only place in the Synoptics where Jesus, or the Messiah, is called the Holy One of God. For the demonology of the age, see *Jewish Encyclopædia*, ' Demonology '; and Conybeare, ' Christian Demonology,' in *J. Q. R.* Vol. VIII. 576–608, IX. 59–114, 444–470, 581–603.

25. Jesus bids the demon be silent. He does not wish his secret to be betrayed. Originally, the shrieking of the demon was a mere shriek. If Jesus said, ' Be still,' this may have meant, ' Cease to rage, and leave the sufferer.' Doubtless Jesus himself believed that the cause of epilepsy and other nervous disorders was demoniac possession. The shrieking cries were afterwards in some cases supposed to have been intelligible words, or to have included them. The origin of such a tale as that here given may lie in the facts that—

(a) Jesus did sometimes order the patient (to his mind, the demon) to be quiet;

(*b*) He may sometimes (though hardly when, as in this case, the cure took place in a synagogue) have urged the cured man not to spread abroad the news of his cure, in order that he might not be besieged and importuned by an inordinate number of patients.

I feel rather doubtful about (*b*). First of all, it was very unlikely in the loquacious East that such a command would be observed ; it was *so* unlikely, that Jesus could hardly have thought it worth while to give it. Secondly, as one of the objects of his mission was to heal the afflicted, why should he have wished to hide his powers under a bushel ? I think it more likely that all the orders about silence are due to theorizing. Even though silence is ordered, the report of the marvels wrought spreads more and more ! It may be noted, moreover, that this miracle, like many others, is wrought quite openly before a large number of persons. Most ingenious are Prof. Burkitt's arguments for the naturalness and historicity of the ' orders for silence,' but me, at all events, they hardly convince. (*The American Journal of Theology*, April 1911, ' Historical Character of Gospel of Mark,' pp. 186–193.) So too Cadman tries to prove the historical character of the orders for silence. ' It was not the mere publication of His " miracles " that Jesus was primarily concerned about, for these were a verification of His message of the Kingdom ; He anxiously sought rather to leave no room for an inference from " miracles " to Messiahship. This may reasonably be taken to be the underlying thought of the several prohibitions. In the fact that powers of exorcism were exercised by others, without, we may doubt-less suppose, Messiahship being thought of, He would have found occasion for believing that the orders of silence would have the desired result ' (*The Last Journey of Jesus to Jerusalem*, p. 75, n. 1). A too subtle explanation, I fancy.

That Jesus worked many great cures can hardly be doubted. Whether many of his cures relapsed we are not told. We must always remember that we are dealing with a biography—if we can call it so—of unmixed eulogy. Only light is allowed to fall upon the hero. Allowance must be made for exaggeration : as the op-ponents are drawn too black, so Jesus himself is, perhaps, drawn too white. The lineaments of the true historic Jesus can never be fully known. We only hear of the last year of his life, and that is set in a golden glow, a haze of pious adoration and glory.

The limits of the influence of a pious and lofty mind upon certain kinds of diseases and nervous disorders are, I suppose, scarcely to be fixed. There are some interesting remarks about war-cures and the cures of Jesus in Dibelius, *Formgeschichte*, p. 100.

It has been rightly pointed out that the healings wrought by Jesus were the outflow of his pity. He cared not only for the soul, but also for the body. He was better and greater than a mere exorcist. The diseased people whom he sought to help were doubly and trebly objects of his pity. (1) They were in themselves miserable or unhappy. (2) Many were more or less regarded as outcasts, smitten by the hand of God. (3) Some were 'possessed' by demons; *i.e.* sick spiritually as well as bodily. He did not merely want to show his power; he pitied, and yearned to heal.

The belief in demons who dwell in man and exercise a malignant activity from within him was then quite general; it was far more widely prevalent than in the older period. The prophets seem quite free from this belief. In this respect they were more 'modern' than Jesus.

So far we have still not been told of any incident or word which is of value for us to-day. For this we have to wait for some time.

29–34. THE MOTHER-IN-LAW OF SIMON PETER— MANY HEALINGS

(Cp. Matt. viii. 14–17 ; Luke iv. 38–41)

And forthwith, when they had come out of the synagogue, they entered into the house of Simon and Andrew, with James and 30 John. But Simon's wife's mother lay in bed with a fever, and 31 they told him of her. And he came and took her by the hand, and raised her up ; and the fever left her, and she waited on them.

32   And in the evening, when the sun had set, they brought unto him all that were diseased, and them that were possessed with 33 demons. And all the city was gathered together at the door. 34 And he healed many that were sick with divers diseases, and cast out many demons ; and he permitted not the demons to speak, because they knew him.

29. Another healing story (and this time of the sickness type which is not created by a demon), and then a general statement or summary. It may be noticed that according to Mark's arrangement both the healing in 26 and 30 take place on the Sabbath, yet no objection is made, and no comment. On the other hand, it is expressly stated that the healings in 34 are worked after the sun had set and the Sabbath was over. It is possible that the two first stories were not originally supposed to have taken place on the Sabbath.

The beautiful, patient, detailed investigations of Professor

Turner into the linguistic usages of Mark as compared with those of Matthew and Luke lead him on to very conservative conclusions which may, or may not, be justified, but for which, at any rate, the evidence is clear and incontestable. For instance, he shows how here and in many other places Mark has a sort of impersonal plural followed by the singular (*i.e.* he, Jesus, did so and so), whereas Matthew and Luke have often the singular throughout. Again, Mark often, when he uses the singular (of Jesus), adds a mention of the disciples or the Twelve. Why does this happen ? ' Why then did our earliest Evangelist tell his story in the plural, not being himself one of the company who went about with Jesus, save because he is repeating the story of one to whom the plural came natural as being himself an actor in the events he relates ? " We went across, and, as he left the boat, there met him. ..." " We come again to Jerusalem : and as he was walking up and down in the Temple. ..." The mixture of nominatives is less glaring between the first person and the third—" we " and " he," instead of " they " and " he " : and that may perhaps be the reason why St. Mark so rarely writes " Jesus." Peter would be content with " He " : there could be no question who was meant. In one passage in particular, i. 29, " they left the synagogue and came into the house of Simon and Andrew with James and John," the hypothesis that the third person plural of Mark represents a first person plural of Peter makes what as it stands is a curiously awkward phrase into a phrase which is quite easy and coherent. " We left the synagogue and came into our house with our fellow-disciples James and John. My mother-in-law was in bed with fever, and he is told about her. ..." So too, i. 16, " He saw me and Andrew my brother " ' (*Journal of Theological Studies*, xxv., April 1925, p. 226). I notice, however, that Professor Turner is not original here. His observations as to this passage have been anticipated by Zahn, Schmidt (*Rahmen*, p. 56), and Klostermann.

31. Jesus touches the sick patient. This is the usual procedure in Mark.

34. The demons are again ordered to keep silent for the same reason as in 25.

35–39. FURTHER ACTIVITIES IN GALILEE
(*Cp.* Matt. iv. 23–25 ; Luke iv. 42–44)

35 And in the morning, very early, before the dawn, he rose up, and left the house, and went to a solitary place, and there prayed. 37 And Simon and his companions pursued him. And when they

38 found him, they said unto him, ' All seek for thee.' And he said
unto them, ' Let us go elsewhere, into the neighbouring villages,
39 that I may preach there also : for to that end I came out.' And
he went and preached in their synagogues throughout all Galilee,
and cast out demons.

35. What was the reason for the action of Jesus ? Some think
that Jesus wished to avoid the crowd and the ' Jewish ' desire for
miracles. Is there adequate evidence for this ? One object of his
leaving the house early was to pray, as his wont was, out of doors
in a lonely place. And if he then, instead of returning to the
village, goes elsewhere in Galilee, he goes on a preaching tour in the
district and expels the demons. There is no sign of any wish to
avoid publicity. He does not want to be detained in Capernaum,
it is true, but he does want to preach and heal elsewhere.

Other commentators take other views. One, for instance, draws
a sharp distinction between ' healings ' and exorcisms. Jesus was
always ready to do the latter ; they belonged to his mission.
' Healings ' hindered it ; for preaching was his real work. He
therefore takes flight in order to resume his preaching. Some think
(as I have suggested above) that he merely meant that Capernaum
must not selfishly monopolize his attention. The commentators
forget that we have no stenographic report, and that we cannot put
any reliance on casual phrases, all the more as Mark has his theories
and his theology. There may be some intention to indicate that
the Messiahship might be prematurely revealed if Jesus remained
too long in one place. The desire and practice of solitary prayer
are to be noticed : they are doubtless authentic. But the words of
Jesus in 38 are probably secondary or redactional. For 35-39 is a
passage which, in contrast to the older tradition, contains no
' single scene ' story or definite saying, but is either arranged as a
transition, or describes habitual practices of Jesus—his solitary
prayers and his constant moving about from place to place
(Bultmann, p. 94). Schmidt, however, thinks that only 39 is
redactional (p. 59).

38. ἐξῆλθον. ' I came out.' What does the word mean ?
According to Harnack, the immense probability is that it merely
resumes the same word in 35 (ἐξῆλθεν). ' Jesus left the house or
city.' Luke, however, saw in the word a deeper meaning : he
substitutes for ἐξῆλθον the word ἀπεστάλην. If Luke's substitution
be right, ἐξῆλθον would mean, ' For this end have I come forth,
have I been sent out.' This, says Klostermann, is certainly what
Mark intended the word to signify.

40-45. THE HEALING OF THE LEPER

(*Cp.* Matt. viii. 1-4 ; Luke v. 12-16)

40 And there came a leper to him, beseeching him, and kneeling
down to him, and saying unto him, ' If thou wilt, thou canst make
41 me clean.' And Jesus, moved with compassion, put forth his hand,
42 and touched him, and said unto him, ' I will ; be cleansed.' And
immediately the leprosy departed from him, and he was cleansed.
43 And he sternly charged him, and forthwith sent him out, and said
44 unto him, ' See thou say nothing to any man : but go, shew thyself
to the priest, and offer for thy cleansing what Moses commanded,
45 for a testimony unto them.' But when he went out, he began to
publish it much, and to spread the story abroad, so that Jesus
could no more openly enter into any city, but he remained outside
in lonely places : and they came to him from every quarter.

Can leprosy be conceivably healed in this psychic fashion ? On
the reply would depend whether the story is to be regarded as
historic or legendary. See also Abrahams, *Studies* I. chap. xiii.

41. The leper apparently enters a house in which Jesus is.
(It is improbable that a synagogue is intended.) In doing so he
violated the law, but Jesus, before he deals with that, shows, first
of all, compassion. He too, apparently, violates the law in as much
as he touches the man in order to heal him. Here we begin to catch
the new note in the ministry of Jesus : his intense compassion for
the outcast, the sufferer, who, by his sin, or by his suffering, which
was too often regarded as the result of sin, had put himself outside
respectable Jewish society, who found himself rejected and despised
by man, and believed himself rejected and despised by God. Here
was a new and lofty note, a new and exquisite manifestation of the
very pity and love which the prophets had demanded.

43. ' Sternly charged.' So R.V. M. (ἐμβριμησάμενος). The
explanations are endless. Does the word mean merely a solemn
order, or does it imply annoyance or anger ? It is possible, moreover, that the true reading in 41 may not be σπλαγχνισθείς, ' moved
with pity,' but ὀργισθείς, ' moved with anger,' some think at the
flattery involved in ' if thou wilt.' See on the whole matter,
Rawlinson's note, p. 256. If anger, at what is Jesus angry ?

(1) Does he rebuke the man because he violated the Law by
entering the room ?
(2) Is he annoyed because he is afraid that endless lepers

will be brought to him for healing, and that his preaching and proper ministry will be interfered with ? or

(3) Is the ' stern charging ' merely meant to accentuate the usual order of silence ?

Another explanation can be read in Goguel, i. p. 314, n. i.

44. 'For a testimony unto them.' This may mean (a) that they may know that the man is cured, or (b) that they may see that Jesus wants the healed man to observe the Law, and does not himself desire to transgress it, whenever no higher duty is involved, or (c) that they may realize that the new Teacher has received a divine commission for the healing of disease.

45. Jesus is reported here to avoid all cities and villages. This is scarcely historic. It is on a par with those orders for concealment, which, constantly repeated, and as constantly disobeyed, are part of the theory and conception which control the Gospel of Mark. Schmidt does not agree. He would take 45 as belonging to the original story ; at the most he would exclude from $\overset{\sim}{\omega}\sigma\tau\epsilon$ to $\mathring{\eta}\nu$. The word $\phi\alpha\nu\epsilon\rho\hat{\omega}s$ is odd, and the $\mathring{\alpha}\lambda\lambda'$ $\overset{\prime}{\epsilon}\xi\omega$ seq. is really in contradiction to it, for if he could not enter a city $\phi\alpha\nu\epsilon\rho\hat{\omega}s$, he ought to enter it stealthily. It may be a later addition to smooth over the difficulty (tant bien que mal) that in ii. 1 Jesus is again in a city (p. 66).

In the leper story we have the first (or, counting the call of the four disciples, the second) of the many stories in which Jesus does actions which are either like, but excelling, actions attributed to Elijah and Elisha, or which are in marked contrast to their actions. It is not to be inferred that the stories are, therefore, historically baseless, but it would be no less exaggerated (in my opinion) to declare that the Elijah and Elisha stories have had no influence upon the form of the stories as we now possess them in the Gospels.

CHAPTER II

1–12. HEALING OF THE PARALYTIC MAN

(*Cp.* Matt. ix. 1–8 ; Luke v. 17–26)

1 And when, some days after, he returned to Capernaum, it was
2 reported that he was in the house. And many collected together,
so that there was no room to hold them even before the door ; and
3 he spoke the Word unto them. And some came unto him, bringing
4 a paralysed man, who was carried by four. And as they could not
bring the man up to Jesus on account of the crowd, they took him
on to the roof of the house where Jesus was, and having made a hole
through it, they let down the bed whereon the paralysed man lay.
5 When Jesus saw their faith, he said unto the paralysed man, ' Son,
6 thy sins are forgiven thee.' But some scribes were sitting there,
7 who argued in their hearts, ' Why does this man speak thus ? He
8 blasphemes. Who can forgive sins but God alone ? ' And immediately Jesus perceived in his spirit that they so argued within
themselves, and he said unto them, ' Why argue ye thus in your
9 hearts ? Which is easier : to say to the paralysed man, Thy sins
are forgiven thee ; or to say, Arise, and take up thy bed and walk ?
10 But that ye may see that the Son of man has power on earth to
11 forgive sins ' (he said to the paralysed man), ' I say unto thee, Arise,
12 and take up thy bed, and go home.' And he arose, and at once took
up the bed, and went forth before them all ; so that they were all
utterly amazed, and glorified God, saying, ' We never saw anything
like this before.'

A new type of story is here presented, of which there are several
examples. They are the stories which record conflicts, discussions,
or disputes between Jesus and the ' Scribes and Pharisees.' Naturally, in these disputes and conflicts the Rabbis and Pharisees always
get the worst of it. The object of the stories is to show the superior
wisdom, righteousness, or power of Jesus, and in the second place to

prepare the way for the *dénouement* of the whole ministry. On account of these disputes the Rabbis and Pharisees become more and more incensed against Jesus, and ultimately bring about his death. There is doubtless a measure of truth in this conception and representation. Jesus *did* have these disputes and conflicts, and his point of view was often, as we shall see, a more prophetic point of view, and as we should now think, a higher point of view, than that of the Rabbis. Yet whether the conflicts and disputes took the exact shape that Mark gives to them may well be doubted. These stories are idealized memories or traditions, and we may be sure that the part which Jesus took in them is not allowed to be less successful than it actually was, or the part which the Rabbis took in them less shabby or disagreeable ! The hero would tend to be exalted ; the opponents depressed and depreciated. No stenographer accompanied Jesus or his disciples. We depend on memory. Moreover, these stories were not collected and written down for the purpose of a scientific biography. The actual purposes were quite different. The stories were put together in the first instance for the needs of preaching or for the needs of controversy, and even when the ' Gospel ' of Mark was compiled, it was compiled for edification rather than for history. The stories are types : how far each one actually happened can never be ascertained. How far they have been touched up can never be known. One can argue for their authenticity ; one can argue for their unauthenticity. And every conceivable argument has been employed. Some of the stories are more credible than others.

The story in ii. 1–12 is unlike any of the other stories. Most of the stories deal with the attitude of Jesus towards the Law. This story deals with the question of the forgiveness of sins. Jesus apparently claims the power to forgive sins, a power which he never elsewhere claims in Mark, and never elsewhere in the Synoptic Gospels except in Luke vii. 47. (I naturally do not count the parallels to the Mark story in Matthew and Luke.)

There are many questions connected with the story, and all of them are difficult and disputed. In a general commentary it would be necessary to deal with all of them at great length. It is right that I should pass most of them by very briefly.

(1) Is the story all of a piece ? Was the forgiveness of sins originally mentioned at all ? Many think not. If from 5*a*, ' He said unto the paralysed man,' we jump to 11 and continue, ' I say unto thee, Arise, and take up thy bed, and go home,' we get a homogeneous story of healing with which verse 12 fits in better than it fits in with the story as it is now arranged. And there are other arguments for the hypothesis

that 5*b* to 10 are an interpolation, which can be read in the commentaries and in Bultmann. It is not, however, very easy to see why, or for what end, on the hypothesis of interpolation, the interpolation was made. Did the early Christian community make any claim to possess the power to forgive sins ? Was the healing of disease used as the evidence of that power, or was the power inferred as the result of the healing ? And did the community seek to show that this connection between healing and the forgiveness of sin had already been touched upon by Jesus, and that the community was only exercising a power which the Master and Founder had already exercised and had conferred upon his ' church ' ? The question is obscure.

(2) How is forgiveness of sins connected with paralysis and its healing ? If we assume that all diseases were looked upon as the punishment of sin, then a diseased person is *ipso facto* a sinful person. This conception is not elsewhere alluded to in the Synoptic Gospels. In John ix. 2, 3 it is partially combated. Here Jesus appears to adopt it. And if he says to the man, ' Thy sins are forgiven,' it is assumed that the proof of the forgiveness will follow—namely, the man will be healed.

(3) It is, however, remarkable (though I do not think that it has been much noticed), that this is the only healing story in which the opponents take exception to the forgiveness of sin, and yet, on the theory that disease implies sin, every healing would appear to include such forgiveness. On the whole, it would seem that though in *theory* disease implied sin, this theory was not usually applied. Otherwise, why is it alluded to so seldom ? Forgiveness of sin is a much more striking thing than healing of diseases. If the second always brought the first to mind, one would imagine that we should have heard at least as much about the forgiveness as about the healing. Indeed, if every healing necessarily implies a forgiveness, is not every healing a blasphemy ? But the Rabbinic opponents of Jesus never seem to hint at this. Apparently, therefore, in actual fact and life, disease and sin, healing and forgiveness, were not so clearly united together as in theory they should have been. Why has forgiveness of sins been specially connected with this particular man ? In the case of the other palsy cure (Matt. viii. 6, 13) sin is not mentioned.

I need not quote the Rabbinic texts : they are given in Strack-Billerbeck (S. B.), and it must be admitted that the theory that suffering or disease implied sin was the prevailing Rabbinic doctrine, at all events in the later centuries. One Rabbi states categorically (R. Ammi, about A.D. 300) that there is no death without guilt, no (bodily) suffering without sin.

And another, R. Alexandrai (same date), declares that no man gets up from his sickness till God has forgiven all his sins. In practice, however, it would seem that the combination was less pressed, else it would surely have been more often alluded to in the Gospels. Why it is brought forward in this story is unclear. Klausner's interpretation of the passage is peculiar. It says in the Talmud, ' Sufferings (*i.e.* bodily sufferings) cleanse a man from all sins.' Hence Klausner supposes that what Jesus meant was that because the man was suffering, he had *already been* pardoned by God. Jesus merely announces a fact, but the Pharisees misunderstand him. This seems very doubtful (p. 277 *fin.*).

(4) What is implied in the words of Jesus, ' Thy sins are forgiven thee ' ? Does Jesus say this in virtue of his Messiahship ? Does he mean that to him and him alone has this power been given by God ? Or does he mean something more ? Here we touch upon a point which raises a moral question interesting for our own time. Clearly Mark—the writer of the story as we have it—meant us to understand that Jesus ascribed this power to himself because of his special office. He was the Messiah, the Son of God, and to him alone had this power been delegated by God. For the words ' the Son of man ' as here used *by* Mark mean *to* Mark the Messiah. (As to this mysterious appellation, see below.) But when we turn to the version of our story in Matthew, we find as Matthew's equivalent of Mark ii. 12 the following : ' When the crowd saw it, they were afraid, and glorified God, who had given *such power unto men.*' Now Son of man is an admittedly false, though literal, translation of the Aramaic original. Son of man in Aramaic idiom means merely man. If Jesus called himself in Aramaic by the words which the Greek renders by ' Son of man,' he called himself not ' Son of man,' or ' the Son of man,' but ' Man,' or ' the Man.' Further, it is quite possible that in many places where the Greek translators or compilers thought that Jesus was referring to himself, he was not referring to himself at all, but to *man*, to man in general. Thus in Mark ii. 28, it is quite possible that the real meaning of the verse is : ' The Sabbath was made for man, and not man for the Sabbath ; therefore man (man generally, not ' The Man,' *i.e.* Jesus) is lord of the Sabbath.' And here, in our story, Jesus, or even the interpolator, may have meant to say ' That you may see that man (man generally, not merely Jesus) has the power to forgive sins,' etc. He would not mean that every man has this power, but that some men *can* have it, can exercise, can be invested with it.

How, however, on this hypothesis, have ' men ' won or got

this power ? Surely Jesus or the story-teller can only have meant by the permission of God, or as the messengers and announcers of God's will. They could not have meant that men had an independent power, parallel with God's power. It is conceivable that if the passage 5*b* to 10 be an interpolation, that the Christian community is here vindicating its power to forgive sins as shown in the healing powers which were practised by it. The community justifies its own coordination or combination of forgiveness with healing by asserting that Jesus had done the same.

It should be observed that the editors of ' *Beginnings* ' are among those who believe that ' Son of man ' is here a mis-understanding of the Aramaic *Bar-nasha*, and that Jesus was speaking about man and not about himself. They say : ' There is no trace in the story that Jesus was claiming to have power denied to other men, though no doubt the evangelists inter-preted his saying in that way, and therefore perpetuated it. The objection of the Pharisees was that Jesus, being human, was blasphemously arrogating to himself divine power by a claim, unsupported by proof, to forgive sin ; his answer was to cure the paralytic, and allege that this was a proof not that he was divine, but that the claim to forgive sin was within human competence' (p. 379). I very much doubt whether this interpretation can be accurate. Meyer argues strongly against it, and believes that it introduces conceptions about sin and forgiveness which were foreign to both Judaism and Christianity. The power to forgive sin has been delegated by God to the Messiah, but is certainly not inherent in man or in any indefinite body of men (I. p. 104). Yet it is argued that if Jesus used the word ' man,' the Scribes (on the hypothesis that the passage is authentic and an exact reproduction of a scene which happened) could *only* have thought that he meant man gener-ally, or some men, and not himself. For the argument is that (1) Jesus had not thus early in his ministry begun to use the term ' the man ' of himself, or (2) that he used it only secretly and to his disciples, or (3) that he never used it at all, and (4) that it was a later misunderstanding which caused it to be applied to him. Matt. ix. 8 shows, however—so it is argued— what Jesus meant. All these arguments seem to me somewhat doubtful. The words in Matt. ix. 8 (' who had given such power unto men ') may, as Meyer urges, only refer to the healing and not to the forgiveness of sins. And in any case the real point at issue between the Scribes and Jesus was not as to the possible powers of man, but as to the actual powers of Jesus himself. Jesus is not concerned to champion the possible powers and prerogatives of exceptional men as men; he is concerned to champion and prove his own. He wants to prove that he *has* power to forgive sin, and surely not as man (this is too modern an idea), but as the commissioned officer and delegate of God, perhaps even definitely as the Messiah. It is not unreasonable to suppose that, if anything resembling this tale really happened in the early days of his ministry, Jesus should have said, ' To show you that *I* have power to forgive sins, I say to this man,' etc., and that afterwards ' Son of man,' when it became a recognized title for Jesus, was substituted in the written account of the story for ' I.' But it seems improbable that Jesus, at such a juncture and moment, wanted and meant to assert that man, or some men, or specially privileged men, as apart from, or in addition to, himself, possessed the power and the right of forgiveness. Moreover, it should be noted that it is the miraculous power of healing which appears to be used as a proof of the power or commission to forgive sins. Now this power of healing which proves the power of forgiveness can hardly be regarded as within the range of general human capacity. Because *Jesus* is invested with the divine power of working a miracle, therefore it is reasonable that he should claim and possess the power of forgiveness of sins. Hence it would seem as if Jesus grounded his power and right to forgive sins, not on the fact that such a power was within the range of man's capacity and privileges, but because he had special power, above the power of man. The power to forgive sins is connected with the power to work miracles. The latter is the greater power in the eyes of those addressed; it is a power exceeding the usual powers of man, a power only belonging to an exceptional man, and as such he may already have regarded himself. Yet he, Jesus, does not say, ' *I* forgive you your sins,' but (maintaining the exclusive rights of God), ' Your sins are forgiven.' He probably meant to speak as the confidant of God, as the proclaimer of His grace and love, as the bearer of His revelation.

(5) How far were the Scribes justified in saying that Jesus blasphemed ? Let us assume that Jesus said the words—that the story is entirely authentic. He certainly did not mean to ascribe to himself a power independent of God. In all things he acted as God's delegate or commissioner. He acted in a particular way because he believed that God had empowered or inspired him so to act. Therefore, it is not likely that he meant that to men generally, or to some men, had been given this power. In spite of Matt. ix. 8 I think that he meant, ' thy sins have been forgiven thee by God,'

not ' *I* independently, and of my own authority, forgive thee thy sins.' (This is the view, I observe, strongly pressed by Windisch in his admirable pamphlet, *De gegenwoordige stand van het Christusprobleem*, 2nd ed., 1925, pp. 24, 70, 71. Jesus speaks as a prophet. He knows, just because he is God's messenger, that God has forgiven the man's sins. So Nathan knew that God had forgiven David (2 Sam. xii. 13). The Rabbis misunderstood the assertions which Jesus made. The meaning of the historic Jesus in the story as it actually took place was limited to this assertion. Mark, doubtless, meant more, and the story, as he gives it, partly reflects this additional meaning.) If Jesus said Luke vii. 47, 48, then I think that here too he meant the same thing. But the Scribes might easily misunderstand him. For the forgiveness of sins is indeed God's prerogative and God's alone. If a man in the strict theological sense were to say ' *I* forgive you your sin,' then the Scribes would be justified from the Jewish point of view in saying of him, He blasphemes. What, if we press the story a little, and assume it all to be authentic (which I doubt), we may conceive Jesus to have meant was, perhaps, something like this. He recognized and perceived in himself this strange power of healing, which he believed God had granted him for special and peculiar ends. He shared the usual belief that special maladies, such as paralysis, implied previous sin. But he was also filled with compassion for these poor sinners, many of whom were, he thought, more sinned against than sinning, while others had perhaps only violated some difficult ordinance of the ritual law. He looked into their souls and saw, or thought he saw, characters which were not in themselves essentially wicked ; characters which were capable of, as they were worth, a moral and religious regeneration. Combining these factors, we may understand how Jesus came to say, ' Thy sins are for-given '; he says it as the human messenger of God ; he says it because he knows that he can prove it (by his healing), and because he believes that the healing and forgiveness are part of the mission which God has entrusted to him at this supreme moment of the history of his race. We may note again that Jesus does not say : ' *I* forgive you your sins,' but, maintaining the divine prerogative of forgiveness, ' Thy sins are for-given.' (*Cp.* Holtzmann, *Neutestamentliche Theologie*, vol. i. p. 299, n. 3, 1911.) (Doubtless *Mark* means more than a sense of mere delegation. ' *Mark* did not intend that Jesus was a mere announcer of divine forgiveness, but that Jesus of him-self forgave sins ' (Klostermann). He did this because he was divine, not, indeed, divine in the sense of the Athanasian creed, but yet more than a prophet, more than a man, the Son of God, on whom the spirit had descended, in whom it had entered.) But the Scribes could not appreciate all this, nor was it unreasonable on their part to disbelieve it. Even miracles were suspicious, and might have other origins than the will of God. Their integrity need have been no less than the integrity of Jesus, though he could not appreciate them, and they could not appreciate him. Each side called the other bad names, and from one point of view each, and from another point of view neither, was justified in doing so.

For any Christian readers of my book, it may be still worth while to add that it would be false to suppose that the reason why the Scribes were indignant was because they thought that sin could only be forgiven by offering a sacrifice and having absolution formally pronounced by the priest. This misrepresents the Rabbinic religion and even the Priestly Code of the Pentateuch. Deliberate sin could not be forgiven by a sacrifice ; nor did its forgiveness need sacrifice, whether in Jerusalem or in Galilee. The ground of opposition to Jesus was that he claimed to himself the prerogative of God. It had nothing to do with sacrifice. No less absurd is the notion that according to ' the Pharisaic religion ' God himself could and does not forgive from free grace, but requires every sin to be paid off and worked off by good works and expiatory sufferings (so Pfleiderer). This sounds almost grotesque to those who know something about the inner reality of the Pharisaic and ' legal ' religion from the age of Jesus to the present day. It is a calumny to say that what Jesus said and did was in accordance with the religion of the prophets and the Psalms, but in contradiction to the ' legal ' religion of the Pharisees. Nothing can be proved by more abundant and overwhelming evidence than that the conception of God as forgiving from free grace was a fundamental and familiar feature of the Pharisaic and Rabbinic religion, just as it still remains so. The only question at issue between Jesus and the Rabbis was whether any *man* had the power to say, ' Thy sins are forgiven.' That God constantly forgave, that forgiveness was his usual, if exclusive, *métier*, was universally believed. The reader should carefully peruse Dr. Abrahams' *Studies* I. chapters xix., xx., ' God's Forgiveness and Man's Forgiveness.' It is important to note that it is *simply not true* that the Rabbis held that a sinner could not be forgiven by God until he had achieved merit by works of the law, and it is a pity that so great a scholar as Bacon, misled by Weber (how many has he misled !), should repeat that error. (Bacon, *The Beginnings of Gospel Story*, 1909, p. 27.)

(6) Some commentators, theologians, and teachers, however, press the interpretation 'men' further still, and it is just here that a question of modern interest comes in.   Thus Dr. Drummond, the distinguished Unitarian divine, held that Jesus on this occasion did make 'this high claim on behalf of mankind.' The authority to forgive is by Jesus 'included among the prerogatives of mankind, which each man must exercise according to the nature and extent of his gift.'   Dr. Drummond goes on to say, 'The look that pierces the heart, the gentle words of forgiveness, may heal the suffering of a sinful life, even as Christ healed the sinful woman whom the Pharisees, scandalized at this contact with sin and tampering with the rights of God, would have driven to despair and ruin.   How many die in their sins because men take upon themselves not to forgive ?   He who lives with a holy piety in his heart is, wherever he goes, a dispenser of divine grace, and pronounces forgiveness with a God-given authority. .Scribes and Pharisees may call this blasphemy if they please ; but such, I believe, was the thought of Christ.' (' Use and Meaning of the phrase " Son of Man " in the Synoptic Gospels,' *Journal of Theological Studies*, 1901, pp. 539–571). What are we to say to this doctrine ?   I am inclined to think it is too modern.   'Forgiveness' to a Jew of the age of Jesus, and even to Jesus himself, had a human and a divine side.   One man could forgive the wrong which another had done to him.   That side of forgiveness is not here in question. On its divine side forgiveness meant the abrogation of the present or future result of the sin upon the doer.   In some cases, therefore, it meant that man was not to be 'punished' or 'annihilated' after death ; in others, as in the story before us, it meant that the present consequence of sin (in this case the man's paralysis) would be removed.   Either of these meanings lay within the divine sphere.

Nevertheless, Dr. Drummond's remarks may not be wholly without justification.   It is, perhaps, not too modern to suppose that Jesus so profoundly pitied certain kinds of 'sinners,' and that his insight into the recuperative capacities of the soul was so keen, that he was able by his encouragement and sympathy to awaken their sense of the redemptive love of God and hitherto unsuspected powers of moral regeneration. He hated sin, but he loved the sinner.   It is, to some extent, a question of words.   If Jesus said : 'Your sin is forgiven, lead a new life from now,' it meant, perhaps, much the same as if a modern disciple of his were to say, 'Do not think yourself an outcast from God's pity or God's love.   Do not think yourself an outcast from human pity and human love.   You

can lead a better life : God will *help* you to do so. Forget the
evil past, and we will forget too. We will forgive you, so far
as our human action and love are concerned, and if you start
afresh, God, I feel sure, will also forgive your past iniquity.'
If a man spoke thus to-day, and spoke thus from his heart and
not merely from his lips—spoke with all the magic of a strong
and loving personality, would there be so much difference
between his words and what we may conjecture to have been
the meaning of Jesus, if the *kind of* words attributed to him in
verse 5 be authentic ? Dr. Abbott held that Jesus did indeed
give this power unto men. His book, *Through Nature to Christ*
(1877), which seems to me (if I may venture to criticize the
work of a man so many times wiser, abler, and more learned
than I) to be one-sided in its treatment both of the ' Scribes
and Pharisees ' on the one hand, and of Jesus upon the other,
is perhaps nowhere more interesting and suggestive than in the
treatment of forgiveness (chapters XIII. and XVI.). Dr. Abbott
urges that forgiveness means far more than merely giving up a
penalty. The forgiver ' must spiritually lift up the person he
forgives,' and he does this by a certain attitude of his own mind.
He must have a hatred of sin, a love of man, and a faith in God
as the Father of men, a faith in men as the children of God.
By his sympathy, faith, and spiritual force he can confirm and
strengthen the weak and wavering repentance of a sinner. If
such a man is a father, and ' accepts his child's contrition and
repentance, though it be for a sin not committed directly against
himself, and tells the little one that he is forgiven, and that now
he will be a good child and sin no more like that again—is the
father overstepping the bounds of the duties of fatherhood, or
is the child wrong in going its way with its heart at rest and
with a sense of burden lightened and peace restored ? Surely
we are bound to admit that every human being, so far as he
has the powers that naturally go to make up the forgiving act—
I mean love, trust, self-subordination, and hatred of sin—
must also have the power of forgiving sins, not only in his own
name, but also in the name of society, and even in the name of
God Himself. And if this be so between father and children,
then it must be within the experience of all that there are
persons so highly endowed with the spiritual gifts of faith and
love and the hatred of sin that they tower above the ordinary
average man as much as fathers above their children. Such
men must be recognized as specially adapted by nature, that is
by God, for the divine task of forgiving.' Such men's ' hopes
will be purer and higher,' their ' hatred of selfishness and of
meanness will be more intense,' their ' sympathy with the

wretched and sinful more powerful,' their 'judgment at once more just and more charitable than in ordinary men. Now such men as these cannot live without lifting up those with whom they live. You go forth from their presence refreshed, with a distinct sense of having been lightened of a burden of selfishness, with better hopes, better aims, with a wholesome self-reproach leading to a wholesome self-respect. A few such men can make a great nation or a great church. But every one has, or may have, something of this power; and it was this power that Jesus came to give to common men. It might have been described as the power of love, or the power of faith, or the power of hope; but any one of these terms would have been inadequate. Forgiveness supposes and includes them all, and exhibits them all in action.' These suggestive and eloquent words may conceivably give some explanation of the power claimed and exercised by Jesus in the forgiveness of sins. On the whole they seem too modern. They may perhaps apply to some extent to Luke vii. 36–50, but they hardly apply so well to the story before us now. The great point in this story is the miracle. It is this which proves, and indeed *is*, the forgiveness. Jesus does not even say to the man, 'Go, and sin no more.' He seems especially concerned in exhibiting his peculiar and miraculous power, such as he only could exercise. And it should once more be noted that nowhere else in the Gospels is this power of the forgiveness of sins ascribed to 'man' or claimed by Jesus, except in Luke vii. 47. It is never made the ground of any 'Pharisaic' attack upon Jesus. In 12 what amazes everybody is clearly the healing miracle; the forgiveness is not alluded to at all. That seems to point to 5*b*–10 being an interpolation. And, as has been well said by Loisy: 'The remission of sins by the Christ finds its place more naturally in the cycle of Christian ideas than in the teaching of Jesus' (*E. S.* i. p. 476).

(7) Finally, however, we must confess that the difficulties which the story presents can hardly be overcome whatever line of explanation be adopted. This is fully conceded in the new edition of 'Die Schriften des neuen Testaments,' in which J. Weiss's contribution was revised by Bousset (1917). (That distinguished scholar has now also passed away.) Thus (*a*) if Jesus accepted the view that all sickness and bodily evil imply sin, why is this view only here referred to? If, on the other hand, this is an exceptional case (of illness being the result of sin), why is this not mentioned by the evangelist? (*b*) How can Jesus really teach and believe that to heal the body is a greater, harder thing than to heal the soul and to forgive sin? (*c*) If we reject the 'man' explanation, the

story says that Jesus announced forgiveness in virtue of his
Messiahship. But in Mark he does not proclaim his Messiahship till towards the end of his career at the entry into Jerusalem. Not before the scene at Caesarea Philippi does he
even confess it to the apostles. (d) If Jesus claimed here to
be the Messiah and Son of man, and the first because the second,
he and all those present could only have thought of the figure
in Daniel, which by this time had been interpreted to mean the
Messiah, but a transcendent, semi-divine Messiah, who would
come down from heaven upon the earth. Could Jesus have
spoken about himself at this early stage as the Messiah in this
sense ?   And indeed he would not and could not be *this* Messiah
till he had died and risen. But in this sense he was not yet the
Son of man : could he have spoken of himself as the Son of man
in the Future, who exercised authority and power to forgive
sins, because he would be Messiah hereafter ?   Improbability
is here piled upon improbability. If the ' man ' interpretation
be followed, why does Jesus perform a great miracle of healing
in order to prove that ' man ' in general has the power of
forgiveness ?

As a result of all these difficulties the conclusion must be
that the story has been so altered by later theological needs and
reflections (*dogmatisch so stark übermalt*) that the original form
of it can hardly be recovered.

1.   Jesus is again in a city and in a house. The remark in i. 45
that he could not enter into any city is ignored. He takes no
precautions for concealment (Goguel, 1. p. 310).

9.   ' Which is easier.' Apparently the meaning is that the
crucial test is the healing. If Jesus can heal the man, it will be
proved by the very fact of the healing that he has the power to
forgive sins. If the man is cured, it is obvious that his sins have
been forgiven. It is easier to say, ' Thy sins are forgiven ' than
' Take up thy bed and walk,' for the mere forgiveness could not be
tested (apart from the healing no one could say whether the sins
have been forgiven or no), but by what would follow upon the
bidding ' Take up thy bed ' it will immediately be seen whether
Jesus is an impostor or not.

' Take up thy bed.' We must suppose the ' bed ' is a mere light
mattress. The probable or possible combination or mixture of
truth and legend in such tales as the one before us is well dealt with
by Fiebig in his *Jüdische Wundergeschichten im neutestamentlichen
Zeitalter*, pp. 93, 94 (1911).

10.   The awkward construction in 10, indicated by the bracketed

words in the translation, point *pro tanto* to the interpolation theory. Jesus begins, by addressing the Scribes, a sentence which he ends by addressing the paralysed man. The commentators say, remarks Loisy, in his ironic manner : '*Trait pris sur le vif !*' But this supposed 'vivacity' of the narrative is more probably a *gaucherie* of the redactor.

'Son of man.' It is needless for me to enter fully into the interminable discussions which this term has produced, but a note about it is appended to this chapter.

12.   'He took up his bed.' Precisely the same proof of a healing miracle is told by Lucian. See the quotation in Klostermann.

13-17.   THE CALL OF LEVI—JESUS EATS WITH SINNERS AND TAX-COLLECTORS

(*Cp.* Matt. ix. 9–13 ; Luke v. 27–32)

13 And he went forth again by the lake side ; and all the crowd
14 resorted unto him, and he taught them. And as he passed by, he
saw Levi the son of Alphaeus sitting at the tax-house, and he said
15 unto him, 'Follow me.' And he arose and followed him. And it
came to pass, that Jesus sat at table in his house, and many tax-
collectors and sinners sat also with Jesus and his disciples : for
16 there were many who followed him. And when the scribes of the
Pharisees saw him eat with tax-collectors and sinners, they said
unto his disciples, 'Why does he eat with tax-collectors and
17 sinners ?' And Jesus heard it and said unto them, 'The strong
have no need of the physician, but they that are sick : I came not
to call the righteous, but the sinners.'

13.   The call of Levi is related in the same way as the call of the first four apostles. The one story may be a variant of the other.

15.   Here the disciples as a body, first appear, so the editor has to explain that those who 'followed him were numerous.' The scene at the dining-table is apparently supposed to have taken place at Levi's house, not necessarily immediately after the 'call.' Jesus has already many disciples. The story may be historic ; or it may have been invented as a setting to the authentic saying of 17. 'Scribes of the Pharisees' is an odd term. We may note that Scribes or Pharisees appear and disappear, just as the compiler requires them. They are part of the stage-property and scenery,

like ' the house ' and ' the mountain.' Here their presence is very awkward. Did they come unbidden to a banquet ? Matthew and Luke, each in his own way, try to make their presence less difficult. That, however, Jesus may have eaten with tax-collectors and ' sinners ' is likely enough and probably authentic.

Who were the ' sinners ' ? This question is exceedingly important and exceedingly hard. We may, however, suppose that we get sufficiently near the truth if we assume that the sinners were persons who knowingly violated, or were believed to violate, some enactments of the Law, whether ceremonial or moral. The tax-collectors had a bad moral reputation. Useful remarks about them may be read in Klausner, pp. 161, 187. From the Rabbinic point of view to violate a ritual law (e.g. the law not to eat rabbits) was a sin, and to violate a moral law was also a sin. Habitually to violate a ceremonial law when one could fulfil it was a very grievous sin. Jesus, like the prophets of old, put the moral laws far above the ceremonial laws, yet in spite of vii. 15 it is doubtful whether he would have deliberately said to any man : ' You need not bother about the food laws of Leviticus,' and still less, ' You need not observe the Sabbath.' So far then we may suppose that the man who was a sinner in the eyes of the Rabbis and the Pharisees was a sinner also in his. But something more must be added. An impression is given by the Gospels that these violations of the Law were in many cases not violations with a high hand. At any rate, men did not violate the ceremonial laws as a man might do to-day simply because he did not believe that these laws were divine or binding. We have the impression that some sinned consciously, but also, in a sense, regretfully. Moreover, it seems to be implied that their sin, whether moral or ceremonial, had put them out of the pale of respectable society, so that they tended to become yet more hardened in their sin. They tended to become an outcast class, a class apart, for whom the observant and respectable classes did not have any regard, whom they despised and condemned. Thus they became the more wedded to, and hardened in, their ' sinful ' ways. They could hardly change even if they would. Who was there to help them and care for them ? Who was there to urge them to repent and change their method of life ? So they lived more or less to themselves, a fringe upon ordinary society, outside its pale. There are indications in the Talmud that such a class of ' sinners ' may have really existed in the days of Jesus, and that after the destruction of the state, and after the awful revolt and persecution under Hadrian and Trajan, this class disappeared. For after Hadrian no one was likely to remain a Jew who did not *try* at least to follow the Law : a despised fringe would have drifted entirely away. But the subject is extremely obscure and very disputed. Yet for the days and the environment of Jesus something of what I have described must, I think, have existed. The picture in the Gospels both of what Jesus did, and the society among which he moved, was not merely invented. It is in its main features historic. And the saying of Jesus in 17 aptly and historically describes a most important part of his character and ministry. He sought to bring back into glad communion with God those whom sin, whether ' moral ' or ' ceremonial,' had driven away. For him sinners (at least certain types of sinners) were the subject, not of condemnation and disdain, but of pity. *He did not avoid sinners, but sought them out.* They were still children of God. This was a new and sublime contribution to the development of religion and morality. When tenderly nurtured women work in the streets of London, and seek to rescue the degraded victims of deception or cruelty, they are truly following in the footsteps of their Master. But it should be noted that there is nothing anti-Jewish in the bearing and teaching of Jesus in this matter. It is only a development of the best Old Testament teaching, and it fits in with the Rabbinic teaching upon repentance. But to deny the greatness and originality of Jesus in this connection, to deny that he opened a new chapter in men's attitude towards sin and sinners, is, I think, to beat the head against a wall. Nevertheless, the Rabbis would not have condemned Jesus merely because he cared for the outcast, the poor, and the sinner. They too welcomed the *repentant* sinner. And they were intensely eager to relieve distress, to mitigate suffering. Any other description of them is untrue. But the Law of God came first. God came before themselves, and even before their neighbour. As Jesus says that a man for the sake of the Kingdom must on occasion leave his father or hate his mother, so they would have said that all other relationships must be put lower than the Law of God. If your father bids you transgress the Law, do not obey him. The enactments by which they developed the written Law were not a benefit to themselves ; they were honestly intended as a fence and honour to the Law. It is all very well to speak (as even Dr. Carpenter does), of ' legal casuistry,' or of ' restraints of the Law ' *versus* ' human need and human rights.' But should not God go before man ? The Law was perfect, immutable, divine. God must know best ; His commands must be perfect, must be divine. Was Jesus to be commended when he said that a man must on occasion hate his father, and are the Rabbis to be *merely* blamed if they say that a sick man whose life is not in danger must be cured on Sunday and not on Saturday, seeing that his cure involved what they, in all honesty and sincerity, believed to be an infraction of the divine Law ? It is easy to speak of ' their sanctimonious piety ' and of ' long-drawn pretence.' But how far more historic to suppose that Jesus, in his new and passionate enthusiasm, misunderstood his opponents ! Jesus would not have been condemned and hated because he cared for the sick and the suffering and the sinful ; he was condemned and hated because he violated the letter of the Law and justified the violation. For the whole subject see Abrahams, *Studies* i. chap. vii., ' Publicans and Sinners.' It is, as I have said, extremely obscure and difficult, but it is also extremely important. Who are the '*Am ha-'Areç*, the people of the land ? That is the question. It cannot be said that Klausner's remarks about them carry us much further or throw much additional light upon the darkness. Nor are they wholly consistent. See his *Life of Jesus*, pp. 194, 196, 214, 222, 225, 276. He says, for instance : ' Most of the village peasants were '*Ammê ha-'Areç* (ignorant of the law).' ' Among the '*Am ha-'Areç* were to be found " breakers of the yoke " [of the Law] who were such owing to their boorishness, ignorance, and dissoluteness.' ' That the Pharisees lauded it over the common people is due to the bad relations between the " chaber " (Pharisee) or " disciple of the wise " and the '*Am ha-'Areç*.' ' The majority of the peasants on the one side and the " students of the wise " (who were also occupied with some handicraft) were pious, God-fearing people.' ' The ordinary people, the average citizen, and a fair proportion of the village folk (though among them the '*Ammê ha-'Areç* predominated) were Pharisees.' ' Hillel drew round him the simple folk, the pious and the unsophisticated, but repelled the boorish '*Am ha-'Areç* who remained obdurate in his boorishness, and such as indulged in exaggerated piety and foolish pietisticism. Jesus, on the other hand, took pleasure in the boorish and every type of the '*Am ha-'Areç*.' ' Multitudes followed after Jesus from all the surrounding towns and villages. They consisted of the class of untaught Jew, the '*Am ha-'Areç*, simple fisherfolk and peasants and, perhaps, inferior tax-gatherers and officials, labourers and journeymen. The majority of the followers were " ignorant of the Law," '*Ammê ha-'Areç* in the Talmudic sense, yet, at the same time, seekers after God, humble in character and ardent in faith. They were not deliberate " sinners," heretics or dissolute, but they failed in that they did not observe the minutiae of the religious laws as did the Pharisees. (Compare the case of the '*Am ha-'Areç* and tithable property, when the '*Am ha-'Areç* is suspect, not because of evil intent, but through ignorance ; and Hillel's axiom, No '*Am ha-'Areç* can be a pious man.)' No clear picture of the '*Am ha-'Areç* can be got from these passages, which seem to me inconsistent with each other. My dear friend, the late Dr. Abrahams, wrote for my second edition a valuable note upon the subject, which gives much of the available material and is entirely impartial.

17. Some Christian commentators, who have a prejudice against Scribes, Rabbis, Pharisees, Legalism, and the Law, are a little worried by this saying of Jesus. One, for instance, is careful to point out that the question is not raised whether any righteous people really existed. Thus Jesus may have meant it merely hypothetically when he said, ' I did not come to call the righteous '; ' supposing such people existed in the world, my business is not with them.' Another supposes that Jesus only really said up to the word ' sick '; the rest is an editorial addition. Or again it has been supposed that Jesus uses the word ' righteous ' ironically. ' You Scribes and Pharisees think yourselves so very righteous ; I need not call you to repentance; you need no doctor (in your own esteem).' Professor Lake, a model of serene impartiality, says simply : ' I cannot see that we have the least reason to suppose that Jesus was ironical when he spoke in this way ' (*The Stewardship of Faith*, p. 28, n. 1, 1915). Mr. Rawlinson, however, has an ingenious note which is perhaps worth quoting. ' To ask whether the saying of our Lord implies the existence of any " righteous " who needed no repentance is a foolish pedantry which misunderstands the character of the context in which both " righteous " and " sinners " are ironical echoes of the terminology of our Lord's opponents.' But Harnack is more interesting. ' The righteous are the righteous without any irony.' Nevertheless, he speaks of them as they ' welche die kultische Rechtbeschaffenheit besitzen.' Doubtless. But no more ? If the words were spoken without irony, it would be monstrous to assume that Jesus meant only this. Yet there is (as I have indicated already) something to be said for Harnack when he designates Jesus's call of sinners as ' einer der grössten Marksteine ' in the history of religion, and as something entirely new. Harnack naturally objects to Luke's addition, ' to repentance,' for the mere summoning of sinners to repentance was by no neans new. Ezekiel and many another prophet has done the same. The nature and peculiarity of Jesus's call are shown in 16. He does not merely summon sinners to repent : he goes among them and heals them : sin is moral disease. Harnack adds : ' wie dieses Rufen zu verstehen ist, lehrt Matt. xi. 28.' (See his article in the *Zeitschrift für Theologie und Kirche*, xxii. pp. 1–30, 1912. But *cp.* also Bultmann, pp. 55, 93, whose scepticism, if excessive, is yet interesting and ingenious.)

18–22. FASTING

(*Cp.* Matt. ix. 14–17 ; Luke v. 33–39)

18   And the disciples of John and the Pharisees used to fast. And some people came and said unto him, ' Why do the disciples of John

19 and of the Pharisees fast, but thy disciples fast not ? ' And Jesus
said unto them, ' Can the wedding guests fast, while the bridegroom
is with them ? As long as they have the bridegroom with them,
20 they cannot fast. But the days will come, when the bridegroom
will be taken away from them, and then they will fast on that day.

21 No man sews a piece of undressed cloth on to an old garment :
for if he do, the patch drags away from it, the new from the old, and
22 the rent is made worse. And no man pours new wine into old wine
skins : for, if he do, the wine bursts the skins, and the wine is lost
as well as the skins. [But new wine for new skins.] '

18. There is much which is obscure and disputed in 18-20, but
from my special point of view I ought to pass all the obscurities over
without remark. For the passage raises no moral or religious
question of interest or value for us to-day. Yet if my notes ought,
at all events, to enable readers to understand the meaning of the
text and its origin and growth, some compressed words must be said.

As the text stands, the reply of Jesus is an allegory. He is the
bridegroom. Bridegroom and wedding feast are regular figures for
allegorical descriptions of Messiah and Messianic age. Jesus then
is bridegroom-Messiah. While he lives, his disciples rejoice. When
he is removed from them, they grieve, and then fasting may be
legitimate. Such an allusion to his death (and to his Messiahship)
by Jesus at this period of his career is open to grave critical objections. The unlikelihood of authenticity is increased by the fact
that the question raised concerns the disciples only. May we suppose
that after Jesus's death his disciples, in disaccord with *his* practice,
began to observe fasts, and took over from John's disciples baptism,
a fixed formula of prayer and fasting ? Hence the permission to
fast after his death is ascribed to Jesus and put into his mouth.
(So Wellhausen.)

It has been supposed that the first sentence of 18 was added to
the story. So too the oddly formed words ' disciples of the Pharisees.' They are not original to the story, and were added to make
it serve as ' the third conflict.'

The saying of Jesus may originally have only included 19a,
' Can the wedding guests fast, while the bridegroom is with them ? '
If, so contracted, the story is authentic, the difficulty about the
bridegroom remains. Bousset suggests that Jesus regarded himself
and his disciples as the guests at the wedding feast of the new era.
His genuine reply ends with the words, ' Can the wedding guests
fast ? ' (*Kurios Christos*, 2nd ed., p. 41, 1921). A dainty conjecture—
but a conjecture !

The saying may have been current and fitted into the story.

And the story may have been devised by the oldest Christian community to justify their *not* fasting.   When they *did* begin to observe fasts, 19b and 20 were added.

Or, again, the substance of the story may be historical, and the reply of Jesus in 19a may be the *substance* of what he said, but not its *form*.   Fasting was not necessary for those who *had* repented, and who *had* accepted the Good Tidings, and who *were* seeking to live the righteous life.   (*Cp.* Bultmann, pp. 8, 104.)

The fasts alluded to were not the official fasts of the Synagogues, but private and additional fasts, voluntarily imposed upon themselves by individuals or groups.   For 'Rabbinic Fasting' see Abrahams, *Studies* I. chap. xvi.

19.   'Wedding-guests.'   This translation, Mr. Mann points out, is inaccurate.   R.V. has the literal 'sons of the bride-chamber.' 'Friends of the bridegroom' appears to be the real meaning. ('Rabbinic Studies in the Synoptic Gospels,' by J. Mann, in *Hebrew Union College Annual*, Vol. I. pp. 335, 336, 1924.)

It is interesting that Burney shows that 'the addition of ἐν ἐκείνῃ τῇ ἡμέρᾳ throws out the rhythm by adding two stresses to the short two-stress member of the *Kina*-verse, and is not found in Matthew' (p. 141).

21, 22.   In the connection in which these adages now stand they may be supposed to mean that the disciples of Jesus, as the representatives of a new religious tone, temper, and point of view, cannot usefully continue the old forms, such as fasting, which grew out of, and only suit, old and superseded religious views and presuppositions. But in reality the two verses are quite independent of 18–20.   What is their meaning ?   Are they authentic ?   As to the second question the interested reader should consult Bultmann, especially pp. 58, 60, 61.   The sayings may be Jewish sayings current at the time, adopted and adapted by Jesus, or later by his disciples, and fathered upon him.   Their original meaning is dubious.   Is the old preferred to the new or the new to the old ?   'Wird für das Alte oder für das Neue Partei genommen ?'   The first illustration of the incompatibility of old and new is odd.   W. observes : 'The rule that one must patch an old garment with old cloth is not observed to-day, and seems to have been thought odd even by Luke.   The meaning is clear.   A rusty kettle goes wholly to pieces if you try to mend it. The old garment and the old wine-skins can hardly mean anything else than Judaism.   Jesus does not oppose the Jewish people to the Kingdom of God, which comes without human interference, but he contrasts its present condition with that which he holds to be right, and for which he was already working ; he lays down no rules of the

divine activity, but of human action, and more clearly and especially
of his own.   The advanced radicalism of these rules or principles is
very remarkable ; practically he does not apply them.   For, so far
as he is concerned, he holds fast to Judaism and to the Old Testament.   It is also very noteworthy that he declares the creation of
new *forms* to be necessary, whereas in fact he left everything in this
department to be devised by his community after his death.   Yet
we need not for this reason doubt the authenticity of the saying :
there is much in the doings and sayings of Jesus which is for us
inexplicable.'   It is doubtful to me whether these ' rules ' or ' principles ' mean all that W. supposes, if Jesus is their author.   It is
in passages of this kind that some Christian commentators seem to
revel.   They read into them their own feelings and ideas.   Thus,
that admirable scholar, Menzies, says : ' The movement Jesus has
set on foot is a fresh and growing thing ; it is impossible to set limits
to its expansion, irrational to confine it to forms which were not
made for it.   The lofty consciousness of Jesus here finds expression,
that as his gospel is one of joy, it is also one of freedom.   He rever-
enced the forms of the religious life of his time, but he saw them to
be inadequate to the new principle of which he was the herald to the
world.   He set no forms for his followers to observe : they can
appeal to him for principles, but not for forms.'   It is only fair and
right to add that Klausner, the Jewish biographer of Jesus, takes
much the same view of the passage as Wellhausen (pp. 248, 275, 369).
' Whatever change there is must be fundamental, and not gradual
or partial.'   ' A new teaching, the preparation for the coming of the
Messiah by means of baptism and repentance, demands the breaking
up of the old external forms ; otherwise the new teaching itself will
be lost.'   Thus though ' Jesus never ventured wholly to contradict
the Law of Moses and the teaching of the Pharisees, there yet was
in his teaching the nucleus of such a contradiction.'   ' Jesus hints
that, like all their religious observances, the fasting of the disciples
of John is but the grafting of the new upon the old, the sewing of
new cloth on an old, outworn garment, the putting of new wine in
old, outworn bottles : a new content requires a new garb : Pharisaic
Judaism must be transformed from the root, and, to the Pharisaic
ceremonial laws, one should not add yet another in the guise of
repentance and good works to hasten the coming of the Messiah.
We have here a hint towards abolishing the ceremonial laws ; it
was not a hint understood by his disciples, still less by the disciples
of John and the Pharisees.   Jesus himself would never, during his
lifetime, have dared to explain his metaphor of " the piece of new
cloth " and " the old bottles " as pointing to the need for a *new
Torah*.'   Jesus himself ' remained steadfast to the old *Torah* : till
his dying day he continued to observe the ceremonial laws like a

true Pharisaic Jew.' ' Yet, on the other hand, had not Jesus's teaching contained suggestions of such a line of action, the idea would never have occurred to " Saul the Pharisee," nor would he have succeeded in making it a rule of Christianity ' (p. 275). There was in Klausner's view (*cp.* p. 291) a revolutionary and anti-legal element in Jesus's teaching from the outset, but it was never pushed home, and in his own life and in much of his action, and even in much of his teaching, it was not carried out or carried forward.

Meanwhile, whoever spoke it or wrote it, and whatever its original meaning, here is the passage ! And it certainly gives rise to many reflections, not least to Liberal Jews. For it may be argued that Liberal Judaism in any of its forms is an attempt to patch the old with the new, to put new wine into old bottles. Is it, *e.g.*, impossible that many generations can observe the Passover, if men have ceased to believe in the miraculous passage of the Red Sea, or that God ordered the Israelites to eat unleavened bread ? I think a good answer can be found, but the argument is serious, and needs most earnest consideration.

Professor Turner gives cogent reasons for holding that the last six words are genuine : there should be a bracket or dash after παλαιούς and after ἀσκοί. Then we can translate : ' No one pours new wine into old skins (for otherwise the wine will break the skins, and both the wine and the skins are ruined), but new wine into new skins ' (*J. T. S.* Vol. XXVI., 1925, p. 147).

23–28. THE SABBATH

(*Cp.* Matt. xii. 1–8 ; Luke vi. 1–5)

23 And it came to pass that he went through some corn fields on the Sabbath day ; and his disciples began, as they went, to pluck
24 the ears of corn. And the Pharisees said unto him, ' See, how they
25 do what is not permitted on the sabbath day ! ' And he said unto them, ' Have ye never read what David did, when he had need, and
26 he and they that were with him were hungry ? How he went into the house of God, while Abiathar was high priest, and ate the shewbread, which only the priests may eat, and how he gave it
27 also to them who were with him ? And he said unto them, ' The
28 sabbath was made for man, and not man for the sabbath : therefore the Son of man is lord even of the sabbath.'

The fourth and fifth ' conflict ' concern the Sabbath. The fifth seems much more important than the fourth. For assuming that the conduct of the disciples was in violation of a Rabbinic law as regards Sabbath observance, yet the justification which Jesus gives for the conduct of his disciples is a strange one, for there is nothing to show that they were in real straits for food. The analogy seems, therefore, strained. (The reference is to the story in I Samuel xxi. 1–6. Abiathar is a mistake for Ahimelech. The argument is *not* that if David acted in a certain way, and so violated the Law, *a fortiori* may a greater than David do so.) If the disciples acted justifiably, one would have to believe that they were in real and urgent need of food. But this is not indicated in the story.

Is the tale authentic ? Bultmann thinks that this is very doubtful, especially because it is the conduct of the disciples which is criticized, not that of Jesus. His words on pp. 7, 24, 25 deserve weighing, but are by no means conclusive. In this story there is the only indication of a date till we get to the Passion narrative. The incident must have happened between April and the end of June. But Schmidt argues that we have no reason to assert categorically from Mark that the ministry of Jesus must have lasted only about a year, and that this story must have taken place some ten months before the crucifixion (pp. 90–92).

27, 28. The addition of the words, ' And he said unto them ' show pretty clearly that we have here an independent Logion (saying) which has been added to our story. The second justification of the disciples is very different from the first. As the Evangelist understood it, it means that Jesus, as the Messiah, is allowed and empowered to violate, upon adequate occasion, the regulations about Sabbath observance. For the Sabbath was given to man for man's sake, for his benefit and joy ; it was not intended that man should be the slave of the Sabbath, and suffer because of it.

The argument is supposed by some commentators to become more logical if we assume that originally ' Son of man ' in the conclusion meant merely ' man.' ' So man is lord of the Sabbath.' The same questions are raised here as in ii. 1–12, but the argument that Son of man here is a mistaken rendering for ' man ' is much stronger. (Even Meyer, p. 106, n. 1, acknowledges this, though here too he clings to the Messianic interpretation as intended from the first.)

The καί in 28 is best rendered by ' even.' The Messiah includes in his authority power over the Sabbath. Or, according to the other interpretation, ' even of so important an institution as the Sabbath man has, or may have, control.' I do not think that the argument is *necessarily* illogical even if Jesus did here use ' Son of man,' or rather ' the Man,' to mean himself as the Messiah. For if the Sabbath was made for man, it is reasonable enough that ' *the* man,' the divine or semi-divine or divinely commissioned ruler of men, should be its arbiter and lord. If Jesus did not use the term ' Son of man ' to mean himself, did he then say : ' Therefore *I* am lord of the Sabbath day ' ? This is improbable, and we must in that case assume that the whole sentence (*i.e.* verse 28) is later than Jesus. And, indeed, this last supposition seems, perhaps, on the whole the most probable. 27 (' The Sabbath was made for man, and not man for the Sabbath '), is authentic ; 28 is added and un-authentic. For if ' son of man ' in 28 means merely ' man,' why is ' son of man ' not used instead of ' man ' in 27, or ' man ' instead of ' son of man ' in 28 ? Again, while 27 continues the thought of 26, 28 does not. Because the Sabbath was made for man, therefore the violation of it mentioned in 26 was justifiable (as the Rabbis say, ' God's commands were given for man to live by '). The general principle of 27 confirms and explains the example of 26. From the fact that man was not made for the Sabbath, it follows that man can be dispensed from its observance, when that observance, instead of doing him good, would do him harm, not that the Messiah has the right to dispense men from its observance. Jesus does not appear to claim authority over the commands of the Law in virtue of his Messiahship. He seems to allow to every man the right to interpret the Sabbath law like himself. I think Mr. Rawlinson is right in observing, ' Our Lord would not have been likely to say that " man " was " lord of the Sabbath," which had been instituted by God. On the other hand it is almost equally unlikely that He would have emphasized His personal lordship of the Sabbath.'

So far as we can gather, Jesus's attitude towards the Sabbath was something like the attitude of Liberal Judaism to-day. It must be observed rather in the spirit than in the letter. The regulations for its observance must not be allowed to destroy its intention. Directly the Sabbath becomes a burden, the object of the Sabbath is frustrated. The aim is the important point : how precisely we carry out the aim is less important. Nevertheless, one must not push the antithesis between Jesus and the Rabbinic teaching too far. Gould, for instance, goes too far when he says : ' The old religion attempted to regulate conduct by rules and forms, the new by principles and motives, and these are foreign one to the other. . . . Judaism is a system of rules, Christianity of principles. And so far as the Sabbath is a rule, that is, so far as it is Jewish, Jesus does abrogate it in these words.' Judaism is not without principles, however much Christianity may be devoid of rules. The antithesis reads nicely, but is, in point of fact, untrue.

It is, moreover, a remarkable fact that, in spite of the many restrictions and regulations, the Sabbath was upon the whole a joy and a blessing to the immense majority of Jews throughout the

Rabbinic period. Yet this fact does not detract from the greatness and originality of Jesus. His teaching is an excellent counterbalance to that casuistic minuteness which is the danger of legalism. It is emancipating ; it enables one to breathe freely. In modern times, at any rate, and with modern ideas, the Sabbath can hardly be observed except on the lines suggested by Jesus.

It is, however, to be noted that Jesus does not say that the law forbidding a man to pick corn upon the Sabbath was merely Rabbinic, and not Biblical. He does not say that to pick corn is not ' work.' He does in a subsequent passage distinguish between the Biblical laws and the Rabbinical or traditional laws, but here he takes higher ground. He seems to concede that a breach of the Law has taken place ; only it is an excusable and proper breach, and may be taken to illustrate the higher principle according to which the Sabbath should be observed.

Verse 27 is only found in Mark. The Rabbinical literature contains an almost identical saying : ' Unto you is the Sabbath given over, and you are not given over unto the Sabbath.' As to the meaning and origin of the saying, and as to the whole subject of the Sabbath in Rabbinical literature, with a very careful comparison of the Rabbinic teaching with that of Jesus, showing that the difference between them was not as great as Mark's ' conflicts ' would make us think, see Dr. Abrahams' *Studies* i. chap. xvii.

Note on the ' Son of Man.'

It may be desirable to append here some general remarks upon the important term ' the Son of man,' and upon its meaning and usage in the Synoptic Gospels. The subject is one of fascination and of difficulty. For the meaning of the term is greatly disputed, and quite a large literature has come into being about it. It is impossible to give more than a bare outline of the discussion and of the problem (which has far-reaching implications) in this place.

The term ' the Son of man ' is in the New Testament (with one exception, Acts vii. 56) only found in the Gospels, and there it is exclusively put in the mouth of Jesus as a designation of himself, or, possibly, of the Messiah or of some mysterious, heavenly Being. It is never used of Jesus by anybody else or by the Evangelists themselves.

The term as used in the Gospels undoubtedly often goes back to, or has some relation with, a famous passage in Daniel vii. 13. There in one of the visions of the Day of Judgment, which are found in that earliest of the apocalyptic writings, it is said : ' And behold there came with (or " on ") the clouds of heaven one like unto a son of man, and he came even unto the Ancient of Days, and they brought him near before Him. And there was given him dominion and glory and a kingdom, that all the peoples, nations, and languages should serve him ; his dominion is an ever-lasting dominion, which shall not pass away, and his kingdom that which shall not be destroyed.' The book of Daniel was written about 165 B.C., during the persecutions of Antiochus Epiphanes. Before Daniel we find the prophet Ezekiel addressed over and over again as son of man. In this usage it is merely a poetical synonym for ' man.' It is intended to emphasize the frail humanity of the prophet in contradistinction to the God who addresses him. It is as much a synonym for ' man ' as when we read in the eighth Psalm, ' What is man that thou art mindful of him, and the son of man that thou visitest him ? ' In Daniel too ' one like unto a son of man ' means merely ' one like unto a man,' but the equation is all the more certain in the Daniel passage, because Daniel vii. is one of the chapters of Daniel which is written in Aramaic, and in Aramaic (see below) ' son of man ' is the regular way of saying ' man.' For where in Hebrew you speak of 'the man,' in Aramaic, or in most varieties of Aramaic, you speak of ' the son of man.' Such is the Aramaic idiom. And whereas in Ezekiel and the Psalms we are justified in translating the Hebrew ' ben adam ' literally by ' son of man ' we should not do so in Daniel's Aramaic. Here we should translate simply ' one like unto a man,' and *not* ' one like unto a son of man.' Who is this figure ' like unto a man ' ? The most probable, and the most generally accepted, explanation is that the mysterious Figure is the people of Israel ; some scholars believe that it represents an angel, or, specifically, the angel Michael, the guardian angel of Israel. However this may be, it is pretty obvious that this mysterious Figure exercised in certain quarters a great attraction, while it is also possible (see below) that he had antecedents. Whatever the writer of Daniel meant by the figure, he soon became more definitely personalized. He became distinct from Israel, and was regarded as a mysterious semi-divine figure to whom God assigned, or would assign, special functions and powers at the Judgment Day. We next meet Daniel's Man in a section of the apocalyptic book of Enoch, often called the Similitudes, extending from chapter xxvii. to lxxi. The date of this section, according to Dr. Charles, a high authority on the subject, is between 94 and 64 B.C. We have to remember that we are dealing with a trans-lation of a translation, that is, we possess the book in Ethiopic, and the Ethiopic was translated from the Greek, which was trans-lated from the original Aramaic or Hebrew. The text, as Prof. Lake says, may have suffered by interpolations and alterations. The son of man is introduced thus : ' There I saw One [*i.e.* God] who had a head of days [*i.e.* the everlasting], and his head was white like wool, and with him was another being whose countenance had the appearance of a man, and his face was full of graciousness like one of the holy angels. And I asked the angel who went with me, and showed me all the hidden things, concerning that Son of man, who he was, and whence he was, (and) why he went with the Head of Days ? And he answered and said unto me : This is the Son of man who hath righteousness, with whom dwelleth righteousness, and who revealeth all the treasures of that which is hidden, because the Lord of Spirits hath chosen him, and whose lot hath the pre-eminence before the Lord of Spirits in uprightness for ever. And this Son of man whom thou hast seen shall put down the kings and the mighty from their seats [and the strong from their thrones] and shall loosen the reins of the strong, and break the teeth of the sinners.' Again it says of him : ' And at that hour that Son of man was named in the presence of the Lord of Spirits, and his name before the Head of Days. Yea, before the sun and the signs were created, before the stars of the heaven were made, his name was named before the Lord of Spirits. He shall be a staff to the righteous whereon to stay themselves and not fall, and he shall be the light of the Gentiles, and the hope of those who are troubled of heart. All who dwell on earth shall fall down and worship before him, and will praise and bless and celebrate with song the Lord of Spirits. And for this reason hath he been chosen and hidden before him, before the creation of the world and for evermore. And the wisdom of the Lord of Spirits hath revealed him to the holy and righteous ; for he hath preserved the lot of the righteous, because they have hated and despised this world of unrighteousness, and have hated all its works and ways in the name of the Lord of Spirits. For in his name they are saved, and according to his good pleasure hath it been in regard to their life.' He is called the Elect One. ' The Elect One standeth before the Lord of Spirits, and his glory is for ever and ever, and his might unto all generations. And in him dwells the spirit of wisdom, and the spirit which gives insight, and the spirit of understanding and of might, and the spirit of those who have fallen asleep in righteousness. And he shall judge the secret things, and none shall be able to utter a lying word before him ; for he is the Elect One before the Lord of Spirits according to his good pleasure.' Again : ' In those days the Elect One shall arise, and he shall choose the righteous and holy from among them : for the day has drawn nigh that they should be saved. And the Elect One shall in those days sit on my throne, and his mouth shall pour forth all the secrets of wisdom and counsel : for the Lord of Spirits hath given (them) to him and hath glorified him.' Then again he is once more alluded to as the Son of man thus : ' From the beginning the Son of man was hidden, and the Most High preserved him in the presence of

his might, and revealed him to the elect. And the congregation
of the elect and holy shall be sown, and all the elect shall stand
before him on that day. And all the kings and the mighty and the
exalted and those who rule the earth shall fall down before him on
their faces, and worship and set their hope upon that Son of man,
and petition him and supplicate for mercy at his hands.' ' And the
righteous and elect shall be saved on that day, and they shall
never thenceforward see the face of the sinners and unrighteous.
And the Lord of Spirits will abide over them, and with that Son of
man shall they eat and lie down and rise up for ever and ever.'
' That Son of man has appeared, and has seated himself on the throne
of his glory, and all evil shall pass away before his face, and the
word of that Son of man shall go forth and be strong before the
Lord of Spirits.' ' This is the Son of man who is born unto
righteousness, and righteousness abides over him, and the righteousness of the Head of Days forsakes him not.' (As regards the last
passage, see Lake, *Beginnings*, i. p. 371 and n. I and n. 2.) I have
quoted these passages at such length because, if they were really all
in existence in this form by 50 B.C., and if Jesus and his followers
knew them, they may have had very great influence upon the conception of ' the Man ' as we find it in the Gospels. It would seem that
the writer had abandoned the old merely human Messiah of Isaiah xi.,
and substituted for it this other conception of the Man, to whom he
gives some of the very qualities which Isaiah gives to his Davidic
offshoot in his eleventh chapter. The Man does not, strictly
speaking, inaugurate a Messianic or earthly kingdom : he only
appears to inaugurate the Final Judgment and the New Age.   In
the so-called Fourth Book of Ezra, which is later than Mark, there
would seem to be a conflation between the old Messiah figure and
the figure of ' the Man.'   He comes up from the sea with the clouds
of heaven, and is perhaps pre-existent : he is God's Son ; he seems
more than ' mere man,' even as the Man in Enoch is more, yet he
lives on earth in the kingdom which he establishes for 400 years only,
and then dies, and what happens to him then is not stated.   Lake,
however, perhaps overstresses the difference between the two figures
when he says : ' It is therefore plain that the writer of 4 Ezra was
thinking of the judgment of destruction on the heathen and the
prosperity of Israel in the period known to the Rabbis as " the days
of the Messiah," not of the final judgment which, as he says elsewhere,
will usher in the age to come.   This is the great difference between
" the Man " of 4 Ezra and " that Son of man " who is the Elect One
of Enoch.   The Elect One of Enoch ushers in the End and the Age
to come : " the Man," who is the Anointed One, the " Son " of 4 Ezra,
ushers in the limited " days of the Messiah ".'   The distinctions
in these apocalyptic writers are less clean cut than this.   The

conceptions of the Messianic Age and of the more supernatural Age to come tend to flow into one another. In any case, the loftier conception of the Man in Enoch is earlier—so far as uninterpolated—than the conception in 4 Ezra. Some scholars, indeed (*e.g.* Dr. Carpenter), hold that the Enoch passages are ' under strong suspicion of interpolation by Christian hands.' But this is not the prevailing view. Professor Toy says : ' The conception of the heavenly man in Enoch is one of the most grandiose in literature. A splendid being of heavenly origin stands by the side of God, and is by him invested with supreme authority in the world. He was chosen before the foundation of the world, has existed from the beginning, but is to be revealed to men only when the time of consummation shall arrive, when he will intervene to judge the world, to punish the wicked, and to establish the righteous in perfect, never-ending felicity. He is a man, but a glorious celestial man, the renewer and regenerator of the world, the introducer of the final age of perfection when all the inequalities and ills of life shall be abolished for the righteous. With this description the portraiture of the Son of man in the Gospels literally agrees. He sits at the right hand of power, and at the decisive moment comes in clouds of glory, gathers his chosen ones from all the world, dispenses rewards and punishments, sums up human history, and ushers in the final scheme of things. Such passages in the New Testament testify to the fact that in the generation following the death of Jesus he was identified with the Enoch figure, the Enoch eschatology was attached to his person, and utterances in accordance with this conception were put into his mouth. At the same time he was identified with the Old Testament Messiah, and his purely human experiences were interpreted as fulfilments of Old Testament predictions. From these two sources the person of Jesus, as it appears in the Synoptic Gospels and in certain other New Testament writings, was constructed.' Prof. Toy thinks that it is unlikely that the conception of the Heavenly Man in Enoch is of Christian origin. Its starting-point is Daniel vii., but in Enoch the celestial figure is represented much more distinctly as an individual, and ' as far above any angel.' ' Such divinization of man ' [does it really go so far ?] ' is probably to be ascribed to the Greek atmosphere in which the Jews of the first century B.C. lived. It was not adopted by the Judaism of the succeeding time ' (' What Christianity owes to Judaism,' in *Addresses before the New York State Conference of Religion*, Series VI. No. I, Feb. 1908, pp. 29–32).

The muddle of conflation in 4 Ezra, though later than Mark and Jesus, may still be used as an illustration how conceptions such as Messiah and ' the Man,' the earthly and the heavenly

Redeemer, could tend to be mixed up with one another.   And it is not impossible that Jesus might have fastened his attention upon the conception of the heavenly Man more than upon the conception of the Messiah.   He may conceivably have disliked the idea of an earthly conqueror, a ' political ' Ruler, a mundane monarch, and preferred that of a supernatural, semi-divine judge, who would at once, without the intermediate stage of a strictly Messianic kingdom, usher in the New Age, and the more final and everlasting Kingdom of God.   And, just possibly, he may have come to identify himself with the Heavenly Man, or to believe that, somehow or other, he, after his death of suffering, would be invested with the office of the Man, and would reappear upon earth as ' the Man ' whom Daniel had foreseen.   This, however, is to anticipate possible conclusions.

Meanwhile as to the use of the term ' Son of man ' in the Synoptic Gospels there are two main theories.

The first is that the historic Jesus never used the phrase of himself, and that the Gospel usage is inaccurate and unhistoric. The second is that he did use it of himself, though by no means necessarily in all the places in which it is at present ascribed to him.   A third theory is that he used the phrase, but not of himself.

We have seen that the Son of man is an inaccurate, too literal, Greek translation of the Aramaic original, which meant, and signified to those who heard it, just simply ' the Man.'   Now it is to be noted that in Mark Jesus uses it some thirteen times ; in the corresponding passages in Matthew the phrase occurs twelve times out of the thirteen.   In addition, twice, where Mark does not have it, Matthew does.   Then it is found in some thirteen other places, eight of which may come from Q.   Total for Matthew, twenty-nine.   In Luke three of the passages where Mark has it are wanting ; of the other ten, Luke has nine ; in one of Mark's passages he has ' I.'   In addition, he has the phrase in some seventeen other places, of which seven may come from Q.   Total for Luke, twenty-six.   Thus we see that the two later Gospels employ the phrase more frequently than the earlier one.   But what is far more important than this observation is a second one, namely, that in Mark, of the thirteen times in which Jesus uses the phrase only two occur before the famous scene in Cæsarea Philippi, that these two can easily be explained away, and that of the eleven others, two refer to his betrayal, one to his sufferings, one to his death, one to his resurrection, three to his sufferings, death, and resurrection, and three to his Parousia (coming, or return, for judgment and in glory).   Generally, it may be said that, of the eleven passages, eight refer to the Passion, or to the Passion and its immediate sequel, and three to the Parousia.   Jesus never employs the word as a *mere* synonym for ' I ' except in ii. 10

and ii. 28. There (see the notes) the original may have meant or
said not 'the Man' but 'man,' or if it did not, one passage or both
passages may be easily regarded as additions or as editorial. It is true
that of the eight Q passages three (or perhaps four) are earlier than the
Cæsarea Philippi episode, and in three of these the phrase may be
regarded as equivalent to 'I' or 'me,' but one is bound to say that
here is one of the cases where Mark is probably more primitive or
more accurate in his terminology than Q. (The passages are almost
all enumerated and classified in Lake, i. pp. 375, 376.) To Mark,
Son of man (or 'the Man') undoubtedly meant Messiah, but it does
not follow that to Jesus, if he used the term of himself, it was
identical with Messiah. Another observation to be made about it
is that Jesus never explains it, and its use causes no surprise. The
disciples are represented as puzzled by some of his phrases : this
one causes them no surprise at all. But if he had used it, *would* it
have caused no surprise ? If the disciples knew that he was referring to a Being something like the figure in Daniel or Enoch,
would they not have been amazed at his apparently identifying
this Being with himself ? Did, then, Jesus use the phrase ('the
Man') to mean, not himself, but the Heavenly Being who would
inaugurate the Kingdom and preside at the Judgment ? In Mark
viii. 38 Jesus says : 'Whoever shall be ashamed of me and my
words in this generation, of him the Son of man shall be ashamed
when he comes in the glory of his Father.' Of this verse it is not
unreasonable that Lake should say 'the natural interpretation
would surely be that the speaker, who is using the first person,
cannot be the same as the Son of man of whom he speaks in the
third.' Again, ' In Mark xiv. 62 Jesus admits that he is the Messiah,
speaking in the first person, and goes on to speak of the Son of man
in the third person : but whether he identifies the Son of man with
himself is not clear. In xiii. 26 there is nothing, except the tradition
of exegesis, to show that Jesus meant himself when he said that the
last sign of the end would be the appearance of the Son of man in
the clouds' (p. 377). But there are several arguments, too detailed
and delicate to go into here, which make this third hypothesis unlikely. That Jesus admitted that he was the Messiah, but distinguished between Messiah and 'the Man,' is improbable. It is
more likely that if he used or adopted the conception of 'the Man'
at all, he substituted it for that of the Messiah, or that he confounded
the one with the other, preferring the theory of the heavenly
Messiah, if one may call him so, to that of the conquering king
Messiah of Isaiah xi.

There are, however, many difficulties in the hypothesis that
Jesus ever used the term to mean himself, just as there are many
difficulties in the hypothesis that he did not. One has to choose

between these difficulties. In the Mark passages 'the Man' appears, as we saw, very frequently in passages where the Passion is spoken of. Now suffering was in no wise a characteristic of the figure in Daniel and Enoch. Was not then the whole attribution of the term to Jesus a product of the event, a product of the Passion, and unknown before it ? Again, it is very strange, to say the least of it, that Jesus should have thought that he would become after his death the Enochian 'Son of man'—the heavenly being, the semi-divine Man, who was to be the Judge at the Great Assize. Nor does he ever say distinctly that he is going to *return* as the Son of man. Again, 'the Man' in Enoch is pre-existent. He already existed in heaven. Did Jesus come to think that *he* (Jesus) had already existed in heaven, and that he *was* the Son of man from heaven sent down to be born from human parents upon earth, and then, after suffering and death and resurrection, soon to enter upon his supreme rôle as Judge and Inaugurator of the Kingdom of God ? That is very difficult to believe. And the argument that the figure of the Son of man was more congenial to him, because it was less 'political' and 'Jewish' than the figure of the old Messiah of Isaiah xi., is largely the product of modern Protestant prejudice— the wish, at any cost, to make Jesus as un-Jewish as possible. On account of all these difficulties, scholars such as Wellhausen and Bousset and Schmidt and Lietzman and others have maintained, more or less confidently, that Jesus never used the Son of man to mean himself, or that he never used the phrase at all. But why, then, has it been put into his mouth, and why do the Evangelists never use it of him, but only make him use it of himself ? Different theories as regards this problem have been put forward. Schmidt's answer in the *Encyclopædia Biblica* is that in certain passages in an old apocalypse, fathered later upon Jesus, there was a prediction (based upon Daniel vii. 13 : ' There came with the clouds of heaven one like unto a son of man ') of a mysterious Man coming on the clouds at the Day of Judgment or at the advent of the Messianic age. Mark xiii. 26 is the primary reference (' Then they shall see the Son of the man coming in clouds with great power and glory '). This apocalyptic prediction was in the Greek translated ' the Son of the man,' partly under the influence of the mysterious figure of Daniel, and partly because it was believed that the more elaborate translation heightened the mystery. In the Septuagint translation of Daniel, ' Son of man ' has no articles, either before ' Son ' or before ' man,' and this may have been the case originally in the apocalypse which is the basis of Mark xiii. But this apocalyptic ' Son of man ' was rapidly identified with Daniel's ' Son of man,' and then with Jesus. Hence the starting-point was given for Jesus to be made to call himself the Son of man. Moreover, as Jesus had spoken of man

generically in startling terms on some four or five occasions, it was
believed that what he had said of man (*bar-nasha*) he could only
have meant of *one* man—*i.e.* of himself. Hence in these passages
' Son of man ' (with the implication that ' Son of man ' was a title
which he called himself) was used to replace ' man.' If, in four or
five passages, ' Son of man ' was used to mean ' Jesus,' it was easy
to extend the number. In genuine utterances of Jesus, the Son of
man could and would be substituted for the personal pronoun, while
in unauthentic passages, more especially in mysterious and apocalyptic predictions, the term would be all the more willingly used.
It would heighten the mystery. Bousset's theory is that the Daniel
and Enoch passages make it likely that in certain Jewish circles a
conflation occurred between Messiah and ' the Man.' When it was
obvious that Jesus, because of his failure and death, was not the
old earthly, ' political,' human Messiah, and when, nevertheless, as
a recoil from despair and unbelief, faith in him had returned to his
disciples, induced and strengthened by ' appearances ' of the risen
Jesus to Peter and others, he was identified with the heavenly
Messiah, with ' the Man ' who was to come on the clouds from
heaven. Who else, indeed, could he be ? And if he had himself
denied that he was the Davidic Messiah, and if he had had any
thought that he might be, or become, the heavenly Messiah, the
identification would be all the more likely. And then, though the
early writers would not in ordinary cases speak of Jesus as
' the Man,' they might precisely begin to do so in places where he
was made to speak of his sufferings, his death, his resurrection, and
his Parousia. For the sufferings and death and resurrection were
the necessary preliminaries to his Parousia, and it was at the
Parousia that he assumed the office of ' the Man ' and discharged
his functions. (*Kurios Christos*, 2nd ed., pp. 5–19.)

Wellhausen stresses the difficulties which I have already
mentioned. His own theory is that the disciples, after the re-
establishment of their faith through the resurrection appearances,
substituted for the ordinary Jewish Messiah quite another conception. Then they made Jesus himself make this change of conception, and they did this specifically in the prophetic passages.
It was not merely that the mysterious name suited the prophetic
style, and enabled the writers to avoid making Jesus say : ' *I* shall
be crucified and shall rise.' The chief point was that the new name
was definitely intended to correct the Jewish conception of the
Messiah. It denotes the heavenly Messiah of the Christians in
contrast to the earthly Messiah of the Jews. And that, at last, Jesus
is made to use it just simply instead of ' I ' may be due to those
two passages in Mark (ii. 10 and 28) where it really means no more
than ' man.' When the Greek rendering ' son of man ' made it

possible to believe that it could only be Jesus who was meant in these passages, because only the Messiah can forgive sins, or may break the Sabbath, it may have led people to think that Jesus must have called himself ' son of man ' from the very beginning of his ministry. (*Einleitung*, 2nd ed., pp. 128, 129.)

But it must be confessed that the difficulties of this theory are considerable. For that the term should have been put exclusively into the mouth of Jesus, and never used of him, that we find it in all four evangelists (though never elsewhere in the N.T. except in Acts vii. 56), used in the same way, and that, nevertheless, it was never used by Jesus himself, seems exceedingly odd. We may fully admit that there is a growth in its usage even within the Synoptics themselves (as we have seen). Thus in Luke vi. 22 where Matthew has ' me,' Luke has ' Son of man,' and so in Luke xii. 8 as compared with Matt. x. 32. And in Mark viii. 27 Jesus says : ' Who do they say that I am ? ' (and so in Luke ix. 18), whereas Matthew has ' Who do they say that the Son of man is ? ' And, contrariwise, it is quite possible that Matt. x. 32, 33, with its ' I 's ' and ' me 's ' is the original of such passages as Mark viii. 38 with their ' Son of Man.' Nevertheless, that Jesus *never* used the term remains a hard saying. Professor Burkitt says : ' I find it difficult to believe that Jesus never Himself connected His anticipations of suffering and rejection with the figure of the Son of man ' (*Beginnings*, p. 33). What immediately follows on that sentence may be contrasted with a passage in Bousset to show how two of the very greatest N.T. scholars can differ from each other.

BOUSSET (p. 7)	BURKITT (p. 33)
' The command of Jesus that the disciples are to say nothing about the Transfiguration till the Son of man has risen from the dead is obviously a secondary addition, and was put in (*cp.* xvi. 8) to explain why the story was only known at a later date. And ix. 12*b* destroys the good connection between 12*a* and 13, and is a disturbing interpolation from Matt. xvii. 12*b*, which itself is a secondary addition to Mark.'	' In particular the passage Mark ix. 9–13, so abrupt, so unliterary, so obscure in detail, however clear may be the general meaning, reads to me like reminiscences of a real conversation. I gather from it that Jesus did speak of suffering and of the Son of man, and that it was by the conjunction of the two things that Peter and his companions were puzzled.'

Perhaps the cautious view of Knopf (*Einführung*, p. 277) may be wisest : ' We have no right to declare categorically that Jesus never used the term of himself, but in which of the Synoptic passages it is authentic it is impossible to say.' The puzzles connected with its use in the mouth of Jesus are very fairly stated by Knopf on p. 278.

It is easier to believe that Enoch's figure was known to Jesus and his disciples because modern research has made it clear that the figure of the heavenly Man was far older than Daniel. He was originally ' the Cosmic Man—the " Urmensch," who, endowed with supernatural gifts, fights and overcomes the monster of Chaos, and so liberates the Cosmos from the tyranny of Chaos.' (*Cp.* Box, *Ezra Apocalypse*, p. 283, 1912, and the references to Gressmann and Gunkel there given.) Here too may be the origin of Paul's ' second man from Heaven ' (I Cor. xv. 47) where, as Lake says, he may be thinking of the *bar-nasha* of Enoch, which *he* was ' too good a Grecian to translate by Son of man ' (p. 380). ' The Man ' may be a shortened form of some longer original ; perhaps ' the first man.' ' The ' is emphatic : ' The Man ' is the well-known, mysterious, heavenly Man, with special functions predetermined for him at the Last Judgment. He is not of Jewish origin, but borrowed by Jewish writers from foreign apocalyptic material and tradition. He is a parallel figure to the Messiah, but of quite different origin. The Messiah is an earthly, the Son of man a heavenly figure. Yet they could easily become identified or confused with each other, just as in Daniel the Son of man is identified with Israel. As the functions of the Messiah at the Last Judgment and in the new age became more exalted, it was all the easier to identify or combine him with the apocalyptic figure of the ' Son of man,' or rather of ' the Man.'

If all this be accurate, the following deductions emerge. If Jesus spoke about ' the Man,' he might have been understood by all who had heard of the current apocalyptic traditions and conceptions. He may have used the term to signify a being other than himself, or he may have used it of himself as the Messiah. If he did not believe himself to be the Messiah, or before he had come to the conclusion that he was the Messiah, he may have distinguished ' the Man ' from himself, and a reflection of this usage may perhaps be still seen in those passages where in one clause he uses the personal pronoun, in the second the Son of man (as if he and the Son of man were not identical). But if and when he felt himself to be the Messiah, he can only have meant by ' the Man,' when and if he used the term, himself.

The whole question is closely allied to the further, no less difficult, question as to the Messianic consciousness of Jesus, and as to his conception of the Messiah. If Jesus (as I believe), in some sense or other, claimed to be the Messiah, we may, perhaps, suppose that, in the later months of his short ministry, he may have come to believe not only that God had invested him with a lofty office (though it was the greatness of service), but also that if in the discharge of that office he must encounter death, he would be transformed, or raised, after death into the veritable Son of man of the apocalyptic seers. There is a certain attractiveness in Schweitzer's theory that Jesus gradually identified himself with the heavenly Son of man, who was also the Messiah, and that he believed he would be transformed into that super-earthly being. But it is surely going too far to say that at that time the Messiah was *generally* regarded as an ' übernatürliche Persönlichkeit.' What we may, however, perhaps, say with safety is that there were very various views about the Messiah's nature floating about in the age of Jesus, and that these ranged from the old purely human conception of Isaiah xi. on the one side, to the conception of him as a heavenly and semi-divine being, on the other.

In his excellent and informing pamphlet, *The Messianic Consciousness of Jesus* (1907), H. J. Holtzmann investigated the subject anew. We see from his book, and from the survey of opinions which he gives, how widespread is the desire to dissociate Jesus from anything Jewish. The Jewish Messiah is depressed and depreciated, and Jesus is magnified and exalted. He must, so far as possible, be kept free from all contact with what is Jewish, and specially from the contamination of the Jewish conception of the Messiah. For the Jewish Messiah is a mere conquering king, a political, particularistic figure, whose sole function it is to cause the Jews to triumph over their enemies and to make them the supreme world-power. Far better Daniel's man who comes upon the clouds than the Jewish Messiah with his selfish Jewish empire, his odious Jewish triumphs. The anti-Jewish bias, the desire to press to the utmost the difference between Jesus and Judaism, to depress the one and to magnify the other, is constantly apparent. No one would imagine in reading Merx, for example, or others of his stamp, and even Holtzmann himself, that there was any ethical or spiritual side to the ' Jewish ' Messiah. The *Judenmessias* would appear to be a sort of Napoleon, protected and inspired by the narrow ' Jewish ' God.

The impartial historian will not deny that there was a ' particularist' and ' national' side to the Jewish Messiah, which was sometimes more and sometimes less prominent. But it is not impartial to deny or ignore that there was another side also. Jesus had not to go beyond Isaiah for a conception of the Messiah which was both Jewish and ethical, far more ethical, indeed, than the ' Man ' of Daniel vii. 13.

Holtzmann himself clings to the view that Jesus regarded himself as the Messiah, but not as the ' Jewish ' Messiah, or Son of David. The remarkable passage in Mark xii. 35-37, the significance of which cannot be denied, sufficiently proves this. On the other hand, the trial proves that a Messiah in some sense Jesus did claim to be. If Jesus (*a*) believed that the Kingdom was soon to come, (*b*) that

he was to bring about, or be closely connected with, its coming, and
(c) that he was invested by God with a special mission, how could
he help drawing the conclusion that he was the Messiah ? 'He
was bound to think Messianically.' Only, as there were many
varieties and kinds of Messianic conceptions then current, some
more ethical, others less, some more national, others less, some more
apocalyptic, others less, some more 'supernatural,' others less, there
was no reason why Jesus should not fasten upon the particular
conception which suited his own ideas and character best, or which
seemed most in consonance with his mission and his destiny. This
conception he might himself develop and modify.

On the whole, perhaps, the soberest and safest view of the Son
of man problem is that taken by M. Loisy, who says :

'However purely religious and moral was his conception of the
Kingdom, Jesus did not any the less on that account regard himself
as the Messiah promised to Israel, and the future king of the elect.
If he applied to himself, on very rare occasions, the titles of "Son
of God" and "Son of man," these formulas were for him but
synonyms of Messiah, and we are the less authorized to seek in them
for special shades of his thought and the personal expression of his
inmost feelings, because it is quite possible that the majority of the
passages in which they occur belong to the traditional gloss upon
his teaching' (*E. S.* i. p. 192).

'If he sometimes made use of the title "Son of man" borrowed
from Daniel, in order to apply it to himself, he must have attached
no other meaning to it than that of Messiah ; and it seems very
hazardous to discover a special significance in it, related to the idea,
personal also, which Jesus is supposed to have formed of his mission.
Such a hypothesis could be accepted only if Jesus had made use of
this formula very frequently or by preference. Now it is the
Evangelists who show the preference, and its use by Jesus, except
in a very restricted measure, does not appear probable. The Evangelical texts seem to establish a special relation between this title
and the idea of the suffering Messiah ; but the relation and the idea
belong only to tradition' (*E. S.* i. p. 243).

'The first generation of Christians contended with the Jews on
the right of Jesus to the character of Christ, and to the glorious
royalty announced by Daniel in the famous passage relating to the
"son of man," who represents and introduces the reign of the Saints.
Men were never weary of repeating, or of ascribing to Jesus, the
assertion that he was the "Son of man" whom Daniel had seen in
spirit, the Christ of the *parousia*, he for whom the Christians were
always waiting, and whose legitimate claims Caiaphas had failed to
recognize. The repeated use of the title "Son of man" in the discourses of Jesus is the result of this preoccupation of the compilers

with this idea. The comparison of the texts suggests that it has been introduced into the written tradition, and does not usually belong to the oldest redaction of the Gospel discourses ' (*E. S.* i. p. 193).

If this be correct, the controversy is reduced in importance. When Jesus used the term, which was not often, he meant by it the Messiah, but he did not put into it special meanings of his own. The great theologian Harnack also thinks that Jesus used the term occasionally of himself, and that he meant by it the Messiah. It will be convenient if I here add a summary of Harnack's view both of the Son of man problem, and, more generally, of the Messianic consciousness of Jesus and of his conception of the Messiah. This view is partly based upon his elaborate study of Q. In his reconstruction of that document the Son of man occurs some seven times : Matt. viii. 20, Luke xii. 8 (perhaps, *cp.* Matt. x. 32), Matt. xii. 32, Matt. xi. 19, Luke xi. 30, Matt. xxiv. 44, Matt. xxiv. 39. Three or four of these passages are not connected with Last Things or Judgment. Clearly, says Harnack, Q meant by the term the Messiah. And the great theologian adds : ' It is still very probable to me that the term in Jesus's mouth had never any other meaning. In each individual case where Q makes Jesus speak of himself as the Son of man, one cannot be certain that he did so. But that he *did* use the term of himself and to mean the Messiah, this Q makes enormously probable ' (*Sprüche und Reden Jesu*, p. 166, n. 1, *E. T.* p. 239, n. 1). The whole document of Q, as it can be picked out and pieced together from Luke and Matthew, is dominated by the theory that Jesus was the Messiah. Harnack, however, thinks that one cannot follow the compiler of Q the whole way. One must remove the Messianic consciousness implied in the story of the baptism and the temptation. One must neglect the use of ' the Son of man ' in the earlier period of the ministry. If one does this, then one can obtain from Q a very early conception of Jesus which, as Harnack thinks, is historic and accurate. I will quote Harnack's own words, but before I do so I would like to point out that those words are controlled by the, as I believe, unhistorical theory that Jesus felt himself to be (of course only in a spiritual and moral sense) the special Son of God, with a knowledge of God and a realization of sonship such as none had possessed or felt before him. Hence Harnack's desperate efforts to maintain the authenticity of Matt. xi. 25–30. The consciousness of sonship was earlier than the consciousness of Messiahship. The first was the preparation for the second. For the consciousness of Messiahship never meant anything else than a consciousness of something which he would *become*. Hence the consciousness of what he *was* had to precede the consciousness of what he was *going to be*, and only if this prior consciousness had reached the height of the 'Sohnesbewusstsein' could it have formed the bridge to the consciousness of Messianity.

The notes on Matt. xi. 25–30 will show how doubtful this whole theory is, and on what slender support it rests. And, indeed, a Jewish admirer of Jesus cannot help hoping that he never believed that no pious Jew in his own age or before him had a sense or a knowledge of God equal to his own. To a Jewish mind, if Jesus believed that he was nearer to God and felt God nearer to him than other men, such a belief would have meant that he was in truth removed from Him. Jesus, like the prophets of old, may, indeed, have believed that his teaching was inspired and indubitably right. Such certainty is not inconsistent with humility. He may have regarded obedience to his commands as equivalent to the doing of God's will, but his Jewish admirers will cling to the hope that he did not believe that he was a better, wiser man, with a fuller knowledge of God, than anybody who had ever lived. And this is what Harnack's view of him seems to imply. The true Jesus is, one hopes, better revealed in the humility of Mark x. 18 than in the self-assertion of Matt. xi. 27. However this may be, the following is the great theologian's view as to the development of Jesus's conception of his Messiahship, which, as he thinks, Q either reveals or does not contradict. It is, in fact, deduced from both Mark and Q, and thus has the greater claim to be regarded as accurate and historical : ' We now have before us a compilation of sayings in which the speaker is a teacher, a prophet, one who is more than a prophet—*the final decisive Messenger of God* ; but so surely as he demands unconditional *obedience* to His commands, in which the will of God is expressed, and calls upon men *to follow Him*, so little does He do this with the expressed self-witness : " I am the Messiah." Rather He points simply to His miracles and His works (in so far as He does not count upon the self-evidence of His commands in their appeal to the hearts of His hearers). If one therefore neglects the term " Son of man "—which was certainly used by our Lord, though we cannot be sure that it is genuine in any particular saying —Jesus first asserts His claim to the Messiahship in the sayings at the close of the source, *but only in connection with, and under the imagery of, the Second Coming* ; He who already in His present state of existence is more than a prophet and greater than John, He who is the *Son*, will be the coming King and Judge.

' Critical investigation of the accounts in St. Mark seems to compel us to the conclusion that our Lord, during the first and longest period of His ministry, does not speak of Himself as the Messiah (because He at first neither regarded Himself as Messiah, nor indeed could so regard Himself) and even rejected the title of Messiahship when it was applied to Himself, but that, on the other hand, He was possessed by the strongest conviction that, as a messenger of God, He was entrusted with a mission of decisive import, and that He knew God as none other knew Him—a conviction to which He again and again gave expression ; and that at a later period after He had accepted at Cæsarea Philippi the confession of the disciples : " Thou art the Messiah "—*i.e.* " Thou wilt be He," He from henceforth (though indeed still with reserve until the entry into Jerusalem) called Himself the Son of man, and with growing confidence proclaimed His Parousia, *i.e.* His Messiahship. There is nothing in the compilation of discourses in Q, if only we neglect the introduction, which can be alleged to be discrepant with this picture of gradual development. We cannot, it must also be acknowledged, derive from Q certain testimony to the detailed accuracy of this picture, because Q pays such slight regard to chronology ; nevertheless Q also bears witness to the main position, in that in the sayings collected in Q the Messiahship is only clearly expressed under the form of the Parousia, and in that in these sayings our Lord claims faith not because He is the present Messiah—this is unthinkable—but because He works the works of God and proclaims His Commandments ' (*Sayings of Jesus*, English edition, p. 244, original German, p. 169). It may be stated that the use of ' our Lord ' in the English version is no exact translation of the German. Harnack simply says Jesus. Again, where the English version has St. Mark, St. Matthew, &c., Harnack has simply Mark and Matthew. The English capital H's in the pronouns, ' he,' ' his,' &c., when these pronouns refer to Jesus, are also no feature of the German original.

Some further reference to recent works by one or two scholars who maintain that Jesus used the term ' Son of man ' or ' the Man ' to mean himself may be permitted. E. Meyer is one of these. He would claim that there is no original confusion of Son of man for man even in Mark ii. 28 any more than in ii. 10. He thinks the term just suited Jesus, because it not only was ' non-political,' but was ' esoteric and mysterious.' ' Through the dark, unexplained expression Jesus hints at his Messianic claim without openly avowing it. The term retains its esoteric character : it indicates the Messianic office without openly making a claim to it ' (Vol. ii. pp. 337, 345). One objection to this is that the disciples show no astonishment at the use of the title. But if they knew what Jesus meant by it, why are they not amazed at the audacity of the claim : for the Man was a much greater being really than the Messiah ? If they did not know, why are they not puzzled ?

Professor Peake is a thorough-going advocate of the early Messianic consciousness of Jesus and of the authenticity of the title of Son of man (or the Man). But though he declares that it is ' difficult to conceive a case much stronger on its positive side than that for the application of the title to Himself by Jesus,' though ' to question the use of the title by Jesus is to fly in the face of all our testimony,' it can hardly be said that he brings forward any new arguments in support of the hypothesis, or perhaps that he quite sufficiently weighs the importance of the arguments upon the other side. ' If,' he urges, ' Jesus really predicted His suffering and death, there is full justification for believing that He connected the idea of the Son of man directly with His passion. He may have combined with it the idea of the Servant of Yahweh. This would be natural as soon as He had realized that He could come as Son of man on the clouds, only if He had first passed through suffering, death, and resurrection to the right hand of God. The Passion is thus taken into His vocation as Son of man. A title which had originally a purely eschatological reference, so far at least as manifestation on earth was concerned, received an extension backward into the earthly career of Jesus. This being so, we need not hesitate to recognize a still further extension, and to admit that Jesus used the term where neither the return in glory nor the Passion was in question. It has been held by several scholars that Jesus did not regard Himself as Messiah or Son of man during His earthly life. He believed that He was to be the Messiah, but was not so yet. This, however, does violence to the documents. The confession of Peter at Cæsarea Philippi and Jesus's own confession at His trial, imply that He was already Messiah. If so, there is no insuperable objection to the view that Jesus, conscious of His present identity with the Son of man, should have used the term of Himself in connections where neither the eschatological nor the Passion reference was involved ' (*The Messiah and the Son of man*, p. 28). This last quotation does, indeed, allude to the undoubted difficulties involved in the theory that Jesus believed that he *was* to be the Messiah, but was not so yet, but it does not clear up the fresh difficulties which arise on the assumption that he believed himself to be the Messiah all along since the Baptism. So even the latest researches about the Son of man still leave the matter wrapped in mist and uncertainty. Lastly, mention should perhaps be made of Reitzenstein's discussions about the ' Son of man ' in his book, *Das iranische Erlösungsmysterium*, pp. 116–125. Reitzenstein combines his views as to the non-Jewish origin of the figure of ' the Man ' with somewhat conservative views as to the undoubted usage by Jesus of this mysterious term to designate himself and as to why he chose it. See especially pp. 118, 119.

CHAPTER III

1–6. Healing on the Sabbath

(*Cp.* Matt. xii. 9–14 ; Luke vi. 6–11)

1 And he entered on another occasion into the synagogue ; and
2 there was a man there who had a withered hand. And they kept
watching him, to see whether he would heal him on the sabbath
3 day, so that they might accuse him. And he said unto the man
4 who had the withered hand, 'Stand up and come forward.' And
he said unto them, ' Is it permitted to do good on the sabbath rather
than to do evil ? To save life rather than to kill it ? ' But they
5 held their peace. And he looked round on them with anger, being
grieved for the hardness of their hearts, and he said unto the man,
' Stretch out thine hand.' And he stretched it out : and his hand
6 was restored. And the Pharisees went out, and straightway took
counsel with the Herodians against him, how they might destroy
him.

The fifth conflict, and the second Sabbath story. Over and
above his reproduction of this story from Mark, Luke has two
other variants (xiii. 10–17 ; xiv. 1–6).

2. It would have been more natural to mention the Sabbath in
verse 1.

Who are ' they ' ? It may be a sign of the antiquity of the
story that the opponents are not named as Pharisees or Scribes.
Cp. verse 6.

4. The meaning seems to be : ' On the Sabbath day should
one not rather do good than evil, rather save a life than kill it ? '

To heal is regarded as an instance of doing good. Thus, not to
heal is equivalent to doing evil, for if the life is not saved, it is killed.

But the reasoning of Jesus seems to be casuistical. More than
once it seems as if he wished to win a dialectical victory without
really meeting the objections squarely. He seems to evade the

argument by a counter argument, which, however ingenious, is not really to the point. Sometimes, too, it seems as if he would not give a straight answer to a straight question, but sought to elude the question by an ingenious parry. How far these evasions and dialectical puzzles are historical, and how far, if so, they were morally justifiable, are difficult points. Jesus seems to take the line that the critics were insincere, and only sought to entrap him. He was therefore justified in avoiding their snares by puzzles, counter problems, and evasions. He is only frank to those who are frank.

The casuistry here is that it could not be argued that the man with the ' withered hand ' was in any danger of his life. The healing could very well have been put off till the morrow, had Jesus been so minded. Yet, even though there was no question of life or death, Jesus thought himself justified in not postponing the cure. Apparently his real view was that any good action, or any kind of healing, should not be postponed for the sake of the Sabbath. This view would lead, if pushed home, to very wide consequences. The truth is that each case must be judged upon its own merits.

Assuming, as I do, that miracles, in the ordinary sense of the word, were not wrought by Jesus, the question arises : Does the sudden healing of a withered hand fall within or without the limits of the possible ?

5.   Note the strong expression ' with anger.' He considers their heart hard because they do not believe in him and do not recognize the force of his argument. Of course the Evangelist tells the story, like all his other stories, to make all our sympathies go with Jesus, and to put the Pharisees in the worst possible light. Hardness of heart does not mean callousness of feeling, but unsusceptibility of mind. The two parties could not understand each other. Their point of view was different. Jesus could not understand them ; they could not understand him ; and so each was unjust to the other. Here, as always, the words of Jowett are true and in point : ' We only learn the true lesson to be gathered ' from these stories ' when we place ourselves above them.' We must be independent before we can be just ; or, in other words, before we can draw near to the truth.

6.   Does this verse belong to the original story ? It is more probably redactional. Mark prepares the way for a new chapter in Jesus's life. ' He no longer preaches in the synagogues, except once, and that unsuccessfully, in his own home at Nazareth. His aim is no longer the rousing of the multitudes ' (how about vii. 14 ?), ' but the instruction and training of his own disciples. He now begins

to organise his followers into an organisation, which was destined to develop into the Christian Church.' (Burkitt, *Gospel History*, pp. 68, 69, 80, 81, and elsewhere.) We may suppose that Mark believed the story of the public life of Jesus to have developed somewhat in this way. Whether it really did so is another matter.

The Herodians are the functionaries and agents of Herod Antipas, the tetrarch of Galilee. Mark apparently brings them in to explain thus early who the men were who, in his opinion, were responsible for the death of Jesus. These were the Pharisees as the representatives of orthodox Judaism, and the Herodians, as the opponents of every one who might be dangerous to Herod's house. Is it likely that Pharisees and Herodians plotted together thus early in the career of Jesus ? Or did this story happen much later on in his ministry ? (Schmidt, pp. 100, 101.) The authors of the death of Jesus were the Romans and a certain section, doubtless, of the Jews. You cannot attack people as Jesus did, you cannot call them vipers and children of hell, without consequences. Doubtless, at the end, after allowing him much latitude of speech in accordance with the custom of the time, some of his opponents and the ruling authorities, both priestly and lay, were not sorry to find a way in which to compass his destruction. But it is doubtful if they could have done this if it had not been for the claim to be Messiah. And that is one reason why, in this matter, the Gospel story as it stands, summed up finally in Mark xv. 26, is, in all probability, quite historical. It should be stated and noted that Meyer sees nothing improbable in the Herodians coming in here. ' This statement is very significant, and certainly quite authentic. The strict religious party of the Pharisees joins hands with the representatives of secular authority, the adherents of Herod Antipas—for Jesus is the subject of Herod—to whom Jesus is as suspicious as John had been formerly ' (i. p. 107).

Who collected the stories in ii. 1–iii. 6 ? Was it Mark ? Schmidt thinks not. Mark found the collection already made. ' In the course of its propaganda and of its discussions with the Jews, the Christian community needed such a series of stories, and it put them together for practical purposes ' (p. 104).

7–12. MANY HEALINGS

(*Cp.* Matt. xii. 15–21 ; Luke vi. 17–19)

7   But Jesus with his disciples retired to the lake ; and a great multitude from Galilee followed him ; and from Judæa, and from
8 Jerusalem, and from Idumæa, and beyond Jordan, and about Tyre and Sidon, a great multitude, who had heard what great things he

9 did, came unto him.   And he tuld his disciples to have a boat ready
10 for him, so that he might not be crushed by the crowd.   For he
had healed many, so that all who were afflicted pressed upon him
11 in order to touch him.   And the unclean spirits, when they saw
him, fell down before him, and screamed, saying, ' Thou art the
12 Son of God.'   And he rebuked them much that they should not
make him known.

From here till viii. 26 the order is very confused.   It is difficult
to discern the plan or framework upon which Mark arranged his
material.   The present editorial section may have been drawn up
by Mark to prepare for the dispute (in iii. 20–30) about the source
from which Jesus draws his power of exorcism.   But verse 7 may
be the conclusion of the preceding story (Schmidt, p. 107).

The crowds from distant parts, the inconvenient pressure, and
the charges to the unclean spirits, must all be taken with many
grains of critical salt in order to reduce the incidents here spoken of
to their real historical proportions.   Jesus's commandment to the
unclean spirits not to make him known, with their instant recognition of him as the Son of God, are part and parcel of Mark's theology
and scheme.   Thus many critics argue that Mark is not the mere,
simple narrator.   He has a theology, to suit which the facts must
be expanded, modified, and interpreted as may be required in each
case.

7.   Mark seems to imply that Jesus seeks to avoid useless disputes with his adversaries.   He no longer preaches in the synagogues.
See the quotation from Prof. Burkitt above.   But the impression
that Jesus avoids his adversaries either because he knows they are
plotting to destroy him (iii. 6), or because discussion is useless, is
illusory.   He remains in Capernaum, and even voluntarily engages
his opponents in a most provocative dispute (iii. 23).

9.   Of this boat no use is made till iv. 1.   Professor Turner
points out that Mark, unlike Matthew and Luke, uses the word
(crowd) only in the singular.   (The one exception is x. 1, which
refers to the ' gathering together of crowds from different quarters.')
He does this ' because he or his informant visualizes as a single
whole the body of people who came together to hear Jesus, and
according to their numbers on each occasion, describes them as " a
crowd " or " a big crowd " or " a considerable crowd " or " a very
big crowd."   Mark never uses the definite article in the nominative,
ὁ ὄχλος, πᾶς ὁ ὄχλος (at any rate till the scene shifts to
Jerusalem), except in relation to an indefinite " crowd " mentioned
just previously.   They are not a fixed quantity, so to say, not

ὁ ὄχλος, but ὄχλος, a necessary element in the picture, but a variable and varying one.   To the other Evangelists, or at any rate to Matthew, they are a stereotyped but vague generality, " the multitudes ".'   ' Luke can use ὄχλος of disciples : Mark never does.   " Disciples " are always to Mark a limited company ' (*J. T. S.* XXVI., April 1925, pp. 227, 238).   The implications of all this are obvious.   Mark reflects the eyewitness, his informant.   I can only here draw attention to the discussion in the same article of Mark's use of the verb ' follow ' (ἀκολουθεῖν) in contradistinction to its use in Matthew and Luke.   Here, too, Mark consistently reproduces the literal facts, what actually happened, and his words are chosen, either carefully or unconsciously, to do this in a clear-cut, unexaggerated way.   Thus Mark never uses the verb ἀκολουθεῖν in the sense ' of the crowds " following " Jesus more or less as his disciples ' (in iii. 7, above, the word has been inserted from Matthew iv. 25, and is wanting in several good MSS. and versions).   He hardly ever uses the word in its literal sense of the Twelve or of the disciples (and yet the literal sense of the word is elsewhere frequent).   For the disciples did not ' follow,' but accompanied Jesus ; ' their normal position was at his side, he in the midst of them : it was exceptional that they should be behind him.'   The exception, x. 32, is carefully noted.   Again, then, we have the eyewitness before us !

11.   When Mark says that the unclean spirits fell down before Jesus, he means that the *men* who were possessed with these spirits fell down.

There is no good and convincing evidence that Son of God was a current Messianic title at the time of Jesus.   Israel had been called God's son for a long while, and the great kings, such as David and Solomon, had also been metaphorically so called.   The ' Son ' in Psalm ii. was interpreted (perhaps rightly) to be the Messiah, and here we find the famous phrase : ' Thou art my Son ; this day I have begotten thee.'   If Jesus was called Son of God while he lived, he, just conceivably, was called so as being the Messiah, not in any metaphysical sense.   He could be man, Messiah, and Son of God in one.   But the pre-existence of the Messiah in heaven had also become a floating Jewish conception by this time.   If the Messiah was pre-existent, he was semi-divine, or angelic, and this is the conception which Paul had of him, perhaps even *before* he identified the Messiah with Jesus.   To Mark, the Messiah Jesus was no mere man.   He had received the spirit, and, in this way, *become* the Son of God, and so, in a sense, divine, at his baptism.   Mark shows no trace of any knowledge of the doctrine that Jesus had no human father, while Paul and the author of the fourth Gospel seem either not to know of the virgin birth or not to accept it.   Another early conception was that Jesus only became the Son of God in any real sense at his ascension into heaven. He was the Messiah, but his Messiahship was latent. He was made and appointed Messiah and Son of God by his resurrection and ascension. ' God has made him both Lord and Messiah, this Jesus whom ye crucified ' (Acts ii. 36). And Paul says that Jesus was ' declared ' (or appointed) to be the Son of God in power by his resurrection (Romans i. 4). That Jesus regarded himself as divine or semi-divine is improbable. He would, at most, only have acknowledged himself to be ' Son of God ' in a simpler Messianic sense, or he may have believed, towards the end of his ministry, that he would be transformed into a higher kind of being (the ' heavenly man ') after his death. The phrase ' Son of God ' represents a further stage beyond the saying ' Thou art my Son,' even if this were interpreted messianically. It is probable that nobody called Jesus ' Son of God ' in his lifetime, and that he did not call himself so. This step was quickly taken by the Christian community, possibly under Hellenistic influences. See Bousset, *Kurios Christos*, 2nd edition, pp. 52–57, an excellent discussion. For another, to my mind much less probable view, see Burkitt, *Christian Beginnings*, pp. 25, 26. The discussion in *Beginnings*, i. pp. 392–403, must on all accounts be carefully studied.

It is not difficult to see that the transition from speaking about Israel and the righteous and the Messiah as God's sons or son to calling the Messiah definitely the Son of God was very easy. But in Mark the usage is not frequent, and the development has not gone far. The demoniacs twice call Jesus Son of God, the High Priest uses the phrase ' Son of the Blessed One ' (*cp.* Ecclesiasticus iv. 10), the centurion at the crucifixion declares that Jesus was truly a (or the) Son of God. The divine voice at the baptism merely says ' Thou art my beloved Son,' and the voice at the Transfiguration says much the same. We have also 'the Son' used in a very special and marked sense in the exceptional sentence xiii. 32, where Jesus himself speaks of himself as ' the Son.' In Q ' Son of God ' is put into Satan's mouth in the narrative of the Temptation, and then there is the remarkable passage in Matt. xi. 27, of which there will be so much to say in due course. The redactors of Matthew and Luke had doubtless a more advanced conception of Son of God as applied to Jesus than Mark. ' Without doubt they took it to express a unique relation between God and Jesus, who was supernaturally conceived, born as the Davidic Messiah, and recognized ' (not only appointed) ' by the voice from heaven at the Baptism.' After the stories of the Birth ' Luke does not specially emphasize the Divine Sonship of Jesus.' And Matthew ' prefers to draw attention to the special relation between Jesus and God by making Jesus speak of God as his Father, rather than by referring to him as God's son.'

In all the Synoptics the disciples (except in Matt. xvi. 16) do not seem to speak of Jesus as the Son of God, and Jesus, as we noted, does not use the title himself.   Indeed, the special Sonship of Jesus is not much ' emphasized in the earliest strata of the Gospels.   In Mark and Q there is very little about it ; it played no part in the public teaching of Jesus, and it does not seem to have been a favourite figure for expressing the disciples' belief that Jesus was the Messiah.   In the Synoptic Gospels it is only Matthew who in any way emphasized this idea, which he does by frequently intro-ducing the phrase " My Father " into the sayings of Jesus.   This characteristic is found throughout the Gospel, and may therefore be certainly regarded as due to the Greek editor who made the final recension rather than to his Jewish sources.   By it the editor clearly implied a special relationship of Jesus to God ; but his exact mean-ing is more doubtful.   He may have meant by this phraseology to imply Jesus's consciousness that he was the Davidic Messiah, or that he was the Son κατ' εὐδοκίαν [by appointment at the Baptism], or that he had been miraculously born as God's son, or possibly, though not probably, that he stood in a special, metaphysical relation to God ' (*Beginnings*, i. pp. 400–402).

13–19.   THE TWELVE APOSTLES

(*Cp.* Matt. x. 2–4 ; Luke vi. 12–16)

13   And he went up on to the mountain, and called unto him whom
14 he desired ; and they came unto him.   And he appointed twelve
15 to be with him, and to send them forth to preach, and to have
16 power to cast out demons.   So he appointed the Twelve, and Simon
17 he surnamed Peter.   And (he appointed) James the son of Zebedee, and John the brother of James, whom he surnamed Boanerges,
18 which is, sons of thunder, and Andrew, and Philip, and Bartholomew, and Matthew, and Thomas, and James the son of Alphaeus, and
19 Thaddeus, and Simon the Cananæan, and Judas Iscariot, who betrayed him.

An inner ring of disciples is now specially marked out, and their functions are described.   They are to spread or carry on what Mark regarded as Jesus's own mission.   (1) Preaching, *i.e.* pro-clamation of the Kingdom and its imminence, (2) expulsion of the evil spirits.   The people referred to in 13 are meant to be these Twelve Apostles.   Levi is not named.   The first Gospel supposes that he is identical with Matthew, but though this identification is generally assumed, it is not by any means certain.   Doubtless Jesus

had both an inner and an outer ring or circle of disciples. Whether
the number of the inner ring was twelve, and still more whether Jesus
specially chose out twelve, is dubious. Yet though the number
twelve is clearly symbolic of the twelve tribes, it may conceivably
be historical. Why and when Jesus gave to Simon his surname Peter
(or Rock) is obscure, and if there be any truth in the tradition that
Mark depended upon or embodied Petrine reminiscences, it seems
hardly adequate to account for the omission of the meaning of the
surname by the argument that Peter did not think it worth while to
give it. Meyer strongly believes in the complete historicity of the
appointment of the Twelve by Jesus. Would Judas have been
stated to have been one of the Twelve if he had not actually been so ?
Therefore the Twelve must be historical. Whether they were
appointed for the purpose of preaching, whether they were ever sent
off on a missionary journey, is another matter. Meyer doubts it.
He points out that two different purposes are indicated in Mark :
(1) that they are to be with Jesus as his regular companions, (2) that
they are to go out on preaching missions. The appointment, moreover, is stated twice over. He thinks that these phenomena point
to two different sources. The appointment of the Twelve was a
symbolic act : they represent the twelve tribes, and imply a
Messianic claim. Loisy also thinks that the Twelve are historical.
If the number be symbolic, yet ' il ne laisse pas d'être historique.'
On the other side the arguments of W. and of J. Weiss in *Schriften*
should be read. For my purpose it is needless to discuss the
question at greater length. The mountain in 13 is merely one of
Mark's ' stage properties,' and can hardly be supposed to have had an
actual existence. The references in Meyer are to Vol. i. pp. 136,
137, 264-280, 291-299. Schmidt, who is pretty conservative as
regards the historicity of the separate stories, finds insuperable
difficulties in accepting the section 13-19, or of allocating it to any
particular period of the ministry. The general tradition of the
twelve apostles after the death of Jesus, and the existence of a
' college ' of Twelve, would account for the story. ' There was a
desire to date and localize this institution more or less accurately,
and this desire created the story. It may be due to the evangelist
Mark, yet it may already have been created before him ' (p. 110).
Klostermann (ed. 2) also agrees that if the Twelve were appointed
by Jesus, it would imply a claim of being the Messiah, for the
Twelve represent the Twelve Tribes over whom Jesus will be the
King. Professor Turner points out that Mark (and Luke) use the
phrase ' the Twelve ' : Matthew does not. He says indeed, ' One
of the Twelve,' but otherwise only, ' The Twelve Disciples.' Once
he says ' these Twelve,' referring back to ' the Twelve Apostles.'
Mark uses the ' apostles ' only once (in iii. 14 Prof. Turner thinks

its use is an insertion from Luke vi. 13 ; many MSS. omit it).
The one occasion when he uses ' the apostles ' is in vi. 30, when the
Twelve return from the missionary journey. ' In other words
" apostle " has not lost with him its original sense of missionary '
(*J. T. S.* xxvi., April 1925, p. 232).

14–16. The text is uncertain. In 16 I have followed R.V. M.

18. ' Cananæan ' ; so as R.V. ; not as A.V. ' Canaanite.' An
Aramaic word is transliterated meaning ' Zealot.' See Luke vi. 15.
This Simon was therefore probably ' of the party known as the
Zealots, fanatically patriotic, fiercely opposed to foreign domination.
If so, his continued fidelity to Jesus is a tribute to the Master's
power ' (Bartlet).

20–30. ATTACK AND DEFENCE

(*Cp.* Matt. ix. 32–34, xii. 22–32, 36, 37 ; Luke xi. 14–23, xii. 10)

20 And he went into an house. And a crowd collected together
21 again, so that they could not even eat bread. And when his
relatives heard of these things, they set forth to lay hold of him :
for they said, ' He is out of his mind.'
22 And the scribes who came from Jerusalem said, ' He has Beel-
23 zebul, and by the ruler of the demons he casts out demons.' And
he called them unto him, and said unto them by way of parable,
24 ' How can Satan cast out Satan ? And if a kingdom be divided
25 against itself, that kingdom cannot endure. And if a house be
26 divided against itself, that house cannot endure. And if Satan
rise up against himself, and be divided, he cannot endure, but
27 comes to an end. No man can enter into a strong man's house,
and plunder his goods, unless he first bind the strong man ; and
28 then he can plunder his house. Verily I say unto you, All the sins
and blasphemies wherewith the sons of men blaspheme, shall be
29 forgiven them, but he that blasphemes against the Holy Spirit has
30 no forgiveness for ever, but is guilty of eternal sin.' Because they
said, ' He has an unclean spirit.'

A section raising many critical questions of great interest, on
which I, however, can be brief, because there is nothing in the section
which has any value for us to-day. It opens with the beginning
of a story about Jesus's family who seek to put him under
restraint. But the story is no sooner begun than it is suddenly

interrupted by another story (22-30), so that the original tale is not resumed till 31. The true explanation of these phenomena is not by any means certain. In one other place Mark has a story within a story, but there the interposed story is inserted with propriety, and even with artistic effect. Here, on the contrary, it would seem that there is a real interpolation. At what stage did it arise, and whence was it taken ? The authorities differ. One question at issue is whether the verses 22–30 are taken by Mark from Q. Many scholars think so, for example Goguel, but I hardly think that his arguments are of much value, except perhaps his point that Matthew's and Luke's introduction of the Beelzebul charge by a miraculous cure is much more natural than Mark's omission of any such incident. ' He gives no reason for the accusations levelled against Jesus. The insinuation of the Pharisees that he drives out the demons with the help of Beelzebul is only explicable as an artifice employed by them in order to destroy the impression which the healing of the " possessed " man produced on the people. True, the healing is here so presupposed and required by the context that one might entertain as an hypothesis the possibility that both Matthew and Luke filled in spontaneously what was an obvious gap in the tradition. This hypothesis, however, would explain neither the identity of the two cures in Matthew and Luke, nor the other close points of contact between their two versions. It is also in conflict with the fact that a comparison of Matt. ix. 32–34, which is a " doublet " of Matt. xii. 22–24 shows that the association between the cure of the man who was possessed and the accusation of " possession " is not due to the evangelist.' [This argument is poor. Matt. ix. 34 is wanting in D and S.S. and has been inserted from xii. 22.] ' The suppression of the story of the cure by Mark was no doubt determined by his intention to bring close together the accusation of madness levelled against Jesus by his relations (iii. 20–21) and the charge of " possession " made by the Pharisees' (Introduction, I. p. 260). Streeter (p. 189), who denies that Mark used Q (early though Q was), denies also that 22–30 are an interpolation. He ingeniously renders ἔλεγον γάρ by ' for people were saying,' and explains 22–30 as a digression intended to explain the action taken by the family. It was not they who said that Jesus was beside himself ; they came to apprehend him because they had heard the report. The Scribes from Jerusalem had even gone so far as to say that he was Beelzebul. This theory of Streeter's is ingenious, but hardly tenable, for the digression has all the appearance of a separate and distinct story. It is too long and independent to be regarded merely as a digression intended to explain the action of the family. Professor Turner, however, in his article on the ' Impersonal Plural in Mark ' argues well for ἔλεγον meainng here ' people said,' ' it was reported.'

(*J. T. S.* Vol. xxv., 1924, p. 384.) Nevertheless, it is unlikely, and one perceives well enough that the desire is to avoid the trouble that Jesus's own mother and brothers thought him hardly sane. (Some of the amazing shifts and interpretations to which orthodox Roman Catholic commentators are driven are given by Schmidt in an amusing note on p. 121. It is worth reading.) Schmidt points out that though οἱ παρ' αὐτοῦ of 21 are certainly identical with ' mother and brothers ' of 31, yet that the two very different phraseologies suggest two different traditions (p. 122 *fin.*, 123 *init.*)

20. An editorial verse upon which 21 follows awkwardly. For it was not because Jesus was unable to take his food on account of the crowd that his family said he was mad. What his family hear about is his preaching and his miracles : but when they arrive from Nazareth they are made to find the circumstances stated in verse 20.

21. ' Out of his mind.' Madness in our sense is not intended, but rather a state of spiritual exaltation and excitement of which we might say, ' The man is beside himself.' ' It is only our familiarity with the story which prevents us from being amazed that it has retained a place in the official documents of the Christian Church. Our Lord's family think He has lost His senses, and they stand outside the house where He is, and send for Him. No wonder, in the circumstances, that He ignores them. Here surely, if anywhere in the Gospels, we are listening to the unaltered reminiscences of an eyewitness ' (Burkitt in *J. T. S.* Vol. xvii., 1915, p. 11.)

22. The connection in Matthew is much better. Here the interpolation of 22–30 between 21 and 31 is very strained. The relations of Jesus say : ' He is out of his mind ' ; the Scribes say : ' He has Beelzebul.' His madness is a demoniac possession ; thus only can it be accounted for. But originally 22–30 was a quite separate and independent story.

As a man possessed by a demon, he is the demon's slave or ally. Jesus shows that the supposition is ridiculous. He who was the demon's slave or partner neither could nor would expel a demon from a man. Satan would not be divided against himself, for that would be the very way to bring Satan's rule to an end. The original story perhaps ended at 26. 27 may have been a separate saying, 28 and 29 may be separate again, while 30 attempts clumsily to connect them all together. The process of the agglutination of the separate sayings is well explained and illustrated by Bultmann. The Scribes, as usual, are to hand whenever wanted.

26. The wording ought to be : If Satan *were* divided against himself, he *would* not be able to stand, but he *would* come to an end.

But instead of that we have : ' If Satan *is* divided against himself, he *is* not able to stand, but he *comes* to an end.' The reason for this logical inexactitude is that, as a matter of fact, Satan *is* coming to an end, though for a different reason. The reason is given in the second parable, in the next verse. Satan's power is falling, not because there is division in the Satanic kingdom, but because Satan has encountered a power stronger than his own.

27. The implication is that Satan has been bound, for he is the ' strong man.' Who has bound him ? Is it Jesus ? There are difficulties in such an assumption. Bousset (*Kurios Christos*, p. 41, 2nd ed., and *Schriften*, 3rd ed., on Matt. xii. 28) argues well that the binder is more probably God. For in Matt. xii. 28 the dawning of the Kingdom is brought into connection with the binding. God has bound Satan, and by inspiring Jesus to expel the demons he pillages Satan's house.

28, 29. These verses with their parallels, Matt. xii. 31–32, Luke xii. 10, are difficult, and raise many questions of priority, origin, etc., which are delightful to the critic, but which I shall pass over in silence. There are two forms of the saying ; we have one in Mark ; the other (from Q) in Luke ; while Matthew appears to give a sort of mixture or conflation of the two. Mark's version would seem to be the more original. Jesus did not speak about blasphemies against himself as such, but only about blasphemies against the Holy Spirit in whose name and by whose power he worked his miraculous cures. It would make the sense easier if we could believe that the words τὰ ἁμαρτήματα καὶ αἱ βλασφημίαι were a needless, late addition to the text from Matthew. Then the saying would only have to do with blasphemies : ' All that the sons of men blaspheme shall be forgiven them.' The unforgivable blasphemy is to deny the results of the divine Spirit and to ascribe them to Satan. The Jews admit that the works of Jesus can only be due to supernatural power, but this power they declare to be not divine, but Satanic. Such a view Jesus holds to be not only irrational (for Satan would and could not expel Satan), but also blasphemous.

The expression ' the sons of men ' is odd. One explanation is this. It is supposed that the text or saying ran originally ' to the son of man ' ; what was meant (according to the Aramaic idiom) was just ' man.' But Jesus sometimes called himself, or was supposed to have called himself, Son of man. Hence the saying took the form which we now find in Luke xii. 10 ; and in Mark ' Son of man ' was altered to ' sons of men ', in order that it might not seem as if the absurd meaning were that the sins of Jesus were to be forgiven.

' Eternal sin.'   ' No forgiveness for ever.'   Very definite statements, which can hardly be whittled down to mean ' for a long
period.'   Dr. Bartlet attempts such whittling.   He seeks to show
that the Greek οὐχ ἔχει ἄφεσιν εἰς τὸν αἰῶνα and ἔνοχός ἐστιν
αἰωνίου ἁμαρτήματος is the equivalent of the Hebrew *l'olam*, ' to
an age,' or ' for age long time.'   The Hebrew points neither to a
definite end to the long time, nor, on the other hand, to the ' age '
[or ' long time '] being strictly endless.   ' Hebrew thinking and
speaking were not couched in such terms at all, and had no notion of
" eternity " or " everlastingness " in relation to any created thing,
but only to God—from the very nature of the case.   The phrase
here, then, means " never " during time, as man reckons time, as
distinct from some day during the limited time of opportunity for
moral change and forgiveness which the individual's life on earth
affords ; in a word, " never " for practical purposes of such reckoning, never within all the human horizon of time.   Beyond that
Jesus's words simply do not look, any more than did the thoughts
of his hearers, or of Jews generally in such a connexion.'   The
further ' question whether or not the capacity for repentance and
forgiveness can be restored by some change in conditions by God's
act ' is left unsettled.   It is safe to say that if similar words in a
Talmudic tractate were edited by Dr. Bartlet or any other Christian
scholar, we should not have found a note of this kind.   The words
may be taken to mean ' without any end,' and Jesus, like the
Rabbis, undoubtedly, to my mind, believed that it was compatible
with the goodness of God that certain sinners would or could never
be redeemed and forgiven.   Dr. Bartlet thinks that Mark may have
made the original words of Jesus too strong.   ' That the phrase in
Mark's context, however, meant something final, and so strictly
" everlasting," is quite likely.   For it is to be noted that the whole
clause, " but is guilty of an eternal sin," emphasizing the force of
the foregoing one, is peculiar to Mark ; and it is very possible that
it is an addition to the tradition of Jesus's words in their most
primitive form, parallel to, and having the same significance as, the
different forms it assumed in Matthew and Luke.'   Happily, however, these discussions are for us of little importance.   We are not
bound by any statement of Jesus or Rabbi ; it matters little to us
whether they taught the doctrine of unforgivable sin or no.   For to
us, who have been taught from our childhood the infinite mercy of
God, there can be no sin for which there can be no forgiveness or no
redemption.   We do not believe in eternal punishment or in eternal
deprivation from the blessedness of the hereafter.

I wrote this note remembering, and deeply influenced by, the
simple and excellent religious teaching of my childhood.   It was a
wise and right thing to make the children recoil in horror before the

conception of a loving God who yet consigns his frail children to everlasting penalties and pains. Nothing does modern Judaism greater credit than its passionate antagonism to this pitiless dogma. At the same time I see the justification from another, perhaps more philosophical, point of view, of Dr. Carpenter when he writes bidding me remember that : ' Forgiveness is something much more than remission of a punishment. I doubt whether in the highest morality punishment can be remitted. Forgiveness to be complete is the act (and state) of more than one person. It takes two : (1) the person who forgives, who restores the condition of moral harmony, sympathy, and love, on his side ; and (2) the person who repents and re-enters the life of obedience and affection. The condition of (2) is essential to the whole process. As long as he remains wilful and unloving, he cannot be forgiven ; the injured father, husband, friend—God in the heavenly world—may be all ready and longing, but they cannot forgive one who does not want to be forgiven. The person who is in a state of blaspheming the Holy Spirit is self-excluded from forgiveness : God's love does not reach him. How this condition is to be changed, what energies of grace may be required, what start in a new life under fresh conditions, how many lives of discipline and patience may be needed, we cannot tell. Ultimately the divine love will win ; but of the process and the time we know nothing. How far Jesus realized what we call " eternity," it is impossible to decide ; but I do not think that *this* passage, truly understood, implies eternal punishment, as *against* the infinite mercy of God. The ultimate punishment is Ezekiel's remembrance and loathing, which we shall not desire to abridge, knowing its purifying power.' But the enormous difference between the views here put forth and the ordinary view of Rabbinic Judaism (shared in all probability by Jesus) is this : According to the old view there was rarely, if ever, any *effective* repentance after death, even if the sinner wished it. Thus punishment was merely penal or retributive, not purifying.

31–35. JESUS AND HIS FAMILY

(*Cp.* Matt. xii. 46–50 ; Luke viii. 19–21)

31 And his mother and his brothers came, and, standing outside,
32 sent unto him to call him. And a crowd was sitting round him, and they said unto him, ' Behold, thy mother and thy brothers are
33 outside and seek thee.' And he answered them, saying, ' Who is
34 my mother, or my brothers ? ' And he looked at those who sat
35 around him, and said, ' Behold my mother and my brothers. For

whoever does the will of God, he is to me brother, and sister, and mother.'

The narrative begun in verse 21 is now resumed. The action of his family depends upon their opinion that he is ' possessed ' (21). This also explains, and perhaps partly justifies, his sarcastic reply. They send to fetch him away and take him home. He has to choose between his work and his family : he therefore chooses his work and rejects his family. He cannot abandon the mission which God has entrusted to him.

It has also been urged that the harsh bearing of Jesus towards his mother and family may be explained and justified on the grounds (a) that his family did not understand or believe in his mission, (b) that his whole soul was so filled with this mission that there was no room in it for family ties and interests, and (c) (the most important of all) that his special work implied and demanded a separation from, an abandonment of, all worldly connections and occupations. A placid attachment to the peaceful atmosphere of family life could not easily be united with his passionate yearning for, and devoted service to, the Kingdom of God.

Yet when all is said, there is a certain violation or *froissement* of Jewish sentiment as to parents in this passage, and it is strange to find Jesus, who acts so dubiously towards his own mother, afterwards reproaching the Pharisees with not honouring father and mother ! Even if the explanations of his conduct given above are adequate, Jesus might have explained matters to his mother and family quietly and in private, whereas he, in order to score a point, put them to open shame and humiliation. If we are bidden to regard the Gospel stories as authentic and historic, and if upon *their* slender basis Jesus is set up before us who are Jews as the ideal character for all times and ages, then *we* have also the right to take them literally as well ! And no Jew, who remains a Jew, can well believe that the conduct of Jesus in this story, however justified in its essential issues, was justified in detail, blameless and exquisite in method. The defence in the late Dean of Carlisle's delightful and informing book, *Conscience and Christ*, seems to me hardly satisfactory. It is quite true that the words in 33 were ' provoked ' by the conduct of his mother and brothers in ' trying to keep Him back from His mission on the ground that He was mad.' But should perfection be ' provoked ' to say something which would give a mother pain ? (*Conscience and Christ*, by Dr. Hastings Rashdall, p. 178 (1916).

32. The omission of his father must not be attributed to the fact that Mark knew the story of the virgin birth. Probably the

father was already dead.   At any rate, if the mother had known that her child had been miraculously born, and that he was the ' Messiah of God,' she would hardly have acted as she is here represented. Some MSS. add ' and thy sisters.'   But the sisters have probably been deduced from verse 35 and vi. 3.

CHAPTER IV

1–20. THE PARABLE OF THE SOWER

(*Cp.* Matt. xiii. 1–23 ; Luke viii. 4–15)

1 And he began again to teach by the lake side : and there was gathered unto him a great crowd, so that he entered into a boat, and sat therein on the lake ; and the whole crowd was by the lake on the 2 land. And he taught them many things in parables, and said unto 3 them in his teaching : ' Hearken : behold, there went out a sower to 4 sow. And it came to pass, as he sowed, some seed fell on the way 5 side, and the birds of the air came and devoured it up. And some fell on stony ground, where it had not much earth : and it sprang up 6 quickly, because it had not depth of earth. But when the sun rose up, it was scorched ; and because it had no root, it withered away. 7 And some fell among thorns, and the thorns grew up, and choked it, 8 and it bore no crop. But some seed fell on good ground, and bore a crop which sprang up and increased, and yielded thirty, and sixty, 9 and even an hundred fold.' And he said unto them, ' He that has ears to hear, let him hear.'

10 And when he was alone, they that were about him, together with 11 the Twelve, asked him concerning the parables. And he said unto them, ' Unto you is given the mystery of the kingdom of God : but 12 unto them that are without all is said in parables ; in order that seeing they may see, and not perceive ; and hearing they may hear, and not understand ; lest they should return, and be forgiven.'

13 And he said unto them, ' Ye understand not this parable ? how then will ye understand all the other parables ?

15 ' The sower sows the Word. And these are they by the way side : there the Word is sown, and when they have heard it, Satan comes immediately, and takes away the Word which was sown in 16 them. And these are they who are, as it were, sown on stony ground, who, when they have heard the Word, immediately receive

17 it with gladness : but they have no root in themselves, and so
endure but for a time : afterward, when affliction or persecution
18 arises for the Word's sake, immediately they fall away. And
these are they who are sown among thorns ; these hear the Word,
19 but the cares of the world, and the deceitfulness of riches, and
the other desires enter in, and choke the Word, and it remains
20 unfruitful. And these are they who are sown on good ground ;
who hear the Word and receive it, and bear a crop, thirty, and
sixty, and even an hundred fold.'

A fresh section, containing parables ; specimens of the *teaching*
of Jesus, extending to iv. 34. The original narrative seems interrupted after 9. The section 10–20 is probably secondary, and in it
verses 11 and 12 form a further interpolation. It may also be
argued that 21–25 would not be where they are if 26–29 had
originally followed 20. The addition of the extraneous sayings in
21–25 can only be understood if the main theme is finished and is
not subsequently resumed. The second parable (26–29) appears in
fact as a mere variant of the first ; the third (30–32) may, perhaps,
betray its later date by a conception of the Kingdom of God which
is more usual in Matthew than in Mark, but this count in the
argument is disputed.

We had already a short 'parable' in iii. 23. As a rule the oldest
parables and those which are most likely to be authentic are not
allegories. The true parable illustrates its point as a whole ; each
detail is not to be explained separately. In the allegory every
single detail has its specific reference.

I cannot enter here into the vexed question whether Mark took
his parables from Q, and whether the Q which Mark used was a
much smaller and earlier Q than the Q from which Matthew and
Luke drew so much of their material. I may, however, notice the
argument (for what it is worth) that Mark by his very wording
shows that he means only to give specimens of the sayings or the
teaching of Jesus. He is supposed to indicate this by his phrase :
' he taught them many things in parables, and said to them in the
course of his teaching' : ἐν τῇ διδαχῇ αὐτοῦ. So too in xii. 1,
' He began to teach them in parables ' ; one parable only is given
as an example. In xii. 38 it is said, ' He said in the course of his
teaching ' ; ἐν τῇ διδαχῇ αὐτοῦ ἔλεγεν. Here, says Dibelius, it is
' perfectly obvious ' (?) that the few sentences which follow are a
mere quotation from what Mark calls the Teaching of Jesus (pp. 68,
69, 78, 79).

Nor can I touch on the relation of the parables of Jesus to the
parables in the Rabbinical literature. Doubtless Jesus may often

have used a current story or parable, and have altered it for his own purpose. Some of the parables and stories attributed to him have a wonderful fragrancy and grace. The reader should consult Dr. Abrahams' chapter on the Parables (xii.) in *Studies*, I. pp. 90–107.

1. The boat mentioned in iii. 9 is now used. But the situation is scarcely to be regarded as historical. How many people could hear what a man said from a boat ?

2. 'In parables,' *i.e.* in a parabolic way. 'In his teaching,' *i.e.* in the ' course of his teaching.'

3–9. The first parable. The parable of the Sower. It has been suggested that the parable of the sower comes first, ' not only because tradition associated with it an explanation of the general aim of the parables, but because it is the parable of the Word, and because it had of itself an almost universal character which marked it out as the typical parable. It must have occupied the first place in the oldest collection of parables, even before speculation on the mysteries of teaching by parables and on the special reasons why Jesus chose that method of teaching had begun ' (Loisy).

What was the original meaning of the parable ? This is by no means certain. The explanation in 14–20 need not necessarily be correct. Here the Word, which must be spelt with a capital, is either the teaching of Jesus concerning the Kingdom of God, or his teaching as a whole. But *was that* the meaning of the ' seed ' in the parable ? Is the parable, Bultmann asks, intended to console any man if not all his labour bears fruit ? Or is it a sort of half resigned, half grateful monologue of Jesus about his own work ? Is it an exhortation addressed to the hearers of the word of God ? Or of the preaching of Jesus ? Or of the preaching of the community ? (p. 125). The very fact that such questions *can* be asked shows that all is not so simple as it seems. If a monologue, why should it be addressed to a crowd ? And if it deals with the teaching of Jesus, is it prophetic or retrospective ? If an exhortation, it seems wrongly framed ; it is not the seed which should get spoilt or ruined, but the places which did not receive it fruitfully. In any case the parable remains obscure. If it is merely meant to explain the diverse, actual results of Jesus's teaching and preaching, it could not have been spoken very early in the ministry, if it is authentic. Jesus feels that it is his duty to scatter the seed. He knows that it will fall mostly upon unfruitful soil, yet in some hearts it will bear fruit. In spite of failures, he looks for, and is sure of, success in the end.

For it is God who has commissioned him to sow.   If the parable be
authentic, what strikes one as odd about it is that Jesus does not
seem to speak and think as if the old order, the natural world, were
soon coming to a violent end.   He speaks rather as if there were to
be a long process in which righteousness should, as it were, gradually
come by its own.   The Kingdom of God upon earth, the reign of
goodness and truth, will surely come, but only gradually.   His own
person is not the centre of all things.   The drama does not consist
of his life, his death, his resurrection, and the Last Judgment—all
closely following each other—but it consists in the gradual reception
of his teaching by a dull and reluctant world.   Can this second, and
more modern conception have existed in his mind *as well as* the more
eschatological and apocalyptic conception ?   Perhaps he did not
perceive their inconsistency.

5.   Bacon thinks that the meaning of the parable is, ' The farmer
is not discouraged because part of his seed goes to waste.'   The
explanation in 15–20 allegorizes, fixing attention on the crops which
the seed produces or fails to produce.   ' Its moral is : Do you,
hearers of the word, take heed not to let it remain unfruitful '
(*Beginnings of Gospel Story*, p. 49).

10–20.   The explanation of the parable.   A later and secondary
section, which is itself interpolated by 11, 12, two still later verses,
that interrupt the connection.   If 10, 13–20 are ' secondary,' these
two verses are ' tertiary.'   One may safely assume that even 10,
13–20 are not authentic.   But it is another question how they came
to be where they are.   Are we to regard them as later insertions
into Mark, though already inserted in the Mark which lay before
Matthew and Luke ?   Or did Mark himself insert these passages
(of which 13–20 may have lain before him, and 10–12 he may have
himself composed) into his narrative ?   So Schmidt (p. 131).   But
there is a little difficulty about 11, 12.   These verses at least, it
might be argued, are interpolated, for 10, which may at first have
had ' parable ' in the singular, seems the direct introduction to 13–20.
I may note here that Schmidt is exceedingly cautious in pronouncing
anything in Mark (which is not sheer framework) to be unhistorical.
At this very point he utters a solemn warning against too hasty
verdicts of ' impossible,' ' psychologically inconceivable,' ' unhistorical.'   The saying : ' Wrede and his adherents have paid too
little consideration to the " tensions " (*Spannungen*) which exist in
Jesus,' is true (p. 132).   That is to say, Jesus was not always consistent, and there were ' tensions ' working within him, which may
have pulled him in different directions, and produced, in moments of
excitement, variously coloured sayings.

It might be argued that 11, 12 are in keeping with Mark's general conception.   To him the people of Israel *were* supernaturally blind.   It was of God that they could not see ; they were not allowed to see or to understand : Jesus hides his Messianity from them ; he reveals the whole mystery of the Kingdom and of the method of salvation only to the disciples, and to them only mysteriously, so that they too do not understand !   They do not even understand the symbolism and meaning of his miracles (viii. 21).   So we may, perhaps, paradoxically and whimsically, defend the real Markan origin of 11, 12 as well as of 13–24.   And we may, perhaps, agree with Dibelius that while Mark created the arrangement of the boat (iv. 1), he neglected and forgot it when he wanted to introduce the private interpretation of the parable and the theory of the parables as a whole.   Mark is a theologian and a full believer in the divinity of his hero ; his Gospel is the book of secret revelations or epiphanies of the Son of God, and yet Mark is also a faithful collector of tradition, which includes pictures and sayings of Jesus quite authentic and very different from the theories of the evangelist (pp. 60–66).

10.   ' His companions as well as the Twelve.'   Were they all in the boat ?   Or has Jesus landed ?   But in 35 he is still in the boat.   The Twelve had not, so far, been specially mentioned.   The plural ' parables ' is odd.   Only one had been, so far, spoken.   In fact, at this point there is intercalated a general statement embodying a theory about the parables as a whole.   We may suppose that an original singular has been, on account of the interpolation of 11 and 12, changed into the plural.

11, 12.   ' The mystery of the Kingdom.'   A strange term.   The word ' mystery ' is only found here in the Synoptics.   For the term and the whole saying, see Bacon (pp. 142, 266 of *The Gospel of Mark*).   The word ' mystery ' is common in Paul.   ' Yet the idea of the " hiding of the mystery " (of the divine revelation), the real point of resemblance, belongs rather to the Hellenistic Wisdom literature than specifically to Paul.'   The rendering of Isaiah xxiv. 16 by Theodotion, ' My mystery is for me and for those who are mine,' is curious.   Bacon thinks that this rendering and the phrase in the Talmud (Sanhedrin, 94 *a*), ' a *bath kol* (divine voice) resounded, saying, My secret is mine, my secret is mine,' ' prove the currency of the idea in Jewish circles.'   The strange Sanhedrin passage refers also to Isaiah xxiv. 16, and the Talmud, like Theodotion, translates by ' my secret,' ' my mystery' (referring to the delay in the appearance of the Messiah).   In our Mark verse we may explain : you, my chosen companions and disciples, are alone permitted to be taught and to understand the laws and constitution of the Kingdom, the conditions of entering it, and so on. But the word 'mystery' suggests that there is a reference here to Jesus's own position in the Kingdom as well as to the Kingdom itself. His Messiahship is the mystery which is to be revealed to the disciples—in spite of their obtuseness—but hidden from the world at large till death and resurrection reveal it. In any case we may be sure that these verses are much later than Jesus. Esoteric teaching would seem to be wholly alien to the historic Jesus : he did not regard and present the Kingdom as a mystery. He pities the multitude, and would not wish to darken, but to enlighten them. Moreover, iv. 21 contradicts these two verses, and the parable itself contradicts them. For all *understand* the Word, but not all take it to heart. Jesus may have used parables to make people think, and even to test intelligence, but surely not to keep his meaning dark except to a few special disciples.

Professor Burkitt is quite ready to defend and champion the historical character of 10–12 and of 13–20. All fits in well : no need to posit 'two distinct sources'; one writer only is required and 10–12 are as early and as authentic as 3–8. But his defence depends upon more than one doubtful hypothesis : it especially depends upon the view that the historic Jesus taught a new doctrine about the Kingdom of God, namely, its 'gradual growth' comparable 'to the growth of a plant,' so that 'it was like a man sowing his seed, which then grew from stage to stage naturally and silently, until at last the harvest was ripe' (*Gospel History*, pp. 86, 87). I have often had to point out the doubtfulness of this theory of the Kingdom in Jesus's view of it. Not least doubtful is it in Burkitt's modified form : to him the 'gradual growth' was apparently only the period between the date of the sayings in Mark iv. and the crucifixion. Jesus, we are told, 'alone knew that a period of gradual growth was necessary before His disciples, even those most attached and devoted to Him, would be strong enough to count the cost intelligently and follow him to the end.' Something much more than all this is involved in 11, 12, something much more theological and Pauline. And whatever the Parable of the Sower may mean, it surely does *not* mean that the Kingdom has to grow gradually until the disciples are strong enough to follow their leader to the end. If there is anything in the parable of gradual growth, it means that the End of the Age would not come for a long while. *Cp.* Bacon, pp. 142, 143. His dubious theory is that 11 is a Markan prosaic version or distortion of the Q Logion Matt. xi. 25. It also rests on such passages as Romans xi. 7, 8, and 1 Cor. ii. 7.

14. The disciples are always represented by Mark as obtuse.

But as we have seen, the parable was really not very clear.   Or, at any rate, if clear to those whom Jesus addressed it, it had become unclear to a later age.   And an explanation may have been requisite how it was, or why it was, that the teaching of Jesus had not been accepted by all.   (11, 12 represent a further stage.   The rejection of the teaching was intentional ; God had willed it so ; the parables were intended not to enlighten the ' outsiders,' but to deepen their darkness.)

15. The explanation is awkward.   The Word is the seed ; the crops should not be *men*.   The hearers should be represented—if the parable is turned, as the explanation turns it, into an allegory—by the different sorts of soil, not identified with the crops.

Satan is here made the general cause of evil issues.   He is no special evil, like the cares of the world, and therefore is not typified by the birds in the same way as the thorns typify the cares.   The introduction of Satan is, however, on the way to the view taken in 11 and 12, and another step is taken in Luke viii. 12, ' that they may not believe and be saved.'   Satan comes to those who are predestined to an evil end.

17.   The explanation now obviously reveals itself as late, for the Christian community is established, and the era of persecution has begun.   And some have fallen away from lack of firmness or for other reasons (19).   *Cp.* Bacon, *Mark*, p. 141.

21–25. The Hidden and the Revealed—Measure for Measure

(Cp. Matt. v. 15, x. 26, vii. 2, xiii. 12, xxv. 29 ; Luke viii. 16–18, vi. 38, xi. 33, xii. 2, xix. 26)

21   And he said unto them, ' Is the lamp brought in to be put under the bushel, or under the bed ? and not rather to be placed on the
22 stand ?   For there is nothing hid, which shall not be revealed ; neither was there anything kept secret, but that it should come to
23 light.   Who has ears to hear, let him hear.'
24   And he said unto them, ' Take heed what ye hear : with what measure ye mete, it shall be measured to you, and even more shall
25 be added thereto.   For he that has, to him shall be given : and he that has not, from him shall be taken even that which he has.'

A collection of more or less disconnected sentences which reappear, some more than once, in different connections and environments in Matthew and Luke. Each of the four sentences may have been a saying by itself, and the original meaning is hard to discover. The authenticity of the sayings can neither be proved nor disproved. To Goguel (p. 265) this section establishes ' nettement ' the dependence of Mark upon the Logia (Q). And the parallels ' show ' that Mark has here ' compiled ' material borrowed from that collection. This seems clear to him and to other scholars too. To yet others (I agree with them) it is very far from ' clear.'

21. What is the lamp ?   To Mark we may take it to mean the teaching of Jesus.   Contrast verses 11, 12.

22. In this verse it would appear as if something *had* been kept dark, or reserved for a few, for a period, but that this temporary withholding was only provisional. The final intention was that all should see.

Did Mark understand by this the early reserve of Jesus as to his Messiahship ?

What the saying originally meant it is not easy to ascertain.

24. The word ' hear ' in 23 may have brought about the juxta-position of 24 in which ' hear ' occurs again. As to the meaning of the verse one can ask : (*a*) what did Jesus mean by it ? (*b*) what did it mean to the compiler of the source whence Mark took it, assuming that he did so ? (*c*) what did it mean to Mark ? As regards (*c*), some suppose that the meaning has to do with the measure of attentiveness which the disciples pay. According to their attentive-ness will be the measure of their gain. But if they attend well, they will find in the words of Jesus more than they could have suspected. Or, again, it may mean : if they act according to the teaching, they will be abundantly rewarded. The original meaning may be the same as the parallel in Matt. vii. 2 : God will show to man the same measure which man shows to his neighbour. Jesus attacks the doctrine of tit for tat in some of its forms, but in others he maintains it.

25. Probably once more an independent saying which has been used in the Parable of the Talents in Matt. xxv. 29 and again in xiii. 12. To Mark, in the connection in which he places the adage, it may mean : ' If you attend to the teaching—to what you hear— your knowledge will increase and increase ; if you do not attend, you will soon even forget what you have heard.' Originally the meaning was probably more general. We may apply the adage still. He who does not advance falls back. He whose knowledge

or goodness is alive and real necessarily improves in knowledge and goodness ; he whose knowledge or goodness is conventional or sterile has no real grip upon either knowledge or goodness ; his possessions are no real possessions, and what he falsely has he will actually lose. Rabbinic parallels can be read in S. B.

26-29. THE SEED THAT GROWS OF ITSELF

(Mark only)

26   And he said, ' The kingdom of God is as if a man should cast
27 seed into the ground ; and he sleeps and arises, night and day,
28 and the seed sprouts and grows up, he knows not how. For of herself the earth brings forth her crop ; first the blade, then the
29 ear, after that the full corn in the ear. But when the crop permits, immediately he sends forth the sickle, because the harvest has come.'

Some regard this section as following originally on 9. For as the hearers from 10 to 25 are the disciples, ' it almost follows that 26-32 which presupposes the " crowd " (cp. 33) originally followed 1-9 ' (Moffatt). The striking parable in 26-29 is only found in Mark. Why Luke and Matthew passed it over is disputed. Good and interesting suggestions can be read in Streeter, pp. 171, 172. The meaning is supposed to be fairly clear, though the warning of Bultmann (p. 125 fin. p. 106 fin.) that we are by no means sure (a) that the parable may not have existed before its combination with the ' Kingdom,' and (b) that we really do possess its exact signification, is not entirely superfluous.

The Kingdom of God is compared to a process. The seed is sown ; though some of it is wasted, some is successful. But it needs time ; yet, once sown, the good seed is bound to ripen and bear its fruit. Jesus preached the Word ; the perfect Kingdom of God will appear in its season.

Jesus can only do the part given to him by God. Nor is it for him to tell when precisely the Judgment and the Kingdom will come. Directly the seed he has sown has ripened, God will begin His harvest. As the farmer sows and then waits, so only can Jesus fulfil his mission : preaching, collecting, preparing. He cannot force the advent of the Kingdom, any more than the farmer can force the appearance of the fruit. Many of his adherents probably urged him to take more forcible action, but he speaks with disapproval of those who would seek to obtain the Kingdom by violence (Matt. xi. 12). The actual bringing of the Kingdom is not the work of man, and not his work ; it is God's work ; he (Jesus) has to proclaim that God will rule, and that man must prepare himself for that rule and make himself worthy of it. This is quite good Pharisaic, Rabbinic doctrine, as opposed to the violent policy of the Zealots.

29. ὅταν παραδοῖ ὁ καρπός, 'when the fruit is ready' or 'when the fruit allows': a difficult phrase, says Mr. Rawlinson. He notes, with some approval, an emendation, which could be translated, 'when the time allows.' *i.e.* καιρός for καρπός. ἀποστέλλει τὸ δρέπανον, ὅτι παρέστηκεν ὁ θερισμός. *Cp.* Joel iii. 13 ἐξαποστείλατε δρέπανα, ὅτι παρέστηκεν τρυγητός. The quotation or reminiscence is obvious. Has this any bearing upon the date or origin of the parable ? Or is verse 29 not a part of the original parable ? It is clear that the divine Judgment is alluded to.

The parable gives rise to certain difficulties. If it is authentic, can Jesus have believed that the end would come so quickly, that the new era had in fact begun ? For in the new era there is no actual development. On first thoughts it might rather seem as if the parable sprang from those who saw the young Christian community before them, and believed that a long and glorious future lay in front of it. But against this view there is the difficulty that, as Dr. Carpenter says, the early Christians were all convinced that the end was at hand. Perhaps, then, Jesus had both ideas in his mind and gave expression to them upon different occasions. Dr. Carpenter says : ' I agree ; and in this respect there was, I think, a change, not for the better (from our point of view). Jesus became more eager, not for his own personal triumph, but for God's, and so he became more apocalyptic.' But the parable may really not contain any idea of a long development. The Kingdom is already imminent in the preaching of the Word. The harvest follows not long after the seed. We must not, it has been rightly said, press the view that in 'this parable, as in other parables of growth, Jesus meant to indicate the view that the Kingdom was to arrive gradually by development, rather than suddenly by the act of God. The prophetic ministry was, it is true, to prepare the way for that last act. But the act itself was very near at hand ; it would burst on the world before the disciples had gone over the cities of Israel. If there was a pause before the final act, it was not strange ; the same thing happened in the natural world in the case of the sower ' (Menzies). The idea of a long process or development may be entirely lacking.

30–34. THE MUSTARD SEED

(*Cp.* Matt. xiii. 31, 32 ; Luke xiii. 18, 19)

30   And he said, ' Whereunto shall we liken the kingdom of God ?
31 or with what parable shall we represent it ?   It is like a grain of
mustard seed, which, when it is sown in the earth, is less than all
32 the seeds that are in the earth.   But when it is sown, it grows
up, and becomes greater than all the plants, and throws out
great branches : so that all the birds of the air can lodge under the
shadow of it.'
33   And with many such parables spake he the Word unto them, as
34 they were able to understand it.   And without a parable spake he
not unto them : but when they were alone, he explained everything
to his disciples.

The third parable.   The mustard seed would appear to be the
Kingdom as represented by, and existing in, the Christian community.   From small and lowly beginnings it is destined to become
the greatest thing on earth, to include all humanity in its embrace.
Whether the fulfilment is to come soon is not stated, but it is, on
the other hand, not implied that it is far off.

One can imagine that in the humble beginnings of the Christian
community the parable would be encouraging and suggestive.

In this parable the Kingdom—here only in Mark—is not the
Kingdom of the future which on a renovated earth God will himself
establish, it is not the perfected Divine Rule of the new era, but
it is the growing Kingdom as represented by the Christian community.   And the seed is not the Word, but the Kingdom.   It may
therefore be questioned whether this parable was really spoken by
Jesus.   Of the thirteen places in which, in Mark, Jesus speaks of
the Kingdom, this is the only passage where it seems definitely to
mean the growing Christian Church.   In i. 14, ix. 1, 47, x. 23–25,
xiv. 25, its eschatological sense seems clear.   iv. 11, 26 do not
contradict that sense.   For the other three passages, x. 14, 15 and
xii. 34, see the notes *ad loc.*   But one must not be too sure about
the meaning of the parable (*cp.* Bultmann, p. 125).

32.   There is a reminiscence of Ezekiel xvii. 23.   The Messianic
Kingdom which is here predicted is of the same kind as that of the
old prophets in their larger, quieter, and more universalistic moods.
It is to be a Kingdom of peace and righteousness and of the knowledge of God.   Jesus, we have to remember, takes up again the
wider messages of Isaiah, and even of Ezekiel too, it may be said,

in such momentary phases of his teaching as are reflected in xvii. 23, where, under the shadow of the Tree of Israel, all the birds of every wing shall dwell. *Cp.* also Ezekiel xxxi. 6 ; Dan. iv. 12, 21.   But quite probably the wide extension of the Christian community among the heathen had already begun, and the words of 32 reflect it. *Cp.* Holtzmann, *Neutestamentliche Theologie,* I. p. 496, 2nd ed., 1911.

33.   This verse seems to indicate that Jesus used parables to help his hearers to understand his meaning.   To the author of verse 33, the parables were spoken to be understood by all who heard them, so far as their capacities admitted.   34, on the contrary, follows the point of view of verses 10 and 11.   It is the work of the latest redactor, who thinks that the object of the parables was to darken or harden the Jews, and who even forgets that Jesus spoke much to the people which was not in parables at all.

35-41. STORM AT SEA

(*Cp.* Matt. viii. 18, 23-27 ; Luke viii. 22-25)

35   And the same day, when the even was come, he said unto them,
36 'Let us cross over unto the other side.' And when they had dismissed the crowd, they took him, even as he was, in the boat.
37 And other boats were with him.   And there arose a great storm of wind, and the waves beat upon the boat, so that it became full.
38 And he was in the stern of the boat, asleep on a pillow : and they awoke him, and said unto him, 'Master, carest thou not that we
39 perish ? '   And he arose, and rebuked the wind, and said [unto the sea], 'Peace, be still.'   And the wind dropped, and there was a
40 great calm.   And he said unto them, 'Why are ye so fearful ? Have ye still no faith ? '   And they feared exceedingly, and said
41 one to another, 'Who is this man, that even the wind and the sea obey him ? '

A fresh series of tales and miracles is now begun, reaching to the end of Chapter v.

35.   It is not explained what the motive was for this departure to the other side of the lake.   Was it to gain some repose, or to carry the Tidings to other centres ?   On the other side of the lake there were indeed many Jews, but they dwelt amid a large number of pagans.   'On that day' may be editorial, but the late evening hour belongs to the original story.

36. Jesus is still in the boat. The disciples ' take him with them,' just as he was, without further preparation. These words, however, are due to the redactor. Originally the story must have meant to imply that Jesus was on land, and that he determined to cross over to the other side of the lake (*cp.* Matt. viii. 18, 23 ; Luke viii. 22). ' They take him with them ' is an odd phrase, if Jesus is already with them in the boat ; ' as he was ' is added to mask the difficulty.

The remark that there were other boats present too has no bearing upon the story, and may therefore point to a real historic tradition.

39. The MS. D omits ' the sea,' perhaps rightly. It is the wind which is regarded as a spirit, not the sea.

41. Was Jesus justified in charging them with want of faith ? Hardly, I think. It may be said that a man in a storm at sea should not be afraid, because he should not fear death, but it cannot be said that faith in God will of itself prevent the wreck of the ship and the death of the passengers. Faith should make one willing either to live or to die. It cannot prevent death.

Dr. Carpenter wrote dissenting. ' The want of courage is traced to lack of faith, with the implication that the man who feels himself in God's hands will not be afraid of shipwreck or death or anything. He can meet catastrophe calmly.' Is not this too modern ? The narrator clearly meant that they should have faith that God would not suffer them to perish. He did not mean that they ought to have shown fearlessness or faith in God, *even though* they were to be drowned.

How far the story, which, as it is written, clearly embodies reminiscences of Jonah, may be historical is dubious. It may have some historical basis. Jesus goes to sleep in a boat. A squall comes on. The disciples are afraid and wake him up. He rebukes them, and, as a fact, the wind soon drops. Here were the historic materials at hand for a supernatural tale. For us it does not matter a straw if some history is here mingled with legend or no. But the anxiety of some Christian critics to preserve, and argue for, some historical substratum is almost pathetic. For the interesting parallel story of R. Gamaliel (who also by his prayer causes the storm to cease), see *S. B.* p. 489 *fin.* Klausner says that ' the Lake of Galilee frequently becomes rough suddenly and as suddenly becomes calm again.' He himself ' witnessed such a change while sailing on the lake in the spring of 1912. Yet for the Galilæan fishermen, with their craving for marvels, it was a miracle which Jesus had performed ' (p. 269).

CHAPTER V

1–20. THE GADARENE SWINE

(*Cp.* Matt. viii. 28–34 ; Luke viii. 26–39)

1 And they came unto the other side of the lake, to the country
2 of the Gadarenes. And as he landed from the boat, immediately
3 there met him [out of the tombs] a man with an unclean spirit, who
dwelt among the tombs. And nobody had been able to bind him
4 even with a chain : for he had been often bound with fetters and
chains, but the chains had been torn asunder by him, and the fetters
broken in pieces : and no one was strong enough to subdue him.
5 And always, night and day, he was in the mountains and in the
6 tombs, shrieking, and cutting himself with stones. But when he
7 saw Jesus afar off, he ran and fell down before him, and cried with
a loud voice, and said, ' What have I to do with thee, Jesus, thou
Son of the most high God ? I adjure thee by God, that thou
8 torment me not.' (For Jesus had said unto him, ' Come out of the
9 man, thou unclean spirit.') And Jesus asked him, ' What is thy
name ? ' And he answered, saying, ' My name is Legion : for we
10 are many.' And he besought him much that he would not send
11 them away out of the land. Now there was there upon the
12 mountain a great herd of swine feeding. And they besought him,
saying, ' Send us into the swine, that we may enter into them.'
13 And Jesus gave them leave. And the unclean spirits went out,
and entered into the swine : and the herd rushed down the cliff into
the lake (they were about two thousand) ; and they were drowned
14 in the lake. And the swineherds fled, and told the story in the city
and in the country. And the people came out to see what had
15 happened. And they came to Jesus, and saw him that was possessed
with the demon, sitting down, clothed and in his right mind : and
16 they were afraid. And the eyewitnesses told them what had
happened to him that was possessed with the demon, and also

110

17 about the swine. And they began to entreat him to depart out of
18 their territory. And as he was getting into the boat, the man who
had been possessed with the demon entreated him that he might go
19 with him. Howbeit Jesus permitted him not, but said unto him,
' Go home to thine own people, and tell them what great things the
Lord has done for thee, and how he has had compassion upon thee.'
20 And he departed, and began to proclaim publicly in the Ten
Cities what great things Jesus had done for him : and all were
amazed.

A strange story. It is clear that a popular folk tale has been
somehow or other caught up, and attributed to, or brought into
connection with, Jesus. This sort of thing constantly happens even
to this day. Stories that have no particular hero, or no historic
hero, become attached to a definite person. And stories which
originally were told of one man become transferred to another.
Dr. Jowett, Master of Balliol from 1870 to his death in 1893, of
whom a quantity of stories, some true and some apocryphal, were
related, told me that stories or sayings were attributed to him
which in *his* undergraduate days were attributed, some truly and
some falsely, to the *then* Master, Dr. Jenkyns.

1. The inhabitants on the east side of the lake were mixed.
There were many pagans as well as Jews. Hence the herd of
swine.

2. The ' possessed ' person is, in this case, a violent madman.
He is represented as dwelling among the tombs, inasmuch as he
avoids all human intercourse, and also because the popular belief
was that demons liked to haunt cemeteries.

9. As the unclean spirit is to go into a herd of pigs, there
must be more than one spirit. This verse makes and explains the
transition from the singular to the plural. Perhaps Jesus asks for
the name, because, in the popular idea, in order to lay a spirit
effectually, it is desirable or even necessary to know its name.
It was also part of the popular belief that demons live in herds of
beasts, and that a whole number of them can reside in a human
body. A demon does not like to mention his name, for if you know
his name, you gain power over him. That is a very old and widely
diffused superstition. A name is no mere vocable. What's in a
name ? the ' ancients ' would never have said. *Cp.* Genesis xxxii. 29
and elsewhere. Did the demon forget himself and give his name too
carelessly ? Or, in the original story, was the name got out of the

demon by some spell or trick, and was this feature of the tale dropped when it was fathered upon Jesus ?

10.   The unclean spirits do not want to go back to their own place (the desert or hell) ; they can easily leave the human or animal body in which they have taken up their abode for some other of the same sort.

12.   Dr. Bartlet's note is interesting, and not least the last sentence. ' This suggestion implies the common popular belief that demons, as incorporeal beings, must have an animal organism of some kind, but not necessarily a human one, if they are to remain contentedly (Luke xi. 24, " seeking rest ") on earth as distinct from some incorporeal sphere, whether above (in " the air," *cp.* " the prince of the jurisdiction of the air," Eph. ii. 2) or below (" the abyss " of woe, Rev. ix. 1 f., xx. 3). It is premature consignment to the latter, " before the time " (Matt. viii. 29), that these demons are represented by Luke as fearing. The whole story is *told* in terms of popular beliefs, not necessarily all of them shared by Jesus, nor even part of the episode as enacted.'

13, 14.   The spirits are disappointed. Their wish is granted, and yet they are dispossessed of their chosen new home. The unclean pigs are drowned, and their heathen owners lose 2000 beasts.

17.   They ask him to leave, partly, perhaps, because they do not wish to lose any more property, partly because the presence of so powerful a miracle-worker makes them afraid.
We are to gather that they are not Jews, but pagans. Whether the man who is cured is a Jew or not is uncertain. Jesus carries out their wishes and returns to the Capernaum side of the lake. Have we here a sort of veiling of the fact that this attempt at preaching the Kingdom on the other side of the lake was for some reason or other a failure, and that Jesus had to return ?

19.   Jesus refuses to allow the man to become one of his disciples ; he does not desire to have a stranger among his own immediate followers. At any rate, whatever the reason, he bids him go home and tell his family what the Lord (here meaning God) has done for him. If the man was a pagan, this might mean that he was to convert his family to the knowledge of the one true God, the Lord (Jehovah, Yahweh).
It is generally supposed that this bidding of Jesus constitutes an exception to the usual command of secrecy and silence. It is, how-

ever, doubtful whether it is so, for the man is only bidden to tell his *family*. He is to keep within the privacy of his house, whereas, instead, he publishes the wonderful cure all over the Decapolis, but Jesus had not suggested or ordered this. On the contrary, the words of the order look rather as if he wished the man to keep among his own household. The order, therefore, is probably no exception to the rule. It is, perhaps, fair to mention another view which, for example, is thus stated by Dr. Bartlet. ' The reason for the difference lay in the different conditions. For this was Peræa, and in that remoter district, where also Jesus would be less known, there might be less risk from publicity ; while the man's testimony would give those ready to hear to purpose a chance of knowing enough to lead them to seek him out, if they so desired. He was to be a sort of forerunner for Jesus himself (*cp.* vii. 31), possibly in non-Jewish circles (*cp.* 7).'

20. ' Decapolis, the ten city district, is the name applied to the cities, east of the Jordan, liberated by Pompey from Jewish rule, which united in the ten city alliance. These cities had been Hellenistic since the Syrian conquest, had been conquered and subjected to Jewish rule by the Maccabees, and were finally liberated by Pompey ' (Gould).

As the highest portions of the Synoptic Gospels excel the *average* teachings of the prophets, so the lowest portions fall beneath them. How pure and free the prophets are from the superstitious ideas about demons and demoniac possession to which Jesus, like many others of his time, was a victim.

21–43. THE DAUGHTER OF JAIRUS AND THE WOMAN
WITH AN ISSUE

(*Cp.* Matt. ix. 18–26 ; Luke viii. 40–56)

21   And when Jesus had crossed over again in the boat unto the other side, a great crowd gathered unto him, and stood by the edge
22 of the lake. And, behold, there came one of the rulers of the synagogue, Jairus by name ; and when he saw him, he fell at his
23 feet, and besought him greatly, saying, ' My little daughter lies at the point of death : come and lay thy hands on her, that she may be healed, and may live.'
24   And Jesus went with him ; and a great crowd followed him, and
25 pressed around him. And a woman, who had had an issue of blood
26 twelve years, and had suffered much from many physicians, and had spent all her fortune, and was not benefited, but rather grew worse,

27 having heard the tales about Jesus, came up in the crowd, and
28 touched his garment from behind. For she thought, ' If I only
29 touch his clothes, I shall be cured.' And straightway the source of
her issue dried up ; and she felt in her body that she was healed of
30 her affliction. And Jesus, realizing immediately that power had
gone out of him, turned round in the crowd, and said, ' Who touched
31 my clothes ? ' And his disciples said unto him, ' Thou seest the
crowd pressing around thee, and thou sayest, Who touched me ? '
32, 33 And he looked round to see who it was that had done it. But the
woman, fearing and trembling—for she knew what had befallen her
34 —came and fell down before him, and told him all the truth. But
he said unto her, ' Daughter, thy faith has cured thee ; go in peace,
and be healed of thy affliction.'

35 While he yet spake, there came some men from the ruler of the
synagogue's house, and said, ' Thy daughter is dead : why troublest
36 thou the Master any further ? ' But Jesus overheard the word that
was spoken, and said unto the ruler of the synagogue, ' Be not afraid ;
37 have but faith.' And he allowed no man to go on with him, except
38 Peter, and James, and John the brother of James. And they came
to the house of the ruler of the synagogue, and he heard an uproar,
39 for they wept and wailed loudly. And when he had entered in, he
said unto them, ' Why make ye this uproar, and weep ? the child is
40 not dead, but sleeps.' And they laughed him to scorn. But he
drove them all out, and took with him only the father and the
mother of the child, and his companions, and entered in where the
41 child was lying. And he took the hand of the child, and said unto
her, ' *Talitha cumi* ' ; which is, being interpreted, ' Maiden, I say
42 unto thee, arise.' And straightway the girl arose, and walked ;
43 for she was twelve years old. And they were utterly beside themselves with amazement. And he strictly ordered them that no man
should know it ; and he told them that something should be given
her to eat.

The stories are vividly told. The ' realistic ' touches are mostly
omitted by Matthew, who either did not appreciate them, or thought
them 'worldly' and secular, or (in 29, 30) materialistic. Not *touching*
Jesus, but the woman's faith, healed her. In 36 the words ' Fear
not ; only believe,' have a wonderfully solemn effect. Whether
such a faith was reasonable need not here be discussed. It could
not lightly or easily be answered. The whole story is told with
consummate art.

Note that here only we find a story within a story. (*Cp.* however, iii. 20.) The interval and necessary pause between the departure of Jesus to see the dying girl and his arrival at the house are admirably filled up by the incident of the woman with the issue. Excellently as the tales are told, the several features of the two miracles are typical in the miracle stories of the age. *Cp.* Bultmann, pp. 132, 135–150.

The historical basis of the stories it is impossible to recover or to fix. We are left to mere conjectures, of which there are a number, especially as regards the child. Was she not really dead? Was it a case of apparent death? Did Jesus realize this? Or did Jesus all the time think she was dead? Did *he* think that he had performed a great miracle, and had he not really done so? (So Thompson, *Miracles in the New Testament*, p. 45, 1911.) It is pretty certain that both stories have some real basis. The first may be a case of auto-suggestion. The woman really believed that if she touched Jesus, she would be healed. And healed she was. But Jesus tells her that it is not the touching which is the *ultimate* source of her cure, but her *faith*. Meyer says rightly : ' The healing power flows from him automatically ; he, however, notices it, and inquires who has touched his garment ; he is, therefore, not omniscient. This story is entirely realistic, and quite similar incidents can be observed at any time among mediæval saints, and, in modern times, at processions, during " revivals " among certain American sects, or in the world of Islam. When the woman tremblingly confesses her action, Jesus declares that her faith has saved her. As in all similar occurrences, down to " Christian Science " or faith-healing, the inward receptiveness is the main thing ' (i. p. 109).

Verse 30, which Matthew objects to, and the sequel 31–34 may have had a simpler form in the reality. In the second story the great faith of Jesus is also historic. His faith in his own God-given power to heal, in the power of faith generally, is not invented. And if this story of the child has some historic basis, it can only be explained upon the strength of this faith, which other stories equally reveal. This faith was a fundamental feature of his character. It was a sort of inspiration, which overcame him with overmastering power. So far as we know, this faith, during the period of his brief ministry, did not play him false, except perhaps at Nazareth. Whether xv. 34 means a disappointment of faith is disputed.

21. εἰς τὸ πέραν. Elsewhere this phrase always means ' to the east side,' not back again to the west side of the lake. Schmidt conjectures that we have here originally a second story about an incident which happened the other side of the lake (p. 145). As to the interweaving of the two stories, he thinks there can be only one

true and legitimate explanation : 'Here actual reminiscence has preserved an historical fact. The cure of the woman by Jesus took place on his way to the house of Jairus' (p. 148).

28. 'The woman seeks to be cured in this surreptitious way because of her uncleanness' (Gould).

29. ἴαται. The perfect passive. 'The conviction flashed through her mind : I have received a permanent cure' (Swete).

32. Literally, 'what woman had done it?' Not that Jesus knew that it was a woman: the writer is responsible for the gender.

34. 'Thy faith has cured thee.' 'In x. 52 this is apparently to be taken literally, but after the words about the power issuing from Jesus (30) it can only mean here that her faith has led her to the true agency of cure' (Menzies).

J. Weiss points out that if the story is historical, the cure could only have been due to 'auto-suggestion.' The excitement and faith of the woman cause the blood to cease flowing. But then the explanation of Mark, and Jesus's feeling that 'power' had gone out of him, must be abandoned. Prof. Bennett sought to put the miraculous or semi-miraculous incidents in such a way that (a) they become more credible, and (b) that they redound to the unique greatness of his hero. Thus here he says : 'He was sensitive to influences which did not affect others. In this incident He distinguished the woman's timid touch amid the pressure of the jostling crowd, as a mother, even in her sleep, singles out her infant's feeble cry from a babel of loud noises. There was, so to speak, an emotional circuit set up between Him and her, so that He felt the shock of her importunate demand for healing and the immediate drain upon His mysterious forces. By such an experience even He was startled' (*Life of Christ according to St. Mark*, p. 77).

36. παρακούσας. The meaning is not quite certain. It may mean simply 'overheard.' On the basis of the usage of the word in the Septuagint, Swete explains that Jesus heard, but heeded not. He spoke as if he had not heard, passed the words by in silence, and followed his own course.

42. 'For she was twelve years old': *i.e.* she was old enough to be able to walk.

43a. Editorial. Mark's theory as usual. And the order for concealment is here more incredible than ever. How could Jesus

have imagined that it would be obeyed ?   Moreover, there was the
child alive and well, whom everybody had supposed to be dead.
In the *E. S.* Loisy attempted to defend the reasonableness (and so,
perhaps, the historicity) of the prohibition.   ' Jesus is not desirous
that people should believe that he has come to raise the dead, as
he heals the sick, and he fears lest the fame of such an extraordinary
prodigy should excite an untimely movement in public opinion.   A
considerable number of persons had heard that the daughter of
Jairus was dead, but only a few had entered the child's room, and
what Jesus himself had said might have aided the belief that she
had only swooned.   If the parents did not speak and Jesus was
absent, soon nothing more would be thought of the matter ' (*E. S.* I.
p. 825).   In his later brief commentary on Mark he is much more
sceptical (p. 166).

43*b* connects with 42.   The order to give the child something to
eat seems a charming human touch, but it is more probably a
typical feature.   No surer proof of the girl being alive again if
she can eat like any ordinary person (Bultmann, p. 133; Klostermann, ed. 2).

CHAPTER VI

1–6. The Cold Reception of Jesus at Nazareth

(*Cp.* Matt. xiii. 53–58 ; Luke iv. 16–30)

1   And he went out from thence, and entered into his native city ;
2 and his disciples followed him.   And when the sabbath day was come, he began to teach in the synagogue : and many, hearing him, were astonished, saying, ' Whence has this come to him ? what wisdom is this which has been given unto him ? and have such miracles been
3 wrought by his hands ?   Is he not the carpenter, the son of Mary, the brother of James, and Joses, and Juda, and Simon ? and are
4 not his sisters here with us ? '   And they took offence at him.   But Jesus said unto them, ' A prophet is not without honour, except in
5 his own city, and among his kin, and in his house.'   And he could not perform there a single miracle, save that he laid his hands upon
6 a few sick folk, and healed them.   And he marvelled because of their unbelief.

    Jesus is now reported to have attempted another missionary enterprise. He will essay to preach the good tidings in his own native village. But for different reasons his venture at Nazareth is as much a failure as his venture on the other side of the lake.

    2, 3. 'Astonished.' The verb is elsewhere used as nearly equivalent to wonder and admiration. It is possible that what the Evangelist means to suggest is that they were half amazed, half annoyed. They are half inclined to marvel and believe, but this very half-belief makes them the more irritated and incredulous. His teaching seems very wise ; but yet how could this man, whose family they know so well—just ordinary people—say such wise things ? He was no Rabbi by profession, and had not frequented any Rabbinic school. It is impossible. This seems true to human nature. They do not *want* to believe. If Jesus *were* a veritable prophet, it would be annoying. ' We are as good as he, but we could not teach as he does, and we could not do the wonders which

118

he is said to have done.   Therefore, after all, his teaching is *not* wise, and he did not do the wonders ! '

3.   The ' carpenter, the son of Mary ' in Mark as compared with the ' son of the carpenter ' in Matt. xiii. 55 and ' son of Joseph ' in Luke iv. 22, is very noteworthy.   Perhaps it rests upon a later manipulation of the text.   The Mark which Matthew and Luke knew perhaps had a reading more like theirs.   Why should they have changed it ?   Indeed, there is some evidence, drawn from the Armenian and a MS. of the old Latin translation, that the earliest form was ' the son of the carpenter Joseph and of Mary.'

5.   This strong expression, ' He could do no wonder there,' is only found in Mark.   To perform his miracles Jesus usually needed a predisposition of faith, and a certain excited expectation of success.   The few healings are apparently not regarded by the narrator as miracles.   Did Jesus try and fail ?   If so, it can be argued that in this record of failure there is good evidence for the historical character of Mark's narrative.   ' It makes a deep impression of historical accuracy (verse 5) when we hear how, in the face of such unbelief, even Jesus's power to perform miracles fails.   It became exhausted, as soon as the indispensable conditions which call out his consciousness of power are wanting ' (Holtzmann).

Probably 5*b* is an editorial gloss intended to save the situation to some extent.   Jesus could not be allowed to have done nothing at all.

In contrast with the argument that 1–6 is historical may be mentioned the view of other scholars that the story has been woven out of a saying.   For in the *Oxyrrhynchus Papyri* there is a Logion attributed to Jesus which runs : ' A prophet is not received in his own city, and a doctor works no cures upon those who know him.'   The saying gradually obtained a setting.   The story was spun out of the Logion.   It is curious that the family of Jesus, here in their own city, play no part.   Where were they ?   (*Cp.* Bultmann, p. 15 ; Preuschen in *Z. N. W.* 1916, ' Das Wort vom verachteten Propheten,' pp. 33–48).   But it does not follow according to the latter scholar that the rejection in Nazareth is a mere and pure invention.   Some actual fact may lie at the bottom of the story.

7–13. The Sending of the Twelve

(*Cp.* Matt. ix. 35–38, x. 1, 5–16, xi. 1 ; Luke ix. 1–6, x. 1–12, xiii. 22)

7   And he went about the villages around, teaching.   And he called unto him the Twelve, and began to send them forth by two and

8 two ; and he gave them power over the unclean spirits ; and he commanded them that they should take nothing for their journey, save
9 a staff only ; no bread, no wallet, no money in their purse. They
were only to be shod with sandals ; and they were not to put on
10 two coats. And he said unto them, ' Wheresoever ye enter into
11 an house, there abide till ye depart thence. And whatever place
will not receive you, nor hear you, depart thence, and shake off
12 the dust under your feet, as a testimony against them.' And they
13 went forth, and preached that men should repent. And they cast
out many demons, and anointed with oil many that were sick, and
healed them.

Jesus is not daunted by his failure at Nazareth. He proceeds
to the ' villages round about,' and sets forth his teaching to their
inhabitants. Of what happens there, and how he fared, we are
told nothing. The narrative passes on to quite different matters.
The section is mainly editorial. (Schmidt, p. 164.)

We are informed that Jesus determines to make his chosen
disciples partners in his work. It is too large for one man. The
Great Day might dawn, the Kingdom might come, and how few
Israelites—even in Galilee—would have had an opportunity to
repent and be saved. Therefore let six small companies traverse
through the land, warning and healing. Was the mission of the
Twelve also due to the growing difficulties and opposition which
Jesus had experienced ? This may be so. We cannot tell. The
instructions to the Twelve are given at much greater length in
Matthew and Luke, and some scholars think that Mark's version
is an extract from the common source (Q). Even if we accept the
historical character of the Sending of the Twelve, the *instructions*
most probably belong to a later generation, and reflect subsequent
experiences of the early Christian community. (So, *e.g.*, Bultmann ;
and even Klostermann thinks this view the more probable. Ed. 2.)

7. ' He gave them power over the unclean spirits.' (This is enlarged in Matt. xi. by the addition ' and to cure every malady and
sickness.') What are we to suppose that Mark meant by this, and is
the assertion historical ? Neither question is easy to answer. I cannot
help feeling dubious as to the historical character of the statement.
That Jesus felt that he had been given power by God to expel demons
is likely enough. But that he felt that he could delegate or pass on
this power, seems far less probable. Was it not a power to be won
from God by faith rather than handed on as by magic ? For how
can we assign any meaning to what Jesus is here said to do, except
one which is at least semi-magical ? If the disciples were to expel

and cure by invoking the name of Jesus, what is this but naked supernaturalism or magic ? But this does not seem in keeping with the character of Jesus.

8. The apostles are to take no luggage or provisions with them ; even their attire is to be most simple ; one coat must suffice. Not even copper money are they to carry. The order is similar to the custom of the Essenes when they travelled. See Abrahams, *Studies*, I. chap. xiv.

11. In each place the apostles are to choose one house and keep to it. ' For a testimony unto them,' *i.e.*, to indicate to them that all intercourse with them is utterly cut off. No attempt is to be made to convert the unwilling. He who will not hear must be left to his fate. There is no time for delay. Before the Kingdom has fully come, there is ever so much still to do.

13. Anointing with oil is only here mentioned in the Gospels (*cp.* James v. 14). ' Although such anointings were of frequent use in ancient medicine, the reference here is not to a purely medical prescription, since it is presumed that the cures are miraculous. On the other hand, the oil cannot be regarded as merely a symbol of the supernatural power of the apostles, for it forms a real means by which the healing is achieved. In that age and in that environment, the idea of purely natural medicine did not exist, and the art of healing was more or less confused with magic, the remedies being charms. The anointing of which Mark speaks partakes at once of the nature of a religious rite, as the exorcism by which the demons are driven out, in so far as a divine virtue is supposed to be attached to it, and of a remedy, in so far as real efficacy in healing was attributed to the element itself ' (Loisy).

14–29. JESUS, HEROD ANTIPAS, AND JOHN THE BAPTIST
(*Cp.* Matt. xiv. 1–12 ; Luke ix. 7–9, iii. 19, 20)

14 And king Herod heard of him ; for his name became known. And some said, ' John the Baptist is risen from the dead, and there-
15 fore miraculous powers are active in him.' Others said, ' It is Elijah.' And others said, ' He is a prophet, like one of the prophets.'
16 But when Herod heard of him, he said, ' John, whom I beheaded, is risen from the dead.'
17 For Herod himself had sent and seized John, and bound him in prison on account of Herodias, his brother Philip's wife : for he

18 had married her. For John had said unto Herod, ' It is not lawful
19 for thee to have thy brother's wife.' Therefore Herodias hated
20 him, and would have killed him, but she could not : for Herod
feared John, knowing that he was a righteous and holy man, and he
protected him ; and when he heard him, he was much perplexed,
21 and yet he heard him gladly.   Now on an opportune day, when
Herod on his birthday gave a banquet to his lords and high captains,
22 and to the chief men of Galilee, the daughter of Herodias came in,
and danced, and pleased Herod and his guests. And the king said
unto the damsel, ' Ask of me whatsoever thou wilt, and I will give it
23 thee.' And he sware unto her, ' Whatsoever thou shalt ask of me, I
24 will give it thee, even unto the half of my kingdom.' And she went
forth, and said unto her mother, ' What shall I ask ? ' And she
25 said, ' The head of John the Baptist.' And she went in straightway
with haste unto the king, and asked, saying, ' I wish that thou give
26 me forthwith the head of John the Baptist on a dish.' And the
king was exceeding sorry ; yet on account of his oath, and on
27 account of his guests, he did not like to refuse her. So the king at
once sent an executioner, and ordered him to bring John's head :
28 and he went, and beheaded him in the prison, and brought his head
on a dish, and gave it to the damsel : and the damsel gave it to her
29 mother. And when his disciples heard of it, they came and took
away his corpse, and buried it in a tomb.

The section 14–29 is obviously intended to fill up the time and
occupy the attention of the reader between the departure of the
Twelve and their return.

But, perhaps, originally, this was not so.   Perhaps in an earlier
form of Mark, or in Mark's source, Herod was not merely used
to fill up a gap.   He was not dragged in merely to give an opportunity for telling the story about the Baptist's death.   Herod may
have belonged to the proper connection of events ; his appearance
at this juncture in the story of Jesus must have had some point and
importance.

Now in vi. 45 Mark makes Jesus leave the territory of Herod,
and go on to ground where Herod had nothing to say ; he appears in
the Decapolis, in the territory of Philip, and in the neighbourhood
of Tyre and Sidon ; afterwards he passes through Galilee, but
secretly (ix. 30), and only on the way to Jerusalem.

According to the oldest tradition the reason for all this may have
been his fear of Herod Antipas. And therefore Herod's ' hearing '
of Jesus may have formed a turning-point in Jesus's life.   There

may have originally been some indication at this point of a threat
at Jesus's life.   If this is now omitted, the answer may conceivably
be elicited from Luke xiii. 31.   There Jesus is advised to depart,
because ' Herod would fain kill thee.'   He answers that he must
indeed soon depart, not because of Herod, but because he must die
in Jerusalem and not elsewhere.   Perhaps it was not liked that the
motive of Jesus's departure from Galilee should be his fear of Herod.
Hence it was desired to cancel the hostility of Antipas against John
and Jesus altogether, and to turn the villain into a good man.   In
Mark (17–29) he likes to listen to John, and is miserable that he
cannot save his life.   The guilt of John's execution is, as far as may
be, removed from him and assigned to Herodias.   In Luke xxiii. 15
he says that Jesus is guiltless.   And whereas in Luke xiii. 31 he
wants to kill him, in Luke ix. 9 he desires to see him.   Meyer accepts
these conjectures of Wellhausen.   (I. p. 110.)

14.   'Heard.'   What did he hear ?   Either of the dispatch of
the apostles, or, more probably, if 14–16 is really independent of
the preceding passage, of Jesus himself, of his doings and reputation.
   It must have been believed that John worked some miracles in
his lifetime, or the conjecture that miraculous powers were active
in him after his death would hardly have been thought of.

15.   That Jesus was a prophet like the old prophets seems to
have hit the mark most nearly.   His freshness and originality, his
power and confidence, his assurance of direct divine inspiration, are
all points of resemblance between him and them.   Like them, ' he
spoke with authority, and not as the Scribes.'   It is important to
note that none suppose him to be the Messiah, though some think
that he is Messiah's precursor.   So far, then, Jesus could have made
no Messianic pretensions ;   his secret, if the secret had yet dawned
upon him, had not been discovered.
   It would be naïve to believe that we have in 14 or 16 an historical
report of what Herod actually said.   In spite of Schmidt's objection
(p. 174), 15 seems a sort of anticipation of viii. 28.   So Loisy:
' All the various opinions here expressed have really been copied
from, or are a doublet of, what we read in the introduction to the
confession of Peter, and, perhaps even, not all at once.   It would
seem as if a first redactor had inserted the opinion of the Tetrarch in
order to narrate (by way of explanation) the death of John.   Then a
second redactor appended the two further hypotheses about Jesus
which, just because they are an addition, necessitate a repetition of
what Antipas had said before the story about the death of John.
In any case, the words of the Tetrarch imply that the fame of the
Galilæan preacher and his preaching only arose after the death of

John (*L'Évangile selon Marc*, p. 180). Loisy accepts the reading 'he said' in 14 instead of 'they said.'

16. Some think that 14*b* and 15 have been inserted from viii. 24. Originally the words ran, 'And Herod heard of him, for his name became known, and he said 'John,' etc. Wellhausen (ed. 2) and Klostermann (ed. 2) think that what is meant may be not that John has *literally* risen from the dead, but that Jesus is another John. 'Er gleicht ihm wie sein alter ego.'

17-29. Now follows a sort of footnote or appendix, explaining how Herod came to hold the view he did about Jesus, and how John had met his end. The story of John's death is full of historical improbabilities, and may be regarded as legendary. But *cp.* Meyer i. p. 88. Herodias was not the wife of Herod's brother Philip, but of another brother, also called Herod. The real reason of Herod Antipas's fear of John is indicated in Josephus (*Ant.* xviii. 5. 2).

18. For this law, *cp.* Leviticus xviii. 16, xx. 21.

30-44. The Return of the Apostles and the Feeding
of the Five Thousand

(*Cp.* Matt. xiv. 13-21 ; Luke ix. 10-17)

30 And the apostles gathered themselves together unto Jesus, and
31 told him all that they had done and taught. And he said unto them, 'Come ye by yourselves into a lonely place, and rest a while.' For there were many coming and going, and they had no leisure so much
32 as to eat. And they went away by boat to a lonely place by them-
33 selves. But many saw them departing, and noticed whither they were going, and they hurried thither on foot from all the cities,
34 and arrived before them. And Jesus, when he disembarked, saw a great crowd, and he was moved with compassion toward them, because they were as sheep without a shepherd : and he began to teach them many things.

35 And when the day was now far spent, his disciples came unto him, and said, 'This is a lonely place, and the hour is already late.
36 Send the people away, that they may go into the farms and villages
37 round about, and buy themselves something to eat.' But he answered and said unto them, 'Give ye them to eat.' And they said unto him, 'Shall we go and buy two hundred shillings worth of
38 bread, and give them to eat ? ' He said unto them, 'How many

loaves have ye ? go and see.' And when they had found out, they
39 said, ' Five, and two fishes.' And he bade them make them all sit
40 down by companies upon the green grass. And they sat down in
41 rows, by hundreds and by fifties. And he took the five loaves and
the two fishes, and looked up to heaven, and said the blessing ; and
he broke the loaves, and gave them to his disciples to set before
42 them ; and the two fishes he divided among them all. And they
43 did all eat, and were satisfied. And they took of the broken pieces
44 twelve baskets full, and also of the fishes. And they that ate of
the loaves were about five thousand men.

The apostles return, and report to Jesus their experiences.
But there seems to have been no tradition as to what these were.
Mark, at least, says no word upon the subject.

31–33 form an elaborate, rather cumbersome and improbable,
connection with, and preparation for, the feeding miracle story.
These verses are mainly editorial (Schmidt, pp. 187–189). The
miraculous story required a desolate place, a large number of
people, Jesus and his disciples. And the editorial link supplies
all these.

34. In the original story the compassion (cp. viii. 1) was
probably for their physical hunger. But Mark knew some saying
about the shepherdless sheep, and this he introduced here, and made
Jesus teach the sheep ' many things.'
How far there were really and truly in the days of Jesus many
persons in a state of spiritual destitution is uncertain. All depends
upon the vexed question of the am ha'aretz, the number of such
people and their religious and moral condition.
Has the miracle any historic basis ? Some scholars think that
some story how Jesus with kindly thought gave some food to some
of his auditors got exaggerated into a miracle. More probably,
while there may be some historic reminiscence, the story is partly
built up of O.T. parallels, and is partly a sort of anticipation of
the common meals and of the celebration of the eucharist in the early
Christian community. Christian usages were foreshadowed by the
miraculous powers of the Saviour. As regards the O.T. the story
in 2 Kings iv. 42–44 has clearly been of marked influence. As
usual, Jesus has to cap and surpass whatever marvels Elijah and
Elisha performed.

39. ' The green grass.' Interesting remarks in Schmidt,
p. 191.

41. 'Bei der Speisung sind Blick zum Himmel und Gegenspruch wunderkräftige Mittel' (Dibelius, p. 49).

46–56. Jesus walks on the Lake

(*Cp.* Matt. xiv. 22–36)

45   And straightway he made his disciples get into the boat, and cross over to the other side, unto Bethsaida, while he dismissed the
46 people.   And when he had sent them away, he departed unto the
47 mountain to pray.   And when evening was come, the boat was in
48 the middle of the lake, and he alone on the land.   And he saw them distressed in their rowing; for the wind was against them.   And about the fourth watch of the night he came up to them, walking
49 upon the lake, and he meant to have passed by them.   But when they saw him walking upon the lake, they supposed it was an
50 apparition, and cried out : for they all saw him, and were troubled. But he immediately spoke to them, and said, ' Take courage ; it
51 is I ; be not afraid.'   And he went up to them into the boat ; and
52 the wind dropped.   Then they were utterly beside themselves with amazement, for they had not understood about the loaves : for their heart was hardened.

53   And when they had crossed over, they came unto Gennesaret,
54 and moored the boat there.   And when they got out of the boat,
55 straightway the people recognized him.   And they ran through that whole region, and began to bring those that were sick on beds
56 to wherever they heard that he was.   And whithersoever he entered, into villages, or cities, or farmyards, they laid the sick in the open places, and besought him that they might touch if it were but the border of his garment : and as many as touched him were healed.

45. The ' crowd ' and disciples have both to be sent away as a preparation for the miracle.   But it is rather awkwardly managed.

48. A ' storm ' miracle, an obvious variant of iv. 35–41, seems to have been mixed up with the walking on the sea miracle.   There are other difficulties, such as : how could Jesus see them in the boat at night in the middle of the lake from a mountain ?   But one must not ask these questions of a legend.

Is there any basis for the story ?   Is it a case of a story growing

out of a saying?   A materializing of symbols?   'The emblematic
language of the Hebrew Scriptures was constantly in the hearts
and upon the lips of the Christian believer.'   We know how often
the metaphor of the great waters and an escape from them meets
us in the Hebrew Bible.   The Christians would have faith even
amid stormy waters :   for Christ could save them.   'Out of some
such utterance of trust has probably come the story of the disciples
in their passage across the lake, distressed by a contrary wind'
(Carpenter).   Mr Rawlinson thinks it probable that the 'kernel of
the story reflects some actual historical reminiscence, the details of
which cannot now with any certainty be recovered.'

καὶ ἤθελεν παρελθεῖν αὐτούς.   What does this mean?   It has
been variously explained.   Dr. Bartlet says : 'made as though he
would pass them : Jesus would test them and train their faith.'
Wellhausen says Jesus had intended to walk straight across the lake
(miraculously) to catch up the disciples, and to surprise them by
being at the other side before them.   Holtzmann says Jesus meant
to pass them and to show himself, in thus passing them, as the Lord
of the water as of the land.   Klostermann (ed. 2) says that we
perhaps have in the words a remnant of an old legend already
misunderstood in 48a.   Jesus walks across the lake miraculously
but in a sense naturally too, as the Lord of the elements, and not in
order to show himself as such to the disciples : it is their danger
which makes him change his plan, and reveal himself and the miracle
to them.   It must be allowed that not one of these explanations is
quite satisfactory.   There is another highly ingenious explanation
by Windisch in *Nieuw Theologisch Tydschrift*, 1920, pp. 298–308,
which is worth reading by the curious, and yet another by Völter
in the same magazine, 1921, pp. 28–35, but I will not set them forth,
for they too fail to convince.

52.   Mark's persistent attribution of spiritual blindness to the
disciples becomes here exceedingly awkward.   The greatness of the
miracles of the feeding and of the walking upon the water could not
have escaped their notice.   What, however, he perhaps wishes to
indicate is that the 'mystery' of the Kingdom, though 'given' to
the disciples, was not apprehended by them till after the resurrection.
Tradition, indeed, told of some definite recognition of Jesus as the
Messiah at Cæsarea Philippi, but the deeper nature of the Messiahship, and the realization that its true manifestation was only to
come after Jesus's death and resurrection, were still hidden from
them.   The 'hardness' of their heart was as divinely wrought as
Pharaoh's.   Or we may explain, more generally, that Mark means
to say that the deeper meaning of the miracles, their inner and
spiritual signification, were at first unknown to those who were

nevertheless their eyewitnesses. They did not (till after the resurrection) understand what had been going on before their eyes.

53–56. 'Clearly editorial; "schematic" representation; the work of a redactor; the multiplication of the marvellous is a sure sign of later origin.' Thus I might sum up the view of Bultmann and others about these four verses. With which contrast Dr. Bartlet: 'This brief paragraph bears on every line the signs of a transcript from the report of an eyewitness' (*i.e.* Peter)! Schmidt mediatizes, not to say, wobbles. But he is interesting as always, especially about the landing in Gennesaret instead of Bethsaida (p. 195).

CHAPTER VII

1–23. THE WASHING OF HANDS; FALSE AND TRUE
PURITY

(*Cp.* Matt. xv. 1–20)

1 And the Pharisees, and some scribes who came from Jerusalem,
2 gathered round him. For they had seen some of his disciples eat
3 bread with unclean, that is to say, with unwashed hands. For the
Pharisees, and all the Jews, observing the tradition of the elders,
4 do not eat without first often washing their hands. And when
they come from the market, till they have washed, they eat not.
And many other customs there are which they have received
and observe, such as the washing of cups and pots and brazen
5 vessels. So the Pharisees and scribes asked him, ' Why walk not
thy disciples according to the tradition of the elders, but eat bread
6 with unclean hands ? ' He said unto them, ' Well did Isaiah
prophesy of you hypocrites, as it is written, This people honours
7 me with their lips, but their heart is far from me. And vainly do
they worship me, teaching as their doctrines the commandments of
8 men. So ye, neglecting the commandment of God, observe the
tradition of men.'

9 And he said unto them, ' Ye do well to reject the commandment
10 of God, in order that ye may keep your tradition ! For Moses said,
Honour thy father and thy mother ; and, Whoso reviles father or
11 mother, let him die the death : but ye—if a man say to his father
or mother, That by which thou mightest have been benefited from
12 me is Corban—(that is, an offering)—ye no longer permit him to
13 do anything for his father or his mother. Thus ye make the word
of God void through your tradition, which ye hand down ; and many
such like things ye do.'

14 And he called all the people again unto him, and he said unto
15 them, ' Hearken, all of you, unto me, and understand : There is

nothing outside a man, which entering into him can make him unclean ; but the things which come out of a man, these are what make him unclean.'

17 And when he had entered into the house away from the crowd,
18 his disciples asked him concerning the saying. And he said unto them, 'Are ye, too, so unintelligent ? Do ye not perceive that whatever enters into a man from without cannot make him
19 unclean ? For it enters not into his heart, but into the belly, and goes out into the privy.' [Thus spake he, making all foods
20 clean.] And he said, 'That which comes out of the man, that
21 makes the man unclean. For from within, out of the heart of men,
22 come the evil thoughts—unchastity, thefts, murders, adulteries, covetousness, wickedness, deceit, lasciviousness, envy, blasphemy,
23 pride, foolishness : all these evil things come out from within, and they make a man unclean.'

This section is of profound significance and value ; it raises questions of the deepest importance. Indeed, from the point of view of Liberal Judaism it might be said that this section is the most important section in Mark, and that its salient and outstanding feature is verse 15. For here Jesus enunciates a doctrine which appears not only to be new and emancipating, but which seems to constitute one of the two chief justifications or reasons for the main way in which Liberal Judaism looks at the old ceremonial law. For first of all came the old prophets of the eighth and seventh centuries B.C. They said : The true service of God is not ceremonial, but moral ; God desires love and not sacrifices, the knowledge of Him rather than burnt offerings. Or again, as the Psalmist, upon the basis of this prophetic teaching, declared : 'Thou desirest not sacrifice else would I give it ; thou takest no pleasure in burnt offering. The sacrifices of God are a broken spirit ; a broken and a contrite heart, thou, O God, dost not despise.' This teaching is resuscitated by Jesus ; we have already met with it, and shall meet with it again. But here he says something which is akin to the prophetic doctrine, but is yet novel. There were two aspects of the old ritual and ceremonial practices, two sides to them. Some of them were supposed to affect God, and some of them were supposed to affect man. The prophets dealt mainly with those which were supposed to affect, please, or propitiate God, and they tell us that God does not care for them : it is not so that he is propitiated or pleased. In this section Jesus deals with those which were supposed to affect man, and these were mainly rules and customs about clean and unclean, which again depended upon conceptions—very old, widespread conceptions—about clean and unclean. Just as the prophets upset the old ideas about the service of God, so here Jesus upsets old ideas about clean and unclean. As the prophets moralized and inwardized men's ideas about the service of God, so Jesus moralizes and inwardizes men's ideas about clean and unclean. In a religious sense it is only man who can be clean and unclean ; nothing else. Only man can make himself clean and unclean ; outside things cannot make him clean or unclean. The conception of ritual or Levitical purity and impurity is overthrown and abolished. Upon these two doctrines, the doctrine of Hosea, upon the one hand, the doctrine of Jesus, upon the other, the new attitude of Liberal Judaism towards the ceremonial Law depends. But let this also be noted. Liberal Judaism does not stop there. It knows and realizes that human nature needs forms and ceremonies, and that a religion which is to satisfy human nature needs them too. After it has cleared up the matter theoretically, after it has established the prophetic truth about the true service of God, and the no less essentially prophetic truth about clean and unclean, it can, in its freedom, bring back, reintroduce, or retain, such forms and ceremonies as it may think good. We may compare what Plato does in the *Republic* as regards true righteousness. He first shows that righteousness is the well-being of the soul, and to be desired apart from all rewards, and in spite of all ulterior and unhappy consequences, but having done that, when the cause is decided, when pure injustice has been weighed against pure justice and has been found wanting, then there is no harm, and indeed it is only fitting, to enumerate ' how many and how great are the rewards which justice and the other virtues procure to the soul from gods and men both in life and after death ' (*Republic*, p. 612). So when the true religion—the true service of God and the true nature of purity—has been adequately defined and understood, there is then no harm, and indeed it is only fitting, to show and bring forward the advantages and utilities of external forms and ceremonies.

The section that we are considering is of high interest from many points of view, critically, historically, and religiously. And we have to distinguish in it several different things. (1) There is the original teaching of Jesus, so far as it is discoverable. What did he say ? And what did he mean ? (2) There is the section as we have it now : what do its various parts and paragraphs mean as they stand ? What did they mean to the compiler ? (3) Does the section, so far as it deals with Jewish customs and laws, deal with them accurately ? Does it reflect customs which obtained at a later period, but which were not yet prevalent in the days of Jesus ? (Here the question alludes specifically to verses 2–4.) And is the attack upon the

Rabbis both in 8 and 9–13 historically inaccurate, or may we suppose (as regards 9–13) that what would be false and inaccurate as regards Jewish law and Jewish practice, as we know them from the Mishnah and the Talmud, may conceivably have been true as regards some Galilean and Judæan Rabbis in the days of Jesus ? These questions and the replies to them cannot be kept entirely separate and treated separately one after the other ; but in our minds we must remember how different they all are. And it may be added that several of them are obscure : in other words, not to all the questions can assured and confident replies be given.

The section appears to be interpolated ; it does not connect with vi. 56 or with vii. 24, whereas vii. 24 can be easily connected with vi. 56. Scene and time are quite uncertain. It has been conjectured that it was placed here as a suitable preliminary to the journey of Jesus on to pagan soil, and perhaps also there was a desire to show the facilities offered by Christianity to the conversion of the Gentiles.

The section is built up of many separate portions, and the relation of these portions to each other, and their history, is disputed. We have (1) 1–8, (2) 9–13, (3) 14–15, (4) 17–19, (5) 20–23. Which if any of these portions is historical ? It has been argued that 1–8 is the only one which is so : that 9–13 is really a variant of 1–8 (God's commandment *versus* human tradition), and that the other sections in their present form, like 9–13, are none of them reproductions of scenes which actually took place. Yet 15 may be an authentic Logion. It has even been argued that 1–8 is doubtfully historic. Why is the conduct of the disciples attacked, and not Jesus's own conduct ? Wherever this happens, it is suggested by Bultmann that we have the discussions or conflicts of the community thrown back into the form of a conflict between Jesus and the ' scribes.' Again, there is no real argument. Instead of any argument, all that Jesus does is to quote Isaiah. In the genuine conflicts, he makes a real retort ; he brings forward a counter argument ; here he does not. 14–15, so it is sometimes argued, had originally nothing whatever to do with 1–8 ; Mark or the compiler of 1–23 added it on here because of the similarity of subject, as it seemed to him (Uncleanness). 18b, 19 is a later commentary upon 15 which Mark joins on to 15 by 17, 18a. To this as a further explanation 20–23 is again added. However all these critical problems may be decided, it is hard to believe that 15 is anything less than a genuine saying of the historic Jesus. It is true that we cannot argue from the greatness of a saying to its authenticity. Some of the biggest things in the prophets are not authentic. But verse 15 is in every way characteristic of Jesus and of his teaching. There is no reason whatever why he should *not* have said it, and much reason why he should. To doubt its authenticity seems scepticism run wild. And Fascher has made me feel that some of Bultmann's scepticism may be rightly so characterized.

1. The Pharisees and Scribes from Jerusalem are to hand as usual. After 13 they appear to be forgotten. Matthew tries to bring greater order and likelihood into the whole section by various devices, and he attempts also to give a sort of artificial unity to the section by making the end reflect the beginning.

2. It is necessary to make a long pause here and to deal with the alleged Rabbinic ordinance to wash the hands before eating, and especially with its relation to outward or ritual cleanness and uncleanness.

The whole question of ritual purity is very intricate, both in itself and as regards the dates at which, and the persons to whom, it especially applied. Ritual purity in the age of Jesus seems to have been mainly a matter for priests, and indeed the very conception of it was a priestly conception, or had become such. It belongs to what we may justly regard as the priestly, as opposed to the prophetic, conception of religion : it is a part of outward holiness as opposed to inward holiness, though this statement must not be taken to mean that outward and inward holiness could not, and cannot, be successfully harmonized and combined. But it has also to be frankly stated that outward holiness depends upon certain definite conceptions which are really and essentially anti-prophetic. Outward holiness ultimately depends upon very ancient ideas relating to bodily conditions or to material substances which, from our modern point of view, even as from the purest 'prophetic' point of view, must be regarded as superstitious. Things connected with the divine are to be looked upon as sacred or dangerous : they must not be approached or handled except in a special bodily condition of outward purity ; otherwise, unfortunate results may ensue : the gods or the spirits may vent their wrath. Again, certain bodily conditions or substances, *e.g.* blood, and especially a special sexual sort of blood, are highly dangerous and 'unclean' : or again, certain foods are 'unclean' : or again, corpses are dangerous and 'unclean,' whether of men or of certain animals. It is clear that modern thought has entirely freed itself from all such conceptions ; there is neither holiness nor 'uncleanness' (the *two* ideas are merely two sides of *one* idea) which is outward or material. And the very idea of outward impurity is essentially anti-prophetic and priestly. It was the priests who took up, maintained, developed, and put into practice, these conceptions of outward purity. But they are fully recognized by the Pentateuch, and the Rabbis (unfortunately) recognized them too. Nor did they drop them when the Temple was destroyed. On the contrary. They continued to maintain and develop them, and in such matters as the ritual, or, as it is often called, the levitical impurity of the hands, and the ritual washing of the hands, they seem to have made what was hitherto, in Palestine at least, only obligatory upon the priests (but upon the laymen only when entering, or bringing sacrifices at, the Temple in Jerusalem) obligatory upon all alike—laymen as well as priests. The Talmud shows that the Rabbis gave up an enormous amount of time to the whole subject of clean and unclean in its various manifestations and departments. How, *e.g.*, an unclean bit of matter, such as a dead mouse, can in certain circumstances defile another bit of matter (*e.g.*, an earthenware vessel); how such a defiled vessel can, under certain circumstances, make certain foods unclean for certain persons at certain times, is elaborated, discussed, set forth, and laid down. Distinction is added to distinction, rule is piled upon rule. The Logion of Jesus that there is no such thing as *religious* impurity attaching to things and material objects, that religious impurity concerns only the spirit and soul and mind and heart of man—that purity is an inward and not an outward conception—takes rank with Hosea's declaration, ' I desire love and not sacrifice,' and places him who uttered it in the true succession of the Prophets.

As regards the subject of the washing of hands before meals in order to bring them into a condition of ritual or levitical purity—to make them (not clean in our sense, but) *religiously* clean in the priestly sense—the question of dates is of great importance. In the story in Mark the question is asked, Why do the disciples eat bread κοιναῖς χερσίν? which Mark explains to mean with ' unwashed hands.' But the use of the adjective κοιναῖς and of the verb κοινῶσαι in verse 15 seems to make it clear that Mark and the story teller are thinking of religious uncleanness in the technical and priestly sense. The opposition in verse 15 between true and false religious uncleanness scarcely allows of any other interpretation. When, then, was it made a rule—a tradition of the elders, an ordinance of the Oral Law—that *all* Jews must ritually wash their hands before meals ? When was the principle and rule established that ritually unwashed hands made the food with which such hands were brought into contact unclean ? (It will be observed that in this chapter of Mark, unlike Matthew xxiii. 25, Luke xi. 29, the dispute between Jesus and the Rabbis refers directly only to the ritual washing of hands and to their defiling power. The pots and pans question, in its relation to ritual impurity, is not touched upon in the dispute or alluded to by Jesus. Therefore I do not propose to deal with it here. It is discussed in the commentaries and also by Brandt.)

Now as to the hands and their ritual washing and religious defilement and defiling power, it is maintained by Dr. Büchler, with a tremendous wealth of learning, that in the age of Jesus the law that the hands must be ritually washed before meals was only incumbent upon priests. A few 'pietists' voluntarily elected to live, so far as outward purity was concerned, as if they were priests. But laymen generally, and even Rabbis and their disciples, had no obligation to wash their hands before meals. The first allusion to the rule being made obligatory upon laymen is hardly earlier than the age of Rabbi Akiba—that is about A.D. 100.

The importance attached to priests having ritually pure hands before they ate their food was closely connected, not merely with the eating of the sacrifices, but also with their eating of *Teruma* (portions of vegetable produce : see, *e.g.*, Gray's long note on Numbers xviii. 11–13, pp. 223–228 in his commentary in *I. C. S.*) which was reserved for the priests, and which had to be eaten by them, *wherever they might be*, in a state of ritual purity, according to the law of Numbers xviii. 11. For reasons which remain obscure and have been inadequately explained, the Rabbis laid enormous stress on the observance of all the rules and regulations about Sacred Food (tithes, teruma, etc.). But these rules only concerned the priests. The ordinary layman had not to concern himself with questions of religious defilement unless he was about to enter the temple and make a sacrifice. He could touch a dead mouse, and had no need to wash, not even if he were about to eat his meal. Only, as I have said, some thirty or forty years after the fall of the temple was the rule of washing the hands before meals made obligatory, as a religious duty, upon laymen.

The Rabbinic evidence is thus in sharp disaccord not only with the editorial note in Mark, but even with the story itself. For the disciples of Jesus were not priests. How, then, could they be reproached for eating with unwashed hands ? But, then, if we were fully to follow out the results of Dr. Büchler's Talmudic investigations, we should be compelled to declare, not only that the story in Mark (though not necessarily the Logion in 15) cannot be authentic, but that it could not have arisen—that it could not have grown up or been devised—till about A.D. 100, or even till about the period of the death of Akiba (A.D. 130). Now such a conclusion would be absurd. Mark, as we have it—omitting, say, such an editorial note as is contained in verses 3 and 4—was *at the latest* produced about A.D. 80, certainly long before the death of Akiba. Here, then, we have a regular contradiction. Dr. Büchler's Talmudic evidence—his most learned, long, and laborious marshalling of it— and his conclusions from it, seem irrefutable. That the date of Mark is not later than 80 seems also assured. It is, perhaps, earlier.

And the *story* of the dispute about the hands, even if unauthentic, was certainly not invented by *Mark*. He found it and adopted it. It must, I should think, be ten or even twenty years earlier than the composition of Mark—say, therefore, A.D. 70 or A.D. 60. A.D. 60 seems to me more likely than A.D. 70. How, then, is the contradiction to be solved ?

The difficulty is got over in various ways by various scholars.

(1) Dr. Bartlet argues thus. He alludes to Dr. Büchler's contentions, according to which ' *transferable* defilement, from hands to food and again to the eater, applied only (*a*) in the case of Aaronic priests, in virtue of their priestly duties, and (*b*), even then, only in relation to " some real levitical impurity," not to mere presumptive impurity—to meet which ritual washing was introduced by Hillel and Shammai shortly before Jesus's day.' He then proceeds as follows : ' This admits the *idea* of " impurity " as transferable from hands, through food, to persons eating the food. The only question at issue then is, was there in Jesus's day a tendency prevalent in Pharisaic circles to extend this ideal of religious " purity" even to others than priests, to practise it themselves, and to judge the piety of those who laid claim to be specially religious—such as Rabbi Jesus and his disciples—by that higher standard, one not expected of all Jews ? Büchler and Jewish scholars generally deny it on the ground that the Talmud makes no reference to such a stage or phase of Pharisaism. But the argument from silence is precarious, especially in face of the analogy of the current Essene view of the highest type of ritual purity as binding on all Jews, as God's priestly people, and of the specially sacred or quasi-sacrificial nature of food consecrated with prayer (according to Jewish custom), of which they partook only after bathing. It is quite possible, then, that a similar feeling was strong in Pharisaism at the period in question, and led to ritual demands upon the pious generally, and not only on priests, which were afterwards silently dropped as impracticable ' (p. 212). But the argument is dubious. The Talmudic evidence seems fairly clear that in Jesus's day the washing of hands before meals was only obligatory upon priests, and that the rule was, later on, not ' dropped as impracticable,' but extended to all. It seems hardly possible to get over the trouble or solve the puzzle in the way suggested by Dr. Bartlet. The ritual washing introduced by Hillel and Shammai appears to have been a washing only for priests in relation to the eating of the Terumah. Dr. Box, indeed, says : ' Ritual hand-washing before (and after) meals was not an O.T. requirement ; for some time its obligation was a matter of controversy between the Pharisaic schools. Its great champions were Pharisees of the school of Shammai, who ultimately enforced their view upon the Sanhedrin with great violence, in the stormy

years that immediately preceded the revolt against Rome (A.D. 66–70). The obligatory duty of ritual hand-washing was one of the " eighteen articles " which this party carried on this occasion against their opponents. Thus at the time of Jesus it was a party question, and Jesus here (as elsewhere in the Gospel) is opposing the Shammaite view. Büchler holds that the Pharisees here mentioned must have been *priests*, as at this time the obligation of ritual hand-washing before meals was not incumbent upon *laymen*. If this was so, how could they expect Jesus's disciples to conform, unless they were priests ? The truth of the matter seems to be that the stricter Pharisees insisted that this duty rested upon laymen as well as priests. The pious were expected to follow the example of the priests in this matter' (p. 244). But Dr. Büchler would reply that there is no evidence that ' the pious' were expected to ' follow the example of priests in this matter' in the days of Jesus in Galilee. On the contrary, he holds that the Talmudic evidence points the other way.

In his article in the *Expository Times*, Vol. XXI. (1909–1910), pp. 34–40, he wrote that the words of Jesus in 15 would seem to show that ' the Pharisees taught that unwashed hands defiled the food, and the food in turn defiled the body inside. If this inference be correct, it is contrary to early rabbinical law. The assumed impurity of unwashed hands is of a slight force, and though it can be transferred to food touched, the food defiled cannot in its turn transfer the impurity to the body of him who eats it. This rule is clearly laid down in the Mishnah, and in all the passages dealing with assumed impurity of the hands. Everywhere the technical term פוסלין is used for this impurity, which can be transferred once and no further, as opposed to מטמאין. At the same time it is stated that the impurity of the hands applies only to priestly dues. And Ilfa, a Rabbi, at the beginning of the third century, points out (Sab. 14*b*) that when this assumed impurity of the hands was first introduced by Hillel and Shammai, it was instituted to apply to priestly dues only. And the same is repeated in other Baraithas quoted in the discussions there. This, again, leads to the conclusion that Mark's statement about the defiling force of the unwashed hands applied only to Aaronites on account of their priestly dues, and not to the lay Jew and his food. And, secondly, since the impurity of the hands is described as defiling food to such a degree that the food in turn defiles a man, the hands must not only have been unwashed, but also actually defiled by some real levitical impurity. In fact, Mark's wording clearly confirms this inference. His source in vii. 2 reported : The Pharisees saw some of Jesus's disciples eat bread κοιναῖς χερσίν and a later editor interpreted this by τοῦτ' ἔστιν ἀνίπτοις. Was he

correct in this interpretation ? κοινός is used in this chapter
several times (though only as verb κοινόω), and in all these
cases it means " defile " and not " to be unwashed." Consequently,
the adjective in the source must have meant the same : " defiled
hands " and not " unwashed hands." When the wrong interpretation was inserted in Mark's report, the usage of considering unwashed hands as defiling had developed among the Jews, and the
author of that insertion simply attributed to an earlier generation
the usage of his own times.'

(2) To Dr. Büchler's arguments in the *Expository Times* the Rev.
G. Margoliouth (Vol. XXII., 1910–1911, p. 22) replied thus : ' Let it
be granted that full ceremonial uncleanness, such as required strict
codification at the time in question, applied only to sacred things
and priests' dues, so that lay Israelites would be exempt from it,
unless they voluntarily submitted themselves to severer forms of
legalistic discipline than was in law required of them. But would
it follow from this that a minor degree of uncleanness, not yet fully
recognized in the codified system of ordinances, but nevertheless
generally avoided by pious laymen with considerable strictness, did
not attach also to ordinary articles of food if touched with unwashed
hands, and also, under certain circumstances, to various kinds of
vessels, etc., kept in the house of non-priestly Israelites ? Dr.
Büchler agrees that the ordinances in question were, during the few
generations that followed the destruction of the Temple, extended
to ordinary persons and things. But does not this very fact prove
the correctness of the theory here advocated ? The strict codification of an ordinance is very often merely the final step in a course
of development ; and one has a right to assume that the formal
extension of these rules of purification to the laity would not have
been introduced, if they had not already taken root in the consciences
and the conduct of the more pious of the people.

' The Talmudical records, though partly confused and uncertain,
do show that the full and strict codification of the traditions, referred
to in Mark vii., applied in the time of our Lord only to priests in
relation to the more or less sacred things which they had to handle.
But both on the authority of Mark and from the inference to be
drawn from the Talmudical records themselves, it is equally true
that pious Israelites generally did, even in those early days, observe
the same laws of purification as a matter of religious duty, though
not yet strictly enjoined to do so by codified ordinances. They no
doubt thought—and, from their point of view, rightly so—that
what a priest might not do in a matter of this kind, a pious Israelite
should not do either. All we have to admit is that the meaning of
the word πάντες (all) in vii. 3 must not be pressed. The customs
referred to were no doubt—as for the most part they are among

the orthodox Jews of the present day—general rather than universal.'

(3) Brandt attempts a different solution. He holds that a custom—borrowed from the Greeks and Persians—arose of washing the hands before meals, not because the hands were technically and ritually unclean, but from motives of cleanliness and propriety. It must be remembered that most Jews (apparently not all, see the odd story in *Nedarim* 49*b*) used no forks : they dipped their hands into the dish : they took bits of bread, dipped them into milk or sauce or vinegar, and then ate the soaked bread. Gradually this custom of washing the hands was regarded as a religious duty ; it became invested with a religious sanction. A story told about Shammai seems to show that it was already a religious duty for observant laymen in his day. The other sort of ritual washing became, later on, amalgamated with this custom of propriety.

But how could the hands make food unclean ? Something, of which the law forbade the eating, might adhere to unwashed hands, and so make bread and legally permitted food unclean and forbidden. But would the eating of such food make the eater unclean ? Brandt holds that there is sufficient analogy with other cases to permit the belief that it could have been held that, broadly speaking, a man was defiled, and made unclean, by eating food which had itself become ' unclean.' It is true that, in the more technical sense, it was quite permissible for a layman to be unclean, but that the disciples of a Rabbi and a Teacher ought to object to any kind of easily avoidable defilement might seem reasonable enough to the Rabbis generally. ' Rabbi ' Jesus ought to have enjoined them to wash their hands. (It is not here said that Jesus *himself* did not wash his hands, though this *is* noted about Jesus in Luke xi. 38.) But, in the opinion of Jesus, bread, which becomes unclean by some unclean substance attaching to the hands getting detached from the hands and attached to the bread, does not defile the man. Though such an opinion seems to conflict with passages such as Lev. xi. 40 and xvii. 15, it may be (as will be again stated later on) that Jesus was really thinking of the possible small defilement passing from the hand to the food, and was led on to make the grand utterance of 15 on that account. He was not therefore brought face to face with the deliberate question : ' May I eat a rabbit, or may I eat a sheep which has been found dead ? ' He did not directly contemplate the overthrow and violation of these definite Pentateuchal laws. I understand, from what Dr. Büchler, with very great kindness and patience, has tried to explain to me by letter and verbally, that, in his opinion, Brandt's solution will not work. The words κοιναῖς χερσίν and κοινῶσαι in Mark show that *ritual* washing is alluded to—ritual washing to remove uncleanness in the technical and outward-religious sense. It is not a case of mere propriety and cleanliness. The Logion in 15 shows this also. The story about Shammai on which Brandt lays stress does not prove what Brandt wishes it to prove. For (a) it is not Shammai who eats, but the child. (b) it is not a case of ritual defilement or uncleanness, as Brandt himself acknowledges (p. 29. *Cp.* too Büchler, *Der galiläische Am-ha-aretz*, p. 133, n. 3). It was a case of ' gewöhnliches Abwaschen ohne das keine Speise berührt werden soll.' (The technical term *medeechah* in the story about Shammai is not one of the three technical terms for that ritual washing of the hands which underlies the story in Mark.)

'No Rabbinic statement,' writes Dr. Büchler, ' of the first century knows anything of the layman's duty to wash his hands before eating ; it is the priest's special duty in connection with the *Teruma.* Shammai ought to have washed his hands *on rising from his bed in the morning*, not on account of any ritual or levitical defilement, but on grounds of cleanliness—or of superstition. With unwashed hands *after the night* nothing ought to be touched. But this one washing sufficed for the whole day. As, owing to the prohibition to wash on the Day of Atonement, Shammai had not washed, he refused to feed his child. But Shammai was neither " clean " nor " unclean " in the levitical sense. The washing of the hands in the morning is quite irrespective of any food to be eaten in the course of the day, and the story should not be used in relation to Mark vii.'

(4) I would, however, venture to suggest that as there *did* exist ' ein gewöhnliches Abwaschen ohne welches keine Speise berührt werden soll,' that Mark might perhaps have confused one sort of washing with the other. If no food could be touched without washing the hands in the morning, is not this, perhaps, enough to have produced the story in Mark ? Might it not even be substantially authentic ? It is conceivable that what is at the bottom of it is that the Scribes had found out that the disciples had not washed their hands on getting up in the morning. For this violation of the law they are rebuked. The Logion in 15 may be explained either (a) on the hypothesis (see below) that it was not connected originally with the story, or (b) that the word κοινῶσαι must not be interpreted too technically. Or, again, Dr. Büchler admits that the custom of washing the hands before meals was discussed in the Rabbinical colleges between A.D. 50 and 120. He adds : ' Über die Pflicht des Händewaschens selbst aber bestand keine Meinungsverschiedenheit mehr ; wenn auch die Frage über seine Stellung in der Reihenfolge der einzelnen Handlungen beim Mahle dafür spricht, dass der Brauch selbst eben erst eingeführt wurde und den bestehenden

Sitten angefügt werden sollte.   Vor der Verwendung dieser Erörterung als Beleg für unserer Untersuchung ist die wichtigste Frage die, ob es sich in נטילת ידים wie der Ausdruck es nahelegt, um die religiöse Sitte, oder, was nicht ausgeschlossen ist, um ein allgemein übliches, von keinem Religionsgesetze, sondern von der Gesellschaftssitte gebotenes Händewaschen handelt' (p. 134). Perhaps, then, we may infer that it was some specially particular Shammaitic Rabbis who started the discussion with the disciples. Even an 'allgemein übliches, von keinem Religionsgesetze, sondern von der Gesellschaftssitte gebotenes Händewaschen' might, perhaps, serve as a historic basis of the story, which might then be authentic even possibly for so early a date as A.D. 28.

(5) I gather that Dr. Büchler, who in 1909 explained the story in Mark by assuming that the censured disciples of Jesus were priests, or again by hinting that Mark must be dated very late (which all N.T. scholars would regard as out of the question), would now suggest another explanation, which he has been kind enough to tell me verbally.   He thinks that some, or even many, Jews in the Diaspora—just because of the necessities (as they regarded it) of their condition—in order to prevent intercourse with heathen, in order to keep themselves free from heathen impurity, etc.— devised and practised rules which *in Palestine* were unknown.   He has discovered various evidence for this.   For example, Judith's ablutions in xii. 7 cannot be made to depend upon, and cannot be explained by, any Talmudic ordinances.   Is it not, then, possible that in the Diaspora, outside Palestine, to wash the hands before meals in the most technical sense was already a religious duty many years before it became so according to the Talmudic evidence ? Outward religious defilement may have been taken much more seriously outside Palestine—at least here and there—than inside Palestine, and at a much earlier date.   May not then the story in Mark have arisen outside Palestine ?   In this case the *story* would (1) not be authentic, though (2) the *Logion* might be.   And this is the view of Bultmann, who (from totally different reasons) considers that the story is secondary, while the Logion is most authentic. The Logion is one of Jesus's most daring utterances, dealing as it ' undoubtedly ' does with unclean food—that is, with foods forbidden by the Pentateuchal law.   Jesus, in the hot inspiration of the moment, does not realize the full import of his words.   He does not mean to go as far as to say, ' Eat rabbits ' ;   all he says is—we can make up, but cannot know, the occasion—' no *food* can religiously defile.'   ' *Things* cannot religiously defile.'

(6) As another somewhat different explanation, we might assume that while to become unclean was no religious offence for the layman, nevertheless, to become unclean through eating

forbidden food was a very different thing. The point at issue, though masked by the language, may perhaps have been the possibility of becoming unclean, in this deeper sense, by the unwitting consumption of a forbidden substance which had become attached to the hands that were dipped into the dish. I can well believe that, while Jesus would himself have shrunk from definitely and consciously eating some lobster or hare, he may have been indifferent whether, in spite of this possibility, his disciples ate, or did not eat, with unwashed hands, and indifferent also himself.

Most of us moderns, from mere motives of cleanliness, like to wash our hands before meals, but we do not think it by any means a religious duty to do so always. Among the Rabbis there grew up a distinct liking and regard for cleanliness and decency and politeness and good manners, even apart from religion and ritual laws ; nevertheless, there was a tendency for the one sort of rules to coalesce with the other. But it may fairly be supposed that a Galilean teacher from a simple carpenter's family would have had much less scruple in eating with unwashed hands. Perhaps, even though by many ' town ' Jews of the age of Jesus washing of the hands was not regarded in the least as a religious duty, but only as a custom of propriety, cleanliness, and good manners, yet, to the *particular* persons who questioned Jesus upon the subject, it was not a mere custom of propriety but, or, but also, a religious duty. After all, there may have been some Rabbis in the age of Jesus of whose stricter tendencies and habits even the Talmud itself is ignorant or has left no record. Jesus in his Logion undoubtedly regards the matter from a religious point of view. Applying the teachings of the Prophets to the Rabbinic customs of his own age, he declares that religious impurity should be a purely spiritual and moral conception, and that bodily religious impurity does not, or need not, exist at all. He may indeed—this man of the people—have offended (Luke xi. 39) against legitimate rules of decency, propriety, cleanliness, and good manners : but, at all events, he helped to break down and abolish the conception of bodily, *religious* impurity, which has played so painful a part in so many religions, and even in the religion of the Rabbis. For even though the elaborate rules and regulations about ritual purity applied only to priests, or to laymen when they wanted to enter the temple, or to ' pious ' and ' holy ' laymen, who chose voluntarily to live their lives in the condition of priests—and of priests when qualified to eat ' holy ' food—yet, even so, they imply an unprophetic conception of religion, just as they go back to, and depend upon, primordial superstitions. Religious defilement is essentially moral and spiritual. It is not physical, and cannot adhere in material substances, or be transferred by them to men and women. Jesus, with the prophet's intuition, realized this truth, and gave it utterance.   He did not perceive—as we may believe—the relation of this truth to definite Pentateuchal laws.   He thought only of the Rabbinic regulations or customs which caused him to give expression to the new truth.   He put himself in line with sundry Greek 'high utterances' quoted by Dr. Farnell in the *Attributes of God* (p. 196), *e.g.*, 'If your mind is pure, your whole body is pure too' (καθαρὸν ἂν τὸν νοῦν ἔχῃς, ἅπαν τὸ σῶμα καθαρὸς εἶ), or, ' The temples of the gods are open to the righteous, nor is there any need of purification ; no defilement can cleave to virtue' (ἱρὰ θεῶν ἀγαθοῖς ἀναπέπταται, οὐδὲ καθαρμῶν χρειώ· τῆς ἀρετῆς ἥψατο οὐδὲν ἄγος).

It is not denied that the primordial superstitions about clean and unclean, and the taboos and restrictions involving these conceptions and based upon them, have had some beneficial effects.   There is no need to deny that *our* conceptions of cleanliness may be historically due to, and the result of, these superstitions and taboos.   Our cleanliness may be the outgrowth of ritual cleanliness, of the ' cleanliness ' against which Jesus spoke.   But we can now maintain the result without maintaining the origin.   This is a case in which it is legitimate to kick down the ladder by which we have climbed. Again, there is no need to deny that the Rabbis had reached a stage in which ritual cleanness and our cleanliness were closely mixed up together.   The Rabbis seem really to have been careful and keen about ' cleanliness ' as well as about ' cleanness.'   The story about Hillel—how he bathed as a religious duty, keeping clean the shell in which dwells the spirit of God—is repeated by modern Jewish scholars *ad nauseam*, but it is pleasant and significant.   Dr. Abrahams, who always made the best of it for the Rabbis, and brought out every possible grace and beauty that he could (of him it may be truly said that he wore his apologetics with a difference), speaks of ' the unique Pharisaic rules regarding the physical life of man, especially the conjugal intercourse of the sexes, rules of a wonderful refinement, in which the bodily and the spiritual are syncretized ' (*Studies*, ii. p. 112).   There is doubtless truth in that, and yet the other truth has also to be emphasized that it was time to break, once and for all, with the conception of priestly uncleanness and cleanness, and this it was which Jesus did.   Remnants of this priestly conception of cleanness clings to orthodox Judaism to-day, over and above the dietary laws, as when, *e.g.*, those orthodox Jews, who are by tradition ' priests,' refuse to enter a house in which there is a corpse.   That taboo is an excellent example of priestly cleanness, and it depends upon superstitions of very great antiquity connected with the dead.

As regards the editorial note in 3 and 4, it may well be a late insertion into the text.   Bacon in his earlier work on Mark observes

(R is the ' editor ' or compiler of the Gospel) : ' The description of Jewish lustrations is of course intended for readers unfamiliar with them.   R himself, however, is either ill-informed or prejudiced, or both.   Such narrow ceremonialism was far from characterizing " all the Jews " or even the best of " the Pharisees."   R's statement better deserves the name of a travesty or caricature, applying at best to the narrowest circles of synagogue orthodoxy.'   ' The Jews' reluctance to defile themselves by " eating with the Gentiles " had been the great bone of contention in the Church.   Jewish exclusiveness is here depicted as specially concerned with lustrations before eating.   Parallels can be adduced from the Talmud for some points in special cases, but as a characterization of contemporary Judaism the representation is misleading.'   But this remark, however kindly meant to the Rabbis, is not wholly satisfactory.   The *real* defence of the Rabbis is always the same, namely, that, at their best, they managed to combine extreme outward scrupulosity with fine inward spirituality in a manner and to a degree which *to us* seems amazing, but was, nevertheless, a fact.   Moffatt's note (p. 232, n. 1), may be used to substantiate Dr. Büchler's hypothesis.   ' The inaccuracies of Mark vii. 1–4 upon Jewish purifications show that the source here has been edited by some Gentile Christian, who, unlike Peter and John Mark, was unfamiliar with local conditions.'   But speaking generally it appears true to say that Christian scholars, such as Box, Bartlet, etc., seem to take Dr. Büchler's arguments somewhat too lightly.   They cannot be easily disposed of.   I have tried my best to do justice to them, and at the same time to remember that Mark, unlike the Talmud, is a work of the first century A.D.   But when all is said and done, the matter remains obscure.   The immense importance and significance of the noble Logion justify, I trust, the inordinate length of this note.

3 and 4 are an editorial parenthesis.   The main sentence is resumed (with irregular construction) in 5.   Dr. Bartlet holds that the words ' and all the Jews,' being an obvious exaggeration, are ' probably an addition by some early copyist or editor of Mark's Gospel.'

3.   πυκνά, ' diligently ' (R.V.), or ' scrupulously ' (Bartlet). Another rendering is ' frequently.'   There is also another reading : πυγμῇ, ' with the fist,' which some explain to mean ' carefully ' or ' vigorously.'   A possible explanation of ' frequently ' is given by Brandt.   The real meaning of πυγμῇ is quite uncertain, but πυκνά may be an ' easier ' and therefore less original reading.   See also Schulthess (Z. N. W., 1922, pp. 232, 233) who thinks that πυγμῇ is undoubtedly original.   It may mean ' with a handful of water.' There is also another possibility discussed by Schulthess and

mentioned by Klostermann in his ed. 2, namely, that it refers to the ' Licenz einer trockenen Abreibung '—a rubbing of the hands together.

ἡ παράδοσις τῶν πρεσβυτέρων, 'the tradition of the elders.' This tradition Jesus in 8, applying Isaiah, calls ἡ παράδοσις τῶν ἀνθρώπων, 'the tradition of men,' and in 9 and 13, addressing the Pharisees and Scribes, he calls it ἡ παράδοσις ὑμῶν, ' your tradition.' Cp. Josephus, Antiquities, XIII. 10. 6.   What was known later on as the Oral Law—the Rabbinic Code—is referred to, which was then really unwritten, and in a more or less floating and formative condition.

4. As to the alleged ' tradition ' or ordinance about the washing of cups, pots, etc., this does not concern us here, for it does not enter into the argument, and the same is true as regards the ablutions on returning from the shops of the market-place.   I may, however, add that the supposed ablutions after coming from the market-place seem quite erroneous.   ' All efforts to prove this a custom even of the strictest Jews must fail ' (Büchler).

6. If we take 1–15 together, and assume that 14, 15 refers also to 1–8, we might say that in his reply Jesus takes a double line. The first is that this human tradition, which he is blamed for disobeying, has become the means whereby his questioners have transgressed the commands of God.   The observance of these ritual enactments has led to the neglect of the moral laws of God.   Hence (it is implied) it is surely not unreasonable that Jesus should disregard this human tradition.   The second line of reply relates to the act itself of which the disciples are accused.   This second ' line of reply ' does not come till 14.   The first line is contained in a double form, 6–8 and 9–13.   For both these two short sections deal with the relation of the ' tradition ' to the ' commandment of God.' It is implied in the one section, and asserted in the other, that through the observance of the ' tradition ' the ' commandment of God ' is annulled or violated.   These two sections are thus independent of each other.   They are parallels.   But as 14, 15 were originally perhaps, or rather as the Logion or saying in 15 was originally perhaps, independent of 1–8, and had no reference to the washing of hands at all, we must consider each paragraph or subsection separately and by itself.

Jesus, then, in 6–8 maintains that the observance of the human tradition has led to the violation of the commands of God.   But something further lies at the back of this.   What would appear to be in the mind of the speaker or writer is that the human commands or tradition are outward and ceremonial ; the divine commands are inward and moral. The standpoint is the old prophetic one, but the argument (if it can be called such) does not work. For the commands of God (if the Pentateuch is opposed to the Oral Law) contain a whole mass of ceremonial and outward commands, while the Oral Law also contained many moral and inward commands. If the attack and reply in 1-8 go back to Jesus, if he said 6-8 in reply to 5, we must assume that in the heat of conflict Jesus forgets the exact facts. To him, in that conflict, it seemed as if the only real commands of God were, and could only be (as to the prophets of old), moral and inward commands. But the prophets were in a position of vantage : in their day there was no Pentateuch and no ceremonial Law which was universally accepted (and stood *outside* the conflict) as authoritative and divine. In Jesus's day there was. He, if you had quietly asked him : Is the Pentateuch the word of God, is it authoritative and divine ? would, I think, assuredly have answered, Yes. It is only in the heat of conflict that he is driven to positions and arguments such as Mark x. 5. But if the Pentateuch is really divine and authoritative, Jesus was logically and dialectically always at a disadvantage with his antagonists.

Again, 6-8, by itself, is not strictly any proof whatever that the observance of the tradition *causes* the violation of the Law. It is a mere assertion, which assumes what has to be proved. Let us take it that the ' commandment ' which is violated for the sake of observing the tradition is the fundamental commandment that God is to be honoured from the ' heart '—loved with all thy heart, as it says in Deuteronomy. If, then, the Pharisees who observe the tradition are the people of whom Isaiah speaks, they *do* violate the Law. But this is only asserted ; it is not proved. It is not *proved* that the ' observance ' *causes* the violation. Did Jesus, we may ask, in spite of Matt. xxiii. 3, really take up a position of definite antagonism to the ominously increasing number of cere-monial enactments of the Rabbinic Law ? I think that we may safely say that he did. It is a somewhat different question whether he opposed ' tradition,' as merely ' human,' to the Pentateuchal Law (' the commandment of God ') as divine. We may, indeed, argue that in the *second* sub-section (9-13) the commandment of God which is violated by the traditionalists is not merely a Pentateuchal law ; it is an injunction of the Decalogue. It is just conceivable that Jesus would have unhesitatingly recognized the divine authority of the Decalogue, and yet have had his doubts about the divine and binding character of the Pentateuchal legislation as a whole. And it may, indeed, be argued that in verse 15 Jesus virtually abrogates a most definite and elaborate Pentateuchal law. But he does not, as we shall see, do this directly, and it may even be that the full consequence of the great principle laid down in 15 was not present to his own mind, or that he did not desire that his disciples should practically draw out those consequences in their own lives. It cannot be assumed offhand that Jesus himself transgressed the dietary laws of Leviticus and Deuteronomy, or even that he would have approved of his disciples transgressing them. Such deductions must remain uncertain, one way or the other. It is true, as Dr. Carpenter says, that ' 15 cuts athwart the whole scheme of dietary laws ; and this principle, together with that of man's lordship over the Sabbath, seems to me to amount to a complete breach with the Law on its ritual and institutional side.' But it does not follow that Jesus recognized this ' cut ' himself, or realized the fulness of the ' breach.' His practice may not have squared with his theory. Indeed the ' Judaic ' church of his first followers in Jerusalem after his death, and the dispute as to the obligations of the Law on the subject of food, would be scarcely explicable if it had done so.

9–13. The second sub-section. It is added on to 1–8 by the usual device, ' And he said unto them.' Both 1–8 and 9–13 quote a sentence from Scripture to prove the same thesis or allegation. Here, however, the argument is much better, or rather, there is a real attempt at a proof : the Rabbinic or human command, so it is alleged, contradicts the divine command. He who observes the first of necessity violates the second.

9. καλῶς is usually here taken in an ironical sense to mean ' excellently,' ' thoroughly.' In an interesting article in the *Theologische Studien und Kritiken*, 1914, pp. 434–444, Horst shows that 6–9 cannot refer to 1–5, but only to the Corban matter. No Pentateuchal command contradicts, or is at variance with, the practice of washing the hands before meals. The Corban story must have been, however, a separate one originally, of which occasion and setting are lost. Again, the Logion of 15 is also no reply to 1–5, for it has clearly to do with food. How can ' enter into a man ' refer to washing ? The water with which he washes does not enter into him ! The setting and occasion of the Logion have also been lost. Mark has combined three stories. He argued : ' You eat with unclean hands. Therefore the food becomes unclean. Therefore you become unclean.' Nor are 18–22 authentic. In verse 19 the deep spiritual meaning of the Logion is misunderstood and cheapened. The real reply to the question in 1–5, now lost, may, perhaps, be found in Luke xi. 40, 41. But here Horst resorts to omissions and other changes, and he thinks that what Jesus said was probably something like this : ' Is not everything which God has made clean ? Behold, all shall be clean to you.' Jesus

daringly denies that anything can be unclean, for God is the creator of all. *Cp.* Acts x. 16, ἃ ὁ θεὸς ἐκαθάρισε, σὺ μὴ κοίνου.

11, 12. The translation of the Revised Version is correct. It preserves the broken construction of the Greek. The construction would be mended if λέγετε be omitted : ' But ye, if a man,' etc., ' no longer suffer him,' etc.

' Corban ' is literally ' sacrifice ' ; here it means the oath used on the occasion of a particular kind of vow.

' Ye no longer suffer him to do aught ' : he is not allowed to benefit his parents. The words are ironical. The meaning is : ' he need no longer benefit them ' ; he *need* no longer, he even *may* not any longer, use that which is now ' Corban ' for the benefit of his parents.

The passage is very difficult. It is difficult (*a*) because the rule which Jesus here attributes to tradition is in flat contradiction to the law as laid down by the Mishnah, as commented on by the Talmud, and as universally accepted and interpreted by all the Jewish codifiers ; (*b*) because the assertion that the Pharisees violated the Law of God in order to maintain, or in maintaining, their own rules is not proved by the instance quoted. On the contrary, the instance fails just at the crucial point.

First of all, what is the usual interpretation of the passage ? It is that the son, in order to annoy his father, dedicated or vowed for the use of the Temple a given part of his property. That part is, therefore, interdicted from his father, who may not benefit from it, or use it. If the son repent, he may, nevertheless, not let his father profit from, or use, the property thus vowed. The Scribes will not let him off his vow. It is, I presume, implied that the Scribes and the priests were in collusion, and because of the advantage which accrued to the Temple, they refused to annul the vow. (Mr. McNeile, however, says : ' Its *actual* dedication is not really contemplated ; it was dedicated (*i.e.* unavailable) only as regards the parent, or other person, who hoped to receive it.' Thus there was no collusion, ' for the " gift," not being really offered, the priests received no advantage from it.') The duty to the Temple is made to take precedence of the duty to parents. But this usual interpretation of the passage is inaccurate. To begin with, ' Corban ' does not mean that the property was dedicated to the use of the Temple. The word is used as a mere oath. When I say, ' Corban, if you shall ever eat anything that is mine,' this does not mean that my eatables are dedicated to the use of the Temple, in which case neither I nor you might eat them, but merely that, so far as you are concerned, they are ' dedicated ' ; you may never eat what is mine. I should sin in letting you eat any of my food, so long as the vow stands, and you, if you ate, would sin also. The Temple does not come in.

We might, however, attempt to save the passage and the accuracy of the argument in the following way. What the Scribes will not allow may be the annulment of the vow. At all costs the vow must be maintained. For example, in a fit of passion I vow, with the oath and formula of Corban, that my father is never to eat at my table, or to receive any of my property. I then want to be absolved from my vow. The Scribes will not let me. *They* gain no profit, and the *Temple* gets no profit one way or the other. But they say, as you have made the vow, you must abide by it.

Now if Jesus had said that the Scribes and Pharisees maintain what is less important and neglect what is more important; that they are anxious to observe the sanctity of vows, but in doing so, they are willing to let the more sacred duty of the fifth command- ment go to the wall, the passage would, so far, be intelligible. But how can it be regarded as a case of Scripture versus tradition ? Where does it say in the Pentateuch, where does ' Moses ' say, that vows which conflict with a more important demand may and should be annulled ? Nowhere does it say so. *The annulling, not the maintenance, of vows, was the work of tradition.* It is to the Pharisaic tradition that are owing all the elaborate rules for annulling vows, and by a curious irony of fate the Pharisees have been constantly assailed just on the ground that they so readily allowed dispensation of vows. Hence the illustration does not seem to fit the thesis. The particular instance is not a case where the word of God is abrogated by tradition. Deut. xxiii. 21–23 speaks of fulfilling vows, not of their annulment. So too Numbers xxx. where the only exceptions are certain vows of certain women. Otherwise : ' When a man voweth a vow unto the Lord, or sweareth an oath to bind his soul with a bond, he shall not break his word; he shall do according to all that proceedeth out of his mouth ' (Numbers xxx. 2). Hence, one could attack the Scribes, perhaps, for not abrogating one ' word of God ' in favour of a more important ' word of God,' but certainly *not* for abrogating the word of God in favour of *tradition*. The only possible explanation would be to suppose that Jesus forgot that a ' word of God ' and ' a law of Moses ' were as much in question on one side as on the other, and that, in his moral enthusiasm, he regarded the decision of the Scribes that the vow could not be annulled, even though the parent suffered, as Scribe law and not Mosaic law, human law and not divine law.

But the difficulties of the passage are not yet over. For the odd thing is that according to the Rabbinic law as codified in the Mishnah, and commented on in the Talmud, the Rabbis are on the side of Jesus, and take his very line. Even Schürer, whose inter- pretation of the Mishnah is inaccurate on the whole, admits that

' so far the practice blamed by Jesus goes further than the law as codified in the Mishnah ' (*Geschichte des jüdischen Volkes im Zeitalter Jesu Christi*, 4th ed., Vol. II. p. 577, n. 112). That is to say, if a man make a vow from which his parents would suffer, then the vow can be annulled. The passage in the Mishnah is clear, though it has been frequently misunderstood by Christian commentators. Yet the Talmud and all the Jewish mediæval commentators are in no doubt as to its meaning. It occurs in Nedarim viii. 1 : ' Rabbi Eliezer said, The door is opened for a man on account of the honour of father and mother. But the Chachamim (literally, wise men, the majority of the Rabbis) forbid it.' By which decision the Chachamim mean this : Suppose a man has made a foolish vow (in general, from which his father does *not* materially suffer). If he reflects : What disgrace I bring upon my father by this foolish vow, or if it is said to him, would you have made this vow had you reflected that people would say to your father, ' What a son is yours ; what hasty vows he makes ' ; then these arguments are not enough to cancel the vow. It cannot be annulled. He, and even his parents, must bear the consequences of his rash action. That this interpretation is correct seems certain by what follows. ' Nevertheless, where the vow *has to do with* his father or his mother, there the Rabbis agree with Rabbi Eliezer that the door is opened to him on account of the honour of father and mother.' Precisely, therefore, where parents would suffer from the vow, would and could the vow be annulled. Thus we have the further difficulty that Jesus and the Rabbis do not here differ ; they agree. One can only get out of the difficulty by assuming that Jesus came in contact with some Rabbis who held that, even when the Law directly affected the parents, it must, nevertheless, be upheld, and that even here it could not be annulled. For this view Dr. Abrahams tells me that there is no direct evidence, but it is not at all improbable that so vast an innovation as the annulment of vows met with opposition at first. We should thus have here an instance, not of a general antagonism between Jesus and the Pharisaic law, but of the participation of Jesus in the discussion of the application of the Law to life. Sometimes Rabbinic opinion finally formed itself (as here) on the side which Jesus approved ; sometimes it took a turn in a direction different from the opinion of Jesus. In any case the passage cannot be used to prove the dangers and moral evils of legalism. It cannot be proved to show that ' the Rabbis ' taught that by a convenient vow a man might easily find a way of disobeying the fifth commandment. The truth is that the Rabbis taught a tremendous respect and reverence for parents. In this matter they are perfectly sound ; indeed, on family relations they are keener than Jesus.

For a different view of the whole passage see Mr. Hart's intensely interesting article ' Corban,' *Jewish Quarterly Review*, Vol. XIX. pp. 615–650.   See also Mr. McNeile in his commentary on Matthew, p. 225, who argues that perhaps the higher, more moral view of the Rabbis of the Mishnah and the Talmud did not prevail in the time of Jesus.

The suggestion which I made in the first edition of my book and which I have retained here as above, that the ' annulment of vows met with opposition at first, etc.', is commented on by Dr. Bartlet. I remarked that the Rabbis of the Mishnah and the Talmud agree with Jesus, and that this agreement constitutes a difficulty, to which Dr. Bartlet retorts thus : ' This difficulty exists only for those who, like Montefiore, habitually assume that the witness of the Mishnah, the written form of which dates from a century and a half after Jesus' ministry, is better evidence to the prevalent thought and usage of Pharisaism in Jesus' day than the Synoptic Gospels them-selves.   The fact is that it is most probable that the balance of Rabbinic thought changed on this (and other matters) as between the two periods in question.'   Well, ' most probable ' is rather stiff. I went as far as I could when I said ' not at all improbable ' : it might perhaps have been better to have said ' not impossible.' But what is much more serious to remark in such notes as those of Dr. Bartlet, and indeed of many other Christian commentators (for Dr. Bartlet is by no means the worst offender) is this.   It is assumed that the hypothetical Rabbis who would not allow the rash vow to be cancelled, even when the father would suffer from the vow, were men dead to all decent moral feeling.   They were odious creatures who ' played fast and loose with the chiefest of ethical principles under the perverting influence of their professional and formal bias in things religious.   Such practical inconsistency made void their professed zeal for honour to parents, a moral principle of the first rank, and reduced their " honouring " of God in this crucial case to mere words, and themselves to " play-actors " in the matter.'   Their ' developments of scribal or traditional law had so perverted moral feeling that it had come to be a recognized thing that to declare any possession to be *Corban, i.e.* " dedicated " *by vow* to some special purpose, even though a selfish one, left one free to refuse—nay, made it wrong not to refuse—to use it for the help even of a parent.'   Now be it observed that there is very little evidence except the admittedly biassed evidence of the Gospels, the evidence of bitter enemies and antagonists, that these exceedingly bad Rabbis existed at all.   Secondly, we have the enormous mass of positive evidence reaching back to the age of Jesus that the Rabbis laid the most enormous stress upon the honouring of father and mother.   Is not the deduction fairly clear

that if any Rabbis held that a vow, even if a parent suffered
from it, could not be annulled, this opinion was a purely legal
decision, had absolutely nothing to do with their moral feeling,
and is no evidence whatever that 'they played fast and loose
with the chiefest of ethical principles'?   Have not English
judges had sometimes to interpret the law as it stands, even
if it involves 'hard lines' upon an innocent person?   Here was
a vow which rested upon a Pentateuchal ordinance.   It needed
some courage to annul such a vow.   Those who declared that
they could not see their way to annul it might yet have had
the most excellent moral feeling, and may have been just as
keen for the honour of parents, and as little willing to put them
to open shame, as Jesus himself, and, if Mark iii. 31-35 be
authentic, even keener.   The instance selected for this attack upon
the Rabbis is indeed, for every reason, singularly ill-chosen.   It is
no wonder that ordinary Jewish readers who know well how the
love and honour of parents have always been a real feather in the
Jewish cap, and a veritable feature of every sort of Judaism
throughout the ages, should feel irritated by Mark vii. 1-13.   For
they remember the statement that he who hates not his father and
mother cannot be a disciple of Jesus, and reading these words literally, just as Dr. Bartlet reads Mark vii. 1-13 literally, and knowing
or allowing no explanation of them by which they can (as I think)
be justified, just as Dr. Bartlet knows or allows no explanation or
extenuation for the alleged moral evil attacked and reprobated in
Mark vii. 1-13, it is no wonder that they should cry out with some
bitterness, 'Physician, heal thyself!'   Let us hope that 9-13 is
not authentic !

13. παρεδώκατε.   This tense is odd.   One would expect
either 'which ye hand on' (παραδίδοτε) or 'which ye have
received' (παρελάβετε).

'Many other such things ye do.'   Jesus mentions no other, and
even the Christian commentators do not, so far as I know, supply
the deficiency.

14, 15.   The third sub-section with the great Logion.   Why
πάλιν?   The Evangelist alludes to similar situations and similar
convocations.   If 15 refers to the question in 5 (*i.e.*, to the unwashed hands), then we have to assume that the meaning must
be that in dipping the hand which held the bread into a dish, or
even in holding the bread, some particles of forbidden matter would
be eaten, and thus make the eater unclean.

Some authorities think that the Logion had originally nothing
to do with 1-8 and the question of the unwashed hands.   In either

case it seems to refer to food, and, if logically and systematically interpreted, is exceedingly daring and revolutionary. For undoubtedly it goes right against fundamental conceptions and assumptions of the Pentateuchal law. The Law describes certain foods as in themselves unclean. ' They are unclean unto you ; of their flesh you shall not eat and their carcase ye shall not touch ; they are unclean unto you.' Creeping things shall not be eaten : ' Ye shall not make yourselves unclean through them.' If clean animals die of themselves, their carcases become unclean : ' he that eats of the carcase shall wash his clothes and be unclean until the evening.' The Logion declares that nothing outside a man can make him unclean. The *principle* of the Logion goes beyond its actual wording. It would apply to *touching* the carcase of an ' unclean ' animal. It would apply to being in the presence of a human corpse. It could be made to apply also to bodily ' issues ' and sores. In fact, it destroys the whole conception of *material* or ritual uncleanness in religion which extends through any number of races and religions, and which fills up such long, intricate chapters of the Pentateuchal and Rabbinic law. Ritual washings, ablutions, taboos, are all abolished by it, for there is no such thing as ritual impurity. It is one of the greatest sayings in the history of religion. Jesus—and there seems to me to be great reason to believe that in 15 we have his own words—lays down the principle that there is no such thing as *religious* impurity in a material sense. Religious impurity can only exist within the moral and spiritual sphere. A man cannot be religiously defiled except by an offence committed in the sphere of religion. Now to Jesus the sphere of religion was the inward realm of the spirit. Inward defilement, the defilement of the heart by the sins of the heart, is the only possible religious defilement.

Only that which goes out of a man can defile a man, that is, make him religiously unclean. Matt. xv. 11 interprets the principle a little too narrowly. What goes into the man from without cannot defile him religiously. ' Going into ' refers to the mouth, but ' going out of ' does not exclusively refer to the mouth, for a man's deeds as well as his words are alluded to. What comes out of the man comes from the heart, and the heart is the seat of religious uncleanness as it is the seat of religious purity. THINGS cannot be *religiously* either clean or unclean ; only PERSONS. And *persons* cannot be defiled by *things* ; they can only be defiled by themselves, by acting irreligiously. We have, however, to note that a voluntary physical action may defile a man. A voluntary sexual defilement, or a voluntary gluttonous deed, is physical, but it is an impure action in a religious sense. A purely involuntary defilement is not.

With the qualifications noted in my remarks on verse two, it is true to say that neither the practice alluded to in verse 5 nor the Logion in 15 is primarily concerned with *cleanliness*, nor can we properly defend ancient ritualistic practices by saying that it is dirty to eat with unwashed hands, that cleanliness is next to godliness, and so on. That is not the issue involved. The question is one of *religious* defilement. It is the same question which is at the root of all the dietary laws. A rabbit is in itself unclean, and to eat it makes you unclean. A chicken is in itself clean, and if it be properly killed, to eat it does not, therefore, make you unclean. According to the principle laid down by Jesus, no *thing* can make you unclean. You can only make yourself unclean by sin.

The principle seems profoundly true. It destroys with a prophet's blow the terrible incubus from which all ancient religions suffered, that certain objects or physical states are in themselves taboo or religiously unclean. Doubtless our modern conceptions of clean and dirty may have had a religious origin ; doubtless, too, there is a certain moral duty in physical cleanliness, a certain interconnection between the material and the spiritual. But this is a totally different thing from the theory of *religious* uncleanness. That rested upon very ancient superstitions, which, again, themselves depended upon polytheistic or ' animistic ' conceptions of still greater antiquity. Ritual religion (which made up a considerable part of priestly religion) was largely concerned with practices which turned upon, or were developed out of, these superstitious conceptions. The reason why dead bodies, or a woman at certain moments in her life, were in themselves ' unclean,' or produced religious uncleanness, was not because they were dirty. It was because the dead body and the woman were the seat, or belonged to the province, of certain hostile or dangerous spirits. It is these ideas which are also at the root of the dietary laws. Religious uncleanness either means being connected with alien, hostile, or dangerous spirits and influences, or, secondly, it means being in a condition to which your god objects, and when it is therefore dangerous to approach him. And this condition is physical, and itself probably related to the former cause of uncleanness. In any case the god is regarded as moved to pleasure or wrath by physical objects or conditions, whereas the God of the prophets is so moved by moral considerations only (reckoning idolatry for the moment as a part of morality).

The old, outward conception of religious uncleanness as caused by things, and not only by immoral acts, is still present in the Pentateuchal laws ; it was maintained and elaborated by the Rabbis. It is the motive of an immense number of their laws about women, and is doubtless also the motive of their laws about ablutions. But it has to be noted that there are two kinds of cleanness : there is (1) the ' cleanness ' which every layman must observe ; there is (2) the cleanness of the priest, which the layman has only to observe, and that partially, when he enters the Temple at Jerusalem, or performs some specific religious act. The second was far more onerous than the first. Christian commentators frequently confuse the two together, and burdens are assigned to the ordinary life of the lay Jew from which he was entirely free. Nevertheless, the *principle* of ritual uncleanness was not disputed, though the old superstitions, and the more ancient conceptions upon which it ultimately rested, had *entirely* disappeared. Ritual uncleanness had no more anything to do with spirits or hostile influences. It existed because it was in the Law, because God had ordained it. The prohibition of rabbit and hare was regarded either as due to the fact that these were sacred animals in heathen religions, or, simply, as due to the fact that God, for some good, if unknown and unknowable, reason, thought it better for the Israelite not to eat these animals. So with regard to all the other taboos and with regard to the ordeals. What really defiled was violating God's law ; what really purified was not the water, but God. And in the case of the forbidden animals feelings of disgust soon grew up concerning their flesh. Hygienic motives also played their part. The holy God was supposed to regard physical as well as moral foulness with disgust, and the Israelite, who must be holy like his God, was to keep himself free from the one foulness as well as from the other. There was a tendency to pass from the old conceptions of ritual uncleanness to the newer conceptions which are expressed in the proverb, ' Cleanliness is next to godliness.' Spiritual purity may not unreasonably be symbolized or typified by material purity. A dirty church or synagogue strikes us as peculiarly inappropriate and undesirable. But all this is a very different thing from technical religious uncleanness in the legal sense. For the other sort of uncleanness, which the proverb speaks of, we need no ritual laws or casuistical enactments. Common sense, and cultivated feelings of decency and propriety, are safe and adequate guides.

Jesus was, therefore, I think, quite right in the great principle which he lays down in Mark vii. 15. It is the same principle as that involved and implied in the superb saying of Theano, the wife or daughter of Pythagoras. Θεανὼ ἐρωτηθεῖσα ποσταία γυνὴ ἀπ' ἀνδρὸς καθαρεύει ' Απὸ μὲν τοῦ ἰδίου, εἶπε, παραχρῆμα, ἀπὸ δὲ τοῦ ἀλλοτρίου, οὐδέποτε. ' Theano, on being asked how soon a woman was clean after intercourse with a man, replied, ' In the case of her own man (*i.e.* husband, for the Greek ἀνήρ, like the German *Mann*, can mean both man and husband), at once : in the case of another man, never.' Such a saying lifts a load, and removes a nightmare, from the human mind and thought. A mass of ritual superstitions is made superfluous. So too with the saying of Jesus. The world is profoundly indebted to Jesus for his liberating and clarifying words. They are spoken in the very spirit of Amos and Hosea. The true province of religion needed to be defined. It was made the greater and the purer by being limited to the realms of spirit and personality. Moreover, the dietary laws and the laws of clean and unclean have doubtless occasionally led, as they led in the days of Jesus, to formalism, hypocrisy, self-righteousness. Outward ' cleanliness ' can occasionally mask inward corruption.

Yet, though all this be so, it was impossible for the Jews to accept the saying, nor can we safely say that Jesus was consistent in asserting it. For though the occasion which (as Mark tells the story) drew it forth was a *Rabbinical* law, though it was only a Rabbinical law which the disciples transgressed, yet the great principle laid down by Jesus runs, as we have seen, directly counter to the laws of the Pentateuch.

Now the Pentateuch makes no difference between some laws and other laws. It does not say that the moral laws are divine and eternal, the ritual laws are human and temporary ; it ascribes the same divinity and immutability to them all.

From the Pentateuchal and Rabbinic point of view, the dietary laws, the laws about women, the laws about corpses and ablutions, were as much given by the wise and righteous God as were the laws about honouring our parents or loving our neighbours. If the one set of laws is divine, so is the other set. It was illogical for Jesus, on one occasion, to appeal to the 'Law of God,' violated by Rabbinical enactment, and to enunciate a principle antagonistic to that Law on another. It is true that Jesus is not recorded to have said, and he probably would not have dreamed of saying, that the Pentateuch was not in all its parts the Law of God. It is more than doubtful whether he would have urged his followers to partake of rabbits and hares. Nevertheless, his great Logion (whatever occasioned its utterance) flies in the face of the dietary laws which are ordered in the Pentateuch by God. But if the wise and perfect God has ordered them, they too are wise and perfect. If the wise and perfect God has said that what enters into man's mouth can and does defile him, then *He* must be right and Jesus must be wrong.

How far Jesus was conscious of his own inconsistency is doubtful. How far in his own mind he separated the moral from the ritual law, and thought that God *had* ordered the one, but had *not* ordered the other, we do not know. But we *do* know that he never enunciated the principle of such a separation and difference of origin. Moreover, there are a few indications that he himself obeyed, and urged others to obey, the ritual laws of the Pentateuch. But all the same he promulgated a principle which invalidates them.

If, however, Jesus was unaware of his own inconsistency, the Rabbis must have perceived it well enough, and they were quite justified in denying his principle and the authority of him who uttered it.

The truth is, as we have already seen, that Amos could have uttered the principle without inconsistency, because in his day there was no perfect, divine, immutable Mosaic Law in existence ; and we, to-day, can consistently utter the principle because we no longer believe in such a Law—because we *do* separate the moral from the ritual—but Jesus could only utter the principle at the cost of an inconsistency, which does not, indeed, lessen the greatness of the principle or of him who spoke it, but which justifies, exonerates, and explains the opposition and disbelief of the Rabbis and Pharisees, who saw more clearly than Jesus whither the principle must tend and how much it implied.

Prof. Burkitt has an excellent paragraph as to the quarrel between Jesus and the Rabbis. He says : ' The real cause of quarrel between our Lord and the Scribes seems to me to be that it was a quarrel between erudition and intuition, between traditionalism and originality. With us the word " originality " tends to be used for mere cleverness, but in its true sense it is the very word for the great characteristic of our Lord's ·teaching, especially as compared with the principles of the Scribes. It was, in fact, so original as to be superficially inconsistent. The tradition of the Elders (said He) is inconsistent with the Word of God, the Law revealed to Moses : well then, the tradition of the Elders must go. But in the matter of Divorce it is the Law of Moses itself that was given for the hardness of men's hearts ; well then, the Law of Moses must go. In the matter of the Sabbath it is the very Law of God, which, according to the Jewish view, God Himself has kept from the beginning, that comes into conflict with duties of kindness and beneficence ; well then, even the Law of God is to be broken, as David did. What does all this mean, but that the supreme sanction lay not in any Code or set of Rules, however promulgated, but in an enlightened conscience, a mind really in harmony with the mind of the Father in Heaven ? We have learnt the lesson so well that we do not see the difficulty. Our difficulty is to know what enlightenment is, but that was not the difficulty of the Scribes. They did not doubt that it was worse for a man to be paralysed than to be sound ; they doubted whether it was worse for a man to be paralysed or for the Sabbath to be broken ' (*Gospel History*, pp. 174–176). I do not know that I have much to differ from in this suggestive way of putting the problem. In a sense it is true that if you believe that a given Law is the direct command of God who, *ex hypothesi*, is perfectly wise and perfectly good, it is better

to be paralysed than to violate it. But that was *not*, I venture
to think, the question at issue in the particular story to which
Professor Burkitt alludes. The question at issue was : May not
the healing wait for twenty-four hours ? The man had presumably
been paralysed a long while. It would not have greatly mattered
had he remained so one more day. Then the man could have been
healed, *and* the law of God could have been maintained unbroken.
The principles of Liberal Judaism are entirely in harmony with
what the Professor says about the 'enlightened conscience,' etc.
But I am still doubtful whether, if I absolutely believed (1) that
God had given the Sabbath law *in the same sense and manner as the
Rabbis believed it*, and (2) that healing was a violation of that law,
I should agree with the Rabbis or with Jesus. There seems to me
a regular *impasse*. The way out is, I think, in (2). The Rabbis
were wrong in thinking that healing could be a violation of the
Sabbath law. But that is not the way out apparently suggested
by Professor Burkitt. He seems to suggest that even if one
believed both (1) and (2), one ought to realize that the Law should
be broken. And at that I stumble. I remain doubtful and un-
convinced.

Dr. Bartlet has a most interesting 'appended note on the issues
in vii. 1-23 ' (pp. 226-231 of his Commentary). He naturally likes
and agrees with all I said in my first edition in praise and recognition
of the great saying in verse 15, but he denies that there was any
inconsistency in Jesus's attitude. He urges that Jesus simply
adopted and expanded the Prophetic point of view. ' The whole
matter was one of a spiritual *perspective* in judging religious values,
and so of *relative* obligation under varying conditions. Under some
conditions the maintenance of the ritual or lower values in the
system of precepts embodying the Divine will for human, that is,
physically conditioned life, involved, while in others it did not
involve, the sacrifice of the higher or moral values—just as there
was a certain competition between these themselves in the practice
of daily life. Everything, then, depended upon the motive or spirit
expressed in the choice made between the competing duties, moral
and ritual.' He then proceeds to quote the remarkable story only
found in the MS. D (Codex Bezae) after Luke vi. 4 (I have quoted
it in my notes on Luke vi. 1-11), and he adds : ' This story, whether
historical or not, preserves the authentic spirit of Jesus' attitude ;
and it is one which puts out of court Montefiore's criticism as applied
to Jesus' own thought. On the other hand, by calling such emphatic
attention to the " higher criticism " of the Mosaic Law implicit in
Jesus' attitude to it, Montefiore brings out not only the bold
originality of the Prophet of Nazareth, but also the transcendent
authority he thus claims for his own spiritual consciousness.' Again,

he says that ' Jesus ever refers to the prophets as his forerunners
in spirit (Matt. xxiii. 29 ff. ; Luke xi. 47 ff.) ; and in claiming to
" fulfil " the Law and the Prophets, he meant that he fulfilled the
Law as understood by and in the light of the Prophets, and not as
read apart from them or in a way alien to their interpretation of its
Divine intention or spirit, as in the current Rabbinical reading and
developments of the Pentateuchal code.'   But is not all this somewhat too ingenious and modern ?   In any case, why, if the Law is
only to be observed where it does not conflict with the principles
of the prophets, did Jesus not more fully explain and justify his
attitude ?   It would have been so much kinder and clearer.   Why
did he not say : ' You have erroneously thought that the Law was
superior to the prophets. You are wrong. The prophets are superior
to the Law, and before observing any enactment of the Law, you
must always ask : Does the observance of this enactment, in this
particular instance and at this particular time, conflict with a
prophetic principle ? '   Even if he had, the Rabbis could not have
believed him, for the Law states that nobody is to be believed who
argues against its validity. But he would have made his own position
much clearer.

This point, however, I need not discuss further. But the great
saying of vii. 15 stands in quite a different category. For here it
is not a question of an observance of the Law being in conflict with
a prophetic principle, as one might argue that the observance of
the Sabbath law conflicts with the prophetic principle of loving-
kindness, if, being able to heal a man on Saturday, you ask him
to wait till Sunday. For here no question of loving-kindness comes
in. There is no conflict. The principle of vii. 15 does not say
that ritual is secondary ; it sets up a counter principle which really
cuts the ground from under a whole set of Pentateuchal enactments.
That is its new greatness. Dr. Bartlet says that for Jesus ' the Law
(even in its details, so Matt. v. 18 seems to imply) had for him
abiding value until the end of this age or dispensation of God's
providence, i.e. until the Kingdom of God was actually come
(cp. Matt. xi. 13–15 ; Luke xvi. 16).' But the logical deduction from
vii. 15, though Jesus did not realize it, is that the principle upon
which a big section of the Law depends (that material things can
make men and women religiously unclean) is a mistaken principle.
We can see that ; we know the origin of all these laws. Jesus did
not. You cannot have it both ways. It is true that the Rabbis
did bravely attempt to get rid of the superstitious element in many
Pentateuchal laws by turning them into arbitrary ukases of the
perfectly wise and good God. ' It is not the water which purifies :
it is God's law, which, because he is perfect in goodness and wisdom,
it is your duty to obey, even as he has bidden you.' That is also, in

its way, a bold and sublime utterance, but it leaves the problem of outward cleanness and physical defilement unsolved. Yet I cannot see that the Rabbis were wrong in their opposition to vii. 15. If the Law is throughout Mosaic, perfect and divine, then it must be obeyed throughout. But a saying like vii. 15 would imply that God made a mistake. In ordering Moses to bid the children of Israel observe *for ever* certain laws about food, etc., God apparently meant that there *was* such a thing as outward defilement. He meant that some things which go into the mouth or which touch the body, or some bodily conditions or impurities, do or can, as a matter of fact, religiously defile and make religiously unclean. And so believing, he ordered Moses to proclaim the observance of certain laws which depend upon that opinion. Jesus in vii. 15 practically declares that the divine opinion was wrong. And yet the Law as a whole was divine, divine throughout (he never said the contrary), and to be observed even 'in its details.' Is not this inconsistent? The inconsistency does not, indeed, matter *for us*. The splendour of vii. 15 remains as before. But I do not see how it can be contended that there is *no* inconsistency, and, if so, from their point of view, not only were the Rabbis justified in protesting against and rejecting the new doctrine of vii. 15, but they could observe the laws of outward cleanness, and *yet* be *also* keen on inward purity as well. The two things can go together. The two purities can be, often were, and often are, combined. If one is sufficiently detached, one can appraise the truth and splendour of vii. 15 at their right level, and yet perceive that no hypocrisy and no blame of any kind attach to the Rabbis. In fact, one can be just to, and one can admire, *both* Jesus *and* the Rabbis. Jesus attacked the Rabbis; the Rabbis attacked Jesus. Both (I am not dealing here with the bad Rabbis) were blameless. But the inconsistency of Jesus was grander than the consistency of the Rabbis. It was more prophetic. It has, moreover, been proved to have been more true.

It may be also be observed that it is quite possible for a modern Jew to observe, and justify his observance of, dietary laws, while yet admitting the truth of the principle of Mark vii. 15. He can be quite free from the old superstitious idea that any material thing is religiously unclean, but he may yet maintain that the discipline and self-restraint and self-sacrifice involved in (*e.g.*) observing a number of dietary laws among an environment which does not observe them may have useful ethical results. He will not maintain that the laws are from God, but he will argue that they form a useful bond for 'keeping Jews together,' for 'maintaining a connection with the past,' and that for these reasons, as well as for their ethical value as a discipline, he chooses freely to obey them freely. Moreover, he may justify and cling to the dietary laws on the ground of hygiene. He may even, though perhaps somewhat fancifully, argue that the connection between the moral and physical nature of man is subtle and obscure, and that allegiance to dietary laws may have some undefinable, but real, moral influence. Such an attitude is justifiable but modern. It does not touch or affect the question as it presented itself either to Jesus or to the Rabbis.

14. The 'people' (τὸν ὄχλον) are at hand for Mark when he wants them no less than the Scribes. We may assume that when Jesus uttered the saying, he did not mean it to possess an esoteric character. He must have wished to be understood, and he probably gave such explanations as made it entirely plain. In fact the substance of 18b, 19a, 20–23 may go back to Jesus himself. Mr. Rawlinson says : ' The scrupulosity of the Pharisees, who showed themselves so anxious to avoid even the bare possibility of cere-monial defilement, was in danger of resulting in a serious distortion of moral judgment. To avoid ceremonial pollutions arising from without was comparatively easy : to avoid the defilements of sin, which arise from within, was at once harder and much more im-portant. The Semite, it has been pointed out, knows no comparative degree. He can only express the thought " A is more important than B " by saying " A matters, and B does not." So our Lord puts His thought in the form of an antithetical epigram, the primary meaning of which is simply that pollutions from within are more serious than pollutions from without.' Cp. the famous words of Hosea vi. 6, ' " I desire mercy and not sacrifice," the meaning of which is simply that mercy is more important than sacrifice ' (p. 96). I am so keen about the great Logion that I cannot help hoping that Jesus really meant that outward uncleanness does not matter ! I ought, perhaps, to add that Bacon (Beginnings of Gospel Story) explains the Logion much in the same way as Mr. Rawlinson. He observes : ' The saying is indeed capable of very sweeping application, but cannot have been understood by the Twelve as intended to abolish the Mosaic distinctions of meats. The Semite knows no comparative degree. Hence to express the thought : Inward (spiritual) purity is more pleasing to God than abstinence from prescribed meats (cp. Matt. v. 8), the natural mode of expression is as in verse 15. In substance at least it is a parallel to the Q saying on cleansing the inside (Luke, of the man ; Matthew, of the dish) rather than the outside (Matt. xxiii. 25, 26 = Luke xi. 39–41). R is more radical than the saying or practice of Jesus really warrants, in declaring that by this utterance he abolished all the Mosaic distinctions of meats.' But I think we may well believe that, in the urge and inspiration of

the moment, Jesus did really mean that there is no such thing as outward religious defilement.

17-19. The fourth sub-section. Mark, true to his theory, assumes that the Logion of 15 was not understood even by the disciples, and required to be specially explained to them. He may have found 18*b*, 19 as a commentary on 15 already in his source, but he provides it with a special introduction.

The disciples call the Logion a Parable. It is hardly even ' a dark saying.' The Hebrew *Mashul*, however, means not only parable, but also adage, proverb, etc., and perhaps ' parable ' is used in a similar extended sense in this passage. The only way in which 15 can be interpreted as a parable in a strict sense would be to assume that its meaning is that, even according to the Law, a man is defiled, not by what enters into him, but by what goes out from him, *i.e.* by morbid issues, by leprosy, eruptions, and so on. Then the spiritual interpretation or application would follow in 17-23. But this explanation is unlikely, first, because to press legal points of this kind does not seem in Jesus's manner; secondly, because of the difficulty as to forbidden food, which, if eaten, does enter *into* the man and does make him unclean. It is inadequate to say that the foods which the Law forbids are not thought of or referred to, because to eat them is a deliberate sin. In fact, the whole explanation would be too subtle, and by what enters into the man the hearers could only understand food.

A slight difficulty may be said to remain as regards 15, over and above the mere fact that the Logion is called a parable, but it seems rather far-fetched. It is this : the first part of the declaration seems to speak of what is material ; the second would speak of what is spiritual. ' The things which go in,' go in literally ; ' the things which go out,' go out metaphorically. Words and thoughts, and the sins of the heart, do not ' go out ' of a man in the same way as food ' goes in.' Yet this irregularity is after all not very awkward, and to admit and accept it gives far the best sense. Brandt does not seem justified, because of this irregularity, in calling the great saying a paradox, and then in denying that paradoxes have much substantive value. (' The value of the actual *content* of paradoxes is slight. They do not lend themselves to serious instruction. They are plays on words, and their only advantage is that they are easily remembered.') The saying, paradox or no, is surely one of the greatest and most original in all the Gospels. On the other hand, there is no doubt that, as Brandt says (*Jüdische Reinheitslehre*, p. 60), the saying in 15 directly contradicts the words of the Law. Brandt quotes Leviticus xi. 40, xvii. 15, xx. 25. Perhaps most significant is xx. 25. Certain beasts and birds are unclean, and it is distinctly implied that he who eats of their flesh becomes, by such entrance of unclean flesh into his body, himself unclean and unholy. Brandt considers that this deliberate contradiction of the written law cannot be credited to the teacher who, after all, was the Master of the apostles of Jerusalem (p. 63).   And then he gives his own view as to how the great saying about Inward and Outward, material and spiritual, purity came to be coined and inserted, as a portion of the teaching ascribed to Jesus in the Gospel. For my part I see no adequate reason for this scepticism. Jesus need not have realized in the moment when he gave vent to his great utterance that he was flying in the face of Pentateuchal conceptions and enactments. And there is surely every reason to believe that the more conservative of the Jerusalem apostles did not realize this either, and never realized it even afterwards. This saying of Jesus is to me not only bold and original, but also very precious and very dear. And, perhaps, I feel the same reluctance to question its authenticity, and the same desire to defend it, as the orthodox Christian feels about Matt. xi. 25–30.

Bacon, as usual, regards the great saying of 15 as borrowed from Q, and ' reproduced by Mark with his usual freedom.' ' The importance of the Logion to Mark is apparent from his extensive elaboration of it.   The particular application he would give it appears from the setting.   It forms the prelude to Jesus' departure " into the borders of Tyre and Sidon," where he extends to the believing " Gentile woman " the divine help at first reserved for " the children " only (vii. 24–30).   It is thus for Mark an equivalent for the story in Acts x. 1–11, 18, of how Peter through the vision on the house-top was taught that the Mosaic distinctions of " clean " and " unclean " are not of God but of men (Acts x. 15), and how thereafter Peter carried the gospel to the Gentile household of Cornelius.'   The doctrine ' goes even beyond Paul in the persuasion " that there is nothing unclean of itself," since it omits the saving clause that " to him that accounteth anything to be unclean to him it is unclean." ' ' Mark is a Paulinist of the type of those in Corinth, who needed to be reminded that Paul imposed voluntary restrictions on his own perfect liberty, for the sake of the overscrupulous ' (*Gospel of Mark*, p. 147).

18.   Virtually repeats 15*a*.

19.   Only the heart or will or mind can be defiled.   The verse is grammatically hard.   The nominative participle καθαρίζων seems to agree with the accusative ἀφεδρῶνα.

The word ἀφεδρών, only found here, is usually translated ' privy,' though why the ' privy ' can be said to cleanse food is not quite easy to see.   Perhaps it is said to do so, because it receives and removes all those parts of food which the human body cannot assimilate and which are unsuitable for the maintenance of life.   W. says that ἀφεδρών means bowel (*Darmkanal*).   The bowel purifies food, in that it ejects what is ' unclean.'   Suidas says that ἀφεδρών signifies τὸ μέρος τοῦ σώματος τὸ περὶ τὴν ἔξοδον.   The manuscript D has ὀχετός, which means the intestinal canal.   The S.S. has a different, and, as Merx thinks, a truer reading, which would mean that food does not cause impurity, inasmuch as it simply passes through the body, is evicted, and does not enter the heart.

Some commentators have thought that καθαρίζων refers back to λέγει.   ' Thus spake he—making all foods clean.'   And I have so translated.   But καθαρίζων seems somewhat far off to go with λέγει, though it makes fine and trenchant meaning if so interpreted.   It is thus taken by R.V.   The words ' making all things clean ' may, thus regarded, be a note by an editor who sees the wide effect of Jesus's words.   (*Cp.* Turner in *J. T. S.*, 1925, Vol. XXVI. p. 149.)

20–23.   The fifth sub-section added on by, ' And he said.'

20 repeats 15*b* as 18 repeats 15*a*.

21.   From the heart spring evil passions and impure thoughts, which result in evil words and impure deeds.   These ' go out ' from a man and defile him.

22.   The list of vices is Hellenistic.   We may compare the list in Gal. v. 19–21 and Rom. i. 29–31.

It would not be denied by Jesus or the Evangelist that gluttony and drunkenness are sins.   Jesus is not thinking of these, but only of the ceremonial observances and abstentions.   The doctrine in any case is still correct, for it has been justly said that ' excess in eating and drinking comes from a perverse will, and it is not for what he takes, but for the excess committed when he takes it, that man is to be blamed ' (Loisy).

Looking back upon the whole incident after 1900 years, we see that while both parties had a certain right upon their side, though neither could persuade the other, Jesus was more profoundly right and more essentially true.   The future was with him, not with the Rabbis and Pharisees.   His principle would gradually win the day. It represented a higher and purer conception of religion than the opposing principle which is embodied in the Pentateuchal Law. Liberal Judaism has consciously accepted it.   Jesus himself, with his keen moral and religious intuitions, went straight to the essential truths of religion.   He probably did not realize the conflict between the principle, which he had laid down with such clear conviction, and the teachings of the Law.   Such conflicts between new and old are often invisible to those who, while ardently possessed of new creative truths, have not thought out their relation to old doctrine in which they still partially believe.   In this respect the Rabbis saw, likely enough, more clearly than Jesus.   But for all that, his conception of religion was in this point, just because the Rabbis were tied to the perfection and divineness of a heterogeneous code, profounder and truer than theirs.

Pfleiderer, I notice, says much the same.   He holds that Jesus was unaware of the implications of his own principle, and that he did not consciously intend to attack the *Pentateuchal* law. ' It is the nature of all, and especially of religious, heroes and reformers (think of Luther !) in the most exalted moments of their struggle against the old to utter thoughts, the far-reaching range of which is concealed even from themselves, and compared with which the conservative moods of their quiet days lag far behind. Hence the manifold contradictions in the life and thought of the men, in whose mind two epochs struggle against one another ' (Pfleiderer, *Urchristentum*, 1. p. 356).

Returning to the subject after a long interval, I would like to add the following.   The usual modern Jewish criticisms of vii. 15 is that it is at bottom untrue : what goes into the mouth does or can defile.   One must not say : it cannot religiously defile, for this is to separate religion from life, which is the very thing that it is un-Jewish and wrong to do.   If a man overeats and overdrinks, he is morally defiled and religiously defiled.   The dietary laws are merely amplified rules for temperance and discipline in eating. Moreover, there are certain kinds of food which the higher feelings or opinions of mankind have justly and fitly come to regard as disgusting.   The dietary laws are extensions or illustrations of such feelings and opinions.   However much I try to do justice to ' the other side,' I cannot believe that the defence is cogent.   It is true that, in a certain sense, the glutton and drunkard are religiously defiled, but it is none the less true that the particular kind of religious defilement which the dietary laws imply and refer to is a fiction. The actual pieces of food which the glutton eats are quite clean. Or, we may more truly say that they are neither clean nor unclean. Whereas the doctrine of the dietary laws is that some foods are in themselves unclean.   This they are not, for no *things* are in themselves religiously unclean, whether it be pig's flesh or excretions or particular sorts of blood.   It is true that the feelings of civilized mankind may have come to regard certain foods as disgusting, and to consider that a man who, for example, ate putrid cats' flesh with relish was in some, half-æsthetic, half-moral, sense a depraved or unnatural person. But it is only in a very far-fetched sort of way that such a man can be said to have committed a religious offence. Moreover, the dietary laws are needless for us even from this point of view. Our own society has created and creates its own social standards of good taste. We do not need to retain the taboos of two thousand years ago (and much more) as our standards of repulsion to-day. We do not need the dietary laws as discipline. It is idle to say that we cannot be temperate in food and drink unless we obey them. As to actual hygiene, our modern doctors know much better than the compilers of Leviticus. It is impossible to get away from the fact that these laws rest (a) upon ancient and now superannuated taboos, (b) upon a conception of outward religious purity which is priestly and unprophetic. The great principle of vii. 15 is, I think, untouched by Jewish criticism. It is worthy to stand side by side with Hosea vi. 6, and is to my own mind one of the most truly original sayings, if not the most original saying, in the Synoptic Gospels.

24–30. THE NORTHWARD JOURNEY AND THE PHŒNICIAN WOMAN

(Cp. Matt. xv. 21–28)

24 And from thence he arose, and went into the district of Tyre, And he entered into an house, and wished that none should know it :
25 but he could not escape notice. For, straightway, a woman, whose young daughter had an unclean spirit, and who had heard of him,
26 came and fell at his feet : (now the woman was a heathen, a Syro-phœnician by race) ; and she besought him that he would expel
27 the demon from her daughter. But Jesus said unto her, ' Let the children first be filled : for it is not meet to take the children's
28 bread, and cast it unto the dogs.' And she answered and said unto him, ' Yes, Lord : yet the dogs under the table eat of the children's
29 crumbs.' And he said unto her, ' For this saying go thy way ; the
30 demon has gone out of thy daughter.' And when she came to her house, she found her daughter lying upon the bed, and the demon had departed.

It is possible that Matthew had an older version of this story before him than Mark, or Matthew may have reproduced in some respects a common source more faithfully than Mark. Some think that Matt. xv. 24 is a very old and authentic saying, and that Matt. xv. 26 is more primary than Mark vii. 27.

24. ' Thence ; ' that is, probably, from Gennesaret. The section vii. 1–24 is interpolated. What is the motive for this journey ? It has been variously interpreted. Was it to enable Jesus to be alone with his disciples, and to teach them especially as to the lot which was to befall their Master ? This seems very doubtful, in view of their subsequent amazement and incomprehension. Was it to avoid the plotting Pharisees, who sought to kill the innovating teacher ? This is conceivable, but not probable. Did he seek for rest and quiet to meditate upon his future prospects and chances ? Or was the journey undertaken to avoid attracting the attention of Herod ? It is noticeable that, instead of going to Bethsaida, as we are told in vi. 45 that he intended to do, he changes his route and goes north. Another view is that the journeyings are apocryphal. There was a story about Jesus meeting a Gentile woman and healing her child. An appropriate geographical setting was given to it. In 31 Jesus returns again to his own country. The whole northern journey, on this supposition, would be a fiction (Bultmann, pp. 19, 20, 35). An elaborate defence of the historic character of the journeyings of Jesus, with a full discussion of the geographical details and a useful map, can be read in Burkitt, *Gospel History*, pp. 89–98.

How far the story in 25–30, or the parallel story in Matt. viii. 5–13, have an historic basis is uncertain. Perhaps the two stories are variants. They are the only instances of healings from a distance in the Synoptics, and it is not very likely that such healings actually occurred.

26. The woman was a Phœnician by race and nationality, a Greek, *i.e.* a heathen, by religion.

27. Jesus very clearly, and, apparently, somewhat roughly, states that his mission is restricted to the Jews. We can hardly believe that, had he not said so actually, had it not been clearly known that he had said so, and that as a matter of fact his activities *were* confined to his own people, such a saying as this would ever have been reported, least of all in Mark.

' Dog ' was a term of abuse and contempt perhaps occasionally used by Jews about Gentiles. If it be true that κυνάριον means the house, or domesticated, dog, it is improperly put into the mouth of Jesus. The language of the statement is assimilated to that of the reply, where it is in place. Did Jesus use the word ? It appears to be untrue that Jews ' habitually ' or even frequently spoke of ' Gentiles ' as ' dogs.' See Dr. Abrahams, *Studies*, Second Series, p. 195. Dr. Bartlet attempts to get out of the trouble in the following ingenious way. ' It is not the usual term for " dogs " that is used, but a diminutive form which softens the harshness of the word and suggests the little house-dogs, one of which may have been in sight at the time. The words, too, were perhaps uttered in a kindly humorous way, both in tone and expression of eye, which showed that he was testing her, to see something of her spirit, since she was making an unusual type of demand. The effect of the diminutive would best be conveyed by rendering it by the homely Scotch "doggie." This reading is the more likely that Jesus speaks in terms of a household, inclusive of its domestic animals. He says virtually : "You are venturing much in making such a request to a Jew. Why should you expect a response, seeing that you know how Jews view people like you, as their common way of speaking implies ? What would you say, if I put it so ? " This gave an opening to the woman, of which she in like spirit availed herself.' But there is not much reason to suppose that κυνάριον meant ' doggie.' More probably the diminutive has no significance here, and κυνάριον merely means ' dog.' See *Zur Sprache der Evangelien*, by Schulthess, *Z. N. W.*, 1922, p. 222, n. 1. Klausner says not untruly that Jesus's reply is ' so brusque and chauvinistic that if any other Jewish teacher of the time had said such a thing Christians would never have forgiven Judaism for it.' Yet it is historical, because ' the Gospels were written at a time when the disciples of Jesus included many non-Jews, and when no one would have put in Jesus's mouth so harsh a sentiment ' (pp. 294, 295).

' Let the children be satisfied first.' Not in Matthew. The words were, perhaps, added later. They anticipate the woman's reply, and were suggested by it. They give a theoretic basis for the later view that, while the Jews were to be offered the gospel first, the Gentiles were to receive it next. The food of salvation is destined for them also. The probable attitude of the historic Jesus to the heathen world is excellently stated by Meyer (II. p. 426).

28. Only here is Jesus called κύριε in Mark. It is a heathen woman who calls him so. The appellation, however, *may* mean no more than our ' sir.' Or perhaps we should translate ' milord.' So Burkitt, *Christian Beginnings*, pp. 46, 47. For the real meaning of the word mistranslated ' crumbs ' (rather ' bits of bread ') see note on Luke xvi. 21. The admirable reply of the woman is both touching and brilliant : ' there is a place for dogs in the household, and there is a place for Gentiles in God's world ' (Gould).

29. Jesus is moved by her humility and courage. He declares that her request has been granted because of her noble reply. Matthew makes Jesus praise her faith, the greatness of which induces

(and perhaps enables) him to grant her prayer. The emphasis upon faith some authorities regard as specifically characteristic of Matthew.

Attempts have been made to argue that we can strip the story of its miraculous character, and yet preserve it as historical. ' The girl, as a matter of fact, happened to be found resting quietly upon her bed after her last attack when the mother returned. It is only Matthew who speaks of an immediate and permanent cure.' Is not this an example of false rationalizing ? And are we to suppose that somebody sent a reporter to the woman's house to find out what had happened ?

Some Christian commentators are much exercised by this story. ' It is sad enough,' says one, ' that a Jewish Christian was still capable of inventing it.' It is ' incredible ' that Jesus would have hesitated to help anybody on the ground that he or she was not a Jew. But whether the story be historic or no, it is tolerably certain that the principle which it illustrates is historic. Jesus felt himself called to serve the ' lost sheep' of the house of Israel, and them alone. To Israel, not to the Gentiles, did he preach repentance and the coming of the Kingdom of God.

True or only *ben trovato* the story is one of great beauty and charm. Whence this wonderful attractiveness of so much of the Gospel narrative, this marvellous combination of power and simplicity ? Whence this impression of *first-classness*, of inspiration ? Surely because the Gospels are the early result of the impression produced by a great and inspired personality. However uncertain it may be whether what we read in any single passage was really said or done by Jesus, only a real Jesus could have caused the Gospel. Without Jesus, no Mark.

' The sublime figure of the Christ, portrayed to us by the first three Evangelists, was, in a certain sense, created by the Church. But if, in turn, we ask what was the moral and religious power by which the Church was created, only one answer is possible : it was the personality of Jesus, his faith, his truth, his love ' (*First Three Gospels*, p. 326).

Nevertheless, do we know enough of the life of Jesus to speak of his character in the customary terms of absolute and unqualified eulogy ? We read that his life was a perfect exhibition of divine love, that it was one long and perfect sacrifice, in fact that it was a perfect life, the product of a perfect character. And so on, with endless variations. And yet we have to remember that Jesus lived only thirty-three years or so, and that of this short life we only know the events of a year or a year and a half. In the Galilæan period we do not know of much which required great sacrifice. There is no reason to suppose that Jesus lived a life of great pain, difficulty, and renunciation. A religious teacher who made a great impression upon many was well looked after. He had no difficulty in obtaining food and lodging.

Again, of the events of this year many are historically dubious, many are mixed up with incredible miracles. We do not know (to pass on to the Jerusalem period) whether Jesus went up to the capital to conquer or to die. Let us assume that he went to die, that he felt that his own death was the necessary preliminary for the full establishment of the Kingdom. It was a fine determination. Nobody would wish to detract from it, but even this act of self-sacrifice scarcely entitles us to say of his character that it was the *most perfect* character, and of his life that it was the *most perfect* life, that has ever been. It is a life

(*a*) Of which we know very little, and only during some eighteen months in all ;

(*b*) Of which the incidents are very few ;

(*c*) Which is very uncertain, and much mixed up with miracle and legend ;

(*d*) Which is recorded by biographers who seek to eulogize and exalt to the utmost of their ability.

While, therefore, willing to pay my tribute of admiration to the life and character of Jesus, so far as we know about them or can ascertain them, I cannot see any reason to speak of them as the acme and embodiment of every conceivable perfection. He was doubtless a great teacher and a noble man, whom we must greatly admire : our *adoration* must be reserved for God.

Yet through the mists of miracle and legend we see a character not indeed perfect, for his attitude neither to his mother nor to his opponents seems to me without question, but yet noble; a character, moreover, finely balanced and tempered. Jesus was virile, but gentle ; severe, but pitiful. He was confident, yet humble. Aloof from the world, yet not gloomy. What a grand grip he had upon essentials, upon the fatherhood of God, and upon the service of God in the service of man. How positive was his goodness. How he hated shams, meanness, hypocrisy, self-righteousness. These hatreds reveal the sort of man he was, filled with pity for the outcasts of society, with scorn for the respectably virtuous who so carefully avoided evil and yet performed so little good. I can quite realize that it is easy, and to those brought up in a Christian environment justifiable, upon the basis of what we know about Jesus, to conjecture and amplify and idealize. 'An ideal,' says Jowett, 'necessarily mingles with all conceptions of Christ.' This ideal, which varies from age to age, 'may be conveniently spoken of as the life of Christ.'   But this ideal is not the actual character or actual life of the historic Jesus, 'of a person scarcely known to us,' as Jowett admits, whose biographies are full of doubt and uncertainty (*Life and Letters of Benjamin Jowett*, Vol. II. pp. 151, 445).

I feel that, though it is extremely unpleasant to seem to cheapen and cavil at one of the accepted great spiritual heroes of the world, there is yet much truth in some incidental words of M. Loisy which he wrote in a review of Prof. Deissmann's book on Paul.   He said : ' At the first words one comes up against an assertion which is meaningless to the historian : Jesus and Paul are not first and second ; " Jesus is beyond all comparison in human history, and Paul is the first after this Unique Being or, in Pauline language, 'within' him."   One day it will at last be perceived that this idea of the Christ is the mirage which the dogma of the divinity of Jesus has left in the minds of liberal Protestants.   Jesus, in so far as he is recognizable, was a grand and simple soul, but not altogether beyond the greatest.   Prophetism produced similar characters.   Some appear to be less eminent, because we do not idealize them to the same extent ; others, Jeremiah, for instance, because we see them more clearly.   In his age Jesus incarnated and renewed the spirit of the Prophets, the best of Judaism ; there we have his grandeur. He did not, however, create the ideal which he represented.   His death, and also the singular chance that this death was the means whereby he became the divinity of a new religion, have raised him above his fore-runners' (*Revue d'histoire et de littérature religieuses*, 1912, p. 569).

31–37. Healing of a Deaf and Dumb Man

(*Cp.* Matt. xv. 29–31)

31   Then he left the district of Tyre, and came by way of Sidon unto the lake of Galilee, through the midst of the district of the
32 Ten Cities.   And they brought unto him one that was deaf and stammered ; and they besought him to put his hand upon him.
33 And he took him aside from the crowd, and put his fingers into his
34 ears, and touched his tongue with his spittle, and looking up to heaven, he sighed, and said unto him, ' *Ephphatha*,' that is, ' Be
35 opened.'   And straightway his ears were opened, and the fetter of
36 his tongue was loosed, and he spoke plainly.   And he enjoined them to tell no one ; but the more he enjoined them, the more did they
37 proclaim it.   And they were exceedingly astonished, saying, ' He has done all things well : he makes the deaf to hear, and the dumb to speak.'

31. This verse would indicate, if it is accurate, that Jesus took a very extended journey before returning to the Lake of Galilee. He would have gone far northwards, and then eastwards and back again to the south. But so protracted a journey seems improbable. It is conceivable that Mark wanted to place the miracle that follows upon heathen soil for the sake of a certain symbolism. It is wrought as Jesus passes through the Decapolis on his way back to the lake. Does it symbolize the salvation of the Gentiles to whom the gospel is also to be rendered ? But Klostermann (ed. 2) points out that in this miracle (unlike in 30) Mark does not appear to have any such intention. He may have meant only to indicate, by the insertion of miracles such as this one, that the Messianic age had arrived. (*Cp.* Isaiah xxxv. 5.) Some think that Sidon is a misrendering of Saidan, which was a variant for Bethsaida. The geography of Mark is somewhat confused, and gives rise to much discussion in the commentators, which I pass over in silence. *Cp.* also what was said on 24.

33. The healing process is here conducted in what would seem to us moderns a strange, half-magical way. One wonders what is the measure of historical basis for this curious tale. Spittle was regarded in antiquity as possessed of healing properties. Tacitus records that Vespasian cured a blind man in Alexandria by wetting his eyes with his spittle (*Histories*, IV. 81).

34. He ' sighed.' The word here means, perhaps, that he was praying. For the prayer, *cp.* Elijah in 1 Kings xvii. 19–21 or Elisha in 2 Kings iv. 33–35. But the ' sighing ' may be part of the method of cure. So Dibelius, *Formgeschichte*, p. 47.

36. Jesus would not have been the ' Menschenkenner ' he was if he had thought that such a miracle, wrought in public, could remain unknown. All these prohibitions are part of Mark's theory, and, like enough, have little historic basis.

These stories are partly told, and partly made up, with an eye to the fulfilment of prophecy. *Cp.* Isaiah xxix. 18, xxxv. 5, 6.

CHAPTER VIII

1–9. FEEDING OF THE FOUR THOUSAND

(*Cp.* Matt. xv. 32–39)

1 In those days there was again a great crowd, and they had nothing to eat. And Jesus called his disciples unto him, and said 2 unto them, ' I feel pity for the people because they have now tarried 3 with me three days, and have nothing to eat : and if I send them away fasting to their own homes, they will faint by the way : 4 moreover, some of them came from far.' And his disciples answered him, ' Whence can one satisfy these men with bread here in the 5 wilderness ? ' And he asked them, ' How many loaves have ye ? ' 6 And they said, ' Seven.' And he bade the people to sit down on the ground : and he took the seven loaves, and spoke the blessing, and broke them, and gave them to his disciples to set before the 7 people ; and they did so. And they had a few small fishes : and he spoke the blessing, and told them to set these also before the 8 people. So they did eat, and were satisfied : and they took up of 9 the broken bits that were left, seven baskets full. And they who had eaten were about four thousand.

The feeding of the four thousand is a close variant of the feeding of the five thousand in vi. 31–44. Mark must have found two ' feeding ' miracles in his sources. It has been noted that the Greek words for baskets differ in the two stories. This difference seems to point to two *written* sources. Mark had two groups of stories before him, representing the same tradition in two forms. He took them to be separate stories relating to different events, and so he incorporated and used both. There are thus two feedings, two crossings over the lake, and two miracles of healing (the one, it is true, of a blind man, the other of a deaf man, but note the identity of the healing procedure). There are insertions in the first group which mask the parallelism. Oddly enough, within the first

173

group is inserted a variant of the earlier story of the storm. (*Cp.* Wendland, p. 264.)

10–12. A SIGN REFUSED

(*Cp.* Matt. xii. 38–42, xvi. 1–4 ; Luke xi. 29–32)

10 And when he had sent them away, straightway he entered into a boat with his disciples, and came into the district of Dalmanutha.
11 And the Pharisees came forth, and began to dispute with him, demanding from him a sign from heaven, in order to tempt him.
12 And he sighed deeply in his spirit, and said, ' Wherefore does this generation demand a sign ? verily I say unto you, There shall no sign be given unto this generation.'

As viii. 1–9 is a variant of vi. 34–44, so viii. 10 is a close variant of vi. 45. In both cases, after a miraculous feeding, Jesus enters a ship and crosses over the lake.

11. As the first miracle of the loaves is followed by the disputation with the Pharisees about ablutions, so the second is followed by a quarrel about ' signs.' To the gospel, the true nurture of souls, is opposed the false Judaism, which is ' outward ' and demands ' signs.' The Pharisees are represented, as usual, in the worst light. They ask Jesus for a sign in order to tempt him. Apparently this means that they knew that Jesus ought to refuse them—*i.e.*, that he ought to refuse to substantiate his special powers or his Messiahship by miracles. Or does ' tempting ' mean that they believed he could not perform a miracle on a grand scale, and that they tempted him to try so that he might fail ? Dr. Carpenter, however, holds that ' trying ' or ' testing ' him (πειράζοντες) is Mark's interpretation. The demand was a trial to Jesus because *he* felt *he* ought to refuse it. This is what Mark wishes to indicate, without reference to the purpose of the Pharisees.

In any case, they are the bad people in asking for a ' sign ' ; Jesus is the good man in refusing them. At the best they suffer from ' incurable *Wundersucht*.' But is not this unjust ? Jesus, in the narrative as we now have it, had already performed two gigantic miracles, which were surely ' signs,' and are treated as such in 17–20. Moreover, he had appealed to his miracles of healing, yet, by his own admission, there were Rabbinic exorcists as well as he. And successful ones too ! Hence, when Jesus made assertions implying the imperfections of the Law, was it unreasonable to ask for a *special* miracle in order to prove these bold assertions contradicting the letter of that Law, which it was a dogma of faith to regard as true and perfect from beginning to end ?   Perhaps Deut. xiii. 1–3 should have made the Pharisees refrain, but the passage scarcely applies, for Jesus, at all events, was not suggesting the worship of ' other gods.'   It is right to remember constantly that there is much to be said for the Pharisees and Rabbis, whose relations with Jesus we only hear of from their bitter enemies, who wanted to depict the Master as all light and his adversaries as all darkness.

The reason why Jesus refuses the miracle, according to other commentators, is because he perceives in the demand the unbelief, the mockery, and the hatred of his opponents.   To demand a sign is the proof of their ineradicable ' superficiality and outwardness.' The faith that Jesus required is of a quite different kind.   To a modern Christian commentator who disbelieves in miracles, this may be very comforting.   But the superficiality is proved none the more.   In the days of Jesus everybody believed in miracles, and Jesus was only too glad when people believed that his miracles were divinely ordered.   His teaching and his miracles went together. But that teaching seemed sometimes to run counter to the written and to the oral Law.   Now the Law itself had foretold that prophets might arise who would ' dare to speak in God's name what God had not commanded.'   Was it not likely that Jesus, who spoke against the Law, was such a prophet ?   The words in Deut. xviii. 20–22 may have moved many to reflection.   If, however, Jesus were to announce and work some sign which ' followed and came to pass,' then, perhaps, it might be safe to think that God, who of old had said that the Law was to be a ' statute for ever throughout your generations,' had really changed his mind.   The ' sign from heaven ' is a miracle over and above mere exorcisms and healings. Was Isaiah superficial and ' outward ' when he urged Ahaz to ask for a sign ?   ' Came forth.'   From where ?   The original meaning, or Mark's meaning, is not ascertainable.

12.   What is the meaning of the question ?   Is it (1) ' They ask for signs from a wrong motive ; therefore I will not give them ; therefore God will not grant them ; ' or is it, (2) ' They do not really want a sign ; they ask but to tempt me.'   In any case we appear to have here one more example of the fact that neither Jesus nor the Pharisees could understand each other.   From their point of view the Pharisees were justified in showing the utmost caution towards, and the utmost suspicion of, a teacher who either violated, or taught by implication the violation of, the Law.   A sign from their point of view was reasonable enough.   But though the Pharisees may have been justified in asking, it does not follow that Jesus was not right in refusing.   The miracles of Jesus were

' uses of divine power, but not displays of it ' (Gould). He refused
to prove his power by empty marvels *ad hoc.*

13–21. THE LACK OF BREAD

(*Cp.* Matt. xvi. 5–12 ; Luke xii. 1)

13 And he left them, and entering into the boat again, crossed
14 over to the other side. Now they had forgotten to take bread with
15 them, and they had not in the boat more than one loaf. And he
enjoined them, saying, ' Take heed, beware of the leaven of the
16 Pharisees, and of the leaven of Herod.' And they argued with one
17 another, ' We have no bread.' And Jesus perceived it, and said
unto them, ' Why do ye argue that ye have no bread ? do ye not
18 perceive or understand ? is your heart hardened ? Having eyes,
see ye not ? and having ears, hear ye not ? and do ye not remember ?
19 When I broke the five loaves among the five thousand, how many
baskets full of fragments took ye up ? ' And they said, ' Twelve.'
20 'And when the seven loaves among the four thousand, how many
baskets full of fragments took ye up ? ' And they said, ' Seven.'
21 And he said unto them, ' Do ye still not understand ? '

A very obscure section. It appears to have been built up
round the Logion in 15 ; yet it has also been suggested that this
verse is an awkward later insertion in 14, 16–21. The trouble is
that the exact meaning of 15, especially its *original* meaning, is
hardly possible to ascertain. Is the leaven the teaching of the
Pharisees, or is it their false piety, or is it their evil disposition ?
And what is the leaven of Herod, and did the saying originally only
refer to the Pharisees, and has the ' leaven of Herod ' been added ?
Then the Greek words τί διαλογίζεσθε, ὅτι ἄρτους οὐκ ἔχετε, are not
very clear. Do they mean : ' What is this discussion of yours about
having no bread ? ' And how is, (16), διελογίζοντο πρὸς ἀλλήλους,
to be translated ? Does it mean : ' They argued with one another
that what he has just said to us (in 15) must mean that we have no
bread.' Or does it mean, ' They discussed with each other the fact
that they had no bread ? ' Or, ' Why does he talk to us about leaven,
seeing that we have no bread with us ? ' Prof. Turner says that
ὅτι is here used, as Mark often uses ὅτι, interrogatively ; it is the
indirect interrogative. (Direct interrogative with ὅτι in ii. 7, 16,
viii. 12, ix. 11, 28.) The meaning he takes to be, ' They discussed
with one another why they had no loaves ' (*J. T. S.*, 1925, Vol.
XXVII. p. 59). The reply of Jesus in 17 would seem to depend

upon Mark's theory of the spiritual obtuseness of the disciples.   As
the passage stands, it appears that Jesus is meant to suggest that
the miracles of the five and of the four thousand had spiritual
meanings.   What the disciples fail to understand is, not that Jesus
can always supply them with bread by miracle, and that therefore
there is no need to worry about the lack of it (which is what the
passage may have meant originally if 15 did not form part of it),
but the spiritual meaning and lessons which underlie the two feeding
miracles.   Professor Turner holds that 15 is a parenthesis, but not
an interpolation.   The meaning of the words of Jesus is simply
that 'his disciples showed grievous want of perception in not
recognizing, after the miracles of the multiplication of the loaves,
that their Master had at command a power from God to provide,
if need were, their necessary food.'   But the word 'bread' reminded
Mark 'of the saying about the leaven of the Pharisees and Herod,
and he inserted it here, though strictly speaking it was foreign to
the context.   In other words, it must be regarded as a parenthesis,
an extreme example of Mark's naïve and non-logical construction
of his narrative.   A modern writer would have put it in a note at
the foot of the page, and introduced it with the phrase " compare . . ."   The ancients, lacking such devices, were shut up within
the alternatives of intercalation into the body of the text and
omission.   The modern editor of an ancient text, in which such
intercalations occur, can only guide his readers by the typographical
expedients of the dash and the bracket' (*J. T. S.*, 1925, Vol. XXVI.
p. 150).

If the leaven of the Pharisees means their false piety, and
if the disciples are made to misunderstand the metaphor (though
how could they *conceivably* suppose that a warning against the
leaven of the Pharisees had anything to do with their having
taken no bread on board the boat ?), then Jesus may be supposed
to hint in his reply that the miracles of the multiplied loaves
had a symbolic meaning.   The multiplied loaves are a symbol of
the salvation offered to the Jews and the Gentiles.   And the intense
stupidity of the apostles is once more shown to be 'a thesis
of the Evangelist, rather than a fact of history.'   It nevertheless
symbolizes a reality, namely, that the disciples during the lifetime
of Jesus never suspected certain facts which afterwards became
apparent, *i.e.* the universal destination of the gospel, the abrogation
of the Law, the institution of a new community of which Jesus was
the centre, and of which the breaking of bread was to be both the
symbol and the bond.   But the whole theory of symbolism in
Mark has received very hard knocks from Werner and others.   The
verses which give 15 its setting seem written from the same point of
view as those which give the explanation of the parable of the

sower and the explanation of the saying of the true defilement. And note that the language recalls previously used expressions. *Cp.* iv. 12, vi. 52, vii. 18. In any case the whole passage depending as it does upon the *two* feeding miracles is clearly editorial, late and unhistoric, though the obscure Logion in 15 may be authentic. (For the use of the metaphor ' leaven ' in Rabbinic literature see Abrahams, Studies I. chap. vi.) Burkitt, however, speaks of 11–21 as ' a narrative which it is impossible not to regard as derived from genuine historical reminiscence' (p. 73). But J. Weiss says: ' There is something here of the mysticism and sym-bolism of John, and in the measure that there is this, the solid ground of historic reality is lost. It is outside the limits of psychological possibility that the disciples who had been with Jesus for so long already should misunderstand so palpably his parabolic manner of speech. . . . Here we have the latest layer of evangelical tradition' (*Schriften*, pp. 143, 144). Schmidt, however, thinks that the conversation may rest upon a genuine historical tradition (pp. 204, 205). But Wendland says (p. 265), ' The source of Mark can at most have supplied him with a saying of Jesus referring to one feeding. But this saying itself could only have been produced by groups of stories beginning to be formed.'

22–26. A BLIND MAN HEALED

(Mark only)

22 And they came to Bethsaida ; and they brought a blind man
23 unto him, and besought him to touch him. And he took the blind man by the hand, and led him out of the village ; and he spat into his eyes, and put his hands upon him, and asked him if he saw any-
24 thing. And he looked up, and said, ' I perceive men, for I see them
25 like trees, walking.' Then Jesus put his hands again upon his eyes, and he looked steadfastly, and was restored, and saw everything
26 clearly. And he sent him away to his house, saying, ' Go not into the village.'

Here, finally, is the variant to vii. 31–37. It is noticeable that in this version of the miracle, the healing takes place by steps, gradually. As to the possible reasons for this, see Bultmann, p. 138. The minutely described procedure and the ' verisimilitude ' of 24 does not necessarily make the miraculous tale more likely to be historic. The critical questions raised by the variants in the section vi. 30–viii. 26 are exceedingly complicated, and have led to very different conclusions and hypotheses. Was Mark interpolated ? That is, was Mark as originally issued, shorter than the Mark which we now possess ? Or again, did Mark himself insert into his book variants from different written sources ? Or only from oral tradition ? I cannot enter into these questions. They are discussed by Bartlet, by Wellhausen, by Streeter (pp. 172–176), who is dead against any Urmarcus theory, by Meyer (I. pp. 130–132), who thinks Mark combined and edited two written sources, and by many others.

26. ' Go not into the village.' There is a most delightful bit of textual criticism on this verse by Professor Turner (*J. T. S.*, 1924, Vol. XXVI. p. 18). By a comparison of the readings in different MSS. and versions, and on the basis of the proved fact that Mark often uses εἰς to mean ' in,' he argues that the original reading was not μηδὲ εἰς τὴν κώμην εἰσέλθῃς, but μηδενὶ εἰς τὴν κώμην εἴπῃς, ' Tell it to no one in the village.'

viii. 27–ix. 1.   JESUS THE SUFFERING MESSIAH : JESUS AND PETER : THE CONFESSION AT CÆSAREA PHILIPPI

(*Cp.* Matt. xvi. 13–28 ; Luke ix. 18–27)

27 And from there Jesus went, with his disciples, into the villages of Cæsarea Philippi : and on the way he asked his disciples, saying
28 unto them, ' Whom do men say that I am ? ' And they answered, ' John the Baptist ; and others, Elijah ; and others, One of the
29 prophets.' And he asked them, ' But ye—whom say ye that I am ? ' And Peter answered and said unto him, ' Thou art the Messiah.'
30 And he sternly admonished them that they should tell no man of him.

31 And he began to teach them that the Son of man must suffer much, and be rejected by the elders and the chief priests and the
32 scribes, and be killed, and after three days rise again. And he spoke the word quite openly. And Peter took him aside, and began to
33 rebuke him. But he turned round, and looking on his disciples, he rebuked Peter, saying, ' Get thee behind me, Satan : for thou thinkest not the thoughts of God, but of men.'

34 And he called the people unto him together with his disciples, and said unto them, ' Whoever would follow after me, let him deny
35 himself, and take up his cross, and follow me. For whoever would
36 save his life shall lose it ; but whoever would lose his life for my sake and the gospel's, he shall save it. For what can it profit a

37 man to gain the whole world, and to forfeit his life ? For what
38 can a man give as the price of his life ? For whoever shall be
ashamed of me and of my words in this adulterous and sinful
generation, of him also shall the Son of man be ashamed, when he
IX. 1 comes in the glory of his Father with the holy angels.' And he
said unto them, ' Verily I say unto you, There are some of those who
stand here who shall not taste death till they see the kingdom of
God come with power.'

Here begins a new section of the gospel story of the greatest
importance and also of great complexity. It may be noted in passing
that there would seem to be a correspondence between vi. 14–vii. 26
and vii. 27–x. 52. Both sections open with the question : Who
really is Jesus ? Both end with a blind man being healed. Is this
more than an accidental correspondence and parallelism ?

Wellhausen's remarks as regards the change of tone and subject-
matter in this section are worth quoting. ' Now only begins the
gospel as the apostles proclaimed it ; before this one does not perceive much of it. The determination to. go to Jerusalem causes a
remarkable change. A transfigured Jesus stands before us, and the
two miracles of healing, which are inserted, seem almost out of place.
He no longer teaches general doctrine, but prophesies about himself. He speaks to his disciples rather than to the people. To them
he reveals his nature and mission. But he does this esoterically.
They are not to tell it to any one till the predictions are fulfilled, and
even they themselves do not till then understand it. The opportunity to reveal the secret is given by the confession of Peter, " Thou
art the Messiah." Jesus induced that confession, and he accepts it
with a ·correction ; he is not the Messiah who is to restore the
kingdom of Israel, but quite another Messiah. He does not go to
Jerusalem to restore the Jewish kingdom, but to be crucified.
Through suffering and. death he enters into glory, and only thus—
through this same path—can others follow him thither. The
Kingdom of God is no Jewish kingdom ; it is only intended for
certain chosen individuals, *his* disciples. The idea of the possibility
of a general repentance of the whole people is entirely abandoned.
Instead of a summons to repentance addressed to all, we have the
demand, " Follow me," the demand of discipleship, which only very
few can fulfil. And the conception of discipleship itself assumes a
new and higher meaning. It no longer merely implies following and
accompanying Jesus in his lifetime, but, mainly, following him in his
death. Discipleship as imitation is possible even after his death,
and, indeed, it only then properly begins. His cross is to be carried
after him. For the Kingdom's sake the disciples are to abandon

people and family ; they must sacrifice everything which binds them to life ; they must sacrifice life itself. Reform is impossible ; the enmity of the world cannot be overcome. A violent breach with the world is demanded, leading to martyrdom. Thus the situation and the mood of the early Christian community is here reflected beforehand in Jesus, as he goes forward to meet his fate. Upon this depends that lofty pathos in which the introduction to the Passion even excels the Passion itself.'

On the other hand Holtzmann pointed out that we must not exaggerate. The section in Mark viii. 37–x. contains incidents with such markedly historical character as those of the epileptic child (ix. 14–29), the quarrel about precedence (ix. 33–37), the strange exorcist (ix. 38–40), the lesson on divorce (x. 1–12), the danger of wealth (x. 17–27), and the regret of the sons of Zebedee (x. 35–45). Wellhausen has rightly laid stress on the number of new technical expressions and conceptions in this christological Messianic section. Yet these new terms and ideas are, at least largely, the natural result of the great turning-point which had actually occurred in the situation of Jesus and his disciples at the time of the confession of Peter. ' The effect of this turning-point can still be discerned in the retrospect contained in Luke xxii. 35, 36, where the setting is most uncertain, but where the saying of Jesus itself is certainly old ' (*Archiv für Religionswissenschaft*, Vol. x., 1906, and *Protestantische Monatshefte*, Vol. x., 1906).

We may briefly enumerate the new topics dealt with in this section as follows :

(1) For the first time Jesus is spoken of as the Messiah. The word—ὁ χριστός, the Anointed One, the Messiah—has not been used since the opening verse : ' The beginning of the gospel concerning Jesus Christ (Jesus Messiah), Son of God.' At the baptism Jesus had been addressed by the heavenly voice as ' my beloved Son.' The unclean spirits, calling out from the men whom they ' possessed,' had addressed him as ' the Holy One of God,' ' the Son of God,' ' Son of the Most High God.' He has been supposed by various human beings to be John the Baptist *redivivus*, or Elijah, or a prophet. He himself has twice spoken of himself as ' the Man ' (Son of man), but, as we have seen, both passages are open to grave critical doubts. But now the apostles, by the mouth of Peter, declare their view, and their view the Evangelist would have us believe is the truth, which Jesus acknowledges, though he bids them keep it dark. ' Thou art the Christ.' ' Thou art the Messiah.'

(2) Jesus appears to acknowledge that the apostles are right, but he proceeds (for the first time) to predict his own imminent and predestined suffering, death, and resurrection.

(3) He had before said to Simon and Andrew, 'Come ye after me' (δεῦτε ὀπίσω μου) and to Levi, 'Follow me' (ἀκολούθει μοι). But this 'following' was a physical following; he now proceeds to define what following means and implies. Nor does he apparently limit the meaning of following to mere attendance upon himself, to mere physical following. One can follow Jesus spiritually. This following must be one of self-sacrifice, even unto death. Even as the Master was ready to suffer and die, so must be the disciple, the follower.

(4) Jesus announces a judgment, at which apparently he, the Man (Son of man) is to be the presiding judge. He apparently announces that this judgment is to come very soon, and that with it, or immediately after it, the Kingdom of God would be effectively inaugurated.

All these subjects are full of problems, especially (1), (2), and (4). Disputed points abound. Bultmann has recently argued that the whole story at Cæsarea Philippi is unhistoric. Jesus never regarded himself as the Messiah. Peter first held him to have been the Messiah, or to have become the Messiah, after his resurrection. It was Peter's vision of the risen Jesus which started the whole theory. In the story before us the community throws its own Messianic belief back into the life of Jesus. Bultmann's essay in Z. N. W. (XIX. pp. 165–174) is very clever, but it is unconvincing. Its scepticism goes too far. It is easier and more reasonable to believe that the story has a real historic foundation than that it has none. Bultmann's arguments are answered with much common sense and caution by Mundle in Z. N. W. (XXI., 1922, pp. 299–311). And I am inclined to agree with Schmidt, who finds in definite geographical localities marks of good tradition. 'Here we reach the ground of the oldest tradition. A genuine fact, which has been remembered, has here been preserved' (p. 216). Mr. Rawlinson says, with regard to the whole section viii. 27–x. 45, 'The probability is that both sayings and events are in substance historical, though the impression now made by these sections as a whole is in large measure due to the manner in which they have been edited.' 'The predictions of the Passion have very likely been glossed in the light of events, and as they now stand are perhaps more explicit and detailed than when the Lord spoke them. The sayings about discipleship in like manner reflect here and there the terminology and conditions of early Church life. But just as it is likely that the Lord anticipated death for Himself, so also it is likely that He anticipated persecution for his disciples' (p. 110).

The section 27–ix. 1 falls into at least three sub-sections, of which it is possible that the last may be the original continuation of the first—(1) viii. 27–30; (2) 31–38; (3) ix. 1.

27–30. In this section is comprised the first of the four subjects mentioned above: Jesus and the Messiahship. Opinions range from those who consider that the section is absolutely historical, dependent upon the vivid memory of Peter, and those who consider that it is entirely legendary.

27. The disciples had been away from Jesus, and had returned to him (vi. 30). Both during their absence and since their return they had had opportunities to hear what was said of him by the people with whom they came in contact. Jesus wishes, therefore, to know whether his Messiahship has been recognized. This seems the more obvious meaning of the question. He finds out that though some think him the forerunner, he is not supposed to be the Messiah. Then Jesus pushes the matter further. Do the disciples rest content with the opinions of others? Have they guessed no better? Such must be the meaning of Mark in this conversation. So too we may explain the verse on the assumption that what we have before us is authentic history.

28. 'A prophet'; that is, probably, not a prophet risen from the dead, but a new prophet on his own account. Luke, on the other hand, understands the words to mean a risen prophet, and it must be confessed that this makes a better parallelism. The three alternatives are precisely the same as those given in vi. 14–16.

29. If Jesus had already spoken of himself as 'the Man,' and if 'the Man' (Son of man) was currently known as a synonym for the Messiah, the question would be absurd. The disciples must already have known the truth from his own lips.

30. The word ($\epsilon\pi\iota\tau\iota\mu\acute{a}\omega$) occurs in 32 and 33 also (cp. also i. 25 and iii. 12). There it means 'rebuke'; here it seems to mean 'sternly admonish.' This verse in its curt brevity raises the whole question. Did Jesus think he was the Messiah? If so, when did he begin to think so? If so, in what sense? Those who think that he never claimed to be, or believed himself to be, the Messiah can only interpret verse 30, if it be historical, to mean what it neither says nor implies, namely: Jesus forbade his disciples to say that he was the Messiah, because he himself did not believe that he was. But though this view would explain many difficulties, it would also create fresh ones and greater ones. The whole story and fate of Jesus are difficult to understand if in some sense or other he did

not claim to be *a* Messiah, or *the* Messiah, *a* king, or *the* king, of the Jews. If, then, he thought he was the Messiah, we may, if we choose, hold that the belief came to him gradually in the course of his ministry. More important is the question what sort of Messiah did he suppose himself to be ?

But first, why did he demand secrecy ? If this order is historic, and is not due to Mark (who has pressed his theory of silence and secrecy from the beginning of the ministry), we may suppose that Jesus knew the imminent danger which a proclamation and acknowledgment of his Messiahship would involve. He was determined at whatever risk to proclaim his Messiahship at Jerusalem, but he would not do so before. Or perhaps he thought that God Himself by some sudden act would reveal it, and that he must not anticipate the divine revelation. We may regard the order for silence here as probably historic. See especially J. Weiss in *Schriften*, ed. 3, 1. p. 147, and also Cadman, p. 75, whose note, however, upon the other orders of silence is extremely doubtful, though very ingenious. But Cadman seems right in saying that if it be true that the disciples did hold that Jesus was the Messiah, the undoubted fact of their silence becomes inexplicable unless they had been laid under a charge of secrecy (p. 74). A more frequent view is that the prohibition is to be taken in connection with the theory that Jesus believed himself to be the Messiah, but in quite a new sense. He was a purely religious Messiah, who would have nothing to do with politics. He would not restore the Jewish kingdom. He was the Messiah in the sense that he was about to introduce the Kingdom of God. By his new teaching a certain number of persons were to be made fit for that Kingdom, while those who rejected him were to be excluded. Or, again, it is argued that he felt himself to be the servant-Messiah of Isaiah xlii. and liii. Only after suffering and death would his true Messiahship begin. There is, perhaps, some unconscious prejudice in the intense desire on the part of very many Christian commentators to prove that the Messianic conceptions of Jesus were new, spiritual, and un-Jewish. They emphasize and reiterate that the Messiah whom Jesus believed himself to be, and the Messianic age which he was going to inaugurate, had nothing to do with the ' impure ' political aspirations of the Jews. Jesus, then, does not desire to be known as the Messiah, so that the people may not think that their hopes are to be fulfilled and the yoke of the Romans shaken off. But if Jesus believed himself to be the Messiah in this new sense, why did he not say so plainly ? It is certain that the bulk of the people connected with the Messiah with political independence, with a condition of liberty, righteousness, and prosperity. So much, at any rate, was still adhered to in the predictions of the prophets and in their delineations of the Messiah. If Jesus believed that this Messiah of the prophets was 'impure' and false—that this Messiah would never appear— why did he not say so? Why did he dally with the Messianic idea at all and permit others to dally with it? He might be a far higher person than the Jewish Messiah; he might even be the Son of God in a special sense; but why did he claim and believe himself to be the Messiah, or at any rate allow himself to be called so by Peter, if he did not fulfil the ordinary conditions, nay, if those very conditions were 'impure,' political, and never to be fulfilled?

The clearest picture of the old prophetical Messiah in the Old Testament is Isaiah xi. But if many commentators are right, the prediction of Isaiah xi. is 'impure' and 'political.' Moreover, Jesus never intended to fulfil it. One cannot help wondering what Jesus thought his own relation was to the Messiah described by Isaiah, or whether he definitely thought that Isaiah was wrong? Was there only to be a Messiah, like the Servant in Isaiah xlii. and liii., who would suffer and die, and come again, and inaugurate a purely spiritual kingdom? Even so, the Romans were surely not to be the rulers in the new age after the Parousia and the Judgment. But, in that case, was there not a political element in the expectations of Jesus after all?

On the other hand, all that we know of Jesus makes it not unreasonable to suppose that he did frame a conception of his Messiahship which was, to some extent at any rate, novel. The 'spiritual' elements would be likely to have exceeded the 'material' elements, and to have made them of small, or comparatively small, account.

Dr. Carpenter remarks that it is a curious testimony to the ingenuousness of the records that it is possible to ask so many questions of them. If they were the result of *reflective* imagination, there *would* be answers, or suggestions of answers. No one is in any doubt as to the view of Rome and its fate in the Book of Revelation. As it is, one is wholly without clue to Jesus's politics. In fact, one cannot say that he had any; the interruption of the world-order by a great divine display is not a political conception, though it may destroy an empire. Thus on general principles it is doubtless right to say that there would be no Roman suzerainty in the new age. But this is not so much a political as a religious expectation. The overthrow of the Roman power would be by some dramatic *coup* from heaven. There is no question of revolt, or organized effort, in the sphere of politics. [I may mention that this 'dramatic coup from heaven' is the prevailing idea of the Rabbis in the Talmud as to the coming of the new age.] The same distinguished scholar describes the growth of the Messianic consciousness of Jesus, as we find it delineated in Mark, in the following words : ' The preacher who begins by announcing that the King-dom of God is at hand is forced by degrees to consider his relation to it. So far from claiming the Messianic function at the opening of his career, he only slowly realizes it ; and even when he finally accepts it, he resolutely refuses to make it known. This repre-sentation appears to be far more in accordance with historical prob-ability—outward and inward—than that of Matthew ' (in whose narrative Jesus is Messiah to himself and to others from the begin-ning of his ministry). ' It is not likely that Jesus would have been long allowed to proclaim the royal dignity which the assumption of the Messianic character involved both in the eyes of the people and of their Roman over-lords. Nor does it seem consistent with his early teaching about the Kingdom that he should have taken up at the outset any sort of official connection with it. The title which he at length accepted was rather thrust upon him by circum-stance than deliberately chosen. It was adopted with reluctance, and an anxious avoidance of publicity ; it involved so much which he could not share ; it failed to express so much that he desired ; yet no other designation spoke in the same way to his own soul, or to the heart of his time ' (*First Three Gospels*, p. 208). Dr. Carpenter has a wonderful way of making his conception of Jesus intensely plausible ! My readers, however, will remember the dubious and meagre evidence for several of the above admirably worded sentences.

We may suppose that the compilers of the life of Jesus had every reason to suppress, so far as possible, any words of Jesus which would show too clearly that his anticipations or predictions were falsified by the event. Again, they were concerned to show that he suffered unjustly : the charges against him were false. The Roman authority need not have yielded to the importunities of the Rabbis and the Pharisees. They would be glad to show that Jesus's conception of the Messiah differed very widely from the ' political ' conception of the Jews. Again, the human element in the Messiah had in certain quarters become less. The Messiah was rather a semi-divine being than the purely earthly king of Isaiah xi. All the facts might be accounted for if we held that Jesus believed himself to be the Messiah, through whom, whether before his death or after his resurrection, God would inaugurate the New Order, the New Kingdom, in which as God's vicegerent Jesus would occupy a pre-eminent position. The enemies of God would be annihilated ; the righteous and the converted would ' live happily ever after,' for death too would be destroyed, and the tears off all faces would be wiped away. This conception is not without its elements of severity : but the Kingdom is so etherealized ; its nature is so other, whatever its *locale*, than an ordinary kingdom

of earth, that it can hardly be called ' political.' Yet it has its
connections and affiliations with O.T. conceptions, and in its funda-
mentals has resemblances with many conceptions of the Rabbis.
A certain amount would depend upon whether 33 is historic or no,
and how much is implied in it. Did Peter only protest against the
idea that suffering and death were to precede the establishment of
the Kingdom, or are we to suppose that Jesus rebuked him because
Peter perceived that Jesus was teaching and aiming at a spiritual
kingdom, whereas he, Peter, wanted a material, political kingdom,
and that Jesus claimed to be a spiritual Messiah, whereas he, Peter,
wanted a political Messiah ? But what is a spiritual kingdom ?
Jesus certainly never contemplated a kingdom of disembodied
spirits. On the other hand, it is most doubtful whether he contemplated a sort of Church within a world which, in its political
aspect, was to go on as before. If he thought that he would first
have to die, and then would reappear and establish the Kingdom
upon a renovated earth, surely upon that renovated earth the
wicked would be annihilated, or dispatched to Gehenna, and the
righteous alone would remain. If so, Rome would disappear. We
cannot imagine that he conceived that the Jews, even after the
Parousia, would be subject to the domination of Rome. And it is
necessary to press this argument home. For it is acknowledged
by many critics, who are all for separating the conceptions of Jesus
about the Kingdom from the political, ' impure ' conceptions of the
Jews, that Jesus's missionary outlook did not extend beyond Israel.
He may, doubtless, have believed that many Gentiles would enter
the Kingdom, but they would come in as proselytes, even as the
Prophets before him had believed. The saying in Matt. xix. 28,
if authentic, gives us a vivid insight into his anticipations of the
future : ' When the Son of man shall sit on the throne of his glory,
ye who have followed me shall also sit yourselves upon twelve
thrones, ruling the twelve tribes of Israel.' In such a picture, has
the continuance of the Roman domination a place ? If Jesus
believed in a regenerated Israel with himself as its King, an Israel
to whom a large number of Gentiles would be joined, an Israel who
would not oppress or be oppressed, an Israel righteous and pure,
from whose midst and around whom all wicked persons, whether
Jews or Gentiles, would for ever have disappeared, what is this but
the old prophetic picture, purified indeed, but yet essentially the
same, even though it be upon a new earth, and even though many,
or most, of that earth's inhabitants have risen from the dead, and
there is among them no marriage and giving in marriage, no death,
and no old age ? Yet we, perhaps, can find even in this interpretation a place for the rebuke to Peter. For we can conceive that
Jesus thought more of peace and righteousness than of victory and

turning the tables. There would indeed be a judgment, and the wicked would disappear. But they would be divinely judged ; there would be no human battles and human victories; no reversal of destiny in the ordinary sense, the Jews oppressing, the foreigners oppressed. The wicked foreigners, like the wicked Jews, would indeed be sent to Hell, and with this change Peter should have been content.

Neither Wellhausen nor Edward Meyer can produce a consistent conception of the meaning of Jesus. The former thinks that it is difficult to say how he himself felt towards the view of others that he was the Messiah. In the first edition of his *Einleitung* he said : ' With the refutation of the idea that the Messiah according to the Scripture must be the son of David, he seems, indeed, also, to refute an objection against the possibility that he himself is the Messiah. And according to all the indications he did not object that others saw in him the predicted one who was to fulfil the hopes of Israel. He had indeed no intention of establishing the kingdom of David, as they expected him to do. In rejecting kinship with David he, at the same time, also rejected all political aspirations. His Jewish adversaries ascribed these intentions to him on account of the title of Messiah, but Pilate recognized his harmlessness. He did not wish to fulfil any patriotic desires. Not the rule of the heathen, but the weight of a deadening tradition, he felt as a yoke. He led no opposition against the Romans, but against the High Priests and Scribes, and it was they who brought about his downfall. Jesus wanted to prepare the way for a religious rebirth of his people, although not only by gaining the allegiance of individuals, for to do that would not have necessitated journeying to Jerusalem. As a regenerator he might indeed accept the title of the Jewish " restitutor in integrum," though he removed from it any political taint. It was, it must be allowed, a compromise ' (p. 93).

In the second edition of the Introduction (p. 83) these sentences are altered to the following, as if the distinguished scholar could not get to a definite conclusion : ' At the trial before the Sanhedrin and before Pilate his silence is very noticeable; if he finally acknowledges that he is the Messiah, he does not do so freely and without hesitation. And some doubt remains over as to whether he acknowledged it at all. The question as to his authority (Mark xi. 28) he skilfully and purposely evades. In spite of all this, however, he must have presented to his enemies some actual ground or occasion for denouncing him before Pilate. A revolt against the Romans, indeed, he did not plan; he did not intend to free his people from foreign dominion. He wanted to liberate them from the yoke of the Priests and the Rabbis. For this purpose he appeared, not only as a teacher, but perhaps also as an agitator; he claimed for himself the Messianic right of rule in internal affairs, or at least made it look as if he did. When he purified the Temple, he did not shrink from violence; his disciples were armed, and endeavoured to fight when they were surprised. Traces of these facts are still preserved in the gospel narrative, others may have been removed. Up to a certain measure Reimarus may have been in the right.'

This second passage is quoted with only partial approval by Meyer. According to him Jesus believed and declared that he was the Messiah, but what he intended and desired to do was to bring about a spiritual kingdom of God in a spiritual community. ('Das ausserweltliche Gottesreich in der geistigen Gemeinde, die er schaffen will, zu verwirklichen.') All political objects were utterly removed from him. He felt that the attempted accomplishment of his desire would bring him into great danger, but he probably did not realize how the establishment of such a community as he wanted, and its separation from the politically organized synagogue and from the State, would lead of necessity to a conflict with Rome (1. pp. 164, 165). With all respect to the great historian, from whom one differs with much diffidence, this conception seems to me most unlikely. Jesus went to Jerusalem, not merely to increase the body of his disciples, not merely to form a spiritual community, but to change the face of the world, to bring present conditions to a sudden and final close, to establish something new, permanent, and complete.

As to Rome, I would like to add here the sober words of Knopf: 'Jesus does not anywhere expressly say that the empire of the Romans will cease in the new world-order; yet this is most certainly his expectation. For how could there be room for the Roman Imperium by the side of, or in, the Kingdom of God? But Jesus clearly left it to God *how* God would make an end of the Roman dominion' (*Einführung*, ed. 2, 1923, p. 252). And note this. It is true that Jesus nowhere in the Gospels definitely says that the Roman Empire would come to an end with the establishment of the Kingdom of God. But have we a record of all that Jesus said? What reason have we to suppose that he never definitely said it? And we have every reason to see that if he did say it, that was not one of his sayings which a compiler or evangelist would wisely admit into his book. One more of the numerous efforts to combine the admission that Jesus did claim to be the Messiah with the usual keen desire that there should be nothing 'theocratic,' 'outward,' 'political' about his conception of the Messiahship can be read in Bacon, *Gospel Story*, p. 107 *seq.* It is about as probable, or perhaps I should rather say, about as improbable, as all the others, and it rests, moreover, on dubious statements as to the growth and nature of the Messianic idea. If Jesus regarded himself as the Messiah, why should he not also have supposed that he would ' reign ' over a regenerate Israel as the deputy of God ?   If king and subjects are all righteous and pure, what is there evil in the relationship, even though it is also ' political,' ' outward,' ' theocratic ' ?   What Jesus thought would be the relation of Israel to the Gentile world in the Messianic Kingdom we have no means for determining.   It is safe to say that he was no eager nationalist, and had no desire for Israel's supremacy or for its vengeance over its national foes, but it is going too far to suppose that he did not conceive the new era as a ' theocratic ' kingdom, with himself as its divinely appointed king.

31–38. The second sub-section, of which 34-38 may again be separate from, or may have been added to, 31–33.

31. Some scholars hold that 31–33 is not the old and original continuation of 30. Loisy, *e.g.*, thinks that ix. 1 connects much better with 30 than 31–33. Again, many commentators believe in the historic and authentic character of 27–30, but disbelieve in the historic and authentic character of 31–33. For here we get (in verses 31–33) the definite prediction by Jesus of his own suffering, death, and resurrection. This prediction occurs three times in Mark : here, and in ix. 30–32, and in x. 32–34.

It will be observed that Jesus makes no use of the word ' Messiah,' to which Peter had given utterance immediately before. To the Evangelist, indeed, Son of man is equivalent to Messiah, but it is not entirely certain that the two terms were synonyms to Jesus. At any rate, Jesus not only ignores the word Messiah, but he even says nothing of the Messianic Kingdom. He says indeed that he will rise again, but as to what will happen at that ' rising ' he is silent. Certainly it is a very odd sequel to the last words of 29.

Every sort of possible opinion has been hazarded as to what was in the mind of Jesus when he took the decision to go to Jerusalem. Did he go fully expecting to die ?   Did he go in the full belief that only after his death would he return and inaugurate the Kingdom, that only after death would he become in visible actuality and power the Danielic Son of man ?   Or, quite the contrary, did he go to Jerusalem fully believing that the Kingdom would be inaugurated in his lifetime, that his Messianic office would be conferred upon him without suffering and without death, that the Son of man would be invested with glory soon after his arrival in the capital ?   Or is an in-between view the true view ?   He went up to Jerusalem to establish the Kingdom, but he realized the risk he was running. He thought that he might perhaps fail, and be put to death, but that he must nevertheless go forward, and that God would somehow or other vindicate him at the end.   And did this 'somehow or other' include the possibility that he would triumph and establish the Kingdom after death by being 'raised up' by God for that special purpose and end ?   If we adopt the first view, then the predictions of suffering and death may have been made more detailed and precise, but are substantially accurate.   If we adopt the second view, then the predictions are unhistoric, and have been constructed *post eventum*.   If we adopt some form of the third view, then the predictions are expansions and elaborations of some vague expressions of fear, or of possible disaster, of ' hope for the best, but prepare for the worst,' which Jesus may have uttered to the disciples.   ' I am going to witness, and to help in, the establishment of the Kingdom. I am going to Jerusalem, even if it be at the risk of my life.'   Thus some scholars think that Jesus realized or believed that his Glory, the assumption of the Messiahship and its recognition, would only take place after his death by a voluntary martyrdom, and after a speedy and miraculous resurrection.   It was idle to proclaim his Messiahship now.   It would be proclaimed *for* him, but only after his resurrection.   Others think that he went up to Jerusalem in the full belief that there the Kingdom would be inaugurated, and that God would then openly invest him with his Messianic office and glory.   Others think that, though he went to Jerusalem hoping to triumph, hoping for the Kingdom and its inauguration, he yet realized the immensity of the risk.   Or again : the Kingdom was certain and his own Messiahship.   His duty was equally certain : to go to Jerusalem and proclaim the Kingdom.   Whether, however, the Kingdom would come before, or without, his death, or whether he would have to die as its condition precedent, and to ' rise ' for its fulfilment, *that* he left to God.   Whatever befell, his own course was clear, and the ultimate triumph of his message assured.

One could, did space allow, quote interesting passages from scholars illustrating all these various views.   Thus for the view that Jesus did not anticipate death but victory, the words of Schmiedel (*E. B.* II. Col. 1887) might be cited.   ' The confession [of Peter] must have been one of the supreme moments in the joyous consciousness of Jesus—the discovery that he was finding recognition as the Messiah and winning his battle.   Suffering and death are the very opposite of all that is looked for in the Jewish Messiah, and what Jesus at that moment could have looked forward to for himself.'   For the view that Jesus did anticipate and predict his death, J. Weiss would serve.   Why should he not have foreseen that the bitter opposition of the Scribes, the fickleness of the people, the fears of the authorities, would make this end inevitable ?   Sometimes he may have hoped that he would succeed without martyrdom ; even at Gethsemane he prays that

this may be possible; but usually his mood and conviction are
different. The details of his Passion—these have been filled in
after the event—he did not foresee, but only the hard necessity of
ultimate triumph being prepared and made way for by suffering,
conflict, and death. For through, and in spite of, death the prophecy
of Daniel will be fulfilled. 'Somehow or other his fate is also
included in the prophecy of Daniel. But how it was exactly to be
realized Jesus will have left to God.' (In this sense Weiss holds
the prediction both of the Passion and of the Resurrection to be
historic.) 'In some such way we might be able to reconstruct
the historical background of the prophecy. It is more certain
that, in its present form, the prophecy contains the chief item
of what the primitive Palestinian community proclaimed to the
world. In looking back the riddle of the crucifixion was revealed
to them' (*Schriften*, 3rd ed. I. p. 150). One form of the in-
between view is expressed in these few words of Loisy. 'Jesus
did not go to Jerusalem to die there; he went there, at the risk
of his life, to prepare and bring about the advent of the Divine
Kingdom' (*E. S.* I. p. 214). And Meyer, vigorous as he is for the
full authenticity and historical character of the 'confession,'
strongly urges that both 31 and 34–ix. I are secondary. As to
the confession and as to the substance of 33, he says: 'This
scene, which is vividly described, obviously rests upon an
authentic tradition. Jesus designates Peter, who has only just
before acknowledged him as the Messiah, harshly as Satan, the
enemy of the Kingdom of God: this cannot have been invented.
But it is impossible that Jesus can have predicted the minute
details of his fate, however obvious it would have seemed that he
should have done so to the Christian community. That the same
fate awaited him as so many other prophets he might have felt and
expressed: the exact details, however, no one could have foretold.
The scene with Peter, therefore, has been placed in a false light:
in reality, Peter must have put forward the demand that Jesus
should now prove the truth of his claims to supernatural powers,
and should accomplish the rôle of Messiah in the way in which
Jewish eschatology had conceived it; and that demand Jesus
rejects emphatically and harshly' (i. p. 117). Yet Meyer admits
that the sayings of 35 and 36 (why not also 37 ?) may be perfectly genuine. But they are used in an unauthentic connection.

It is interesting that on the whole question scholarship has
hardly advanced beyond the temperate words in which Strauss
summed it up over ninety years ago. 'If Jesus in any period of
his life thought himself to be the Messiah, as to which there can be
no doubt, and if he called himself the Son of man, he was bound,
it would seem, to expect that " coming on the clouds " which was

predicted of the Son of man in Daniel : the only question is if he thought of this as a transfiguration (*Verherrlichung*) which would happen during his life, or as something which would only befall him after his death. According to statements like Matt. x. 23, xvi. 28 [Mark ix. 1], one might conjecture the prior alternative ; yet it is always possible that if, later on, his death seemed certain to him, his conception assumed the latter form, from which point of view Matt. xxvi. 64 [Mark xiv. 62] would have been spoken' (*Das Leben Jesu*, II. p. 373, first ed.).

Δεῖ, ' must.' Why ' must ' ? In the eyes of the writer, doubtless because the divine purpose in sending Jesus to earth could only be fulfilled by his death.

The ' elders and the chief priests ' represent the clerical and lay aristocracy in Jerusalem

' After three days,' so in ix. 31, x. 34. In Matthew and Luke, ' on the third day,' which is not necessarily the same thing. The origin of ' the third day ' some find in Hosea vi. 2. It is less easy to see how ' after three days ' can be accounted for, except by the Jonah sign : Jonah i. 17, Matt. xii. 40. The two different expressions may imply variants in the reckoning of the resurrection, but they may conceivably mean the same thing. The first and third day need not be taken as full days. In order to maintain the thesis that Jesus predicted his resurrection, but did not predict anything so precise as when it would exactly happen, the theory has been suggested that ' after three days ' means merely ' in a short time,' ' soon after death,' and that, after the event, the phrase was altered by oral tradition to ' on the third day.' So, for example, Goguel I. p. 296. But in Matt. xii. 40 it is said that Jesus will be in the heart of the earth for three days and three nights, which could not be equated therefore with the third day. If three days and three nights, or three days, had been meant originally as a brief period only, Matt. xii. 40 would seem to show that, when a more precise date was desired, or when the general expression was turned into a precise reckoning, we ought to have had ' on the fourth day,' not ' on the third day.' For a careful discussion of the whole matter, including the origin of the legend of the empty grave, see Clemen, pp. 96–105. He comes to the conclusion that ' the third day ' is due to some heathen legend or cult. ' Again we have a case before us, where foreign influence on primitive Christianity has been of the greatest importance.' Johannes Weiss, in the very interesting section on the Resurrection upon the Third Day (*Das Urchristentum*, pp. 60–75), thinks that, on the whole, it is safest to assume that the Hosea passage seemed to reveal a prophecy about the death and revivification of the Messiah, and that the entire story of the

bodily resurrection on the third day or after three days is due
to this passage. However this may be, it would seem highly
probable that the assertion of the resurrection on the third day is
later than the belief in the appearances of the risen Messiah, and
that it does not rest on any basis of history.

32. παρρησία. Usually the word means 'openly,' and some
think that it means this here, but perhaps it only means 'clearly,'
'definitely,' 'deliberately.' τὸν λόγον. Surely this must mean
here the teaching about his suffering, death, etc. (Against Klostermann.) 'Peter takes him aside.' But why, if no 'crowd' is
present? That is why the view has been held that παρρησία
must be translated 'openly.' Mark forgets the order in 30, or thinks
that it has nothing to do with the contents of 31 ; he assumes that
the 'crowd' in 34 is already present. If we render παρρησία by
'clearly,' and do not allow 34 to influence our exegesis, we must
suppose that Peter takes Jesus aside in order not to rebuke his
Master in the presence of the other disciples.

For what did Peter rebuke him? It would seem that Peter is
appalled at the revolutionary idea of a suffering and dying Messiah.
He wants to lead Jesus away from such thoughts. A Messiah who
does not conquer, but is himself conquered, who does not overcome
others, but is himself overcome, is to him a monstrous impossibility,
a contradiction in terms. Away with the thoughts and conceptions
and policy which could make the Master's career issue in such a
shameful end. Thus he is a tempter, like the devil in Matt. iv. 10,
and is so called. There is a connection between the two passages,
which makes the authenticity of 33 as it stands somewhat doubtful.
Klausner's view of 32, 33 is peculiar and improbable. He holds that
' it is most probable that, immediately after his disciples' recognition
of his Messianic claims, he spoke of the sufferings which he must
undergo. To deny this would make the whole history of Christianity incomprehensible. If, after the crucifixion, the disciples
believed in a suffering Messiah, then Jesus must, while still alive,
have spoken of such sufferings: (a) he had seen the fate of John the
Baptist; (b) he was, at the time, persecuted and suffering in a foreign
land; (c) the coming of the Messiah was impossible without " the
pangs of the Messiah." It is true that the " pangs of the Messiah "
are not, in the Talmud, explained as sufferings affecting the Messiah
himself, but as the sufferings of the Messianic age : but this " Son
of man " who found himself persecuted by the Pharisees and Herodians, and who did not expect to realize his claims by victorious
warfare, must have begun to imagine that, before his victory, such
sufferings must befall him, himself. And these sufferings must
come about in Jerusalem ' (p. 300). This implies that at ' Cæsarea

Philippi, therefore, Jesus told his disciples that he was about to
go to Jerusalem, where he should suffer greatly, but would, in the
end, be victorious, and be recognized by the crowds of people who
had come to celebrate the Passover, as the Messiah' (p. 302).
Thus Jesus predicted suffering, but he did not predict his death.
'The whole idea of a Messiah who should be put to death was one
which, in Jesus's time, was impossible of comprehension both to
the Jews and to Jesus himself' (p. 301). While this view is
possible, it seems very unlikely that what Peter objected to was
not the suffering, as opposed to the victorious, Messiah, but running
into danger and going to Jerusalem at all. 'If Jesus and his
disciples had been so persecuted and had run such danger in
Galilee, how could he dare to go to Jerusalem, the centre of civil
and religious authority, where the danger which threatened them,
simple Galilæans, was seven times greater!' (p. 302). I hardly
think that the historical character of Peter's rebuke and Jesus's
reminder can be thus maintained.

33. Jesus in his turn rebukes Peter. Peter's ideas that a
Messiah must be a fighting conqueror, and that to suffer and die can
be no part of a Messianic programme or rôle, is to think humanly.
God sees and wills otherwise. The throne of glory must be reached
by suffering and death. Such is divine 'thinking.' Such is the
divine will. Jesus must not be 'tempted' to shrink away from,
and not to submit himself to, this divine will. To the Evangelist,
Son of man is itself a Messianic title, whatever Jesus, if he used it,
may have meant by it. It is needless to add that if 31 is unhistoric,
32, 33 are no less so. To Mark the connection between 27–30 and
31–33 is clear enough, and it was therefore that he added the second
paragraph to the first. Jesus agrees that he is the Messiah, but
explains that this Messiahship must be still hidden. For the
Messiahship does not truly begin till, after suffering and death, the
risen Saviour enters into his glory. For the wording οὐ φρονεῖς,
etc., we may compare Romans viii. 5. Meyer would like, as we have
seen, to believe that 33 in substance is quite authentic. Peter
wants the political Messiah ; Jesus is only a spiritual Messiah. In
that case we have to assume that Jesus said something of the sort
to the disciples, though not what we now have in 31. Here we move
in a cloud of conjectures, none of which, as it seems to me, can be
of very much value. I might mention, perhaps, the conjecture of
Schmidt. The rebuke addressed to Peter may have been an isolated
logion, and Mark may have given to it this suitable setting (p. 220).
The words ὕπαγε ὀπίσω μου do not mean, it is supposed, ' get
thee behind me,' but ' away from me,' ' leave me.'

34–38. In this sub-section is comprised the third subject

mentioned above: and for us this sub-section is the most important of all. Originally these sayings were probably not connected with 31–33. Moreover, they were probably not originally connected in themselves. 34 was probably not originally connected with 35. and 36 may not have been connected with 35 ; 36 and 37 probably go together, but not certainly ; 38 again was not originally connected with 34–37. Verse 34 occurs, over and above the corresponding passages in Matthew and Luke, in a somewhat different form in Matt. x. 38, Luke xiv. 27. Verse 35 occurs in a slightly different form in Matt. x. 39 and in Luke xvii. 33. That these sayings occur thus separately and more than once in Luke and Matthew shows that they were originally distinct, separate Logia. They wear the appearance of being in substance, not necessarily in any of their exact wordings, authentic. Verse 38 too is reproduced in Matt. x. 33 and Luke xii. 9.

Cadman accepts the order and sequence of 31–38 as historic. Jesus expects death at Jerusalem ; and he not only expects to die there himself, but that any disciples who might accompany him to the city would die there with him. This anticipation 'was not verified by the course of events.' The anticipation of death for the disciples as well as for himself, if they came with him to Jerusalem is implied in 34, 35. Nor did Jesus predict his resurrection as apart from his parousia. Verse 30 is not *exactly* what Jesus actually said. It is unlikely that Jesus ever drew a ' distinction between resurrection and parousia. His only return would be for judgment and the Kingdom ' (p. 79).

34. The introduction of the crowd is very perplexing, not so much only because it is unexplained as to where it came from, or how it suddenly appeared (for this does not matter to Mark, who, as it were, keeps Pharisees and Scribes and crowds as part of his editorial stage machinery, to be used as required), but because Jesus is really addressing the inner ring. The demands he now makes are *not* for all ; they are for full disciples only. It has been suggested that the ' crowd ' was added mistakenly by a still later redactor, who perhaps was thinking of Luke xiv. 25. This view is pressed by Cadman, who points out that the crowd are wanting both in Matthew's version and in Luke's. ' Doubtless some revising hand, after Matthew and Luke had employed Mark, rewrote the introductory verses in Mark, and inserted the reference to the '' crowd.'' The redactor's desire would have been to make his readers understand that the teaching was applicable to them too.' Cadman thinks that this same redactor added the words ' and he spoke the word openly, or clearly ' in 32, which are also wanting in Luke and Matthew (pp. 62, 65).

In the form in which 34 is now worded, it can hardly go back to Jesus. For to what does the cross refer ? It can hardly refer to anything else than to Jesus's crucifixion ; the disciples are to suffer martyrdom willingly. This metaphorical application of the crucifixion, which has not yet happened, is most peculiar at this place and time, for it must have been wholly unintelligible to his hearers. The cross appears here already as the symbol of Christianity. But Jesus has not carried it for all : each must carry it after him. There is indeed one possible method of saving the authenticity even as the verse stands, and that is to assume that ' the cross ' was already a traditional and familiar metaphor for suffering and sacrifice. Some think Luke xiv. 27 is probably a more original form of the saying than Mark viii. 34. Is it not also possible that the saying ran first of all : ' If anybody wishes to follow me, let him deny himself ' ?

The word ' follow ' as used the second time has a somewhat fuller meaning than as used the first time. ' If you want to follow me, you must be prepared for a following indeed, a following of pain and death.' Or we may paraphrase, ' If you deny yourself, and take up your cross, then, indeed (or then only), shall you follow me.' So Klostermann, who, for the construction, compares Luke vii. 7 and xiv. 27,

' Let him deny himself,' ἀπαρνησάσθω ἑαυτόν. These great words are apparently only found here, and in the parallel passages, in the New Testament.

35. The saying is in all probability not originally connected with 34, and indeed it might almost be said that the pure altruism and lofty spirituality of 34 are, if anything, impaired by the reason and justification given for them in 35. For though the words in 35 have been refined and spiritualized by later interpretation, they meant originally, and they certainly meant to the editor who put them in their present connection, just this : He who finds martyrdom in this life will live again in the world to come, or in the Kingdom of God. He who avoids martyrdom, and thus saves his life in this world, will lose it in the next world. For the passage 35–37 is purely eschatological. It does not mean that to gain the higher life we must forgo the lower life. Nor do any of the parallels in the Synoptics, Matt. x. 39, xvi. 25, Luke ix. 24, xvii. 33, mean this. Perhaps John xii. 25 may have this signification, but the Synoptic passages have not. The parallel in the Talmud (Tamid 32a) seems to have a less distinctly eschatological meaning. How early, we would like to know, did the saying of Jesus receive a purely spiritual signification, *without reference to anything which may happen to us after death* ? It has been suggested that the

verse gives the impression of a popular saying which was either used by Jesus with an adaptation, or was given a Christian adaptation and put into his mouth. Another view is that the saying is authentic fundamentally, but that the words ' for my sake and the gospel's ' have been added. Others accept ' for my sake ' as authentic, but think that the words ' and the gospel's ' were added to make the saying applicable even after Jesus's death. In Luke xvii. 33 we actually have the saying without the words ' for my sake and the gospel's,' and it is more likely that the words were added than subtracted. Matt. x. 39 has only ' for me.' Harnack insists that ' for the sake of the gospel ' means what it says, ' for the sake of the glad tidings of the coming of the Kingdom,' and that the words are not, as W. thinks, equivalent to ' for my sake.' He seems to think that both are authentic. (*Constitution and Law of the Church*, E. T. pp. 280–282.) Burney believes that the metrical Aramaic original enables us to say pretty definitely that ' and the gospel's ' has been added. It ' overweights the clause.' Moreover, as ' it is improbable that both Matthew and Luke should have improved upon the form of Mark's parallelism by excision of the words καὶ τοῦ εὐαγγελίου, we must infer that they depended upon a source of information superior to Mark, *i.e.* probably Q ; in other words, the passage is an indication that Mark knew and used Q, and in this case has glossed it to the detriment of the parallelistic form of the antithesis ' (p. 74, n. 4). *Cp.* also p. 142, n. 1. It may be that for metrical reasons ' for my sake ' should also be omitted (p. 85, n. 1).

36. The thought of 35 is given another turn in 36, which originally, in much probability, was a separate saying. If one became for this life the lord or emperor of the whole world, but were excluded from the next world, it would be bad business ; loss instead of profit. The immortal life is worth more than the whole material world. The grandest life on earth is purchased dearly if it be at the cost of the life of the great world to come, the life after the reappearance of Christ, or the life of the New Jerusalem and the Messianic Age.

37. This verse is an echo of Psalm xlix. 8, and hence we may account for the word ' give ' where ' receive ' would make a better sense. For the meaning is, what can a man obtain in exchange for giving up his true, eternal ' life ' ? In both 36 and 37 ' life ' means the life of the coming age, or of the world to come. Originally these sayings must have been coined with a less exalted meaning. We know that as regards 37, for it depends upon Ps. xlix. 8, where ' life ' does not refer to the life of ' the world to come.' And in 36

we may suppose that originally the saying only meant : riches will not help in the hour of death. *Cp.* Luke xii. 20.

38. The verse raises many critical questions of the greatest interest, which may not unfortunately be discussed at any length here. The interpretation of the verse, and any view as to its relation to the parallel passages in Matthew and Luke, must largely depend upon whether we hold that Jesus did call himself the Son of man, or ' the Man,' or that he did not. And was the Son of man originally—*e.g.* in this very verse as first spoken or written—distinguished from Jesus, or were the two always identical ?

The parallels in Matthew and Luke over and above Matt. xvi. 27 and Luke ix. 26 are Matt. x. 32, 33 and Luke xii. 8, 9. Which is primary ? Is the personal pronoun in Matthew older than the Son of man in Mark ? Or is Son of man the older version, and were the Son of man and Jesus distinguished from one another ? It may be observed that the rôle and position of Jesus in Matt. x. 32, 33 appear less exalted than in Mark viii. 38. In Matthew Jesus is a sort of witness : he gives evidence. In Mark viii. 38 (if he *be* the Son of man) he is the Judge, and comes down ' in the glory of his Father ' from heaven.

It is conceivable that Jesus thought that he would be called upon by God to give evidence at the Judgment, and that the test to be applied would be the measure of heed and obedience that men had given to his message, and the measure of acceptance that men had given to his mission and his inspiration. If Jesus did not call himself Son of man, and did not believe himself to be the Messiah, he may yet have used words such as we now find in Mark viii. 38. The Son of man, Daniel's ' Man,' is then the Judge, not Jesus. If, again, Jesus believed himself to be the Messiah, it is not impossible that he also believed that a great office and function would be bestowed upon him at the Judgment. He may have believed that what is foretold in Daniel vii. 14 would be realized in him. All is conjecture, and not very profitable conjecture. It has, for instance, been argued that the perhaps transitional phraseology whereby Jesus is partly distinguished from, and yet partly identified with, the Son of man is further illustrated by the strange use of ' Father ' in the phrase ' in the glory of his Father.' The Son of man is here modelled upon the Son of man in Daniel, but the words ' in the glory *of his Father* ' would not fit that figure. On the other hand, except in xiii. 32, Jesus never (in Mark) calls God *his special* Father. He never uses such a phrase as ' in the glory of my Father.' Once only does he address God in the vocative as Father, but the meaning there is the same as in the Lord's Prayer (*cp.* Luke xi. 2, ' Father,' not ' Our Father ').

As to what *Mark* thought there is no doubt. The Son of man is the Messiah, the Messiah is Jesus.

'Ashamed' is the equivalent of 'deny.' And the meaning, though not definitely stated is clear. He who has accepted Jesus and recognized him as divinely sent, and his words as good and inspired, is admitted into the Kingdom ; he who has refused to accept and recognize him and his words is rejected. A narrow test ; the origin of much intolerance and grievous persecution. Cadman holds that Mark's 38 is secondary in relation to Matt. x. 32, 33 and Luke xii. 8, 9 (Q). The fact that the bit in Mark, 'and my words in this adulterous and sinful generation,' is absent from Q makes against its authenticity, and for the same reason 'when he comes in the glory of his Father with the holy angels' is probably an editorial supplement (p. 72).

ix. 1.   Another saying, added on to the foregoing by the familiar, 'And he said.' Two interpretations may be given of it. If, as some think, ix. 1 is the original sequel of viii. 30, then we should have to suppose that Jesus announces here that the Kingdom will soon be inaugurated in the lifetime of many of those then present. He says nothing of his suffering and death. But in that case 'some of those' is strange. Jesus expected the *dénouement* soon. One would surmise that he must rather have said, 'Those who stand here,' not 'some of those who stand here.'

Or we may assume that viii. 38 meant originally that the End and the Judgment were coming in the lifetime of the sinful generation, so many of whom refused to accept Jesus (or who had caused his death). But the Judgment and the Second Coming of Jesus (the Parousia) delayed. So a word was added. Though there *was* delay, yet *some* persons at any rate would yet live to witness the Coming. Note that the Kingdom of God in Mark has become in Matthew the Kingdom of the Messiah, the Kingdom of the Son of man. 'Taste death.' For the phrase, *cp.* Bacon, p. 165 and 2 Esdras vi. 26. The metaphor is also Rabbinic.

Whatever the date when 38 and ix. 1 were written, in one important respect they do not greatly misrepresent the dominant thought of Jesus. The Kingdom was near—the Kingdom in its true eschatological sense.

'The coming of the Kingdom of God in power : ' ἐν δυνάμει means the Kingdom in its completed development ; in the full realization of its strength. The Kingdom in one sense has already begun ; it exists potentially. The final and perfect realization will take place at the Parousia.

I have tried to be brief about this section, but it has been difficult to be so. For us the real importance of the section lies in

34–37, and more especially in 34. To this verse we owe the great conception of ' following Christ ' : the conception of leading a life of hardship and poverty, of purity and sacrifice, for his sake—for the sake of goodness, for the sake of man, for the sake of God. Jesus kindled an unceasing personal devotion for himself ; but he also has represented the other terms. To follow him has meant for endless noble souls to labour and renounce for the sake of goodness, for the sake of man, for the sake of God. No one can fail to recognize what a rich addition to the moral and religious store of the world this following of Christ has been and has brought about.

Its distinctive and novel note was upon the active and positive side. For it might be said that from the Maccabæan age (Psalm xliv. 22) the Jews have suffered and renounced and undergone martyrdom and persecution, for the sake of truth and for the sake of God. And this is quite true. But the Jewish devotion has been rather passive than active. Sooner than give up or abandon the truth, sooner than renounce the Law and the Unity of God, they would suffer or die. The new note in the following of Christ is its activity. The best disciples have wanted not merely to endure, but to battle with, evil, to win proselytes, to transform the world, to redeem the fallen, to cure the sick, in the name, and for the sake, of Christ.

And then come the two simple Greek words, ἀπαρνησάσθω ἑαυτόν, ' let him deny himself.' Here again we have what is practically a new conception. Self-denial was not unknown before Christ ; but the *clear conception* of it and the ideal which it suggests *were*, I think, new, and they in their turn have exercised an immense influence for good upon men's thoughts, aspirations, and actions. More restricted, but not less intense, has been the effect of the next words : ' let him take up his cross.' The true follower of the Master, in proportion to the perfection of his discipleship, must endure and renounce, suffer and die. Jews cannot accept the verse as it stands ; they must substitute God for Jesus. ' He who would follow God upon earth, let him deny himself.' So worded, is not the adage true also for them ? As to 35–37 the original meaning was strictly eschatological. One can reduce them to the rather bald statement : he who would enjoy eternal life must be willing to abandon this earthly life, or even to suffer martyrdom. But though this be the original meaning, the words were soon more liberally and variously interpreted. And even if we keep to the original meaning, we may give the verses a higher as well as a lower significance. For if the life of the world to come be indeed not merely longer in duration, but in all the good of the spirit greater than this world, then it is not a question of reward, and not a question of punishment ; it is simply a question of choosing the nobler and better, and rejecting, where needful, the cheap and the poor. There is nothing selfish in such a doctrine ; nothing of mere investment. It *is* supremely worth while to reject the less good for the more good ; still more, the false for the true ; the glitter for the gold ; the impure for the pure. So far then as this passage (35–37) has made men realize that what we may call the things of the spirit—truth and righteousness—are not only rather better than the things of sense, but on a different plane, better in kind, it can only have done good. Or, again, so far as it has made men realize that the ultimate right thing for each one of us is to develop his own best self to the utmost, that in the long run the cultivation of the soul is the final end of all education and development, it has lifted men above temptation, and nerved them to higher things. The doctrine it preaches is the same as that preached by Plato. To him the only thing a man should care for is his soul. Her he must, as his true life's work, seek to array ' not in some foreign attire, but in her own proper jewels, temperance and justice and courage and nobility and truth—in these adorned, she is ready to go on her journey to the world below when her hour comes.' It is quite true that on the hypothesis of a future life, or even perhaps without it, it cannot profit a man to gain the world and lose his soul, foregoing the highest of which he is capable.

It may, indeed, be questioned whether the passage (35–37) and some others like it have not helped to induce the false individualism which has sometimes marred certain phases of the Christian life— that false individualism whereby the religious life has sometimes been set in antagonism to the life of the family and the life of the State. There may be such a thing as a selfish or even morbid anxiety about the saving of one's soul, leading to exaggerated asceticism, hermitlike withdrawal from the world, or neglect of the closest duties of man. Judaism has never sanctioned or admired a double kind of religious life. Its ideal is that a man should be in the world, though not *of* the world. To neglect, abandon, or disobey your parents for the sake of the state or the community may be, under certain circumstances, advisable and justifiable ; to do so for the sake of your soul is extremely dubious. Again, the saving of one's soul is sometimes a little like happiness ; it is best found when least sought. It is not always the safest, surest, and healthiest way to save one's soul to think too much about it.

But these reflections do not make us admit any the less the noble religious and moral effects which 35–37 as well as 34, though 34 probably much more than 35–37, have produced in the history of the world.

I may add here that Cadman's theory is that ix. 1 is unhistorical, while the substance of viii. 27–38 is historical both in fact and in

order of time. He thus actually reverses the view (of Loisy, *e.g.*)
which has been mentioned above. Verse 34 relates to the disciples
only. They must be prepared for martyrdom, like their Master.
Jesus will return after suffering and death as the Danielic Son of
man. But the words of Jesus ' about the fate of the disciples were
not verified by the course of events ' (p. 86). The working out of
the theory is wonderfully ingenious, but probably too ingenious.

[For the view that the statements in Mark that Jesus foresaw
and predicted his death are trustworthy, *cp.* the interesting article
by Eisler, in *Z. N. W.*, 1926, pp. 26, 27. 'Dass Jesus seinen Tod
nicht habe voraussehen können, beruht auf eine ganz ungenügende
Einsicht in die geschichtliche Sachlage . . . Wer im Kampf gegen
Herodes und die jerusalemitische Hierarchie—von der düster im
Hintergrund drohenden Macht des römischen Weltreichs gar nicht
zu reden!—so weit gegangen war, ohne selbst eine geschlossene
Macht hinter sich zu haben, konnte dem Tod durch die Hand seiner
Feinde nur durch ein unmittelbares, wunderbares Eingreifen Gottes
zu entgehen hoffen.' Strictly speaking, Eisler would, however, re-
gard such predictions as much more probable after Mark xi., xii.,
with their provocative incidents, than before them.]

CHAPTER IX

2–8. The Transfiguration

(*Cp*. Matt. xvii. 1–8 ; Luke ix. 28–36)

2   And after six days Jesus took with him Peter and James and John, and led them up on to an high mountain, apart by themselves.
3 And he was transfigured before them, and his raiment became shining, exceeding white, so as no fuller on earth could whiten it.
4 And there appeared unto them Elijah with Moses : and they talked
5 with Jesus.   And Peter said to Jesus, ' Master, it is good for us to be here : let us make three tents ; one for thee, and one for Moses, and
6 one for Elijah.'   For he knew not what he should say ; for they were
7 sore afraid.   And a cloud arose and overshadowed them : and a voice came out of the cloud, saying, ' This is my beloved Son :
8 hearken unto him.'   And suddenly, when they looked round, they saw no one any more, except Jesus only with themselves.

The Transfiguration was originally, so many scholars suppose, one of the stories of the resurrection.   (For the mountain, *cp*. Matt. xxviii. 16.)   The story was somehow moved forward and made an incident in the earthly life of Jesus.   In the place where we now find it the tale is probably intended to give a miraculous confirmation from heaven of the Messiahship : it is also a sort of confirmation by way of anticipation of the predicted resurrection.   The story partly depends upon Exodus xxiv. 12–18 (' six days,' the Cloud). The Transfiguration in verse 3 caps and excels the shining of Moses' face in Exodus.   The story (2–8) appears to be intercalated here. Verse 11 may connect with verse 1.   Verses 9, 10 are an editorial link.

It is very interesting to find that Meyer strongly defends the historical character of the Transfiguration.   The story goes back to, and comes from, Peter himself.   As the rebuke administered to Peter in viii. 33 ' could only have been reported by Peter himself,' so the Transfiguration, which is closely connected with the Confes-

sion by the unusual and definite statement ' after six days,' is the
record of a vision which Peter experienced and which Peter told.
It is a true reminiscence of Peter.   The vision is no more and no less
real than many other excellently accredited visions throughout the
ages, and not least, as Meyer urges, some of the visions experienced
by some of the Mormons.   In fact, so far from the Transfiguration
vision being a mere reflexion or adaptation of the Resurrection
visions, the truth is exactly the reverse.   ' The resurrection and
the appearances of the risen Jesus grew out of the Transfiguration,
which is the ultimate root of Christianity.   The Transfiguration
accounts for the fact that Peter, James, and John are the " Pillars "
and the first heads of the nascent Church ' (p. 156).   By these words
Meyer does not mean that Peter did not see, or, rather, did not
think that he saw, the risen Christ after the crucifixion, but that it
was the first vision which caused him to see the second.   The same
line is taken by Harnack in his deeply interesting essay, ' Die Ver-
klärungsgeschichte Jesu,' in the *Sitzungsberichte der preussischen
Akademie der Wissenschaften,* 1922, pp. 62–80.   The story is
authentic.   The ' six days ' is not due to Exodus xxiv. 16, but
is a true piece of Peter's reminiscences.   (' Wer hat die präcize
Zeitangabe gegeben wenn nicht Petrus selbst ? ')   ' He knew not
what he said.'   Who could have been the author of this unsparing
criticism except Peter ?   ' It is well that we are here,' (for so, says
Harnack, must we translate).   This foolish remark is also authentic
and characteristic.   ' Dieses vorschnelle sich selbst In-den-Dienst
Stellen ist für Petrus charakteristisch, und die Verkennung der
Eigenart der Messianität Jesu in der Tat gedankenlos töricht, weil
jüdisch subaltern.'   [I do not exactly know what ' subaltern ' means
here ; it is obviously not complimentary to the Jews.]   Peter *was* a
visionary, and all conditions for a hallucinatory vision were present
and fulfilled.   There was the excitement produced by the confession
of Cæsarea Philippi and by what Jesus had there said :   Peter was
on a lonely mountain ; probably he had not eaten or drunk for some
hours, and had been exposed for long to the sun's rays and heat.
Probably it was only Peter who saw the vision ; probably the other
two saw nothing.   That Peter thought he saw Elijah and Moses is
also very likely.   He saw Elijah and Moses because he still thinks
of the *Jewish* Messiah.   He still thinks that the earthly kingdom is
soon to be established, and that Elijah and Moses will help Jesus to
establish it.   That Elijah and Moses were seen as well as Jesus
shows that the Transfiguration vision really happened to Peter : in
the Resurrection vision there were no Moses and no Elijah.   The
Transfiguration vision is a root of Christianity only in the sense that
Peter would not have had the vision of the risen Messiah (which was
the *first* of the resurrection visions) unless he had already seen (as

he thought) the Christ in his glory during his lifetime and before his death upon the Cross. The conditions which psychologists and theologians describe in order to account for Peter's resurrection vision are inadequate. Something more is needed, and that something more is the recollection, the constant memory, of the vision of the Transfiguration of the Messiah in his glory before his earthly death. (It must be understood that Harnack does not mean that there was any objective reality behind the visions. Peter was deluded, if the word is rightly to be used here, on both occasions.) Thus the Transfiguration is the root of all the stories of the risen Christ after the crucifixion and entombment. For all these visions were started by Peter's vision, and Peter's vision was started by his earlier experience. Harnack, however, always presses the fact that Peter believed that Jesus was the Messiah *before* he had any vision of him *as* the Messiah. And this recognition of Jesus as the Messiah was the result of the impression which the personality and the actions of Jesus made upon Peter (and upon others), and so this recognition of Jesus as the Messiah, depending upon the personality and deeds of Jesus, is the ' ultimate root ' of Christianity.

It seems strange that London scholars should apparently have taken little notice of Harnack's article which, like the article on ' Thou art Peter and on this rock, etc.,' whether right or wrong, is of absorbing interest. Yet when I read the two articles in the British Museum on May 14, 1926, the pages of both were uncut.

In a very interesting study of the Transfiguration story by E. Lohmeyer in *Z. N. W.*, 1922, pp. 185-214, the writer comes to conclusions very different from those of Harnack. He argues strongly for the complete independence of the two stories—Transfiguration and Resurrection. The historic character of the former he denies. It is a combination of two stories—the transfiguration itself in verse 3 ; the heavenly pronouncement with the appearance of Moses and Elijah in 4-8. This second story gives, in the form of a vision, a piece of old Christian apologetic, showing that Jesus is the Messiah who brings and consummates the Messianic Age. The Transfiguration story is hellenistic : here is a case where ' extrem jüdisches ' (in 4-8) and ' extrem heidnisches ' (3), a manifestation of a divine personage in his heavenly form, have been welded together. But I cannot say anything further about Lohmeyer's interesting essay. Certainly in spite of Harnack's brilliant arguments, it is not easy to believe that much or anything that is historic underlies the whole story.

Moffat writes : ' The twofold apologetic motive of the transfiguration story is fairly obvious : viz., to meet the objection raised by the Elijah tradition, and to explain how the crucified Jesus could be the Christ of God ' (p. 224). Mr. Rawlinson says, ' It seems likely that there may have been a basis of genuinely historical reminiscence as well.   The remark of S. Peter (verse 5) is precisely the kind of remark—half-related to the supposed situation, semi-reasonable, and yet fundamentally foolish—which might be made by a man in a dream, or in the strange, half-hypnotic condition in which men see visions (and hear voices)' (p. 118).

2.   Note ' after six days.'   In Exodus xxiv. 16 we may probably find its origin ; not in historical exactitude.   Note that Jesus takes with him Peter, James, and John as in v. 37 and in xiv. 33.   Different critics draw different conclusions.

3, 4.   Moses, like Elijah, is supposed not to have died as other men.   He is in heaven, not in Sheol.   There is an old apocalypse called the Assumption of Moses.   But there is another reason for the choice of these two men.   Their joint appearance with Jesus is to show that the great representatives of the Law and of prophecy recognize Jesus as the Messiah, and do him homage.   The possible implications of the word μετεμορφώθη are discussed and set forth by Lohmeyer.

5, 6.   Is this a later addition—an awkward attempt to give the apostles something to say ? ' It is good for us to be here ' means, it would seem, ' it is pleasant here ; it is glorious for us to be here ; let us remain.'   Or the meaning may be : ' It is well that we are here, for we can build tents for you and Moses and Elijah.'   Lohmeyer may usefully be consulted as to the exact meaning and full bearing of Peter's suggestion to ' make tents.'   For these beings from heaven ' tents ' are the fitting abode.   Lohmeyer shows why. ' Rabbi' instead of the usual Greek διδάσκαλε.   So xi. 21, xiv. 45.

6.   Some would explain that Peter and his colleagues do not understand that Jesus must die in order that the prophecies may be fulfilled.   Peter wants to see the Messiah in his glory all at once ; he does not understand the mystery of salvation through the cross. For the transfiguration is, some think, connected with the predictions of the Passion ; it justifies and explains them.   But others think that the story is not connected with the Passion predictions.   It is intended to be the divine confirmation of Peter's ' confession.' The Glory which belongs to Jesus is momentarily revealed to the disciples.   In that case the inappositeness of Peter's remark may be just that heavenly beings need no earthly tents and dwellings (Klostermann).

7.   ' Them ' is Jesus, Moses, and Elijah.   Another reading is ' him,' i.e. Jesus.   At the Baptism God had spoken only to Jesus

as to his sonship; now the disciples are also informed. It is possible that 'Son' here goes beyond 'Messiah' and means more. 'The Son' is on his way to becoming metaphysically, and then physically, connected with the Father. The cloud is the supernatural cloud which in the Pentateuch conceals and reveals the presence of God. The divine words imply that the Kingdom, the new era, has indeed begun. If the reappearance of Moses and Elijah herald its approach, in Jesus it finds its consummation: he is the Messiah. The second half of the divine words depends on Deut. xviii. 15.

8. Moses and Elijah vanish. Before the new authority, the higher revelation, Law and prophecy must yield and give place. The glory of the Christ makes the glory of Moses and the prophets disappear.

9–13. Elijah and the Son of Man

(Cp. Matt. xvii. 9–13)

9 And as they came down from the mountain, he commanded them that they should tell no man what they had seen, till the Son of man had risen from the dead.
10 And they kept the command, but among themselves they dis-
11 puted what 'rising from the dead' might mean. And they asked him, saying, 'Why do the scribes say that Elijah must come first?'
12 And he answered and told them, 'Elijah verily comes first, and puts all things in order; yet how then is it written of the Son
13 of man, that he must suffer much and be despised? But I say unto you that Elijah has come already, and they have done unto him whatsoever they wished, as it is written of him.'

9, 10 connect 11–13 not very cleverly with 2–8. Originally 11–13 appear to be connected with verse 1. In accordance with the general theory of Mark the full revelation and affirmation of the Messiahship are only to be made known after the resurrection. If even the other apostles are not to be told of the Transfiguration, that explains why no one but the Three had ever heard of it before the death of Jesus. Different deductions can be drawn from this fact according as the critic looks at the whole story. Thus Loisy says: 'To the historian the matter is as clear as day. No one before the death of Jesus had ever heard of the Transfiguration. Why? Because the story grew up out of the resurrection story; it is a product of the later tradition.' And yet Meyer is a great *historian,* and he entirely accepts the Transfiguration story as historic and ' Petrine ! ' As to the prohibition in 9 he says : ' The formulation obviously grew out of the later occurrences. But before the crucifixion the Three would certainly not have spoken about the Vision.' [Why, if there was no prohibition ?] ' But all the more will they have thought and worried about it (*grübeln*) when the execution of the Messiah seemed to ruin all their expectations ' (p. 156). According to Schmidt 11–13 is an entirely fresh section without any original connection with 2–10. Verses 9, 10 belong to the Transfiguration story from the beginning. In 11–13 the questioners may originally have been ' some people.' Or perhaps even, the questioners may originally have been the Pharisees (p. 226).

10. ' They kept the saying : ' *i.e. either* they observed the command that they were not to talk about the transfiguration, *or* they kept hold of and remembered this saying about his resurrection.

' Questioning among themselves : ' *i.e.* discussing among themselves. The apostles are made very obtuse whenever required by the theory. But Mark can hardly mean that they did not know what ' rising from the dead ' means. The words must rather be interpreted to mean that they had never heard of a Messiah who was to die and rise.

11. The question is not connected with 9 or 4, but rather with viii. 29 or ix. 1. If the Kingdom is to come so soon, how about Elijah ? For according to a Rabbinic tradition, before the Messiah arrives, and the Kingdom is established, Elijah is to appear (Malachi iv. 5, 6) and he is to restore the hearts of the fathers to the children and the heart of one man to his neighbour. (So the LXX. The Greek word is ἀποκαταστήσει, as in 12.)

12, 13. Jesus's reply is obscured by the words ' and puts all things in order,' which appear to be a confusing and useless quotation from Malachi, and by 12*b* which appear to be an awkwardly interpolated adaptation of Matt. xvii. 12*b*, where, however, the words can make sense. Here they seem out of place. If we remove these additions from Jesus's reply, it is clear and cogent enough. Yes ; Elijah was indeed to come first. But he has come already in the person of John the Baptist. John was really Elijah, who was murdered even as was foretold.

A difficulty is contained in the words ' as it is written of him.' Where is the martyrdom of *Elijah redivivus* predicted in Scriptures ? It has been suggested that the reference is to 1 Kings xix. 2, 10, or to some apocalyptic writing such as underlies Rev. xi. 6*f.*

It may be noted that in verse 12 we have the important statement that the sufferings of the Son of man (who must here equal the Messiah) are predicted in Scripture. This is the only passage in Mark in which such a prediction is alluded to. The allusion can only be to Isaiah liii. It was only gradually that this chapter assumed its christological importance. If the historic Jesus had really thought that he was not the ordinary Messiah, but the Servant of Isaiah xlii. and liii., should we not have had more allusions to, and quotations from, these chapters in the oldest Gospel? Would not Jesus himself have quoted them, and would not his citations have been remembered and chronicled? But we see in the statement that what happened to John and Jesus was all predicted the way in which the Christian community met the objections of its antagonists. It is true that neither John nor Jesus did what Elijah and the Messiah were commonly expected to do. But all happened according to the divine will, which for those who can look deeper is revealed in the Scriptures. Other explanations of the passage are given in my first edition and in the various commentaries. See also notes on Matthew.

It may be added that Burkitt, always so intensely keen to vindicate and champion the historical character of Mark, observes : ' I find it difficult to believe that Jesus never himself connected his anticipations of suffering and rejection with the figure of the " Son of man." In particular, the passage Mark ix. 9–13, so abrupt, so unliterary, so obscure in detail, however clear may be the general meaning, reads to me like reminiscences of a real conversation. I gather from it that Jesus did speak of " suffering " and of the " Son of man," and that it was by the conjunction of the two things that Peter and his companions were puzzled ' (*Christian Beginnings*, p. 33).

14–29. THE EPILEPTIC CHILD

(*Cp.* Matt. xvii. 14–20 ; Luke ix. 37–43, xvii. 5, 6)

14 And when they came to the disciples, they saw a great crowd
15 around them, and some scribes disputing with them. And straightway all the crowd, when they beheld him, were greatly amazed,
16 and running up to him, welcomed him. And he asked them, ' What
17 are ye disputing with one another ? ' And one of the crowd answered and said, ' Master, I brought unto thee my son, who is possessed by
18 a dumb spirit ; and wherever the spirit seizes him, it tears him : and he foams, and gnashes his teeth, and wastes away : and I
19 asked thy disciples to cast it out, but they could not.' Then Jesus

answered and said to them, ' O unbelieving generation, how long
shall I be with you ? how long shall I bear with you ? bring him
20 unto me.'   And they brought him unto him : and when he saw
Jesus, straightway the spirit convulsed him ; and he fell on the
21 ground, and rolled about, foaming.   And Jesus asked his father,
' How long ago is it since this has happened to him ? '   And he said,
22 ' From childhood.   And ofttimes it has thrown him into the fire,
and into the water, to destroy him : but if thou canst do anything,
23 have compassion on us, and help us.'   Jesus said unto him, ' If thou
canst, sayest thou ?   All things are possible to him that believes.'
24 And straightway the father of the child cried out, and said, ' I
25 believe ; help thou mine unbelief.'   When Jesus saw that more
people kept running up to him, he rebuked the unclean spirit,
saying unto it, ' Thou dumb and deaf spirit, I command thee, come
26 out of him, and enter no more into him.'   And the spirit shrieked,
and rent him sore, and came out of him : and he was as one dead ;
27 insomuch that many said, ' He is dead.'   But Jesus took him by the
hand, and lifted him up ; and he arose.

28   And when Jesus had gone into the house, his disciples asked
29 him privately, ' Why could not we cast it out ? '   And he said unto
them, ' This kind goes not out except by prayer [and fasting].'

The setting of the miracle seems to have been partly influenced
by the narrative in Exodus xxxii. 1-6.   The Israelites wrangle
with Aaron while Moses is still upon Mount Sinai.   If they behave ill
in the absence of Moses, the disciples, too, are helpless without their
Master.   Schmidt argues that the whole *mise en scène* of the story
' must go back to authentic tradition, and, it may be added, to correct
reminiscence and to history.'   But it does not follow that it originally belonged to its present place.   Jesus often separated himself
for a while from his disciples.   He comes back to them, and this is
what he finds.   The reading of some MSS. ἐλθών and εἶδεν may
therefore be correct.   ' He came, he saw ' (pp. 227-229).

14.   The Scribes are very out of place, and probably a later
addition.   The crowd is at hand as usual, because required.

15.   ' Amazed.'   Why ?   Some commentators say, because
Jesus arrived so suddenly and just at the appropriate moment.
But are not others justified in thinking that the wonder is rather
due to visible remnants of the Transfiguration still clinging to the
face and form of Jesus ?   *Cp.* Exodus xxxiv. 30.

16.   The usual interpretation of the verse is that Jesus asks the crowd : What are you disputing about with the disciples ?

18.   If the story has an historical basis, it is a case of epilepsy.

19.   To whom is Jesus's outburst addressed ?   Who are they who have awakened his anger ?   It is not easy to say.   The request of the father showed no incredulity : on the contrary.   Does he specially address the disciples, because their lack of faith had made them fail to cure the child ?   Would Jesus have said of them before the crowd that he longed to be quit of them ?   Or did he address himself to the crowd, either because they wanted to try the powers of the disciples without believing in them, or because they were always anxious for a miracle ?   Both the last explanations seem very strained and unlikely, and to be without any justification in the text.   On the whole, the lack of faith in the disciples seems the best explanation.   Jesus generalizes, and includes in their want of faith the whole generation of which they form a part.   The exclamation of Jesus, difficult from the point of view of actual history, is explicable from the later point of view of the Evangelist who marvels at and condemns the lack of faith which Jesus had experienced.   And the father is included in the rebuke, so far as he represents the unbelieving crowd.   In the primitive story, the incapacity of the disciples was, perhaps, explained by the especial maliciousness of the demon or the peculiar difficulty of the malady, and neither father nor crowd may have been blamed.   The words put into Jesus's mouth are doubtless intended to indicate that the ministry is drawing to a close.

23.   Note the insistence of Jesus upon the sovereign power of faith.   According to what has been said before about the lack of the disciples' faith in the powers of healing which Jesus had granted to them, the exclamation, ' If thou canst ! sayest thou ?   All is possible to him who believes,' should refer to Jesus himself.   ' I, at all events, have enough faith ; therefore I can heal.'   But this is not what Jesus means here.   He means : ' If you (the father) have enough faith, then I, Jesus, shall be able to heal your son.'

It may be noted here that the noun πίστις (faith) occurs some five times in Mark, the verb πιστεύω some ten times, while ἀπιστία occurs once, and ἄπιστος twice.   The faith which Jesus possesses and demands is trust in God and in the powers which God has given. Here, for instance, the father has to have faith that God has really granted to Jesus the power to heal (or to expel demons).   Jesus did not primarily ask for faith in his own person as such, or in his Messiahship.

It was Paul who first made this faith—faith in Christ as redeemer—
the test of salvation.   He changed, as Professor Wahrmund rightly
says, the words ' Follow me ' into ' Believe in me.'   And thus the
first significant step was taken on that road which led from inwardness to externalism, from liberty to servitude.   Jesus sat at table
with sinners and tax collectors :   in the circle of Pauline Christianity,
the question is already raised : ' What has the believer to do with
the unbeliever ? ' (*Religion und Klerikalismus*, p. 14).

24.   One cannot but be struck with the nobility of the outcry,
' help thou my unbelief ' : *i.e.*, if my belief is still not adequate, help
me to increase it.   The beseeching request to help his unbelief is
itself a confession of faith.   But it is possible that the words should
be taken to mean : ' what is wanting in my faith do thou helpingly
supply ' : *i.e.*, though I do not believe enough, nevertheless help me.

25.   ' Running up.'   Apparently this means (not that Jesus
had taken father and child apart, and that the people are running
up to them, but) that the crowd keeps becoming greater.   To put
an end to their importunity, Jesus waits no longer, but proceeds
to work the miracle.   On the other hypothesis, Jesus cures the child
before the crowd, eager to see the wonder, has arrived.   For 27 *seq.*,
cp. Chapter v. 39–42.   The one passage may have been imitated
from the other.

28.   An appendix to the story.   When Jesus gives private
explanations, we suspect that the Evangelist himself is at work.

29.   The power requisite for such healing can only be obtained
by earnest and assiduous prayer.   Some MSS. add also καὶ νηστείᾳ,
' and through fasting ' (Matt. xvii. 21).   Here the position taken up
in 23 seems changed.   It is not faith that works the miracle, or
gives the power to work it, but prayer.   To combine the two views
one would have to say that the prayer produces the faith.   But the
natural order is for the faith to produce the prayer.   The reply is
in any case obscure.   ' Does Jesus mean to reproach the disciples
with having omitted to pray, and relied instead on the mere magical
power of working miracles ? ' (Klostermann, ed. 1).   It is strange
that whereas Mark's usual view is that the Messiah has power to
evict demons, or to delegate that power, here the eviction is made
conditional upon the use of special means (Kl. ed. 2).
What are we to say of the faith preached and praised in this
story ?
It seems at first remote from us because it is so connected with
the miraculous.   We certainly do not believe that faith can work

miracles in the ordinary sense of the word ; and it seems almost impossible to believe that, through the faith of A, B, who is unaware of that faith, can be healed. We do not clearly see why, if Jesus could miraculously cure the epileptic boy, so that he never had epilepsy again, and fully and permanently recovered his speech, he could not have done so whether the father of the child believed in his miraculous powers or not. It may, however, be argued that the faith of A, who is intensely interested in the cure of B, may help C to perform it.

But we are in truth attempting the impossible in such inquiries. We can never know what measure of historical truth underlies the tale. So with regard to Peter walking on the water, we neither believe that the story happened, nor that such a thing could happen. No amount of faith that he would be able to walk on water would enable a man to do it.

But because we cannot use the sayings of Jesus about faith literally in the form in which we have them, it does not follow that they are valueless or false. The power of faith and the value of trust are still enormous. Jesus as the prophet of faith and trust has still a message to the world.

30-32. SECOND PREDICTION OF SUFFERING, DEATH, AND RESURRECTION

(*Cp*. Matt. xvii. 22, 23 ; Luke ix. 43-45)

30 And they departed thence, and passed through Galilee ; and
31 he desired that none should know it. For he taught his disciples, and said unto them, ' The Son of man will be delivered into the hands of men, and they will kill him ; and after he has been killed,
32 he will rise after three days.' But they understood not the saying, and were afraid to ask him.

The journey to Jerusalem now begins. ' Thence ' is the North, the territory of Philip, where Cæsarea Philippi was situated. Jesus ' passes through ' Galilee as quietly as he can. What he tells the disciples in 31 is made the reason. He wants to give up all his time to teaching and preparing the Twelve or the disciples for the coming Doom. But the more probably true reason, if this journey be historical, has been indicated in the notes on Chapter vi.: Jesus wants to avoid attracting the attention of Herod Antipas. Perhaps in the oldest source what is now found in ix. 1, 11, 12*a*, 13, 30, 33 were closely connected. The death predictions are repeated three times. They are inserted without any close connection with their context, nor do they refer to each other. The predictions can only in the most limited sense be historical. Is an older scholar right in thinking that Jesus's entry and action in Jerusalem, as well as his last words upon the cross, give the undoubted impression that he went to Jerusalem not to die, but to fight and conquer ? Defeat and death may have crossed his mind as a possibility, but not more than this, just as they cross the mind of a general upon the eve of battle (Pfleiderer). As to ' the third day ' the following remarks of Loisy are, perhaps, worth quoting. ' The feature of the third day was not in all probability taken from the Bible, but from the popular idea according to which the body and the soul of a dead person are definitely separated from each other at the end of three days. After this interval the resurrection would have been inconceivable ; before it the actual death might have seemed doubtful. Faith in the resurrection of Jesus did not become assured till some time after his death, and it is probable that not a single one of his disciples had the least idea of it three days after the crucifixion. But it is easy to perceive that the first need for the acquired belief in the resurrection was to fix the time when Jesus had ceased to be dead and had become immortal. The number of three days imposed itself, but tradition seems to have hesitated for some while as to how the number was to be applied. Was it after being dead three days or on the third day after his death that Jesus returned to life ? According to the first hypothesis, the story of Jonah and the whale could be regarded as a typological prophecy of that which God was going to do for the Messiah. According to the second, a passage from Hosea (vi. 1) offered a basis for argument. The fixing of Sunday, the second day after the death, as the day of the resurrection does not seem to have its origin either in a traditional reminiscence or in a biblical text, but in the custom which, from very early times, used the first day of the week as the day for Christian reunions and the day of the Messiah. This custom itself got its use, not perhaps only from the fact that the first believers were induced to choose for their meetings the first free day after the Sabbath, but from the fact that the day of the Sun became as it were quite naturally the day of the Saviour for those Christians who had just come over from paganism. Thus may be explained the singular anomaly of the Gospel narratives declaring that Jesus rose on the *second* day after his death, and yet wishing to find therein the fulfilment of predictions which placed the resurrection at the end of three days' (*E. S.* 1. p. 177).

32. The disciples, as usual, are obtuse. In ix. 11 they ask questions ; here they are represented as afraid to do so.

33–50.   Who is the Greatest ?—Of Service, Stumblingblocks and other Matters

(*Cp.* Matt. xviii. 1–9 ; Luke ix. 46–50, xvii. 1, 2)

33   And they came to Capernaum : and when he was in the house,
he asked them, ' What did ye discuss among yourselves on the way ? '
34 But they held their peace : for on the way they had argued among
35 themselves who was the greatest.   And he sat down, and called the
Twelve, and said unto them, ' If any man desire to be first, let him
36 be last of all, and servant of all.'   And he took a child, and set him
in the midst of them : and he embraced him, and said unto them,
37 ' Whoever shall receive one of these children in my name, receives
me : and whoever receives me, receives not me, but Him that
sent me.'

38   And John said to him, ' Master, we saw one casting out demons
in thy name : and we sought to prevent him, because he did not
39 follow us.'   But Jesus said, ' Prevent him not : for no man who
40 does a miracle in my name, will readily speak evil of me.   For he
41 that is not against us is for us.   For whoever shall give you a cup
of water to drink because ye belong to Christ, verily I say unto you,
42 he shall not lose his reward.   And whoever shall cause one of these
little ones that believe to stumble, it were better for him that a
millstone were hanged about his neck, and he were cast into the
43 sea.   And if thy hand cause thee to stumble, cut it off : it is better
for thee to enter into Life maimed, than having two hands to go
45 into hell, into the fire that shall never be quenched.   And if thy
foot cause thee to stumble, cut it off : it is better for thee to enter
47 lame into Life, than having two feet to be cast into hell.   And if
thine eye cause thee to stumble, pluck it out : it is better for thee
to enter into the kingdom of God with one eye, than having two
48 eyes to be cast into hell : where their worm dies not, and the fire
49, 50 is not quenched.   For every one shall be salted with fire.   Salt is
good : but if the salt have lost its saltness, wherewith will ye season
it ?   Have salt in yourselves, and keep peace with one another.'

A very complicated section raising many interesting critical
problems which have been, and can be, dealt with in many ways ;
it is, however, impossible for me to deal with these problems.   Some
of the sayings here collected occur more than once, and have more

than one setting, in the Gospels, and some may have been altered in their wording from their original form.

The section can be split up into three or four sub-divisions, but these are not clearly indicated. We may mark off 33–37, 38–41, 42–48, 49–50. There is a certain parallelism between 33–37 on the one hand, and x. 35–45 and x. 13–16 on the other. The lesson given in ix. 35 is almost verbally the same as that given in x. 43, 44, and it has therefore been inferred, with much probability, that different settings have been given by Mark to one and the same saying which he has taken from his source. Again, the incident with the children is twice repeated. It occurs in ix. 36 and x. 16. Doubtless it is one and the same incident which has suggested both forms of the story. The occasion and setting of the lesson given in ix. 35 and x. 42 may have been a single incident which the Evangelist has doubled.

33. Is Capernaum in place here ? See Schmidt (p. 230). ' The house ' ; is this Peter's house, or is it the editorial house, as one might almost say, ready to hand for private discussions between Jesus and the disciples ? The saying in 35 was originally, in much probability, older than its setting, and independent of it.

34. ' Who was the greatest ? ' But the words may mean not greatest now, but who *will* be greatest in the Kingdom. So Matthew (xviii. 1), and, what is very important, so the S.S. *Cp.* also, for the wording, Luke xxii. 24, which may be the original form of the opening of the story. *Cp.* Mark x. 43, 44.

35. ' He called the Twelve.' This would appear to be a later editorial insertion. In 33 Jesus is indoors with his disciples. Why need he ' call the Twelve ' ? Yet there seems no distinction to be made between the Twelve and those disciples who have been mentioned in 33. To Mark ' the disciples ' are the Twelve (Bultmann, p. 210).

Jesus is here supposed to read the hearts of the disciples. He knows about what they have been talking. In Matthew the disciples directly ask him the question, which is more natural.

The great saying on Service does not occur in the parallel passages in Matthew or Luke. In Mark it is repeated in x. 43, 44 in another connection where Matthew has it also. In Luke it occurs in still another connection in xxii. 26. There is no reason why it should not have been a favourite saying with Jesus, or why he should not have used it on many occasions and with different incitements. It occurs yet another time in Matthew xxiii. 11.

True greatness is service : service is true greatness. And not merely service, but humble service. In the eyes of God the humblest may be the greatest. The servant of all and last of all may be in truth the first of all. A grand paradox. In such simple and yet profound sayings is, perhaps, best reflected the ethical teaching of the historic Jesus. The saying about Service is apparently new. The Rabbis were never weary of preaching humility and its greatness. In that there is nothing new. But the combination of humility with *service* would seem to be new. Lovingkindness, the doing of deeds of charity and love (*gemiluth chesadim*), are indeed familiar enough in the Rabbinical literature. But I do not think I am wrong in supposing that this touch of eager personal service, especially towards the sinner and the outcast, was a special character-istic of the religion of Jesus, and a new thing when he preached it.

More generally, I might here observe that it is hard to see why the finest and most original sayings which are attributed to Jesus do not represent ethical and religious gains to be fitly added to the great ethical and religious stores in the Old Testament. And even if it could be shown that all the great sayings of Jesus were verbally and textually contained in the Talmud, it might still be justly argued that the lack of familiarity with the New Testament is a loss to the Jews. For most Jews do not know the Talmud. Their religious literature is usually confined to the Old Testament and the Prayer-book. And in the huge bulk of the Talmud the great passages are overwhelmed and lost to view by the mass of second-class matter. Moreover, no collection of Rabbinical sayings that I am acquainted with can quite rival the sayings of Jesus in im-pressiveness, profundity, and power. To have been familiar with them from childhood must surely be an important ethical and religious asset in people's lives. To the Christian—even to the Unitarian Christian—the teaching of Jesus can never be separated from the life and the personality of Jesus. The two form a whole. We are constantly told that the teaching is almost as nothing if kept, or looked at, apart from him who gave the teaching. The Jew, however, is bound to make this separation. It is not that he doubts the ' historicity ' of Jesus. The Jew who doubts that is as foolish as the non-Jew who doubts it. Nor need he be wanting in admiration for the character and personality of Jesus, so far as they can be discerned through the mists of legend, of miracle, of exiguous report, of calculated hero-worship and exaggeration. What looms through these mists is noble, original, and great. Nevertheless, as he keeps his head cool, and refuses to worship any man, to call any man his Master, or to believe that any man was perfection, the Jew can no more refuse, and is no more unable, to distinguish between teaching, on the one hand, and character and personality, upon the other, than in the case of any other prophet or ' rabbi.' Even if Jesus had never existed, the teaching would still be there ; the words attributed to Jesus are for the Jew—just otherwise than for the Christian—much more important than the life. Of the life little is known, besides its noble and pathetic close, besides the one great act of heroism and sacrifice at its conclusion. But of the teaching a good deal is known, and it may even be said that the noblest and fairest elements in the teaching are also, on the whole, those which there is most reason to regard as authentic. Not that the value of any bit of teaching is diminished if it is editorial, or the product of the ' Urgemeinde ' and not of the Master. Nevertheless, in its most characteristic and highest flights, the teaching probably proceeds not merely from the inspiration of Jesus, but from Jesus himself. And it is with that teaching that I am here primarily concerned.

36, 37. The connection of 37 with 35 is artificial. For what 36 and 37 say is how others are to be treated by the disciples, not how they are themselves to behave. The child is not here a type of humility and ' Anspruchslosigkeit ' (as in x. 15), but the type of the poor and the simple who are to be welcomed and served in the name of Christ. A forced connection of 37 with 35 is to say that the servant of all, who is the greatest of all, is also he who receives the smallest and humblest for the sake of Christ.

36. The child incident is more naturally given in x. 13–16. Here it may be an editorial introduction to 37.

37. In 37 reference is made to a deed of kindness to a child ; in 41 to a deed of kindness to the apostles or disciples ; in 42 to a deed of unkindness to ' little ' or humble believers ; in Matt. x. 40 to deeds of kindness to the disciples ; in Matt. x. 42 to deeds of kindness to ' little ones.' In Matt. xviii. 5 and Luke ix. 48 we have once more the child. It would appear as if the children were primary. The kindness shown to a little needy child is equivalent to a kindness shown to Jesus or to God. That charity shown to man is reckoned by God as if it were done to Himself is quite a Rabbinic sentiment. The children were subsequently turned into the disciples or into lowly members of the Christian community.

  ' In my name.' Added by Mark. Not in Matt. x. 40. Are the words a translation of the Hebrew idiom, meaning ' for my sake ' ? Or do they mean : ' because I desire it,' ' as a part of Christian duty ' ? Or do they mean ' invoking my name,' ' calling upon my name ' ? (Those who wish to pursue the subject further should read Heitmüller's excellent book, *Im Namen Jesu*.)

  ' Receives me.' If the service is done for the sake of the Master, and because he desired it, it is reckoned as if it had been done to the Master himself. The dynamic effect of this saying has been enormous. All social service wrought in Christ's name and spirit is wrought to him. Who can measure or count the deeds of sacrifice and love to which this saying has prompted ?

' Him that sent me.' What are we to make of this ? Is it part of a unique self-assurance in Jesus, part of his consciousness that he was a superior being, the Messiah, the Son of God, perhaps himself divine ? There seems no absolute necessity for this. Isaiah, no less than Jesus, believed that God had ' sent ' him. Doubtless Jesus believed that he was sent by God, and he probably held that he was the Messiah. Yet the saying, which Mark records, ' Why callest thou me good ? Only God is good,' shows that he did not ascribe to himself a sinless pre-eminence of perfection. Social service is the right service of the Messiah, and it is also the right service of God. If Jesus said this verse, I would venture to think that he did not mean that *any* service rendered to himself was a service rendered to God, but rather that the *service of the poor* was service both to himself *and* to God.

' Receive.' In what sense is the word used ?

The literal meaning need not be pressed. To receive the child may mean to serve it, to show it kindness. But in what sense can Jesus himself be ' received ' ? In what sense can God be ' received ' ?

Do the words mean more than that a good deed done for the sake of Jesus is like a good deed done to him, and that a good deed done for him is like a good deed done to God ?

But the use of the word ' receive ' suggests mystical meanings. The indwelling spirit of Christ or of God may be said to be ' received ' through goodness, self-sacrifice, and love. God and Christ may both be said to ' dwell ' in man or be united with man. If the verse occurred in the fourth Gospel, that would be its meaning, but it is scarcely likely that this mystical meaning is the correct interpretation of a passage in Mark. In Matthew x. 40 ' receive ' would seem to have even a literal meaning, for it would refer to showing hospitality to the apostles in their missionary journey.

38-40. These three verses appear to be intercalated and to break the connection. Why they were here inserted is hard to say. Perhaps they were hung on to 37 because of the words ' in my name ' occurring in both. But note that ' in my name ' means in 38 and 39 something very different from what it meant in 37, if in 37 it meant ' for my sake.' In 38 and 39 it means merely the utterance of the actual name, as part of an exorcist's formula. It has here its old and regular meaning of ' invoking the name by saying it aloud.' The ' name ' of Jesus was believed to possess as strong a power in protection or exorcism as the name of God.   There is no difference in meaning between the two different Greek prepositions in 38 and 39.

The situation suggested by 38 could hardly have happened in Jesus's lifetime.   It reflects a later age, when the reputation of the Christian community was great enough to tempt outsiders to try their fortune as exorcists by using the name of Christ.   Such people are not to be checked ;   perhaps one thing may lead to another, and they may become full members of the new brotherhood.   (*Cp.* the story of Eldad and Medad in Numbers xi. 26–29.) The statement that a man, who is no disciple of Jesus, nevertheless exorcises demons by the name of Jesus, is extremely peculiar and interesting.   We are intended to suppose that the exorcisms were successful.   The ' name ' is enough.   It has a magical force, and compels the demons to yield to its power.

Whatever the first meaning and origin of the saying, ' He who is not against us is for us,' it was soon capable of extended applications.   It can, indeed, be used for most broad and liberal interpretations.   Swete says :   ' The man who is not a declared enemy of the Christian brotherhood may be provisionally regarded as a friend.'   And one can go further still.   The man who is in sympathy with the fundamental teaching of Jesus is his true follower, whether he acknowledges him or no.   Or again :   all men who love goodness and God belong to the same religion and are allies in the same cause. Professor Turner regards 42 as closely connected with 37.   Mark has ' interwoven with one another sayings originally independent, though very probably belonging to the same cycle of teaching.' 38–41 form a sort of parenthesis.

In 40 Wellhausen accepts the reading of D, namely ' you ' for ' us.'   The passage really reflects the earliest apostolic age.   Those who exorcise demons in the name of Jesus are not to be regarded as heretics, even though they do not accept the full authority of the Twelve.   Professor Turner objects to any doubt being cast upon the authenticity of the whole passage, but his arguments seem inconclusive.   That Jesus ' contemplated preaching in his name after his death ' is doubtful.   There is nothing improbable or unlikely in the assumption that many a saying attributed to Jesus is later than Jesus.   If in itself any saying is more likely to be later than Jesus, its mere attribution to Jesus is of no great counter importance (*J. T. S.*, 1925, Vol. xxvi. p. 152).

41.   This verse would appear to connect with 37.   According to the hypothesis mentioned above, ' you ' is not original. ' Children ', or indigent, humble people would be original.

' Because ye belong to Christ ' would be a late explanation of ' in my name.'   *Cp.* 1 Cor. iii. 23.   Matthew has ' in the name of a disciple,' which means the same thing : ' he who does the loving deed for my sake, and because he is doing it to a Christian.'

42. This verse seems connected with 37. Originally children were probably referred to, and τῶν πιστευόντων is an editorial gloss. *Cp.* Matt. xviii. 10. It is not quite easy to say what to cause a child to stumble, or to cause little ones, humble ones, to stumble, originally meant. Are we to suppose that it meant to injure the innocence of children, to lead them astray ? Did it mean merely to do them some unkindness, *not* to help them in trouble or difficulty or poverty ? It is perhaps partly the perplexity of deciding what ' scandalizing ' as applied to children meant (without giving it too *modern* an interpretation) which has induced many commentators to hold that Mark's addition ' that believe ' is a correct explanation. Humble believers *they* think were referred to even originally. But Luke xvii. 2 has only ' one of these little ones.' Matthew (xviii. 6) has ' one of these little ones who believe in me,' which is perhaps earlier than Mark's version, for the absolute use of ' believe ' to mean the Christian believer is secondary and late.

σκάνδαλα and σκανδαλίζειν are expressive words, for which, as Wellhausen points out (on Matt. xiii. 41), there is no precise German (or English) equivalent. ' Cause to stumble,' ' seduce,' etc., are none of them quite satisfactory renderings for the verb, nor will ' stumbling-block ' do well for the noun.

To seduce others from their faith is the greatest of sins. The Rabbis thought the same. To them Jeroboam was the type of the greatest sinner, because he not only did evil himself, but ' caused Israel to sin.'

43–47. These verses are mechanically added on to 42 because of the catch-word σκανδαλίζειν, but deal with quite a different subject. The temptations here referred to are not brought to others, but occur, through the weakness of the flesh, to oneself. These verses occur in the Sermon on the Mount (Matt. v. 29, 30) as well as in Matt. xviii. 8, 9.

The advice which Jesus here gives is clearly not to be taken literally. But the form of the maxims rests upon the conception —still widely prevalent—that in the life of the resurrection a man's outward form will be the same as that which he had when he died. If you die with one eye, you will only have one eye when you ' rise.'

The term ' life ' is used as equivalent to the ' Kingdom of God.' It has a somewhat late look used thus absolutely : the term is not used in Matt. v. 29, 30, though we find it in Matt. vii. 14, where it is, however, used in contrast to ' destruction.' ' The fire that shall never be quenched' seems added as an explanation of 'Gehenna.'

The 'life,' and therefore the Kingdom, are thus regarded as future, not present. When were the hearers of these maxims supposed to enter the Kingdom ? Apparently after death, at the resurrection, when Jesus in his risen glory appearing upon earth again, would admit the good into the full beatitude of the perfected Kingdom, and send the bad to everlasting hell.

The advice which Jesus here gives is that we are not to provoke danger and call it forth. Far better to nip it in the bud, and to pray, 'Lead us not into temptation.' The word 'Gehenna' only occurs here in Mark. For the origin and Rabbinical use of the word see *Jewish Encyclopædia.*

48. The reference is to Isaiah lxvi. 24. The worm is the decomposed body, which is to continue to feel pain, and to be burned with constant fire. The quotation, wanting in Matthew, seems to be added here only in order to make a verbal connection for the following verse. 'The reference here is to an eternal fire ; whether eternal pain for the condemned is thought of as connected therewith is uncertain.' So J. Weiss, who adds, 'This is the foundation passage (*Grundstelle*) for the doctrine of the everlasting pains of hell, a doctrine which is, indeed, consonant with the outward Jewish dogma of retribution, but not with the gospel of the God whose nature is love.' Yet Christianity has made much greater use of the doctrine than Judaism, and Judaism has freed itself from it more easily and completely than Christianity. The doctrine of divine forgiveness is so fundamentally Jewish that it was quite easy for Judaism to see that the doctrine of eternal punishment was in flagrant violation of its own clearest and chiefest teaching. It is amusing to think that from the Jewish pulpit, under which I sat for many years, the doctrine of eternal punishment and eternal pain was habitually referred to as characteristically Christian. So apt are we to attribute opinions which we dislike to our neighbours ! It is needless to tell my Jewish readers that J. Weiss's words are merely the product of prejudice. His scholarship is, I hope, reflected in what follows, which I trust is true, though I feel very doubtful. 'Happily,' he says, 'it is very unlikely that Jesus himself gave any occasion (*Anlass*) to this horrible doctrine. For the judgment of fire, according to Jesus, is a rapid process, which leads to annihilation. In the Judgment it is a question of *death* or of life.'

If 43–49 and Matt. x. 28 were reported as the saying of any other man in the world except Jesus, should we find a sober and highly intellectual commentator observing about them that they leave 'the whole question of the fate of the wicked absolutely open' (Bacon *Gospel Story*, p. 136). But Jesus must be cleared of unpleasing doctrines at all cost !

49. Many attempts have been made to connect 49 with the preceding passages, but they have not been very successful. The 'eternal fire' seems to have suggested the idea of purification by another sort of fire. 'The salt and fire are both divine.' So Coleman (see on 50). The Holy Spirit will purify as by fire.

The verse has been taken to mean that everyone, or every disciple, must be purified by the fire of tribulation. But this seems somewhat strained. Loisy takes it to be a sort of false connecting link between 48 and 50, and to refer to the final crisis of the world, the universal conflagration, in which the wicked would perish, but which the just would pass through purified and unharmed (*E. S.* II. p. 84). Many MSS. add : 'And every sacrifice shall be salted with salt,' which seems to mean '*just as* every sacrifice is purified (salted) by salt.'

50. This verse, again, seems merely outwardly hung on to 49. Indeed, the two halves of it seem to have been originally independent. For the first half *cp.* Matt. v. 13 ; Luke xiv. 34. The salt in Mark, as in Matthew and Luke, is meant to be the disciples. They are to season and purify the world. If the purifying condiment has lost its purifying quality, its environment cannot freshly season or purify it. The hope of the world lies in the disciples : if they become proud and impure, who can make them pure and humble ?

The second half of the verse uses the metaphor in a different way. The disciples themselves are not salt (as towards the world), but they are to *have* salt in themselves, and to be at peace one with another. This may mean, perhaps, that they are to be pure and humble, uncontaminated by the soilure of the world. But perhaps it means that they are not to quarrel, the end of the long section returning to the subject with which it opened (33). There is a very interesting article on these two verses in *J. T. S.*, 1923, XXIV., pp. 381–396, by N. D. Coleman. He thinks that in 50*a* ἅλας means salted fish or salted food, and that the passage should be translated : 'Salted food is excellent. But if the salted food loses its saltness how shall you season it ? ' You are led to infer that you may just as well throw it to dogs or cast it into the fire as try to pickle it again. See also the article on ' The Salt of the Earth,' *J. T. S.*, 1924, XXV. pp. 167–172, by W. S. Wood, which freely admits the great difficulty of the ' salt ' sayings.

CHAPTER X

1–12. Of Divorce

(*Cp*. Matt. xix. 1–12)

1   And he arose from thence, and came into the district of Judæa beyond the Jordan : and crowds collected unto him again ; and he taught them again, as he was wont.

2   And the Pharisees came and asked him, in order to test him : 3 ' May a man divorce his wife ? '   And he answered and said unto 4 them, ' What did Moses command you ? '   And they said, ' Moses permitted him to write a bill of divorce, and to send her away.' 5 And Jesus said unto them, ' To suit the hardness of your hearts 6 he wrote you this precept.   But from the beginning of the creation, 7 He made them male and female : therefore shall a man leave his 8 father and mother, and cleave to his wife ; and they two shall be 9 one flesh : so then they are no more two, but one flesh.   What therefore God has joined together, let not man separate.'

10   And in the house his disciples asked him again about this matter. 11 And he said unto them, ' Whoever divorces his wife, and marries 12 another, commits adultery against her.   And if the woman divorce her husband, and marry another, she commits adultery.'

A very important section which has had far-reaching social and ethical consequences for good and happiness, but also in some measure for trouble, perhaps even for evil.

Jesus in his prophetic rôle has opposed the teaching of the Rabbis as regards certain features of Sabbath observance, as regards conceptions of clean and unclean.   He has probably come near to an antagonism to Pentateuchal ordinances in his attitude towards the dietary laws.   Now he is apparently to come into conflict with both Rabbinic and Pentateuchal law in his attitude to divorce.

The Pentateuchal and Rabbinic laws about divorce depend upon Oriental conceptions of marriage and women, which are very different from our own. Rabbinic divorce moves within those Oriental conceptions, but provides many safeguards for the protection of the woman. How far divorce was of frequent occurrence in the first century it is impossible to say. For a very temperate statement of the whole matter the reader is earnestly recommended to peruse chapter ix. (pp. 66–78) in Dr. Abrahams' *Studies* (first series).

Rabbinic divorce, however mitigated in practice and in theory, rested upon two fundamental improprieties. (*a*) Divorce was the act of the man. Though the woman in certain circumstances could claim it, her claim, if the man was obstinately contumacious, could not be enforced. In the last resort, the man could divorce his wife ; the woman could not divorce her husband. Thus Rabbinic divorce rests upon inequality. The man has a power which the woman has not. Whether Jesus felt and attacked this inequality, this inferiority of the woman to the man is not entirely certain.

(*b*) But what did obviously arouse the antagonism of Jesus was the second impropriety. A man could divorce his wife, according to Rabbinic law, for many reasons over and above infidelity. The Rabbinic law starts from Deut. xxiv. 1. It is doubtful what this verse precisely means. What is the ' unseemly thing ' which, if a man find in his wife, he may divorce her ? In the first century there was a dispute about the matter. ' The schools of Hillel and Shammai,' says Dr. Abrahams, ' differed materially ; the former gave the husband the legal right to divorce his wife for any cause. . . . The school of Shammai limited the right to the case in which the wife was unchaste. The " schools " or " houses " of Hillel and Shammai belong to the first century. It is uncertain whether this particular difference of opinion on divorce goes back to Hillel and Shammai themselves, and thus to the very beginning of the Christian era ' (*Studies*, p. 71). Most unfortunately the school of Hillel carried the day, and Rabbinic practice and law followed it, and so the matter has remained even unto the present day. Orientalisms— as we may call them—as regards its laws about women and divorce still remain a sore spot in orthodox Judaism. Fast bound in the bondage of a code, from which it cannot shake itself free without losing its own identity, orthodox Judaism (like other ' orthodox ' creeds) is in a difficult and unenviable position. On the other hand, it is a remarkable fact that, both in ancient and modern orthodox Judaism, woman has usually received a high place of honour. It has been held that the duties of wifehood and motherhood were in themselves sanctioned and sanctified by God, and thus rightly dispensed a woman from many ritual enactments. Her place within the family has always been high and revered. ' Comparisons are odious,' but it is pretty certain that among the very poor the Jewish woman is not less honoured in her home than is her Gentile neighbour in hers. So true it is, as Dr. Abrahams has said, that ' Judaism is the great upsetter of the probable. Analyse a tendency of Judaism, and predict its logical consequences, and then look in Judaism for consequences quite other than these.' [This quotation is from the author's remarkable little book, *Judaism* (Constable, 1910), p. 69.]

In his antagonism to the divorce laws of his environment, Jesus went, perhaps, to the other extreme, and took up the view that divorce should be forbidden altogether. If he only meant, as some would now suppose, that in an ideal society there would be no divorce, his teaching did not go beyond the best Rabbinic teaching. ' " I hate divorce, says the Lord " (Mal. ii. 16) was a verse much honoured in Pharisaic thought, and Malachi's protest gave rise to the pathetic saying : " The very altar sheds tears when a man divorces the wife of his youth," and to the sterner paraphrase, " He that puts her away is hated of the Lord " ' (*Studies*, p. 69). But it is not impossible that he meant more. How far the debate in Mark goes back to him, and how far it reflects the position and conflicts of the young community, recalling as best they can the teaching of the Master, is uncertain. The version in Matthew of the discussion differs materially from that in Mark, and more closely reflects the actual question at issue between the two Rabbinic parties. For in Mark, the question is asked quite generally, May a man divorce his wife ? In Matthew, the question is, May a man divorce her for any cause ? (In other words, does Jesus side with the Hillelites or with the Shammaites ?)

There is one interpretation of Mark according to which the difference between his version and that of Matthew's is overcome. It assumes that Jesus did not mean to say that, even if a woman had committed adultery, she must not be divorced, and that in the lifetime of that guilty woman the guiltless husband must never marry again. It supposes that adultery was not in question. For though the ' school ' of Shammai held that unchastity ought to be the only ground for divorce, there is no reason to suppose that the ordinary custom and law from the earliest period onwards had not been in accordance with the opinion of the ' school ' of Hillel, namely, that a man was able to send his wife away for a number of reasons unconnected with unchastity. Adultery was a separate affair, which was not dealt with by anything so mild as a mere bill of divorce. The penalty of adultery was death. The reply of Jesus in 10–12 refers to all other causes for divorce except adultery. So Wellhausen. But Dr. Abrahams shows that the death penalty for adultery ' can never have been frequently enforced.' It was hedged round with difficulty to start with, for it needed eyewitnesses of the very act. And for this and other reasons the question whether

Mark and Matthew do, or do not, seriously differ is still uncertain. If we take 2–9 by themselves, and without 10–12, as we have a right to do (for those three verses are clearly an addition, though they may rest upon an authentic saying), it is impossible to say how far they are intended to go. Do the last words mean : ' Let not man lightly separate. Let not man separate for any reason of his own ' ? It may be held that in the case of adultery, the union has *ipso facto* been dissolved. The woman has broken the union. The man has not ' sent away,' or separated himself from, the wife. The wife has, by her own act, separated herself from the husband. The question remains obscure.

1. ' He arose from thence,' *i.e.* from Capernaum. See ix. 33. It is assumed that a period has just elapsed during which Jesus had withdrawn himself from the people. He now resumes his public teaching. But he finally leaves Galilee. Prof. Bennett says : ' Jesus left Galilee, and crossing the Jordan came to the eastern districts opposite Judæa. He now felt safer than in Galilee. The eastern borderlands were less settled : the population was largely of Gentiles, and was more directly under the government of Rome. There was less opportunity for official persecution or popular fanaticism, and the desert offered a refuge from danger. Hence Jesus resumed his public ministry ' (p. 144).

Some think that the καὶ after Ἰουδαίας should probably be omitted. So in the MS. D, in the S.S., and in the parallel verse in Matthew. Peræa would thus be described as ' the Judæan land beyond Jordan.' Others think that Jesus preached first in Judæa, then in ' Peræa,' whence he made his way to Jerusalem for the Passover.

2. ' The Pharisees.' To hand as usual. But in the MS. D and in the Sinaitic Syriac (S.S.) they are omitted. But see also Schmidt, p. 240.

' In order to test him.' What does this mean ? Was the question asked because the answer was anticipated ? Did the questioners anticipate that Jesus, the austere moral preacher, would say something definitely against the Law ? Or did the conversation arise from no such intention, but casually ? The words ' testing him ' *may* mean no more than that they wanted to see what attitude he would take up on a difficult and disputed subject. A test ; not a temptation. But if the question, as *Mark* suggests, was about divorce generally, and not about the *reasons* for divorce, as in Matthew, the second explanation is less likely.

3. The version of the debate in Matthew may have been merely

altered from Mark without other authority, but it has, some think, much more verisimilitude.   They argue that it was very unlikely—unless we assume that unusual teaching from Jesus as to women had become known and bruited about—that anybody would have asked the question as Mark has it : ' May a man divorce his wife ? ' It was quite likely that they would ask Jesus which line he took as to the point at issue between the two rival ' schools.'   Moreover, the debate as constructed in Mark is considered by some to be very improbable.   It is unnatural that Jesus would have replied as he is made to reply in 3.   Verses 3 and 4 should both belong, as is practically the case in Matthew, to the questioners.   It is too subtle to suppose that Jesus was deliberately leading the Pharisees, or whoever the questioners were, into a trap, and that he intended to defeat Moses by Moses—that he was thinking all the time of the passage in Genesis by which to overthrow the passage in Deuteronomy.

The question whether Mark is more original than Matthew in this divorce section is exceedingly difficult.   It depends on a variety of disputed points.   The student should by all means read Dr. Charles's vehement pleading in his little book, *The Teaching of the New Testament on Divorce* (1921), and the reply by Dr. Box and Dr. Gore, *Divorce in the New Testament* (1921).

A good deal turns on the meaning of πειράζοντες.   If it means nothing more than ' testing,' then that is so much in favour of the view, so vigorously championed by Dr. Charles, that the version in Matthew is more primary and more historical.   The questioners are anxious to know what line Jesus takes upon an important matter in dispute between the followers of Hillel and of Shammai. Does he adhere to the strict view of Shammai or to the lax view of Hillel ?   And then, even though Matthew's famous qualification μὴ ἐπὶ πορνείᾳ be an admitted addition and gloss, yet Dr. Charles and others may be right in holding that adultery was not in question. In adultery the woman herself has broken the bond : it is not the husband who does so by divorcing her ; it is not the court who does so by sanctioning the divorce.   These but confirm what the woman has already done.   The marriage bond has been broken by her, and divorce follows automatically.   But where the woman has not broken the bond by infidelity, there it remains as a divine bond, and no man, whether the husband or another, has the right to break it. Jesus would range himself with the Shammaites, though for a higher reason.   He does not base his view upon an interpretation of Deut. xxiv. 1, but upon the higher and more fundamental principle of marriage contained in Genesis.

If, however, πειράζοντες means something more than merely ' testing,' if the questioners ask in order to make Jesus say something against the Law, if the 'testing' is a sort of temptation, then Mark's version becomes *pro tanto* more probable than Matthew's. One would then have to suppose, with Klostermann, that the Pharisees anticipated that this severe teacher, who took so strong a line on many moral questions, would probably disapprove of the law in Deuteronomy, which made concessions to the weakness of human nature. For if it is a temptation, this is the only way in which the question can be interpreted. Whether Jesus sided with Hillel or with Shammai could not be a 'temptation.' It would not have been dangerous for Jesus to have expressed approval with either one or the other. The only danger or trap was to get into a conflict with the Law. And this is what the Pharisees hope to bring about.

The next trouble is as to the condition of affairs among the Jews, in the period of Jesus's ministry, about adultery. If it could be shown that every proved adulteress was always put to death, then Dr. Charles's view would at once be established. For then obviously the only question would be as regards divorce for something less than adultery—as regards the power of *free* divorce according to a man's pleasure. Adultery would settle itself! But we have seen that, in any case, adultery was only punishable by death when there were eyewitnesses, when the woman was caught in the very act. And Dr. Abrahams holds that 'there is no doubt that the death penalty was neither pronounced nor inflicted for adultery in the time of Christ.' If that be so, the question whether adultery on the woman's part should be followed by her divorce was still a possible one. The Jewish law as codified in the Mishnah compelled the husband to divorce his guilty wife. Did Jesus sanction this law, or cancel and disapprove of it? According to Mark, if πειράζοντες means 'tempting,' it would seem that he denounced it, and condemned all divorce absolutely. Those who uphold the priority and the accuracy of the Mark version, and interpret it, not as Wellhausen and Charles do, but as forbidding all divorce, have also a reply to the objections made above in verse 3. Jesus, 'by his supernatural knowledge' (Klostermann), but quite possibly by his human quick intelligence, sees the object of the question. He takes the bull by the horns, and himself asks about, and brings in, Moses and the Law. Nor can it be said that Moses did not 'command,' but only 'suffered' or 'permitted.' For the permission is a command in the sense of a 'law.' The question put by Jesus is merely an equivalent to: 'What is the Mosaic Law?' 'What is the Pentateuchal law upon the subject of Divorce?' Dr. Charles's bright pages (pp. 87–89) about the antithesis between command and permission, and the suitability and propriety of the words as allocated to Pharisees and Jesus in Matthew's

version, and their unsuitability and impropriety in Mark's version,
are hardly convincing. ' What is the Law of Moses ? ' asks Jesus
boldly. The Law of Moses is that divorce is permitted, is the reply.
Then Jesus argues that this law was a mere (temporary) concession,
and is contradicted, and now by him superseded and abrogated,
by the higher and older law of Genesis. One cannot deny that, so
interpreted, the passage reads connectedly and logically. But it
is impossible to come to any firm conclusion. The arguments are
too well balanced. It is noticeable that the interpretation of Deut.
xxiv. 1 is never in question. The words in dispute in that verse
are not quoted. This omission seems to me a further argument
pro tanto on the side of those who think that Jesus objected to all
divorce, even for adultery. For it is not said : ' What does the
unseemly thing mean ? ' This is not said even in Matthew. The
words used are just the mere general statement : ' Moses permitted
him to write a bill of divorce and to send her away.' If the question
had been : ' Should divorce be permitted when there is no adultery,
why should not Jesus have said that, in addition to the statement
in Genesis, the law in Deuteronomy is no less emphatic (Shammai's
line), and that there is no contradiction between them ? Both
would (in this hypothesis) really assert that where the woman herself does not break the bond by her own unchastity, the bond can
be broken by no man and by no number of men. See also notes
on Matthew.

5. As the discussion stands we have to suppose that the expected reply having been given to his question, Jesus then proceeds
to state that the ' command ' in Deuteronomy was only given in
view of the Israelite ' hardness of heart.' ' σκληρός [here] means
hard, in the sense of *rough* or *coarse*, rather than *unimpressible*.
καρδία is the common word for the inner man generally in the New
Testament. The whole word [σκληροκαρδία, ' hardness of heart ']
denotes the rude nature which belongs to a primitive civilisation '
(Gould).

The Mosaic law was in certain cases a kind of second best. The
highest law could not, or would not, have been obeyed. So there
was a concession made to human weakness or ' hardness.' The
divorce enactment was not a law, but a dispensation. This is a
fine interpretation of much of the Mosaic law, and may be compared
with Maimonides's view of sacrifice. Both are equally unhistorical,
though, from a sort of universal or world-historic point of view,
one can see that Jesus was in the right.

6. ' But from the beginning of the creation, male and female
made he them.' So R.V., literally. Klostermann says we must

translate, ' but at the beginning of the creation ' (story, he wrote),
' male and female made He them,' *i.e.* Moses wrote so.   And it is
true that the correction of Moses by Moses would come out more
clearly if we might render : ' In the beginning of Genesis (Moses
wrote) : Male and female created He them.'   In any case Jesus cites
Genesis to overthrow the law of Deuteronomy.   The fundamental
law of marriage was not, he holds, destroyed by the dispensation of
divorce.   That was but a temporary concession.   The true and abiding law of God is indicated in Genesis : ' Therefore shall a man leave
his father and mother and cleave unto his wife, and they two shall
become one flesh.'   As one flesh they form a unity, and this unity is
divinely ordained.   What therefore God has joined together let not
man separate.   Monogamy, as in Genesis, is assumed.

9.   Man has no right to sunder what God has joined together.
The ' man ' who sunders would be the husband when he gives the
letter of divorce.   But those who would attempt to reply to Jesus
by asserting the divineness of the Pentateuchal law, would doubtless
urge that it is not man who sunders, but God ; for if God, through
Moses, gave the command, it is God who permits and sanctions the
sundering divorce.   Nowhere more than here does Jesus go nearer
to denying the absolute divinity, permanence, and perfection of the
Law : that is, if he forbade divorce absolutely.   Yet one can see
that he was not himself conscious of doing so.   Or, at any rate, the
theory of the hard heart was devised to soften the blow, to preserve
the inspiration of the Law, while at the same time maintaining its
ethical inadequacy.   Whether, however, when the woman has by
adultery herself ' sundered ' the unity, Jesus would have assumed
that the man is free, still remains uncertain.   But it is possible that
he would not have held that the man was tied to the woman, even
though the woman had left the man.   Dr. Bartlet feels confident
that neither Jesus nor Mark intended anything different from, or
more severe than, the teaching in Matthew.   Therefore : ' Much of
the modern use made of Christ's teaching on Divorce is not strictly
relevant or warranted.   In particular the case of adultery or unchastity, which by general consent was held *ipso facto* to dissolve
the oneness of man and wife, and so make a formal act of divorce
a duty, does not seem here in question, even in verse 9.   Such a
a deed *per se* " puts asunder " the unity provided for by God's ordinance, which " joined together " man and wife as " one flesh " apart
from any human ordinance of judicial " putting asunder." '   It is
therefore, he thinks, wholly illegitimate to maintain on the strength
of the words of Jesus in Mark that ' so long as the divorced wife is
alive, however guilty she may have been, the husband cannot marry
again.   This goes quite beyond the intention of Jesus's words here.'

10–12. As in vii. 18, Jesus gives a further explanation to the disciples privately. These two verses have, therefore, to be put on the same level as the explanations of the ' sower ' and of spiritual defilement. Nevertheless, the saying they enshrine may be old and authentic in substance. With the Logion here must be compared not only Matt. xix. 9, but also Matt. v. 32 and Luke xvi. 18. There seems no reason why the teaching in one or other of its forms should not be authentic. The form most likely to be authentic is that of Luke xvi. 18. According to that version, Jesus throughout refers to the man, and deals only with him. And Jesus teaches the highly novel doctrine that a man commits adultery if (a) he divorces his wife and marries another woman, or if (b) he marries a woman who has been divorced by another man. Some argue that Luke's version makes it likely that Jesus is throughout not thinking of cases where the woman has committed adultery. By Jewish law, when the woman was not put to death for adultery, she could marry again (except her paramour), but it was thought very unrespectable conduct for a man to marry a woman divorced for licentiousness.

11, 12. In these verses Jesus appears to add something new. To divorce your wife is a sin, but that sin is not adultery. If, however, in addition to divorcing her, you marry another woman, then to the sin of divorce you add the fresh sin of adultery. But Harnack does not think that this distinction between (a) the sin, which is *not* adultery, of divorce, and (b) the sin, which *is* adultery, of divorce *plus* remarriage, is intended by Mark. He says (a) this view contradicts the context of 1–9, (b) is artificially introduced into the wording of the passage, and (c) ignores the fact that in Oriental life remarriage regularly followed divorce.

μοιχᾶται ἐπ᾽ αὐτήν, he commits adultery in respect of his first wife. The assertion of adultery following on remarriage after divorce occurs four times in the Synoptics, but in each of the four passages there are varieties in detail. Mark predicates adultery (a) of the *man* who, having divorced one woman, marries another, (b) of the *woman* who, having divorced (or being divorced from) her husband, marries again. Matt. v. 32 predicates adultery (a) of the *woman* who, being divorced, marries again, (b) of the *man* who marries a divorced woman. [Mark's second case is the same as Matthew's first case, though Matthew assigns the evil to the man who by his action causes the woman to sin.] Matt. xix. predicates adultery (a) of the *man* who, having divorced one woman, marries another, and there is no second case (b) mentioned. Finally, Luke predicates adultery (a) of the *man* who, having divorced his wife, marries another, and (b) of the *man* who marries a divorced woman. There

are thus three different cases, *A*, *B*, and *C* : two in which adultery
is predicated of men (*A* and *B*), and one in which adultery is
predicated of woman (*C*).   Mark has *A* and *C*, Matt. v. has *C* and
B, Matt. xix. has *A*, Luke has *A* and *B*.   The case of the woman
is mentioned twice ; the case of the man divorcing and marrying
again thrice ; the case of the man marrying a divorced woman
twice.

As I have said above, I believe that the oldest and most original
form of the saying is Luke's.   Jesus spoke to men, and where
women are not specially before him, it is probable that he would
allude to man's sin rather than to woman's.   Moreover, it is man
who divorces, and it is man's divorcing that Jesus blames and
would stop.   Hence it seems likely that he should predicate adultery
for each remarrying possibility, *i.e.* whether you yourself divorce,
and then marry another woman, or whether another man having
divorced, you marry the divorced wife.   Jesus gives a tremendous
extra weight to his attack upon a man divorcing his wife (apart
even from the question of unchastity) by asserting that he commits adultery by marrying another woman, his original wife
having been improperly divorced from him, and that if a man
marries such an improperly divorced woman he too commits adultery,
because, in Jesus's eyes, she is still the wife of another man.

12.   The preceding verse is clear and intelligible.   But the 12th,
according to the usual and most authorized text, gives rise to great
difficulties.   It says : ' And if the woman divorce her husband,
and marry another, she commits adultery.'

But, according to Jewish law, the woman could not divorce
the man.   It is this disparity which is the second great blot
in the Jewish law of divorce.   The woman, in true accordance
with Oriental conceptions, is the subordinate of the man.   The
Jewish law—to its credit be it said—made some improvements in
her insecure and unequal position ; but she remained, and remains,
religiously and legally, the inferior.   Her husband can divorce her,
even if she has not committed adultery ; she cannot, by her own
direct act, divorce him, even though he has committed adultery.

In these circumstances it seems inconceivable that Jesus could
have made a statement so inconsistent with Jewish law and life.
It is hardly likely that Mark could have written such a statement
(as to 1 Cor. vii. 13, Paul often writes as if he had never been familiar
with the Jewish religion).   But the important MS. D (Codex Bezæ),
upon which W. so often relies, reads καὶ ἐὰν γυνὴ ἐξέλθῃ ἀπὸ τοῦ
ἀνδρὸς καὶ ἄλλον γαμήσῃ : *i.e.* If a woman is divorced from her husband
and marries another man, she commits adultery.   And this reading
may very likely be original.   If the divorced woman marries again,

she commits adultery as well as the man.   But if this reading is correct, it would then follow that the case of the woman who had *already* committed adultery must be excluded.   For if she had been divorced for adultery, it could not be said that she commits adultery if she marry again.   The reason why the oldest form of the teaching, namely Luke, was altered to the (older) form in Mark may have been that a desire was felt to have a decision about the woman as well as for the man.   The later Mark form (*i.e.* that found in most MSS.) is due to an alteration made to suit other social and legal conditions than those of the Jews.   Mark had Gentile readers, and among them the wife could claim divorce as well as the husband, and so the text was altered to meet their case.

Thus Jesus breaks away from and condemns the prevailing and dominant Jewish law of divorce.   According to the one interpretation, he associates himself with the ' school ' of Shammai in asserting the inviolability of marriage except where the woman has committed adultery.   And he goes further than the ' school ' of Shammai, because he says that not only should it be forbidden for a man to divorce his wife except for adultery, but that if he does so, and if either he or his wife marry again, both he and she are themselves guilty of adultery.   According to the other interpretation (which holds that the qualification made by Matthew, ' except for unchastity,' misrepresents the Master's teaching), Jesus rejects all divorce, whether for adultery or for any other cause whatever. He meant to urge that the marriage bond is inviolable.   The one flesh can never be made two.   This is the interpretation which the Roman Catholic Church has given to his words.

Prof. Burkitt holds that there is a special allusion to a special case in x. 12.   The *exact* wording of the text may not represent what Jesus said, because a woman, according to Jewish law, cannot divorce her husband.   But suppose the words ran more like this : ' If a woman leaves her husband and marries another, she commits adultery.'   Such a case had happened.   Herodias had left her first husband, Herod (erroneously called Philip in Mark vi. 17), in order to marry his half-brother Antipas.   Prof. Burkitt supposes that this famous case was alluded to by Jesus (*op. cit.* pp. 98–101). Dr. Charles argues vigorously against Professor Burkitt's view on p. 28 and pp. 122, 123 of his little book.   He also rejects the reading of D in 12.   For ἐξέλθῃ cannot mean ' has been divorced by her husband,' but only ' has deserted her husband,' and even that not certainly, and if she had deserted her husband, she could not, in any case, by Jewish law marry another man until she was divorced by her first husband (p. 76).

The Sinaitic Syriac version puts the woman before the man ; it reads : ' The woman who leaves her husband and becomes the wife of another does indeed commit adultery, and that man who leaves his wife and takes another does indeed commit adultery.' Here the man and woman are put on the same level. And the doctrine of the one flesh may be taken to imply that the same conduct which is invalid and wicked and illegitimate in a woman is invalid and wicked and illegitimate in the case of a man. If a woman cannot and may not divorce or leave her husband, a man cannot and may not divorce his wife. This reading of the S.S. is in accordance with the reading of the MS. D quoted above.

If Jesus absolutely forbade divorce, he went further than most of us can follow him. We may even hold that the rigid interpretation of his words has been, and is still, productive of grave evils. For his fine defence of the teaching of the 'school' of Shammai, we can but be grateful to him. It is true that many of us would entirely approve of divorce in some cases where adultery is not in question (*e.g.* incurable madness). (Of these cases it is interesting to note that some are specially mentioned in the Jewish law as now codified.) Nevertheless, as a protest against the undesirable doctrine of the 'school' of Hillel, the doctrine and practice of the Judaism of his age, and of Rabbinic and orthodox Judaism ever since (albeit with cautions, provisos, and restraints), the words of Jesus are memorable and of much importance. They have surely done more good than harm. They are a great and notable contribution to the history of morals.

13–16. JESUS AND THE CHILDREN

(*Cp.* Matt. xviii. 3, xix. 13–15 ; Luke xviii. 15–17)

13 And they brought young children to him, for him to touch
14 them : and his disciples rebuked those that brought them. But when Jesus saw it, he was indignant, and he said unto them, ' Let the little children come unto me, and prevent them not : for of
15 such is the kingdom of God. Verily I say unto you, Whoever shall not receive the kingdom of God as a little child, he shall surely not
16 enter therein.' And he embraced them and blessed them, putting his hands upon them.

A touching section, the humanity and grace of which are somewhat injured by Matthew. As we have seen, it has been used, as it were, beforehand by Mark in ix. 36. Verse 15 was perhaps a separate Logion inserted here. Matthew omits it ; he has a parallel to it in xviii. 3.

13. *Cp.* 2 Kings iv. 27. Is there a magical element about the Master's mere ' touch ' which is unsympathetic to Matthew ? With him the touch is turned into Jesus putting his hands upon their heads. But probably Mark meant by ' touching ' much the same (*cp.* verse 16). Putting the hand upon the person's head was a regular accompaniment of the act of blessing (*cp.* Genesis xlviii. 14). It is reasonable enough to suppose that Jesus was genuinely fond of children. At the same time there is here, as so constantly in all the stories about him, the curious parallel with, or contrast to, the stories of Elijah and Elisha. Compare Mark x. 13–16 with 2 Kings ii. 23. But Dr. Abrahams has shown that Jesus's loving regard for the young was in full accordance with Rabbinic feeling and teaching. See his *Studies*, 1. chap. xv. Klausner quotes the saying : ' Little ones receive the presence of the Shechinah.'

14. ' Of such.' Does Jesus refer to real children as well as to those who have a pure, child-like mind ? Quite possibly. The indignation shown or felt by Jesus is mentioned by Mark only. The earliest Evangelist is not afraid or unwilling to indicate that the Master was a man who could be moved by strong emotions.

The child symbolizes or represents the temper in which the Kingdom must be received. Humble trust, a complete lack of assertiveness, no consciousness of ' merit ' or desert, simple confidence and purity—these are the qualities which Jesus means to indicate in the character of the true child. The Kingdom can only be entered by those who can approach it in such a spirit. To those who do, the highest good, as the direct gift and grace of God, can and will be given.

Wellhausen aptly points out how Shakespeare has felt the contrast between this section and the section which follows it. For *here* the Kingdom is a gift which one must accept as a child, *there* it is only to be won by effort and self-denial.

The passage from Shakespeare occurs in the famous soliloquy of Richard II. just before his death (Act V. Scene v.) :

> . . . No thought is contented. The better sort,
> As thoughts of things divine, are intermixed
> With scruples, and do set the word itself
> Against the word :
> As thus, ' Come, little ones,' and then again,
> ' It is as hard to come as for a camel
> To thread the postern of a small needle's eye.'

15. The Kingdom appears to be both present and future, but what is meant is rather that he who does not accept the announcement of its coming, the conditions for entering it, and its spirit and

constitution in simple faith and trust, will not be allowed, or will not be able, to enter it.   The Kingdom must be won by faith and truth.   Those who accept the teaching have, as it were, entered into the Kingdom by anticipation.   They have, in Jewish phrase, received its yoke upon themselves.   They have received its spirit. They are members of it beforehand.

16.   The 'embracing' is peculiar to Mark.   *Cp.* ix. 36.

The picture of Jesus embracing and blessing the children has rightly sunk deep into the human heart.   It would be unjust to contrast with it, as has sometimes been done, the picture of 2 Kings ii. 23.   For in the one picture the children are brought to Jesus to be taught ; in the other they mock at the prophet on the road.   Yet the beauty, the significance, the ethical force, and the originality of the Gospel story, as of the great saying in 15, can also only with injustice be overlooked, cheapened, or denied.

17-31.   The Danger of Riches—Wealth and the Kingdom

(*Cp.* Matt. xix. 16-30 ; Luke xviii. 18-30)

17   And as he set forth upon his way, one ran up, and knelt and asked him, ' Good Master, what shall I do that I may inherit eternal life ? '
18 And Jesus said unto him, ' Why callest thou me good ? no one is
19 good except God alone.   Thou knowest the commandments, Do not commit adultery, Do no murder, Do not steal, Do not bear false witness, Defraud not, Honour thy father and mother.'   And
20 he said unto him, ' Master, all these have I observed from my youth.'
21 Then Jesus looked at him, and felt love for him, and said unto him, ' One thing thou lackest : go thy way, sell whatsoever thou hast, and give it to the poor, and thou shalt have treasure in heaven :
22 and come, follow me.'   But he was sad at that saying, and went away grieved : for he had great possessions.
23   And Jesus looked round about, and said unto his disciples, ' How difficult is it for them who have riches to enter the kingdom of God !
25 It is easier for a camel to go through the eye of a needle than for a
24 rich man to enter the kingdom of God.'   And the disciples were astonished at his words.   But Jesus spoke again and said unto them, ' Children, how difficult it is to enter into the kingdom of
26 God ! '   And they were appalled beyond measure, saying among
27 themselves, ' Who then can be saved ? '   But Jesus, looking at

them, said, ' For men it is impossible, but not for God : since for God all things are possible.'

28   Then Peter began to say unto him, ' Lo, *we* have abandoned all,
29 and have followed thee.'   And Jesus answered and said, ' Verily I say unto you, there is no man who has abandoned house, or brethren, or sisters, or father, or mother, or children, or lands, for my
30 sake, and the gospel's, who shall not receive back an hundredfold : now in this age, houses, and brethren, and sisters, and mothers, and children, and lands, though with persecutions ; and in the world
31 to come eternal life.   But many that are now first shall be last ; and the last first.'

The section consists of three well-marked subdivisions, 17–22, 23–27, 28–31.   The story in 17–22 had, we may presume, originally no special place or time.   Mark gives it a setting in 17*a*.

17. ' Inherit.'   A Hebraism.   It means no more than ' obtain.' That which in ix. 43 had been simply ' life ' is here called ' eternal life.'   Both are equivalent to, and identical with, the Kingdom of God (ix. 47 and x. 14, 15).   Here the Kingdom is clearly something which man must seek to obtain, and can obtain, by his own right-doing.

18.   The reply of Jesus is of the utmost significance.   It is obvious that no divine being would or could have answered thus. Jesus knew himself to be a man.   The verse is naturally extremely inconvenient to orthodox Christian commentators who think that Jesus was God or was divine.   It is interesting to see how they deal with it.   It appears that one traditional way out is to say that ' Jesus, as often, answers from the point of view of the questioner.' So Schanz, the capable Roman Catholic commentator, who honestly insists on the correct translation of the verse, but adds that the words do not exclude ' dass Jesus seiner höheren Natur nach selbst zu diesem göttlichen Wesen gehören kann.'   It is pleasant to know that Jesus was a better and purer monotheist than Schanz would have him to be.   Even Mr. Allen, though he honestly acknowledges that the changes in Matthew are ' probably intentional,' says that the meaning in Mark ' seems to be : Why go out of your way to call one whom you regard as a human teacher good ? '
    Another method, and a more legitimate one for getting out of the difficulty, is to insist that good, both to questioner and respondent, means here not ' morally excellent,' but beneficent.   *Cp.* Dalman, *Worte Jesu*, I. 277, and Strack-Billerbeck, *ad loc.* ; also Windisch, *De tegenwoordige stand, etc.*, pp. 23, 24.   In that case, Jesus says only

that beneficence must be ascribed to God alone ; he does not deny his own moral perfection and sinlessness.   One would have thought that ' beneficence ' was also an element in moral perfection.   Whether ' good ' means here ' beneficent ' or not, or whether it is (as is more probable) used in an ordinary general sense, the reply of Jesus is clearly the reply of one who felt himself to be a man, and no more than a man.   The Jesus of Matthew xi. 27 would and could not have replied thus.   The historic Jesus would, I think, have been much disconcerted at the idea of sinless moral perfection being ascribed to him.   The simplest meaning that can be attached to the word ' good ' is also the truest.   Jesus meant no more and no less than what any unsophisticated and unprejudiced reader would understand him to mean.   ' Merit lives from man to man.'   Only God is good in the sense of faultless.   If Jesus was in the human sense ' good,' he was also humble, and where, in the Gospel narratives, he is represented as least humble, he seems least good.   The divine being may know himself sinless ; a *man* can only sin in fancying that he is without sin.   We know too little of Jesus to describe his character fully ; his eulogistic biographers do not allow anything which seems to them a fault to obscure their hero.   The invectives of Jesus against his opponents and those who differed from him in religious opinion are to his biographers wholly admirable.   We shall judge otherwise.   Yet it is a noble character that peeps through the fragmentary and one-sided records—none the less noble because we may be sure that of Jesus, both in fact and in his own estimate of himself, the adage was true : ' there is no man that sinneth not.' Mr. Rawlinson argues with great ability that I go here much too far.   But I very much doubt if he would have argued as he does had the story been about some Indian or Mahommedan saint.   But, as always, what he says is well worth considering.

19.   The order of the commandments seems strange.   No less so that ' thou shalt not covet ' is omitted, and ' thou shalt not defraud ' put in its place.   But the S.S. omits ' thou shalt not defraud,' which appears to be not original.   It is perhaps specially introduced as suitable for a rich person.

The reply of Jesus may appear strange.   We should have supposed that it would have been more in keeping with his usual line if he had quoted positive rather than negative commandments, even though these form part of the famous Ten.   Had he quoted Deut. vi. 5, Lev. xix. 8, it might have seemed more natural.   But Jesus had no prejudices.   He was much freer than some of his Protestant German commentators.   He did not anxiously divide up the commandments into positive and negative, and tilt against the negative ones.   He probably meant to indicate that the old commandments were good enough for men's salvation, if only they were followed.   How far such a teaching is consistent with the teaching of the Sermon on the Mount is another question, which may be elsewhere considered.   Matthew's interpretation of ' one thing thou lackest ' in 21 may, perhaps, be accurate.   It is not necessary to be ' perfect ' in order to enter the Kingdom.   The tests of ' perfection ' or of ' discipleship ' go beyond the requirements of admission into the Kingdom.   But this view has also difficulties in its turn.   See below.   Does not Prof. Bacon press the difference between Mark and Matthew too far ?   For ' thou knowest the commandments ' Matthew (xix. 17) has the imperative, ' keep the commandments.'   ' Could anything,' says Bacon, ' more flatly contradict both spirit and letter of the original ?   Mark has the definite, distinct declaration that the keeping of these commandments *leaves lacking* the essential thing, which is the doctrine of the cross, life through death, the world to come by surrender of this world.   And Matthew, by the alteration of a phrase or two, states the contrary.   Eternal life is the reward of keeping the commandments ' (*Gospel Story*, p. 132).   Nor can I see that the ' one thing thou lackest ' is equivalent to ' self-surrender by faith ' as opposed to ' works of the law.'   Prof. Bacon would perhaps hold that a morality and religion which honestly preach salvation by means of works of the law are a poor morality and a poor religion ; and yet it is not unlikely that no religion and no morality have produced a higher percentage of saintly lives and martyrs than these. ' On that essential issue the Gospel of Mark here shows itself no less squarely Pauline than on the practical one of the Mosaic distinctions.'   If in both these cases it is ' squarely Pauline,' is it also authentic ?   Can we have it both ways ?

20.   Some MSS. read, ἐφυλαξάμην, *i.e.* ' I have kept myself from doing these things ' ; if this is right, we may suppose that the command ' Honour thy parents ' has been interpolated.   Some read, ἐφύλαξα, ' I have observed.'

The man is disappointed.   He had expected Jesus to say something new.   Moreover, though he has kept the ordinary commandments, he does not feel by any means sure that he has ' deserved,' or that he will attain, eternal life.   He is conscious that he has done nothing out of the common.   He has made no great or special effort. He ought to do something more if he is to obtain the great gift or guerdon.   It is in order to know what this something more should be that he has come to question Jesus.   So, perhaps, one may interpret, and fill up, the reply.

21.   It may be argued that one must not make a general principle

out of what Jesus here says. The reply is relative (a) to the particular individual, (b) to the particular epoch. The man's morality had been somewhat negative ; he had committed no wrong, but he had attained to no high standard of right. He had injured no man, but he had not benefited many. His abstentions from wrong-doing had made no great calls upon him. He had not shown much self-sacrifice and self-denial. He was, perhaps, dimly conscious himself of this inadequacy or imperfection. Not all was right within him, though he had done no wrong. It is not unwarrantable to suppose that Jesus realized this. The old commandments, of which Jesus selects a few as typical or as examples, are sufficient for salvation if they are fully and actively carried out. It all depends upon the 'how' ; it all depends upon the will and the heart. Jesus, therefore, to test the real ethical quality of the man, bids him make a big and complete sacrifice. Let him give up his fortune and private ties, let him become a disciple. If he will do that, there is no doubt that his heart is keen on goodness, his will powerful enough to put the desires and ideals of his heart into operation. If he will do that, there can be no doubt, and he need feel none, that he has fully kept the commandments, and that he will inherit eternal life. The above seems the more probable explanation of what Jesus says here. But it is not without difficulty, It has to read in a good deal into what is actually said. Are we to assume that Jesus knew the man already ? In that case, I suppose, the reply in 19 is merely provisional, and even before it was uttered, Jesus had something more in his mind. Or was the reply in 19 meant quite seriously, but did Jesus come to the conclusion as he spoke that it was not adequate for this particular case ? Or were the words of 21 caused by the reply in 20 ? Anybody who can say that he *has* fulfilled God's commands can most assuredly never have fulfilled them. Or, again, did Jesus mean, even in the Mark version of the story, to set forth a double morality : one—not in itself inadequate for the attainment of the Kingdom—for the general mass ; another and a higher, for full disciples ? Another difficulty in the explanation is the second sub-division. If, indeed, the reply in 19 to the question in 17 is meant to be serious, if the saying in 21 is only meant for the particular case, can we harmonize with such a view the statements in 23, and still more the statement in 24 ? For no indication is given that it is *so* difficult to observe the commandments that, without the grace of God, hardly anybody could enter the Kingdom. It is quite possible to take that view ; Paul took that view ; but it does not seem elsewhere as if Jesus took it, and there is no clear reason to believe that it is applied in 19, which would then be rather an ironical than a sincere reply. See further on 23–31.

Still, taking the story as we find it, it is not a fair criticism of Jesus's words to suppose that he here lays down the one means or canon of salvation for everybody throughout the ages. It is also a false criticism when the counsel of Jesus is condemned because it would not be to the benefit of existing society if all of us were to give all we possessed to the poor. The point here is not what would benefit society, but what will be a difficult thing for the individual. And who can deny that for the average excellent citizen it would be a hard sacrifice to sell all he has and give it to the poor ? The questioner did not refuse to comply with the advice which Jesus gave him because the advice was ' quixotic ' or ' impracticable,' or ' not for the benefit of society,' or ' not even good for the poor,' but because he did not want to give up his possessions and make the sacrifice. Jesus divined where the shoe would pinch. If the man was really keen about goodness, let him make the one great sacrifice which would prove his keenness. Or was he merely a professor ? It does not seem unreasonable to say that the words of Jesus in 21 are not a general counsel of perfection, but a test of obedience and faith which he saw ' to be necessary in this particular case ' (Swete).

Then, too, one must remember that Jesus believed that the end of the existing order was imminent. In the new order there would be no need of wealth and no social inequalities. But, lastly, Jesus, as we see from what follows, and as we gather from other passages, did apparently regard personal poverty as something in itself desirable, either as a mark of self-sacrifice, or as a condition little likely to lead into temptation and sin. At the same time, what was said for a particular purpose at a particular time to a particular individual must not be turned into a universal rule, and then laid to the account or charge of him who said it. As to the effects in history of Jesus's words, that is another matter. The effects have been immense, and both for good and for evil.

The fragment from the Gospel of the Hebrews is interesting. How can a man be said to have fulfilled the commandments of the Lord when he lives in comfort and wealth, and so many of his brethren are in distress ? ' And the Lord said to him : how canst thou say I have fulfilled the law and the prophets. For it is written in the Law, Thou shalt love thy neighbour as thyself, and behold many of thy brothers, children of Abraham, are covered with filth, and thy house is full of good things, and nothing goes from it to them.'

' Treasure in heaven.' See Matt. vi. 20. The human touch that Jesus felt an affection for the man, who was honest, if narrow, is omitted by Matthew and Luke.

The ' one thing which was wanting ' was an enthusiasm or passion for righteousness. The man possessed, if one may say so, ordinary morality ; he could not rise to ideal morality.   So, perhaps, we are to interpret.   But are we also to add, that, while to be a *follower* or disciple of Jesus in the stricter sense demanded complete self-surrender, a full breaking away from the ordinary ties and interests of the world, Jesus, nevertheless, believed that God in His mercy would not refuse ' salvation ' to those who obey the fundamental commands of morality ?

23–27. This paragraph gives the impression of being less authentic than the preceding one. It may have been built up around two Sayings about riches. The Sayings may be authentic, but not the dialogue. In any case there is no need to suppose that the connection between 7–22 and 23–27 is historic, or more than editorial. At any rate, the point of view of 23–27 seems harder and sterner than that of 17–22. In 17–22, as we have seen, Jesus does not seem to teach that eternal life or the Kingdom of God is only to be won by God's grace, or that the keeping of God's commands does not go a long way towards its acquisition. He does not seem to teach that wealth as such is an immense bar to obtaining the Kingdom. But now the conditions which in a previous chapter were laid down for true discipleship seem almost to be required for all—if they would enter into the Kingdom. Jesus declares first that it is very difficult for the rich to enter the Kingdom. And not satisfied with that, he declares that it is very difficult for anybody to win acceptance into the Kingdom. For how many, for how generous a proportion of the living, the saving clause of 27 would make exception it is impossible to say. But the increase of severity from 17–22 to 23–27 seems hardly to be denied.

The following words from Wellhausen seems worth hearing. ' In spite of the words " one thing thou lackest," Jesus regards the fulfilment of the commandments as adequate for the acquisition of eternal life (*cp.* Luke xvi. 29).   Only for his disciples and followers does he demand something more, or rather something totally different : a complete severance from the world. But finally he declares that this complete discipleship, with its abandonment of all earthly ties and goods, is the general and indispensable condition for everyone who would enter into the Kingdom of God. That is a tremendous increase of demand. The distance from the one stage to the other is so great that it only becomes intelligible on the supposition that a historic development lies between the two (*unter Voraussetzung eines dazwischen liegenden Prozesses*).' (The last sentence is omitted in the second edition of the commentary.)

23–25. In verse 24 the A.V. and R.V. have : ' How hard it is for them that trust in riches to enter into the Kingdom of God.'

But the best MSS. have quite generally : ' How hard it is to enter into the Kingdom of God,' a very different and a very terrific proposition. In verse 23 Jesus had said, ' how difficult it is for the rich to enter the Kingdom.' Are we to understand that, in spite of the omission of the qualifying words ' for the rich,' 24 means the same as, and no more than, 23 ? This seems to be the opinion of some commentators. If, on the other hand, 24 is general, and is to be compared with such statements as Matt. vii. 13, 14, then there is much to be said for those who, with the Codex Bezæ (D), would transpose 24 and 25. We then get an intelligible intensification. Jesus first speaks of the difficulty of the rich (in 23 and 25). The disciples are ' astonished.' Not satisfied with this, Jesus begins again, and makes the statement general : ' how difficult for all men it is to enter the Kingdom.' At this they are amazed still more, and say, ' *Who* then can be saved ? ' Such a question would have far less force and meaning if, as in the ordinary text, it immediately followed the verse about the rich and the camel.

There are thus two statements to be considered :

(1) How hard it is for the rich to enter the Kingdom.

(2) How hard it is for any one to enter.

As to (1), it seems a fact that Jesus had a certain inclination in favour of associating the higher or ideal life with poverty. We find in the Psalms a certain bias against the rich and in favour of the poor. Humility and poverty seemed to some Psalmists to go together ; riches and pride. Perhaps Jesus thought the same. One has to criticize the statement of Jesus differently according as one interprets the Kingdom to mean (*a*) the life of ' heaven,' ' salvation,' and the like, or (*b*) the highest life on earth. If it means the former, we should (to my mind) justly regard the saying of Jesus as harsh, unjustifiable, and presumptuous. It is not for man to know the manner and the laws of the life beyond the grave. But to exclude whole classes, or indeed permanently to exclude any, from its blessedness conflicts with our conception of the goodness of God. The horrible doctrine that most men are ' lost ' and that few are ' saved ' seems to have been held by Jesus as well as by the author of the fourth book of Ezra. The latter had natural qualms against the odious doctrine, which do him the highest honour. It remains a mournful religious puzzle that Jesus, if such verses as Matt. vii. 13 were said by him, with all his pity and love for the sinner and the outcast, had no such qualms.

On the other hand, if the Kingdom merely means the highest life on earth, then there is a good deal to be said for Jesus's statement. It *is* a difficult thing for a rich man to lead the highest life.

But there is little reason to suppose that Jesus meant this. For Rabbinic views on riches and poverty see Abrahams, *Studies*, I. chap. xiv.

The second and wider statement, ' how hard it is for anybody to enter the Kingdom,' cannot be discussed here. It would take too long. One must, at any rate, distinguish. It *is* hard for any one to live the highest life. Goodness is *not* easy. But we may also say that, by his own actions, it is hard for *any one* to ' merit ' the blessedness of eternal life. For ' merit lives from man to man,' and not from man to God. The eternal life must be a grace granted, not a guerdon won. Yet the hope is universal, and any dogma which would permanently exclude many, or even any, from a blessedness to be allotted to some is (as Jews to-day think) both repugnant in itself as well as flagrantly inconsistent with the goodness of God.

The reading of the S.S. agrees with that followed by the A.V. and R.V. If it were correct, Jesus was not speaking about the general difficulty of entering the Kingdom at all. Nor even was he speaking of wealth without qualifications. Only those who *trust* in their wealth have these difficulties. We should have then to believe that the text was more than once altered in an ascetic direction. On the other hand, it is even more probable that the reading of the S.S., which was adopted by A.V. and R.V., was a deliberate attenuation of the old drastic assertions. *Cp.* the interesting brief article by J. Weiss in *Z. N. W.* for 1910, pp. 79–83, with its trenchant questions as to the meaning of Matthew and Luke's shorter versions of Mark's story and their bearing upon the question of an Urmarcus.

27. Jesus qualifies his own statement. It is hard, but not impossible. By his own effort the rich man, or any man, can ' hardly ' enter ; by God's grace he may. Here we have the same antinomy as is alluded to by Shakespeare : the highest exertion is demanded, but the result is due to the grace of God. At least to some extent, Jesus here gives back what he had before taken away. In our modern Jewish faith we go yet further. By God's grace we hold that all human souls shall ultimately enter the Kingdom of Heaven. We are convinced ' Universalists.'

Burney says : ' This example offers another instance in which Mark is clearly inferior to the other Synoptists. The typical form of antithesis (as witnessed by numerous other examples) is that given by Matthew :

> With man this is impossible,
> But with God all things are possible.

This has been somewhat paraphrased by Luke :

> The things which are impossible with men
> Are possible with God,

a form in which the strict parallelism of the two antithetical statements is modified so as to produce a *single* statement—still, nothing
is added.

'In Mark, however, we read :

> With men it is impossible,
> But not with God ;
> For all things are possible with God.

Here the insertion of " But not with God," which is really redundant
by the side of the following line, has the effect of marring the sharp-
ness and balance of the antithesis.   Clearly the addition is a gloss '
(p. 75, n. 1).

28, 31. A separate Logion in 29, 30 is artificially connected
with 17–27 by 28. The Logion was not, we may suppose, originally
a reply to an ejaculation of Peter.

28. Peter's interjection means that he and his fellow-apostles,
who *have* divested themselves of everything for the sake of Jesus
and his cause, ought, therefore, surely to inherit the life eternal.

29. To this Jesus replies that they will. All who have made
the sacrifice of family ties and of personal property for the sake of
the gospel will receive their reward.
The Logion seems to have been a good deal changed about. *Cp.*
the versions in Matthew and Luke. Originally it ended with
' hundredfold,' and the reward was purely a reward in the Messianic
Kingdom, or in the ' eternal life ' : later on a distinction was made,
and the reward was divided between this life and the next life, or
between this age and the next age. Even in this world the faithful
disciples will receive, in lieu of the property or family they give up,
their place and their share in the Christian community, although
this collective property and family can only be shared in amid
persecutions. (*Cp.* Acts ii. 44, ' All that believed were together,
and had all things common ; and they sold their possessions and
goods, and parted them to all, as any man had need.' So, too,
iv. 32, Romans xvi. 13, ' Salute Rufus ... and his mother *and
mine* ; ' and *cp.* 1 Cor. iii. 22, iv. 15 ; 2 Cor. vi. 8–10.)
Notice the omission of the ' wife.' Is it implied that one may
and must at the gospel's call abandon brother, sister, mother, child,
but that one's wife one must not abandon ? Or is it possible to

speak of receiving back a hundredfold in a spiritual sense mothers and children and brothers, but hardly wives ?

The verse is an interesting confirmation of Acts ii. 44, but was surely said and written in the first period of persecution of the infant Church, many years after the death of the founder. But note that the words ' with persecutions ' are wanting in the parallel passage in Luke and Matthew. ' They seem to betray the later hand of one who had, indeed, found anew in the hearts and homes of believers the dear relationships which he had himself surrendered, but who knew likewise at what price of danger and suffering they must be won' (Carpenter, *First Three Gospels*, p. 210).

30. ' In the world to come eternal life.' An interesting combination. The words ' in the world to come ' are omitted by Matthew, and are really unnecessary. If a man enters the world to come he of necessity obtains eternal life. If a man obtains eternal life, he does so because he has entered the world to come, the Kingdom of God.

31. The saying may be authentic. It may also be a formula of Jewish apocalyptic writing. It occurs in Matthew xx. 16, Luke xiii. 30, as well as in the parallel places in Matthew and Luke to Mark x. 31. Its position in Mark is in all probability editorial, and even if Jesus said 29 and 31, he probably did not say them at the same time on the same occasions and together. The verse would seem to declare that many persons who are now rich and prominent shall in the life to come be last—*i.e.* excluded ; while many who are now poor, in the world's view last, shall be among the first and the most prominent in the life to come. The disciples who have ' lost ' all on earth shall be foremost in the Kingdom of God. *Cp.* for other uses of the saying Matt. xx. 16, Luke xiii. 30. From another point of view there is to be no pre-eminence of station or merit in the ' Kingdom.' ' Whosoever would be first among you let him be the servant of all ' (x. 43, 44).

32-34. THIRD PREDICTION OF SUFFERING AND DEATH

(*Cp.* Matt. xx. 17-19 ; Luke xviii. 31-34)

32 And they were on the way going up to Jerusalem ; and Jesus went on in front of them ; and they were amazed ; and they that followed were afraid. And again he took the Twelve aside, and
33 began to tell them what would happen unto him. ' Behold, we go up to Jerusalem ; and the Son of man will be given up unto the

chief priests and unto the scribes ; and they will condemn him to
34 death, and will give him up to the heathen.   And they will mock
him, and spit upon him, and scourge him, and kill him : and after
three days he will rise again.'

32.   Here, for the first time, Jerusalem is distinctly stated to
be the goal of the journey and the scene of the final catastrophe.
One must assume that, in addition to the Twelve, there were others
who also accompanied Jesus upon his fateful path (*cp*. x. 1.)

The phrasing of the Greek is odd, and suggests that the wording
has not come down to us in its original form.   Are the ἀκολου-
θοῦντες the same people as the subject of ἐθαμβοῦντο or not ?
If they are not, then the subject of ' they were amazed ' may be
the Twelve, while those who followed and were afraid would represent a wider group of disciples.   Mark seems to lay some special
stress upon Jesus walking in front of the others.   The Messiah
has to proceed upon the fateful journey in dignity and alone.   Is
Bartlet reading too much into the words when he writes : ' Jesus
withdrew as it were within himself for a time from the immediate
companionship of the Twelve, and contrary to his habit moved on
ahead, alone, with set face : see Luke ix. 51, " he stedfastly set his
face to go to Jerusalem," ' and again (' for " amazed " better render
" were lost in awed wonder " ') : ' Something in the way in which
Jesus went before them—the rapt abstraction of his gaze or the
resolved bearing he assumed—awed the Twelve with the sense of
the fatefulness of this movement towards Jerusalem.   But there
is not enough, either in the form of the original (where " they "
is not expressed, and therefore cannot afford any contrast to " but
they that followed ") or in what we know otherwise of the Twelve
at this stage, to warrant the usual view of the passage, one contrasting the attitude of the inner and outer circles of Jesus's following on this occasion.   Hence we seem bound to accept the conjecture of Dr. C. H. Turner that we have here a primitive corruption
of Mark's true text, which perhaps read " and *was* lost in awed
wonder " (*cp*. xiv. 33) ; so that this feeling, reflected in Jesus's
bearing, caused those following to be afraid.   The non-use of this
sentence by Matthew and Luke is perhaps significant of the difficulty
which it presented to early readers of Mark.'   As to those who
were afraid, Dr. Bartlet thinks that they are not meant to be ' a
body of " disciples " in a wider and looser sense than the Twelve
(just alluded to as themselves " awed "), going up to the Passover
in Jesus's company or caravan (as most suppose) ; but Jesus's
followers generally.   They all felt vague fear at his manner as he
walked ahead, manifestly filled with agitating thought and emo-
tion.'   ' Again ' must refer to ix. 31.   Quite probably, however, 32,

introducing the unhistorical prediction of 33, 34, is itself the un-authentic composition of the Evangelist (Schmidt, p. 218).

34. It is strange that each prediction is, as it were, independent of the other. Jesus here tells what is going to happen to him as if he had never mentioned the subject before. That the prediction in its present detailed form is a *vaticinium post eventum* needs no proving. Yet Jesus may have had some dark ominous feeling that he was destined to suffer and die in Jerusalem. That he had more is also possible, but far from sure. For though the cry on the cross can be explained away, it is upon the whole somewhat more likely that the great *dénouement*, which, in the Gospel story, Jesus is represented as expecting to happen soon after his death, at his Parousia, he really expected to happen after his arrival at Jeru-salem, and without the necessity of his death. It has been suggested that these predictions in Mark are founded upon a narrative in which the eventuality of death was merely indicated, and when the hope of a near triumph was more predominant. Jesus went to Jerusalem, led by a great hope, but without dissimulating to him-self the possible danger. The disciples saw chiefly the danger; Jesus encourages them with hope. This was the real historical situation, which 32 still faintly shows (Loisy).

35-45. THE SONS OF ZEBEDEE

(*Cp.* Matt. xx. 20-28 ; Luke xxii. 24-27)

35 And James and John, the sons of Zebedee, came unto him, saying, 'Master, we wish that thou wouldst do for us whatever we
36 ask thee.' And he said unto them, 'What do ye wish that I should
37 do for you ? ' They said unto him, 'Grant unto us that we may sit, one on thy right hand, and the other on thy left hand, in thy
38 glory.' But Jesus said unto them, 'Ye know not what ye ask : can ye drink of the cup that I am to drink of ? and be baptized
39 with the baptism that I am to be baptized with ? ' And they said unto him, 'We can.' And Jesus said unto them, 'Ye shall indeed drink of the cup that I am to drink of : and with the baptism that
40 I am to be baptized with shall ye be baptized : but to sit on my right hand and on my left hand is not mine to give ; but it shall be for them for whom it is destined.'
41 And when the ten heard it, they began to be indignant with
42 James and John. But Jesus called them to him, and said unto them, 'Ye know that they who are supposed to rule over the

nations lord it over them ; and their great ones play the tyrant
43 over them.   But it is not so among you : and whoever wishes to
44 become great among you, let him be your servant ; and whoever
45 of you would be the first, let him be the slave of all. For the
Son of man came not to be served, but to serve, and to give his
life as a ransom for many.'

As the second prediction of suffering and death was followed
by a dispute between the disciples as to who was or should be the
' greatest,' so the third prediction is followed by a similar incident.
But I cannot pursue the critical deductions to which this observation may give rise. The section 35–45 is composite. 41–45 is an
appendix dealing with a kindred, but not identical, subject. For
35–40 deals with precedence in the Messianic Kingdom ; 41–45
deals with precedence in the Christian community. Again, 35–40
may have been enlarged. It may have originally consisted of
35–37, 40 (' To sit on,' etc.). These verses may rest on some
recollections or traditions of an actual conversation between Jesus
and the Apostles. It is noteworthy that in Matt. xix. 28 Jesus
promises to the Twelve that they *shall* sit upon twelve thrones,
judging the twelve tribes of Israel, ' when the Son of man sits on
the throne of his glory.' Mark omits this verse, and here Jesus
refuses to commit himself as to thrones and as to nearness to himself
in the Kingdom. It seems clear that 38, 39 are *vaticinia post
eventum*. They not only predict the martyrdom of Jesus, and
declare that the path of martyrdom is the road to glory, but also
predict the martyrdom of James and John.

37. It is not said that the ' glory ' referred to is the ' glory ' of
the Parousia after the death and resurrection. But we must
suppose that this is assumed.

38. The verse implies that such distinctions as they ask can
only be obtained through martyrdom. The cup is used in the Old
Testament as a metaphor for affliction ; *cp.* Isaiah li. 17 ; Jer. xlix.
12, etc. The waters of affliction are also familiar, especially in
the Psalms.
    The question means : Can you face the pain and the death such
as I am about to undergo ? Can you face martyrdom ? It is a
baptism of death, which will usher in the everlasting glory.

39. In this passage martyrdom seems predicted for both James
and John. If only James had been martyred (Acts xii. 2), the
prediction that both would die the martyr's death would perhaps

not have found a place in the gospel.   Hence this passage suggests doubts as to the trustworthiness of the tradition that John died peacefully at a very advanced age.   On the other hand, those who would like to maintain the authenticity of the passage plead that we have here a real prediction of Jesus which was only half fulfilled, and was therefore omitted by Luke.

41–45.   Authentic words or authentic teachings of Jesus may lie at the bottom of this section which were expanded and put by the Evangelist into an artificial connection with the preceding story. In that case we need not be surprised that the reply which Jesus makes to the ten does not seem in keeping with what he had to reply to.   The ten are irritated that James and John had asked for a special place in the perfected Kingdom.   What Jesus says is that within the community there must be no question of ruler and servant.   Within the community the only pre-eminence to be sought for and acknowledged must be a pre-eminence in service. He who serves best is by that very fact the greatest.   The question of what is to happen after death or at the Parousia is neglected.

43.   *Cp.* ix. 35.   It has been well argued that these parallel verses make it probable that the noble saying and teaching about humility and service and the greatness of service were originally uttered by Jesus as of general application.   They were then used by Christian tradition to refer specifically to the Christian community.   42 is a foil to 43, and the example of Jesus is added at the close (Bultmann, p. 86).

A comparison of 42–45 with Luke xxii. 25–27 makes it probable that Luke's version is older than Mark's, or, that Luke has preserved a common source more accurately.   In each verse Luke's language is more simple and more ' concrete ' than Mark's, and in Luke nothing is said of the redemptive or vicarious death, and the term Son of man is not employed.   The ' rule ' of the best Christian disciples in the Kingdom must be quite different from the external, ordinary, tyrannical rule of Gentile rulers over their kingdoms. They rule for their own advantage, but their rule is no true or genuine rule.   Outward rule and outward subjection are the marks of the Gentile.   οἱ δοκοῦντες ἄρχειν τῶν ἐθνῶν, ' they who are supposed to rule ' ; for these words mean that the Gentile rulers are, as Plato would say, not true rulers.   But they may merely mean : ' they who are accounted or known to be rulers.'

διάκονος is a servant who waits at table.   In the Messianic banquet the greatest is he who is the lowliest.   Greatness among the citizens of the Kingdom—among the members of the Christian community—is only to be won by service and humility.   Hence

among them there must be no dispute about primacy or ranks.
The present ' is ' seems to include the future. And the future (ἔσται)
' shall be ' seems used for the imperative. ' Among you ' refers
not to the Kingdom, but to the Christian brotherhood (cp. ix. 35.)

Pre-eminence in service, greatness in humility—these were
noble conceptions which Jesus introduced to the world. And
though humility and charity were well-known ideals among the
Rabbis, the particular form and combination in which we find them
here are, I think, as highly original as they certainly were highly
stimulating and productive.

One true meaning of the verse is, indeed, that the disciples of
Jesus are not to seek after rule, but to find their life's purpose in
service.   Yet it would be false to say that this teaching runs counter
to a fundamental conception of Judaism.   For Jesus is not here
speaking of national rule.   It is quite true that many Jews did yearn
for rule over the heathen.   They did desire that the tables should
be turned.   But that is not the rule which is here opposed by Jesus.
He does not allude to it one way or the other.   A man might be
keen that his oppressed nation should rule over its oppressors, and
yet in his private life exhibit the most devoted service.   But this
is not to detract from the originality of Jesus.   That he could
regard his life—at any rate his earthly life—as a service, that he
could see in this service his mission and his Messiahship, was indeed
a triumph of moral grandeur and of religious inspiration.   To
Mark, Jesus, as J. Weiss says, is Messiah, not in spite of suffering,
but because of suffering.   The ' mystery ' of the cross can only
be understood by those who are themselves prepared for sacrifice,
suffering, and martyrdom (*Urchristentum*, p. 541).

45.   The Lord of the Kingdom came to serve.   Therefore his
life can be the pattern for all.   The first part of the verse may be
quite authentic, and most probably is so.   Jesus, however, may
have used the first person, and not said, ' The Son of man came,'
but ' I came.'   The originality and genius of Jesus are revealed in
the saying.   Not unjustly does Harnack speak of it as containing
an ' Umwertung der Werte.'

The conception of the λύτρον, ' the ransom,' is different.
Only here do we find it placed in Jesus's mouth.   The idea of life
given as a ransom belongs, it has been argued, to another current
of thought than the idea of a life spent in service.   It is true that to
give your life for others is the highest possible service (McNeile),
but the word ' *lutron* ' seems to imply something more.   Cp. 4
Macc. vi. 29, xviii. 22, i. 11, 2 Macc. vii. 37.   God somehow makes the
death of Jesus help in the salvation of others.   It is in this more
special sense that Jesus gives his own life for the sake of many lives.

'Aντί does not here mean 'in the place of,' 'in the stead of,' but 'for the sake of.' But the idea that the life or death of Jesus is a substitute for that of others is closely approached. Those who believe in him receive the benefit of his death, and join him in 'eternal life.' In Luke xxii. 27 the ransom idea is wanting. The passage seems to show the influence of Isaiah liii. Mr. Rawlinson says : ' The kindred Greek words rendered "redeem" and "redemption" are used in the New Testament and in the LXX to express the idea of a "deliverance" wrought by God on behalf of His people, without any special emphasis on the idea of a *ransom*. It is probable, therefore, that in the case of our Lord's saying here the idea of the "ransom" metaphor ought not to be rigorously pressed (*i.e.* that *ransom*=simply "means of deliverance" or of redemption). The phrase sums up the general thought of Isa. liii., and expresses the idea of a vicarious and voluntary giving of life, with the thought also implied that the sacrifice was in some way mysteriously necessitated by sin. Jewish Christians would eventually understand it as meaning that the death of the Messiah was the means of redemption for Israel. Gentile readers would understand it as meaning that by the death of Jesus Christ they had been set free from their old sinful life and from the power and dominion of the demons.' Though the whole passage in its present form may be later than Jesus, the ethical conception of greatness realized in lowly service may surely and safely be ascribed to him. Moreover, Jesus may conceivably have realized that his death would be to the advantage of many ; that many would enter the Kingdom as an effect of his death. This is a possible view, though not a very likely one. It may be added that the theology or soteriology of 45 is not fully Pauline, though connected with Pauline ideas. See Werner's book, *Der Einfluss paulinischer Theologie im Markus-Evangelium* (1923), pp. 69, 70, 116, 191.

46–52. BARTIMÆUS, THE BLIND MAN, HEALED

(*Cp.* Matt. ix. 27–31, xx. 29–34 ; Luke xviii. 35–43)

46 And they came to Jericho : and as he went out of Jericho with his disciples and a large crowd, a blind beggar, Bartimæus, the son 47 of Timæus, sat by the way side. And when he heard that it was Jesus of Nazareth, he began to cry out, and say, ' Jesus, son of 48 David, pity me.' And many rebuked him that he should hold his peace : but he kept on crying all the louder, ' Son of David, pity 49 me.' And Jesus stood still, and said : ' Call him.' And they called

the blind man, saying unto him, ' Be of good cheer, rise ; he calls
50 thee.'   And he, casting away his cloak, sprang up and came to
51 Jesus.   And Jesus answered and said unto him, ' What wouldst
thou that I should do unto thee ? '   The blind man said unto him,
52 ' Master, I would that I might see again.'   And Jesus said unto him,
' Go thy way ; thy faith has healed thee.'   And immediately he
received his sight again, and followed Jesus on the way.

The division viii. 27–x. ends with the healing of a blind man, just
as the section vi. 14–viii. 26 ends with the healing of a blind man.
The name seems a late addition, as in the case of Jairus (cp. Bultmann, 132, 148).   In Luke no name is given.

47.   Jesus does not here make any open objection to being
called the son of David.   In Mark he has not been so called before.
Undoubtedly, ' son of David ' is, to Mark, a mere paraphrase for
' Messianic King.'   But one must not make too much of an epithet.
How can we be sure, if the Bartimæus episode happened at all (and
be it remembered its essence is a miracle, which ' suggestion ' can
hardly account for), that Bartimæus used the appellation ' son of
David ? '   In 51 the blind man calls Jesus only ' Master.'

48.   Why did ' they ' censure him, and who are ' they ' ?   Some
of the disciples ?   Some of the general crowd ?   Is the case parallel
with x. 13 ?   Then we must assume that it was in order not to trouble
Jesus on his journey, or that their march might not be interrupted.
Or did ' they ' bid him be silent in order that their secret may not
prematurely be revealed, for only at the entry into Jerusalem do
they propose to proclaim Jesus the son of David, or Messiah.   This
explanation seems less likely.   Bartimæus is no real separate name ;
it means merely ' son of Timæus.'

52.   Jesus, in contrast with viii. 22–26, heals by his mere word.
The story is told with rare simplicity and grace.   Cadman (p. 112)
has an elaborate explanation of the ' rebuke,' which yet assumes the
historic accuracy of the cry ' son of David.'   The explanation is
most ingenious, but to my thinking strained.   It is very interesting
that Meyer regards the story as substantially authentic.   He says :
' Manifestly this scene which is related most vividly is derived from
the best tradition, and is historical in all its essentials.   Such miracles,
which, under similar conditions, occur at all times, can be considered
as historical in the same sense and to the same extent as those which
take place during pilgrimages to Lourdes and to the Holy Garment,
and are told by believing eye-witnesses ' (p. 114).   Cp. Tacitus,

Histories, iv. 81, describing how Vespasian, against his will, heals a blind man, and a lame one. ' Persons actually present,' says Tacitus, ' attest both facts, even now when nothing is to be gained by falsehood.' The whole chapter is very well worth reading. Schmidt says : ' The story of the blind Bartimæus presupposes that the blind man already knows something about Jesus. If we ask how that can be possible, we shall have to say : already at a former time Jesus would seem to have been active in this district ' (p. 301). A very doubtful hypothesis.

CHAPTER XI

I–II. The Entry into Jerusalem

(*Cp.* Matt. xxi. I–II ; Luke xix. 28–38)

1 And when they came nigh to Jerusalem, unto Bethphage and Bethany, at the mount of Olives, he sent forth two of his disciples,
2 and said unto them, ' Go to the village before you : and immediately as ye enter it, ye will find an ass's colt tied, whereon no man has yet
3 sat ; loose it and bring it here. And if any man say unto you, Why do ye this ? say ye, The Lord has need of it, and he will send it back
4 again here at once.' And they departed, and found the colt tied by the door outside in the open place ; and they loosed it. And
5 some men who stood there said unto them, ' What do ye, loosing
6 the colt ? ' And they said unto them even as Jesus had commanded :
7 and they permitted them to take it. And they brought the colt to
8 Jesus, and laid their cloaks upon it ; and he sat upon it. And many spread their cloaks upon the way : and others strewed herbs
9 which they cut from the fields. And they that went before, and they that followed, kept crying : ' Hosanna ; blessed be he that
10 comes in the name of the Lord : blessed be the kingdom of our father David that is coming ; Hosanna in the heights.'
11 And Jesus entered into Jerusalem, and into the temple : and when he had looked round at everything there, as the hour was late, he went out unto Bethany with the Twelve.

Here begins the last section of the Gospel. It can be divided into two parts, the first telling the story of the entry into Jerusalem, the conflict with the authorities and the apocalyptic discourse, and extending over chapters xi., xii., and xiii. ; the second recording the story of the Passion, the entombment and the resurrection (xiv. to end).

1. According to Mark, Jesus is in Jerusalem three days before

the events narrated in xiv. *seq.* occur.   The first day extends from
xi. 1 to xi. 11 ;   the second from xi. 12 to xi. 19 ;   the third from
xi. 20 to xiii. 37.   Thus the third day is by far the fullest.   It is
another question whether these chronological notices have any
historic value, or even whether all the stories and sayings belong
to this period of Jesus' ministry.   See Schmidt, pp. 275 and 287–300.
Whether Jesus had already friends in Bethany, which was a village
on the south-east side of the slopes of the Mount of Olives, is
uncertain, but it seems likely.

2.   The young ass is the ass—' the colt, the foal of an ass '—of
Zech. ix. 9.   Jesus here implicitly proclaims himself as King and
Messiah.   If this tale be true, Jesus is, to say the least, not afraid
to take action which would imply that he regards himself, and
wishes others to regard him, as the ' political ' Messiah predicted by
the prophets.

3.   Klostermann prefers the rendering ' What is this that ye are
doing ? '   ' The Lord.'   Jesus here for the first time gives himself
this name.   The sub-intention is ' the Messiah.'
  ' At once,' *i.e.* Jesus will send the ass back as soon as he has done
with it.

4.   πρὸς τὴν θύραν ἔξω ἐπὶ τοῦ ἀμφόδου.   Dr. Moffatt renders :
' outside a door, in the street.'   It is at least strange that Justin says
that the ass was attached to a vine.   Have we here a fulfilment of a
Messianic prophecy, and was ἀμφόδου originally ἀμπέλου ?   The
Septuagint of Genesis xlix. 11 runs : δεσμεύων πρὸς ἄμπελον τὸν
πῶλον αὐτοῦ, καὶ τῇ ἕλικι τὸν πῶλον τῆς ὄνου αὐτοῦ.   Strauss
suggested that the origin of the tied ass is to be sought here
(*Leben Jesu*, 1st ed., ii. p. 294).

8.   A crowd accompanies him to the gates of the city.   They
strew leaves and herbs upon the ground.   στιβάδες are not branches ;
R.V. M. has ' layers of leaves ' ;   Kl. has ' grüne Büschel.'   For the
garments, *cp.* 2 Kings ix. 13.

9.   Psalm cxviii. 26.   The right translation is : ' Blessed in the
name of the Lord be he that comes.'   Yahweh is invoked and asked
to bless.   But, perhaps, though this is the correct translation of the
Hebrew, the Evangelist took it to mean ' Blessed be he that comes
in the name of (*i.e.* as sent by) the Lord.'   ' He that comes ' is
almost a technical term for the Messiah in Matt. xi. 3.   ' Hosanna '
is the Hebrew ' save,' with the enclitic ' na ' added to the imperative.
It is an appeal for help to the king (*cp.* 2 Sam. xiv. 4 ; 2 Kings vi. 26)
or to God.

In *J. T. S.*, 1916, XVII. pp. 139–149, Burkitt has an interesting discussion about Mark xi. 9, 10.   He points out that the business with the ' branches ' followed by the Hosannas suggest ceremonies connected with Tabernacles and not with Passover.   He quotes Wuensche's observation made as long ago as 1878 that the passage is either a confusion of Passover with Tabernacles, or a deliberate and intentional transference of a Tabernacle ceremony to Passover. S.-B. do not appear to appreciate the difficulty, just as I fully admit that I had not appreciated it, and deserve with other commentators Professor Burkitt's scolding (p. 142).   Clearly Mark regards the actions and exclamations mentioned in 8–10 as intended to point to, and welcome, the coming and entry of the Messiah into his chosen city, to indicate the inauguration of his Kingdom.   But (*a*) were these actions and words distinctly Messianic ?   Were they commonly associated with the advent of Messiah ?   The evidence produced by S.-B. to the effect that they were is slight and late ; (*b*) does not this very paucity of evidence show that the deeds and words were not directly Messianic, and must have, if historic, some other explanation ?   It is this other explanation which Burkitt essays to give.   He shows that in 2 Macc. x. 6 it is stated that the rededication of the Temple was celebrated in the manner of Tabernacles with green boughs and branches.   Next he shows by a quotation from the Aramaic Targum to Esther that the green boughs were called Hosannas, in all probability because Hosanna was shouted when they were used.   He then makes the deduction that it was a fresh Dedication which was in the mind of Jesus and of the Galilean crowd at the coming to, and the entry into, Jerusalem.   I can imagine that this might perhaps be the case as regards Jesus, but I find it much more difficult to accept this view as regards the crowd. Burkitt points out that the entry was followed by the cleansing of the Temple.   ' It is true that according to Mark it did not take place till the next day, a postponement which is so little in accordance with romantic effect that we cannot fail to accept it as sober fact.   But notwithstanding the delay, the Cleansing takes place.   It must have been a remarkable scene ; no wonder the authorities sought some way of bringing the Galilæan Prophet to grief.   And it is difficult to believe that the personal ascendancy of a single stranger would have compelled instant obedience with such summary commands, if unsupported by a large body of those who already sympathized—more than sympathized, expected something striking and astonishing.   Mark xi. 18*b*, in fact, tells us that the action of Jesus was supported by the crowd.   We need not even suppose that πᾶς ὁ ὄχλος xi. 18 means the crowd who had shouted *Hosanna* yesterday, but if those who had shouted *Hosanna* told others that their Prophet was coming as the messenger of the covenant to purify the sons of

Levi just before the great and terrible Day of the Lord, that Pass-over-Multitude would be far more ready to let Him do what He would, for a time.   A new Dedication—that is the connecting link between the Entry and the Cleansing.   On the next day begins the tragedy : Jesus still has the shout of *Hosanna* in mind ; but things go on as usual.   The end has not come, and He thinks of Himself as the Stone which the builders have rejected.   Before the end of the day the hot-heads among the Galileans will have learned that their Prophet is willing after all to pay tribute to Cæsar.'   This sounds fairly cogent in Burkitt's persuasive words.   But even though Jesus has the Cleansing in his mind, there is no reason to suppose that he had told of his intention beforehand.   As to the one crowd telling the other that Jesus was ' coming as the messenger of the covenant to purify the sons of Levi just before the great and terrible Day of the Lord,' that is merely to make a second conjecture support a first. Bartlet more or less adopts Burkitt's hypothesis, but his long note on verse 9 hardly makes things much clearer.   The narrative still remains obscure.

Lake and Jackson observe that in Mark xi. 9 there is no neces-sary implication in the words of the populace that they regarded Jesus as the Messianic King : he may have been welcomed solely as the herald of the approaching kingdom of David.   The words in Matt. xxi. 9 seem Messianic ; yet in the next verse, when the same speakers are asked who Jesus was, the reply is merely that he is the prophet from Nazareth of Galilee.   The Messianic interpretation is only made quite plain in Luke xix. 33 (*Beginnings*, Vol. I. p. 7, n. 1).

10.   ' Save in the heights ' is scarcely an explicable Hebrew or Jewish phrase.   Help should come *from* heaven, rather than be established in heaven.   Kl. supposes that it is a shortened phrase for ' Give salvation, O Thou who dwellest in the heights.'   Perhaps Mark, like Matthew and Luke, misunderstood the meaning of Hosanna.   They supposed that it meant praise or glory to Jesus the Messiah.   Hence Mark adds ' in the heights ' on the lines of Psalm cxlviii. 1, ' praise him in the heights,' where the Septuagint has ἐν τοῖς ὑψίστοις as here.   Jesus, according to Mark, is welcomed by this cry as the Messianic King.   ' Hosanna ' becomes equivalent to ' Hail.'   If, however, the cry was merely ' Save now, O God. Blessed in the name of the Lord is he that comes,' perhaps nothing Messianic was intended.   ' The teacher and wonder-worker of Nazareth was greeted with joyous cries and benedictions.'   The entry received its Messianic colouring a good while after the event occurred (Dalman, *Die Worte Jesu*, 1. pp. 181, 182).   So Burkitt in *The American Journal of Theology*, April 1911, pp. 180–183, and Lake, *The Stewardship of Faith*, p. 42.   ' The disciples do proclaim

the Kingdom of David, which is Messiah's Kingdom, the Kingdom
of God ; they proclaim this Kingdom to be at hand, just as Jesus
and John the Baptist had done.   But they do not proclaim the
Prophet of Galilee to be the Messiah.   And what is the conclusion
of the Entry according to Mark ?   Is all the city moved ?   Does
Jesus proceed at once to cast out the buyers and sellers from the
Temple, while the children cry Hosanna to the Son of David ?   No ;
Mark says : He entered into Jerusalem, and having looked round on
everything, it being now late, he went forth to Bethany with the
Twelve.   I find it difficult to believe that this is the voice of a
dogmatic historian : it sounds to me more like that of the interpreter
of Simon Peter, the chronicler of Simon Peter's reminiscences '
(Burkitt, p. 181).   In his later article in *J. T. S.*, already quoted in
the note on 9, Burkitt attempts to explain the phrase ' the Kingdom
of our father David.'   He says that the collocation ' our father
David ' is unparalleled elsewhere.   He thinks it is a sort of telescop-
ing together of two separate cries (*a*) ' Kingdom of our Father '
meaning ' Kingdom of God,' (*b*) ' Kingdom of David.'   I doubt this.
Jewish scholars are right in saying that the idea of the Fatherhood
of God was not unfamiliar in the days of Jesus, but I do not think
that ' Father ' would have been used in this sort of ' absolute ' way
by a crowd.   ' Kingdom of our Father ' does not strike me as having
a very likely ring.

As to ' Hosanna in the heights ' Burkitt observes that ' as the
phrase is unparalleled elsewhere it seems to me possible that it is
based altogether upon a misunderstanding, and that it represents
הושענא לעילא, " Hosanna upwards," *i.e.* " Up with your wands ! "
It was at the moment when they waved their Hosanna boughs (or
palm-branches, if they had them) that the actual cry of *Hosanna !*
was made.'   ' We may then, I venture to suggest, reconstruct the
cries of the crowd at the Entry somewhat thus : They escorted the
ass and its Rider with shouts of " Hosanna ! "   " Blest be He who
comes ! "—" Our Father's Kingdom ! "—" The Kingdom of David ! "
—" Up with your palms ! "   And if the general argument here
followed is sound, the best English equivalent for *Hosanna,* when it
does not mean the green boughs, will be " God save Israel ! " used
more or less as we are told they use " God save Ireland ! " over the
water.   I mean that *Hosanna* is a festal shout in the form of a prayer
to God to give a good turn to the affairs of the nation.'

11.   Jesus, as a new-comer, on this, perhaps his first, visit to
the capital, inspects the Temple and its surroundings.   Jesus may
have been at Jerusalem before, at former festivals, though Mark's
words would seem to exclude any previous visit since the opening
of the ministry.   We can, if we like, explain his ' looking round ' by

assuming that he is making his own observations and preparations
for the next day's work, but this is somewhat strained. The explanation is, however, adopted by Rawlinson, who thinks that it is ' quite
arbitrary,' and ' almost certainly unhistorical to assume,' that Jesus
had not visited Jerusalem before. Apart from the question of the
duration of the ministry, the point is of no importance.

The entry is clearly Messianic as described in Mark. But it is
also miraculous as dependent upon supernatural foreknowledge.
We may, therefore, assume that, in the exact form in which it is
related, it is unhistoric. Perhaps Jesus did enter Jerusalem upon
an ass, no uncommon method of journeying, amid the acclaims of
his disciples and the wondering concourse of the inhabitants :
' Here is the great teacher and miracle worker from Galilee,' and
the Messianic character of the entry was afterwards added. It has
been observed that the Messianic entry is not referred to at the
trial. If any hailed him as the Messiah, it was his *entourage*, not
those to whom he came. It is, at any rate, highly remarkable that,
in Matt. xxi. 11, upon the question being put by the excited populace,
' Who is this man ? ' the reply is given, ' It is Jesus, the prophet of
Nazareth.' It is not said : ' It is Jesus the Messiah.' But one
has also to remember that Jesus was put to death because of his
Messianic claim : if he had denied that he was the Messiah, Mark
xv. 26 is inconceivable, and there is every reason to believe that
Mark xv. 26 is historic. Hence it is also possible that a ' Messianic '
entry in some shape or form really took place. But it may have
been much less provocatively public than is described.

Burkitt is quite ready to defend the historicity even of the story
of the colt. ' The events related in 2–6 and in xiv. 13–16 do hint
at previous acquaintanceships and arrangements in Jerusalem,
but surely if the evangelist had intended the colt tied by the way-
side, and the man bearing the water-pot to have been there by
miracle, or have been known to have been there by miracle, he
would have given some indication of it. We are not told that the
disciples "marvelled," or said, " Who then is this ? " ' (*American
Journal of Theology*, April 1911, p. 182). (*Cp.* also Schmidt, p. 302.
All points to previous visits of Jesus to Jerusalem.) As against this
Wellhausen's words are perhaps worth adding: 'Rationalizing is here
unpermissible. Jesus did not order the ass beforehand, and make a
previous arrangement with its owners. He foreknows the chance coincidence, because God, who directs what is apparent chance, is with
him. The ass serves no ordinary purpose ; it is *the* ass of Messianic
prophecy. Thus Jesus proclaims himself as the Messiah. According
to Zech. xiv. 4, Yahweh was to appear on the Mount of Olives, and
popular Jewish faith held that the Messiah would appear there.

' Yet this imposing demonstration has no effect. Neither

priests nor Romans pay any attention. And yet the Romans might have been expected to take umbrage. Hence one can hardly believe that Jesus was the responsible author of the incident. If it took place, it must have happened without his intention and have possessed no special importance. It is conceivable that the populace in a moment of excitement acclaimed him as Messiah, and it is also not improbable that he made no actual protest against their doing so.

‘The Gospel tradition lets us see that Jesus's journey was no mere harmless pilgrimage, but that there was a special reason for it and a special purpose. He must have arrived there some while before the Passover. Mark tries to limit the period between his entry and his death to a week, but the material can hardly be fitted into so short a time. He seems to have acquired acquaintances and connections in Jerusalem, and these cannot be accounted for on the strength of previous visits, when ’ [if such took place] ‘ he would not have been known as the great prophet from Galilee. In Bethany he seems to have laid the foundations of the subsequent Christian community in Jerusalem. In xiv. 49 he says : “ I have been daily with you in the Temple, teaching ” ; two days would not justify “ daily.”

‘ Thus the concourse of people who accompanied him from the borders of Judæa (x. 1), who passed by Jericho (x. 46), and descended the Mount of Olives with him, did not go with him because of the festival, but because of himself, in expectant anticipation of what he might do in the metropolis. It seems very likely that the people were inclined to regard him as the Messiah, and to interpret his journey to Jerusalem messianically. The step from prophet to Messiah was easily taken ; false prophet ($\psi\epsilon\upsilon\delta o\pi\rho o\phi\acute{\eta}\tau\eta s$) and false Messiah ($\psi\epsilon\upsilon\delta\acute{o}\chi\rho\iota\sigma\tau os$) in Josephus and the Gospels mean much the same thing ’ (*Commentary on Mark*, ed. 1).

The story of the Entry, if it be accepted as, in essentials, historic, makes the theory of the purely spiritual Messiahship very difficult. For the awkward question has to be faced : why, if his Kingdom was to be so purely spiritual, so unlike that of the Messiah of the prophets, did Jesus nevertheless seek to fulfil the Messianic prophecies ? Why did he raise the very expectations which he thought outward and wrong, which he did not desire to fulfil ? Gould grasps the nettle boldly, but his words are unconvincing. He says : ‘ The acceptance of him as King, and not merely as prophet, was what he demanded.’ His entry was ‘ a public proclamation of his Messianic claim.’ But his programme remains unchanged. He will still only be the teacher and benefactor. His Kingship is service, and so remains. ‘ The multitude who followed him thought that with the announcement of the claim the programme would change.   But the unchanged programme means that Jesus, just as he was, claimed Kingship and would be King only by spiritual enforcements.   The distinct claim to be a King is followed immediately by the revolutionising of the whole idea of Kingship.'

Professor Peake says (*The Messiah and the Son of Man*, 1924, p. 11) : ' We need not insist that Jesus instigated the popular enthusiasm by any disclosure of what the act meant for Himself. It is quite conceivable that He desired no popular demonstration. The main intention of the act was to conform to the Messianic rôle as the prophet had depicted it.   The consequences of the action did not so much concern Him.   It is not quite clear, in fact, that the demonstration was designed as a welcome to the Messianic King. In our oldest source the acclamations are reported in this way : " Hosanna ; Blessed is he that cometh in the name of the Lord : Blessed is the kingdom that cometh, the kingdom of our father David : Hosanna in the highest."   This need not imply more than that Jesus was regarded as a harbinger of the Kingdom.   The later documents definitely make the identification with the Messiah, Matthew using the term " Son of David," Luke, " the King," John, " the King of Israel."   But John adds the significant words, " These things understood not his disciples at the first : but when Jesus was glorified, then remembered they that these things were written of him, and that they had done these things unto him " (xii. 16). The difficulty in regarding the triumphal entry as a Messianic demonstration is that the authorities took no action upon it ; and apparently no reference was made to it at the trial of Jesus, though it would have greatly strengthened the case against Him.   But, whatever the attitude of the people may have been, and however the disciples regarded the action of Jesus, it seems to be clear that in His own mind the action was imposed upon Him by the necessity of fulfilling Messianic prophecy ; and that he felt the pressure of this necessity, and acted in accordance with it, demonstrates that He believed Himself to be the Messiah.'   Meyer says : ' After the Confession of Peter Jesus let himself be known to his adherents as the Messiah, and with this behaviour the entry into Jerusalem corresponds. . . . The demonstration recorded in Mark xi. 8–10 does not proceed from the population of Jerusalem or its environment, but from those who accompany Jesus and from Jesus himself (*cp*. Luke xix. 37).   The Purification of the Temple next day is in accord with it.   The claim to be the Messiah is quite unmistakable. By a great demonstration from his adherents he obviously hoped to carry away and gain to his side the populace of the capital (who had already heard of his activities) and to obtain the leading position in the city ' (pp. 162, 163).   Cadman rejects the Messianic interpretation of the Entry.   It was made to appear so by ' later embellishments.' The procedure at the trial is unfavourable to the Messianic interpretation. Cadman realizes the difficulty to which I have called attention above. 'At the Confession scene Jesus announced His Messiahship to the disciples in a sense (the apocalyptic "Son of man") which the reports of the entry are incapable of bearing' (p. 115). Goguel has an interesting theory that the anointing in Bethany, the sleeping at Bethany, the careful division of the time into days, and the cursing of the fig tree, are secondary additions to Mark which were known to Matthew, but not to Luke. If in 11a, we pass on from 'And Jesus entered into Jerusalem and into the temple' to 'and he began to drive out' (15), and again, from 'he went out of the city' (19) to 'and they came again to Jerusalem' (27), we get a connected narrative, and the difficulty about 'these things' (28) disappears. Moreover, Jesus, as in Luke, would sleep always on the Mount of Olives, and not at Bethany (xxi. 37). 'If Jesus, having spent the preceding nights at Bethany, had been at Gethsemane for the first time on the night of his arrest, it does not seem clear how Judas could have led thither those who came to arrest him. Everything, on the other hand, is perfectly straightforward if the place to which Judas leads his band is the one where Jesus spent every night. The indication given by Luke probably corresponds to the records of the early tradition. The question, however, is not settled by this correspondence, for it is not inconceivable that Luke corrected the story he found in Mark by making use of a direct or indirect acquaintance with the earlier tradition' (I. p. 300). Wellhausen suggests another explanation. That there is some confusion and a mixture of traditions seems clear.

12–14.   THE BARREN FIG TREE

(Cp. Matt. xxi. 18, 19)

2 And on the morrow, when they left Bethany, he was hungry :
3 and seeing a fig tree afar off having leaves, he went up to it to see if he should find anything on it : and when he came to it, he found
4 nothing but leaves ; for it was not the season for figs. And Jesus spoke and said unto the tree : 'Let no man eat fruit of thee again for ever.' And his disciples heard it.

A great deal has been written about this story, which finds its continuation in 20–25. Has it any historic basis whatever ? Has a parable, such as that of Luke xiii. 6–9, been turned first into an allegory, and then externalized into a miracle ? For the purpose of this book it is needless to discuss these very hypothetical questions. The story has, in any case, no moral or religious value for us to-day.

14. For the question as to the date when figs ripen in Galilee and Judæa reference must be made to the larger commentaries. Jesus bids the fig tree be barren for ever. It seems a strange thing to do, for the tree was not in fault. If the story has any historic basis, we cannot imagine that Jesus acted in so irrational a way as this. At the least the story must have been greatly perverted from what actually took place.

Burkitt is even ready to champion the historic character of the fig-tree story. As Mark tells the story it is credible enough. He says : ' Of all current explanations, surely the most improbable is the often repeated theory that Mark's narrative is a distorted version of the Parable of the Fig Tree in Luke xiii. 6–9. I cannot but suppose that the story in Mark, so odd, so unmoral, so unlike conventional ideas of what Jesus ought to have done and said, does really rest upon reminiscence, however inaccurate, of an actual occurrence. I do not profess to know what caused the fig tree to be withered twenty-four hours after Jesus had spoken, but the final verse about forgiveness—quite unexpected, quite unlike what a mere compiler would have added—suggests to me a genuine saying, corresponding to a change of mood in Jesus himself. It was not Jesus, but Peter, who noticed the tree this second morning. On the previous day Jesus was crossing over to set the Temple in order. He is now convinced that his word has doomed the tree ; does it warn him to forgive his adversaries in Jerusalem ? ' (ib. p. 180). The curses of Rabbis and their results are an unpleasing feature in Rabbinic literature. Cp. S.-B. on Matt. xxi. 19. There is even a saying of a Rabbi to the effect that ' even the groundless curse of a wise man is fulfilled.' The Rabbis took themselves much too seriously.

15–19. The Purification of the Temple

(Cp. Matt. xxi. 12, 13, 17 ; Luke xix. 45–48)

15 And they came to Jerusalem : and Jesus went into the temple, and began to drive out them that sold and bought in the temple, and he overthrew the tables of the money-changers, and the seats 16 of them that sold doves ; and he would not allow anyone to carry a vessel through the temple.

17 And he taught, saying unto them, ' Is it not written, My house shall be called a house of prayer for all nations ? but ye have made 18 it a den of thieves.' And the chief priests and the scribes heard it

and sought how they might destroy him : for they feared him,
19 because all the people were amazed at his teaching. And when
evening was come, he went out of the city.

The Purification story may depend upon a well-founded report,
and may be, to some extent, historical. For the facts about the
Temple and what went on there we can now read, and depend on,
Abrahams, *Studies*, I. chap. xi.

There was a market within the precincts of the Temple for the
purchase of animals and birds, and for sacrificial purposes. The
‘ thieves ’ may refer to the cheating practised by sellers, or the
reference may be more general : the Temple has become a meeting-
place of scamps. If this story is historical, we may have to assume
that Jesus at first occupied a position of some power in Jerusalem.
His followers are numerous enough to execute his orders in the
Temple, and important enough to allow him and them to be un-
disturbed in their unusual and high-handed proceedings. Of his
teaching no specimen is given. The Scribes and priests are afraid
to lay hands on him, though they would fain get rid of him. Again,
we may ask whether the action of Jesus, if historic, was due to
some sudden outburst of anger, or was it a first display of Messianic
authority ? How was the action described in 15 carried out ? By
the disciples ? By other supporters ? We are accustomed to the
story, but it raises a good many difficulties. How had Jesus the
power to do what Mark says he did in 16 ? A possible view is that
what Jesus did was something much smaller than is here represented.
Everything tends to be magnified in the Gospel report—the miracles,
the opposition, the attention excited, the renown, the doings, and
all. If the Gospel narratives were accurate and unexaggerated,
the silence of Josephus would be a little odd. On the other hand,
Prof. Lake sees in the event ‘ the immediate cause of the crucifixion.’
The priests ‘ were in possession of a commercial monopoly ’ both
as regards buying animals and changing Roman money into Jewish
money, which alone was accepted. ‘ It was against this commercial monopoly that Jesus protested when he spoke of a den of
thieves. The den of thieves retaliated by accusing him of rebellion
against the Romans, and in spite of his teaching of non-resistance to
persecution, they secured a conviction by making use of the information that Jesus regarded himself as the coming Messiah, who would
reign in a Kingdom which would take the place of the Roman
Empire. By a curious, but intelligible, process Christians came
in the next generation to put on the Scribes, and their successors,
the Rabbis, the guilt of the judicial murder of Jesus. That is
because the controversy between the Christians and the Jews was
primarily a matter which concerned the Scribes. It centred in the

exposition of the Law, and the interpretation of Scripture, especially the Messianic passages. It was natural to connect the existing Jewish opponents with the death of Jesus. But it seems to me that financial interest rather than theological hatred was the real cause of the accusation of the priests, though they dressed it up in a partly political, partly religious, form. I do not think that history gives us reason for supposing that the financial interests of a wealthy class are an inadequate explanation of a failure of justice ' (*The Stewardship of Faith*, 1915, pp. 38, 39). Abrahams clearly proves that to suppose that the Temple had become an habitual den of thieves, and that there was constant ' terrible desecration ' going on, or that the money-changing was in itself illegitimate, or that all the priests were always rapacious, is illegitimate, and unwarranted by the evidence. All we can say is that ' certain rapacious priestly families were detested by the people *and by the Pharisees*,' and that there might have ' been occasions on which indignation such as that of Jesus ' would have been justified. Both the reasons for Jesus's action and the action itself probably need a good deal of watering down. The Gospel narrators do not spoil any chance for showing their enemies in an unfavourable light. But the ordinary reader and the ordinary commentator do not bear this in mind. They take every attack upon Priest, Scribe, and Pharisee at the foot of the letter. In one sense it does not matter. All the actors are dead long ago ; but history suffers. Cadman's view of the story is ingenious, but too dependent upon his whole elaborate theory (pp. 116-118). Bacon also probably exaggerates the importance of the incident (*Beginnings of Gospel Story*, p. 161).

There is an interesting article on the ' cleansing ' and on Mark xiv. 58 by Burkitt in *J. T. S.*, 1924, Vol. xxv. pp. 386-390. He contrasts this action of Jesus with the tenor of his words on the following day. ' On the Monday He goes into Jerusalem to set the Temple right, relying on the power of God to carry His programme through. Nothing shall be impossible to Him, and woe to anything that disappoints His expectations ! The next day, when Peter is inclined to gloat, his Master tells him to trust in God—and to forgive if he have any grievance ! Was Jesus beginning to repent of His violent action of yesterday ? Did He think *He* had been too hasty ? In any case, the action of Jesus that day is quite different from that of the day before. He parries the question about His authority, he does *not* give countenance to rebellion against the Roman taxes. We hear no more of any attempted changes in the arrangements of the Temple, and the Parable of the Husbandmen leaves the coming change of government to God. I think that from that Tuesday morning, perhaps as early as the evening before, Jesus despaired of Jerusalem. His action on the Monday morning, the

Cleansing of the Temple itself, shows hope displayed in vigorous, if rather impracticable, action.   But He, Jesus, is the first to see that it is no good.   It did not touch the disease, and those who were most active in backing Him up were probably least in sympathy with His aims and ideals.   The first sight of the chafferers and marketers while He was surrounded with a crowd of Galilean followers, who were at least enthusiastic if not very intelligent, had moved Him to attempt a change, something which should at least indicate the worship which God desires, but it is not long before He is convinced that the whole spirit of Jerusalem is against Him.   He feels it to be a doomed city.'   I wonder if it is that I lack imagination, but I always feel so sceptical about these attempted peerings into the mind of Jesus—these imaginative reconstructions.   I feel as if it is only too probable that in another ten years some one will come along (though he would have to be a *very* unusual person if he were Burkitt's equal), and make a fresh reconstruction quite different from this one.   Still these attempts from a brilliant mind have indubitably their value and their attraction.

16.   Mark only.   Not to permit any one to carry a vessel through the Temple shows Jesus in an unexpected light.   If a Rabbi were so particular, the German theologians would call it externalism.   When an external act shows a lack of reverence for the House of God, Jesus is rightly keen to condemn it.   It is usually supposed that what was objected to was the use of the Temple as a short cut from one quarter of the city to another.   This had already been prohibited by Jewish law.   Josephus says that no one was allowed to carry a vessel into the Temple (*Against Apion*, II. 8).

17.   The allusion is to Isaiah lvi. 7 and Jeremiah vii. 11.

20–25. THE FIG TREE AND FAITH

(*Cp*. Matt. xxi. 20–22, xvii. 20, vi. 14, xviii. 35)

20   And in the morning, as they passed by, they saw the fig tree
21 dried up from the roots.   And Peter remembered, and said unto
    him, ' Master, behold, the fig tree which thou cursedst is dried up.'
22, 23 And Jesus, answering, said unto them, ' Have faith in God.   For
    verily I say unto you, that whoever should say unto this mountain,
    Lift thyself up, and hurl thyself into the sea ; and did not doubt
    in his heart, but believed that his word would come to pass : to
24 him it would come to pass.   Therefore I say unto you, What things
    soever ye pray for and ask, believe that ye have received them, and

25 they will be yours.   And when ye stand and pray, if ye have aught
against any one, forgive him, that your Father who is in heaven may
also forgive you your trespasses.'

Utterances of Jesus about faith, separately and independently
current Logia, are appended by Mark to the conclusion of the fig-
tree story.   They come in here very awkwardly.   To draw from the
success of Jesus's imprecation a lesson on faith is putting it to strange
uses, and giving a bad example of what faith can do.   To say that
the success of the imprecation was due to Jesus's faith in God, his
conviction that God would fulfil his prayer, suggests strange uses of
faith and prayer.   Is the believer to ask for, and to see accomplished
any miracles which come into his head—to make the vine which
gave no grapes sterile for ever, or to remove mountains, which he
might like better to see elsewhere ?   Only those miracles which the
interests of faith justify can be referred to.   Yet the other sayings
of Jesus on the efficacy of prayer have a form almost as absolute as
23, 24 (Matt. vii. 7–11).   Rawlinson quotes with approval J. Weiss,
who says, ' The phrase *believe that ye have received them, i.e.* that your
request has been granted before ever your prayer is uttered, deserves
to be noticed.   The prayer, then, is after all not so much an attempt
to bring influence to bear, so as to determine or alter God's purpose,
as a trustful self-submission to God's hand.'   But can we legitimately whittle down the saying to that ?   A Jew of the first
century who had not the slightest idea of any law of nature and knew
nothing of science, who had no difficulty whatever in conceiving
God working any miracle if He chose, must necessarily have thought
about petitionary prayer very differently from ourselves.   Why
should we wish to make him think as we think, or to conceal the
gulf that lies between us ?   We, at least, who have no apologetic
purposes to serve, like Mr. Rawlinson and J. Weiss, can be more
historic.

24.   Again one must notice the immense (and probably historical)
stress which Jesus lays upon faith.   We cannot to-day accept the
doctrine as here laid down.   As to the power of faith on the one hand,
and of prayer on the other, there can be no doubt.   Nevertheless,
even though the wording of 23 is merely metaphorical, we shall be
compelled to admit that there are limits to faith, which Jesus would
not have recognized or allowed.

25.   An addition which is out of place.   It is perhaps an insertion due to Matt. vi. 14.   The expression, ' Father in heaven,' is
only here found in Mark.

27-33. THE AUTHORITY OF JOHN

(*Cp.* Matt. xxi. 23-27 ; Luke xx. 1-8)

27   And they came again to Jerusalem : and as he was walking in
the temple, the chief priests, and the scribes, and the elders came
28 up to him and said : ' By what authority doest thou these things ?
29 and who gave thee this authority to do these things ? ' And Jesus
answered and said unto them, ' I will also ask of you one question ;
do ye answer me, and I will tell you by what authority I do these
30 things.   The baptism of John, was it from heaven, or from men ?
31 answer me.'   And they deliberated among themselves, saying, ' If
we say, From heaven ; he will say, Why then did ye not believe
32 him ?   Or shall we say, From men ? '   But they feared the people :
33 for all held John to be really a prophet.   So they answered and said
unto Jesus, ' We do not know.'   And Jesus said unto them, ' Neither
do I tell you by what authority I do these things.'

Here we have a story, which was doubtless originally a separate
story without any particular setting or time, given a particular place
in the whole.   Scribes, Elders, and Chief Priests are at hand and
together as usual.   In the connection in which we find the story
' these things ' probably refers to the purification of the Temple, so
that 27 would continue 18.   But the question may originally have
been much more general.   ' What is your authority for your
teaching ? '   Its object is apparently to make Jesus declare himself.
If he let others acclaim him as Messiah, why will he not definitely
himself say of himself that the Messiah is he ?   Or, at any rate,
is his mission of God ?   Does he claim special divine inspiration ?
Has he a direct mandate from God ?

29.   True to the policy of silence and semi-evasion which Jesus
is represented as adopting towards the outer world (whether he
really adopted it is another matter, about which no one can know
for certain), he asks his questioners a counter-question, which, from
his vantage-ground of knowing the inward thoughts of his adversaries, he foresees will not be answered.   Under the word ' baptism '
we must include John's activity and teaching as a whole.

30.   It is possible that the original reply to 30 has been changed,
and that 31-33 are later additions.   For the reflection of the chief
priests : ' If we say, From heaven, he will say, Why then did ye not
believe him ? ' is unnatural.   They ought to have reflected, ' If

we say, From heaven, he will say, So too is my authority from heaven.' Verse 30 is written from the point of view of John's 'heavenly' authority being acknowledged by both sides ; 31, 32 is written from the later standpoint according to which it was held that the Jews had rejected the message of John (the foretelling of Jesus) and had denied his heavenly authority (Bultmann, p. 9).

32. They know, like 'the people,' that his authority was divine.

35. Jesus takes advantage of their confusion and hesitation to continue his policy of silence. He had prepared an ingenious trap, and his antagonists fell into it. It would be interesting if we could have some records of conversations between Jesus and his antagonists drawn up by *them*! Is there any reason to believe that he *always* had the best of it ?

CHAPTER XII

1–12. THE PARABLE OF THE VINEYARD

(*Cp*. Matt. xxi. 33–46 ; Luke xx. 9–19)

1   And he began to speak unto them in parables. ' A man planted a vineyard, and set an hedge around it, and dug out a wine press and built a tower. And he let it to husbandmen, and went abroad.
2 And at the proper time he sent to the husbandmen a servant, that he might receive from the husbandmen his share of the fruit of the
3 vineyard. And they seized him, and beat him, and sent him away
4 empty. And again he sent unto them another servant ; and him
5 they wounded and reviled. And again he sent another ; and him they killed. And he sent many others ; and some they beat, and
6 some they killed. But he had still an only and well-beloved son : him he sent last unto them, saying, They will have respect for my
7 son. But those husbandmen said among themselves, This is the
8 heir ; come, let us kill him, and the inheritance will be ours. So they seized him, and killed him, and cast him out of the vineyard.
9 What will the lord of the vineyard do ? he will come and destroy the husbandmen, and will give the vineyard unto others.

10   ' And have ye not read this passage in the scripture : The
11 stone which the builders rejected is become the corner-stone. This is the Lord's doing, and it is marvellous in our eyes ? '

12   And they sought to take him prisoner, for they realized that he had spoken the parable against them : but they feared the people, so they left him, and went their way.

It would appear more than doubtful whether this parable can be ascribed to Jesus himself. In its present form, at any rate, it reflects a later situation, and assumes his death. Nor is it quite easy to see what form it could originally have had, if it was spoken by Jesus. Moreover, it is not a parable, but an allegory. God is the owner of the vineyard. The servants are the prophets. The husbandmen are the Jews or their leaders. Finally, the son is Jesus. While Loisy, Wellhausen and others argue cogently that the parable is later than Jesus, Burkitt champions its authenticity, for is it not in Mark ? The parable is ' a genuine historical reminiscence of words actually spoken by Jesus. If it were the " product of later Christian reflection " it would contain a reference to the resurrection.' (Loisy replies that the author could not mention this without abandoning completely the whole framework of the parable.) Burkitt argues also that ' the forecast of the parable was not fulfilled. For after A.D. 70 the vineyard in the literal sense was not given to anybody else at all ; it was desolate.' But one need not suppose that the parable, even if later than Jesus, was written after 70. And, in any case, the vineyard was given to the Romans. What it does suggest is that the position of vantage relative to God, held before by the Jews, is now to be held by ' others,' *i.e.* by Christians. Burkitt holds the view that Jesus not only foresaw his death, but regarded it as the divinely appointed means for hastening on the Day of Judgment, and thus for bringing in the Kingdom. Hence he presses the authenticity of the conversation appended to the transfiguration, in spite of its suspicious environment. ' For even in the transfiguration, we have practically a narrative of what St. Peter thought he remembered having seen,' while Mark ix. 9–13 is 'a piece of true historical reminiscence.' Just as the herald had to suffer and die, so too does Jesus discern that he, the Messiah, must suffer and die likewise. In John's fate he reads his own, ' even though no Scripture seemed to indicate it.' So too with Mark x. 45. There is no Paulinism here. All that the verse says is that the death of Jesus will bring ransom and redemption to many—to the true Israel. The wicked husbandmen will be slain, the sinners will perish, ' but the true Israel will be delivered from their enemies and God will reign over them. He will come and visit his vineyard.' Just so does Jesus say in xiv. 24, that his blood will be poured out ' for many '—to the advantage of many. And this result of his death was to happen very soon (Burkitt, ' Parable of the Wicked Husbandmen,' in *Transactions of the Third International Congress for the History of Religion*, Vol. II. pp. 321–328. Mr. Rawlinson seems to work himself into a crescendo of belief that Jesus foresaw and predicted his sufferings and death. On p. 110 such predictions are ' probable ' ; a little later they are ' likely ' ; on p. 114 ' they may well be historically based ' ; on p. 143 the ' specific details ' (of the third prediction) are probably *ex eventu*, though, as Mr. Wood says, ' Mark's view that Jesus more than once foretold the Passion may still correspond with facts.'

On p. 161 (*fin.*), however, it is ' morally certain ' that Jesus ' foresaw and anticipated ' his death, and so the parable is authentic. It is obvious how important it is for a Christian to believe that Jesus had this prevision and expressed it in words. But the commentator who happily is ' above the facts ' will, I think, refuse to go beyond the view that there are arguments on both sides, and that certainty, even ' moral certainty ' (whatever that may exactly mean), is unobtainable. The balance of probability is against authenticity.

1. The vineyard parable quotes and follows Isaiah. ' Jesus was not wont to draw from the Old Testament the matter of his stories ' (Loisy). The vineyard is, in one sense, Israel, in another, the Kingdom. Its owner is God. The absence of the owner, demanded by the development of the allegory, is unsuited to God. The husbandmen are, partly, the leaders—priests, Scribes and Pharisees—as representing the people ; partly, the people themselves. The parable is not quite consistent.

2–5. The various servants represent the prophets whose messages Israel refused to hear.

6. The son is Jesus. The Kingdom is his. Hence he may be called the ' heir.'

9. Who are ' the others ' ? This is not clearly indicated. Some think that the poor and the outcast, the repentant tax-collector and sinner, are intended. More probably, as in Matthew, the ' others ' are the Gentiles. Klostermann says, ' other leaders of the people.'

10, 11. Some think that these verses are an addition, and that the true close to the parable is 9. The stone is Jesus. ' This is the Lord's doing,' *i.e.* the stone came from God. Rejected by the Jewish religious authorities, the stone has become the chief stone of the world's spiritual edifice. Or, perhaps, Jesus, rejected by the Jews, is now seated at God's right hand in heaven. ' This is the Lord's doing,' *i.e.* this change, this reversal.

12. The editor constantly suggests and prepares for the *dénouement*. But the phrasing of the verse is odd. The translation has transposed the words and inserted a ' but ' to make better sense.

13–17. 'Give unto Cæsar'

(*Cp.* Matt. xx.i. 15–22 ; Luke xx. 20–26)

13 　　And they sent unto him certain of the Pharisees and of the
14 Herodians, that they might entrap him by his words.　And when
they were come, they said unto him, 'Master, we know that thou
art truthful, and hast regard for no man : for thou respectest not the
person of men, but teachest the way of God in truth.　Is it lawful
15 to give tribute to the Emperor, or not ?　Should we give it, or should
we not give it ? ' But he, perceiving their deceitfulness, said unto
them, ' Why tempt ye me ? bring me a silver coin, that I may see it.'
16 And they brought it.　And he said unto them, ' Whose is this image
and superscription ? ' And they said unto him, ' The Emperor's.'
17 And Jesus, answering, said unto them, ' Pay to the Emperor what
is the Emperor's, and to God what is God's.'　And they marvelled
at him greatly.

　　13.　The series of questions, which was begun by the priests in
xi. 27–33, is now, after the interruption of xii. 1–12, resumed and
continued till xii. 34.

　　The place of the ' Herodians ' is rather in Galilee than in
Jerusalem, but Mark wants, and therefore supplies, them here, so
that friends and foes of Rome are to unite in the question, and
Jesus may be endangered whether he says yes or no.　' The
Herodians, upholders of the native monarchy, were averse to any
political disturbance, which might complicate the relations between
the Roman government and that monarchy, and could not desire
any Messiah to succeed ' (Menzies).　Or we may suppose that they
desired that Judæa, instead of being governed by the Romans,
should be under a prince of their own family.　In that case both the
questioners would be supposed to be hostile to Rome.

　　14. They flatter him in order to induce him to give a direct
answer.　The fiercer party among the Jewish nationalists held that
it was not permissible to pay tribute to Rome (*cp.* Josephus, *Ant.*
Book XVIII. ch. i. 1 ; Acts v. 37).　If Jesus said it was permissible,
how could he claim to be the Messiah ?　Was not the Messiah to
usher in the era of national independence ?　Or if Jesus said it was
permissible, ' the Pharisees will denounce him to the people ' (Wood).
If he said it was not, there would be trouble for him with the
authorities.　Or, again, we may even assume that the question
could have been asked even if Jesus had not manifested any Messianic

pretensions. It was a question which concerned any religious
teacher. I observe this note in Bacon. 'Jesus himself and the
Church afterwards on all political questions were strictly Pharisean,
they confined their efforts to the practice of righteousness, leaving
to God the establishment of the Messianic Kingdom in his own time
and in his own way' (*Gospel Story*, p. 170). Quite so. But then,
what was the huge difference between Jesus's conception of the
Messiah and that of the Pharisees ? Was not the second less crudely
'political,' the first less immaterially 'spiritual,' than is usually supposed ? And have we not to remember Prof. Bacon's useful warning
that 'records written when Christians were concentrating every effort
to prove the political inoffensiveness of their faith . . . must be
subject to discount' ? And this effort began much before the era
of the Fourth Gospel.

15. ὑπόκρισις, 'dissimulation.' Jesus recognizes that he is not
being asked for the sake of getting at the truth, but in order to trip
him up. They 'tempt' him to deny the authority of the Emperor
by boldly declaring his Messiahship. The purpose of the question
is either to entangle him with the Roman authorities, or to lower
his prestige and popularity with the 'crowd.'

Jesus has no money. He asks for a silver *denarius* (worth about
8½d.). These coins were not made in Palestine. The copper coin
which alone was made there bore no head or figure on it, on account
of Jewish susceptibilities. The *denarius* would have on it the head
of the deified Augustus.

Jesus, says Rawlinson, 'expresses no opinion as to the theoretical
rightfulness or wrongfulness of Cæsar's rule. According to the
ancient way of thinking, the authority of a ruler was co-extensive
with the circulation of his money as *de facto* " coin of the realm,"
and coins were regarded as being ultimately the private property of
the sovereign whose image they bore. Since Cæsar's coins were in
actual circulation, our Lord argues, the Jews in paying tribute were
only giving to Cæsar that which was his own. There was no conflict between that and their duty to God. It is probable that at the
time our Lord did not mean more than this' (p. 165).

17. What are we to say of this famous answer ? It implied
that there was a field in which the Emperor had authority, but that
religion, without interfering with the legitimate rights of the
Emperor, could exist in its fulness notwithstanding. The rule of
Rome need not interfere with the practice of religion.

It is very important to notice that the bulk of the Pharisees
took much the same line. The Scribes and legalists at all events
were by no means keen to raise the standard of revolt. They

expected God to destroy Rome, just as Jesus did. There was no great difference in this respect between them. The commentators ignore this agreement or deny it. It is inconvenient, perhaps, but the evidence seems to show that it is true. The importance of the saying is diminished when we remember that Jesus, in any case, believed that the rule of Rome was only going to last quite a short time. For either before his death, or after it and at his reappearance, would come the new age and the perfected Kingdom, and then the Roman dominion would disappear. The rule of Rome was to disappear by God's agency, not by man's. Not by revolt and force of arms, but when the Son of man comes down from heaven will the heathen domination cease.

As a matter of fact, the answer was primarily intended to be non-committal. It maintains the policy of caution. Once more Jesus cleverly avoids a dilemma. W. holds that no more was intended, though a denial of the theocracy may be found as the *implication* of his reply. He sets up no principle by which one can clearly sever the claims of God from the claims of the Emperor. He only asserts that each has his rights and claims, which we may legitimately satisfy. We cannot use his answer as a solution of any of our own difficulties, except in so far as it may seem to assert that state and religion are two separate and not connected territories. And W. seems to me right when he calls Ranke's opinion that our passage is the most important and far-reaching of the words of Jesus, ' etwas profan und recht verkehrt.'

Loisy's remarks upon the passage seem judicious and sensible. Jesus means, he says, that ' civil obedience, attested by the payment of the tribute, no more contradicts than it abolishes the obedience which is due to God. The first of these duties does not interfere with the second. The first is trivial in comparison with the second. Let men observe it without attaching greater importance to it than it possesses, and let them give their minds above everything to the essential duty, which is moral and religious duty. Jesus emphasizes the lawfulness of political power and of tribute much less than the insignificance of these things in comparison with the Kingdom of heaven. It is implied that the Kingdom of heaven is not to be established by violence, by a rebellion against the established order ; in the interval before its coming one should pay to Cæsar the tax which attests his sovereignty, and it would be foolish to believe that God and His reign would gain anything by the rejection of an obligation of this kind. Let the things of this world be esteemed according to the smallness of their value, and let these duties be discharged according as there is necessity ; but let men know above all that the greatest thing lies elsewhere, in fidelity to the heavenly Father. It would be to falsify the thought of Jesus to suppose that the debt to Cæsar is on the same plane, or that it has the same absolute and definite character as the duty towards God. Nothing was farther from his thoughts than to establish a principle in accordance with which the boundaries of the domains of God and those of Cæsar might be rigidly defined' (*E. S.* II. p. 336).

I do not see that a Rabbi could not have given this prudent reply. It is certainly one which would not have been given by a Zealot. But the majority of the Rabbis were opposed to the Zealots. Most of them were not by any means anxious to revolt against Rome, if the Roman authorities would but allow the Jews to pay unto God what is God's, *i.e.* to observe the Law. What tended to bring about the revolt was that the division was not clearly made. The Rabbis would have been ready to give unto Cæsar what is Cæsar's if he had never made them also give unto Cæsar what was God's. The whole matter is fully discussed in Dr. Abrahams' *Studies*, I. chap. viii. Klausner says : ' The answer convinced the people that Jesus was not their redeemer, and that he was not come to free them from the Roman Edomite yoke. He thus lost some of his popularity.' ' When we notice that the people *supported* him when he entered Jerusalem as the Messiah and purified the Temple, but did nothing to save him three days later when he was crucified—the change is hard to explain unless we assume that his answer about the tribute money proved to the people that not from this Galilæan Messiah could they hope for national freedom and political redemption' (p. 318). This is doubtful. ' They marvelled '—at the ingeniousness of his reply, and how well he had avoided the pitfall prepared for him.

THE WOMAN TAKEN IN ADULTERY

(John vii. 53—viii. 11)

53, 1   And they went, each one, to his own house. And Jesus went
2 to the Mount of Olives. And early in the morning, he returned to the temple, and all the people came unto him, and he sat down,
3 and he taught them. And the scribes and Pharisees brought unto him a woman taken in adultery, and putting her in the midst of
4 them, they said to him, ' Master, this woman was taken in the very
5 act of adultery. Now Moses commanded us in the Law that such
6 women should be stoned ; what then sayest thou ? ' And they said this to try him, that they might have something with which to accuse him. But Jesus stooped forward, and wrote with his finger
7 upon the ground. But when they continued asking him, he raised his head, and said unto them, ' He that is without sin amongst you,

8 let him be the first to cast a stone at her.' And again he stooped
9 forward, and wrote upon the ground.   And they, having heard that,
withdrew one by one, beginning with the eldest ; and Jesus was left
10 alone, and the woman, where she was, in the midst.   And Jesus lifted
his head, and said to her : ' Woman, where are they ?   Has no one
11 condemned thee ? '   And she said, ' No one, Lord.'   Then Jesus said,
' Neither do I condemn thee.   Go, and from henceforth sin no more.'

According to many critics it is probable that in the oldest story
of the life of Jesus in Jerusalem there followed between the ' Give
unto Cæsar ' incident, and the question of the Sadducees, the tale
of the woman taken in adultery.   Why this tale dropped out of the
Synoptics, and why it found an incongruous and unsatisfactory
home in some MSS. of the Fourth Gospel, are questions upon which
I need not enter here.   Some regard the story as apocryphal.
Others think that it is authentic.   The internal difficulties of the
story are great, and these difficulties make me incline somewhat
towards the first opinion.   But if it is not true, it is at least *ben
trovato*, and quite in keeping with some of the moral statements,
paradoxical, searching, exalted, but elusive, of the historical Jesus.
In any case it may usefully be included here.

2.   Thus this story, if authentic and put in its right place,
makes and marks a fresh day in the Jerusalem ministry.

3.   How and why was the woman taken and brought before
Jesus ?   Did her accomplice escape ?   Did the ' Scribes and
Pharisees ' seize her in order to bring her to justice—to a court—
and was the Temple near where she was seized, and did the idea
strike these Scribes and Pharisees to see if they could use this woman
as a snare for the Galilæan teacher ?   And why should Scribes and
Pharisees have been present, and in such convenient numbers ?   All
these quite unanswerable questions give rise to suspicion.
Again it is a very dubious matter whether adultery was, or
could be, at that time, punishable with death.   Many great scholars
think that it was not.

5.   Another difficulty.   The law does not say that adulteresses
are to be stoned except in the special case mentioned in Deut. xxii.
23.   Was this woman betrothed ?   If not, the Rabbinic law
arranged that when the Pentateuchal ordinance fixed no particular
kind of death, the guilty person should be strangled.

6.   What was the ' temptation ' or ' test ' ?   Probably this.

Jesus was supposed to be merciful to sinners, perhaps especially to women. If, then, his opinion were asked, and he were tempted to urge that this woman, if she repented, should be forgiven, then he could be brought into conflict with the letter of the God-given Law.

Jesus guesses what they would be at. Perhaps he is morally wroth that this woman in her shame should be used for such a purpose. He refuses to look upon them or upon her; he will not add to her shame. At any rate, be her guilt what it may, it does not concern him; it is not for him to decide and condemn her. He therefore abstractedly makes marks in the dust on the floor. So one may interpret his action. One need not ask: What did he write?

7. Forced to reply, Jesus once more raises another issue. He neither condemns nor acquits. What does he mean? It is easy to admire and vaguely to paraphrase his words; it is less easy to understand them. It would be ludicrous that no one should judge criminal cases who was not himself 'sinless,' conscious of no sin. In that case there would be no judges or juries in the world. The words of Jesus are relative to his questioners. Do they imply:

(1) It is not for any one except the regularly constituted tribunal to condemn this woman. It is not for you, therefore, or for me, to condemn her.

(2) 'Judge not.' You seem glad to condemn. But should one not be sorry and reluctant? Perhaps too: was it for *you* to seize her? Are *you* guilty of no sins, whether sins of the flesh or others, for which *you* should not be seized?

(3) Should this woman's shame be used as a means with which to entrap me?

(4) Is it conceivable that the very absence and escape of the probably greater culprit makes Jesus the more scrupulous about condemning the woman? Is not society always readier to punish the woman than the man? Was not Jesus the champion of womanhood?

The words make a deep impression upon us even though we cannot be wholly certain as to the precise meanings they are intended to convey.

9. It seems doubtful whether this dramatic retirement is historically likely. The gloss of some MSS. 'convicted by their own conscience' is what is intended. Again 'beginning with the eldest,' to which some MSS. add 'even unto the last,' is very obscure and doubtful. It raises suspicion. It was no regular court: why

then should the eldest have been the first to sneak off ?   The narrator
thinks of a court with a regular order and precedence.   He falls out
of his narrative, and thus casts doubt upon the whole.

11.   The final scene between Jesus and the woman is impressive
in its brief simplicity.   His point of view is that of Ezekiel xxxiii. 11.
'Repent and live.'   He was sent to call sinners to repentance and
to save them.   He is no judge in the ordinary sense of the word.

18–27.   THE LIFE OF THE RESURRECTION

(*Cp.* Matt. xxii. 23–33 ; Luke xx. 27–38)

18   Then came unto him some Sadducees, who say there is no resur-
19 rection ; and they asked him, saying, 'Master, Moses wrote for us,
     If a man die, and leave a wife and no child, his brother must marry
20 his wife, and raise up seed unto his brother.   Now there were seven
21 brothers : and the first took a wife, and dying left no seed.   And
     the second married her, and died without leaving seed : and the
22 third likewise.   And all seven left no seed : last of all the woman
23 died also.   In the resurrection, therefore, when they rise, whose
     wife will she be of them ? for all the seven had her to wife.'
24   And Jesus answering said unto them, 'Does not this prove that
     ye err, and that ye neither know the scriptures nor the power of
25 God ?   For when they rise from the dead, they neither marry nor
26 are given in marriage ; but are as the angels in heaven.   But as
     regards the dead, that they rise : have ye not read in the book of
     Moses, in the story of the burning bush, how God spoke unto him,
     saying, I am the God of Abraham, and the God of Isaac, and the
27 God of Jacob ?   He is not the God of the dead, but the God of the
     living : ye do greatly err.'

18.   After the Pharisees have had their 'test' comes the turn
of the Sadducees.   Their question is put in order to show that,
whatever answer be given, the theory of resurrection leads to
absurdity.   If Moses ordered the so-called Levirate marriage
(Deut. xxv. 5), he cannot have believed in the resurrection.
    Jesus shows that no absurdity is involved.   The conditions of
the resurrection life are unlike those of the present life.   There
is no marrying or giving in marriage.
    Though the popular view may have been that the ordinary life
on earth, interrupted by death, would be resumed at the resur-

rection, this was not the official doctrine of the Rabbis.   The *locus classicus* on the subject is Berachoth 17 *a*, and runs thus : ' Rab used to say : In the world to come there is no eating or drinking or marrying or envy or hate ; but the pious rest with crowns upon their heads, and are satisfied with the glory of God.'   This passage is much later than the first century, but I see no reason why we may not believe that Rab's teaching would not have been accepted by Hillel or Tarphen.

Doubtless there was also some lower teaching prevalent among the Rabbis as well.   But what we read about Rab's saying in S.-B. (p. 888) is not, I think, accurate.   *Cp.* Dr. Abrahams' *Studies*, I. chap. xxi.

24. ' Your very question with the dilemma you suppose involved, and your consequent denial of the resurrection, show the measure of your error.   They show that you know neither the Scriptures (which prove the resurrection) nor the power of God (who makes the resurrection life to differ from, and be higher than, the life on earth).'   The second point is taken in 25 ; the first point in 26.   There is a certain parallelism of words and phrase with I Cor. xv. 33, 34 dealing with the same subject.   οὐ διὰ τοῦτο. The question and the argumentation of the Sadducees are referred to in the τοῦτο.

26.   The proof of the resurrection is of the usual fanciful kind when proofs from Scripture are attempted.   As God is (as *all* admit) the God of the living and not of the dead, and as He calls Himself to Moses the God of Abraham, Isaac, and Jacob (who had died long ago), these patriarchs must still live ; and this, again, can only mean that they will ' rise ' or have ' risen.'   Is it assumed that they are now in ' heaven ' ?   Or are they only potentially alive, while, at the resurrection, they will live fully once more ? The idea apparently is that the dead are waiting for the resurrection, not asleep, but with full consciousness, whether of pleasure or pain. But only the righteous dead are thought of, or referred to, in this passage.

28–34.   The Greatest Commandment

(*Cp.* Matthew xxii. 34–40 ; Luke xx. 39, 40, x. 25–28)

28   Then one of the scribes who had heard them disputing together, and had perceived that Jesus had answered them excellently, came up and asked him, ' Which commandment is the first of all ? '

29 And Jesus answered him, ' The first of all the commandments is,

30 Hear, O Israel, the Lord our God, the Lord is One : and thou shalt
love the Lord thy God with all thy heart, and with all thy soul, and
31 with all thy mind, and with all thy strength.   And the second is
this, Thou shalt love thy neighbour as thyself.   There is no other
32 commandment greater than these.'   And the scribe said unto him,
' Excellently, Master, thou hast said the truth, that He is One, and
33 there is none other but He : and to love Him with all one's heart,
and with all one's understanding, and with all one's strength, and
to love one's neighbour as oneself, is much better than all burnt
34 offerings and sacrifices.'   And when Jesus saw that he answered
intelligently, he said unto him, ' Thou art not far from the kingdom
of God.'

It is pleasant, at last, to come once more upon a passage of
religious value for us to-day, which we have not had since x. 44.   One
more question is put to Jesus.   He has triumphantly answered priest,
Pharisees, and Sadducees.   Now an individual Rabbi comes upon
the scene.   His question, however, is not asked in any hostile spirit,
nor with insidious intent.   Therefore it is frankly answered.   This
paragraph shows us Jesus as the true successor of Amos and Isaiah ;
he speaks as they would have spoken.   And here, too, Mark allows
us to see for once that there were good men even outside the
followers of Jesus and even among the Rabbis.   Such a concession
is somewhat too arduous for Matthew.

But in Luke it is the Scribe, and not Jesus, who gives the answer,
and declares which commandments are the greatest, and this version
of the story may be the more original.   Dr. Abrahams' excellent
chapter in *Studies*, i. pp. 18–29 should be read here.   Meyer, commenting on this section of Mark, observes, ' The inner freedom to
which Jesus has attained, even with regard to the Law, places him
far above all his Jewish predecessors.   A full metamorphosis of
the Law into a religious ethic was only effected by Jesus.   It had,
indeed, been striven after by his forerunners, and had been
announced by them to the heathen as the true content of the Law ;
but they were not able to achieve it fully on account of their lack of
power and courage to shake off the shackles of ritualism ' (p. 431).
Here we have once more the old confusion.   The Prophets, the
true predecessors of Jesus, said the same thing as he, but they had
not the divine Law before them, so that with them—Amos, Hosea,
Isaiah especially—the question does not apply.   They were not
able to show ' inner freedom ' towards the Law, for there was no
Law.   As regards the Rabbis, it is not a question of inner freedom ;
it is not a question of power and courage.   If you believe that a

given code is perfect and divine, you must, if you are logical, draw
the consequences. The Rabbis had a greater faith than Jesus in
the perfection and divinity of the Law, and they were more trained
logicians. This faith and this logic hampered them: not the
lack of courage.

29. The reply of Jesus is very significant. Like the good
Jew he is, he at once quotes the *Shema* as the first and highest
commandment. The love of the one God is the supreme ordinance.
Next to it he places Leviticus xix. 18. The bringing together of
these two commandments is highly striking and suggestive. They
are to this day the main part, though not the complete whole, of
the Jewish religion.

It is going too far to say with Dr. Bartlet: 'In Leviticus the
word "neighbour" is used with reference to fellow-Jews. In the
N.T. it has the widest possible extension of meaning; for Jesus
lifted it at once and for ever out of its more limited application
by his parable of the Good Samaritan (Luke x. 29-37).' For (*a*)
even if the Hebrew word for 'neighbour' meant when Leviticus
was written 'fellow-Jew,' the commandment of Lev. xix. 18 was
immediately followed by the commandment of xix. 34, and if,
again, the Hebrew word 'ger' meant not 'stranger,' but 'resident
alien,' yet the resident alien was certainly not a fellow-Jew. And
(*b*) even if the Hebrew word 'rea' meant fellow-Jew in 500 B.C.,
it does not follow that it was understood to mean fellow-Jew in
A.D. 28, and there is, indeed, some evidence to show that it was not.
And (*c*) in the exquisite parable of the Good Samaritan it is by no
means sure that 'Samaritan' was part of the parable in its oldest
form. And (*d*) is it not rather dangerous to make the teaching of
Jesus about the connotation of 'neighbour' depend upon one
parable only found in one Gospel?

Wellhausen's note runs thus: 'Jesus answers with two sayings
of the Law, which the Rabbi also acknowledges to be its flower and
kernel. Only here does Jesus (using the words of the Old Testament)
speak of the love of God and of one's neighbour; usually he does
not give verbal utterance to them. Monotheism is no theory;
it is a practical conviction; it is the spring of inward character
and the motive of our conduct to our neighbour. It is, in other
words, the motive of morality; and morality, according to the
right supplement of the Scribe, belongs to the service of God and
is the right worship of Him; it is of more value than all sacred
actions which are specially rendered to God and are of no use to
anyone else. The combination of the two sayings, which in the
Law occur in different places, is very important for the understanding of the whole passage; the combination was first effected

in this way by Jesus.' Perhaps this last statement is somewhat too categoric; it may not be true. But I cannot go into this question here.

32. Has the Rabbi heard rumours that Jesus arrogates to himself some vague sort of quasi-divinity, and is he, therefore, delighted with his frank confession of pure, unadulterated monotheism? It looks almost as much, for the Rabbi proceeds to emphasize the doctrine of the One God with renewed intensity. The verse is spoken to the heart of every Jew. It contains the essence of Liberal Judaism in a nutshell.

33. The conclusion of the verse recalls Hosea vi. 6 and the many similar prophetic passages.

34. Again it is well to quote Wellhausen's note: ' Thus one can be, already on earth, in the Kingdom, or near it, or far from it. The conception is less markedly eschatological here than in x. 17-31. Nor does Jesus say to the Rabbi, " Abandon everything, and follow me." The love of God and one's neighbour is not the same as the renunciation of the world. The decalogue may indeed be excelled (x. 21), but the monotheistic faith, as represented in the combination of Deut. vi. 4, 5 with Leviticus xix. 18, cannot be excelled, not even by discipleship and martyrdom.'

But the words ' Thou art not far from the Kingdom of God,' which seem at first sight simple, contain several problems and difficulties. First of all do they imply that the Kingdom is present? If so, this is already a difficulty, for in Mark the Kingdom is almost always future. And for Jesus himself the Kingdom was only imminent, hardly already present. Yet the words ' Thou art not far from the Kingdom' seem certainly to imply that the Kingdom *is* present. They can hardly mean, ' You *will* nearly enter the Kingdom, though never quite.' They must rather mean, ' You are at present very near something which already exists.' Here, then, we must admit is one of the rare instances in which in Mark the Kingdom is spoken of as something which already exists. But there is another trouble about the words, at least if Wellhausen (*Einleitung*, 2nd ed. p. 93) is right in pointing out that what is implied is that morality is not enough to secure the entry into the Kingdom. ' He who knows that the love of God and one's neighbour is the sum of the Law is, however, only " not far from the Kingdom of God," and he who has kept all the commandments from his youth up, still lacks the chief thing, and even John the Baptist lacks it. [The reference is to Mark x. 21 and Matt. xi. 11.] And this chief thing is the acknowledgment of Jesus, the imitation of him, and the adhesion to his body of disciples—an adhesion which is not bound up with his life, but starts most effectively with his death.'   But would the historic Jesus have taught such a limiting conception ?   At any rate, if Wellhausen's view be accurate, the words of 34 start a new particularism, worse and more rigid than the much abused particularism of the Jews and of the Rabbis.   For that national particularism was constantly broken through, and even for the Gentiles morality became in Jewish opinion the test for the admission into the beatitude of the Life to Come.   The particularism of the Rabbis showed itself much more in denying that heathen or idolater could be good than in denying that, even if he were good, he would not enter into the Kingdom of God.   But the second denial is far worse and far more shocking than the first.   And it is this second denial which is heralded in verse 34, and becomes full-blown in the later Christian teaching.   No particularism can be more odious than that which asserts that morality is not the adequate condition for entry into the Kingdom of God, or into 'heaven.'   The particularism based upon right belief (characteristic of Christianity) is much more objectionable than the particularism of descent (characteristic of Judaism).   The old Jews said frankly : The heathen in the lump are bad.   This was narrow enough, but at all events there was a certain naïve and healthy narrowness about it.   It still preserves the supremacy of morality, and renders it possible for a Rabbi to urge that the righteous of every nation shall be ' saved.'   But if morality is not the test for heaven—can there be a worse particularism than this ?   Be as good as you please, and yet you shall not enter in unless you believe that Jesus is the Messiah, or some other dogma quite outside morality—this is surely a particularism more immoral and more dangerous than any foolish pride of race.   Let us hope that Jesus was free from it.

I am now inclined to think that Jesus, if he said the exact words attributed to him, meant that the man *would* enter the Kingdom when the Kingdom arrived.   He did not mean that he still lacked something (unlike x. 21).

35–37.   WHOSE SON IS THE MESSIAH ?

(*Cp.* Matt. xxii. 41–46 ; Luke xx. 41–44)

35   And no man ventured to ask him any more questions.   And Jesus went on teaching in the temple, and said : ' How can the 36 scribes say that the Messiah is the Son of David ?   For David himself said in the Holy Spirit, The Lord said to my lord, Sit thou 37 on my right hand, till I make thine enemies thy footstool.   David

himself calls him lord ; how is he then his son ? ' And the mass
of the people heard him gladly.

The section is of little interest to Jewish readers. The introductory words come awkwardly. They would find a better place
after xii. 27. The meaning of the section seems clear, but the more
clear the meaning, the stranger does it become. Jesus certainly
seems to say : How can it be asserted that the Messiah is the son of
David, if David in Psalm cx. regards himself as inferior to the
Messiah ? A father would not call his son ' lord,' but David calls
the Messiah ' lord.' (Jesus shares the ordinary belief of his time
as to the authorship of the ' Davidic ' psalms.) Apparently this
must imply that Jesus claims to be the Messiah, though he be *not*
the descendant of David. (The genealogies in Matthew were made
up later to prove that he was.) Jesus seems not to *wish* to be
regarded as the ' son of David.' But how could he be the Messiah
if he was not the Messiah of prophecy ? If the Old Testament was
wrong, and the prophets spoke falsely, why did Jesus not say so ?
Why did he not say, ' There will be no Davidic Messiah, but I am
something far higher than the mere Davidic Messiah of the prophets ? '
The puzzle is that Jesus wants both to refute and to fulfil the Old
Testament and its prophecies. He is the predicted Messiah ; and
he is not the predicted Messiah. One asks in vain : (1) Did he
really take up this illogical position ? (2) Was he conscious of the
illogicalness ? To say that Jesus thought he was the Servant-
Messiah of Isaiah xlii. and liii., but not the Messiah of Isaiah xi., is
not an adequate answer. Dr. Carpenter thinks that the explanation
is that the ' Old Testament does not speak with one voice. The
Gospel writers were no more historical critics than Jesus himself. If
they and he fastened on the Servant passages (Messianically interpreted), the only way open to them was to *ignore* the Davidic
king passages.' But the difficulty of this view is (1) that there is
very little evidence indeed that Jesus did ' fasten ' on the Servant
passages, and (2) that Jesus does not here merely ' ignore.' He
goes out of his way to *attack*. He combats the doctrine which the
' Davidic king passages ' emphatically teach. Or shall we suppose
that Jesus had a higher, more apocalyptic, conception of the Messiah ?
As a heavenly being he would, after his suffering and death, descend
from heaven upon the clouds. If he be the Messiah, or rather if he
is to become the Messiah, a miracle from God must raise him upon
his divine throne. He does not want to be a son of David who,
through his legitimate descent, shall become an earthly king. Only
a divine miracle can make Jesus the true heavenly Messiah that is to
be. And the Messiah, as a heavenly being, is not of human descent.
    If the passage is authentic, we must, perhaps, suppose that the

interest of Jesus in the question which he raised was caused, on the one hand, by the conviction that he was the Messiah, and on the other, by his knowledge that he was not descended from David. The common belief that the Messiah must be a scion of David's house stood seriously in the way of his own recognition as Messiah. In any case the story seems to show the inadequacy of the idea that he *consciously* wanted to be quite a different sort of Messiah from the ordinary ' political ' Messiah expected by the populace and the Rabbis. For if he was only a ' spiritual ' Messiah, the question whether the customary belief in the Messiah's Davidic descent was justified or not would have had no interest for him one way or the other. But here we find him implying that he was the predicted theocratic king, even though he was not of Davidic descent. He pits David in the 110th Psalm against Isaiah xi.

Some think that the passage is not authentic, and that the words were never uttered by Jesus at all. I cannot give all the arguments for this view. If Jesus had said 35-37, the belief that he was the descendant of David would hardly have won the day, as it eventually did. The Christian community desired to show (by 35-37) that Jesus as Messiah was something greater than the son of David, namely, the Son of God, or again, it attempted by such arguments as 35-37 to empty the objection that it could not clearly prove that he was the son of David of any value or force (Bultmann, p. 83). There is an interpretation of the passage to which I have not so far alluded, because it is so unnatural and awkward, but which is defended by many scholars in order to get out of the difficulty. According to this interpretation Jesus holds to both the Lordship and the Sonship. He does not disclaim being ' a son of David ' in any sense. 'But what he disclaims, and refutes by showing the impasse to which it led (on their own premises), was the Pharisees' notion of Messiahship *as determined* by sonship to David " according to the flesh," rather than by the divine sonship, or unique spiritual relation to God—which was to Jesus the basis of his own Messianic vocation ' (Bartlet). This view seems to me much too subtle, if not too sophistic, to be probable. Would any Buddhist commentator have ever hit upon it ? Or would any Christian commentator have ever devised it, if a similar passage occurred in some sacred Buddhist book ? The interpretation of the passage in Cadman is ingenious, but, as it seems to me, very fanciful and unlikely. Meyer accepts the historicity of the story.

35. Both here and in 37 we have to translate, according to Klostermann, not ' David himself,' but merely ' David.' *Cp.* vi. 17 where we should translate ' Herod,' not ' Herod himself.' Αὐτός is ' vorweisendes Pronomen nach aramäischer Sitte = er, David.'

37. πόθεν seems here to mean merely 'how.' How can the Messiah be the son of the very man who calls him 'lord' ? Fathers do not call their sons 'lord.'

Klostermann observes : 'Mark himself will hardly have felt, or meant to express, any doubt as to the Davidic descent. He will have understood : the title "David's son" gives to the Messiah too little honour.'

38-40. ATTACK UPON THE SCRIBES

(*Cp.* Matt. xxiii. 1, 6, 7 ; Luke xi. 43, xx. 46, 47)

38 And he said unto them in his teaching, ' Beware of the scribes, who love to walk in long robes, and to be saluted in the market-
39 places, and to have the first seats in the synagogues and at feasts :
40 who devour widows' houses, and for a pretence make long prayers : these shall receive all the heavier punishment.'

These verses would appear to be an extract from a much longer and more elaborate attack which is found in Matt. xxiii. How much Mark had before him of what we find in Matthew is uncertain, but it is possible that he contracted and that Matthew did not merely expand.

The attack must be regarded as directed against some bad Rabbis, not against the Rabbis as a class. If it was directed against the Rabbis as a class, it is almost certainly false. In any case it is the attack of an antagonist, and all attacks of reformers against those who oppose them must be taken with grains of salt. All this would be obvious to, and accepted by, everybody, were it not that these attacks are put into the mouth of one who founded a religion the adherents of which regard the founder as perfect, immaculate, and divine. Hence the words must be strictly true. If he said ' the Scribes of my time were bad,' bad they were. Moreover, Paul devised a theory according to which every one who had lived under the Law, and loved the Law, was of necessity bad. Hence the accuracy of the attack was theoretically proved. Happily, even among the German Lutheran theologians, a more historic and impartial attitude is beginning to assert itself. Critics and theologians are slowly beginning to try to put themselves above the documents, and to judge them as they would if they referred to a teacher and his opponents in Mongolia. There is no reason why there should not have been some bad hypocritical Rabbis in the first century. Jews should not excite themselves, or attempt a general whitewash. That would be as silly as the Christian view that whatever Jesus is reported to have said about his opponents is necessarily accurate. It is neither necessarily accurate nor necessarily inaccurate. Nothing could be better than the tone of Dr. Abrahams, chap. x., ' Widows' Houses,' in *Studies*, I., to which the reader may be referred. Here the rather wild accusations of verse 40 are subjected to a cold and dispassionate criticism. It is possible, though not certain, that in the first century—' an age that was rent by outward collapse and spiritual contradictions,' as Dr. L. Blau calls it—there may have been some larger degree of moral corruption than usual. The theory is attractive; the evidence is inconclusive. The whole question is becoming less interesting than it used to be. When everybody who was not a Jew joined in believing that both Jesus and Paul were necessarily right, and that, both theoretically and actually, all the Scribes and Pharisees, as lovers of the Law, were hypocritical, proud, cruel, and all the rest of it, it was quite exciting to try to prove that Jesus and Paul were wrong. But now that it is becoming more and more admitted that Paul spoke for himself, and that his theory, like many other religious theories, had no close relation to facts, and that Jesus did not mean ' *all* Pharisees and *all* Scribes,' but only ' *some* Pharisees and *some* Scribes,' the interest and piquancy of the controversy are enormously diminished. Whether five per cent of the Rabbis in the age of Jesus were bad, or eleven, is a question (especially as the answer can never be ascertained) about which it is almost impossible to pump up much interest or enthusiasm.

38. τῶν θελόντων, ' who like.' They are accused of liking to walk in long robes, and to be respectfully greeted in the market-place, and to have the best seats at synagogues and banquets. The ' walking in long robes ' Goguel thinks is only intelligible as a ' résumé du développement du premier évangile sur les phylactères ' (I. p. 266). The next verse deals with moral offences. They are hypocrites in prayer, and rob the widow. How the last charge was carried out in practice is not stated. It is perhaps implied that they acquired an authority over women, and let themselves be richly paid for their advice. Some think that they obtained money by offering to pray for them. This charge is not in Matthew. It is peculiar to Mark. These charges, if applied to a whole class, refute themselves by their violence. There were good and bad Rabbis then, as there have always been good and bad priests and good and bad clergymen. We may assume that it was the bad Pharisees and Rabbis (Mark, it is to be noted, does not here mention the Pharisees) who were attacked by Jesus. The Talmud speaks of hypocritical Pharisees, who loved to show off a pretended piety. The Assumption of Moses is believed by some scholars to allude to Pharisees who are pretenders and hypocrites and eat the property of the poor. Josephus usually

praises the Pharisees and dilates upon their good qualities. In one place, however (*Ant.* Book XVII. 2), he speaks of them as a party (μόριον) γεραίρειν τὸ θεῖον προσποιούμενον (making men believe that they are favoured by God), and he says that the women were influenced by them (οἷς ὑπῆκτο ἡ γυναικωνῖτις). There was doubtless some material for attack. Fiebig is not unfair in what he says on p. 69 of his book *Die Gleichnis reden Jesu* (1912). The volume deserves study.

41–44. The Widow's Mite

(*Cp.* Luke xxi. 1-4)

41 And Jesus sat down opposite the treasury, and watched the people throwing money into the treasury : and many that were
42 rich cast in much. And a poor widow came and threw in two
43 farthings, which make a halfpenny. And he called unto him his disciples, and said unto them, ' Verily I say unto you, this poor widow has thrown in more than all who have thrown into the
44 treasury : for all they threw in from their superfluity ; but she from her poverty has thrown in all that she possessed, even all her living.'

41. For the ' treasury ' and its arrangements see *Encylopœdia Biblica, s.v.* ' Temple,' par. 36, and Hastings, *Dictionary of the Bible, s.v.* ' Treasury.' χαλκόν does not mean here probably ' copper money,' ' small change ' literally, but rather ' money ' generally. For rich people were there also, giving much.

42. She puts in two separate ' mites,' though she could have kept one for herself. λεπτὰ δύο, ' two lepta.' The ' lepton ' was half a ' kodrantes ' (*i.e.* the Latin *quadrans*). Thus it was the eighth part of an *as*, and the one hundred and twenty-eighth part of a *denarius*. (The value of a *denarius* was about ninepence.) A lepton was the smallest copper coin in circulation, and less than a third of a farthing. In contrast to the bad Scribes, who ' eat ' widows' property, we have now the tale of the good widow and her sacrifice.

44. ' All her living ' or possessions (ὅλον τὸν βίον) must be understood to mean all that she possessed at the moment. The S.S. omits the words ; they may be a gloss. The moral of the story is quite Rabbinic.

There is a close and famous parallel in the Midrash. I think it is a pity that in the second edition of his Mark Wellhausen omitted the observation that the little story of the widow goes more to one's heart than all the miracles of which the first half of Mark is full.   How far the story is to be regarded as historic is another question.   It has been asked : how could Jesus accurately observe how much each person threw in ?   How could he know that what the widow threw in was all she possessed ? (Bultmann, pp. 16, 29). On the other hand *cp.* Schmidt's reply p. 291, n. 2 ; it is not very successful.

Wellhausen notices that, except for the fig tree, Jesus works no miracles in Jerusalem, and executes no healings or exorcisms. He also presses the difference between the Jesus of viii. 27–x. 45, and the Jesus of xi. and xii.

' The mournful mood which Jesus showed on the way to Jerusalem ceases in Jerusalem itself ; it gives place to a mood of confidence and energy.   Jesus seems buoyed up by the enthusiasm of the multitude.   The near and certain death does not fill his heart or his words ; there is only one prediction of death, and that is in the interpolated parable of the vineyard.   The purification of the Temple brings about a conflict with the chief priests, but Jesus avoids accentuating it ; he bears himself with caution and cleverness against his opponents, and yet without concessions or compromise.   We hear no words about the inevitableness of the cross, not only for him, but also for his disciples, about their having to follow him to death, or about the complete renunciation of the world in view of the near approach of the Kingdom ; the sections xii. 28–34 and x. 17–31, though outwardly alike, are inwardly totally dissimilar.   These deep-going differences are hardly to be explained by the fact that in xi. and xii. Jesus is no longer speaking, as in viii. 27–x. 45, privately to the disciples, but openly before the people at large.   And why in Jerusalem *does* he no longer speak to his disciples, except in the certainly spurious apocalypse xiii., and on the last day ?   He had opportunity enough during the evenings at Bethany to talk to them about himself and the meaning of his imminent sufferings and death, and yet not a word is reported about it.'

The legitimate deduction from these observations, which I presume we are to draw, is that the picture of Jesus in Jerusalem, as given in xi. and xii., is more authentic and more historic than the deviating picture of him as given in viii. 27–x. 45.

CHAPTER XIII

1–37. The End and the ' Parousia '

(*Cp.* Matt. xxiv. 1–36 ; Luke xxi. 5-33)

1 And as he went out of the temple, one of his disciples said unto him, ' Master, see, what grand stones and what grand
2 buildings ! ' And Jesus, answering, said unto him, ' Seest thou these great buildings ? There shall not be left one stone upon another, which shall not be thrown down.'

3 And as he sat upon the mount of Olives over against the temple, Peter and James and John and Andrew asked him
4 privately, ' Tell us, when shall these things be ? and what is the sign when all these things are to be fulfilled ? '

5 And Jesus, answering them, began to say, ' Take heed lest any
6 man lead you astray : for many will come in my name, saying, It
7 is I, and they shall lead many astray. And when ye hear of wars and rumours of wars, be ye not alarmed ; for these things must
8 happen ; but the End is not yet. For nation will rise against nation, and kingdom against kingdom : and there will be earthquakes in divers places, and there will be famines : these are the beginnings of the Pangs.

9 ' But ye—take heed to yourselves : for they will deliver you up to law courts ; and in synagogues ye will be beaten : and ye will be brought before rulers and kings for my sake, to bear
10 witness before them. For the gospel must first be proclaimed
11 unto all nations. But when they take you away, and deliver you up, have no care beforehand what ye shall speak, but whatsoever shall be given you in that hour, that speak ye : for it is not ye
12 that speak, but the Holy Spirit. And brother will deliver up brother to death, and the father his son ; and children will rise up
13 against their parents, and will put them to death. And ye will

be hated of all men for my name's sake : but he that endures unto the end, he shall be saved.

14 'But when ye shall see the Abomination of Desolation, standing where it ought not (let him that reads give heed), then let 15 them that be in Judæa flee to the mountains : and let him that is on the roof not go down into the house, neither enter therein, 16 to take anything out of his house : and let him that is in the 17 field not go back to fetch his cloak. But woe to them that are 18 with child, and to them that give suck in those days ! And pray 19 ye that it may not be in the winter. For in those days there will be affliction, such as has not been from the beginning of the 20 world which God created until now, and will not be again. And if the Lord had not shortened those days, no flesh would be saved : but for the elect's sake, whom he hath chosen out, he has shortened 21 the days. And then, if any man shall say to you, Lo, here is the 22 Messiah ; or, lo, he is there ; believe him not. For false Messiahs and false prophets will arise, and will perform signs and wonders, 23 to cause the elect, if it be possible, to go astray. But take ye heed : behold, I have foretold everything unto you.

24 'But in those days, after that affliction, the sun will be 25 darkened, and the moon will not give her light, and the stars will fall from heaven, and the heavenly powers will be shaken. 26 And then will be seen the Son of man coming on the clouds with 27 great power and glory. And then he will send out the angels, and will gather together his elect from the four winds, from the uttermost part of the earth to the uttermost part of heaven.

28 'From the fig tree learn a parable : when its branch becomes 29 soft, and it puts forth leaves, ye know that summer is near ; so, too, ye, when ye see these things happening, know that he is nigh, even at the door.

30 'Verily I say unto you, that this generation shall not pass 31 away, till all these things shall have taken place. Heaven and 32 earth shall pass away : but my words shall not pass away. But as to that day and as to the hour, no man knows, not even the angels who are in heaven, and not even the Son, but only the Father.

3, 34 'Take ye heed, watch : for ye know not when the time is. For it is as if a man went abroad, and left his house, and gave authority to his servants, and to every man his work, and commanded the

35 porter to watch.　Watch ye therefore : for ye know not when the
master of the house comes, whether at even, or at midnight, or
36 at the cockcrowing, or in the early morning : lest coming suddenly,
37 he find you sleeping.　And what I say unto you, I say unto all :
Watch.'

This apocalyptic oration as a whole is certainly unauthentic.
Much of it is built up upon the familiar lines of Jewish apocalypses
from Daniel (164 B.C.) onwards.　It has very slight interest for us
to-day, and little or no religious value.　Judaism freed itself of
apocalyptic dreamings sooner than Christianity, but both religions
have long advanced beyond them now.

How much of the oration from 5 to 37 goes back to Jesus is very
doubtful.　Verse 32, though not necessarily in its present exact
form, may be authentic.　As regards the rest, the portions which
are of Jewish origin, or of Christian origin, or, lastly, which proceeded
from the mouth of Jesus, can never be distinguished with certainty.
The oldest parts, representing the original Jewish apocalypse, may be
7, 8, 14–20, and 24–31.　Christian editors, including the Evangelist,
will account for what remains.　It is even questionable whether
any part was said by Jesus of what we now possess.　We may
indeed argue that there is no reason why Jesus should not have
conceived of the future upon the ordinary lines of the prevailing
Jewish apocalyptic teaching.　Because people to-day dislike the
fantastic doctrines and conceptions of the apocalyptic writers, that
is no reason why Jesus should not have shared them.　However, as
the chapter is of little or no religious value to us to-day, it is not
necessary for me to discuss the question of origin and source at
any length.　28–37 are additions to 3–27.

1, 2.　Many commentators, perhaps rightly, hold that a very
marked difference must be made between 1, 2 and the rest of the
chapter.　They strongly press the authenticity of 2.　It is possible
that Jesus, like a new Jeremiah, predicted the destruction of the
Temple.　This may account for the hostility felt towards him,
perhaps even for the revulsion of popular feeling.　It is in accordance
with his prophetic character that Jesus should predict the destruction
of the Temple.　It is also in accordance with the spiritual character
of his religion.　It is also a mark of his originality, and of his elevation
above the religious level of his age.　For though it is exaggerated
to say that the Jews believed that God lived in the Temple and not
elsewhere, or that the presence of God among his people was conditioned by the existence of the Temple, the old ideas did still hang
about men's minds, and the continuance of the religion apart from
the Temple, and all the better for its loss, was hard to conceive.

The question is put, and the answer is made, privately ; it is not said that the pronouncement in 2 was said publicly, but some prediction of the kind may have got abroad (*cp.* xiv. 58). Some think that the form of verse 2 is an argument for its authenticity, because the Temple was actually burnt, whereas in verse 2 a different form of destruction appears to be predicted. This argument seems feeble. Another view is that the present wording of the prophecy of 2 has been substituted for the words : ' I will destroy this temple and rebuild it in three days.' Jesus would not have referred in that case to the destruction of the Temple by human enemies, but to his own action after his Glory. The material Temple would be ended, and a ' spiritual ' Temple put in its place. So, for example, Loisy : ' The terms of the prediction, borrowed from the language of the Prophets, give us to understand that the building will be utterly destroyed. The profanation of the temple, let it be re- marked, is foreseen in the apocalyptic discourse ; not, however, its destruction : that is significant. Further on, Jesus is reproached for having said that he would destroy the temple (xiv. 5, 8 ; xv. 19), and that he would rebuild it within three days. The evangelists dare not protest directly against this imputation, and John (ii. 19) does not hesitate to put the prediction into the mouth of Jesus, although he interprets it in his own fashion. The accusations which were brought against Stephen in the Acts (ii. 13, 14) make us suppose that Stephen attributed the saying to Jesus, and that he interpreted it literally as the destruction of the temple by the Christ in his glory. That seems indeed to be the original sense of the words quoted in the Acts. They have a much more original flavour about them than the saying reported here. The prophecy which we now read in the three Synoptic Gospels—somewhat colourless, and, moreover, imitated from the Scriptures—has probably taken the place of the striking oracle which was not fulfilled ' (*L'Évangile selon Marc*, p. 365).

3. It was not unnatural that the anxious desire to know when the End would come should increase after the crucifixion, when the months and years rolled by and nothing happened. The longing for signs of the end increased, and the longing was satisfied. To Jesus, on the other hand, the imminence of the End was assured, and in his most authentic utterances he does not announce any signs of it. His own presence and his miracles were signs and evidence enough.

4. What is ταῦτα (' this ' or ' these things ') ? The first ταῦτα in this verse would seem to mean the destruction of the Temple. But really what the disciples ask is something different. They

want to know what is to be the sign of the body of events which are
to prelude and mark the coming of the End. The second ταῦτα
looks forward, not back. The question is really twofold : When
will the End be ? By what sign will one recognize its imminence ?
What is to be the indication that the End of the existing order of
things is at hand ? When will the Son of man come ? Loisy notes
that the apocalyptic oration is said privately to the four disciples
only—a mark of its secondary character (cp. iv. 10, vii. 17, &c.). It
is not a real speech, but ' a description made to be read.'

5-37. The apocalyptic oration now begins. The old original
apocalypse had perhaps three parts or divisions. In the first were
described certain preliminaries of the great event (5-8) ; in the
second we have the desolation of Judæa (14-20) ; the third told
of the commotion of the heavenly bodies and the appearance of
the Son of man (24-31). Matter which did not belong to the
original apocalypse opens the speech, and is added after each
section. Thus to the first section are added the verses 9-13, to
the second 21-23, to the third 32-37. The additions are mainly
warnings and instructions how to behave in view of or during the
great event ; they teach how one may traverse, without injury to
one's eternal salvation, the troublous days which are to precede
the End of the present order and the coming of the Kingdom.

5. The opening words contained in this verse may be the
composition of the Evangelist. Note βλέπετε four times repeated
(5, 9, 23, 33). There is a practical object in what is to follow.
Mark not only wants to explain the delay in the coming of the
Messiah in glory, but perhaps also to urge that even the troubles
of the period in which he lived (near A.D. 70) were not the signs of
the End. They were at most premonitions.

6. This verse is obscure. It is doubtful whether it comes
from the old apocalypse, or whether it is an addition. As it
stands it can only allude to persons who not only pretended to
be the Messiah, but *Jesus* the Messiah. They are people who
come using the name of Jesus and who say that they are Jesus.
Of such false claimants we know nothing. If the verse belongs
to the old apocalypse, we may explain that the deceivers come
and speak in the name of God. They say, ' I am he,' that is
not necessarily the Messiah, but God's messenger, an inspired
prophet or the like. We know of nobody before Bar Cochba, who
claimed to be the Messiah, but the mere claim of being divinely
sent or inspired might be ascribed to Judas the Galilæan, to Theudas,
to the promoters of the great revolt or even, if the apocalypse is of

Jewish origin, to the initiators of the Christian movement.   But even this explanation is awkward.

7.   What are these wars ?   As the verse comes from the old apocalypse (of which the date may be somewhere between 60 and 70), the wars need not necessarily refer exclusively to the war between the Jews and Rome.   Yet the beginning of the troubles between Judæa and Rome are probably referred to.   The wars are the preliminaries of the End.

Many scholars argue most strongly that there is nothing in xiii. which compels us to assume a date after 70, and that there is much which makes an earlier date (*e.g.* A.D. 60–64) most probable.   So J. Weiss.   To Mark the Temple still stands : it will be destroyed at the End of the Age.   Hence when Jesus is asked about the date when the Temple will be destroyed, he answers with a description of the signs and indications of the end of the Age.   ' Am Horizont des Markus ist das Belagerungsheer der Römer noch nicht erschienen, er denkt sich das Ende nach den Anweisungen der Apokalyptik. Das Datum des Markus ist also vor Ausbruch des jüdischen Krieges, jedenfalls vor Beginn der Belagerung Jerusalems ' (" Das Problem der Entstehung der Christentums," in *Archiv für Religionswissenschaft*, 1913, Vol. XVI. pp. 503, 504).   For Bacon's view see below.

8.   ἀρχὴ ὠδίνων ταῦτα, ' these are the beginnings of the Pangs.' The allusion is to the Rabbinic doctrine of the pains (the travail or labour pains of the Messiah).

9–13.   Mark's supposed addition to the first section of the apocalypse.   *Cp.* the parallels in Matt. x. 17–22, xxiv. 9–14 ;   Luke xii. 11, 12, xxi. 12–19.

9.   The Christians will be persecuted and ill-used by both Jews and heathens.   ' To bear witness before them.'   They witness to the truth of the gospel by their endurance under persecution and pain.   The ' witness ' becomes the ' martyr.'   Matt. x. 18 has, ' To bear witness to them (the Jews) and to the heathen (lit. nations).' Professor Turner thinks that the verb παραδώσουσιν is here used absolutely as, *e.g.*, in i. 14, and that there should be a comma after ὑμᾶς.   ' They shall give you in charge, in sanhedrins and synagogues shall you be beaten, and before governors and kings shall you be made to stand ' (*J. T. S.*, 1924, Vol. XXV. p. 19).

10.   Mark only.   The verse seems to interrupt the sequence. 11 follows closely on 9.   Burkitt learnedly essays to prove by MSS. and other evidence that εἰς πάντα τὰ ἔθνη should really be joined

on to, and read with, εἰς μαρτύριον αὐτοῖς. Then between πρῶτον and δεῖ should be inserted a δέ. Matthew in x. 18 has deserted Q and adopted the wording of Mark xiii. 10. In xxiv. 9-14 Matthew paraphrases Mark xiii. 9-13, for the passage has been used already. The meaning of Mark xiii. 9, 10 is : ' These things *must* be, but the End is not yet. There will be troubles everywhere, as the Prophets have said. And don't think *you* will not suffer : you will be delated to the Beth Din, flogged in synagogues, have to stand your trial before Roman officials (ἡγεμόνων) and the Herods (βασιλέων) for my sake. So you will be a testimony to Jews and to Gentiles. This painful period of delay must be, so that the good news may be proclaimed.' ' Thus the mental horizon is still Palestine, not a formal world-wide evangelization. And consequently the historical critic may believe that the text, with its broken construction and Palestinian outlook, is really a reminiscence of words spoken by Jesus. In Mark xiv. 9 εἰς ὅλον τὸν κόσμον only means " every-where " in a general way. There is no direct anticipation of regular missions ' (*Beginnings*, pp. 139, 145-147). Burney, on the other hand, gives highly interesting metrical reasons for suspecting the originality of verse 10 (pp. 118, 119).

12. A customary trait in the description of the pangs of the Messiah in Jewish apocalypses. For its O.T. basis see Micah vii. 6.

13. εἰς τέλος : ' bis zum letzten Opfer.' He who is ready to endure martyrdom. ' Saved ' : does this mean that he shall obtain salvation without having to pass through death, or that he shall, after death, receive the reward of eternal life ? (Rawlinson).

14-20. Second section of the apocalypse.

14. ' The Abomination of Desolation.' The reference is to Daniel ix. 27, xi. 31, xii. 11. The phrase of Daniel is supposed to signify the altar of Zeus set up by Antiochus Epiphanes upon the altar in the Temple of Jerusalem. Probably the rendering ' Desola-tion ' is wrong. It should be the ' Abomination of Horror,' *i.e.* a horrible abomination. Perhaps the writer of this apocalypse in Mark did not know more than that it was to be a profanation of the Temple. Or did he anticipate that the image of the Emperor would be set up in the Holy of Holies ? Note that it is not anywhere clearly implied that the Temple will be destroyed. Hence the date is presumably prior to 70. It may be that an attack by powers of darkness upon the Temple is meant. There is no allusion to the war with Titus. Some suppose that by the Abomination is meant

the Anti-Christ.   Hence the masculine participle agreeing with the
neuter noun (ἑστηκότα βδέλυγμα).   So Streeter, p. 492.

'Let him that reads give heed'; either an indication that the
apocalypse was *written*, not said, or an interpolation from Matthew,
for there the book of Daniel is directly quoted.   In the second
alternative the meaning is, 'let the reader of *Daniel* mark.'   The
first alternative is more probable.

The inhabitants of Judæa are not to take refuge in the capital,
for things there will be even worse.   These horrors are the true
beginning of the true End.

The apocalyptic chapters in Mark, Matthew, and Luke are subjected to a minute analysis and an elaborate discussion by Bacon
(*The Gospel of Mark*).   As the final object of this analysis is only to
establish the date of Mark as falling after the capture of Jerusalem,
it is needless for me to reproduce Bacon's arguments here, seeing
that the apocalyptic chapters are of no interest to Jewish, or, indeed,
one would imagine, except archæologically, to any modern readers.
Bacon holds that what lies at the basis of Mark xiii. is not any
written leaflet, but orally transmitted apocalyptic predictions.   The
prediction in verse 14 was the product of the feeling in Palestine
in the year A.D. 40 'just before the assassination of Caligula, on
January 24, A.D. 41, when there seemed to be immediate danger that
the megalomania of the insane emperor would issue in a repetition
of the outrage of Antiochus' (p. 56).   But it also depends upon the
conception of the Pauline apocalypse and of the Lawless One—the
Anti-Christ—in 2 Thessalonians.   What we get in Mark xiii. 7, 8,
14, 18–27 more particularly 'is fundamentally an interpretation of
apocalyptic Scripture, more especially Daniel.   What Matthew has
done for Mark in assimilating the prediction to the precise (or almost
precise) words " spoken by Daniel the prophet " had been already
begun by Mark himself.   Paul speaks of " the manifestation of the
Man of Sin " or " the Lawless One."   Mark reverts to Daniel
(though without mentioning the name) and speaks of " the abomination that maketh desolate." '   ' While, for the sake of Scripture
fulfilment, Mark reverts to the Danielic phrase " abomination that
maketh desolate," he does not relinquish the Pauline adaptation,
but retains the Anti-Christ doctrine as the real sense of the Scripture.
The Shiqqutz (*i.e.* the Abomination) according to Mark, will not be
a material object, but a " manifestation of the Man of Sin " or
" of Lawlessness." '   ' The effort of Mark xiii. 13, 14 is to obtain a
justifying exegesis of Dan. xi. 31 under circumstances wherein a
literal fulfilment was no longer possible.   Paul in A.D. 50 has no
difficulty in retaining the literal sense of a manifestation " in the
temple of God."   For some reason Mark finds it necessary to substitute for this perfectly definite location the vague and ambiguous

clause " where he ought not." Matthew naturally finds this very
unsatisfactory, and substitutes " in *a* holy place." But Mark's
helplessness is apparent. In the words of M'Neile, " the reference
is vague and cryptic." The destruction of the temple in 70 will
explain both Mark's correction, and Matthew's correction of the
correction. Mark is forced to be " vague and cryptic." After the
disappearance of " the temple of God " he that read Daniel would
need to " understand " in some peculiar way. Matthew removes
the difficulty by substituting " *a* holy place " for " *the* holy place " '
(pp. 129-131). I do not propose to allude to Bacon's further theory,
according to which, in addition to the Little Apocalypse, Mark also
uses the Special Source of Luke, which source ' has the clearest
predictions by Jesus of the siege and overthrow of Jerusalem, but
no suggestion whatever of a connection between these political
disasters and the end of the world ' (p. 132). Mark ' finds it needful
to explain in just what relation these disasters to Judæa and
Jerusalem really stand to the final catastrophe.' ' While the political
disaster is not to be regarded as the *immediate* precursor of the End,
it does belong among the signs of its coming ' (pp. 131-133).

15. An outside staircase led, it may be assumed, from roof
to street.

18. γένηται. Subject must be ' their troubles ' or the like.
Cp. Matt. xxiv. 20.

20. ' No flesh.' Is the writer thinking only of Jesus, or of all
the world ? For the sake of the elect, the interval between the
beginning of the End and the End itself is made short.
    Almost all the apocalyptic writers are hard ; they delight in
horrors ; many will perish ; few will survive ; many are ' lost ' ;
few are ' saved ' ; these are their cruel and favourite commonplaces.
Dr. Carpenter thinks that the sudden lapse from prophecy to retrospect makes it probable that this verse was a note added later.

21, 22. These verses may also, some hold, be of Jewish origin.
Of false Messiahs, we know of none among the Jews till Bar Cochba
in 131. Are these deceivers supposed to be Jewish impostors,
whose miracles might seduce even the disciples of Jesus ? (*cp.*
verse 6). For false prophets, *cp.* Acts v. 36, viii. 9-11, xxi. 38 ;
Revelation xiii. 11-17.

23. ' The word *ye* in this verse is very emphatic in the Greek.
The Evangelist has been copying a source which spoke in general
terms of *the elect* : he here addresses himself directly to his readers,

i.e. to the Christian community, *sc.* " But do *you* take heed !
The warning of Jesus is meant for you ! He has forewarned you
of everything, so that there is no excuse for being misled ! " '
(Rawlinson, p. 189).

24–27.   Third section of the apocalypse.

24.   The days and the tribulation refer to what was said in
verse 20.   The End, the *dénouement*, is at hand.

26.   The ' Son of man.'   The ' Abomination ' is the sign of the
beginning of the End ; the ' Son of man ' is the sign of its consummation (*cp.* Daniel vii. 13).   Wellhausen's theory is that the
Christian editor found the figure of the Man (Son of man) in the
old apocalypse, and identified him with the Messiah and with
Jesus.   To him Son of man equals Messiah, and Messiah equals
Jesus.   Here, then, we mark the transition to the Christianizing
of the term ' Son of man,' and to its being stamped afresh as a
sort of proper name for Jesus—at first for the Jesus of the Parousia.
This is in accordance with W.'s theory that Jesus himself did not
call himself the Son of man.   If, on the other hand, Jesus believed
that he was, or would, as it were, turn into, the heavenly Son of
man predicted by Daniel and the apocalyptic dreamers, then he
could have adopted such a verse as this, and meant it of himself.

27.   ἀποστελεῖ.   Is God the subject or the Son of man ? The
' elect ' Jews are gathered in from the dispersion.   But to the
editor, to Mark, the ' elect ' are the Christians.   The apocalypse
is here, at all events, pleasantly silent over the final destruction
of enemies and the wicked.   ' From the uttermost part of the earth
to the uttermost part of heaven ' is a queer mixture, made up of
such passages as Deut. xxx. 4 and xiii. 7.

28, 29.   Perhaps an appendix.   What are ' these things ' ?
They are the signs of the End, not the End itself.   They therefore
look back beyond 26, 27 which describe the End itself.   Wellhausen (*Marcus*, ed. 2), on the basis of an article by Schwartz
(*Z. N. W.*, 1914, pp. 80-84), takes quite a different view of these
verses.   He thinks that the fig tree here is related to the fig tree
incident of xi. 13 *seq.*   He and Schwartz suppose that there was
a dried up and withered fig tree in or near Jerusalem, about which
a popular tradition ran that, when the ' harvest,' *i.e.* the Messianic
Age, was at hand, it would sprout again.   What Jesus originally
said was that this withered fig tree would never bear figs again,
i.e. the Jewish hope of *national* glory would never be fulfilled.

Here in 28 the old tradition is used, though it is Christianized and spiritualized. 29 is an interpolation, resting on a false interpretation of 28, while 30 connects with 28, for the harvest in 28, like ' these things ' in 30, is the Parousia and not what precedes it.

30.   Is this a variant of ix. 1 ?   Is it the close of the apocalypse, or does it belong to 27 ?   It declares that though the coming of Christ is delayed, it will happen before the ' generation ' of the writer has perished—*i.e.* before all human beings then living have died—within, at the most, 100 years.   A perilous prediction !

31.   It is not the historic Jesus who would have made a statement of this kind.   So Loisy.   Or have we to assume that Jesus did prophesy the speedy advent of the End and of all which the End implies, and that he here emphasizes the prediction very solemnly ?   (See Klostermann.)

32.   Perhaps a Jewish saying up to the word ' heaven '.   How it found a place here, and whether it was originally related to the apocalyptic discourse nobody can say.   It is, indeed, possible (as some hold) that Jesus announced that the Kingdom was very near, that it would come suddenly, but that only the Father knew the exact hour.   For here all signs and reckonings are abandoned. Nobody knows, except God.   Here only, in Mark, are ' Son ' and ' Father ' used in this specifically Christian sense (*cp.* Matt. xi. 27). The verse is important.   Jesus always proclaimed that the End was near, but it is reasonable enough that he should have said that the exact moment—the day or hour of its coming—was only known to God.   There was all the more reason to be and keep ready, for the Kingdom would come suddenly and unexpectedly.   It is also possible that the verse is unauthentic : the Parousia was delayed, and the verse would explain why no exact date for its appearance had been given.   Or did Jesus himself say : ' Only the Father knows the day and hour.'   And did the Christian editor add the words, ' not even the angels, not even the Son ' ? (Loisy).   Or, again, was the original ending ' not even the angels know it,' and are the words, ' nor the son, but only the Father ' the addition ? (Dalman).   Klostermann's note is very interesting.

33-37.   These five verses draw the moral of 32.   Jesus *will* come again, though none can say when.   Hence let every Christian be prepared : neither impatient nor negligent, but ready.   Let each do his duty faithfully, so that none be caught napping.   The discourse began privately, but the end is obviously addressed to the whole Christian community.

Is the 'doorkeeper' to be pressed in the application of the parable ?   Is he Peter, or the apostles ?

For 'the cockcrowing' (3 A.M.), cp. xiv. 30.   The night is divided into four parts beginning at 9 P.M., midnight, 3 A.M., and the dawn.   This is the Roman method of division and may be due to the Evangelist.   Meyer points out that while the whole discourse (5–37) has 'nothing to do with the historic Jesus,' it is yet very early.   It is a product of the first generation of the Christian community.   The conflicts and persecutions appear to emanate exclusively from Jews.   Nothing is said of the conflict with Rome which began soon after A.D. 60 and of which we hear so much in the Book of Revelation.   Nothing is said of the destruction of Jerusalem.   Its date, not later than 60, is probably not earlier than 50 (pp. 129, 130).

Before entering upon the story of the Passion (= Suffering), let us reflect for a moment upon what we have so far been through. If Mark had been the only Gospel preserved to us, how much teaching of value would there be to add to our Jewish store ?   How far could we speak of a *new* teaching ? (i. 27).   I do not think we could, but then so far as Judaism is concerned, I hold that even when we add Matthew to Mark and Luke to Matthew, we have supplementary teachings of value, but nothing fundamentally new. Nevertheless, some things which we find in Mark are of great value. There is first of all the revival of the old prophetic teaching, the application of it to the needs and circumstances of another day. Here we can gain something from the Sabbath stories, but far more from the great saying, so new and so illuminative, and so entirely in the spirit of the Prophets, 'Whatever enters into a man from without cannot make him unclean.'   Then we have the doctrine of service wedded to the doctrine of humility.   'If any man would desire to be first of all, let him be last of all and the servant of all.'   To which we may add, 'Whoever shall not receive the Kingdom of God as a little child, shall not enter into it.'   Using the teaching of Jesus for the highest earthly life rather than in its primary and directly intended sense, we may find sayings of value in 'If thine eye cause thee to stumble, pluck it out,' or 'How hard it is to enter the Kingdom of Heaven,' but above all, " If any man would be a true follower ' (of Jesus, or, as we should say, of God) 'let him deny himself.'   And again, 'Whoever would save his life shall lose it.' Then we find points of value in the doctrine of Faith, in the saying, 'To him who has shall be given,' in the teaching about Divorce, and in the saying *reflecting the practice*, 'The strong need not the physician, but the sick : I came not to call the righteous, but the sinners.'   All this teaching can well be added on, and wedded to, the fundamental commands of the Pentateuch and the great primary doctrines of the Prophets. Thus there are teachings which it would be foolish for us Liberal Jews to neglect; there is nothing which requires us to leave our banner or to call ourselves by another name. The same conclusion is suggested by what we learn in Mark i.–xiii. about the life of Jesus. And this is important, because it is a critical conclusion of some certainty that while Matthew and Luke have many authentic contributions to make to the teaching of Jesus, they have little to add to our knowledge of his life, or to the story of the ministry. The miracles of which Mark is so full leave us cold. Of them we have nothing to learn. Nor are there any actions in i.–xiii. which are specially heroic. There is no reason to believe that in his short ministry—up to the entry into Jerusalem—Jesus encountered any very serious opposition. Perhaps towards the end he had to be a little careful, but that is all. There is no reason to believe that in the pursuit of his mission he had to endure much hardship, or make any tremendous sacrifices. The life of a wandering teacher in the East at that time was not, I think, a very arduous one. Material wants were not large, and the care of disciples, friends, admirers, even wondering strangers, would easily supply them. With the best will in the world, trying hard to peer through the mist and see the facts as they were, trying hard not to be prejudiced and prepossessed, I cannot see in the life of Jesus as recorded in Mark i.–xiii. anything about which to be lost in marvelling admiration or adoration. The character revealed, so far as *it is* revealed, appears undoubtedly strong and sweet, firm and tender, ardent and compassionate; but the evidence in Mark i.–xiii. for regarding Jesus as the most wonderful and perfect character which ever existed seems to me to be lacking. Thus whether we consider the teaching or the life, Mark i.–xiii. confirms us in our Liberal Jewish position.

CHAPTER XIV

1, 2. THE DECISION OF THE PRIESTS AND SCRIBES

(*Cp.* Matt. xxvi. 1–5 ; Luke xxii. 1, 2)

1   Now it was two days before the feast of the passover and of the unleavened bread : and the chief priests and the scribes sought
2 how they might capture him by craft, and put him to death. For they said, ' Not on the festival, lest there be an uproar among the people.'

The story of the Passion is not only told with consummate distinction and beauty, but gives the impression of a well-ordered and connected narrative. Up to this point the life of Jesus from the beginning of his Galilæan ministry has only been told in the roughest outline. As we have seen, many of the stories are grouped together from a non-chronological point of view ; others seem to possess no true and clear indication of place and time. But for the last few days of the life of Jesus all seems changed ; the connection seems clear and good, one event succeeds in time to another and there are no gaps unfilled. We seem to follow Jesus almost hour by hour from the repast at the house of Simon to the morning of the resurrection. Yet Loisy is probably right in pointing out that this good connection has been artificially obtained, and that here as elsewhere we have, even in Mark, to deal with what he calls ' entrecroisement et superposition ' of traditions. Many difficulties crop up when we question the narrative more closely.

1. ἦν δὲ τὸ πάσχα καὶ τὰ ἄζυμα μετὰ δύο ἡμέρας. What does this refer to ? What is the event which preceded by ' two days ' the festival of the Passover. In the book as we have it now, the reference must be to the story of the anointment. This happened two days before the Passover. But, as we shall see, this story is probably intercalated. The primitive object of the date seems to refer to something more important. The machinations of the priests and the Scribes can also not be intended. For these did not

307

begin at a special fixed time. As the imperfect tenses show, they were going on for some while : ' they were seeking how to kill him.' Some have thought that the reference is to verse 10. It was two days before the Passover that Judas went to the chief priests. But this too has been shown by Loisy to be unlikely. His own hypothesis is that the story of the anointment has taken the original place of the Last Supper. It is this which took place two nights before the Passover (*E. S.* II. p. 491).

But the very meaning of the verse is uncertain and variously explained. The natural meaning would appear to be that the beginning of the Passover was to take place two days after the day at which the story has now arrived. Thus, if the first night of Passover—the opening of the feast—fell on Thursday evening, the day where we now are is Tuesday ; if the first night fell on Friday evening, the day where we now are is Wednesday. But the phrase is in any case an odd one. The ' Passover,' the sacrifice of the Paschal Lamb, is stated in Lev. xxiii. 5 and 6 to fall on the fourteenth day of the month ; the feast of unleavened bread on the fifteenth. The Passover, that is, was sacrificed *towards* sunset, the feast of un-leavened bread began *with* sunset, of the same day, *i.e.*, the beginning of the fifteenth. See more on this subject below.

That Jesus was crucified on a Friday seems pretty certain. Mark xv. 42 mentions this date almost casually. It is not likely that it was invented. A great question in dispute is whether this Friday was the first day of the Feast of Unleavened Bread or whether that first day was Saturday. The former date is the implication of the Synoptics ; the latter the view of the Fourth Gospel. Under ordinary circumstances when Synoptics and Fourth Gospel disagree, there is little hesitation as to which is the more historic. But in this particular case there is reason to hold that, somehow or other, the Fourth Gospel has recorded accurately, the Synoptics falsely. It is true that the more probably accurate date fits in with the theology of the Fourth Gospel. For Jesus is crucified on the same day as the Paschal Lamb is killed. He is in his own person the Paschal Lamb—sacrificed once and for all, and making the observance of the old Jewish imperfect Passover superfluous and unnecessary. Hence we might suppose that the date was arranged to suit the theory. But it would rather seem as if the right date was maintained because it corresponded and fitted in with the theory.

Mark, or at any rate one of the two traditions which he followed, wanted to turn the ' Last Supper ' which Jesus ate with his disciples into a last Passover meal. Hence the probably accurate date, according to which the Friday on which Jesus was crucified was the morning of the day towards the sunset of which the Passover was offered, was changed into the probably inaccurate date according to which Friday (and not Saturday) was the first day of the Feast of Unleavened Bread.

Mark seems to know this double tradition, for xiv. 1, 2 would at least imply that the intention was to get Jesus executed before the Passover began ; nor is it definitely said that the intention was not carried out.   It has even been supposed that the fact that Jesus was crucified the day before the Passover suggested the explanation of the date given in our passage.   Yet there is no word in Mark which seems to depend on the Passover beginning *specifically* on Friday evening.

To put the crucifixion on the first day of the Feast of Unleavened Bread, or to use common language now, the first day of Passover, causes great difficulties.   That the trial should have been held upon the first night of the festival would have been a flagrant violation of Jewish law.   That the Romans would have crucified Jewish criminals upon the first day of Passover is extremely unlikely. J. Weiss thinks that he can discern in the ' Passion ' narrative of Mark two strata of narratives, embodying two traditions, the one older and generally more authentic, which accepted the historic date of the crucifixion, the other later and less accurate, which adopted the wrong date.   To the second stratum he assigns xiv. 3–9, 12–25, and 53–65.

On the Johannine hypothesis, then, the day of which xiv. 1 speaks is Wednesday.   The Passover would begin on Friday at even.

On the other hand, Holtzmann supposes that the Greek phrase μετὰ δύο ἡμέρας (' after two days ') can be equivalent to ' on the next day.'   In that case the day spoken of would, on the Johannine hypothesis, be Thursday.   On the Synoptic hypothesis it would be Wednesday.   But ' after two days ' probably does not mean here ' on the following day ' : it means that a whole day lay in between the day of which it speaks and the day on which the opening of the festival fell.

W. holds that the day spoken of in xiv. 1 is Thursday, not Wednesday.   He comes to this conclusion even though he supports the Johannine hypothesis of the date of Jesus's death, and translates μετὰ δύο ἡμέρας ' after two days.'   For Mark wrote for western readers.   Hence, though for Jewish readers the first day of Passover began on Friday at sunset, for western readers the first day was Saturday.   Therefore, if it is said that the Passover was ' after two days,' the day implied is not Wednesday, but Thursday.   But how can this be accurate when we have the phrase in 12, ' on the first day of the Unleavened Bread,' where the meaning clearly is ' the evening before the first day ' ?   Hence it seems that the day alluded to in xiv. 1 must be Wednesday, not Thursday, which seems also to give more time for 10 and 11.

Strictly speaking, the phrase ' two days before the Feast of the Passover and the Unleavened Bread ' is a contradiction in terms. For the Passover fell on the afternoon of the 14th, the Unleavened Bread on the 15th. Hence two days before the former would be three days before the latter, and two days before the second would be one day before the first. But in view of the phrase in xiv. 12 we may assume that one and the same period is alluded to : *i.e.* the afternoon and evening of the 14th. If this was Thursday, then Tuesday is alluded to, if this was Friday, then Wednesday is alluded to.

2. The more obvious meaning of this verse is that the Jewish authorities desired to get the execution over before the festival. They were afraid that the popular teacher and reformer might have many sympathisers among the people, who heard him gladly. More especially, if Jerusalem became full of festival pilgrims from Galilee and elsewhere, any attempt to put Jesus to death might easily provoke a riot, in which the priests and Scribes would not escape the vengeance of the crowd. Hence it was urgent to seek for some pretext by which the inconvenient Galilæan teacher —or, shall we say, the aspirant to the Messiahship ?—might be quickly got rid of. W. supposes that the ruling priests waited on purpose till near to the festival in order that the sentence might be quickly passed and rapidly executed by the Roman governor.

These two verses of Mark are redactional and ' secondary ' : their historic value is by no means certain. Bertram suggests that ' Not on the festival ' refers loosely to the arrest and not to the death. The Greek word θόρυβος can be rendered ' gathering together,' ' crowd,' ' Auflauf ' : it need not necessarily, he thinks, signify ' uproar,' ' tumult.' The meaning may therefore be : ' Let us not arrest him on the festival, when there will be crowds of people about. It is better, in view of the Romans and the government, to act secretly.' *Cp.* verse 49. (*Die Leidensgeschichte Jesu und der Christuskult,* 1922, p. 13.) Bultmann (p. 159) prefers the reading of the MS. D which has : ' lest there be a tumult on the festival,' *i.e.,* Jesus must be arrested, as he is likely, if allowed to continue his preaching and actions, to cause a disturbance on the festival. He asks what sense can be got out of the usual reading. For it was now only two days before the Passover, and would not the city be already, and certainly on the day before, full of pilgrims ? *Cp.* M'Neile : ' It is strange, however, that they should fear an uproar only during the festival ; since the city was already crowded with pilgrims who flocked to Jesus in the temple (Lk. *v.* 37 f.), the uproar

would take place if He were arrested before the festival began.'
On the other hand, Meyer thinks the words as they stand quite
intelligible. The authorities were anxious to get the whole affair
—arrest, trial, death—over before the actual opening of the festival,
and (on the assumption that the Johannine chronology is correct)
they succeeded. Jesus was crucified early on the morning of the
day on which, at sunset, Passover began (Vol. I. pp. 170, 197).
Prof. Turner thinks that ἔλεγον here, as in iii. 21, is an instance of
the Impersonal Plural, so frequent in Mark. And his interpretation is very interesting, for it would be consistent with the arrest,
like the Last Supper, having taken place not on the festival (Friday evening), but on the day before (Thursday evening). Prof.
Turner says (*J. T. S.*, 1924, Vol. xxv. p. 384): ' Next day was
the Passover : and the chief priests were on the look out for some
underhand way of arresting Him : for it had been urged that an
(open) arrest at the feast might lead to a riot. That is, I think,
what St. Mark means. The emphasis in the second clause is, as the
position of the word indicates, on δόλῳ : and what reason would
there be for any emphasis on δόλῳ, if the point were that they were
going to make *no* arrest during the festival ? But if the conditions
were (1) that the chief priests were determined to arrest Jesus before
He left Jerusalem, (2) that some of the Sanhedrists, to whom they
felt bound to defer in order to secure unanimity, made a timid *caveat*
against any action which might involve the chance of a riot at the
moment of arrest, then the need for δόλος explains itself. An arrest
effected by δόλος would avoid the chance of a riot, whether it was
effected during the festival or no. Hence the value to them of
Judas, and of the information which enabled them to carry out their
coup in the late evening and at a retired spot. It has been suggested
that the mysterious directions given by our Lord to disciples in xi. 2
and xiv. 13, where no names are named, were intended to prevent
Judas from obtaining previous knowledge of our Lord's movements
which he could convey to the Jewish authorities. However that
may be, it seems clear that δόλος meant just the securing of a time
and place for the arrest where popular support for Jesus would have
no opportunity of asserting itself. It is difficult to suppose that it is
intended to imply a contrast between an arrest on Thursday and an
arrest on Friday. And the solitary change which Matthew makes in
copying Mark is in this respect very instructive : for, understanding
ἔλεγον to refer back to the chief priests, he alters ἔλεγον γάρ into
ἔλεγον δέ. The chief priests, that is to say, determined to arrest
Jesus, but determined at the same time that an arrest during the
feast must be avoided. Later exegesis has, as in so many other
passages, interpreted Mark by Matthew. But if Mark's account is
taken as the primary one, ἔλεγον γάρ gives the reason for δόλος. On

the ordinary view, St. Mark ought to have written " Next day being
Passover, the authorities determined to effect the arrest of Jesus
before passover began : for they said, Not during the feast. . . ."
But that is not what St. Mark says. He says, " The feast being now
imminent, the authorities determined to avoid a direct and open
arrest, for the objection had been taken that such methods were too
dangerous at such a time : they had to have recourse therefore to
some secret *coup.*" '

Another interpretation of the verse is that the authorities
meant to let the festival go by, and the pilgrims disperse to their
homes, before they acted, but that their hands were forced by the
unexpected deed of Judas (verses 10 and 11). So, *e.g.* Klausner.
This seems less likely.

Brandt's conclusions (*Die evangelische Geschichte und der
Ursprung des Christentums*, 1893) are more negative. He holds :

(a) That the Synoptic date for the crucifixion is impossible.
Jesus could not have been crucified on the first day of Passover.

(b) The Johannine date is due to the author's theology,
and is not necessarily historical.

(c) That Jesus was crucified on a Friday is certain. The
very existence of the Christian Sunday—(the ' third day ')
on which his resurrection is celebrated—proves that the
crucifixion must have taken place on Friday.

The exact date of the crucifixion relative to the Passover
cannot, Brandt thinks, be now ascertained. It may have been
a few days before the festival, it may have been a few days after
it ; it may have even been in one of the intervening days between
the first day and the last. Brandt is possibly too negative.

In his deeply interesting and quaintly written treatise, *Das
letzte Passamahl Christi, etc.*, Dr. Chwolson attempts to harmonize
the Synoptic and Johannine narratives. Jesus, he thinks, was
crucified on the fourteenth of the month, which fell on a Friday.
The first day of the Feast of Unleavened Bread, or, as we popu-
larly call it, the first day of Passover, synchronized that year
with the Sabbath. So far the date of the Fourth Gospel is right.
But the Synoptics only contradict this date apparently. It is
usually argued that as the Synoptics state that Jesus held a Paschal
meal with his disciples on Thursday evening, they must imply
that he was crucified on the first day of the festival. Chwolson
tries to get over this by showing the probability that when the
fourteenth of the month Nisan fell on a Friday, the Paschal lamb
was slain on the Thursday. In Leviticus xxiii. 5 (*cp.* Exodus xii.
6 ; Numbers ix. 3) it is stated that the Passover is to be sacrificed
' between the evenings.' In later times this odd expression was

interpreted to mean in the afternoon, that is before sunset. In earlier times Chwolson seeks to show that it was taken to mean the first hour or two immediately after sunset. Also, did the killing and washing of the Paschal Lamb conflict with the keeping of the Sabbath? In later times it was held that it did not do so, but in earlier times it was held, Chwolson believes, that it did. Thus when the fourteenth of the month fell on Friday, it was not held to be legitimate to kill the lambs on that evening, and they were killed and roasted on Thursday instead. The Paschal meal could be celebrated on the same evening too, and probably most Pharisees did celebrate it then, although the bread used at such an antedated meal was leavened and not unleavened bread. Thus Jesus was crucified before the seven days' Festival of Unleavened Bread began, and yet he celebrated on Thursday evening the Paschal meal with his disciples.

Klausner follows Chwolson. Moreover, he thinks that the 'Supper' of Thursday was a full Passover meal, and that the bread was unleavened (p. 326). I am unable to accept the views of Oesterley set forth (in defence of the Johannine date) in his interesting book on *The Jewish Background of the Christian Liturgy* (1925) except as to the point of the *Kiddush* in old days having succeeded the Friday evening meal, whereas now it precedes it. But I must not discuss Oesterley's arguments further. Whether the Johannine dates be right or wrong, I do not think they can be established as correct by Mr. Oesterley's pleadings.

Another arrangement is suggested by Loisy. Suppose the event which occurred 'two days before the Passover' was the Last Supper. Suppose this was held on a Thursday, then the Passover would have been held on a Saturday evening. The first day of the Unleavened Bread festival would be Sunday. This date would fit in neither with the Synoptic nor with the Johannine chronology, but it would avoid the difficulty, which Loisy regards as almost as great, of the coincidence of the crucifixion with the day on which all the final preparations for the Passover feast were made.

Loisy further thinks that it is not wholly certain that the day of the crucifixion was Friday. For instead of the day of the resurrection being deduced from the Friday, it is possible that Sunday was chosen as the day of the resurrection, and hence the Friday, reckoning backwards, was invented as the day of the crucifixion (*E. S.* II. p. 491). But probably Loisy's extreme scepticism is unjustified. It remains probable that the crucifixion happened on a Friday.

The main dates of Jesus's life and death are, in any case, fairly sure. He was born before Herod the Great's death (4 B.C.). John the Baptist preaches in A.D. 28; Jesus may have been baptized the same year. He himself begins to preach, say, early in 29, and is crucified in 30. The exact date may just possibly have been Friday, April 8th. The month and day of the year are computed according to an astronomical calculation that there was a full moon on Thursday, April 7th, and to a tradition recorded by Clement of Alexandria.

The attempt by Chwolson to harmonize the Synoptic and the Johannine date of the crucifixion has been followed by another attempt made by S.-B. II. pp. 812–853. S.-B. seek to show that Chwolson's attempt, highly ingenious and plausible as it is, breaks down. A single passage in Philo seems enough, they hold, to discredit it (p. 847). Other arguments against it can be read in Dalman, *Jesu-Jeschua*, 1922, pp. 82, 83. On the other hand, S.-B.'s own attempt seems highly dubious, and is too complicated to be set forth here. Dalman maintains that the Synoptic date, namely, that Jesus was killed on the first day of the Passover festival and that the Last Supper was a Passover meal, is correct : the Fourth Gospel deliberately altered the date, for the sake of the higher spiritual truths which it was thereby enabled symboli- cally to teach. Though S.-B. do not agree with Dalman, they yet hold that many of the objections to the Synoptic date are not conclusive, and can, to some extent at any rate, be got over. Indeed, one may legitimately observe that the Rabbinic evidence is stated and given much more fully, clearly, and fairly by S.-B. than by Dalman. Thus it is shown that such apparent breakings of the law as Jesus leaving the city and walking to Gethsemane, the disciples carrying arms, and the police force sent to execute the arrest also being armed, Simon's coming from the field, the preparations for, and the carrying out of, the interment, can all, more or less satisfactorily, be got over. As to Mark's statement that Joseph bought the linen, see note to verse xv. 46. The holding of the trial on the festival and the execution itself are much greater difficulties, as S.-B. acknowledge more frankly than Dalman. Yet, even here, there are possible ways out. The principle that it is per- missible to violate one Sabbath in order that many Sabbaths might be kept holy may have been brought into play. Certain special offenders *could* be executed on a festival, and there was a view that extraordinary needs and circumstances require extraordinary measures. ' The time needed it ' is a phrase found in the Talmud to justify certain judicial decisions and executions which were against the Law. A Rabbi of the third century said, ' Sometimes the violation of the Law is the establishment of the Law.' May not the enemies of Jesus, whether among the priests or the Rabbis, have acted upon some such principle ?

Nor can it be said that S.-B.'s attempt to harmonize the Synoptic

and Johannine date is in itself unjustifiable. They say : ' A real
contradiction in the tradition about the date of the crucifixion in
the most ancient Christian times seems to us unthinkable. A
solution must be found. Both the Synoptics and John must be
right.' Walter Bauer (*T. L. Z.*, 1925, p. 535) makes merry over
this straining for harmonization as mere apologetic. But this is,
perhaps, hardly fair. It *is* surely rather odd that such a difference
on so important a point should be found in the tradition, and still
odder is it if it is John who is in the right as against Mark.
Meyer is vigorous in support of Wellhausen's arguments that the
Synoptic date is wrong. He assumes that all the bits which transform the Last Supper into a Passover meal are legendary, and do
not belong to the oldest source in its oldest form. His own final
conclusion is that there was no trustworthy tradition about the day
of the week on which Jesus died, or on its relation to the Passover :
the only thing actually known was that the execution took place,
not on the festival, but before it. But it is justifiable that Jülicher
(*T. L. Z.*, 1922, p. 518) calls attention to the contrast between
Meyer's readiness to accept the full historicity of Mark's narrative
in so many respects in the Jerusalem period with his determined
refusal to accept Mark's crucifixion date. And, indeed, Julicher
is not wrong. For Meyer rejects any idea of an Urmarcus. The
book is a unity. How, then, should one who knew Peter, and heard
and wrote down Peter's reminiscences, have made such a blunder
about so important a point, or how should he have accepted this
late legendary addition to the old authentic source ?

Professor Burkitt indeed has, as usual, a most ingenious theory
to explain why Mark went a little wrong. *Cp.* the note on Luke xxii.
15. He supposes that ' Jesus and the Twelve may really have sung
the Hallel or part of it,' even though the Supper was on Thursday,
and Passover did not begin till Friday evening. ' The crowd of
Galilæan sympathizers had shouted Hosanna : this suggests that
Psalm cxviii. was just at this time in the mouth and hearts of the
Disciples.' And though it was not the Passover evening, yet Jesus
had really planned to hold the Passover in that very room. But
there had to be—for danger of separation and arrest was imminent
—a Last Supper *before* the Passover, in which Jesus designed to perform a solemn symbolical act with bread and wine. Mark was an eyewitness of much which happened on that Thursday; he had followed
Jesus to Gethsemane. He witnessed the arrest. He had been at
the house where the supper was held, and that house (it is ' a reasonable conjecture ') was the house of Mary, the mother of John Mark,
where afterwards we find the Christians assembled (Acts xii. 2).
Again, the story in Mark xiv. 13–16 is not regarded by Matthew as
supernatural. Matthew does not regard the rendezvous as in any

way miraculous. We can therefore suppose that an arrangement had been made. Perhaps Mark's uncle, Barnabas, may have been either the man with the pitcher, or the master of the house. ' In that case, if Mark was a young boy about the house, he may actually have remembered the two men coming to his home and the preparation of the room as for a *Seder*. He may have heard the company singing *Hosanna* and other *Hallel* strains before they departed. His acquaintance with Jewish customs, judging from other passages in his Gospel, appears to have been a sort of ignorant familiarity, the reminiscences of boyhood as distinct either from really accurate knowledge or from book-learning.' And Mark is always conscientious and accurate. There were lines of thought which led many to feel that it was congruous that the last Supper should have been a Passover. Mark ' writing thirty years after the event might very well feel that his reminiscences of a Paschal character concerning the Last Supper shewed that it was really a Passover. Even so he writes accurately. He introduces no lamb, and he makes no alteration in the story of the Trial or Crucifixion to suggest that the day was actually the day of the Feast. The details which he actually records may really have happened : what is wrong is the construction which he puts upon his reminiscences.' It is all wonderfully ingenious. But is it not *too* ingenious ? Surely Peter, if Peter was one source of Mark's Gospel, would have very definitely told him one way or the other, that the Last Supper was, or was not, a Passover meal, that Jesus had, or just had not, fulfilled his ardent desire of eating this last Passover with his disciples.

3–9. THE ANOINTING IN BETHANY

(*Cp*. Matt. xxvi. 6–13 ; Luke vii. 36–50)

3   And while he was at Bethany in the house of Simon the leper, as he sat at table, there came a woman having an alabaster cruse of precious ointment of pure balsam ; and she broke the cruse, 4 and poured the balsam on his head. And some were angry, saying among themselves, ' Why has this waste of ointment been com- 5 mitted ? For it might have been sold for more than three hundred pieces of silver, and have been given to the poor.' And they re- 6 proached her. But Jesus said, ' Let her alone ; why plague ye 7 her ? she has wrought a good deed towards me. For ye have the poor with you always, and whensoever ye will, ye may do them 8 good : but me ye have not always. She has done what she could : 9 she has anointed my body beforehand for its burial. Verily I say

unto you, Wherever the gospel shall be preached throughout the whole world, that which she has done shall also be spoken of in her memory.'

In Luke this story is given a different setting, and referred to a much earlier date in the life of Jesus.   How much of it is historical is dubious.   It seems to break the connection between verse 2 and verse 10.

3. Jesus is at table. Whether the meal is in the evening or earlier is not stated. It may be argued that we are to assume that Jesus had been in Jerusalem, and had returned to sleep in Bethany. Simon the leper is spoken of as if he were well known. There seems no reason to doubt that he is a historical character. He is doubtless called the leper because he had formerly been leprous, though he now was cured.

The woman is not named. The older tradition did not know her name. As time went on, the tendency to give names to such anonymous persons grew stronger. Hence, in the Fourth Gospel, the woman is identified and named.

The object of her action is to show Jesus honour, and this she does by using up all the valuable balsam, and even breaking the vessel of alabaster in which it is contained, so that it could never be used again. Perhaps the story has some connection with the beginnings of the worship of Jesus and the doubts and criticisms which it at first aroused. (*Cp.* Bertram, p. 17.) πιστική may mean pure = genuine, or a special sort of balsam called 'pistike.' (See Klostermann.)

4. 'Some' are indignant at the waste. The MS. D turns the 'some' into the 'disciples,' which seems reasonable. This reading is followed by Matthew.

6–9.   There is a double reply.   6, 7 are earlier than 8, 9, though even these verses are hardly to be regarded as historical.   Even verse 7 alludes to the coming death. *Cp.* ii. 20.   In any case the story is beautiful, and the words of Jesus in 6 and 7 are touching and significant. Special occasions justify special actions. An act of love and reverence may justify exceptional and costly means. The teaching of 6 and 7 supplements (and only apparently contra-dicts) the teaching of Matt. xxv. 36–46.   Both are justified in their season, and we can still in their due season make justified application of both.

7. Burney notes that Matthew's more original, 'sharp and

telling antithesis' is 'destroyed in Mark by the insertion after
the first stichos of the words, And whenever ye will, ye can do
(them) good. This must be thought to be a gloss, adding a correct,
but unnecessary, explanation of the implication of the first clause'
(p. 76, n. 1. Cp. also the argument on p. 86).

8, 9. A later addition. The earlier reply finishes with verse
seven. Here the allusion to the death is much more definite than
in 7. The first three Greek words are not quite easy. 'She has
done what she could'—what it was in her power to do. The words,
suitable to a situation such as that of Mark xii. 44, are less so here,
for the owner of the balsam is not a poor woman who gives her all.
The words are sometimes interpreted to mean : she has done what
could only then be done and not again ; *i.e.* as the next phrase
explains, she has anticipated the anointment of his corpse, which
was attempted after his death, but not carried out. This interpretation seems to put into the three Greek words, ὃ ἔσχεν ἐποίησεν,
more than they can contain.

But, in any case, the eight following words definitely make
the curious statement that the woman by anticipation anointed
his body for burial. This may merely mean that she has done it
beforehand, or inverted the order. But it may also allude to, or
have been coined because of, xvi. 1. There, three women go early
on the morning of the resurrection to the tomb, in order to anoint
the Master's dead body. But, as Jesus has already risen, they are
unable to carry out their purpose. The anointing which the three
women tried in vain then to accomplish had already been done in
Bethany by anticipation. It may, however, be noted that the
Greek words are different. In xvi. 1 the verb used is ἀλείφειν. The
material is ἀρώματα. Here the verb is μυρίζειν, and the material
is μύρον νάρδου.

In either *nuance* of meaning the words are hardly conceivable in
Jesus's mouth. He not only assumes his death, but also his burial,
and nobody is astonished.

9. The last portion of Jesus's speech also bears the mark of
a later date. The word 'gospel' (εὐαγγέλιον) would hardly have
thus been used by him. The good tidings here clearly imply the
full story of Jesus's life, and sufferings, and death. (At the same
time the 'proclamation' or preaching is still verbal.) Jesus's
vehement assurance that the woman's deed shall always be included in the gospel story awakens a suspicion that it was not
always a part of it. Surely the woman's name should have been
part of her 'memorial,' and this is omitted. Holtzmann thinks
that the verse in its present form may have been enlarged and

'edited.' Perhaps Jesus said : ' Her deed shall never be forgotten ' ; ' when my story is told, her deed shall always be remembered.' Thus do the commentators weave hypothesis to
hypothesis, and add argument to argument. They play among
the shadows of an irrecoverable past. Happy are they, as to me
it seems, whose religion does not depend too greatly—happiest they
whose religion does not depend at all—upon the historic accuracy
of a half-legendary narrative, written for purposes of edification or conversion by men, pious indeed and devoted, but for
whom the sovereign sacredness of historic fact was a distant
and unknown conception. ' It is difficult to believe that the words
came from the lips of Jesus.' His ' expectation of the immediate
advent of the Kingdom, which in Matt. iv. 23 *is* the Gospel, forbids
us to think that He would speak of a world-wide preaching of the
Gospel, even if κόσμος means οἰκουμένη, the Roman world' (M'Neile).

10, 11. THE BETRAYAL

(*Cp.* Matt. xxvi. 14–16 ; Luke xxii. 3–6)

And Judas Iscariot, one of the Twelve, departed unto the chief
priests, to betray him unto them. And when they heard it, they
were glad, and promised to give him money. And he sought a
good opportunity to betray him.

10. This verse continues the narrative of verses one and two ;
3–9 seems to be an interpolation, or, at all events, a ' parenthetical '
story. There seems no good reason to suspect that the action of
Judas Iscariot is not historical. That a disciple betrayed the
Master would hardly have been invented by legend. Mark says
nothing of his motive. Much has been conjectured. Was he
disappointed that Jesus did not actively assume the Messianic
rôle ? Did he want to force his hand ? Had he been a disciple
for a short time only, and therefore misunderstood the character
and aims of the Master ? (Iscariot is supposed to mean ' the man
from Kariot,' a place already mentioned in Joshua xv. 25. W.
thinks this explanation impossible, and that the name has, so far,
not been capable of explanation). Klausner gives an acute
explanation of Judas's motives. He had come to the conclusion
that Jesus was a false Messiah, who neither could nor would effect
the political redemption of his people. He, therefore, deserved
death (p. 325).
At first sight it might seem that no betrayer was necessary,
for Jesus was by this time well known (*cp.* verse 48). But the
desire of the authorities was to effect a secret arrest, and for this

purpose Judas's offer was convenient and timely. Perhaps Jesus changed his night quarters on purpose. He may have suspected what was planned. To know where he would be on any particular night some espionage or treachery was necessary.

The historical character of Judas Iscariot is confirmed by the further reflection that Jesus would not have wished one of his own disciples to betray him, and we may safely assume that he did not foresee that he would do so. The prediction of 18 was a natural, but later, growth, when an explanation was needed for the fact that Jesus had admitted into the inner ring of his disciples a man who misunderstood and betrayed him. But though the figure of Judas and the betrayal may be historical, the details about him as recorded in the Gospels are very doubtful. Most of them are probably legendary. The promise of the 'chief priests' may have been inferred from what actually took place. And, similarly, as regards all the statements in verse 11. (Bertram, p. 19, Bultmann, p. 159.) The verb παραδιδόναι may contain an allusion to Isaiah liii. 12. Perhaps some allusion is desirable to the modern theories about Judas and the betrayal, such as those of Bacon, Schweitzer, and Cadman. To these scholars the ordinary explanations on the lines of the statements in Mark are inadequate. To them what Judas betrayed was not the mere whereabouts of his Master—for that could have been otherwise discovered—but some secret fact about him, which Judas and the Twelve knew, but which the authorities and the people did not. It may be pointed out that such a view is purely inferential. The narratives in the Gospels give no hint of it ; indeed, they seem almost to contradict it. The secret fact was, according, for example, to Cadman, that Jesus believed and asserted himself to be the Son of man who would sit at God's right hand, and who, so far as Jews generally were concerned, could only be supposed to be the Messiah. He was indeed the Messiah, though not the Messiah as the Jews generally conceived him. Cadman, we must remember, and others who take his line, do not believe in the Messianic entry. Unless, therefore, Judas betrayed the secret, the charge of Messiahship as brought up against Jesus before Pilate becomes inexplicable. The knowledge was not common property ; there is 'ample reason' 'for holding that Judas betrayed it.' Why did he do so ? Cadman supposes that Judas, like Peter, was much shocked that Jesus, instead of going to Jerusalem to conquer, to inaugurate his Messianic reign, and to free his people from their foes, was going thither to die, and was asking his disciples to share his fate. Instead of merely leaving the circle of the disciples and maintaining silence, Judas seems 'to have been bent on ensuring his own safety before it was too late.' All this explains, Cadman thinks, the sudden veering round of the people. Hitherto the people had only regarded Jesus as a prophet, though a prophet of great and peculiar eminence. The Jewish authorities, however, 'we may be sure,' 'noised abroad the findings about the Messiahship at the examination before the High-Priest.' And this would-be Messiah was a prisoner. How could he be other, then, than a mere deluded enthusiast, and, if only that, then also a blasphemer. The Kingdom, the nearness of which he had announced, was no nearer than ever. No wonder that the reaction was violent (pp. 129–136). To myself all these suggestions, however cleverly woven together, nevertheless seem very improbable. Yet the betrayal must always keep its difficulty, though I do not go as far as Dr. Jacks, who holds that, looked at from a purely historical and psychological point of view, the betrayal is ' an inexplicable phenomenon which grows out of nothing that has gone before, and is, strictly speaking, quite unnecessary to account for what follows. The motives of it are undiscoverable, and the conduct of the eleven disciples who, after hearing that Judas was about to betray their Master, take no step to counter his treachery, but let the affair pass without even a protest, is, humanly speaking, as unnatural as could be ' (*Hibbert Journal*, April 1925, p. 425).

Certain more extreme critics have sought to eliminate the figure of Judas altogether, to regard him as wholly the creation of legend and of the half-conscious and half-unconscious attempt to make what occurred the fulfilment of Scriptural passages. It cannot be said that these attempts are very successful. Two articles in the *Z. N. W.* are, however, worth reading, which work on these lines : (1) Schläger, *Die Ungeschichtlichkeit des Verräters Judas*, 1914, pp. 50–59, and (2) Plath, *Warum hat die urchristliche Gemeinde auf die Überlieferungen der Judaserzählungen Wert gelegt?* 1916, pp. 178–188.

11. Having made his arrangement with the authorities, and having received a promise that his treachery would be suitably rewarded, Judas now seeks for a convenient or opportune moment in which the arrest may take place.

But, nevertheless, the arrest does *not* take place before the festival, *if* the Last Supper is the Paschal Meal.

12–16. PREPARATION FOR THE PASSOVER MEAL

(*Cp.* Matt. xxvi. 17–20 ; Luke xxii. 7–14)

12   And on the first day of the unleavened bread, when they sacrifice the passover, his disciples said unto him, ' Whither wouldst thou

13 that we go and prepare for thee to eat the passover ? ' And he sent
two of his disciples, and said unto them, ' Go ye into· the city, and
14 a man will meet you bearing a pitcher of water : follow him. And
into whatever house he goes in, say ye to the master thereof, The
Master says, Where is my chamber where I may eat the passover
15 with my disciples ? And he will show you a large upper room,
16 furnished with couches and ready ; there prepare for us.' And his
disciples departed, and came into the city, and found as he had
said unto them : and they prepared the passover.

12. How far is this section historical ? Some would reject it
altogether, on the ground (a) of its miraculous character, which is
like the equally unhistorical passage xi. 1–7 ; (b) of its supposition
that Jesus ate the opening Paschal meal with his disciples, whereas,
according to the Fourth Gospel he died before Passover began. If
the Synoptic date for the crucifixion be retained, one might assume
that an arrangement which Jesus had made with a householder in
Jerusalem was turned into a miraculous coincidence. Some think
that Jesus had arranged all the details beforehand, even down to
the man with the water-jar, who was to be on the watch for the
dispatched disciples. The danger of arrest was great. The smaller
the number of those who knew where he was to be the better. This
does not seem very probable. The predicted meeting is frequent in
legends. *Cp.* 1 Sam. x. 2–5.

' On the first day of the Unleavened Bread.' This is a loose
expression. What is meant is : on the day the sunset of which
was the beginning of the festival. ' The first day of Unleavened
Bread ' would extend to a Jew from sunset to sunset. The Paschal
meal had to be eaten, say, on the evening of Thursday. On Thursday
morning the disciples ask Jesus where he will eat it. The odd thing
is, perhaps, that no arrangement was made *before* Thursday morning.
But this detail need not be accurate.

To my doubt Mr. Bartlett replies thus : ' Jesus had good reasons
to allow Judas as short notice as possible of his exact plans. This
perhaps explains the very form of Jesus's directions ; while only
the fact that it was the Paschal meal warranted his arranging to be
in Jerusalem after dark.' Chwolson seeks to show that, strictly
speaking, ' the first day of (the feast of) Unleavened Bread ' would
be the fifteenth of Nisan, and could not mean the fourteenth.
In Numbers xxviii. 16 the fourteenth day is called the Passover ;
the fifteenth day is said to be a feast, on and from which the seven-
day festival of Unleavened Bread starts. The same phrases are
used in Leviticus xxiii. 5 and 6. Chwolson's final explanation of
the words in Mark and Matthew is that the original Aramaic ran

ביומא קמי דפסחא. This meant, ' on the day before the Passover,'
i.e. on the thirteenth.   But the word קמי can also mean ' first.'
Hence the translators rendered ' on the first day of the Passover
(festival).'   This reading is still found in some versions and MSS.
It was further altered to ' on the first day of Unleavened Bread,' to
which the words ' when they sacrifice the Passover ' were added as
a gloss (Chwolson, p. 180 of his new edition).

Jesus, against his wont, is in the daytime not in Jerusalem,
but goes there at evening in order to eat the Passover.

13.   The ' man ' is the servant of the owner of the house in 14.
He is known to Jesus, but not to the disciples.

15.   ἀνάγαιον, ' an upper chamber ';   ἐστρωμένον ἕτοιμον,
' furnished and ready,' ' that is, provided with the necessary low
table and carpets or divans ' (Bartlet).   'Εστρωμένον would refer
to the floor being covered with rugs or carpets, including pillows.

16.   *Not* the passover, if the Synoptic chronology is wrong.
M'Neile also supports the Johannine view very strongly.   He puts
some of the arguments very tersely.   (1) ' Details of the Last
Supper make its identity with the Passover very doubtful.   (2)
The Sanhedrin had determined to arrest Jesus before the festival,
yet according to the Synoptic chronology they arrested Him *on*
the festival.   (3) No Jew would carry arms on the festival (v. 51
Mk., Lk.), nor would Joseph have bought linen (Mk. xv. 46).   And
if ἀπ' ἀγροῦ (Mk. xv. 21, Lk.) means that Simon was returning from
work, though that is not necessarily the meaning, it must have
been before the festival began.   (4) Mk. xv. 42 can only mean that
Joseph buried the Body at once, because it was Friday afternoon,
and the hour when the Sabbath would begin (6 P.M.) was near.
Hence (Lk. xxiii. 56) the women could not embalm it at once,
but were obliged to wait till the Sabbath was over.'

17-21.   PREDICTION OF THE BETRAYAL

(*Cp.* Matt. xxvi. 21-25 ; Luke xxii. 21-23)

18   And in the evening he went thither with the Twelve.   And as
they sat and ate, Jesus said, ' Verily I say unto you, One of you
19 will betray me, who is now eating with me.'   And they were
grieved, and said unto him, one after the other, ' Surely not I ? '
20 And he answered and said unto them, ' One of the Twelve, who

21 dips with me into the dish. For the Son of man indeed departs, as it is written of him : but woe to that man by whom
the Son of man is betrayed ! Better were it for that man if he
had never been born.'

17. The prediction of the betrayal is regarded by many critics
as inserted in an older connection. Thus 17 and the opening words
of 18 (' As they sat and ate ') could well be followed by ' Jesus took
bread,' etc., in 22.

' The Twelve.' Here the phrase is used to prepare for verse
twenty. In the preceding paragraph we have Mark's usual expression for those who accompanied Jesus : ' the disciples.' The
Twelve in verse 17 is loosely used, for two of the Twelve were presumably already in the city. (*Cp.* Wellhausen's Introduction,
2nd ed., pp. 138-147.)

18. How much of the incident is due to Psalm xli. 9 ? A
critical view of the story can hardly allow a large amount of historical
basis. May we suppose that Jesus expressed some fear or anticipation that one of his disciples or friends would betray him ? It is
improbable that Judas, after his visit to the authorities, returned
to close intercourse with Jesus. He suddenly reappears upon the
scene in 43.

20. The reply of Jesus in this verse is very peculiar. The
Twelve are present ; yet he does not say, as in 18, ' One of you,'
but ' One of the Twelve,' as if they were not with him, or as if he
were not speaking to them. Is this the effect of an old tradition
that Jesus had said that one of the Twelve would betray him ?

In the second part of the verse the words, ' who dips with
me into the dish,' are not intended to refer specifically to Judas.
It is not implied that, at that very moment, when Jesus was speaking,
Judas dipped his hand into the dish. Judas is not singled out,
for all dip into the dish. It merely means ' one who is dining
with me.' Or the words may mean ' one who has lived in familiar
intercourse with me ' (*cp.* Psalm xli. 9).

In Luke, the prediction of the betrayal takes place after the
communion scene, and the words are still vaguer : ' Behold the
hand of him who betrays me is with me at the table.' If the
prediction is historic, Luke's version seems the best.

The desire for greater definiteness is seen in Matthew's version,
in which Judas asks if he is the betrayer, and Jesus replies, ' Thou
hast said,' which is perhaps equivalent to ' Yes.' The change of
the participle from the present ($\dot{\epsilon}\mu\beta\alpha\pi\tau\acute{o}\mu\epsilon\nu o\varsigma$) to the aorist

(ἐμβάψας) is probably meant also to point and single out Judas (' he who has just dipped ').

That Jesus should have definitely said before the others that Judas would betray him is very improbable. Would Judas then have been allowed freely to leave the table (Mark does not record his departure) and to effect his purpose ?

It is hardly likely that if Jesus knew that Judas would betray him, he would have tolerated him to the last by his side. For he is *ex hypothesi* attempting to guard himself to some extent against his enemies by keeping his exact whereabouts secret.

' The dish.' Is the meal the same meal as 22–25 ? The story may have an independent origin. If the meal is the Passover meal, the dish, as most commentators suppose, might be the Passover dish ' charoseth,' that is, a semi-liquid compound made up of almonds, figs, dates, spices, and vinegar. The participators in the Passover meal dip the unleavened bread and the bitter herbs in this charoseth mixture and eat them.

21. The verse bears all the marks of a later date than Jesus. The expression ὑπάγει (' departs,' ' goes away ') is vague and mysterious. It is used again in the Fourth Gospel (vii. 33, viii. 22).

What is the Scripture reference ? Is it to Isaiah liii. ? Or to Ps. xxii. ? It is very uncertain.

Whatever the historic character of the scene may be, its solemnity and impressiveness cannot be denied.

22–25. THE LAST SUPPER

(*Cp.* Matt. xxvi. 26–29 ; Luke xxii. 15–20)

22 And while they were eating, Jesus took bread, and said the blessing, and broke it, and gave it to them, and said, ' Take, this 23 is my body.' And he took a cup, and spoke the blessing, and gave 24 it to them : and they all drank of it. And he said unto them, 25 ' This is my blood of the covenant, which is shed for many. Verily I say unto you, I shall not drink again of the fruit of the vine, until that day when I drink it new in the kingdom of God.'

These four verses can be dealt with at any conceivable length. To discuss them and their parallels in the other Gospels and in Paul's Epistle to the Corinthians in full detail a whole book, as big as this book and bigger, could easily be written. But immensely important as these verses are in the history of Christian theology —and indeed we might add, in European history—much as they

have contributed to the weal and woe of the mediæval and modern
world, it is unnecessary to dwell upon them at any great length
in a book or commentary intended primarily for Jewish readers.
So far as Jews are interested in them from a general point of view,
they can read about them in the endless works of Christian theologians.   Jews will never commemorate the rite then instituted
by Jesus, if instituted it was ; its precise meaning is for them, as
Jews, one of very minor and secondary importance.   It is of profound importance and interest for them to consider whether, and
how far, and in what, the moral and religious teaching of the Sermon
on the Mount supplements or excels the teaching of the Old
Testament and the Rabbis.   What precisely Jesus meant by the
words attributed to him in Mark xiv. 22-25 does not greatly
concern them.   They need no communion except with God.   They
worship the Father and Him alone, not materially or by the help
of bread and wine, but, to quote the language of the Fourth Gospel,
' in spirit and truth.'

The problems raised by the four verses are very numerous, and
the divergence of the commentators is extreme.

To begin with, was the Last Supper the Passover meal ?
Those who accept the Synoptic date for the crucifixion think that
it was ; those who reject this date, and believe that the first night
of Passover was on Friday, and not on Thursday, think that it was
not.   In the latter case, it need not necessarily have been, and
most probably was not, held in Jerusalem.   The words of Mark
and the words of Paul (1 Cor. xi. 23-25) do not compel one to
believe that it was the Passover meal.   And even if it was the
Passover meal, the rite or actions mentioned in the four verses of
Mark seem to stand, or can stand, out of close connection with the
special rites of the Passover.

But whether the Last Supper was the Passover or no is really
a subsidiary question.   Far more important and far more intricate
and perplexing are the questions :

(a)   What did the words, as we find them in Mark, exactly
mean to Mark ?

(b)   Can we, on the basis of what Mark says, and of what
Paul says, and of what Luke and Matthew say, draw any
conclusions as to what Jesus did and said, and as to what
he meant by what he did and said ?

It will be seen that the answer, at least to the second question,
must be exceedingly problematic.   The differences between Mark
and Paul and Luke (in whom we have to take account of a most
important variety of reading) are sufficiently serious to make it
doubtful as to what exactly Jesus did.   As what he did is doubtful

how can we penetrate with any degree of certainty to what he meant in that which he possibly did ?

The main points in dispute are, first, whether Jesus intended to institute a rite to be celebrated after his death, or whether he did something, or acted some symbol, for the sake of his disciples then present, once and for all.   Secondly, whether what he did was a symbolic rite of communion, or whether it symbolized the offering or sacrifice of himself that he was going to make for the benefit of his community by his approaching death.

As to the second question, there can be no doubt that the conception of the Last Supper as a symbolic or dramatic representation of a sacrifice, even if not intended by Jesus, was soon ascribed to it and to him, after his death.   And as such it is regarded by Mark and by Paul.   But soon the rite was not merely regarded as a dramatic symbol or representation.   The bread and wine were not merely symbols, but in some mystic sense they became that which they symbolized, at least for those who in faith and purity received them.   The process, which culminated in the full Roman doctrine of ' transubstantiation,' began early.   But the other idea of communion was maintained or developed, as well as that of a sacrifice.   And, indeed, the two could pass into each other.   For sacrifice and communion to the ancient world are two aspects of the same thing.   Moreover, the mystic and sacramental idea of the ' elements '—of the bread and wine—was generated or stimulated by the idea of communion.   By means of a joint participation of sacred food the eaters are knit unto the god and to one another.

We may also surmise, with high probability, that though the words which Mark employs do not definitely say that the rite was instituted for repetition, still Mark, like Paul, meant his readers to infer, as he himself believed, that it was.   In his days, when he wrote, the ceremonial was practised, not only as an imitation of the Last Supper, but with the idea that a command of Jesus, then enjoined, was being faithfully carried out.

It is, perhaps, therefore, the more remarkable that Mark, unlike Paul, says nothing about repetition, or as to a rite instituted ' for the sake of remembrance.'   Hence there seems, for this reason, as for others, much to be said for the view held by W. and by others, that the rites mentioned by Mark, as performed by Jesus at the Last Supper, were intended to be something done once and for all as between himself and his disciples.

According to most of those who take this view, what Jesus did was, in anticipation and expectation of his approaching death, to celebrate an act of sacramental communion with his disciples, in order that they might hold together after his death and to some extent supply his place. I will quote a few words from W., in which this view of the rites of the Last Supper is very clearly put forward :

'The ancient idea (then still alive among the Jews) of sacramental union by eating the same food lies at the bottom of the rite (*cp.* I Cor. x. 17). The body of those who have taken part in the same meal is renewed from the same source, and becomes one and the same.' 'The historic Last Supper had for its motive the near death of Jesus. It was a special act through which a society was founded, an act of brotherhood between the twelve disciples, in order that, when their head was gone, they might yet keep together, and in a certain sense represent, and be the substitute for, their chief. The making of a covenant is effected once and for all ; it needs, and can tolerate, no repetition.'

By the act of communion Jesus knits the disciples to one another and to him. He will still be mystically and spiritually present among them after his death till the Kingdom is established and the will of God has been fulfilled.

I have not here altered what I wrote in the first edition. A great deal has been written upon the subject since, but it cannot, I think, be said that any certain or fixed conclusions have been arrived at. It is possible that the last meal which Jesus took with his disciples was not the Passover meal, but that the Johannine date for the crucifixion, which the author of the Fourth Gospel requires for his typology, is also inaccurate. We cannot be sure of the day on which the Last Supper was held or on which Jesus was crucified. While we cannot be sure of the exact relation of either to the Passover, yet the Last Meal and its solemnity are, doubtless, historic. It may be that we can know no more (*cp.* Bultmann, pp. 160, 161, and Bertram, 26–32).

22. 'While they were eating.' Mark does not say that the rite was instituted at any special portion of the meal. To reach the conclusion that the regular meal was finished (whether the Passover meal or no), or that what was now to come was a special addendum or extra, one has to make deductions and combinations which are scarcely legitimate.

εὐλογήσας, 'said the blessing.' The word εὐχαριστήσας, used for the wine in the next verse, means the same thing. Although Jesus had already eaten bread and drunk wine at this meal, and said the blessing over them, still, as he was now going to use bread and wine for a special purpose, he says the blessing over again. We need not assume that we have here to think of the special Passover blessings for bread and wine.

ἔκλασεν, ' broke.' Tremendous conflicts cluster round this word.

Was the breaking a mere detail, a mere necessary preparation or precedent for the distribution, or was a symbolism intended in the action of breaking ?   Many think the latter. 'Even as I break the bread, so will my body be broken by death.' This view is held by those who think that the rite symbolized the coming sacrifice ; but it is not necessarily held by all of them.   The breaking of the bread, says Holtzmann, was 'ein in Form einer symbolischen Handlung gekleideter Anschauungsunterricht.'   But the body of Jesus was not 'broken' by the crucifixion.   Menzies, who adopts the view that the rite symbolized the death of Christ as his final gift for the benefit of others, denies that the 'breaking' is a part of this symbolism.   W., in his usual emphatic style, says that the breaking is 'obviously' only a preparation for its distribution, not a symbol.   So too the wine was not scattered to symbolize the pouring forth of the blood.

'He gave it to them.'   These words involve a further warm dispute.   Did Jesus himself eat and drink ?   Mark does not say that he did so, nor do the other two Synoptics, nor does Paul. Some of those who hold that the rite was a symbol of his death think that he did not do so.   Those who hold sacramental or Roman views of the bread and wine tend to argue on this side. The disciples eat of the sacrifice ; they partake of that which symbolizes it; he who is to be sacrificed cannot partake of himself. Menzies, though his point of view is quite different, yet strongly emphasizes his conviction that Jesus did not eat or drink. 'He cannot drink of the draught he has compared to his own blood ; it is a thing he gives ; it is for others, not for him.'

Those commentators, on the other hand, who see in the rite a communion between Jesus and his disciples are naturally keen to argue that Jesus must himself have eaten and drunk.   The omission to say that he did is merely due to the fact that his own eating or drinking, as obvious, is assumed and taken for granted. Some would see in Luke xxii. 17, 18, a proof that Jesus did not share in the wine which he bade the disciples drink.   W. calls this 'eine unglaubliche Wortklauberei.'   If Jesus did not eat and drink with the disciples, ' dann fiele die ganze Communio dahin ' (cp. Meyer i. p. 179, n. 2).

'This is my body.'   This is the shortest formula as regards the bread which we possess.   Luke and Paul have extra words.   In their brief and mysterious character many see reason to believe that they are authentic.

What did they mean to Jesus ?   Gould seems to me justified when he says that to give them any material or semi-material or 'realistic' meaning is to interpret them in violation of the general teaching of Jesus. ' It would pull down all that he had been at pains to set up throughout his ministry—a spiritual religion.' The words rather mean 'this bread represents my body.' At the most we may assume the idea of communion through the common partaking of the same food. Jesus may be supposed to say, 'regard this bread as my body, and by eating it let us form one society, let us be united to each other ; be you united to me.' Because Jesus himself also eats of the bread which they eat, it is as if they had partaken of him and become one with him.

If Jesus alluded to his death as a sacrifice or gift rendered for the sake of others, we can best interpret 'this is my body,' as Menzies interprets it. 'Even as I *give* you this bread, so I shall give up my body.' But this does not seem a very obvious idea or obvious parallelism.

To ordinary, average Palestinian Jews, such as the disciples may be supposed to have been, the words, 'this is my body,' could have had little meaning. It looks almost as if the Christian communion rite, however it grew up, was here, unhistorically, attributed to Jesus. Yet, perhaps, this is going too far. On the whole, it may, perhaps, be said that Jesus, in dividing and giving the bread to his disciples, and saying ' this is my body,' meant ' this represents me ' : be united with me for ever, whatever may befall me or you. One of the best analyses of the texts in the Gospels and in Paul, and one of the soberest interpretations, is Heitmüller's in the article 'Abendmahl,' in Schiele's useful lexicon, *Die Religion*, Vol. i. (1909).

I must just refer to the extraordinarily interesting article by R. Eisler in *Z. N. W.*, 1925, pp. 161–192. According to Eisler the words, 'This is, or represents, my body, etc.,' are perfectly genuine. They are an application of a portion of the Seder ritual, and their meaning must be taken in conjunction with the words in 1 Cor. xi. 24, 'This is my body which is (to be) broken for you.' The disciples eat the bread which represents the body. And this body is the body of the Messiah. They 'enjoy' the Messiah, that is, they enter into union with him—a sacramental food or bread union, such as was not unknown both in Jewish antiquity and elsewhere. The new interpretation is supported by a wealth of knowledge, and is very clever ; but it seems almost too clever. Moreover, it depends upon the accuracy of the Synoptic statements that the Last Supper was the Paschal meal. If it was not, the whole argument falls to the ground. Noteworthy, too, are Eisler's deductions from the word ' broken,' and his ideas as to the manner in which Jesus thought that he would die (p. 182).

23, 24. We now come to the second portion of the rite, and are at once confronted with fresh puzzles and difficulties.

First, as to the four last words of the verse : ' which is shed (or poured out) for many.' W. regards them as an addition to the more original remainder. The idea of communion is crossed by them with the idea of a symbolizing of the sacrificial death.

There remains, then, if these words are removed, the phrase : ' this is my blood of the covenant.'

Now, J. Weiss points out that the words ' of the covenant ' join awkwardly on to the words ' my blood.' Hence the suspicion is aroused that here too we have an addition assimilating Mark to Paul, and that the oldest form is, ' this is my blood,' in close parallelism to ' this is my body.'

If so, then, to Mark, the meaning of the whole would be : ' as the wine is poured forth from the chalice, so was the blood (or life) of Jesus spilt as a sacrifice.' The wine symbolizes the death of Jesus just as the bread does.

But if Jesus spoke the first four words (*i.e.* ' this is my blood '), he meant by them in all probability much the same as he meant by ' this is my body.' The wine, too, formed part of the communion rite. Because they ate and drank what he ate and drank, there-fore—regarding the bread and wine as symbolizing his body and blood—they had become one with him ; he had knit them to him by a sacramental bond. W. would keep ' of the covenant.' It is an epexegetical genitive : my blood, which is or forms the covenant.

This part of the rite W. regards as semi-sacrificial. The wine recalls the blood of the sacrifice by which communion was origin-ally made. This seems to me very doubtful, as the days in which blood was drunk lay so very far off. But W. says : ' The meal (the bread) sufficed for making a union. But it is only a shadow of the old union (*Verbrüderung*) by sacrifice. This was done, not merely through the sacrificial meal, but more solemnly by the sacrificial blood, which the participants applied to themselves in the same way as to the god (*i.e.* the idol on the altar), by smearing or sprinkling. This sprinkling was a softening down of a more original drinking. Another softening down was the substitution of red wine for blood. Wine is a better means of uniting together than bread ; it symbolizes the blood, which is more important than the flesh, and is regarded as the equivalent of the very life itself, the essence of what is holy and divine. Hence Jesus does not combine the bread and the wine in one act ; he puts the stress upon the wine.'

There is, however, some reason to think that the original rite performed by Jesus was limited to the bread. An important MS. reading in Luke, accepted by many scholars, and one interpreta-tion of that reading, would suggest that the symbolic act in the

Last Supper was confined to the breaking and distributing of the bread, and that the wine was not brought by Jesus into any connection with his blood and with his death. This view is supported by the fact that, in many of the oldest Christian communities, water was used in the celebration of the ' communion ' and not wine. Moreover, this was especially done in the Palestinian communities who kept most closely to the original traditions and were least influenced by Paul.

I would also venture to suggest how difficult it is to believe that a Palestinian or Galilæan Jew could have suggested that in drinking wine his disciples were, even symbolically, drinking blood. For the horror with which the drinking of blood was regarded by the Jews is well known.

Taking the words in Mark as we find them, a reference to the covenant of Exodus xxiv. 8 is pretty clear. Whether Jesus intended such a reference is far more doubtful, even if he spoke part of the verse. But to Mark the new covenant was to be sealed by blood, even as the old covenant which it transcends or supersedes. Some such idea was doubtless in the mind of the writer of I Cor. xi. 25, and of our verse in Mark.

Even if Jesus only said ' this is my body,' we may yet perhaps assume that this communion ceremony was performed by Jesus with the feeling, and because of the feeling, that his death was nigh. W. says : ' Some have doubted whether Jesus was conscious of his approaching death, and whether the disciples could have understood this background of his action. But he knew the danger which threatened him. He passed the night out of doors. The scene at Gethsemane is fundamentally historic : his fear of death, his wish to avoid it, do not fit in with the conception of later writers that he went to Jerusalem with the intent to die there. That the disciples did not realize the seriousness of the situation, and that, therefore, they could not have understood at the moment the allusion at the Last Supper to his death, must be admitted. Yet the words which Jesus then said—his last words to them when together with him—would have remained in their minds, even though not understood, till the very short interval had passed when, after his death, their true significance was revealed to them (ed. I.).'

Thus W. argues that in τὸ αἷμά μου, if not already in τὸ σῶμά μου, one must admit a reference to the imminent death. He adds : ' Nevertheless the two short statements remain dark and mysterious. The only comparatively safe thing to do is to set forth the circle of old ideas from which their explanation must start. In that age of general religious ferment these old ideas were then coming to fresh life in various places.'

'Which is shed for many.' Bartlet says that we should rather render, 'which is being shed on behalf of many.' *Cp.* x. 45 and Isaiah liii. 10, 11. Meyer is sceptical about the authenticity of 'This is my body' etc. That Jesus spoke at the Last Supper about his foreboding of imminent death is hardly to be doubted, but as to the actual words put into his mouth it is very questionable whether any are authentic. (xiv. 25 is the most likely to be so.) Meyer gives his reasons, which are not without some cogency (Vol. I. p. 179).

Cadman rejects the words 'which is shed for many.' Jesus did not, according to Cadman, believe that his Suffering and Death would be for 'many'—that is, not for many of those then alive. Before the betrayal Jesus had, indeed, counted on a mass movement of repentance amongst the Jews by means of his death and teaching combined; after the betrayal he confined the blessings of the Kingdom to a remnant (pp. 137, 139). What Jesus did at the Last Supper was to make a covenant with the disciples through a sacramental rite. He realized that his work in Jerusalem would fail still more completely than in Galilee. Few of his own generation would possess the Kingdom, yet it would come. He makes the covenant with the Eleven. Judas must have left the room before the covenant was made. The agony at Gethsemane was not merely the anticipation of the horrors of the martyr's death. It was also the realization of the consequences of the betrayal; his rejection by the Jews; the guilt they would incur, and their own inevitable rejection at the Judgment. He may have desired that his disciples should, if possible, escape the fate which he had not so long before asked them to accept. Perhaps that is why he admonishes them to pray not to enter into 'trial' ($\pi\epsilon\iota\rho\alpha\sigma\mu\acute{o}s$). Jesus dies not only a martyr, but a disappointed martyr in that he perceives that even his death (like his preaching) would not bring about the repentance of his countrymen, or even 'many' of them. Yet would he return 'upon the clouds' as the Son of Man. God would not in any case be left without a people. Doubtless Jesus shared the belief that the righteous of the past would rise and enter the Kingdom. Such are the weavings together of an ingenious investigator: for each single statement something may be said; yet, as the whole, their probability seems small. It may be added that Cadman holds that Mark x. 45 can be authentic if it be regarded as a saying of Jesus spoken without reference to Isaiah liii., and at some moment between 'the Confession scene' and the Betrayal, *but not afterwards*. It seems strange that such a picking and choosing of Gospel utterances and statements in regard to authenticity, such a free acknowledgment of the difficulties in forming any consistent and intelligible picture of the events can yet consort with an obvious, earnest, and

eager belief in Jesus as ' our Lord.'   Can so shadowy a figure long
remain ' our Lord ' ?   A figure of whose true historical features,
and of the actual details of whose life and death, so little is known,
and that little—just at the most important issues and developments—so disputed and hypothetical ?   Paul could care little for
the Jesus of flesh.   He cared for the Christ.   But to-day, and still
more to-morrow, can and will people still care to worship Christ
if Jesus is wrapped in shadows ?

25.   If Jesus did not himself drink when he handed the cup,
the words must imply that he had drunk before at the meal—the
usual Passover cups, if the supper was the Passover meal—but
that he would thenceforth drink no more, and so did not drink of
the cup which he now hands round to his disciples.   More probably,
however, the words imply that he now drank again, and that
this solemn draught was to be his last.

The words in their general sense are clear.   Jesus says that he
will drink no more till he drinks the new wine in and of the Kingdom
of God.   That is the wine of Isaiah xxv. 6.   The joys of the Kingdom
are constantly referred to in Rabbinical literature under the metaphor of pleasures of food and drink.   Jesus accepts and uses the
metaphor ; indeed, we cannot be sure that it was merely a metaphor
to him, for there might be such a thing in the world of the resurrection
and of the Kingdom as a drinking which is only semi-material.
Jesus's last words are spoken in a tone of proud confidence and
joyous hope, which is very remarkable.

' Καινόν is not the word for new wine, for which νέον is used,
but καινόν denotes a new kind of wine.   In the making of all
things new, the ἀνακαίνωσις (Romans xii. 2 ; Titus iii. 5), there is
to be a new festal meeting and association of Christ and his disciples
—a realization of these earthly feasts and symposia, which are
brought to an end in this Last Supper ' (Gould).

Does Menzies deduce from the verse too much or not when
he writes : ' Jesus knows that his death is at hand, and his drinking
is over for the present.   But he will drink again.   The separation
will be very short to which he is looking forward, and after it he
will be in the Kingdom of God where all is new, the wine as well
as other things. . . . The verse certainly shows that he looked for the
advent of the Kingdom to take place at once ; his death was to be
the signal for its appearance ; he was to return at once out of the
realm of death to take his place in it at the head of those whom by
dying he has enabled to enter it ' ?

In its present connection, the verse appears to indicate a twofold conviction in the mind of Jesus : he is about to die, but the
Kingdom of God will surely come, perhaps even is near at hand.

Though Jesus may have gone to Jerusalem not to die, but to initiate the Kingdom, he may now have realized that this was not to be, and that, even if he was the Messiah, it was probably God's will that he should end his earthly career by suffering death at his enemies' hands : nevertheless he did not waver in his conviction that the Kingdom was coming. By his death, or in spite of his death, the Kingdom would come. His noble faith in God was not weakened by adverse circumstance.

W. lays great stress upon this verse. Whereas Brandt does not hold that its words are authentic (*op. cit.* pp. 288–302), W. considers that there is no saying of Jesus which gives us more the impression of authenticity than this one. But why he thinks so is because he finds certain implications in the saying, which are by no means obviously to be found there. It is true, as W. points out, that Jesus does not speak of his Parousia, of his return in power as the Messiah. But is it not going too far to say that he does not represent himself as the Messiah at all ?   (' Es ist unverkennbar, dass er sich in diesem Augenblicke gar nicht als Messias gibt, weder als gegenwärtigen, noch als zukünftigen.') Is it not going too far to say that he only regards himself as one of the guests at the table, at which the elect are to sit, after the Kingdom, without his agency (*ohne sein Zutun*), shall have come, and that anybody else could have expressed the hope that he would take part in the joys of the Kingdom in precisely the same words ?   It is true he does not speak of his own special resurrection (*seine singuläre Auferstehung*), but is it not going too far when W. seems to imply that this ' most authentic ' utterance of Jesus shows that he did not think that he had any special part to play either in the Kingdom itself when established, or in bringing it about ?

On the assumption that W. and others are right in holding that at the Last Supper Jesus did not institute a rite to be repeated after his death, but performed a rite as between himself and his disciples, once and for all, it may be asked how it came about that the rite was perpetuated and developed into a solemn liturgical practice and ceremony ?   Into this question I cannot enter here. Sufficient for our purpose to say that it is supposed that the rite grew up as it were from a twofold stem. On the one hand, it was the custom of Jesus to share common meals with his disciples ; he broke bread with them habitually. At these meals there may have sometimes been wine ; more usually only water. This practice of common meals was continued after the Master's death, and he was even supposed to be, in a sort of spiritual sense, still present among the disciples (' Die alte Tischgemeinschaft mit dem Meister wurde festgehalten. Das machte sich von selbst, er hatte es nicht ausdrücklich beim letztenmal befohlen.') But the second stem was a conscious imitation of the Last Supper itself, with a modified and more sacrificial interpretation of the communion rite. An immense step in the development of the rite must have been given by the teaching of Paul. Into all this, however, these notes cannot enter.

Loisy differs greatly from Wellhausen. To begin with he holds that all three Gospels mean the same thing in spite of their divergencies. More particularly, Luke, in spite of his difference of order, etc., nevertheless does not mean anything different. The 'institution of the Last Supper' has the same meaning to him as to Mark and Matthew (Loisy accepts the reading of D as the primitive reading of Luke, *i.e.* he includes verse 19 up to 'my body' and rejects the rest of 19 and all 20).

Secondly, he holds that all three go back in idea—not necessarily in language—to Paul. To Paul the eucharist, the sacramental blood and wine, includes the notions of sacramental communion and of the representation of the Christ's sacrificial death. The two are closely and inseparably allied. Just so also the brief words of Mark 'this is my body' cannot merely imply the creation of a sacramental union between the disciples and Jesus. They also refer to his imminent death and to that death as a sacrifice. This is more clearly expressed in the words about the cup and the blood. The breaking of the bread, and the wine in the cup, prefigure and symbolize this sacrifice, and though the words 'do this in recollection of me' are wanting, the Evangelists none the less intend the acts of Jesus to be regarded as the institution of a liturgical rite, commemorating and symbolizing his sacrifice, and securing a perpetual union with him through the eating of bread and the drinking of the wine. The faithful receive mystically his body and blood and so become one with him.

All this is Pauline doctrine and goes back only to Paul. The new covenant supersedes the old covenant of Exodus xxiv. 8.

If Luke does not make Jesus say of the wine, 'this is my blood,' nevertheless he means the wine also to be sacramentally understood. But from his omission of the words 'this is my blood,' we may infer that the reference of the bread to the body of Christ preceded that of the wine to his blood. Paul himself makes Jesus say, not 'this is my blood,' but 'this cup is,' that is, represents, 'the new covenant made in my blood.'

Did, then, Jesus say 'this is my body'? As Loisy thinks that the words cannot be stripped of their Pauline tenor, he is driven to deny this. He largely agrees with Andersen's remarkable article in the *Zeitschrift der neutestamentlichen Wissenschaft* (Vol. III., 1902, pp. 115-134). But there are special indications which tend to the same conclusion. Note, in the first place, the 25th verse of Mark's

14th chapter. Contrast it with 24. The two belong to different
' courants d'idées,' and with a little reflection one can see that only
the words of 25 would have been intelligible to the disciples. The
words of 24 only contain a meaning for those who are already
acquainted with Paul's theory about the redemptive death of Jesus.

Note, in the second place, that in Mark the words ' this is my
blood,' etc. are not said till the disciples have drunk of the cup
(Matthew transposes the order). But these words should precede,
not succeed, their drinking. On the other hand, the words in 25
rightly follow the distribution of the cup. Thus, in the source from
which Mark drew his narrative, the statement in 24 did not occur.
He added the Pauline words of 24, which he did not necessarily
take from 1 Cor. xi. 25, but from the eucharistic rites of the communities founded by the apostle.

Then, as to the words ' this is my body.' They correspond
with ' this is my blood,' and must stand or fall with them, even
though they occur (unlike ' this is my blood ') in the true Luke. The
original for the bread is similar to the original for the wine. As
Jesus said of the wine that he would drink of it no more till he drank
it in the Kingdom, so he said of the bread that he would eat of it no
more till he ate it in the Kingdom. Whether the last meal was the
Passover or not (and this Loisy leaves an open question), the original
saying about the bread is more or less preserved in Luke xxii. 16 as
the original saying about the wine is preserved in Mark xiv. 25.   In
order to find room for ' this is my body ' Luke applied to the entire
meal words which had originally been said of the bread alone.

The sort of isolation in which ' this is my blood ' stands in
Mark, and ' this is my body ' in Luke, the impossibility of explaining
them by the context—while they are so easy to understand in Paul
—tend to show that the body and the blood have been intercalated
in a narrative where bread and wine were only mentioned in relation
to the approaching Messianic banquet and Kingdom.

M. Loisy implies that even if the words were supposed to have
been merely ' this is my blood ' and ' this is my body,' yet they
could not be reasonably attributed to Jesus. He does not think
that they can be limited in their application to the mere idea of
communion (as in W.'s interpretation), or that the idea of the
sacrificial death can be excluded from them. He holds that the
anticipation of the Messianic banquet excludes the remembrance
of the death. It was only the fact of that death, and the faith in
the risen Christ, which interpolated (here as elsewhere) the mystery
of the redeeming death in the gospel of the Kingdom and of ' le grand
avènement ' (E. S. ii. p. 540).

The real words of Jesus, ' I shall not eat or drink again,' may
perhaps imply his death, but they do not announce it. Like all

the other authentic sayings of Jesus, they maintain the point of view of the imminent Messianic advent. They do not imply that a long time will elapse before the Kingdom comes ; nor do they directly say that the death of Jesus must first intervene. They do imply that a radical change is close at hand, and that one cannot depend upon the morrow ; to-morrow the expected Kingdom will perhaps be there, but perhaps, on the other hand, there will be a terrible crisis before the Kingdom, which is nevertheless near at hand, actually arrives (*cp. E. S.* i. p. 219).

How out of the Last Supper as it actually happened was developed the institution of the eucharist is another matter on which I need not dwell here. It probably owes its origin (*a*) to the historic common meals which Jesus was wont to partake of with his disciples, and (*b*) to the inventive genius of Paul. For the common meals continued after Jesus's death, perpetuated his memory, and still united his disciples with him who was yet alive, and yet among them, though invisibly. Paul was the first to conceive and represent this common meal as an institution which commemorates the Saviour who had given up his body and shed his blood for the salvation of the world, and which had been founded by the will of Jesus himself.

Andersen agrees with W. in omitting from the original Luke all xxii. 19. His view is that the original narrative was something like this : ' Jesus spoke the blessing, broke the bread, gave it them, and said, Take, eat. For I say to you, I shall not again eat of it till it is eaten fresh in the kingdom of God (*i.e.* Luke xxii. 16). And he received the cup, and spoke the blessing, and said, Take this and divide it among you (*i.e.* Luke xxii. 17). For I say to you that I shall not drink from this product of the vine until that day when I drink it new in the Kingdom of God ' (*i.e.* Mark xiv. 25). Upon this basis Mark's narrative was constructed and elaborated.

I have, on the whole, thought it best to leave the notes on this section very much as they stood in the First Edition and to add very little to them. Bultmann calls xiv. 22-25 a ' Kultus-legende,' and Bertram's view appears to be much the same. *Cp.* also the condensed and informing notes in Klostermann (ed. 2). The story in 22-24 may be ' eine Kulterzählung die in der Form eines geschichtlichen Berichtes anscheinend die in hellenistischen Kreisen übliche Abendmahlsfeier ätiologisch rechtfertigen soll.' The various possibilities as to what Jesus may have meant, if the story be historic, are briefly and lucidly given. In 25, whereas in ed. 1 Klostermann showed some tendency to ' wobble,' in ed. 2 he takes quite definitely the (to me common sense) view that by the words used Jesus implies that he too had drunk from the cup. As to ' this is my body,' Klostermann says that though the words τὸ ὑπὲρ ὑμῶν διδόμενον (1 Cor. xi. 24) are wanting in Mark, yet Mark meant that Jesus was going to die for the disciples, even as the bread he distributed was given to them.   He *may* have thought that the breaking of the bread was a symbol of the destruction of the body (*i.e.* of death).   ' This is my blood ' may be older and more original than the words which follow.   The wine symbolizes the blood of Jesus—' wird mit Jesu Blut in Parallele gesetzt—weil es als Opferblut zur Besiegelung eines neues Bundes mit Gott für viele vergossen wird.'   In 25 we may possibly see a fragment of an older story which we may connect with Luke xxii. 14–18.   According to this story, at a last meal, and with the sure anticipation of the near catastrophe, as also of the speedy appearance of the Kingdom, Jesus would have predicted to his disciples his coming reunion with them at the Messianic meal in the Kingdom of God, and he would not have spoken of any commemorative act at all, and would not have brought the bread and the wine into any direct parallelism with his body and his blood.   Klostermann rightly leaves all these possibilities open, but seems to incline towards the last.

26–31.   Peter's Denial Foretold

(*Cp.* Matt. xxvi. 30–35 ; Luke xxii. 31–34)

26   And after they had sung the *Hallel*, they went out to the mount
27 of Olives.   And Jesus said unto them, ' Ye will all stumble ; for it is written, I will smite the shepherd, and the sheep will be scattered.
29 But after I have risen, I will go before you to Galilee.'   But Peter
30 said unto him, ' Even if all shall stumble, yet will not I.'   And Jesus said unto him, ' Verily I say unto thee, This day, even in this night, before the cock crow twice, thou wilt deny me thrice.'
31 But he spoke the more vehemently, ' If I must die with thee, I will not deny thee.'   So also said they all.

26.   We may assume that the ' denial of Peter ' is historic, and also the flight or defection of the disciples.   Both are in a sense deprived of their objectionable character by being foretold, and by being represented as the fulfilment of prophecy.   It all had to happen thus and not otherwise.   Verse 26 may belong to an earlier story and have been followed by 32.   And in this section itself 28 and 27b may be secondary, for 29 follows well on 27a. The flight of the disciples is not fully described in Mark as we now have it ; xiv. 50 seems too fragmentary.   Verse 28 prepares the way for the story of the empty tomb ; it also exonerates the disciples ; they go to Galilee after the discovery of the empty tomb,

and not before (xiv. 7), in order to obey the order implied in the prediction and enunciated in xvi. 7.

The definite Passover meal, which had not at any rate been directly alluded to since 16, is now again mentioned. For ὑμνήσαντες seem to mean ' having sung the " Hallel " Psalms,' *i.e.* the well-known festival Psalms cxiii.-cxviii., so familiar to every Jew. These were then sung at the end of the meal. Jesus leaves the city and goes out to the Mount of Olives. He does not go to Bethany. Some think that as it was the Jewish custom to pass the first night of Passover in the city, that Jesus went to the Mount of Olives and not to Bethany, because the Mount was technically regarded as within the city. The question is obscure. For, as we have seen, it is doubtful whether the Last Supper was held on the first night of Passover, and not certain that it took place in Jerusalem.

27. Jesus predicts the defection of the disciples. It is conceivable, though not likely, that he did so. Assuming that certain recollections of Peter were one of the sources of Mark, the words of Jesus in 17–31 may go back to the memory of the disciples and of Peter. It is not inconceivable that Jesus may have felt that his disciples, however ready to share with him in his ordinary life and in his journeys, were not made of adequate stuff to cleave to him if the hopes to which they clung were rudely shattered, and if he, whom they believed to be the Messiah, should be captured by his enemies.

But if the opening words of the verse are authentic, the quotation from Zechariah (xiii. 7) was added later. The words are slightly altered to suit the occasion. (' I will smite ' for ' smite.')

28. Though this verse can obviously not be attributed to Jesus by any thoroughly critical commentator, it is yet of much importance. For it seems to show, what is confirmed by other evidence, that the locality where Jesus was first seen, after his death, by his disciples was Galilee. The verse, as Holtzmann says, interrupts the connection, for 29 follows far better immediately after 27*a*. It is wanting in the Fragment found in the Faijum in Egypt. Peter does not make the slightest allusion to it. Perhaps, it is Mark who himself added the verse to his source.

What exactly does προάξω ὑμᾶς mean ? J. Weiss urges that it means, not, ' I will go before you go to—I will arrive before you in—Galilee,' but ' I will go at your head, and will lead you to Galilee.' (*Cp.* for this meaning of προάγειν Mark x. 32, Matt. ii. 9). He supposes that this verse embodies a very old expectation (or prediction) which was not fulfilled. Mark himself misinterpreted it. He assumes that the apostles first saw the risen Jesus in Galilee, and that the angel ordered them to proceed thither (xvi. 7).   The apostles really remained in Jerusalem, and Peter saw the risen Jesus there.   The ' scattering ' of the ' sheep ' (*i.e.* of the disciples) does not refer to this hurrying back to Galilee, but to their dispersion on the night of the arrest.   *Cp.* Matt. xxvi. 31.   ' On this night,' the night of the arrest, is the ' scattering.'   This view of J. Weiss is set forth not only in *Schriften des Neuen Testaments*, but also in *Das Urchristentum*, pp. 12–18.   It is criticized by Goguel in his essay on ' La Résurrection dans le Christianisme primitif ' in the *Actes du Congrès international d'histoire des religions*, Vol. II. pp. 244–246.

29–31.   Some suppose that the prediction in 29–31 is unhistorical (*cp.* Bertram, p. 42).   But one may also argue that this famous passage must contain an historical basis.   For would Peter have allowed the story to grow up if there were not truth in it ?   The *precise* details and wording are another matter.   The impetuosity and eagerness of Peter are perhaps true to his actual character. Meyer argues strongly and cogently for the completely historic character of the prediction of the Denial and the story of it.   Also for the historic basis of viii. 32, 33, x. 28, xi. 21.   They go back to Peter's own telling, and the story of the denial most assuredly of all (I. pp. 147–152).

30.   ' Before the cock crow twice.'   Only Mark (though not in all the MSS.) speaks of *two* crowings.   It is disputed whether there was a real cock, or whether the crowing has not grown out of the fact that ' cockcrowing ' was used as a technical term to indicate a particular hour in the night—3 A.M.   (*Cp.* Mayo, " St. Peter's Token of the Cock Crow," in *J. T. S.*, 1921, Vol. XXII. pp. 367–370.   Also on the question of the legality of keeping hens and cocks in Jerusalem, S.-B. Vol. I. pp. 992, 993).   In any case, the double crowing is, as we shall see, highly effective in the fulfilment.   The meaning may be that Peter will have denied his Master three times between the beginning and end of the watch (3 A.M.—6 A.M.)—the two crowings marking the two limits of time.   But the source in all probability spoke of only *one* crowing.

The writings of the Gospel maintain a splendid level of dignity and pathos throughout the story of the Passion.   (For Jewish readers is it *quite* unnecessary to add that ' Passion ' is used in its older sense of suffering ?)   Whether Mark xiv. and xv. tell truth or fiction, or whatever combination of the two, in simple sublimity and exquisite pathos they reach the very highest rung of the literary ladder.

32-42. GETHSEMANE

(*Cp.* Matt. xxvi. 36-46 ; Luke xxii. 39-46)

32 And they came to a place which was named Gethsemane : and
33 he said to his disciples, ' Sit ye here, while I pray.'   And he took
with him Peter and James and John.   And he began to be dis-
34 tressed and troubled, and he said unto them, ' My soul is exceeding
35 sorrowful unto death : tarry ye here, and watch.'   And he went
forward a little, and threw himself upon the ground, and prayed
36 that, if it were possible, the hour might pass from him.   And he
said, ' Abba, Father, all things are possible unto thee ; take away
this cup from me : nevertheless not what I will, but what thou
37 wilt.'   And he came and found them sleeping, and said unto Peter,
38 ' Simon, sleepest thou ?   Couldst not thou watch one hour ?   Watch
ye and pray, that ye come not into temptation.   The spirit is
39 willing, but the flesh is weak.'   And again he went away, and
40 prayed, speaking the same words.   And he returned, and found
them asleep again, for their eyes were heavy ; and they knew not
41 what to answer him.   And he came the third time, and said unto
them, ' Sleep ye still and take your rest ?   It is enough.   The
hour is come ; behold, the Son of man is betrayed into the hands
42 of sinners.   Rise up, let us go ; lo, he that betrays me is at
hand.'

Jesus is represented as fully convinced that the hour of his
arrest, the beginning of the fatal End, is nigh.   The narrator
shows him to us almost divinely prescient, but in a moment of
human weakness, turned by faith into new strength.   The details
of the exquisite story must not be pressed, but it may well have
a historic basis.   For the tendency was to turn Jesus from a man
into a God, and a God has no moments of fear or agony, even if he
is about to die.   Thus the author of the Fourth Gospel omits the
scene altogether ; it does not fit in with his theology or with his
conception of the ' divine word ' made flesh.   The disciples may have
seen that Jesus was wrestling in prayer ; they may have perceived
that he was in trepidation and sore mental distress ; they may
have noticed that, at the moment of the arrest, before they left
him, he alone was perfectly collected and calm.   Upon this knowledge, the story, as we have it now, may have been built up.   Yet
one cannot but marvel at the wonderful grace and beauty, the
exquisite tact and discretion, which the narrative displays.   There
is not a word too little ; there is not a word too much.

32.   Gethsemane means ' oil press ' or ' olive garden.'   According to the Fourth Gospel this garden or enclosure was a place to which Jesus had often resorted with his disciples, and where Judas would naturally seek him out.

Perhaps Jesus did not leave the house in which he had supped merely in order to pray.   He feared arrest, and sought to avoid it by passing the night in the open air.

33, 34.   Three special disciples are allowed to accompany him. Though he cannot depend upon them entirely, he does not, perhaps, wish to be quite alone in this dark hour.   Luke says nothing of the distinction between the three and the other eight.   Had Luke a separate source, or did *he* use the source which Mark himself had drawn upon ?   In any case, the three disciples are as doubtful here as in the transfiguration.   ' At the end of the story, no difference is made between the three and the eleven ; Jesus, returning to the three, is found also with the eleven, and is speaking to them when Judas arrives.   No more here than elsewhere does it seem probable that the redactor fills up with special Petrine recollections less precise data of the general apostolic tradition ' (Loisy).

The sleep of the disciples is clearly a supernatural sleep.   The effect of the whole scene and of the isolation of Jesus is greatly heightened by the sleep of the disciples.

Peter and the two others see physical signs of fear and distress. Moreover, Jesus says to them, ' My soul is very grieved, even unto death.'

The word περίλυπος is used in the Greek translation of Psalms xlii. 5, 11, xliii. 5.   It is usually rendered ' very sorrowful.' Menzies has ' in great suffering.'   ' Even unto death ' is a reminiscence of Jonah iv. 9.   *Cp.* also Judges xvi. 16, 1 Kings xix. 4. As to the meaning, it is either, ' I would that I were already dead,' *i.e.* ' I would that the awful experiences I have to go through were over,' or ' My grief is so great that I feel as if death were upon me.'

The words in which Jesus's fear and distress are depicted are very strong : ἐκθαμβεῖσθαι καὶ ἀδημονεῖν, ' to be full of terror and distress,' is Dr. Weymouth's rendering ; ' appalled and agitated ' is Dr. Moffat's.   ' Watch.'   The order to watch, says Bertram, does not reflect an historic situation : it is to be understood as in passages like Matt. xxiv. 42, xxv. 13.   The Christian community must be watchful in all temptations (p. 46).

35, 36 may be doublets.   What Jesus prayed is first told in *oratio obliqua* and then in *oratio recta*.   The hour is the hour of fate, the hour of destiny, the supreme hour, the hour of doom. The cup is the cup of pain and martyrdom.   Jesus asked the three disciples to wait and watch. They were to give him timely notice should intruders appear upon the scene. Or perhaps ' he wanted them to watch with him, to share his vigil, not against human foes, but against the flood of woes overwhelming his soul. If possible, he would have companionship in his extreme hour ' (Gould). He then goes a little way off from them in order to pray. They see him praying, but then fall asleep. It is reasonable therefore to argue that Jesus went far enough off to make them unable to hear what he said even if he prayed aloud. Moreover, if they fell asleep, they would not have heard. The words which Mark gives are a consummately successful attempt to express what the situation demanded—what the fear and despair of Jesus, contrasted with his subsequent calm, suggest that he must have said in his prayer.

Some observations of Klausner are worth quoting. ' Jesus did not *know* that death was imminent ; but the *fear* of death was upon him.' ' Jesus had no foreknowledge of his impending death. He did not know that he would soon be arrested and put to death. But he did know that his enemies among the Pharisees and Sadducees were many and powerful while his own followers were few, and his disciples weak : " their spirit was willing, but the flesh was weak." Therefore the fear of death crept over him.' The words of his prayer up to ' from me ' are genuine. They would not have been invented. ' His prayer is wonderful in its brevity and truly human.' ' The whole story bears the hallmark of human truth : only a few details are dubious. It must have been transmitted to the Evangelists (or their sources) direct from Peter, James, or John, with such simplicity and conviction that even the ideas or tendencies of Pauline times could not obscure their memories. The sorrow and sufferings of the solitary Son of man, profound as they are, leave on every sympathetic heart, be it the heart of the believer or unbeliever, such an impression as may never be wiped out ' (pp. 330–332).

36. The simple and sublime words show prayer at its highest. ' Not what I will, but what thou wilt.' The lesson of Gethsemane speaks to all. If we learn from the lives of heroes, we too have something here to learn. How much strength has the recollection of the prayer at Gethsemane given to endless human souls ! And why should it not, even though for us Jesus is neither God nor Messiah, give strength to Jewish hearts also ? We must restore this hero to the bead-roll of our heroes ; we must read his story ; we must learn from it and gain from it all (and it is not little) which it can give us and teach us.

Bartlet and Turner think that ὁ πατήρ is the Greek equivalent intended to explain the ἀββα for those who knew no Aramaic. Jesus

did not use both words in his prayer—any more than he used Greek
as well as Aramaic when Mark mentions the actual Aramaic and
Hebrew words employed by him. ὁ πατήρ, then, is ' one more of
Mark's parentheses' (*J. T. S.*, 1925, Vol. XXVI. p. 154).   The
phrase ἀββα ὁ πατήρ occurs Gal. iv. 6, Romans viii. 15.   Perhaps
the double term had become a familiar form in prayer among
Greek-speaking and even Gentile Christians (Bartlet).

38*b*. The words are hardly in place. Bultmann is probably
right in calling them ' ein eingeschobenes Wort der christlichen
Erbauungssprache' (p. 162).   Or, perhaps, the saying and command
were both uttered by Jesus upon another occasion.   As the words
stand, they may be explained to mean : be vigilant, and pray that
you do not succumb to temptation (which will soon befall you).
Sudden danger, for which men are unprepared, makes the body
unable to obey the mind when the peril comes ; it seizes the body
and overawes the ' willing' spirit.

39. The triple going and coming are dramatic, but scarcely
historic.

40. *Cp.* ix. 6 and Luke ix. 32.

41. There is some doubt as to the rendering of the opening
words. Some take them interrogatively. ' Do ye still sleep on
and take your rest ? ' Others take them ironically : ' sleep on then,
and rest.' Or they may be taken to mean, ' sleep on : it now matters
not ; I fear no longer ; I do not need your support ; I am resigned,
and you cannot prevent the destined doom, which is the will of God.'
τὸ λοιπόν is odd in any case. Some render ' henceforward ' ; others,
' now.' The words are wanting in the S.S., as also is ἀπέχει.
   ἀπέχει. The meaning is disputed. W., who would bracket
the intervening words as secondary, would connect ἀπέχει closely
with ἐγείρεσθε, *i.e.* ' Enough of sleep ; stand up.' So too Kl.
B. Weiss says it means, ' it is enough : ye can sleep on now.' Jesus
has conquered in the arduous battle ; he needs his disciples ·and
their companionship no more.   The hour is come and he is ready
for it.   Dr. J. de Zwaan (in *Expositor*, 1905, pp. 459–472) has given
a new and interesting explanation of ἀπέχει. He denies that there
is any adequate evidence for the impersonal use, or for the meaning,
sufficit, ' it is enough.' On the other hand, he finds that in the papyri
the word is often used for acknowledgments of money, where it
means, ' I have received.' So too here, Jesus knows that Judas is
meditating his betrayal ; he realizes that this betrayal will have
been brought about for the sake of money, and that money will be

its result. So now, when he catches sight of Judas and his band, he says : ἀπέχει, ' he *did* receive ' (the promised money) ; he *has* succumbed to the temptation. The subject of ἀπέχει is therefore Judas. Deissmann seems to think favourably of this interpretation (*Licht vom Osten*, p. 90, 4th ed.).

' The hour is come.' These words W. would regard as ' secondary,' on account of the use of ' Son of man.' The ' hour ' is the same as the hour in 35. J. Weiss also thinks that the sentence looks like a sort of quotation from ix. 31, or similar passages.

' Sinners.' In what sense is the word used ? W. says ' the " sinners " are, elsewhere, the heathen, who do not fit in here.' But this is rash, for ' sinners ' is also used, as in ii. 15 (in the phrase ' tax-collectors and sinners '), of Jews. Differing from Menzies, I think that ' sinners ' is used here to characterize those who are the enemies of the Messiah.

Bultmann thinks that this story should end with 41 (which would make de Zwaan's view of ἀπέχει impossible), and that it did so end originally. Mark adds 42 to unite the story with what follows. But is this not hypercriticism ?

42. The former verse (from ἀπέχει) possibly, but this one certainly, are spoken under the consciousness, whether through sight, or sound, or both, that the arresting party are at hand. The speech becomes more agitated. It ends hastily.

ἄγωμεν. ' As the hour has come, it must be met worthily. It must not find the disciples lying on the ground, but standing by the Master's side. " Let us go," does not point to flight, but to an advance to meet the approaching party ' (Menzies). And J. Weiss says : ' Jesus feels the presence of the betrayer even before he is there, and goes with his disciples to meet him ; nevertheless the next verse begins as if Jesus were interrupted in his words by the approach of Judas and his band.' We have, then, I suppose, to understand that Jesus sees or hears men drawing near ; he says ' Let us go forth to meet them ' ; but hardly are the words out of his mouth before the men are already upon him.

43-52. The Arrest

(*Cp.* Matt. xxvi. 47-56 ; Luke xxii. 47-53)

43 And immediately, while he yet spoke, came Judas, one of the Twelve, and with him a band with swords and bludgeons from the 44 chief priests and the scribes and the elders. Now the betrayer had given them a token, saying, ' Whomsoever I kiss, that is he ;

45 seize him, and lead him away safely.' So soon as he had come, he
went straightway up to Jesus, and said, ' Master '; and kissed
46, 47 him.   And they laid their hands on him, and seized him.   But
one of the bystanders drew his sword, and smote the servant of the
48 high priest, and cut off his ear.   And Jesus answered and said
unto them, ' Have ye come out to capture me with swords and with
49 bludgeons, as if against a thief ?   I was daily with you in the temple,
teaching, and ye seized me not : but the scriptures must be fulfilled.'
50, 51 Then they all forsook him, and fled.   Yet a young man followed
him, clad only in a linen shirt upon his naked body ; and they
52 seized him.   But he let the linen shirt slip, and fled from them
naked.

43. Some (*e.g.* Bultmann) consider that 43 was originally the
sequel to 31.   Here comes the fulfilment of what Jesus said in 27 :
' Ye will all stumble.'   Jesus is speaking to the three disciples,
according to the strict interpretation of the narrative, but the local
separation of the three from the eight is now ignored.   It is somewhat noteworthy that Judas is explained to be ' one of the Twelve,'
just as if nothing had been said about him before.   But probably no
deductions are to be drawn from this.

Who form the ' crowd ' ?   Not, it is generally supposed, Roman
soldiers (as in John), and not the regular Temple guard, but an
unorganized band hired for the occasion.   If the arrest took place
the night before, and not the night of, the Passover, many difficulties
are avoided.   Then probably the ' band ' (ὄχλος) is incorrect, if it
means an unorganized rabble.   We may much more readily believe
that the arrest was effected by ' the ordinary " police officers," and
if a " band " with their " captains " accompanied the police officers it
was composed of a portion of the temple guard.'   So Husband,
whose section on the arrest is good and worth reading (pp. 70–101)
(*The Prosecution of Jesus : its Date, History, and Legality.*   1916).
The arresting party is purely Jewish ; a small force sent by order of
the Jewish authorities.   The observations of Klausner (p. 337),
and the pertinent quotation from Pesachim 57 a, are interesting.

44. This verse may, or may not, be historic.   The betrayal
with a kiss is not mentioned by the author of the Fourth Gospel.
It is a little difficult that this ' sign ' was necessary in the case of a
man who had been prominently teaching in Jerusalem for some
while ; but it was night time, and we need not suppose that Jesus
was well known to everybody.   ' The sign given by Judas,' says
Gould, ' had nothing unusual about it, but was the ordinary form
of salute.'   He adds : ' The motives of Judas in this extraordinary

treachery are hard to understand.   In judging of them, we have to remember that he was one of the Twelve chosen by Jesus to be his most intimate companions [there may, however, be some doubt as to the length of time he had been with Jesus], and we must not undervalue that choice by ascribing to Judas motives of such utter and irredeemable vileness as would make him an impossible companion for any decent person.   It may be that he had for his purpose in this extraordinary move to force Jesus to assume the offensive against his enemies.   This is, at least, vastly more probable than the mercenary motive hinted at in the Fourth Gospel.'   The ' kiss ' is suspicious, on account of the parallels, 2 Sam. xx. 9, Prov. xxvii. 6.   The kiss might be historic, while the interpretation of its meaning might be due to the evangelist ; or, again, ' der Kuss kann als listige Umgehung etwaigen Widerstandes gedacht sein ' (Klostermann).

46.   In Mark Jesus says no word to the betrayer, and indeed 46 fits on well to 43.

47.   In Luke the attempt at resistance on the part of the disciples takes place before the arrest.   In Mark we have to suppose that they are so appalled and overcome by the sudden onset of Judas and his band that, till the arrest is effected, they are unable to make the smallest movement.

The words εἶς δέ τις τῶν παρεστηκότων, ' one of the bystanders,' are very peculiar.   So far we have not heard of any one else being present at Gethsemane except the Eleven.   One would have expected : ' one of the disciples ' at the least.

' His sword.'   Thus some at least of the *entourage* of Jesus are armed, and, expecting an attack or onset, are prepared to resist it. Jesus does not rebuke the action of the ' bystander.'   (For a further consideration of the subject see the notes on Luke.)

The ' servant ' of the high priest is probably the leader of the band.   It is not said that upon the action of the bystander reprisals followed.   Or, at the threat of this, did the disciples flee ?   We cannot reproduce what exactly happened.   ' Dass nun nicht ein Kampf entbrennt, sondern Jesus das Wort nimmt, und danach die Jünger fliehn, fällt auf ' (Klostermann).

48.   The speech of Jesus is somewhat inappropriate for such a scene of scuffle, confusion, and alarm ; but it is filled with a quiet dignity.   It is addressed rather to those who sent the ' crowd ' than to these men themselves—to the masters, not to their servants. Luke seems to feel this, and makes the authorities present, which is healing one inappropriateness by creating another.

Jesus implies that he would have readily allowed himself to have been arrested in broad daylight in the Temple. The reply of the authorities would presumably have been that an arrest in the city or the Temple might have provoked from the excitable populace effective resistance and riot. The swords of the arresting troop were not unjustified in view of the fact that swords were not absent among the disciples or friends of Jesus.

Bultmann says that the words of Jesus smack of ' Gemeinde-apologetik und -dogmatik.' In fact, in the hurry and confusion of the nightly arrest, what Jesus actually said would hardly be accurately remembered.

49. ' Daily.' The interval between Jesus's arrival at Jerusalem and his arrest must have been fairly lengthy to justify this expression. Mark himself, as we have seen, would apparently confine the interval to three days. If the Last Supper and the arrest happened on a Thursday evening, Jesus entered Jerusalem, according to the Marcan chronology, on Monday (see Mark xi. 11, 12, 20, xiv. 3, 17). Luke seems to have preserved the more accurate tradition in xxi. 37, 38.

' But [this has happened] in order that the Scriptures might be fulfilled '; so literally. Two explanations are possible. Jesus means generally that he resigns himself to the arrest, because his capture and death are part of the divine will and foretold in Scripture. So e.g. Menzies : ' What Scripture had foretold of the death of the Messiah had come to pass, and so Jesus submits to the arrest, protesting against the manner of it, but recognizing in the fact itself the will of God.' In this case the γραφαί (Scriptures) might be Isaiah liii. On the other hand, J. Weiss says that the γραφαί cannot be those ' which merely speak generally of the death of Messiah.' The allusion must be to passages in which the special manner of Jesus's arrest seemed to‧ be portrayed. But what passages the Evangelist had in his mind we cannot tell.

50. Who are the ' all ' ? The disciples ? The Eleven ? Or all ' the bystanders ' ? Whither ' all ' fled is not stated. The general view of the commentators is that Mark implies that before long they all returned to Galilee.

51, 52. Only Mark has this curious incident. Who was this ' young man ' ? A popular idea at present is that it was the Evangelist Mark himself. It is often supposed that Jesus ate his Passover meal in the house of Mark's mother (Acts xii. 12), ' and Mark might have followed the party unseen when they left for the Mount of Olives ' (Menzies). But it is by no means sure that this Mark was the author of our Gospel. And, again, it is not sure that these two verses, ignored by Matthew and Luke, are not a later addition. There are also other arguments against the suggested identification, upon which it is unnecessary to dwell.

συνηκολούθει. The word is rather peculiar, but it occurs in Mark v. 37, and need not imply, as Brandt thinks, that the youth was one of the Twelve. The term εἶς τις νεανίσκος seems intended to exclude the disciples. Kl. translates 'Ein Jüngling wollte ihn begleiten.'

He had only a linen shirt on. Why was this? It does not seem clear. Those who think that he was Mark suppose that when the party broke up late, after the Passover meal, he hurriedly followed them *en déshabillé*. This seems very peculiar and unlikely. But if he did not come from the house in which Jesus had held the Last Supper, where did he come from? Was he a workman or watchman living in some hut in the olive garden? (So some older commentators quoted by Schanz.) Meyer accepts the story as quite historical, though the young man is not Mark. 'Es ist der vortreffliche Bericht einer Augenzeugen, der hier vorliegt, aber keineswegs der des Schriftstellers selbst' (B. i. p. 151, n. 2). Jesus is accompanied not only by the Twelve, 'sondern auch von einer unbestimmten Masse von μαθηταί' (p. 151). Yet the peculiarity of the whole incident lends some little strength to the old hypothesis that it is due to two passages in the Old Testament: Amos ii. 16 and Genesis xxxix. 12. M. Loisy is inclined to share this view. How, he asks, could the incident have become known? Did the youth in his flight meet Peter and tell him the story? But, then, ought we not to know more about him? The Messianic interpretation of Amos ii. 16 may have suggested the entire incident. So Kl. 'wahrscheinlich hat der Schriftsteller die Flucht der gangen Umgebung Jesu noch um ein prophetischer Motiv bereichern wollen.'

For the more orthodox view that the young man was Mark, and that the incident is historic, the reader may be referred to the notes in Bartlet.

53-65. THE TRIAL BEFORE THE SANHEDRIN

(*Cp.* Matt. xxvi. 57-67 ; Luke xxii. 54, 55, 63-71)

53 And they led Jesus away to the high priest : and all the chief
54 priests and the elders and the Scribes assembled together. And Peter followed him at a distance unto the court of the high priest : and he sat with the servants, and warmed himself at the fire.

55 And the chief priests and all the High Court sought for evidence
56 against Jesus, to put him to death ; but they found none.   For
many bore false witness against him, but their evidence did not
57 agree.   Then some rose up, and bore false witness against him,
58 saying, ' We heard him say, I will destroy this temple which is
made with hands, and after three days I will build another made
59 without hands.'   But even in this their evidence did not agree.
60 Then the high priest stood up among them, and asked Jesus,
saying, ' Answerest thou nothing to that which these bear witness
61 against thee ? '   But he held his peace, and answered nothing.
Again the high priest asked him, and said unto him, ' Art thou
62 the Messiah, the Son of the Blessed One ? '   And Jesus said, ' I am :
and ye shall see the Son of man sitting on the right hand of the
63 Power, and coming with the clouds of heaven.'   Then the high
priest rent his clothes, and said, ' What further need have we of
64 witnesses ? Ye have heard the blasphemy : what think ye ? '
And they all condemned him to be guilty of death.
65   And some began to spit on him [and to cover his face], and
to strike him with their fists, and to say unto him, ' Prophesy ' :
and the servants dealt him blows.

It is impossible, and for my particular purpose even unnecessary, to enter with fulness and detail into the many questions
raised by the trial of Jesus—if trial it was—before the Sanhedrin.
We shall never be able to tell or decide with any certainty
what took place in the high priest's house or before Pilate.   We
shall never be able to tell and decide with certainty what share
the Jewish, and what share the Roman, authorities had in the
death of Jesus.   A few general observations may be desirable at
this juncture.

(1) The desire of the Evangelists is clear—to increase the
share of the Jewish responsibility for the crucifixion ; to diminish
the share of Roman responsibility.   Pilate is whitewashed as
much as possible ; the Jewish authorities are condemned.   We
shall see many indications of this desire as we proceed.

(2) It does not follow, because the trial of Jesus before the
Sanhedrin violates Jewish law in many important points, that
therefore the account given of it cannot be true.   There have been
illegal trials at all times, and even the flimsiest legal forms have
sufficed to get rid of an enemy.

(3) Upon the whole it seems probable that the Jewish

authorities no longer had the power of conducting criminal prosecu-
tions which involved the penalty of death. So much Husband's
book seems to make fairly sure. And his conclusion seems the most
likely that what the Jewish authorities did was to draw up a case
against Jesus which they could then present to the Roman governor
and his tribunal. Husband's words are : ' The Sanhedrin conducted an investigation into the charges that were being made
against Jesus, to see whether these were sufficiently well founded
to justify them in preparing an indictment against Jesus for submission to the Roman court ' (p. 135). Or, rather : the Sanhedrin
was convoked to draw up a charge against Jesus which could be
submitted to the Roman court. The details of the proceedings
as we find them recorded in the Gospels are obscure and dubious.

(4) Not only, as we shall see, is the story of the trial before
the Sanhedrin (and also before Pilate) very obscure, but it has to
be remembered that no disciple of Jesus was present upon either
occasion—certainly not upon the former. The disciples, those
who collected and handed down the traditions about the life and
death of Jesus, could only have heard of what took place at second
hand. Some think there must have been many discussions, conversations, questionings, and arguments between friends and foes
of Jesus after his death about the grounds of his condemnation and
the details of his trial. This indeed is not impossible, but it is, of
course, only conjecture.

(5) On the whole, while the details of the trials can never be
ascertained with certainty, the balance of probability strongly
inclines to the view that the Gospel narratives are so far correct
in that Jesus was really put to death by the Romans at the instance
and instigation of the Jewish authorities, and more especially of the
ruling priesthood.

(6) The part played by the ' Scribes and Pharisees ' is very
doubtful. It is noteworthy that no word is said about the Law and
of the attitude of Jesus towards it. The allegation about the Temple
would especially concern the priesthood. We may in fact conclude
that the Sadducean priesthood was at the bottom of the arrest and
of the ' trial,' and that the result of this ' trial ' was adequate to
obtain a condemnation from Pilate. That the Jewish authorities
instigated the Roman trial cannot reasonably be doubted.

53. The whole narrative from 53–65 is full of difficulties and
improbabilities. Bultmann regards it as a secondary expansion
of xv. 1. As Klostermann, expanding Bultmann, observes : ' Wäre
die ganze nächtliche Sitzung mit ihren Unwahrscheinlichkeiten

eine Dublette zu der Verhandlung vor Pilatus (der nicht etwa ein jüdisches Urteil bloss ratifiziert), eingeschoben in die Erzählung von der Verleugnung des Petrus, um zugleich die Juden zu belasten und Jesus von ihnen als Messias verurteilt zu sehen, so könnte der Rahmen der Verhandlung aus xv. 1. übernommen, die falschen Zeugen (*cp*. Psalms xxvii. 12, cix. 2–4, 1 Kings xxi. 10, 13), und das Schweigen Jesu (*cp*. Isaiah liii. 7) dem Weissagungsbeweis entlehnt sein, während der Messiasanspruch Jesu nach christlichem Verständnis wohl die Reaktion der Juden (63, 64) hervorrufen durfte.'

It is curious that the name of the high priest is not given by Mark. The statement that ' all the chief priests, etc., assembled together ' need not be accepted in any case.   It would not perhaps have been so very difficult for a certain number of the Sanhedrin to have been got together, even at night, in anticipation of the arrest.   Twenty-three formed a quorum out of the total number of seventy-three. But then we should have to assume that Judas must have arranged the arrest, or that the arrest must have been arranged, some hours before it took place.   If the arrangement of the betrayal had only been made after the ' supper ' or even during it, the difficulty is greater.   For then one would have to assume that messengers must have been hurriedly sent out at night in order to collect enough members of the Court together.

The illegalities are very great, and if it were the case that the evening on which the arrest was made was the First Night of Passover, they are almost insuperable.   However eager the enemies of Jesus might be to get him put to death, they would scarcely have held a meeting of the Sanhedrin on a festival.   Again, no trial for life might be held at night, and the court which tried such an offence was specially constituted, and consisted of twenty-three members, not of the whole Sanhedrin.

Who are the chief priests ?   Menzies observes : ' There was but one [high priest] ; but the office appears to have conferred an indelible character, and there were always at this period a number of men who, after serving as high priests for a time, and being deposed by the government, still busied themselves with public affairs and exercised great influence.'   More probably Mark means merely the chief priests who constituted the main Jewish authority, or the priestly members of the Sanhedrin.

The house of the high priest was not the right *locale* for the court to meet in.   This is another little ' irregularity ' to add to the account.

If, however, the whole so-called trial was not a real trial at all, but only a preliminary examination, a setting up of an indictment, then the various irregularities and illegalities are of much less significance.

54. The Peter story and the 'trial' story are woven together. They may originally have been separate. 55–65 could be removed, and then 53, 54, 66–72 form one narrative. So Bultmann (p. 163), who regards the Peter story as 'legendary and literary.' The usual view is that the source of the Peter story is Peter himself, and that there is no reason to doubt any part of it.

55. It is impossible to state definitely what actually occurred in the 'trial' of Jesus before the Sanhedrin. Most of the various statements in 55–64 are very doubtful. In verse 55 the 'seeking for evidence' is most unlikely. Surely the 'evidence' would have been prepared beforehand and not left to chance. If false witnesses were obtainable, they would not have been allowed to disagree. The object of the narrator in 55–59 is obviously to show that Jesus was entirely guiltless. Even the statement about the Temple is false. The court is both prosecutor and judge—a further 'irregularity.' In Luke the court does not meet till the morning, which is more probably correct.

The court does not merely hear evidence, but looks for it. We ask, how have the witnesses been obtained at this hour of night ? Where did they spring from ? Were they kept in constant attendance lest their evidence should be suddenly required ? W. says, is true : ' That the witnesses are at hand in the middle of the night need cause no difficulty. The hearing was prepared and there was need of haste.' But if all was prepared, how was it that no satisfactory evidence was found ? The Psalmist says : 'False witnesses are risen up against me' (xxvii. 12), and again : ' Unjust witnesses rose up : they laid to my charge things that I knew not ' (xxxv. 11). Perhaps here we may find the origin of Mark xiv. 56 and 57. It was important for the early Church to show that their Master and Lord had been put to death upon a false charge, and that no consistent evidence could be found against him.

56. As the evidence did not 'agree' or 'tally,' it was equivalent to no evidence. Either we must assume that the statement is inaccurate, or that the 'trial' was more fairly conducted than other verses would lead one to suppose. Thus Holtzmann says that it would seem as if the witnesses were examined separately and not in each other's presence. On the whole, it is more likely that the picture of the witnesses sought out by the prosecuting judges, but giving inconsistent, and therefore obviously false, evidence, is rather imaginary than real.

57. The verse (' And some rose up and bore false witness against him ') reads oddly after 56 (' For many bore false witness against him ').

This looks like two distinct narrations, or as if 57–59 were more secondary than 56.   But though 57–59 may be secondary, they may yet contain history.

At this point the whole big question can be raised : What was the charge for which Jesus was condemned ; or, What was the charge which sufficed for the Jewish authorities to salve their consciences, and to make Jesus, in their opinion, worthy of death ? It does not follow that the charge upon which they were able to condemn him as a Jewish court was the same as the charge which they brought against him before Pilate, but to distinguish between the two causes a difficulty.   Moreover, if the whole object of the investigation before the Jewish court was only to formulate a charge, substantiated by witnesses, against Jesus to be sent up to the Roman authorities, the accusation in regard to the Temple would be of small avail.   For the Roman court would hardly consider that a man ought to be put to death who had made what a Roman judge would consider a silly prediction or boast of this kind.   And yet it seems likely that this charge was actually made in the course of the investigation.   It is to some extent substantiated by xiii. 2, where Jesus predicts the destruction of the Temple.   It is indeed the only charge which is made against him by witnesses.   The confession in 62 in answer to the question of 61 seems independent of the charge about the Temple, for I hardly think that Husband and Bartlet are right in holding that the question in 61 is the *result* of the statement in 58.   (*Cp.* Bultmann, p. 164.) They argue that the assertion that he would destroy the Temple and build another was tantamount to a claim of being the Messiah.

Taking the story as we find it, we observe that the condemnation follows upon the confession of Messiahship, not upon the charge made by the witnesses about the Temple.   Meanwhile, if either, or both, of these matters furnished the pretext for the condemnation, there is the difficulty that neither of them, according to Rabbinic law, constituted blasphemy.

W. takes the line that the charge brought up against Jesus which sufficed for his condemnation before the high priest, was his prediction of the fall of the Temple.   Thus 58 is, in substance, authentic and historical ; 61*b* and 62 are interpolations and unhistorical.

The statement of the witnesses in 58 is, in substance, the same as that made by Jesus in xiii. 2, which W. regards as most authentic and original.   It is alluded to in xv. 29.   Now W. asserts that though such a prediction may not be blasphemy according to the letter of the Mishnah, yet it was blasphemy according to Jewish sentiment and opinion right away from Jeremiah's days (Jer. xxvi.) till the days of Jesus.   For the Temple was the seat of God. To foretell its destruction was blasphemous (*cp.* Acts vi. 13, as regards the case of Stephen). That they bore false witness, and that their evidence did not tally, is Mark's judgment, not that of the Sanhedrin. If their evidence was inconsistent and false, why is it separated from that of the witnesses in 56, and treated differently by the court ? Matthew shows that the text of Mark has been ' edited,' for in his narrative Mark ˙xiv. 59 is wanting, and for ἐψευδομαρτύρουν in 57, Matthew has merely εἶπον. Hence W. asserts that ' this blasphemy ' was the ground upon which Jesus was condemned as worthy of death ; it was proved by consistent witnesses, to whom no objection could be taken, and by his silence Jesus confirmed and acknowledged it.

W. does not seem to have come to this opinion because he wants to deny that Jesus, in one sense or another, claimed to be the Messiah. For he expressly says that he takes no objection to the contents of xv. 2, in which Jesus seems to admit his Messiahship to Pilate. But he thinks it is impossible to believe that the claim to Messiahship constituted blasphemy. He says : ' To the Jews a man who claimed to be Messiah was not a criminal, as he was to the Romans. Even though there can be no doubt that Jesus at the last did give himself out as the Messiah, and was for this crucified by Pilate, yet his condemnation by the Jewish authorities must have had formally another ground. According to Jewish ideas there was no possible blasphemy if a man said he was the Messiah, the Son of God.'

Before this view is criticized, it must be asked why, if the prediction of the Temple's destruction was the real blasphemy, and the real ground of Jesus's condemnation, the Gospel narrative does not say so. The reply is manifold. First, Pilate, anyway, condemned Jesus for claiming the Messiahship. Surely then the Sanhedrin had done the same. Secondly, the Messiahship, when Mark wrote, was the great difference between Jew and Christian. Jesus to the latter was Messiah and Son of God ; to the former he was not. Surely he had been sent to his death because the Jews refused to recognize his Messiahship and his divine Sonship. Thirdly, we can trace in the Gospels themselves a disinclination to allow that the words attributed to Jesus in 58 contained any truth. Thus Mark, or an editor, speaks of the evidence as false and inconsistent, and Luke leaves this charge out altogether. Just because the tradition still accepted to a large extent the Jewish reverence for the Temple, and felt that an attack upon it would have given the Jewish authority the legal pretext they required, did it, half consciously, half unconsciously, seek to get rid of this historic ground of Jesus's condemnation and to substitute for it another.

As to the form of the prediction, it is probable that originally, if the witnesses quoted it, it was nearer to what we read in xiii. 2. J. Weiss points out that the evidence shows that the prophecy in its literal sense was 'unendurable' to the early Christians. In John ii. 21 the temple to be destroyed is explained to be Jesus's body, which is to be destroyed and to rise again. Mark stands half-way. He probably interpreted at any rate the rebuilding of the temple spiritually : the new temple is the Christian Church (*cp.* 1 Cor. iii. 17 ; 1 Peter ii. 5). Weiss further points out that it is not said that Jesus will build up another temple *within* three days, but *after* three days ; that is, after a short interval. The idea is that the building will, through a divine miracle, become ready all at once ; it will descend—like the new Jerusalem—from heaven. Jesus in all probability did not say that *he* would destroy the Temple. Its destruction was part of the divine judgment, and as God would destroy the old Temple, so would God create the new one, or, perhaps, he Jesus, as Messiah, would build the new one ; that the Messiah would build up the Temple again was a Jewish idea after 70. *Cp.* Klostermann's note. 'Made with hands' and 'not made with hands' may be expansions of the original statement.

Nevertheless W.'s trenchant interpretation of the trial whereby the accuracy of 61*b* and 62 are wholly rejected, and the entire weight is thrown upon 58, seems very doubtful. For we must surely believe that the Messiahship claim was at least ventilated, and that it was resolved that Jesus was to be denounced to Pilate upon that ground. It seems somewhat rash in a narrative, the whole of which is so shaky and dubious as xiv. 55–64, to pin one's faith upon one piece, and strenuously to reject another. Lastly, though the prediction about the Temple may have been nearer blasphemy than the claim to be Messiah, still, on the one hand, it was not technically blasphemy according to Jewish law, as later codified ; and, on the other hand, if 'blasphemy' could have been stretched to suit the one offence, it could also have been stretched to suit the other. The claim to be Messiah, without any of the ordinary qualifications of a Messiah—a claim admitted by a solitary prisoner in the full power of his enemies—must have seemed a presumptuous insolence, a kind of taking God's holy promises in vain. It could, perhaps, have been regarded as blasphemy by those who had predetermined to put out of the way a man who challenged the legitimacy of their authority, their claims, their rectitude, and their teaching.

Moreover, if, according to Husband's view, there was no real trial at all, the situation becomes more intelligible. Then the confession wrung from Jesus that he was the Messiah would have seemed enough to the authorities as a basis upon which to bring

Jesus before Pilate and to demand his execution. Luke does not mention a formal verdict and condemnation. Something, too, may be said for the argument that Mark ii. 7 shows that blasphemy was an elastic conception, not confined to the mere pronouncement of God's name (Yahweh). There is also force in Menzies's words : ' If the condemnation was illegal, it may have come about in various ways. A charge of constructive blasphemy was likely to be made against him by those who were familiar with his utterances in Galilee, *e.g.* those as to the forgiveness of sins (said, ii. 7, to be blasphemous) and as to the Sabbath. A condemnation on such a charge lay within the competence of the Sanhedrin, and was likely to impress the mind of the Jews. It is not unlikely that the charge was blasphemy, but the report of the trial cannot be considered full or satisfactory.'

The line taken by Husband is followed by Danby, who also seeks to show that the provisions in the Mishnaic tractate *Sanhedrin* as to criminal trials and as to the action and methods of the Sanhedrin are mostly unhistorical and ' ideal' (Danby, ' The Bearing of the Rabbinical Criminal Code on the Jewish Trial Narratives in the Gospels,' *Journal of Theological Studies*, 1920, pp. 51-76). Certain statements of Danby's are criticized and corrected by Abrahams in *Studies*, II. pp. 129-137. I do not here refer to the theory of Dr. Büchler's that there were two Sanhedrins, one for political cases, one for religious. Though the theory is more or less adopted by Abrahams, it is too problematic and hypothetical to be discussed here. It is set forth clearly and well in the article ' Sanhedrin ' in the *Jewish Encyclopœdia*, Vol. XI., by Lauterbach. Meyer argues strongly that the account of the trial in Mark is historic and reasonable and homogeneous. W.'s theory of interpolation is quite needless and wrong. The blasphemy does not consist in the mere foretelling that the Temple would be destroyed. It consists in the alleged assertion that *he*, Jesus, would destroy it and build up another. By this assertion he implicitly claims to be the Messiah. It is for this that the High Priest tears his clothes (Vol. I. pp. 188-192). ' Even in this their evidence did not agree.' It is not quite easy to see what this means. Are we to understand that though the general sense of their statements was what we are told in 58, yet in details there were conflicting divergencies ?

60. The high priest ' stood up in the midst ' ; so literally. This is usually taken to mean that he got up, left his seat, and stood in front of Jesus. But the phrase may merely mean ' got up.'

61. Jesus makes no reply. This may be quite historic. The judges would not understand his point of view, his aims, his hopes,

or his belief. But one remembers Isaiah liii. 7 ; Psalm xxxviii.
12–14, and one is a little doubtful.

It is, no doubt, highly curious, as W. says, that the high priest
does not say, ' Your silence means a confession,' does not, in fact,
pursue the charge of 58 at all, but raises a totally fresh question.

As to the form of the question, Jewish readers must specially
notice that the high priest's question does not imply that the very
idea of ' the Son of God ' is itself a blasphemy. It is assumed by
him that the true Messiah *would* be ' the Son of God.' Nor was
Mark inaccurate in making the high priest use such words.

The metaphysical or definitely ' Christian ' conception of the
Son of God is not implied. Yet in a *certain* restricted sense it
was universally admitted that the Messiah *was* the Son of God ; in
the Messianically interpreted second and eighty-ninth Psalms he
is actually so called. Moreover, in the age of Jesus the purely
human character of the Messiah was not emphasized by Jewish
teachers as it became emphasized after the development of
Christianity. Room was given for wide speculations and fancies
as to his nature and pre-existence; he stood in a special relation to
God, and was in a somewhat special sense his Son. In the conception of a few he was nearly a divine being, though a separate and
subordinate being, distinct from, and created by, God. But only
in some limited and narrow sense could the high priest speak of
him as God's Son, and only in this sense probably does Jesus mean
that he is Son and Messiah. The ' Blessed One ' is merely a cir-
cumlocution for God. To a Jew, as Loisy says, the phrase ' Son of
God ' would have implied no ' idée métaphysique,' which he rightly
and truly says is more ' conforme à l'esprit de la gentilité ' than to
that of Judaism. The phrase would indeed be blasphemous if it
implied the incarnation of a being ' qui était, pour ainsi dire, quelque
chose de Dieu.'

On the other hand, if it was no blasphemy for the real Messiah
to be spoken of, and to speak of himself, as the Son of God in the
more limited sense, it might not unreasonably be regarded as
blasphemy for a man to claim to be that Son, when he was not.
J. Weiss points out that, when the Fourth Gospel was written, the
Jews are said to be indignant because Jesus called God his own
(ἴδιον) Father, thereby making himself equal with God. And, long
before, when the Wisdom of Solomon was written, the wicked are
said to taunt the righteous man because ' he calls himself the child
of God, he vaunts that God is his father.' They urge, in words
which seem oddly relevant to the trial of Jesus : ' Let us see if his
words be true, and let us try what shall befall him in the ending of
his life. For if the righteous man is God's son, he will uphold
him, and he will deliver him out of the hands of his adversaries.

With outrage and torture let us put him to the test, that we may learn his gentleness, and may prove his patience under wrong. Let us condemn him to a shameful death ; he shall be visited according to his words.' If the judges sought for a plea on which to get Jesus condemned by Pilate, his confession of the Messiahship would surely have sufficed.

Klausner's observations are worth quoting. 'Throughout the entire inquiry Jesus remained silent. At the moment silence was best suited to his frame of mind. Jesus did not resemble in his preaching those other rebel-messiahs of the time, and it was difficult to get at the truth as to his real character. The high priest therefore put the direct question to Jesus himself : " Art thou the Messiah ? " Mark here adds the words, " the Son of the Blessed." This is not a Hebrew expression and must be a later addition : it is scarcely an abbreviation of the habitual " the Holy One, blessed be he." Matthew records the question in more solemn form : " I adjure thee by the living God that thou tell us whether thou be the Messiah, the Son of God ! " The oath is possible, but the words "Son of God" (which become a separate question in Luke) from the mouth of a Jewish high priest, and particularly from a Sadducee, are inconceivable. Jesus was convinced of his Messiahship : of this there is no doubt ; were it not so he would have been nothing more than a mere deceiver and impostor—and such men do not make history : they do not found new religions which persist for two thousand years and hold sway among five hundred millions of civilized people. When this challenge came from the high priest, a challenge which he had already answered affirmatively at Cæsarea Philippi and Bethphage, it was impossible but that the soul and feelings of Jesus—a mystic, a dreamer, and an enthusiast—should be stirred to their depths. There is no doubt that he returned a positive answer.

'According to Mark's version, he answered : " I am he " ; and according to Matthew : " Thou sayest " (derived from the answer of Jesus to Pilate) ; then, according to all the Synoptic Gospels, Jesus added : ' And ye shall see the Son of Man sitting at the right hand of Power and coming with the clouds of heaven." Could his enthusiastic belief in himself have led him to such lengths as to make use of this startling reference to himself ? With an Oriental possessed of such a conviction, it was by no means impossible. The two expressions " Son of Man " (frequently on his lips) and " at the right hand of power " ($\dot{\epsilon}\kappa\ \delta\epsilon\xi\iota\hat{\omega}\nu\ \tau\hat{\eta}s\ \delta\upsilon\nu\dot{\alpha}\mu\epsilon\omega s$, a peculiar Hebrew expression for the Deity) show that the answer is perfectly in accord with Jesus's spirit and manner of speech. To the high priest the answer was sheer blasphemy—a Galilæan carpenter styling himself " Son of man " in the sense of the Book of Daniel and saying that he should sit on the right hand of God and come " with the clouds

of heaven " !   The high priest rent his garments—the custom of the
judge who heard blasphemous words.   According to the ruling of
the Mishnah, Jesus was not worthy of death since " the blasphemer
is not guilty till he have expressly pronounced the *Name*," and Jesus,
like a scrupulous Jew, said ' Power ' instead of ' Yahweh.'   We have,
however, already pointed out (*a*) that this was a court of law mainly
composed of Sadducees whose president, the high priest, was a
Boethusean ; and (*b*) that, even in Jesus's time, the Pharisees had
not yet laid down the rules of procedure in the precise form which
they receive in the Mishnah ' (pp. 342, 343).

62.   The first part of the reply of Jesus is a formal acknowledgment of his Messiahship.   In Matthew and in Luke he does not do
this.   (Compare the parallel passages and the notes to them.)
Some suppose that in this respect Matthew and Luke are nearer the
truth.   The marked divergence of Luke shows that he followed a
different account or version of the trial from that of Mark.   In
Matthew's ' Thou hast said,' some have thought that Jesus means
to say, ' You suggest that I am or claim to be the Messiah, but *I* do
not.'   We have, however, seen reason to believe that Jesus did in
some sense or other claim to be the Messiah.   J. Weiss thinks that
Jesus, as the version in Luke records, refused to answer, because
there was no common ground between accuser and accused.   He
did indeed believe that he was the Son of God, and he did believe
that it would probably please God to effect the transformation
from the one era to the other era, from the old kingdom of sin and
violence to the new Kingdom of righteousness and peace, through
him.   But his conviction that he was the Son of God was a sanctuary
of faith into which he allowed none to enter, about which he would
not speak, which he could not and would not explain to his enemies.
And as to the Messiahship, that, too, in his conception of it, would
be unintelligible to them.   But how subjective all this is, how
conjectural !   It may be more or less true, it may be false.   How
can we hope to guess with any approach to certainty what Jesus
may have *meant*, when we do not even know with any assurance
what he actually *said* ?
    Jesus proceeds not merely to acknowledge his Messiahship
(which is here shown to have been no longer a secret of his disciples)
but he also volunteers a statement that the famous prediction of
Daniel is soon to be accomplished before their eyes.   He combines
with Daniel vii. 13 the equally famous phrase of Psalm cx. 1 : ' The
Lord said unto my lord, *Sit thou at my right hand*.'   If Jesus said
these words we can hardly think that he distinguished between
himself, the Son of man, and the Messiah.   The Son of man must
be the Messiah, and both must be himself.   Though now, as Menzies

says, ' a Messiah in disguise, he is on the point of being invested with all that belongs to the office. The Messiah, as spiritual-minded Jews conceived him, is about to appear. Even his enemies will see Jesus clothed with all the power and splendour of the Son of man, sitting, as that personage was expected to do, on the right hand of the Power, the powerful or Almighty One (Jesus also avoids the divine name), and coming with the clouds to execute His judgment and set up His Kingdom.' If Jesus said the words, this seems their most obvious explanation.

So too Professor Peake in his essay on the Messiah and the Son of Man (1924). In spite of ' the perplexing use of the Son of man alongside of the first person singular, it is difficult to resist the con-clusion that in this context Jesus means to identify the two. He could scarcely in one breath have affirmed his identity with the Messiah and implied his distinction from the Son of man. This is not to say that the Son of man is necessarily equivalent to Messiah ; but if the ideas are distinct, Jesus was conscious that both were fulfilled in him, just as he was at once both Messiah and Servant of Yahweh ' (p. 26). It may also be noted that it is not definitely stated that the manifestation of the Messiahship in Glory would take place after Jesus's death. The view is still tenable, if perhaps, on the whole less likely, that to the very end Jesus expected a miracle and a divine deliverance and transformation while he was yet alive. Bousset is interesting on verse 61 (*Kyrios Christos*, ed. 2, p. 37). He thinks that the trial is looked at, and worked up, from the point of view of the theology of the nascent Christian com-munity. Jesus was already a semi-divine being, and this belief is reflected in the words ' Son of the Blessed One '. The Jewish op-ponents of the Christians did regard such a belief as blasphemous.

W. argues against the historical character of the verse. ' Jesus not only acknowledges that he is the Messiah, but calls himself the Son of man and predicts his Parousia. It is very improbable that he ever did that, but most improbable of all that he did it before the Sanhedrin. . . . The solemn scene is pleaded as proof of authen-ticity. But if Luther's " Here stand I," when half Europe was listening, is not by any means free from doubt, how can these words of Jesus, spoken much less openly, and in the absence of his disciples, be guaranteed by the solemn scene ? ' In truth one's judgment must be left in suspense. But in view of what they had to report to Pilate, it does seem as if the judges would naturally have tried to get some evidence against Jesus, and some confession from himself, as to his rumoured Messiahship. Beyond this we cannot go. I cannot set forth, or enter into Reitzenstein's interesting explanation of 57–59, 61, 62 in *Das mandäische Buch des Herrn der Grösse* (1919), pp. 66–70.

63. The high priest tears his clothes. This was quite in accordance with Jewish law and custom upon hearing a blasphemy. But it may not be meant here in a purely legal sense. To tear one's clothes might also be a sign of horror and grief.

If W.'s view that 61*b* and 62 are later interpolations be correct, then 63 follows on 61*a*. But then, how could the high priest say, 'ye have *heard* the blasphemy'? It is rather lame to argue that Jesus's silence was interpreted by the high priest as a confession, or to point out that, at all events, Mark, unlike Luke, has not the words 'from his mouth.'

The difficulty has been cleverly avoided by Norden through a fresh hypothesis, too elaborate and too hypothetical to be set forth here, but worth reading for its ingenuity (*Agnostos Theos*, 1913, pp. 194–197 and especially n. 2, p. 195). M'Neile argues that what Jesus had said was 'technically speaking, not blasphemy, in the strict sense of saying something against God.' But, with their determination to condemn, the court not unnaturally treated as blasphemy words from a young Galilæan prisoner which implied 'I shall be seated at God's right hand.' It seems to me of importance that a trained historian like Meyer finds Mark's trial narrative 'durchaus anschaulich und einheitlich.' He will have nothing to say to Wellhausen's proposed excision of 61*b* and 62. The exclamation, 'what more evidence do we want,' has no relevancy if it is joined on to the disagreement of the witnesses and to Jesus's silence, and the assertion, 'you have heard the blasphemy,' would be a mere lie. Jesus declares himself to be the 'Son of man,' the Messiah. Meyer holds that the mere assertion that the Temple would be destroyed is no blasphemy. Moreover, the edge of the assertion of the witnesses is not that the Temple would be destroyed, but that *he*, Jesus, would destroy it and rebuild it in three days. Who could do this, and who could even make such an assertion? Only the Messiah, or only he who claimed to be Messiah. It is because the claim to Messiahship is explicit in 58 that the high priest puts the definite question in 61. The Messianic charge and claim are not got rid of by the excision of 61 and 62, for they are implicit in 58. So too Matthew in the sequence of xxvi. 63 on 61. (*Ursprung*, i. pp. 188–194.)

64. Thus Mark records a formal condemnation. It is this which Husband and others regard as unhistorical. It is part of the tendency to throw as much blame as possible upon the Jews, as little as possible upon the Romans. Luke does not mention a formal verdict. It would be enough to assume that an informal meeting of the Sanhedrin or of some of its leading members was held, at which Jesus was interrogated, and perhaps even some evidence taken

against him.   It was considered that enough had been elicited with
which to obtain his successful condemnation from the Roman
procurator.

M. Loisy goes furthest in denying the historical character of
the trial before the high priest.   He supposes that Luke has preserved from the source which both he and Mark used one accurate
point.   The meeting of the Jewish authorities (not a regular sitting
of the Sanhedrin, but a hurried and informal consultation) took place
in the morning.   There were not two meetings, as Mark would have
us believe, but one only.   At this meeting the denunciation of Jesus
to Pilate was arranged.   Whether Caiaphas then interrogated Jesus
is uncertain ;   probably he did not do so.   Probably the whole scene
before Caiaphas is spun (with a particular object), out of the scene
before Pilate, one historical fact, and certain Old Testament passages and predictions.   It is not certain that the Sanhedrin, subject to confirmation by the Romans, could not have condemned a
man to death, but Caiaphas and his friends preferred to denounce
Jesus to Pilate as a false Messiah, because judgment could be
more quickly obtained, while the judicial proceedings would be protected and guaranteed against any popular movement, and upon
the Roman governor would be placed the responsibility of the
condemnation.

As to the scene of the trial before Caiaphas, the saying about
the Temple is taken from words of Jesus which he had undoubtedly
used.   But Loisy holds that the words (Mark xiv. 58) ' made with
hands ' and ' made without hands ' have been added to the text, to
indicate that the Temple of which Jesus was thinking is the Christian
society or church, founded on the faith in the risen Christ.

The second part of the trial deals with the Messianity of Jesus,
and depends upon the historic trial before Pilate.

The object of the whole scene is to fix the responsibility for Jesus's
death definitely upon the Jews.   It was desirable that the founder
of the new religion should not seem to have been condemned by a
just verdict of Pilate.   On the other hand, it was a delicate thing to
accuse Pilate of prevarication, and it was impossible to deny that the
death sentence had been uttered by him.   But the Jews were in any
case the accusers of Jesus ;   they were the enemies of nascent Christianity ;   they were detested in the pagan world.   Nothing then was
more easy than to enlarge their part in the tragedy so as to shift upon
them the entire responsibility of the verdict.   Hence the elaboration
of the trial before Caiaphas.   Pilate has only to confirm a sentence
passed by the Sanhedrin.   Hence too the episode of Barabbas.   The
execution of Jesus was the crime of the Jews ;   the Roman governor
was guiltless (*E. S.* II. p. 610).

Though Loisy holds that Jesus's assertion about the Temple

was not mentioned formally before Caiaphas in the way indicated
by Mark, it may nevertheless have been mentioned to Pilate. For
it may well have been regarded as an evidence of Messianic pretension.

Thus Loisy rejects the scene as it stands as well as W.'s amend-
ment. He also refuses to admit the compromise of Dalman that
the blasphemy was limited to the words about the Son of
God being seated at God's right hand, or the compromises that
the high priest alleged a blasphemy where there was none, or that
the Messianic claim in the mouth of a man as impotent as Jesus
amounted to blasphemy. ' The story of the nocturnal sitting
of the Sanhedrin has been inserted into a narrative (known to
Luke) in which Peter's denial followed the arrival of Jesus
at the high priest's house, and in which the sole meeting of
the enemies of Jesus took place in the morning in order to draw
up the denunciation which was to be submitted straightway to
the Roman governor (i.e., join xiv. 53a, 54, 66-72, xv. 1). The
trial before Caiaphas has been deduced from the trial before Pilate,
the Evangelist desiring to throw upon the Jews the responsibility
of the Saviour's death. Mark is anxious to make the Sanhedrin
pronounce the death sentence. The object of the questioning of
Jesus is to bring about this sentence, and as the Evangelist knew
that such a judgment could not have been obtained in the very early
morning previous to the appearance of Jesus before Pilate, he
devised a sitting at night. The words attributed to Jesus about
the Temple (which Mark has enlarged) may have been borrowed
from the real trial, when the denunciation of the members of the
Sanhedrin and the depositions of the witnesses, which Mark transposes to the nocturnal session, had their proper place. The declaration according to which the Christ is called " Son of God "
corrects beforehand the historic definition of the charge which gave
the motive of Jesus's condemnation : namely, the avowed claim
to the kingship over Israel : this declaration, if understood in the
sense in which the Evangelist understood it, is blasphemous in
the eyes of the Jews, and the blasphemy explains the sentence of
death. The series of outrages which follows the condemnation
seems derived from the mocking scene at the Prætorium and to
have been drawn up to show an accomplishment of prophecies '
(E. S. 1. p. 102).

65. This verse appears to be in the wrong place. If there
be anything historic about it, Luke's version, according to which
the evil doers are the police or temple guard who made the arrest,
is more probable than Mark's. For who are the ' some ' who in
Mark spit upon Jesus and hit him with their fists ?   It is usually

assumed that they are some of the judges. This seems most unlikely. Menzies says : ' Is it some of the councillors who do these
unworthy acts, or others who are there, perhaps some of the witnesses ?
We cannot tell.' Mark distinguishes them from the servants or
attendants, whose turn comes later. ' To cover his face.' Matthew
and Luke explain this by adding to the word ' prophesy,' ' who is it
that struck thee ? ' Others explain that Jesus is to foretell to the
strikers their punishment. Perhaps putting a cover over his face
is only meant to indicate that a prophet must be withdrawn from
the visible world in order to receive his inspiration, or to obtain a
vision. W. thinks that the words ' to cover his face,' which are
wanting in the MS. D, and in the S.S., are interpolated. So too
Streeter. *Cp.* notes on Matthew. Burkitt thinks that the words
mean that the Jewish court regarded Jesus as a condemned criminal,
like Haman (Esther vii. 8) of old (*Gospel History*, p. 53). ' Prophesy ' means merely, ' *We* will teach you to prophesy,' or ' *We*
will make you give up prophesying ! ' Or ' Now prophesy still
more about the Temple.' ῥαπίσματα are apparently blows upon the
cheek. Either ' they received him—took him over into safe custody
—with blows,' or the phrase is a Latinism, and means the same as is
indicated in another reading (ἔβαλον for ἔλαβον) : ' they dealt out
to him blows.'

How far is this verse historic ? It is conceivable that the
attendants or slaves, to whom Jesus was entrusted after the trial,
ill-treated and abused him, though it is not easy to say who could
have reported it. J. Weiss goes so far even as to call the narrative
' an extremely life-like and vivid scene which undoubtedly depends
upon the recollections of an eye-witness.' Menzies is more cautious.
' It is not necessary to suppose,' he says, ' this scene to be formed
on Isaiah l. 6 ; the various incidents explain themselves quite
naturally.' That the members of the highest court of the Jews,
at any rate, should have forgotten their position, and sunk to the
vulgar cruelty attributed to them, seems far from ' natural.' Holtzmann is a little more cautious still. ' As regards the fulfilment of
x. 34, the particular colours (*die Farben im Einzelnen*) may be due
to Micah iv. 14 ; Isaiah l. 6, liii. 3–5 ; 1 Kings xxii. 24.' This has
been shown by Brandt in detail. Almost every word in Mark xiv.
65 is taken from the Greek versions of the Old Testament, in the
passages referred to by Holtzmann. Even the covering of the face
seems to rest upon a mistranslated and misunderstood expression
in Isaiah liii. 3. Finally, the contemptuous summons, ' prophesy,'
seems to depend upon 1 Kings xxii. 24. Thus the historical character of this verse is exceedingly dubious.

66–72.   PETER'S DENIAL

(*Cp.* Matt. xxvi. 69–75 ; Luke xxii. 56–62)

66   Now Peter was below in the court.   And one of the maids of
67 the high priest came, and when she saw Peter warming himself,
she looked at him, and said, ' Thou too wast with Jesus the Naza-
68 rene.'   But he denied it, saying, ' I do not know or understand
what thou sayest.'   And he went out into the outer courtyard.
69 And the cock crowed.   And the maid saw him, and began again
70 to say to the bystanders, ' This is one of them.'   And he denied
it again.   And a little after, the bystanders said again to Peter,
71 ' Verily thou art one of them : for thou art a Galilæan.'   But he
began to curse and to swear, saying, ' I know not this man of whom
72 ye speak.'   And straightway the cock crowed a second time.   Then
Peter called to mind the word which Jesus had said unto him,
' Before the cock crow twice, thou wilt deny me thrice.'   And when
he thought of it he wept.

The admirably dramatic scene of Peter's denial is supposed by
some to rest upon his own honest report and confession, though the
minor details are open to question.

66.   The story takes up the situation in which Peter had been
left in 54.

67.   The fire shines upon Peter's face and reveals him.

68.   He goes further off, to escape detection, into the outer
court.   The first crowing of the cock is only found in Mark, and
not in most of the good manuscripts.   The two cockcrowings are
highly dramatic, but probably not historical.   (*Cp.* verse 30.)

69.   In this outer court there are many persons collected,
' not perhaps members of the household only, but attendants of
councillors summoned to the meeting, and others ' (Menzies).   The
same girl notices him again.   Matthew speaks of a second girl.

70.   They recognize him as a Galilæan, according to Matthew,
from his speech or accent.   This seems probable.

71.   ἀναθεματίζειν.   The verb means ' to call down curses
upon oneself ' (if one is not telling the truth).

72.   The word ἐπιβαλών is hard.   Its meaning must be ' to

call to mind,' ' to become attentive.' Peter, however, had already been reminded by the cock. The word may be corrupt. It is wanting in Luke and Matthew.

Bartlet says: ' " He set to " and wept. This has the support of a usage revealed by an Egyptian papyrus cited in J. H. Moulton's *N. T. Grammar*, and may be what is meant by the old Syrian and Latin versions, " he began to weep," " and he burst into tears " (Moffat). Other suggested renderings may now be dismissed from account. The meaning is " he began to weep with all his might," which suits alike the occasion and the man. It agrees too with Luke's version of the matter, " and going out he wept bitterly." ' W. (ed. 1 only) suggests that Mark originally had only the pregnant phrasing : 'And straightway the cock crowed a second time. And he remembered and wept.' ' Dem Urmarcus sähe es ähnlich, dass er sich hier auf zwei Worte beschränkte : sie verfehlen die Wirkung nicht.' (But *cp.* for the whole passage Prof. Turner on ' Marcan Usage ' in *J. T. S.*, 1925, Vol. XXVI. pp. 344, 345.) The whole scene is indelibly fixed in the consciousness of the Western world. It is full of beauty, and yet awe-inspiring too. It tells its own lessons, and its moral need not be drawn out. Loisy regards the triple denial as historic ; not so the prediction and the recollection and the tears. He thinks the original story which Mark enlarged can easily be picked out of the narrative and restored. The source is followed accurately up to 68*a*. Then Peter is wrongly said to have gone out ' to the outer courtyard ' (or vestibule). This is put in here because in the original story his going out is connected with the cockcrowing. To avoid the natural meaning of ' he went out,' ' to the outer courtyard ' is added, which really contradicts it. Then in 69 one must omit ' saw him ' and ' again,' which are added by the Evangelist. Their removal gets over the difficulty that the same girl seems to speak to the same people among whom Peter had been sitting before, and that the apostle is still there, though he had moved away. In 70 one can omit ' a little after ' and ' again,' intended to lengthen out the incident, and to accentuate the triple denial. Then in 72 the words must originally have run : ' And he went out, and a cock crew,' or ' And he went out,' and it was ' cockcrow,' *i.e.* dawn. Thus the second crowing, the recollection of the prophecy, the apostle's grief, all belong to the work of ' redaction.' For another view, accepting the text as it stands as historic, see Rawlinson. Peter hurried to get away, as he felt himself in peril. Did he make his way at once to Galilee, or did he stay in Jerusalem till the Friday evening ? We cannot say : probably the latter. ' If there is an actual reminiscence from Peter anywhere in the second Gospel it is most certainly in the story of the denial in the form in which it is found in Mark ' (*E. S.* II. p. 618).

CHAPTER XV

1–5. JESUS BEFORE PILATE

(*Cp.* Matt. xxvii. 1, 2, 11–14 ; Luke xxiii. 1–5)

1 And straightway in the early morning the chief priests, with the elders and scribes, and the whole council prepared their decision, and having bound Jesus, led him away, and delivered him 2 to Pilate. And Pilate asked him, ' Art thou the King of the Jews ? ' And he answering said unto him, ' Thou sayest it.' And the chief 3 priests vehemently accused him. And Pilate asked him again, 4 saying, ' Answerest thou nothing ? see, of how much they accuse 5 thee ! ' But Jesus answered nothing more ; so that Pilate marvelled.

' In the story of the trial before Pilate, the formal accusation is wanting at the beginning, and the condemnation at the end. It is hard to see why the governor, without yet knowing anything, asks Jesus if he is the King of the Jews, and why the accusations of the priests, which become useless after the avowal of Jesus, were not made earlier. The transposition has been effected by the redactor (one gets a better connection by reading 3 or 3–5 before 2) either to make the Pilate trial different from the trial before Caiaphas, or to make the silence of Jesus more marked, or, more probably still, to introduce the incident of Barabbas. For the favour, unexplained and inexplicable, which Pilate is supposed to have shown to Jesus has its reason, according to Mark, in the silence of the accused, not in the avowal of his Messianic claim. The episode of Barabbas corresponds (*fait pendant*) with the judgment of Caiaphas ; it is interpolated in the historic tale of the trial before Pilate to make us understand that the governor did not condemn Jesus, but that he merely allowed him to be put to death, in accordance with the sentence of the Sanhedrin, after having in vain essayed to free him from the hatred of his foes ' (*E. S.* i. p. 103).

1. We now pass from a difficult and hardly conceivable trial before the Jewish authorities to a difficult and hardly conceivable trial before Pilate. The historic residue in both cases seems to reduce itself to the bare fact. Some Jewish authorities procured the arrest of Jesus. They found some means of holding or declaring him worthy of death—some charge upon which they could secure his condemnation from Pilate. He was brought before Pilate, and Pilate condemned him to death. The first fifteen verses of Chapter xv. hardly contain anything more historical than the short summary contained in these few words : brought before Pilate, he was by Pilate condemned to death.

Mark's favourite εὐθύς need not cause us difficulty or delay. πρωΐ is enough. Jesus was crucified at 9 A.M. Hence he must have been brought before Pilate very early in the morning.

συμβούλιον ἑτοιμάσαντες. The text is not certain. Some MSS. read instead συμβούλιον ποιήσαντες. The meaning is far from clear. If the first reading be taken—and its authority is greater—the meaning may be : 'having formed a resolution,' or 'having prepared their decision.' If we read ποιήσαντες, 'having taken counsel' or 'having held a consultation' might be the translation, perhaps also 'having taken a decision.'

In either case, the idea is that the court comes together a second time. A second meeting was necessary by Jewish law, but then this second meeting must be held on another day, whereas the sessions at night and at dawn would be both on the same day, according to the Jewish method of reckoning, by which the day begins at sunset.

The expression, 'the chief priests with the elders and scribes and the whole council,' seems too full. The object of the redundancy is to emphasize the wide and general Jewish responsibility for Jesus's death.

It is a further question whether or no the entire responsibility on the Jewish side should fall solely upon the priests. (As to this, see *Encyclopædia Biblica*, art. 'Synedrium,' columns 4841 at bottom, and 4842 at top.) One sees why Jewish scholars are anxious to put the whole guilt upon the priests. For the Sadducean priesthood, though composed of Jews, was not in the same sense Jewish as the Rabbis are Jewish. The Rabbis fashioned traditional Judaism, the Judaism of all the centuries from the age of Jesus to our own time, not the priests. Therefore it would be much more pleasant to think that only the priests—the Temple authorities—instigated the arrest of Jesus and arranged the charge against him, and that the Rabbis had no hand in it at all. But, historically and dispassionately, one does not quite see why this should have been the case. By his teaching Jesus had displeased the Rabbis quite as much as the priests.   Unless one is to argue that all the Rabbis were better and more tolerant men than the priests, and that they would not have sought to compass Jesus's death, however much they might have disliked his teaching, one cannot easily see why Rabbis as well as priests should not have been concerned in the plot against him.   Or were the Jewish authorities—the moving and leading spirits in Jerusalem—in those days exclusively priests ? Is there any reason to believe this ?

Jesus is now bound.   Mark does not add Pilate's office ; Matthew calls him ὁ ἡγεμών—the governor.   It was the custom for the Roman procurator to come to Jerusalem from Cæsarea, his usual residence, at the season of the Jewish festivals.   Apparently this was done as a precautionary measure in case of any disturbance.

2.   The opening of the verse assumes what is not clearly stated, though it may be implied in 1.   The Jewish authorities must have made some formal accusation of Jesus to Pilate.   Whether this was done by word of mouth or by written charge, or both, is not said, and remains uncertain.

Whether Jesus was condemned by the Jewish authorities because of what he said about the Temple, or because of his claim to be Messiah—it must certainly have been the latter allegation with which he was charged before Pilate.   But the term Messiah is translated by the Roman authority into its purely political equivalent : ' King of the Jews.'

Jesus, interrogated by Pilate, replies : ' Thou sayest it.'   This is usually interpreted to mean an absolute confession.   It is alleged that ' Thou hast said ' is a recognized form of affirmation, or a Jewish form of assent.   This is, however, disputed and doubtful. And from what follows it can be argued either way : either that Jesus confessed, or that he practically refused to answer.   No certainty can be achieved.   Anyway, Jesus did not deny the charge.   It would be consistent both with his practice of evasion before hostile critics, and with his own spiritualized conception of the Messiahship and Kingship, if he neither affirmed nor denied. He was not the King of the Jews in Pilate's sense of king ; yet he was, or was to be, their king, in another sense, and even in this dark hour, his faith in *this* kingship, to which God had appointed him, did not succumb or fade away.

Dibelius (*Z. N. W.*, 1915, p. 117) points out that the reply ' Thou sayest,' even though it be an equivalent of ' I am,' allows the scene to be continued.   Had Jesus replied ' yes,' the condemnation of Pilate would have had to follow immediately : now the priests can come in with their charges, even though the content of the charges cannot be given.

3. πολλά may mean ' vehemently ' or (as R.V.) ' of many things.' As was pointed out in the quotation from Loisy at the beginning of the chapter, 3 or 3–5 would apparently come better before 2. Jesus, denounced before Pilate as a pretended Messiah, or as a claimant to Messiahship, does not reply. Interrogated by Pilate, he confesses or does not deny his Messiahship. Condemnation followed. It is true that the charge ought to be made before Pilate's question. But *cp.* as to all these matters the elaborate note of Norden, p. 195 (n. 2)–197. Moreover, what the charge was—the points of the indictment—is left undisclosed. But, as Dibelius cleverly points out in his article ' Herodes und Pilatus ' (*Z. N. W.*, 1915, p. 116), the narrative as it stands shows its primitiveness as compared *e.g.* with Luke. Jesus was condemned by Pilate because of his claim, or alleged claim to be the Messiah, the King of the Jews. That was probably all that a narrator could know of the trial who was not an eyewitness.

4, 5. Pilate presses for a reply to the charge, and Jesus, in accordance with Isaiah liii. 7, preserves silence. Pilate marvels that he does not try to defend himself. θαυμάζειν in the Gospel tradition has almost become a technical term for the impression which Jesus made upon his environment. It is no ordinary astonishment which Pilate is represented as feeling. He has a sort of superstitious and uncomfortable dread. (Bertram, p. 63.)

What we may also imagine to have happened was that upon Jesus's confession or refusal to reply Pilate condemned him out of hand. But for apologetic purposes it was important to show that though Pilate condemned him, he did so reluctantly, unwillingly, and that the true authors of the condemnation were not the Romans, but the Jews. Pilate knew well enough that Jesus was innocent. There was no danger in him. He was no revolutionary, *any more than his disciples and followers.* Pilate yielded to Jewish hatred and clamour. The guilt fell upon the Jews, not upon the Romans. The whitewashing of Pilate and the Romans was most important, not only in order to blacken the hated Jews, but in order to show to the world that the Roman governor would have wished to save Jesus : that in his eyes there was nothing criminal in the founder of the Christian religion. *And if the founder was harmless, equally harmless must be his followers.*

6–15. JESUS, PILATE, AND BARABBAS

(*Cp.* Matt. xxvii. 15–26 ; Luke xxiii. 18–25)

6   Now at the festival, he used to release unto them one prisoner,
7 whom they chose to beg off. And the so-called Barabbas lay

bound with the rioters who had committed a murder in the insur-
8 rection. And the crowd came up, and began to demand what
9 Pilate was wont to do for them. But he answered them, saying,
10 'Do ye wish that I release unto you the King of the Jews?' For
he realized that the chief priests had delivered him up out of envy.
11 But the chief priests incited the people that he should rather
12 release Barabbas unto them. And Pilate answered again and said
unto them, ' What then shall I do with him whom ye call the King
13, 14 of the Jews ? ' And they cried out in answer, ' Crucify him.' Then
Pilate said unto them, ' What evil has he done ? ' But they cried
15 out the more vehemently, ' Crucify him.' And so Pilate, wishing
to content the people, released Barabbas unto them, and delivered
Jesus, when he had scourged him, to be crucified.

6.   The trial is now interrupted by an unexpected incident—
of a very doubtful historical character. Its object is still further
to whitewash Pilate, and to throw the responsibility of the crucifixion upon the Jews. Pilate would have saved Jesus. The Jews
insist upon his execution. They prefer that Jesus should die rather
than Barabbas.

The first two verses of the section are intended to explain what
is to follow. The custom alluded to in verse 6 is wholly unknown.
It is extremely improbable in itself ; and, whatever basis the
Barabbas story may have, this part of its setting is almost certainly
fictitious. We may also doubt whether the Romans would have
pardoned a leader of a revolt. (*Cp.* also Dibelius in Z. N. W., 1915,
p. 116.)

Klostermann (ed. 2) observes : ' eine gelegentliche Einzel-
begnadigung zumal auf Akklamation des Pöbels wäre durchaus
möglich.' And certainly the parallel in Deissmann's *Licht vom
Osten* (4th ed., p. 229) is very striking. An Egyptian papyrus gives
the official account of the trial of a certain Phibius, and it says :
' You deserved to be flogged, but I will make you a present to the·
populace ' (A.D. 85). (ἄξιος μὲν ἧς μαστιγωθῆναι, χαρίζομαι δέ
σε τοῖς ὄχλοις.)

7.   The statements about Barabbas seem very precise, and
suggest that some historical reminiscence is at the bottom of the
tale. Loisy, however, calls them ' très vagues, sous une apparence
de précision ' (*E. S.* II. p. 642). Barabbas lay ' bound with them
who had made insurrection, who in the insurrection had committed
murder ' (so literally). What insurrection is referred to ? Is Mark
quoting textually from his source ? He speaks as if everybody

knew to what he was referring.   Is this, however, merely ' a popular, one might even say childish, way of presenting a fact of which the writer himself knows nothing ' ? (*E. S.* II. p. 642, n. 4).   We are in complete ignorance.

ὁ λεγόμενος Βαραββᾶς.   The phrase is peculiar.   'The so-called Barabbas.'   Was it a nickname ?   For surely the words do not mean merely ' a man called Barabbas.'   Barabbas is supposed to mean ' son of the father,' that is, of the ' master '—the teacher. Was he the son of a known Rabbi ?   We hear of Rabbis in the Talmud called, *e.g.*, Rabbi Samuel Bar Abba, and Rabbi Nathan Bar Abba.   But more probably Abba was a proper name.   ' It is certainly true that in no instance, except Barabbas, can the personal name Abba be cited quite so early.   Yet it is not necessary to suppose that Abba means " father " in this case, seeing that Abba is a well-established proper name, and that early enough. . . . The evidence for the use of Abba as a personal name is quite conclusive ' (Abrahams, *Studies*, II. pp. 201, 202).

Bertram pleads for the historicity of Barabbas and of the incident.   ' The story is drawn in rather thick colours, but it must have an historic kernel.   The figure of Barabbas cannot be merely removed from the Gospel story ' (p. 67).

8.   The crowd appear upon the scene quite independently of Jesus and his trial.   Pilate is sitting in his tribunal at the wonted place and time ;   or the hour was announced beforehand.   It was very early in the morning.   The people came, we may suppose, to prefer their requests and complaints, but more especially, according to the narrative, they came to take advantage of the custom which has just been explained in verse 6.   But 'ni ces détails ni les suivants ne semblent à discuter au point de vue de l'histoire ' (*E. S.* II. p. 643).

9.   Pilate sees his chance.   He would like to release Jesus, and thinks here is his opportunity.   (The historic Pilate was a man of different mould—stern, pitiless, and cruel.)   He suggests that the prisoner to be released should be Jesus.

Pilate's words (' Do ye wish that I release unto you the King of the Jews ? ') are to be regarded as a mixture of pity and contempt. ' Shall I release this harmless simpleton who apparently calls himself your king ? '   The narrative implies that the people know what is going on, and that Jesus has been convicted upon the charge of claiming to be King of the Jews.   Pilate is supposed to think, not unnaturally, that Jesus, though hateful to the priests, is liked among the people at large.

10. Pilate's view is that Jesus is not worthy of death. *His* kingship is not antagonistic to the Roman supremacy. This, at least, is what we may suppose that Mark would wish us to think that Pilate meant. Beyond this we cannot go, for that the historic Pilate had any such opinion as is here ascribed to him is improbable. Mark's Pilate sees through the whole thing. He realizes that Jesus is to be executed, not because, from the Roman point of view, he deserved it, but because he was, for some reason or other, obnoxious to the Jewish priests.

11. The deepest responsibility is the priests'; and here probably the story is true enough. Not the 'Pharisees,' not the 'Elders,' not the 'Scribes,' but the governing priesthood, were the true, or, at any rate, the main, authors of Jesus's death.

Barabbas, it is implied, was well known and popular. Hence the priests suggest to the populace to ask for Barabbas instead of Jesus. Matthew has a different version. He makes Pilate himself proffer the two, and bid the people choose between them.

That the people are now against Jesus is—though probably not historic—not psychologically quite incredible. Jesus had disappointed them. He had played and lost. The hopes which he had aroused in them had been dashed to the ground by his arrest. Let him pay the penalty for his folly. It is also possible that the priestly party had helped to this change of feeling. Loisy is more sceptical : 'That the people, when Jesus was once a prisoner, should have passed suddenly from admiration to hate, that not content with preferring Barabbas, they should have demanded in their rage the crucifixion of Jesus, that Pilate should have lent himself to this furious caprice, or that the priests should have had time (verse 11) between the suggestion of Pilate (9) and the people's reply to change their feelings towards Jesus—all these are traits that belong rather to legendary fiction than to history, and rather resemble a theatrical effect in a melodrama or in a childish play than historical reality ' (*E. S.* 11. p. 644).

12. The rejoinder of Pilate is almost ludicrously inappropriate for a Roman governor. But the motive is obvious. The Jews are to pronounce the sentence, not Pilate. Not thus were Roman governors wont to deal with their prisoners !

Pilate's words again assume that Jesus and his claim are well known. The interrupted trial is to be concluded. But the people and not Pilate are to be the judges. What do they wish Pilate to do with the man whom *they* call their King ? Another reading is rather easier. 'What would ye—say !—that I should do with the King of the Jews ? '

13. The people demanded the punishment of death in its most terrible form. Crucifixion was a Roman method of execution, introduced by them into Palestine, and reserved for the worst offenders and criminals. πάλιν, says W., must here be regarded as equivalent to an Aramaic ' but,' ' thereupon.' Or perhaps it merely refers to verse 11. There the people cry out for the release of Barabbas ; here they cry out again, but this time for the execution of Jesus.

The famous cry, ' crucify him ' is probably unhistoric, but of what oceans of Jewish blood, and of what endless Jewish misery wrought by Christian hands, has it not been the cause. One man was unjustly put to death : millions have been unjustly killed, tortured, hated, because of the one. It may be observed that I do not regard the cry ' crucify him ' as probably unhistoric because crucifixion is a Roman punishment, as M'Neile supposes. That certainly would be no reason ; I regard it as probably unhistoric because the picture of the crowd as now entirely unfavourable to Jesus, and indeed thirsting for his blood, though not incredible, is yet unlikely. When to the antecedent improbability we add the immense advantage and temptation to the authors of the story to whitewash Pilate and to blacken the Jews, the antecedent improbability becomes very great.

14. Pilate is even made to go so far as to urge that Jesus is quite innocent. But the Jews will hear of no defence or exculpation, and Pilate has to give way.

15. Pilate is anxious, or thinks it best, to satisfy the people. Hence he releases Barabbas, while Jesus is condemned to death by crucifixion. Before the sentence was carried out, the criminal was scourged. Note παρέδωκεν. ' The Evangelist tries to avoid saying that Jesus was sentenced and condemned by Pilate. He wants the reader to understand that Pilate was constrained by the Jews to allow the sentence of death pronounced by the Sanhedrin to be carried into effect ' (E. S. 11. p. 645).

W. attempts to preserve a certain amount of the story : ' When Pilate came up to Jerusalem for the festival, he held his court there upon serious cases in which the judgments of the native tribunals needed confirmation : he could occasionally exercise his power of pardon. These circumstances probably are at the bottom of the tale. . . . Pilate does not consider the mere fact that Jesus regards himself as King of the Jews an adequate ground for his condemnation, seeing that he has not broken the peace, or done anything to get the kingdom into his hands.' Not very convincing.

Brandt has a different view. He 'takes the kernel of the story to be that a certain prisoner who had been arrested in connection with some insurrection, but against whom no crime, or at least no grave crime, could be proved, was released on the application of the people, who intervened on his behalf because he was the son of a Rabbi. The incident, even though it was not simultaneous with the condemnation of Jesus, gave occasion in Christian circles for the drawing of this contrast : the son of the Rabbi was interceded for and released ; Jesus was condemned. In the course of transmission by oral tradition the statement of this contrast might gradually, without any conscious departure from historical truth, have led to the assumption that the two things happened at the same time on the same occasion. Finally, the liberation of a seditious prisoner—in any case a somewhat surprising occurrence—seemed explicable only on the assumption of some standing custom to account for it ; this assumption must presumably have arisen elsewhere than in Palestine.' This extract from the *Encyclopædia Biblica*, art. 'Barabbas,' well sums up Brandt's hypothesis, which seems somewhat far-fetched.

A very interesting hypothesis has been offered by Rawlinson, but it is not very convincing. 'How is the Barabbas episode to be explained ? I suggest that it arose as the result of a strangely dramatic historical coincidence. It is pointed out by Meyer (I. p. 195) that the *multitude* who *went up* to interview Pilate about the release of a prisoner (verse 8) are not to be understood as having assembled in order to witness the trial of Jesus : they are a crowd of partisans of Barabbas, who happened to arrive at this point in the proceedings, presumably in order to beg for the latter's release. This view explains what is often felt as a difficulty, viz., the sudden change of attitude on the part of the crowd, more especially on the assumption (often gratuitously made) that it was the same crowd who on Palm Sunday had hailed our Lord as King. There was in fact no change of attitude, since there is no reason to assume that the crowd of Mark xv. 8 was at any time sympathetic towards our Lord. It is, further, worthy of note that in the early " Cæsarean " text of Matt. xxvii. 16, 17 the name " Barabbas " is twice given as "*Jesus* Barabbas," and although A. C. Clark thinks that the reading in question is a blunder due to dittography, it is accepted as genuine by Burkitt, Allen, Streeter, and other authorities, and is probably correct. It is intelligible that early Christian sentiment should have shown itself in general reluctant to recognize that the name " Jesus " was actually borne by the evil-doer Barabbas, but the compiler of Matthew depended at this point probably upon good tradition. The name " Jesus " (= Joshua) was by no means uncommon among the Jews (*cp.* Col. iv. 11), and it is not improbable that the coincidence of the names may afford a clue to the understanding of what actually occurred, viz. that the arrival of a crowd demanding the release of " Jesus " (*i.e.* Jesus Barabbas) was at first mistaken by Pilate for a demonstration of popular sympathy in favour of *Jesus of Nazareth,* of whose harmlessness from the political point of view he was personally satisfied, and whom he at once offers to set free. *The chief priests,* however, *stirred up the multitude, that he should rather release Barabbas unto them* : in other words, the chief priests intervened by making common cause with Barabbas's supporters, and themselves championing the latter's release, in return for the support of the " Barabbas " party in favour of their own demand for the crucifixion of Jesus of Nazareth ' (pp. 227, 228).

16–20. JESUS IS MOCKED BY THE SOLDIERS

(*Cp.* Matt. xxvii. 27–31)

16 Then the soldiers led him away into the courtyard, which is the
17 Prætorium ; and they called together the whole cohort. And they clothed him with purple, and wove a crown of thorns, and put it
18 upon his head, and they began to salute him, ' Hail, King of the
19 Jews ! ' And they beat him on the head with a cane, and spat upon
20 him, and bent the knee, and did him reverence. And when they had mocked him thus, they took off the purple from him, and put his own clothes on him, and led him out to crucify him.

16. Jesus is now at the mercy of the Roman soldiery. He is utterly bereft of friend and earthly hope. To the physical agony of the scourging there is added mockery and insolent contempt. The narrative in its brief intensity is very poignant.

Jesus is led away from the presence of Pilate—(it is not said where he is scourged, or even whether the scourging preceded the scene of the mockery)—into the courtyard of the house where the governor was living.

' Which is the Prætorium ' seems to be a gloss inserted from Matthew, who thinks of Jesus as taken from the governor's house to the barracks of the soldiers. But the meaning of Prætorium in the Gospels is disputed. Matthew probably meant by it the fortress of Antonia, which was the headquarters of the Roman garrison. Or it may be that the trial is supposed by Mark to have taken place at this citadel, to which Pilate had come.

A cohort ($\sigma\pi\epsilon\hat{\imath}\rho\alpha$) consisted of 600 men. The numbers are a detail.

17.   Whether the scene is historic is doubtful.   There are arguments on both sides.   (See below.)   The crown of thorns parodies the royal laurel wreath.

19.   With the mock homage insult and blows are mingled.   The κάλαμος, or reed, is to represent a sceptre.   In Matthew it is first put in his hand, and then he is hit with it.   A stick or cane made of a stout reed is what is meant.

20.   This verse seems to imply that the scourging had already taken place.   His own clothes had been removed from him for the scourging, and after it he is invested with the purple to add insult to agony.   Now his own clothes are put on him once more.

Recent investigations have made it rather less unlikely that the scene of Jesus being mocked by the soldiery may be historical.   There are curious parallels to the Gospel story, into the details of which I cannot, however, enter.   We know about the Persian festival of the Sacæa, at which a prisoner condemned to death was put upon a mock royal throne, invested with royal purple, and allowed to have his royal will for a season.   After that he was flogged and hanged. This practice has many parallels, and goes back to widespread religious ideas and ceremonies, of which the learned author of the *Golden Bough* has so much to tell us.   And Philo records an odd scene once enacted in Alexandria, of which the mock hero was one Carabas, a name that gives us pause.   It is conceivable that the soldiers—possibly Orientals—seeing that Jesus was condemned upon the charge of kingship, may have mocked him in the way in which the hero of the Sacæa and of similar ceremonies and carnivals was mocked.   Some, among whom is Loisy, see here and in what Philo says the origin of the incident of Barabbas.   Does the name Carabas conceal the name of Barabbas ?   Was Jesus delivered up to the soldiers to be crucified ' in the style of ' or ' in place of ' Barabbas, who would then be not a historic individual, but the name of a personage who figured as king in popular festivals parallel to the Roman Saturnalia and the Persian Sacæa ?   (*E. S.* II. pp. 653, 654.)   This is unlikely and needlessly sceptical, yet while the scourging (15) is historic, 16–20 may be a secondary enlargement of the fact, and probably is so.

21–32.   The Crucifixion

(*Cp.* Matt. xxvii. 32–44 ; Luke xxiii. 26–43)

21   And they compelled one Simon of Cyrene (the father of Alexander and Rufus), who happened to be passing by from the country, to

22 carry his cross. And they brought him into the place Golgotha,
23 which is, being translated, The place of a skull. And they offered
24 him wine mixed with myrrh : but he did not take it. And they
25 crucified him, and they divided his garments, casting lots for them,
26 what each man should take. And it was the third hour when they
crucified him. And the inscription of the charge against him was
27 written above him : ' The King of the Jews.' And with him they
crucified two thieves ; the one on his right hand, and the other on
his left.

29   And the passers-by reviled him, wagging their heads, and saying,
' Ah, thou that destroyest the temple, and buildest it in three days,
30, 31 save thyself, and come down from the cross.' Likewise also the
chief priests with the scribes mocked him, saying to one another,
32 ' He saved others ; himself he cannot save. The Messiah ! The
King of Israel ! Let him descend now from the cross, that we may
see and believe.' And they that were crucified with him scoffed at
him.

Until the death of Jesus Loisy supposes that the Evangelist
followed an older source, which he enlarged and embroidered. The
older source contained ' sobres indications ' concerning the departure
from the Prætorium, Simon of Cyrene, the crucifixion, the inscription on the cross, the two robbers, the insults of the passers-by and
of the robbers, the last cry of Jesus, and the exclamation of the
centurion. This older and more historic portions of the narrative
would be 20b, 21, 22a, 24a, 26, 27, 29, 30, 32b, 37, 39 (E. S. I.
p. 104).

21. The statement contained in this verse is, in all probability,
historic. The two men, Alexander and Rufus, were probably
known both to the Evangelist and to many of his readers. They
knew from their father that he had been compelled to carry the
cross (or part of it) upon which Jesus was suspended. ἀγγαρεύειν is
the technical word for ' impress ' (cp. Matt. v. 41).
The usual idea is that Jesus was too exhausted by the scourging
and the mental agony to carry his own cross, as was the prevailing
Roman custom.
Simon came from the country ; not necessarily from work among
the ' fields.' But still, though this is not necessary, the words
would be more natural if the day of the crucifixion were not a holiday
—not the first day of the Passover. However, Simon may have
merely been returning from a walk or visit, such as would have been
permissible on the festival. It is even supposed that if field *work*

had been meant, the Greek would have been ἀπὸ τοῦ ἀγροῦ, and not merely ἀπὸ ἀγροῦ.

22. The place of the crucifixion must have been some hill outside the city walls, which, from its shape, was called ' skull,' or ' skull place.' It cannot any longer be identified.

23. The ' wine ' referred to must have been the concoction which was given to Jews who were about to suffer the penalty of death, in order that they might lose consciousness. The preparation of this drugged wine seems to have been left to the hands of the ladies of Jerusalem, who, doubtless, regarded making and giving it as a deed of piety.

Who offered the wine to Jesus ? We are not told. Was it the women who ' looked on from a distance ' ? (40). It must, anyway, have been offered by Jews or Jewesses.

It was not ' wine mixed with myrrh,' for apparently myrrh would have, if anything, the contrary effect. The Talmud says that it was frankincense which produced the benumbing result upon the consciousness.

Jesus refused the wine. This, too, may be historic. Either he determined to suffer with full consciousness, or he had still not given up hope of a miraculous intervention from God. Some are inclined to think the verse an addition to the ' source ' (a doublet of the vinegar (36), says Loisy, and an incident in which the fulfilment of ancient prophecies was indicated). Note in Greek the present in 22 and 24, with the past tense in 23. In my English translation I have put the past tense throughout.

24, 25. The awful event is narrated briefly, simply, calmly. The division of the garments is an embroidery, in order to show the fulfilment of Psalm xxii. 18 ; but it is a fact that the clothes of crucified persons, who suffered quite naked, were the perquisites of the executioners.

The ' third hour ' is 9 A.M. Some think that verse 25, with its repetition of the fact of the crucifixion, is a later addition. Matthew and Luke do not give the hour.

26. ' The inscription of the charge against him was written aboye him : The King of the Jews.' This, again, may be historical ; for it was customary to attach a tablet, with the crime or charge for which the condemned were to suffer, either to their necks or to the cross itself.

Jesus, then, suffered because he was accused of claiming to be King of the Jews. The brief words were enough to tell the tale.

27. In spite of 28 (see A.V.), which has been inserted from Luke xxii. 37, and is wanting in the best MSS., and, therefore, in spite of Isaiah liii. 12, the statement that two other men were crucified with Jesus may be historical. We need not suppose an intentional, added ignominy. Their execution was due, and it was convenient to crucify the three criminals on the same spot.

29. How far what now follows is historical is doubtful. For it closely follows the expressions of Psalm xxii. 7; moreover, it is not easy to see who could have reported the incidents and the words.

It is natural that W. should regard 29 as historical, for it supports his theory that Jesus was condemned for his prediction about the Temple.

30. The taunt, even if not historic, admirably fits the situation, and augments the horror.

31. The statement about the priests and the Scribes is doubtful. They would hardly have come out on purpose to feast their eyes upon the spectacle of their enemy upon the cross. That kind of thing rather befits the officers of the Inquisition than the members of the Sanhedrin. Brandt thinks the words in 32 are a sort of echo of taunts often made in later days by opponents. ' He, who, as you would have us believe, was the Saviour of the world, the Messiah, could not save himself. Why, if he were God's son, did he not come down from the cross ? ' (Compare the reasoning in Wisdom of Solomon ii. 17–20, which is directly used in Matt. xxvii. 43, and *cp.* above all, Psalm xxii. 8). ' He saved others.' Ironical. ' He pretended to be the Saviour of the world in claiming to be the Messiah.' Equally doubtful are the revilings of the robbers. Who reported them ?

Rawlinson, on the other hand, says : ' The scene has verisimilitude, and there is a nice psychological discrimination made between the taunts of the vulgar, who address our Lord directly, and the derisive comments of the members of the Sanhedrin, who converse with one another ' (p. 234).

33–39. THE DEATH OF JESUS

(*Cp.* Matt. xxvii. 45–54 ; Luke xxiii. 44–47)

33 And at the sixth hour darkness came over the whole land until
34 the ninth hour.   And at the ninth hour Jesus cried with a loud voice,

saying, ' *Eli, Eli, lama sabachthani ?* ' which is, being translated,
35 ' My God, my God, why hast thou forsaken me ? '   And some of the
bystanders, when they heard it, said, ' Behold, he calls Elijah.'
36 And one ran and filled a sponge full of vinegar, and put it on a cane,
and gave him to drink, saying, ' Let alone ; let us see whether
37 Elijah will come to take him down.'   But Jesus uttered a loud cry,
38 and expired.   And the curtain of the temple was rent in twain from
39 the top to the bottom.   And when the centurion, who stood by,
opposite to him, saw that he so expired, he said, ' Truly this man
was a son of God.'

33. Jesus, according to Mark, endured six hours of agony
upon the cross before his death.   Often, before the release of death
came, a much longer interval elapsed.

The darkness which fell upon the face of the land (or earth)
happened at noon.   There can be no ordinary natural eclipse of the
sun at the full moon of Eastertide.   The miracle depends upon such
passages as Amos viii. 9 ; Exodus x. 22 ; Jer. xv. 9.   Moreover,
darkness and eclipses were often supposed to have happened on
specially solemn occasions.   Thus an eclipse of the sun is said to
have taken place upon the Ides of March, at the murder of Cæsar
' at the sixth hour till night.'

34. According to Mark, Jesus only makes one utterance upon
the cross.   He quotes the words of Psalm xxii. 1, applying them to
himself.

Two questions present themselves.   The first is : Did Jesus
really say the words ?   The second is : If he said them, what did
he mean ?

Many scholars think that, like the other borrowings from Psalm
xxii., these words too were borrowed from the same source, not by
Jesus, but by the Evangelist, or by tradition.   Jesus died with a
' loud cry.'   What did he say ?   What had he said ?   Pious
phantasy soon found answers ; hence what we now read in Mark and
Luke.   Jesus was the Messianic hero predicted and represented
in the Psalm.   Therefore, he is made to quote its opening words,
not because those who put these words in his mouth thought that
he was, or that he believed that he was, forsaken of God, but because
they are the opening words of the Psalm—because they were merely
taken to mean an impassioned invocation unto God.   So, for
instance, argue Brandt and J. Weiss.   The latter says : ' The
Evangelist probably did not trouble himself as to the deeper meaning
of the words ; he probably just regarded and used them as a fulfilled

prophecy from a Messianic psalm.' So too Loisy, and *cp.* Bertram, p. 83. If Luke and John disliked to attribute the words to Jesus, that only shows that Christian feeling was more ' affiné ' in the last years of the century than about 70 (*E. S.* II. p. 685). It is argued, moreover, that the only reporters of what happened at the crucifixion were the women who ' stood afar off.' They might have heard the ' loud cry,' but would not have distinguished any words. *Cp.* generally, Feigel, *Der Einfluss der Weissagungsbeweises und anderer Motive auf die Leidengeschichte* (1910), and also Weidel, ' Studien über den Einfluss der Weissagungsbeweises auf die evangelische Geschichte' in *Theologische Studien und Kritiken* (1910) (pp. 265, 266).

Others argue that just *these* words would not have been assigned to Jesus. Why should the dying Messiah have been made to indicate any lack of faith, even though the famous Messianic Psalm opens with these words ? Thus the words are authentic. Luke clearly felt the objection to them. Hence he substituted a quotation from Psalm xxxi. 5.

Those who regard the words as authentic interpret them in different ways. Dr. Carpenter's interpretation has been already alluded to. ' What do the words mean ? ' he asks. ' Do they denote defeat and desolation ? ' Though such an interpretation is natural at first, it ' seems inconsistent with the whole character of Jesus, and especially with the inner history of the fatal night. The possibility of death had been in sight for weeks. He had come to Jerusalem ready to face the worst. As it approached, it proved indeed a trial more grievous than even he had foreseen. But in Gethsemane he had solemnly offered himself to God. Could he flinch when the offer was accepted ? What pain and shame could undo his trust, or sever the fellowship of his spirit with the Father ? It is more congruous, therefore, with his previous attitude, to interpret the cry as a final declaration of faith. The verse opens the passionate pleading of one of Israel's hymns ; but the Psalm which begins with desolation closes with glowing hope (24–28) :

> He hath not despised nor abhorred the affliction of the afflicted ;
> Neither hath he hid his face from him ;
> But when he cried unto him, he heard. . . .
> And all the ends of the earth shall remember, and turn unto the Lord.
> And all the kindreds of the nations shall worship before thee.
> For the kingdom is the Lord's ;
> And he is the ruler over the nations.

' With this last affirmation of the Kingdom Jesus died ' (*First Three Gospels*, p. 393).

Menzies and Holtzmann argue in much the same way.

On the other hand, B. Weiss considers, not without force, that to make Jesus think of the whole Psalm and its close in quoting its opening words is somewhat arbitrary, and introduces into ' a moment of immediate feeling ' ' das Fremdartige der Reflexion.' Jesus believed that God, if he chose, could effect his purpose in another way—all is possible to God—and thus he asks in his agony, why has God refused to him special and miraculous intervention ? Pfleiderer argues strongly on the same side. For such an interpretation fits in with his whole picture of the last days at Jerusalem, and his view that Jesus until the last believed that the Kingdom was to be realized upon earth, and in his own life-time, not through his death. His words upon the cross imply that he regarded his fate as the shipwreck of his holiest hopes. J. Weiss, in his article *Das Problem der Entstehung des Christentums*, argues that the words are unauthentic. ' Gerade hier ist äusserste Skepsis am Platz. Offenbar sind diese Worte nichts als eine ausfüllende Dublette zu dem lauten Todesschrei, mit dem Jesus verschied, und der allein von den Umstehenden vernommen werden konnte ' (p. 460).

For ἐγκατέλιπες (forsaken) some good MSS. and early versions read ὠνείδασας, and Harnack thinks that this is the true reading. Mark felt that what Jesus meant was, not that God had altogether forsaken him, but that he had forsaken him in allowing him to be mocked at and reviled. ' Why hast thou caused me to be insulted or mocked at ? ' Mark knew the LXX and used it. He knew what the real translation of the Hebrew was. But he deliberately put ὠνείδασας in its place, because he felt that it was a less literal, but yet more accurate, rendering of what Jesus really meant. Harnack's exposition of his view is a beautiful specimen of learned and suggestive criticism (*Probleme im Texte der Leidensgeschichte Jesu*, 1901, pp. 11–15).

35. Did Jesus say the words, if he said them, in Hebrew or in Aramaic ? Mark reports them in Aramaic ; Matthew largely in Hebrew. The misunderstanding spoken of in verse 35 requires the Hebrew. ' Eli ' could be mistaken for ' Elijah ' ; not the Aramaic ' Eloi.' Moreover, the bystanders would have understood Aramaic, their own language ; they might not have understood, and hence might have misinterpreted, the Hebrew sounds. Jesus might well have known the Psalms in Hebrew. ' The Aramaic may,' says Menzies, ' be due to a corrector who reflected perhaps that Aramaic, and not Hebrew, was spoken in Palestine at this time.' So, too, Brandt. So, too, Turner, who points out that D and other MSS. imply the Hebrew and not the Aramaic (*J. T. S.* xxvi., 1925, p. 154, n. 2). Klostermann denies that a misunderstanding is intended. It was a Jewish pun in order to taunt the

pretended Messiah yet more.   He calls upon Elijah who was to announce his coming : but Elijah will not save him.

The bystanders must have been Jews, who alone would know about Elijah and his connection with the Messiah.   But that there were Jews present as well as Roman soldiers is, perhaps, a little unlikely.

Elijah was to prepare the way for the Messiah.   Moreover, there is frequent mention of him in Jewish legend as appearing to people in moments of distress and danger.

Weidel denies the historicity of the Elijah verses (p. 265).

36.   On the other hand, if the man who offers the sponge drenched with vinegar was a soldier, a difficulty arises as to the end of the verse.   There are various suggestions.

It seems necessary that the man with the sponge should be one of the group mentioned in 35.   Were they, then, not soldiers, but Jews ?   And was this Jewish bystander allowed to take some of the soldiers' wine and give it to Jesus ?   This seems unlikely.   But if it was a Roman soldier who held up the sponge to the sufferer (by means of fixing the sponge upon the end of a tall cane) in order to relieve the agonising thirst, how could he have said what follows at the end of the verse ?   The difficulty was felt by Matthew, who changes the subject (' but the others said '), and the S.S. does the same in this very verse of Mark.

The meaning of the words apparently is that the giver of the drink wants to prevent his companions from hindering him in his act of mercy.   Hence he affects to follow up what had been said before, and suggests that they should allow him to keep Jesus alive by the drink in order that they might see whether Elijah would come to take him down from the Cross.   All this, however, seems rather strained.

Klostermann denies that an act of pity is intended.   It is a taunt even as the action in 35 is a taunt.   And the allusion is to Psalm lxix.   ' Freilich soll nun dieser römische Soldat mit 36b auch in den jüdischen Spott eingestimmt haben.'   Therefore, for 36b the reading of S.S., " and they said " may be preferable.'

The difficulties are about equally great, whether the giver of the drink is conceived to be a Roman soldier—for then he knows about Elijah, and the ' bystanders ' must also be soldiers—or whether the bystanders and the giver of the drink are all Jews. Hence, W. regards 35 and 36b as later inventions—partly at least upon æsthetic grounds.   ' The impression made by the moving cry of despair is painfully spoiled by the misunderstanding of the onlookers.   Yet it might easily have come into the mind of Christians who talked Aramaic and were ignorant of Hebrew.   They might

readily have thought that the Messiah in the moment of his deepest
need would have called upon the man who was to prepare and
make smooth his path : " Elijah, Elijah, where art thou ? " and
this interpretation would have the more quickly occurred to them
as it removed the stumbling-block of the Messiah thinking himself forsaken by God.' Or perhaps the play upon words was
created by the Jews. The disciples said that Jesus cried out ' Eli,
Eli.' But no ' Eli '—*i.e.* no Elijah—came. There was none to
rescue or intervene.

Whether the episode with the sponge is historical cannot be
decided. Roman soldiers had a drink called *posca*, which was
made of water, vinegar, and egg. There may, therefore, have been
the necessary material present. On the other hand, Psalm lxix.
21 : ' In my thirst they gave me vinegar to drink,' causes suspicion.
Luke uses the vinegar at an earlier period. (*Cp.* Luke xxiii. 36.)
Loisy thinks that the earliest tradition knew of only one ' cry '
before the death. This was interpreted and explained and doubled
in various ways. The ascription of the exclamation in Psalm xxii.
(a fulfilment of prophecy) to the dying Messiah ; the call upon
Elijah, the precursor of the Messiah, grew up independently, and
were then combined. Independent too at first was the fulfilment
of Psalm lxix. The vinegar owes its origin to the Psalm ; it is not
the *posca*. Moreover, this drink ' fait double emploi avec le vin
aromatisé dont Marc a parlé plus haut ' (*E. S.* ii. pp. 684–686).

37. It is implied that Jesus accepted the proffered drink.
But it did not keep him long alive. He gave one last loud cry—
a cry which may have reached to the ears of the women who
watched from a distance—and expired.

A good deal has been written about the loud cry—its possibility
and its meaning. Usually sufferers upon the cross died of slow
exhaustion. Jesus seems to have died after a comparatively short
period of agony. Perhaps some vital organ gave way : there was
a momentary spasm of acutest pain, a loud cry, and then all
was over.

Brandt thinks the ' loud cry ' unlikely to have been invented,
and therefore probably historic. So too Loisy. It is probably the
only detail which comes from the primitive tradition. The women
may have heard the cry ; or Simon of Cyrene (*E. S.* ii. pp. 680,
681).

38. The curtain of the Temple is rent in twain. The symbolic
meaning of the miracle is that, through the death of Jesus, there
was now a complete and unimpeded access to God. ' In the Jewish
Temple God was behind a veil, which was never lifted except once

a year to the high priest ; but Christians have access or admission '
(Menzies). The thought is elaborated and clearly expressed in
Hebrews x. 19–25, ix. 1–12 ; Ephesians ii. 14–18. To Jewish
feeling the ' access ' to the Father, so immediate and intimate in
prophetic and even in Rabbinic Judaism, has been obscured by
the doctrine of the Mediator and of the divine Son. To Jews it
is a curious irony that Jesus, who would (as we think) so intensely
have disliked the idea that he, or any other man, should stand
between the divine Father and his human children, has yet been
made to occupy this position. There was no gulf ; and so no bridge
was required ; yet for the sake of an imaginary evil, a needless
remedy was devised.

Another interpretation of the passage is apparently favoured
by W., and has ancient support. The rending of the veil means
the mourning of the Temple ; it bewails, not the death of Jesus,
but its own imminent destruction.

39. The centurion calls Jesus ' *a* son of God.' On what does
he base his remark, which is not out of place in a heathen's mouth,
for ' son of God ' would merely mean to him a demi-god, a divine
being ? The usual interpretation is that the captain is impressed
by the ' loud cry,' so unusual from those who suffered on the cross.
Instead of languor and prostration, Jesus at the very moment of
death shows vigour and power. Though this view is shared by the
MS. D, which adds κράξαντα to οὕτως, W. called it ' scurrilous
nonsense,' perhaps because B. Weiss, among others, adopts it.

In his 2nd edition he modified his words. The wrong view
is now only ' albern '! He supposes that the οὕτως (' thus ')
means ' under such circumstances,' and refers it to the ' darkness '
mentioned in 33. This seems less likely. Bacon thinks that there
is a gap here. We know not by what the centurion was impressed
in the manner of Jesus's death (*Gospel Story*, p. 195).

' The captain,' says J. Weiss, ' stands at the end of the Gospel
as the type and forerunner of the countless bands of heathen who
have been won over to the message of the crucified one. The conjecture is near at hand that the captain became afterwards a
Christian.' In that case, his utterance might be authentic. In
the Gospel according to Peter he is called Petronius. But Mark
does not know his name, which gives rise to justifiable doubts ;
and Brandt roundly asserts : ' Dass wir mit einer evangelischen
Dichtung zu thun haben, ist offenbar.' There were many motives
which would have stimulated the invention, and it provides a fine
conclusion to the story. The ' loud cry ' was, probably, to the
Evangelist a ' cry as of thunder,' a supernaturally loud cry ; such
as, to the captain's mind, only a god could have uttered at such a

moment, on such an occasion. Loisy also is suspicious. He denies that ' Son of God ' means merely in the centurion's mouth ' divine hero ' or ' demi-god.' Not so did the Evangelists understand it. (And Kl. thinks that this view is probably correct.) We have to do with a regular conversion, a true confession of faith. Perhaps the centurion is intended to represent the first homage rendered by the Gentile world to the world's Saviour.

40, 41. THE WOMEN WHO SAW

(*Cp.* Matt. xxvii. 55, 56 ; Luke xxiii. 48, 49)

40   There were also some women looking on from a distance, among whom was Mary Magdalene, and Mary the mother of James the
41 Little and of Joses, and Salome (who already, when he was in Galilee, had followed him, and attended to him) ; and many other women who came up with him unto Jerusalem.

Here we have a probably historical, and, if so, a valuable, reminiscence. The crucifixion was, though from a distance, actually witnessed by some of Jesus's own female friends. Incidentally, too, Mark makes an important statement that already in Galilee Jesus had been followed and waited on by some women, and that others had joined him on his way to Jerusalem. Luke had made a similar statement at an early stage (viii. 1–3). There can be little doubt that in Jesus's attitude towards women we have a highly original and significant feature of his life and teaching.

Mary of Magdala is so called from her place of birth or residence, near Tiberias. There is no reason whatever to identify her with the woman who had been a sinner, of Luke vii.

The second Mary is said here to be the mother of James the Less and of Joses. ' In xv. 47 she is called *Mary of Joses* and in xvi. 1 *Mary of James*, phrases which, if they stood by themselves, would be most naturally understood as meaning " Mary the daughter of Joses," and " Mary the daughter of James " respectively. Some scholars are inclined to translate the words in the present passage "Mary the daughter of James the Less and mother of Joses," but the rendering is hardly the natural one ' (Rawlinson, p. 239).

' James is called the Little or the Less to distinguish him from the other " celebrities " of the name. But whether it designates him as less in stature, or in age, or of less importance, there are no data for determining ' (Gould). Some conjecture that this James the Less is James the son of Alphæus, the apostle mentioned in iii. 18. The more famous James was the son of Zebedee.

The ' many others ' may be an unhistoric exaggeration. Matthew
does not mention them. Salome was apparently the mother of the
sons of Zebedee, if we may make this inference on the ground that
Matthew, in place of Mark's Salome, puts ' the mother of the sons
of Zebedee.'

Loisy points out that the women are mentioned in this place
to prepare for, and lead the way to, the story of the burial and the
story of the empty tomb. ' Their presence at Jerusalem, accompanying Jesus and his disciples, perhaps even their presence at
Calvary, may well be an historical fact. This fact, however, was a
mere incident in the tradition, which did not make these women (who,
when all the apostles left, may possibly have remained at Jerusalem)
the first witnesses of the resurrection ' (*E. S.* II. p. 708). Bultmann
(p. 166) is equally sceptical. ' As in the story of the resurrection,
women are brought in as witnesses. They are as little historical
here as there : they were needed, because the disciples who had fled
could not be used.' This is simple enough, but is not the scepticism
excessive ?

I cannot enter into the exceedingly interesting and elaborate
arguments with which Bacon (*Gospel of Mark*) seeks to prove that
Mark in the section xv. 40–xvi. 8 drew from, and is dependent on, the
Special Source of Luke, itself, in this portion of its story, composite.
The women are ' strangers in Mark,' and they, with many other
touches, are evidence of an ' almost certain direct literary connection
with the Special Source,' priority being on the side of the Source
(pp. 195–198). xvi. 8 is less original than the Lukan form of the
story, where the women report to the company (not including Peter),
but are disbelieved. ' From the earliest form of all (1 Cor. xv. 1–11)
the incident of the women was absent altogether ' (p. 198). Bacon
thinks that the ' whole Jerusalem episode of Mark, centring as it
does on the story of the Women at Joseph's Tomb, forms an erratic
block in Mark xv. 40–xvi. 8, a block derived from the ' older '
element of Luke's Special Source. The splitting off of the original
ending of the Gospel is probably due to the presence of this unassimil-
able foreign element ' (p. 199).

42–47. The Burial of Jesus

(*Cp.* Matt. xxvii. 51–61 ; Luke xxiii. 50–56)

42   And as the evening was already at hand, because it was the
43 Preparation, that is, the day before the sabbath, Joseph of Arimathæa, an honourable councillor who himself too was waiting
for the kingdom of God, came, and ventured to go to Pilate, and

44 asked for the body of Jesus. And Pilate marvelled that he should have already died, and he summoned the centurion, and asked him
45 whether he was long dead. And when he was informed by the
46 centurion, he gave the body to Joseph. And he bought fine linen, and took him down, and wrapped him in the linen, and laid him in a sepulchre which was hewn out of a rock, and rolled a stone
47 against the door of the sepulchre. And Mary Magdalene and Mary the mother of Joses watched where he was laid.

42, 43. The burial of Jesus, as described in this paragraph, is probably, in substance, historic. As has been pointed out, its main points 'tradition was not likely to have invented.' Isaiah liii. 9 is inadequate for that, and is not quoted in the Gospels. That the body of Jesus was buried is confirmed by Paul in 1 Cor. xv. 4.

The part played by Joseph of Arimathæa (his birth-place or residence is usually identified with Ramathaim mentioned in 1 Macc. xi. 34, or with the locality mentioned in 1 Sam. i. 1) is also probably to be regarded as historic. Mark calls him $\epsilon \dot{v} \sigma \chi \dot{\eta} \mu \omega \nu$ $\beta o v \lambda \epsilon v \tau \dot{\eta} s$, ' an honourable councillor,' which is usually interpreted to mean that he was a member of the Sanhedrin. If so, the obvious question arose : what part had he played at the trial ? and this was answered by Luke xxiii. 51. More probably the words mean merely, as the adjective so applied leads us to infer, a man of high social rank. It is rash to assume, as J. Weiss does, that Joseph was present at the trial, or even that any part of the account of the trial in the Gospels is due to him.

Joseph is said to be also himself expecting the Kingdom of God. This does not necessarily mean that he was a disciple of Jesus, or that he even expected Jesus to bring the Kingdom about. There were Pharisees who eagerly expected the Kingdom—and even expected it soon. Such a one was Joseph. He may have been sympathetic towards Jesus and his teaching, but it does not follow that he was a regular disciple, though it was only natural that Mark's words would soon be understood in that sense. Klostermann thinks that Joseph *was* an adherent of Jesus. The words used mean that Joseph was expecting the establishment of the Kingdom by Jesus. And it seems very unlikely that Joseph was not even in sympathy with Jesus or his teaching, but that he simply acted (more probably as the representative of the Sanhedrin) in order to carry out the law of Deuteronomy. ' Speed was essential ; the law enjoined burial, and it also enjoined the Sabbath rest. The only way of fulfilling the law of burial without breaking the Sabbath law was to use a grave close to the place of crucifixion ' (so Lake, *The Resurrection of Jesus Christ*, pp. 174, 182).

Matthew calls him 'rich.' This addition is probably not due to Isaiah liii. 9, but was suggested by his action and position. ' εὐσχήμων had obtained in vulgar speech the meaning " rich," though it properly means " of good standing " ' (Lake, p. 50).

Only here, for the first time, and quite casually, does Mark mention that the day of the crucifixion was Friday. The words are not without difficulty. Jesus died at 3 P.M. The sun would set between six and seven. Joseph can only have heard of the death some little while after it took place. Indeed, Mark says ' it was already evening.' The word ὀψίας, W. urges, never means an earlier moment than sunset. Hence, W. says that he cannot understand what ἐπεί, ' since,' refers to. It cannot, he contends, imply that because it was not permissible to take a body down from the cross and bury it on the Sabbath, therefore there was no time to lose. For the Sabbath had already begun. Perhaps, however, the meaning may be that Joseph was anxious that as little of the Sabbath as possible should be defiled by the body (or bodies, though we hear nothing of the two thieves, or whether they were yet dead) remaining upon the cross. John xix. 31 attributes this anxiety to the Jews. Perhaps, too, the law of Deut. xxi. 22, 23, had to do with the matter.

In any case, the verse makes the Synoptic chronology very unlikely. For if Jesus was crucified upon the first day of Passover, one holy day was succeeded by another, and the words, ἤδη ὀψίας γενομένης, ἐπεὶ ἦν παρασκευή (' as the evening was already at hand, because it was the Preparation') become quite unintelligible. They have only a meaning if the Friday was not a festival. Loisy continues his scepticism. Even the Friday is to him dubious. ' The Passover of the Last Supper in the Synoptics, and the Passover of the crucifixion in the fourth Gospel, the Sabbath eve of the burial, and the Sunday of the resurrection, are symbolic data, from which it is now difficult for the historian to disentangle the point of departure in the actual facts. Note too that Mark's " for it was Friday " comes as a sort of extra (comme en surcharge). Yet it is only by this sort of gloss—though, one must admit, already known to Matthew, Luke, and John—that the day of the week on which the crucifixion took place has been ascertained ' (E. S. II. p. 700). Lake too suggests that the clause ἐπεὶ . . . προσάββατον (' because it was . . . Sabbath ') may be an addition to the original text. It appears that ἐπεί is nowhere else found in Mark (Lake, p. 52).

Only Mark has ' ventured.' But it is very plausible. For, according to Roman law or custom, the bodies of crucified persons were not buried. They were allowed to rot where they hung.

44. Pilate's wonder is probably invented. He is astonished that death should have supervened so rapidly. It is clear that the early death was looked upon as something of a wonder or a divine mercy. Six hours of appalling agony is little! One shudders to think of such agony prolonged for a whole day, or even longer, as it would appear did occasionally happen.

45. Pilate grants Joseph's request. It is implied that a bribe or payment would not have been unusual; but Pilate sanctions the burial without any such preliminary. It has been suggested that 44 and 45 may have been added later. 'There is a very harsh change of subject which disappears if 44 and 45 are omitted, and the word ἐδωρήσατο is not found elsewhere in the New Testament except in 2 Peter i. 3' (Lake, p. 53).

Only Mark mentions that Joseph bought the linen. It was forbidden to make purchases whether on Festivals or Sabbath. For a possible explanation see S.-B. II. p. 831. Apparently Mark does not realize that the prohibitions as regards Festivals were pretty nearly as severe as the prohibitions about the Sabbath. But the impression cannot be got over that much of the narrative in Mark—apart from the Passover settings to the 'last supper'—seems to ignore any idea that the arrest and capture and trial and death of Jesus took place upon the sacred Passover Festival. But no more, on the other hand, does Mark seem to contain any indication, any *survival* of any idea or recollection that the evening of the Friday on which Jesus died was not only the beginning of the Sabbath, but *also* (as in the Fourth Gospel) the beginning of the Festival of Passover. It is all most obscure and peculiar.

46. The vault in which Joseph places the body may have been near the place of crucifixion. It is not said by Mark that it was his own grave-vault, or that no use had been made of it before. It is not said that it was intended to be the *final* resting-place of the body. The vault was hewn out of the rock, as places for burial are in the East (Menzies). But the details of the tomb may be due to Isaiah xxii. 16, xxxiii. 16 (Septuagint). So, too, the stone which Joseph rolled against the opening may be due to the narrative which follows, or to the stone of Gen. xxix. 2, 3. But, as Menzies says, 'the tomb had to be guarded against wild beasts and against thieves; and this was commonly done in the way here described.' (See the article 'Tomb' in *Encyclopædia Biblica*.)

Joseph appears suddenly, and as suddenly disappears. The following remarks of Brandt deserve consideration: 'There is every reason to believe that the man who buried the body of Jesus did not belong to his regular adherents, that he executed

his pious work as quietly as he could, and afterwards showed
himself no more in Jerusalem. For otherwise, when the Galilæans
returned with the cry, "Jesus has risen," Joseph, whether gladly
or reluctantly, would have had to play a part. Neither the Jewish
authorities nor the disciples would have left him in peace ; friend
and foe would have talked much more about the tomb than is
now noticeable in the tradition. . . . Ramathaim was not far from
Jerusalem. The expression "Joseph of Ramathaim" indicates
that the person so named had not continued to live there ; but
that he was or remained a resident in Jerusalem is not by any
means implied. Perhaps before, or soon after, the disciples returned
to the city he left Judæa and went abroad. Perhaps his very
name first became known abroad, through some accidental combination of circumstances, and then came, through tradition, to
the knowledge of the Evangelist' (*op. cit.* p. 312).

Loisy thinks that the entire story of Joseph and of the
entombment is as unhistoric as the discovery of the empty tomb
itself. 'On peut supposer que les soldats détachèrent le corps
de la croix avant le soir, et le mirent dans quelque fosse commune,
où l'on jetait pêle-mêle les restes des suppliciés' (*E. S.* I. p. 223).
If this scepticism were justified, and the body of Jesus was treated
as Loisy supposes, there would be something wonderfully dramatic
in such a fate for such a corpse. Here is the body of a man who
is to exercise the greatest influence of any man of all mankind
upon the history and civilization of the world, who is to be
worshipped as God by untold millions of men, thrown unregarded,
uncared for, into a common ditch, to mingle undistinguished with
the malefactors' bones which filled it. That would be indeed a
contrast and an irony worthy of the event and its results.

47. The two Marys watch the burial. It is not said whether
they had remained all the time at the same place from which
they saw the crucifixion ; but this is perhaps implied. If the
tomb was near the cross, the women could have seen how the
body was recovered and buried. It is hardly to be inferred that
they went, after the burial, up to the spot and looked at it. The
imperfect ἐθεώρουν rather implies that they watched from their
post the process of entombment. Or if the point is pressed, that
only two women see the entombment, we may assume that these
two leave their former post of observation, and, following Joseph,
draw nearer to the grave.

The second Mary is called Μαρία ἡ 'Ιωσῆτος. W. says this
must be translated ' the daughter of Joses,' which would conflict
with xv. 40. But Swete says : ' sc. μήτηρ,' and so Holtzmann.
The point is unimportant. All the details of the story of the

entombment, says Loisy, are conceived in view of, and to lead
up to, the discovery of the empty tomb. Mark would impress
upon our notice that the same people who saw the entombment
saw also the empty tomb. He only wants to introduce a little
variety in making a considerable number of persons watch the
death of Jesus, while two only of these witness the entombment,
and three the discovery of the empty grave (*E. S.* II. p. 707).

It is hardly desirable to add any general note upon the crucifixion
and death of Jesus. For, if a beginning were to be made, it would
not be easy to stop. Those who believe in a God of Righteousness
can only bow the head in awed and yet trustful submission at the
strangely mixed means which He takes for the progress of mankind, at the painful and involved interconnection of good and evil.
In spite of the endless misery which was to come upon the Jews
because of the death of Jesus ; in spite of the false theology and
the persecutions and sore evils (apart wholly from the Jewish
misery) ; in spite of the wrongs which were to be done to liberty,
to enlightenment, and to toleration, by the Christian Church—one
yet sees that the death of Jesus, even as his life, was of immense
benefit to the world. Christianity, as we know it, and as Paul
made it, was due to his death as much as, if not more than, to his
life. Some fundamental truths of Judaism (though not all of them)
have been taught to a large proportion of the world by Christianity ;
and while in some directions it obscured those truths, in others it
expanded them. That this might be done, the ' chosen people '
has had to suffer. For the law of election seems to go even further
than Amos realized, though what he said was sufficiently startling
and revolutionary. For Amos said : ' You only have I known out
of all the inhabitants of the earth ; *therefore* I will visit upon you
your iniquities.' But even this is not enough. Nineteen centuries
of suffering compel us to realize that for some august reason or
purpose we must say, ' You have I called : therefore ye shall suffer
undeservedly.'

The precise proportion of responsibility which belongs to any
section of the Jews of Jerusalem for the death of Jesus must always
remain doubtful and uncertain. But the probability, as we have
seen, is that the Sadducean priesthood, perhaps backed up by some
of the leading Rabbis, were responsible, together with the Romans,
for his death. Yet what matters this, so far as God is concerned ?
We are disposed to find a difficulty in the 'third or fourth generation '
of the Second Commandment. Yet if the death of Jesus had been
unanimously voted by the entire Jewish people, with votes taken
by plebiscite or referendum, what difference would it make ? Third
or fourth generation ! Why, there have been fifty generations !

And the roll is not yet ended, and there seems no prospect of its close. For in substitution of the Master's command, ' Ye shall love your enemies,' there has been forged another : ' Ye shall hate your enemies to the fiftieth and sixtieth generation.'

But this is the will of God in His scheme for the progress of the world. We do not understand why. But the Jews have ever to realize that they have received the consecration of supremest suffering, and that they still in many lands remain the hunted, hated, wounded, but deathless, witnesses of God.

[The above was written seventeen or eighteen years ago. In some respects things are better now than they were then. But there is still much hatred, and much persecution of one kind or another, and, in the interval between then and now, appalling things have occurred. There has also been much change among the Jews themselves. Old ideals, to the present writer, as fresh and valid as ever, have lost their appeal, and, what is far worse, there has been some falling away from Judaism and from God. ' Who is blind, but my servant ? ' But, nevertheless, if these worthless servants exist, there exist faithful servants as well. We must leave the matter in His hands.]

CHAPTER XVI

IT is unnecessary for the purposes of this book to add lengthy notes to the brief narratives which tell the story of the resurrection. It would suffice, for those who want to gain a very convenient conspectus of the whole subject, to read the article on the resurrection narratives in the *Encyclopœdia Biblica*. There will be found a complete summary of the facts and of the main theories. There, too, is enumerated the full tale of the inconsistencies of the various Gospels with each other, and with the statements of Paul. For the purposes of this book it is the narratives about the life and teaching of Jesus which are of the greatest importance, while those which tell of his death are less important, and those which describe his resurrection are least important of all. Dr. Carpenter, in that splendid chapter of his book which he calls ' The Jesus of History,' says : ' The resurrection is not here discussed, as it belongs properly to the history of the Church.' And this is doubtless correct. But, over and above this reason, there are others which make lengthy notes upon the resurrection chapters unnecessary in this place. For this book is not polemical, and it is also not an apology. It frankly assumes the Jewish point of view. If a Jew were to write a commentary upon the Gospels in order to show why, in spite of them, he remains in religion a Jew, and does not become a convert to Christianity, he would have to show why the resurrection narratives are wholly insufficient for, and do not even help towards, his conversion. He would then have to dwell at length upon their difficulties and inconsistencies ; he would have to show why he ranges himself with those Christian critics, such as the author of the article in the *Encyclopœdia Biblica*, who deny the empty tomb, the material or semi-material risen body, or even the ' objective ' vision. But the author of this book need not enter into these discussions. He writes frankly as a Jew, and, therefore, as one who does not so ' believe in ' the resurrection as would logically compel him to change his creed. He is not concerned either to defend his own faith or to attack the faith of others.

The most probable views of the resurrection stories to the present commentator are based upon the assumption that there is a real foundation for these stories. In other words, that the disciples, or some of them, saw a vision of Jesus which they believed to be a vision of their risen Master. The assumption is that in that sense, and within these limits, the Gospel narratives are historic. It is an assumption, for it can never be proved ; but, all things considered, it seems the most probable assumption—far more probable than the opposite assumptions, that the stories are fabricated, or that the disciples told what they knew to be false, or that the stories are completely legendary, and grew up as legends do grow up, no man knowing how.

If, then, there is historic truth at the bottom of the narratives— though the truth did not include much (such as the empty tomb) which the narratives now contain—that truth can, roughly stated, be one of two main possibilities : *Either* the disciples, or some of them, or one of them, not merely saw a vision of Jesus, but what they saw *was* Jesus in some special supernatural manifestation ; *or,* though the vision was real to them, it was, as we should now say, ' only a vision,' and had no further reality, being exclusively a ' product of the mental condition of the seer.'

The first of these possibilities, again, may be held in the form that the disciples saw what we should call the ' spirit ' of Jesus, either ' in true spirit form or in some kind of acquired visibility,' or, it may be held in the form that what they saw was ' only a visionary image without any real appearance of Jesus,' but that ' this visionary image was produced in their souls immediately by God in order that they might be assured that Jesus was alive ' (*Encyclopædia Biblica*, art. ' Resurrection,' col. 4077). And even in the first form we may hold, as Prof. Lake has pointed out, that the real spiritual being was only perceived by the disciples under the conditions and limitations of their minds and senses. The ' being ' had an objective existence, but what they ' heard ' or ' saw ' was due as much to them as to ' it ' (Lake, pp. 271, 272).

Many persons, both Jews and Christians, would hold that no one could believe the first possibility (in either form) and yet legitimately remain a Jew. I do not myself believe this possibility —(I think the vision was purely ' subjective ') ; but, nevertheless, I do not think that the objective vision possibility could not be held by a Jew. For if we believe in the immortality of the soul, we shall also believe that the spirit of Jesus survived death, and it may have been the will of God that the disciples should be miracu- lously accorded this particular vision. So it may have been the will of God that Mohammed may have been accorded a ' super- natural ' vision. When I think of the gigantic results of both Christianity and Mohammedanism, it seems to me, in some moods and for some reasons, less difficult to believe that they are based upon, or partly built up from, certain special divine interventions than that they are based upon what we call ' illusions.'

But, on the other hand, it is, for other reasons, our scientific duty to do without miracles when we can. If all other miracles are ill-founded, it is probable that this one is ill-founded too.

The whole building up of the resurrection narratives can be adequately accounted for on the subjective vision possibility ; and again, the appearance of the subjective visions to the disciples, or to some of them, can also be accounted for with adequate psychological verisimilitude. Not only has the objective vision hypothesis its own difficulties, but it is also more ' economical ' to be content with the subjective vision hypothesis, if it can be adequately accounted for with fair and reasonable arguments.

No one who accepts the doctrine of ' immortality ' will hesitate for one moment to believe in the ' resurrection ' of Jesus, if by resurrection we mean that his life did not terminate upon the cross. If others ' live again,' then, *a fortiori*, one of the best of men so lives. But to the Jew, and to all those who hold the subjective vision hypothesis, the resurrection of Jesus is not the proof or pledge of general human immortality ; but, on the contrary, the belief in general human immortality is the proof and pledge of the ' resurrection of Jesus.' If we believe already in human immortality, it does not, in one sense, make much difference whether we accept the objective or the subjective vision hypothesis : Jesus, in either case, is alive, whether the disciples ' really ' saw him or not. If, on the other hand, we do not believe in human immortality, we shall still less believe in the objective vision hypothesis. Thus, to those who have not grown up in, or who have not retained, the old Christian theology, the ' resurrection ' of Jesus has no central importance. Their faith does not hinge on it ; the Gospel narrative can neither upset their faith nor confirm it.

A difficulty to my own mind in the subjective vision hypothesis, as set forth and explained, for example, by Schmiedel and Arnold Meyer, is one which, to many minds, will not seem a difficulty at all. It is, perhaps, less a difficulty than a sadness. It is the same difficulty or sadness which presents itself to me when Professor Margoliouth, in the plenitude of his great knowledge, would have me believe that Mohammed was largely a conscious impostor. It is hard to be content that great religious results should have had not quite satisfactory causes. The subjective vision was, in one sense, an ' illusion.' Yet upon this illusion hinged the great religious result which we call Christianity. So, too, it is hard to be content that any dross and error should be mingled with the pure gold of the prophets. But we cannot hope to understand the means which God allows or wills (whichever word may be preferred) in the development and production of human righteousness and knowledge. His will is done. Righteousness and knowledge, which are the only ' proof ' of God, exist and increase. We must not stumble because we cannot understand the means.

The visionary hypothesis is very ably defended and justified from a religious point of view by J. Weiss in his *Urchristentum*, pp. 18–28. He also urges that the depression of the disciples and their disappointment must not be pushed too far. They still hoped ; they still trusted ; they still believed. Weiss holds that we must not assume that the predictions of suffering and death had no foundation. Jesus must have realized the possibilities of his fate, and he probably gave the disciples to understand that his own death might be the necessary preliminary to the establishment of the Kingdom. If the disciples half believed and half doubted, if they had intimations from Jesus to encourage them, the ' vision ' hypothesis is the more likely. They still believed in the greatness, the truth, the trustworthiness, of the Master : they believed that he was yet alive, and Peter, the greatest of them, most of all. In such a mood of expectancy, of faith and doubt, of inward turmoil and agitation, a vision was not unnatural.

1–8. The Empty Tomb

(*Cp.* Matt. xxviii. 1–10 ; Luke xxiv. 1–11)

1 And when the sabbath was over, Mary Magdalene, and Mary the mother of James, and Salome, bought sweet spices, that they 2 might go and anoint him. And very early in the morning of the first day of the week, they came unto the sepulchre, at the rising 3 of the sun. And they said among themselves, ' Who will roll away 4 for us the stone from the door of the sepulchre ? ' And when they looked, they saw that the stone had been rolled away : for it was 5 very great. And entering into the sepulchre, they saw a young man sitting on the right side, clothed in a long white garment ; 6 and they were sore afraid. But he said unto them, ' Be not afraid : ye seek Jesus the crucified Nazarene ; he is risen ; he is not here : 7 behold the place where they laid him. But go, tell his disciples and Peter that he goes before you into Galilee : there shall ye see him, 8 as he said unto you.' And they went out, and fled from the sepulchre ; for they trembled and were amazed : and they said nothing to any one ; for they were afraid.

1. ' In Marcus fehlt heute ein Schluss, der wie xiv. 27 mit einer

sofortigen Flucht der Jünger rechnete, von galiläischen Erscheinungen berichtete, und auf den xiv. 28, xvi. 7 ausdrücklich hinzielen. Statt dessen bringt er die Erzählung vom leeren Grabe, die (*a*) ein Bleiben der Jünger in Jerusalem voraussetzt, (*b*) durch die höchst verwunderliche Absicht nachträglicher Salbung, nicht Embalsamierung, die Frauen an das Grab bringt, und (*c*) durch ihr Streben das Wunderbare zu belegen als jünger erscheint. Der Glaube der Jünger beruht nach 1 Cor. xv. so wenig auf ihr, dass sie als eine spätere Schlussfolgerung des Auferstehungsglaubens erscheinen kann ' (Klostermann).

The second Mary is here called the mother or, as W. thinks, the daughter of James. *Cp.* the statements in xv. 47 and xv. 40.

They make the necessary purchases late on Saturday evening. That the women determine to anoint a corpse which had already been entombed two days and wrapped round in its cere-cloths seems very strange. W. calls it a ' bold thought.' It seems to me more —it seems to me a thought which is not likely to be historic. In any case the women could hardly have thought of anointing the corpse unless they knew that the entombment had been meant to be, and was, of a temporary character only. J. Weiss says : ' How could the women reckon upon the stone being rolled away ? The cause assigned for their visit to the grave is very unlikely.'

2. They arrive very early on Sunday morning at the grave. But the sun has risen.

3. They have no idea or thought that Jesus may have risen. On the contrary, their one preoccupation is the question of the heavy stone at the mouth of the grave. Who will roll it away for them ?

4. The stone has been already rolled away : for it was very big. The second part of the verse seems awkward. That the stone was very big does not prove that it was rolled away. The words would be more suitable after verse 3. In their present place they can only be regarded as a loose way of expressing the implied thought that the rolling away of the stone was something very portentous and remarkable. (So Klostermann.) Who had rolled the stone away ? Is it implied that this was done by Jesus himself ? He ' rises,' rolls away the stone, and disappears. Or has the stone been rolled away by invisible divine power ? ' In any case,' says Loisy, ' it is understood that the stone had to be rolled away in order that Jesus might come out.'

5. The women, finding the stone removed from the mouth,

enter into the vault. Instead of seeing, as they expect, the body
of Jesus, they see an angel. The angel looks like a young man,
but his white (priestly) garments, as well as the mere fact of his
presence in that strange place, reveal his angelhood. (*Cp.* 2 Macc.
iii. 26 ; Revelation vii. 9, 13.) It is also important to note that one
good MS. has merely ' having come to the tomb ' (*i.e.* ἐλθοῦσαι for
εἰσελθοῦσαι). Is this original ? Prof. Lake strongly holds that the
young man is not an angel, but a man. The narrative, in its essence,
is historical.

6. The angel's words : ' Ye seek Jesus, the crucified Nazarene,'
sound a little strange. Menzies says that they are ' in character.
Jesus is not described in terms a believer would use, or with any
reference to his Messiahship, but in such words as might be used to
identify him either to a follower or an unbeliever.'

The angel then announces the fact of the resurrection. Jesus
has risen in his own very body. The angel shows the place where
the body had been put, and this place is empty. The MS. D reads :
' He is risen, he is not here, lo, there is the place where they laid
him.' Is this, as Lake is inclined to think, the original text ? See
below. (Lake, p. 69.)

7. Is there a contradiction here with xiv. 50 ? W. and others
think there is, inasmuch as xiv. 50 supposes that the disciples had
fled, immediately after the arrest, to Galilee (except Peter), whereas
this verse would imply that they are still near or in Jerusalem, and
that the women are to tell them to proceed at once to Galilee. But
it must be admitted that it does not say in xiv. 50 that they fled at
once to Galilee. When exactly they dispersed to their homes,
whether after or before the crucifixion, is not stated. In any case
our verse, like xiv. 28, is meant to account for the fact that the first
appearance of the risen Jesus took place in Galilee, perhaps also
to account for the flight of the apostles and to justify it. Lake
suggests that the true explanation of xvi. 7, by which we can
maintain its consistency with xiv. 50, and yet explain that verse as
implying that the disciples had already scattered to Galilee, is that
the meaning of ' he goes before you into Galilee ' (*cp.* xiv. 28) is, he
will be in Galilee before you. Before you arrive in Galilee, which
will take you some time, Jesus will already be there (Lake,
p. 76).

' There shall ye see him ' ; that is, the disciples, not the women.
The words which the women are to repeat are addressed direct to
the disciples.

According to J. Weiss Mark has misunderstood the old tradition
embodied in xiv. 28, with its prediction which was unfulfilled. *The*

disciples did not disperse to Galilee at all. The usual explanation
is that they only remained in Jerusalem till after the conclusion of
the Sabbath, and that they left for Galilee on Sunday morning,
though not because of any angel's order. Even Mark does not go
so far as this, for according to him the women do not carry out the
order. Only in Matthew are they supposed to have done so. (*Cp.*
Goguel in his essay in the 'Actes,' p. 241.)

Professor Turner says that 'the natural exegesis of the Greek
original of the words "tell his disciples and Peter that he goes
before you into Galilee : there shall ye see him, as he said unto
you," if printed without punctuation or brackets, is that our Lord
had told the disciples that they would see him in Galilee. But
the Gospel contains no record of any such saying. Matthew,
therefore, by substituting the first person for the third, εἶπον for
εἶπεν, changes the sense from a prediction of our Lord's to a
statement by the angel, "You will see him in Galilee : I tell you so
categorically." Luke retains the third person ; but as his Gospel
records appearances of the Risen Christ in Jerusalem and its neighbourhood only, he has to connect Galilee, not with the appearances,
but with the prediction, "He spake yet being in Galilee." But St.
Mark had recorded one prediction by Jesus, uttered as recently as
the Last Supper (xiv. 28), μετὰ τὸ ἐγερθῆναί με προάξω ὑμᾶς εἰς
τὴν Γαλιλαίαν, in language of which the angel's words seem an
obvious echo, xvi. 6, 7, ἠγέρθη . . . προάγει ὑμᾶς εἰς τὴν Γαλιλαίαν
. . . καθὼς εἶπεν ὑμῖν. Apart from the three intrusive words,
ἐκεῖ αὐτὸν ὄψεσθε, the correspondence is exact. Treat them
as a parenthesis after the Marcan manner, place them between
dashes, and all difficulty disappears' (*J. T. S.*, 1925, XXVI. p. 156).
Whether the confident assertion that 'all difficulty disappears' is,
perhaps, somewhat excessive, I will not further discuss in this place.

Klausner has a peculiar interpretation of the words 'I will
go before you into Galilee.' He thinks that 'Jesus had appointed
a prearranged meeting-place (of course, during his lifetime),
telling them that now, as distinct from the time when he had
sent them forth from Capernaum as his Apostles, they would
need purse and wallet and even a sword' (p. 358). 'He had
promised his disciples that he would leave Jerusalem (naturally in
secret), and go before them to Galilee.' (*Cp.* p. 331. A most improbable and far-fetched hypothesis.) That Peter and others of the
disciples had a vision of Jesus Klausner regards as certain. He
says rather finely: 'It is impossible to suppose that there was
any conscious deception: the nineteen hundred years' faith of
millions is not founded on deception. There can be no question
but that some of the ardent Galilæans saw their lord and Messiah
in a vision' (p. 359).

8. It is highly remarkable that the women are expressly stated
to have disobeyed the angel's order. And if they did not obey it,
how did it become known ? Did they go with the disciples to
Galilee and tell them *there*, either before or after the visions of
the risen Jesus had occurred ? But this is a very strained explanation. And, on the other hand, the reason for the women's silence
is far from clear. That the occurrence at the tomb filled them
with awe and fear is reasonable enough ; but that, when they
joined their friends, they still said nothing seems most peculiar.
The trembling and bewilderment are psychologically inadequate.
The only explanation which is possible seems to be that it was known
that the disciples were unprepared for what they saw in Galilee.
The faith in the risen Messiah owes nothing to the discovery of the
empty tomb. No story of the empty tomb had reached the apostles
when that faith was born within them. The empty tomb story
grew up afterwards. Hence it had to be explained why the women
kept silence ; this is done as well as might be. When the story of
the empty tomb became current and accepted, the need was no
longer felt for the silence of the women. Its improbability, on the
contrary, became felt. Hence the change in Matthew and Luke.

J. Weiss has, perhaps, most ably shown the historical sequence
of the resurrection stories. See his sections on these matters
in his *Urchristentum*, pp. 9–28, 60–75. First come the visions.
These we must assume actually took place. Not that Weiss
believes in any objective reality behind them. They were what we
should now call hallucinations, though, as he urges, the modern
Christian believer, who also believes in God's rule in history,
may justly hold that these hallucinations were the will of God.
In any case, however, the visions were in this sense real. But
they were wholly independent of any belief in a resurrection on
the third day, and still more of an empty tomb. A glorified Jesus
—not indeed a wholly immaterial Jesus, but a Jesus who was
endowed or was clothed with a ' spiritual ' body, unlike the body of
earth—may have been conceived as ' resurrected ' at any moment,
even immediately, after death. His earthly body could have
remained in the tomb. The saying in Luke, ' To-day thou shalt
be with me in Paradise ' is an echo of this conception. The body
of the thief hung undoubtedly still upon its cross. First, then,
the visions, which showed that Jesus was not only not ' dead,'
but that he was already with God, that he had begun his true
Messiahship, that he had passed from ignominy to power, that he
was in heaven, sitting at God's right hand, where it was Messiah's
place to sit. But this daring belief needed substantiation from
Scripture. And the substantiation was found in Hosea, and
perhaps elsewhere as well. The Hosea passage suggested ' the third

day.' Jesus had not ascended to God till then. Paul knows of this teaching and accepts it. But he knows nothing of the empty tomb and of the actual material body which had been deposited there having risen out of the tomb. In the earliest stage the risen body was not the material body. It is the glorified body which is manifested to those to whom the vision is vouchsafed. It can appear and disappear. But enemies said that the Visions were merely imaginary : they were hallucinations. And doubters may have said that the Visions, if more than hallucinations, were the appearances of what we call a ghost. The 'spirits' of dead persons might wander about for a while after their death, but such apparitions would not prove that Jesus had risen into heaven (Luke xxiv. 37). Hence came about the materialization of the visions. It was no apparition. The risen Jesus had a real body : he could be touched. He could eat. The stories in Luke show an odd mixture of view. The risen Jesus can miraculously appear and disappear : but yet he has a body of flesh and bones, and he eats. When enemies denied the truth of the visions, the reply grew up, not merely that the risen Jesus, who had shown himself to his disciples, was no ghost, but that he was the very same Jesus who had died on the cross and been put into the tomb. Hence arose the story of the empty tomb, and the developments of it such as we find in Matthew. (The disciples had not stolen the body. It had risen miraculously, et cetera.) The spiritual visions became materialized.

Bickermann (Z. N. W., 1924, 'Das leere Grab,' pp. 281-292) attempts to make a strong distinction between the ideas of a sudden being carried away into heaven (*Entrückung*) and a resurrection. The *Entrückung* idea is the older ; the empty tomb is its proof. The visions also probably depended on the *Entrückung* idea, or suggested it. They would not have suggested the idea of a Resurrection. The Resurrection idea came from another quarter. It came from Hellenistic circles, ' denen die sterbenden und auferstehenden Gestalten der Mysterien wohlbekannt waren. Daher eroberte die neue Auffassung nicht nur die neue Welt, sondern auch die alte der Urgemeinde.' Thus here is one more of the endless theories to which the Resurrection stories have given rise !

The opening word of the verse ἐξελθοῦσαι ' is not represented in the Arabic Diatessaron and in some MSS. is altered to ἀκούσαντες ' (Lake, p. 62).

What follows after verse 8 is from another hand. It is interpolated and late. W. thinks that Mark always ended at 8. It was the intended end. Nothing is wanting. The resurrection is announced and proved. Others hold that the end has been lost, or that the writer was suddenly prevented from concluding his

work.   No certainty on this point is possible.   The present ending
is rather abrupt and awkward.   To end a sentence with γάρ
seems odd.   ‘ It is therefore probable that the sentence originally
ran “ for they were afraid of the Jews ” or some such phrase ’
(Lake, p. 72 *init*.).   But if they had told the truth secretly to the
disciples, why should they have been afraid of the Jews ?   Others
think that the end of Mark was deliberately suppressed, because its
narrative of the resurrection, which perhaps told of the appearance
of Jesus ‘ to Peter and a small group of fellow-disciples,’ was
‘ inconsistent with what was now becoming the dominant tradition,
which Matthew embodies, in favour of an expected and formal
first appearance in Galilee to the eleven ’ (Bartlet, p. 443), and for
other reasons (p. 444).   So, too, Goguel, 1. p. 295.
     The more radical critics reject the story of the empty tomb as
entirely unhistorical.   Attempts have been made to retain the
story and get rid of the miraculous elements.   Thus it has been
supposed that the women did go to the tomb and did find it
empty, but that the reason was that the Jewish authorities had
removed the body.   Or, again, it is conjectured that Joseph had
only provisionally put the body in his own vault, and had had it
removed to another resting-place before the visit of the women.
Or, again, it is conjectured that Mary Magdalene alone visited the
tomb (so John), and that she had a vision, or trance, or seizure
there, and that her vision may have grown into the present story.
But, as Loisy well points out, the story is all of a piece.   The
angel is not added later ; he cannot be removed without destroying
the whole.   In fact, all the above conjectures are very doubtful.
     The best defence of the story is by Bartlet.   ‘ If what the women
found on going to the tomb to embalm the body of Jesus, after its
all too hurried burial by Joseph, was an empty grave and nothing
more—no angel with a message of reassurance as to its meaning,
and no commission to deliver it to the disciples—then they may
well have stolen away in silence, utterly at a loss what to think
of it, and in no mood to hasten to share with others so unwelcome a
piece of intelligence.   Meantime the disciples were “ scattered,”
“ the shepherd ” having been smitten down in death, and were
making for Galilee in order to escape sharing his fate ; and ere the
three women’s story of “ the empty grave ” in Joseph’s garden
reached their ears in Galilee, they had already reached by personal
experiences the triumphant faith that Jesus was living, and was
therefore risen from the dead.   It would be only later, in the
course of the controversy with Jewish denial of the Resurrection—
as based on those first-hand experiences of Jesus’s personal disciples,
especially “ the Twelve ” and the larger circle of “ all the Apostles ”
(to which Paul himself appeals as the final evidence in the matter)

—that apologetic use was made, as in the Marcan form, of the women's experience of "the empty tomb" and the angelic witness seated therein.   To this the Jews probably replied in terms of the explanation "his disciples came by night and stole him away" from Joseph's tomb (Matt. xxviii. 13), which we find worked into the special episode in Matt. xxviii. 11–15, embodying an answer to any such suggestion.   But in any case that answer seems to imply the fact of "the empty tomb"—a point which the Jews could (and had every reason to) disprove, if the belief itself were ground-less.   Accordingly, while the angelic vision in Mark's story of "the empty tomb" can fairly be said to have 'grown up after-wards,' it may well be that there was from the first a story of Joseph's empty tomb, as seen by the women (unlikely to be invoked as witnesses, rather than men) whose names and object in visiting it Mark recounts so circumstantially and naturally ; and that the disciples nevertheless left Jerusalem without receiving word of it ' (p. 440).

For the entirely legendary character of the story it is argued that Paul knows nothing about it.   Secondly, that if the story had happened, the women would not have disobeyed the order of the angel.   Mark's statement that the women said nothing implies that the story of the empty sepulchre was unknown when the disciples had the visions in Galilee of the risen Jesus, and that it is, in fact, a later tradition.   How the story arose on this hypothesis is not easy, but the growth of legend is often difficult to explain. If Jesus had risen, as the disciples believed after the visions in Galilee, then, on current theories of the resurrection, the tomb must have been empty.   'Therefore no hesitation was felt in declaring that (according to all reasonable conjecture) the women who had witnessed Jesus's death had wished to anoint his body, and then had come to know of the emptiness of the grave.   In the fact that, according to Mark and Matthew, this was not alleged regarding the male disciples, we can see still a true recollection that those disciples were by that time no longer in Jerusalem.' So Schmiedel, in *Encyclopædia Biblica*.   The defenders of tradition and miracle may not unreasonably argue that this is rather a poor explanation.   But, nevertheless, the story itself, and the supposi-tion of the empty sepulchre, and of the rolled-away stone, are much more difficult still.   It is better to assume that the body of Jesus remained where it was placed without disturbance or miracle.

After the above paragraph was written Prof. Lake's book on the Resurrection appeared.   His view is rather peculiar.   He holds that there is no reason to believe that Paul was unacquainted with the story of the empty tomb.   (It is in any case difficult to prove a negative.)   Moreover, he thinks that the story in Mark in its essentials is accurate and historic. The women go to what they think is the tomb : they find it open. 'A young man who was in the entrance, guessing their errand, tried to tell them that they had made a mistake in the place. " He is not here," said he ; "see the place where they laid him," and probably pointed to the next tomb.' But the women were frightened at the detection of their errand and fled. They heard very imperfectly, or not at all. Later on, when they were rejoined by the men who had experienced the visions (or when, as others would put it, they rejoined the men in Galilee), they remembered the incident at the tomb. But if Jesus was risen, then the tomb was empty : so they came to believe that the young man was an angel, and that what he had told them was that Jesus had risen and that he had given them a message for the disciples (Lake, pp. 246–253, 193, 199). It does not seem to me likely that this explanation, or 'suggestion,' as Lake calls it, will permanently hold the field. Its ingenuity, however, is undeniable.

Bacon has a peculiar theory to account for the lost ending, and the incompleteness, of Mark. 'Why Mark is incomplete' is the title of a special chapter of his book. I have no space to deal with it, and will only quote the final paragraph. The disappearance of the original ending ' was not accidental, since a merely accidental lacuna would have been quickly remedied. The disappearance of the original ending forms part of the protracted story of adjustment between two conflicting streams of tradition both of which Mark had attempted to combine. The disruptive force came from inside. In respect to the time and place of Peter's vision of the risen Christ Mark retains traces of a better tradition than Luke. But in Luke there are traces of a tradition which is superior to Mark as respects Peter's isolation from the rest when he " turned again." The Special Source of Luke also introduces a new factor, the story of the Women at the Sepulchre, the historical value of which is hard to appraise since it is unknown to, or ignored by, Paul. The vain attempt of Mark to bring this new factor into harmony with his story of an appearance to Peter " and those who were with him " in Galilee (a fusion into one event of the two appearances reported by Paul : " to Peter, *then* to the Twelve ") is responsible for the present condition of the ending of his Gospel' (p. 203, *cp.* pp. 190, 191. The original ending with its contradiction to the Lukan version of the Resurrection appearances in or near Jerusalem was suppressed). The ' disappearance of the original ending of Mark belongs probably to this period of rivalry ; for the two methods of piecing-out still reflect the difference. The disappearance of the original ending was not due, however, to the lack of exemplars, but rather to their too great abundance. It disappeared for the same reason that the account of how "the Lord appeared to Simon" has disappeared.   There were so many improved versions, each requiring to be harmonized with some other, that in the end nothing else but "improved" versions was left' (p. 190).

9–20. LATER VERSION OF THE RESURRECTION

9   [Now after he had risen, early on the first day of the week, he
     appeared first to Mary Magdalene, out of whom he had cast seven
10 devils.   And she went and told them that had been with him, as
11 they mourned and wept.   And they, when they heard that he was
12 alive, and had been seen by her, believed it not.   After that he
     appeared in another form unto two of them, as they were walking
13 and going into the country.   And they went and told it unto the
     others, but they did not believe even them.

14   Afterward he appeared unto the eleven as they sat at table,
     and upbraided them with their unbelief and hardness of heart,
15 because they believed not them who had seen him risen.   And he
     said unto them, 'Go ye throughout all the world, and preach the
16 gospel to every creature.   He that believes and is baptized shall
17 be saved ; but he that believes not shall be condemned.   And
     these signs shall follow them that believe : In my name shall they
18 cast out demons ; they shall speak with new tongues ; they shall
     take up serpents ; and if they drink any deadly thing, it shall not
     hurt them ; they shall lay hands on the sick, and they shall recover.'
19   Now after the Lord had spoken unto them, he was taken up
20 into heaven, and sat down on the right hand of God.   But they
     went forth, and preached everywhere, the Lord helping them and
     confirming the Word through the signs which followed it.]

The Gospel of Mark ends with xvi. 8.   Whether the true end has been lost, or whether xvi. 8 was the intentional—though, to us, oddly abrupt—end, is disputed among scholars.   But the passage which now follows (9–20) is certainly unauthentic.   It is wanting in some of the best MSS.   It is wanting in the S.S.   It is a compilation unlike Mark in style and vocabulary.   It contradicts implicitly, if not explicitly, what Mark had said as to the scene of the apparitions being Galilee.   It presupposes Matthew and Luke and John.   It has allusions to them all, and also to Acts.   Streeter says that 'the author of the Gospel cannot have originally meant to end it without the account of the Appearance to the Apostles in Galilee which is twice

prophesied in the text (Mark xiv. 28, xvi. 7). Indeed, the words
ἐφοβοῦντο γάρ in Greek may not even be the end of a sentence; they
lead us to expect a clause beginning with, "They were afraid, lest
they should be thought mad," or something to that effect.' He
supposes that the loss of the actual ending was a very early one. 'It
would,' he says, 'seem probable that the end of the roll on which it
was written must have been torn off before any copies of it had got
into circulation. Otherwise such a loss would have been repaired
at once from another copy' (pp. 337, 338). The end of the Gospel
was already lost when it was used by Matthew and Luke, but
Streeter conjectures that the author of the Fourth Gospel derived
his Resurrection stories from the lost end of Mark : in other words,
the Ephesian copy of Mark was 'the first ever made,' and was 'made
before the original was mutilated' (p. 352). In an interesting article
in *J. T. S.*, July 1926, Mr. R. R. Ottley shows that the abruptness
and 'oddness' of the ending in γάρ must not be exaggerated. He
points out that sentences do sometimes end with γάρ in Homer, in
the Tragedians, and in the LXX (though the imperfect in Mark
adds to the unusualness). *Cp.* Genesis xviii. 15, ἠρνήσατο δὲ
Σάρρα λέγουσα, οὐκ ἐγέλασα. ἐφοβήθη γάρ. (Except for the aorist
a curiously good parallel.)

9-11. This 'appearance' depends on John xx., but has a few
touches from Luke xxiv.

12, 13. This depends on Luke xxiv. (the Emmaus story).

14. The final 'appearance,' which depends partly on Luke
xxiv. 41-43 and partly on passages in Acts. The words which
Jesus speaks contain many echoes. Thus 15 depends on Matthew
xxviii. 19.

16. *Cp.* Acts xvi. 31 ; John iii. 18.

17. The signs refer to Acts ii., or to the 'tongues' of Paul in
I Cor. xii., xiv.

18. The snake-lifting is curious. Some see an allusion to Acts
xxviii. 3-5. Perhaps it is only another way of putting Luke x. 19.

19. The description of the ascension is suggested by some
verses in Acts. (*Cp.* Acts i. 8-11, ii. 33.)

'The resurrection of Jesus is a Christian belief, not a fact of
Gospel history. And if one were compelled to regard it as a historic
fact, one would be obliged to admit that this fact is not guaranteed

by evidence which is adequately sure, consistent, clear, and precise'
(*E. S.* II. p. 798). With these words Loisy ends his great commentary.

There is also a shorter ending to Mark which, as translated by
Bartlet, runs thus: ' But all that had been enjoined they reported
concisely to Peter and his companions (*lit.* " those about Peter ").
And after these things Jesus himself also appeared to them, and
from East even to West sent forth through them the sacred and
incorruptible proclamation of eternal salvation.'   For this ending,
and for fuller details about the other and longer ending, the reader
may be referred to Bartlet's excellent notes.

END OF VOL. I